INSIDERS' GUIDE® SERIES

P9-DKF-040

INSIDERS' GUIDE® TO

PORTLAND, OREGON

INCLUDING THE METRO AREA AND
VANCOUVER, WASHINGTON

SIXTH EDITION

RACHEL DRESBECK

INSIDERS' GUIDE®

GUILFORD, CONNECTICUT
AN IMPRINT OF THE GLOBE PEQUOT PRESS

The prices and rates in this guidebook were confirmed at press time. We recommend, however, that you call establishments before traveling to obtain current information.

INSIDERS' GUIDE®

Text design by Sheryl Kober
Maps created by XNR Productions, Inc. © Morris Book Publishing, LLC

ISSN 1541-7921
ISBN 978-0-7627-4869-3

Printed in the United States of America
10 9 8 7 6 5 4 3 2 1

CONTENTS

Directory of Maps

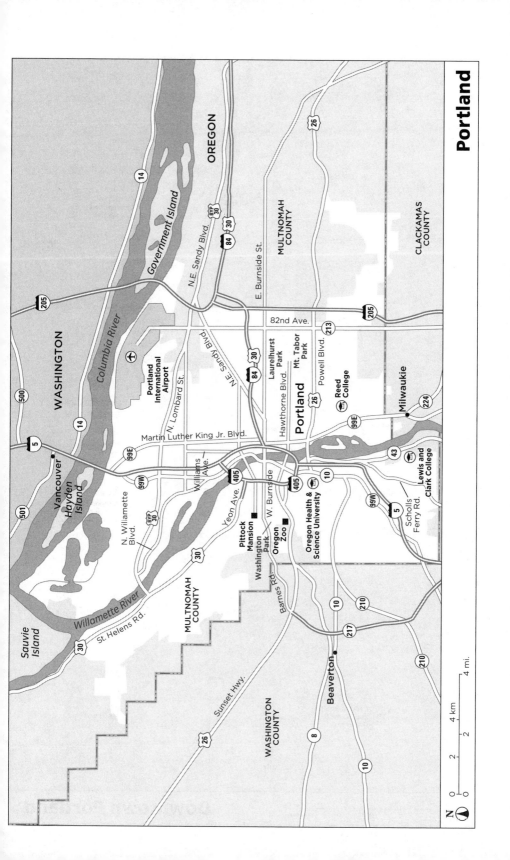

Portland

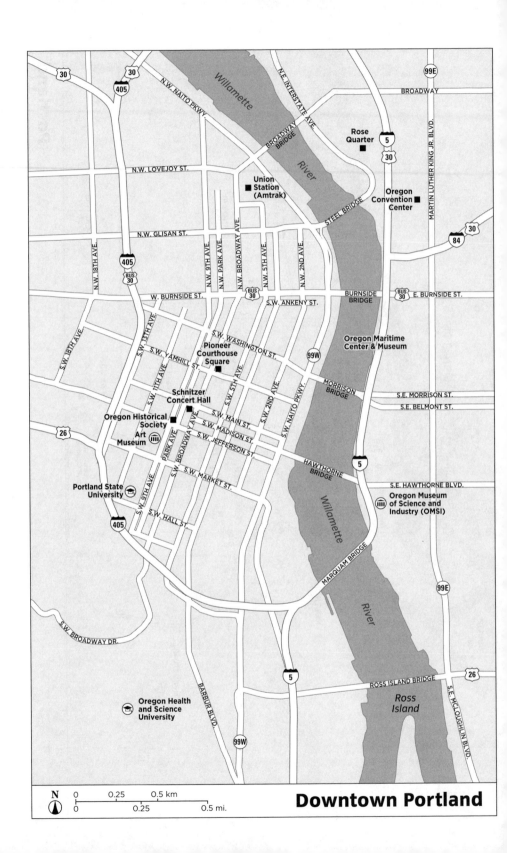

Downtown Portland

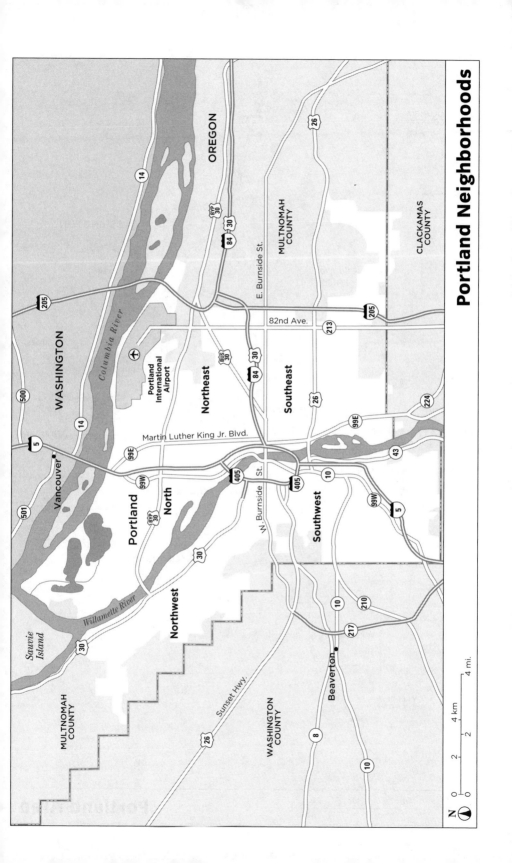

Portland Neighborhoods

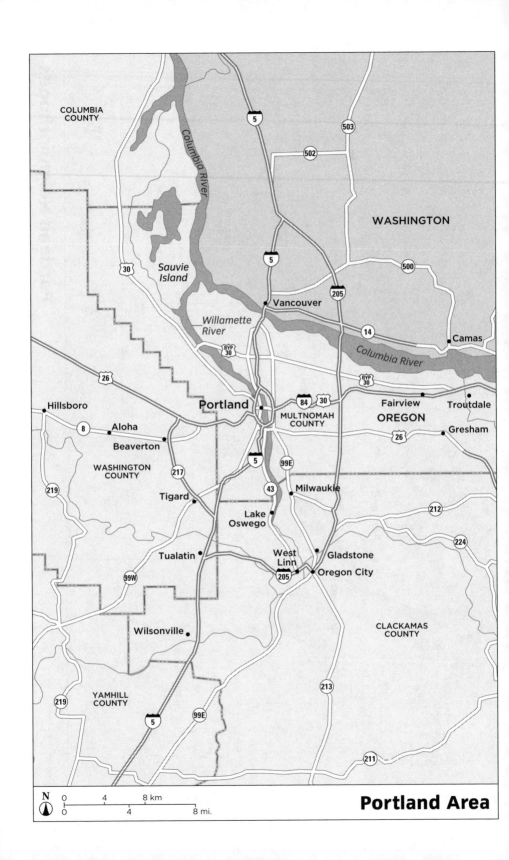

Portland Area

ACKNOWLEDGMENTS

Portland is a city of neighborhoods, so first I would like to thank my neighbors for their insight, witticisms, and generosity over the years. As always, the Banchero, Frost, Forrest, Bolles, and Colwell-Averett families have been especially generous with their time, knowledge, and hospitality. And while the Thomas family lives in a different neighborhood, nevertheless I thank them thoroughly for their wonderful photographs and for sharing their enthusiasms so liberally.

My brother Brian has been an invaluable resource, not only introducing me to this city so many years ago, but also helping me spy the flaws and virtues of this volume. I thank him deeply. Also due thanks are my ever-patient husband, Tom, and my daughters, Flannery and Cleo, who make writing anything a more interesting experience. I thank them for their editorial contributions, great writing, and strong opinions. This book is dedicated to them.

HELP US KEEP THIS GUIDE UP TO DATE

Every effort has been made by the author and editors to make this guide as accurate and useful as possible. However, many changes can occur after a guide is published—establishments close, phone numbers change, facilities come under new management, etc.

We would love to hear from you concerning your experiences with this guide and how you feel it could be improved and be kept up to date. While we may not be able to respond to all comments and suggestions, we'll take them to heart, and we'll make certain to share them with the author. Please send your comments and suggestions to the following address:

The Globe Pequot Press
Reader Response/Editorial Department
P.O. Box 480
Guilford, CT 06437

Or you may e-mail us at: editorial@GlobePequot.com

Thanks for your input, and happy travels!

HOW TO USE THIS BOOK

Compared with cities such as Los Angeles, San Francisco, or even Seattle, Portland is small. But we like it that way. Though Portland contributes its share to cyberspace, it is also concerned with human space. Portland is the home of groundbreaking biomedical research and world-class firms for animation, advertising, and athletic wear. Yet it is also renowned for its amiable, everyday civility, for its dedication to wise planning and public transportation, for its charming neighborhoods, for its bookstores, sidewalk cafes, and pubs. The parks contain more forest than any city in the nation. People ride their bikes or walk to work. The library serves coffee. Portland is a city where the fire department will still come to your block party.

Portland is an attractive city with a friendly skyline in a beautiful region of the country. Its setting, in a fertile valley ringed by mountains and bordered by the Columbia and Willamette Rivers, shapes the character of the city in ways that residents tend to take for granted. But the beautiful country surrounding us and within the city itself commands great loyalty—a loyalty that extends to the way we live and work. Many local businesses, for example, are consciously devoted to growing and creating products that draw from our regional abundance, and many others are devoted to using and promoting these products. We work hard to maintain our quality of life.

But we are also a playful city. Citizens prize their parks and libraries. Neighborhood coffee shops and brewpubs are busy long into the night. Workers may leave the downtown area at 5:00 p.m., but they are soon replaced by recreators attending the theater, the movies, the ballet, the symphony, or the opera, strolling the boulevards, stopping for dinner or a glass of wine. On the weekends, crowds gather at the Saturday Market, at the Farmers' Market, at the river. Or people head up to the mountains or to the coast. We know how to have a good time.

Sometimes we lose our way. But when that happens, Portland rises to the challenge. When our downtown area was dying in the 1970s, the community—the residents, businesses, government—came up with a plan to save it. When sprawl began to threaten farms and forests, we created an innovative regional government to coordinate growth, create places where people want to live, preserve green spaces, and organize public transportation. This feature of Portland life extends to the entire state. When beaches were under siege by acquisitive developers, Republican governor Tom McCall insisted that we keep the entire coastline open to the public, up to the high tide line, resulting in higher property values for owners and sublime beaches for everyone. We have our share of problems, but we do not feel helpless before them, and our efforts to solve them represent an enormous amount of creativity and goodwill on the part of our citizens to try to work things out.

As a result, we have a clean, safe, interesting city. We have a city where you can still send your kids to public schools. We have a city where you can sit on a downtown park bench in peace. We have a city where you can talk to the farmer who grew your vegetables and the brewer who made your beer. We have the largest independent bookstore in the nation and one of the most well-read populations. We have a city where you can escape to the forest on your lunch break. We have space to dream and plan and hope and the resources to make those dreams, plans, and hopes come true.

These are the reasons we love our city, and we think you will love it too. This appealing mixture of nature and culture, of sophistication and friendliness, draws people from all over the world to visit, and sometimes when they have visited, they want to stay. Who can blame them? The population gets bigger, but we retain the small-city values that define us. There's room for everyone.

The *Insiders' Guide to Portland* is designed to allow you to make the most of your time here, however long it is. Our guide is organized into thematic chapters that cover everything from accommodations to well-being. The internal organization of chapters will vary depending on their content. For example, the Festivals and Annual Events chapter is sorted chronologically, but the Recreation chapter is set up alphabetically by topic. Many chapters, such as Accommodations, Restaurants, or Attractions, may be additionally organized into geographic areas for easier navigation. Portland is divided into eastern and western halves by the Willamette River. It is further divided by Burnside Street, which runs east and west, into four quadrants: Southwest, Northwest, Southeast, and Northeast. A fifth "quadrant," North Portland, the portion west of Williams Avenue, extends from the Broadway Bridge to the Columbia River; however, for the purposes of this book, listings in North Portland and Northeast Portland have been kept together. Vancouver, which is immediately north of Portland just across the Columbia River in the state of Washington, is also mentioned frequently in our book, as are the towns that surround the city. Thus you will also find sections for Vancouver and for Outlying Areas, for a total of six basic geographical divisions.

The first chapters are designed to help you orient yourself to the Portland Metro area by giving you information about transportation and history. The next several chapters concern the exigencies of daily living—where to eat and sleep. Then we devote a large number of chapters to various forms of recreation; these range from telling you how to find a nearby brewpub, antiques shop, or climbing park to securing Blazers tickets. We also include a chapter on Day Trips, should you want to go exploring the innumerable attractions of the region beyond the city limits. And after exploring all that the region has to offer, many people who visit Portland find they would like to live here. The final chapters are devoted to the concerns of potential and actual relocaters, from finding a house and school to figuring out which newspapers to read. Within all chapters, you will find frequent cross-references and even, for the sake of convenience, some cross-listings.

> **i** The official state Web site is a rich and exhaustive resource for information on all things Oregon. Here you'll discover the market conditions for starting a business, profiles on communities, details on state historic sites, the locations of good cross-country ski trails, and anything else you might want to know about our beautiful state. You'll find it at www.oregon.gov.

Throughout this book you'll find Insider's Tips (indicated by an **i**), which offer quick insights, and Close-ups, which provide in-depth information on topics that are particularly interesting, unusual, or distinctly Portland.

A few basic maps are included in the guide, but you may also want to purchase a more detailed map of the city and surrounding areas in order to prevent those interesting discussions between driver and navigator about which way to turn.

The Greater Portland Metro area comprises Multnomah, Washington, and Clackamas Counties. You won't notice when you cross from one county into another, but you will need to know which county you are dealing with for the sake of real estate, schools, and government. Where necessary, then, we will point out these distinctions.

AREA CODES AND 10-DIGIT DIALING

Due to a proliferation of telephone numbers, Portland, like most metropolitan areas, has added area codes in recent years. The area codes that serve Portland are (503) and (971). These are also codes for

Salem and northern coastal towns. Area code (541) will give you access to southern, central, and eastern Oregon, including the central and southern coasts.

When you make a call in the Portland area, you will need to dial the area code first—all 10 digits. (It won't be a long-distance call unless you dial a "1" first, which would make 11 digits.) Area code (360) serves Vancouver; calls from Portland to Vancouver, however, are long-distance calls.

LOOKING AHEAD

Don't just take our word for it: Use this guide to explore for yourself the charms of Portland. Our dynamic city is always changing, adding new attractions and business, and closing others down. You may discover some of these changes in your own travels. Let us know about those that ought to be reported in future editions. If, in your journey to becoming an Insider, you find you have something to tell us, please write to us in care of The Globe Pequot Press, Reader Response/ Editorial Department, P.O. Box 480, Guilford, Connecticut 06437-0480, or visit us online at www.Insiders.com.

AREA OVERVIEW

The Portland Metropolitan area comprises Multnomah, Washington, and Clackamas Counties, as well as the southern edge of Clark County in Washington State across the Columbia River to the north. The area is home to nearly two million people, who live, work, and play in one of the most beautiful urban areas in the country—at least, that's what we think.

Portland sits just to the south of the confluence of the Willamette and Columbia Rivers; it is indeed a port city. It is situated approximately 70 miles from the Pacific Ocean and connects to the Pacific via the Columbia River. Its busy shipping schedule makes it the third-leading commercial maritime center on the West Coast. A significant portion of its freight is eastern Oregon grain, barged down the Columbia, loaded into huge grain elevators, and poured into freighters heading for Asia. On the receiving end, Portland is the third-largest West Coast port for ships bringing Japanese cars into the United States.

ECONOMIC DEVELOPMENT

Like many American cities, after the world wars Portland thrived during the 1950s, but by the late '60s the city was faced with serious economic problems. Due to environmental concerns and international competition, its economy, dependent on timber and Pacific fisheries, spiraled downward. The decline of these two major industries affected secondary service and retail businesses. But the city rose to the challenge: In 1973 the city council and planners came up with the Downtown Plan, a vision that reinvigorated local retail, housing, entertainment, and government. A westside freeway was torn down and redirected around town, and the Tom McCall Waterfront Park, named after a popular Oregon governor, was built along the edge of the Willamette River. Another major change that dynamically rearranged Portland was comprehensive transportation planning, including investing in light rail and reestablishing a streetcar line. And key to all has been a commitment to a lively downtown area, anchored by Pioneer Courthouse Square, a central open space for community events.

This commitment to infrastructure has been complemented by robust land-use planning.

An urban-growth boundary was designed as an outer edge for housing developments within the city limits of Portland and its neighboring towns. This strategy, combined with tax breaks and grants for low-income housing, encouraged contractors to "in-fill" within the growth boundary. This plan has worked well—though not without grumbling by some who complain that it's too strict and others who think it's not strict enough. On the whole, however, the urban growth boundary has allowed Portland to become a vibrant city filled with high-density vertical shops, apartments, and other mercantile and living spaces. The result: Portland regularly earns high praise as an exemplar of a city that is planned with the future in mind—a future that offers its residents alternatives to reliance on oil.

A major facet of the local economy is the high-tech sector. Beginning in the 1980s, microchip makers flocked to the area, attracted by cheap electricity generated by dams on the Columbia River, lots of clean water, and tax incentives offered by city and county governments. Sportswear is another important sector. Nike has its world headquarters here, and inspired by its rival, Adidas moved its American headquarters here as well. Columbia Sportswear is a locally

Portland Index

- The Portland Metropolitan area has more than two million people.

- The city of Portland covers 134 square miles.

- The average rainfall in Portland is 36 inches per year.

- Portland residents enjoy an average of 128,618 minutes of sunshine per year.

- Portland has nearly 13,000 acres of parks and open space—15 percent of its land area.

- The number of hens a Portland household may keep without a permit: 3. No roosters, please.

- The median age in the metro area is 37.

- The mean time for commuting to work is 24.5 minutes.

- The largest private employers in the Portland area are Intel (16,500), Providence Health System (13,500), Safeway (13,000), Oregon Health and Science University (11,500), Fred Meyer Stores (10,500), and Kaiser Foundation Health Plan (8,700).

- Portland-area residents drink more gourmet coffee and microbrewed beer than anyone in the nation.

- Portland is the home of Powell's City of Books, the largest independent bookstore in the world.

grown outfit, and Portland is also the home of Langlitz Leather, which supplies Harley gear for anyone willing to pay top dollar for the coveted handmade jackets.

Portland's strongest industry at present is health care, and the areas forecast to grow the most are the service and trade sectors, with slight dips in manufacturing. But that just describes the large employer sectors. Portland's entrepreneurial culture is thriving, and more than 8 percent of area workers are self-employed. It costs as little as $50 to incorporate a business.

THE CITY OF ROSES

But there is more to living in a city than making a living. Portland is known as the "City of Roses," and it possesses the ideal climate in which to grow these lovely flowers. Each June, they are celebrated with a party called the Rose Festival, an event that includes three parades, a carnival, the crowning of a queen, and a visit from a dozen ships from the U.S. Navy, U.S. Coast Guard, and the Canadian Navy and Coast Guard.

Part of what makes those roses grow, of course, is rain. While Portland has 82 days per year when the sky is blue and the sun is shining, it also has, on the average, 82 partly cloudy days and 220 cloudy days per year, with 165 of those coming with at least some precipitation.

Another element that defines the essence of Portland is the 40-mile Willamette River Greenway, a network of pedestrian and bike trails on both sides of the Willamette that will eventually stretch into a 140-mile-long system connecting 30 parks. Currently it is a paved trail that can take you from Oaks Park in Southeast Portland north along the Willamette to the Steel Bridge. From there you can cross the river to Northwest Portland and follow it south through Tom McCall Park to Willamette Park off Macadam Avenue.

Then there are the wonders of nature surrounding the city: the Columbia Gorge; Mount Hood, one of the crown jewels of the Oregon Cascades; and the North Coast, with beaches, jutting capes, and art colonies. (Read more about these in our Day Trips chapter.) And Seattle is just a few miles farther, 173 miles to the north.

Portland's friendly skyline invites reverie. RACHEL DRESBECK

Few things define Portland as much as its neighborhoods, however, and so to these we now turn.

SOUTHWEST PORTLAND

Southwest Portland encompasses the downtown area, stretching west beyond Washington Park and south along the Willamette River. The result is an urban village cradled by a friendly wilderness. The downtown area is composed of short blocks, platted in the 19th century to contain lots of little stores and cross streets, thus limiting the size and height of new construction.

Built on the hills above downtown are affluent neighborhoods with lovely houses lining hillside streets. Down on the plains of the Willamette River, the area has undergone vibrant renewal as new condominiums and businesses are built along the river.

A good place to start a tour of the Southwest is Pioneer Courthouse Square (http://www .pioneercourthousesquare.org/), which is bordered by Yamhill Street, Morrison Street, 6th Avenue, and Broadway. This is the piazza that anchors the city, full of tourists, office workers eating lunch, families with children, and all the characters that city plazas attract. It is also noted for its waterfall fountain, its imaginative sculpture, and an echo chamber—if you face the steps of the small amphitheater while standing on the round marble stone, you can create a cascade of sound by just saying hello.

Depending on the time of year, Pioneer Courthouse Square is also the site of sand-castle contests, cultural festivals, flower gardens, and a huge Christmas tree. The Tri-Met bus information and tickets office is found here, as is Travel Portland, the official visitor center run by the Portland Visitors Association (POVA), with info and tickets to special events (www.travelportland.com/). The center features, in addition to a superabundance of information, a small theater that shows short films about Portland.

Enjoy a visit to Tom McCall Waterfront Park. Along this west-side esplanade are the Salmon Springs Fountain, children's play areas, a monument to the battleship *Oregon*, and a sculpture garden dedicated to the World War II relocation trauma of Oregon's Japanese-American community (see Portland's Parks). You can also get a riverside view of the city's 10 bridges.

If you show up on the weekend, you can peruse hundreds of craft and food booths at another neighborhood attraction: the Saturday Market, 108 West Burnside Street. On the western side of the downtown district, Southwest Broadway is our version of the "Great White Way," with cinemas and performing arts centers. Among these is the Oregon History Center, filled with ongoing exhibits and new shows that combine to tell the story of the state. Across the South Park Blocks is the Portland Art Museum, with European paintings, an exciting Native American art wing, and blockbuster touring exhibits. The Park Blocks are also the home of Portland's cutting-edge farmers' market, from April through November.

Southwest Portland is also the location of PGE Park, home to baseball and soccer teams. Other highlights of Southwest Portland are Washington Park, nestled on the east side of the long ridge called Forest Park, the International Rose Test Garden, the Japanese Garden, and the Washington Park Zoo.

The newest neighborhood in Southwest Portland is the South Waterfront area, a district rising atop old shipbuilding yards along the banks of the Willamette. This neighborhood features sleek high-rises built alongside a verdant greenway. It is the home of one of the campuses of Oregon Health and Science University and the lower landing dock of the Portland Aerial Tram (see the Getting Here, Getting Around chapter for more information on this unique transportation alternative).

NORTHWEST PORTLAND

Northwest Portland is characterized by its creative energy, both in its industrially chic Pearl District and in its beautiful Victorian district, Nob Hill. Northwest Portland is also the home of Old Town on the north side of Burnside Street and Chinatown and the Skidmore District. Chinatown, with its entrance at 4th Avenue and Burnside Street, is an Asian-American neighborhood with grocery stores, restaurants, and art galleries. This small neighborhood was once home to the West Coast's largest population of Chinese Americans, immigrants who mined for gold here and built the railroad. The Portland Classical Chinese Garden, a standout in the district, is one of the few authentic classical-style Chinese gardens in the United States.

Nearby is the Skidmore Historic District, north of West Burnside Street and between Front and 4th Avenues. Once the hangout of unemployed loggers and sailors, this riverside cluster of streets

i Portland has a number of colorful nicknames: the City of Roses, Puddletown, and Bridgetown, as well as PDX, our airport code. And we are still known as Stumptown, from the hundreds of fir stumps left in the streets by hasty 19th-century builders. Hinting at our future commitment to good public transportation, early city officials painted them white to warn wagoneers out after dark.

led to the term "Skid Row," borrowed from "Skid Road," a muddy path of logs leading down from the forests to the river. You may still see folks down on their luck lining up for a Salvation Army lunch here. But this sad reality aside, Skidmore is worth a visit for its charming old buildings and its colorful history.

Northwest Portland is the site of Powell's Books, one of the largest bookstores in the world. Powell's marks the outer edge of the Pearl District, a reclaimed industrial area that is now home to art galleries, luxury condos, upscale shops, art schools, and fine restaurants. Across from Powell's is the historic Blitz-Weinhard Brewery, which is now part of the Brewery Blocks development and home to swanky shops and condominiums. First-Thursday gallery walks turn the neighborhood into one big open house.

The Pearl also hosts the Weiden & Kennedy Advertising Agency (they do ads for Nike and Coca-Cola) and Laika, the animation studio that produced *Coraline* and *Corpse Bride,* among other things. Other film, video, mixed-media companies, and recording studios inhabit this neighborhood as well. The streetcar system links the Pearl to the rest of Northwest Portland, including the excellent shopping districts along Northwest 21st and 23rd Avenues, before it heads back downtown.

Along 21st and 23rd Avenues, you'll find boutiques, antiques shops, and bookstores in renovated Victorian houses. The street life along both avenues is bustling and vibrant, and it's a city favorite for window-shopping and people-watching. The district is also home to some of the city's best restaurants. After exploring the neighborhood at ground level, it's fun to head up to the Pittock Mansion and its 46-acre site, 3229 Northwest Pittock Drive, to capture the bird's-eye view.

SOUTHEAST PORTLAND

Southeast Portland is a sprawling district characterized by parks, funky residential neighborhoods, alternative-lifestyle shops, Reed College, a riverfront industrial area, and an emerging indie business scene. Lower Burnside is the epicenter of new urban energy and its attendant development. The Hawthorne, Belmont, Division, and Clinton Districts are filled with single-family homes and apartment buildings mixed with shops, music stores and bookstores, coffeehouses, microbrew pubs, and restaurants geared to every palate. It's a delightful area for shopping and browsing. Hawthorne Boulevard from 30th to 50th Avenues has been characterized as both the Haight-Ashbury and the Greenwich Village of Portland, but it's too locally inspired for those names to be accurate. Here you will find homegrown books, clothes, music, coffee, and beer—it couldn't be anywhere but Portland.

Further south, Sellwood, a historic district annexed to Portland in 1893, features Antique Row, more than 50 antiques stores tucked into the neighborhood of Victorian homes and turn-of-the-20th-century architecture (see Shopping). Sellwood is south of the Oaks Bottom Wildlife Sanctuary (see our Recreation chapter), a refuge for herons, beavers, ducks, and other marsh animals and birds. Here, the neighborhood floats in houseboats along the river's edge. Westmoreland, north of Sellwood, has its share of fine restaurants and unique shops, as well one of the city's most beautiful parks—a haven for picnickers, joggers, basketball players, and duck feeders. Across McLoughlin Avenue, Eastmoreland's residential neighborhood is tranquil, bordered by the public Eastmoreland Golf Course, the brick campus of Reed College, and Crystal Springs Rhododendron Garden, a riot of color each spring, with seven acres of rhododendrons, azaleas, and hybrids. At the gateway to inner Southeast is the tranquil, historic neighborhood of Brooklyn. Once home to East Coast immigrants working at the nearby rail yard, it is now a pleasant sanctuary, away from chain stores and suburban blight.

NORTH/NORTHEAST PORTLAND

Northeast Portland and its neighbor North Portland are home to the same blend of industry, commerce, culture, and houses that characterize the rest of the city. Beautiful older houses line tree-shaded streets in neighborhoods such as Laurelhurst, Irvington, and Alameda. Attractive shopping areas draw people from around the region. The popular Lloyd Center is the largest single shopping destination in the area (see Shopping). By light rail, Lloyd Center is just minutes from downtown. Around Lloyd Center, the Northeast Broadway Business District is blossoming, and just to the east, the delightful Hollywood District offers a blend of charming houses and retail businesses.

Portland's Convention Center lies between the Lloyd District and the river, its 150-foot-high twin spires stamping their distinctive profile on the city's skyline. The center's walls, lamps, and tiles display handsome detail, and plaques in the lobby carry insightful quotes about Oregon. A Chinese dragon boat is suspended at the base of the center's south spire, while a dramatic bronze pendulum sways below the north spire. Large murals by Lucinda Parker and Bill Hoppe celebrate Oregon's natural bounty, and outside, temple bells from Portland's sister cities Sapporo, Japan, and Ulsan, South Korea, offer friendly greetings to visitors. The MAX line stops outside the center's north entrance and also serves the adjacent Rose Quarter, a 43-acre complex, featuring the Memorial Coliseum arena, the Rose Garden arena, One Center Court entertainment complex, and four parking garages. The Rose Quarter hosts a variety of sports events, including those of the Portland Trailblazers, college basketball, and indoor-soccer teams (for more on these, see Recreation and Spectator Sports). The arenas are also booked with rodeos, circuses, concerts, ice shows, and other spectacles, and they are linked to the nearby Convention Center to accommodate the numerous trade shows and conventions that Portland hosts. Other neighborhoods farther north, such as Alberta, Mississippi, St. Johns, and Kenton, offer their own charms and have been swept along with the tide of urban redevelopment to find new identities. These areas, rich in history and blessed with many well-maintained parks and green spaces, hold some of the city's best-kept secrets.

i Portland's Washington Park station is the home of the deepest light-rail stop in the nation, at 260 feet below Earth's surface. En route to the elevators that take you to the zoo, stop to look at the core rock samples and read about the geology of the West Hills.

VANCOUVER

Vancouver is one of Washington's fastest growing communities, with a population of more than 160,000. This scenic Northwest city, named after British explorer George Vancouver, has 55 parks and playgrounds inside city limits, including the Burnt Bridge Creek Greenway and the Discovery Trail.

But it's the history of this settlement that really puts it on the map. Once the Northwestern headquarters for the Hudson's Bay Company and the oldest settlement in the region, Fort Vancouver—now just Vancouver—was the center of all fur trading in the West. After the United States claimed the Pacific Northwest, the fort at Vancouver became a barracks for U.S. soldiers, including Generals Ulysses Grant, Philip Sheridan, and George Marshall. The Vancouver National Historic Reserve is a partnership that manages of historic sites at Fort Vancouver, Columbia Park, and Pearson Field, one of the oldest operating airfields in the nation.

Vancouver is also known for its celebration on the Fourth of July, when it stages the largest fireworks show west of the Mississippi. Admittedly in the cultural and economic shadow of the big town across the river, Vancouver is reinventing itself as a modern metropolis proud of its vivid heritage.

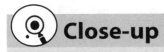

Close-up

How to Talk like a Native

While Oregonians, especially natives, don't have any revealing regional accent, we do have a vernacular. To aid you in communicating effectively here in Portland, we offer the following list of local phrases and pronunciations.

The Banfield: Interstate 84, which runs east from Portland to eastern Oregon and beyond. A major commute route.

City of Roses: A popular nickname for the city of Portland.

The Coast: The beaches along the Pacific Ocean anywhere between Astoria, Oregon, and the California border.

Couch Street: Pronounced "Kooch."

Fareless Square: The area of downtown, including the transit mall and the Lloyd Center on the east side, where rides on buses and light-rail vehicles are free (hence, fare-less).

Freddy's: Any Fred Meyer store.

Glisan Street: Pronounced "Glee-son."

MAX: More formally the Metropolitan Area Express, this is the light-rail system operated by Tri-Met. The system runs from Hillsboro to Gresham, to the airport, and to North Portland. Do not get caught riding MAX (outside Fareless Square) without a ticket or valid transfer.

The Mountain: Mount Hood. If you are looking directly at Mount Hood, you are facing east.

OHSU: Oregon Health and Science University.

OMSI: Oregon Museum of Science and Industry. Pronounced "AHM-zi."

Oregon: Correctly pronounced "OR-uh-gun," never "OR-uh-gone."

PDX: The baggage handlers' and airport code for Portland International Airport. Frequently used as shorthand for Portland.

PICA: Portland Institute of Contemporary Art.

Pill Hill: The complex of hospitals and medical facilities, including the U.S. Veterans Administration Hospital and the hospitals and clinics of Oregon Health and Science University.

Sauvie Island: To sound like a native, call it "So-vee's" Island.

The Schnitz: The Arlene Schnitzer Concert Hall, named after the grande dame of one of Portland's most prominent families.

The Sunset Highway: U.S. Highway 26, which runs west from Portland to the Oregon coast. Another major commute route and perpetual construction zone.

Willamette: The Willamette River. This river divides Portland into east and west neighborhoods before flowing into the Columbia at Kelley Point. Residents on each side have strongly held opinions about the other's attitudes, political perspectives, lifestyles, and personalities. The correct pronunciation is "wil-LAM-et," not "WILL-a-met."

OUTLYING AREAS

You will also find charming towns throughout the greater Portland area, including Beaverton, Lake Oswego, West Linn, Tigard, Tualatin, and Hillsboro on the west side, and Troutdale, Fairview, Gresham, Milwaukie, and Oregon City on the east side. These prodigiously growing communities tend to have more new houses and strip malls than Portland proper, but their rural roots are evident if you know where to look. These towns are technically considered suburbs, but they also have their own distinctive economic centers and personalities.

Hillsboro, for example, is the home of Nike, as well as a regional shopping area for the agricultural workers who live and work west of the city.

Beaverton, too, is not simply a suburb of Portland, despite its location 7 miles southwest of downtown. Its economy is healthy, and the town is a favorite among families because of its strong school system and newer houses. (Though some feel it is straining at the seams; its population now stands at more than 84,000, up from less than 70,000 just a few years ago.) Good golf courses, bike paths, shopping malls, and easy access to TriMet make it an attractive choice for many.

And Gresham, east of Portland heading toward the foothills of Mount Hood, is now the fourth-largest city in Oregon, with nearly 100,000 residents. Gresham is the home of Mt. Hood Community College and is known for its excellent jazz festival (see the Festivals and Annual Events chapter). It is the eastern outpost of the MAX light-rail line. Here, too, you will find new malls and housing developments for young families.

These areas and others are profiled in greater detail in the Relocation chapter.

PORTLAND'S BRIDGES

Portland is a city of bridges: More than 10 span the Willamette River, from the St. Johns Bridge at the north end to the Sellwood Bridge at the south. Because Portland is a deepwater port, the five bridges in the heart of downtown are drawbridges, letting large ships pass through. Each bridge has singular characteristics. The Hawthorne Bridge, for example, is the oldest operating vertical-lift bridge in the nation, while the Steel Bridge is a rare example of a bridge with twin decks capable of independent movement. Besides being useful, Portland's bridges are beautiful: They add charm to the cityscape, especially when viewed from the Eastbank Esplanade. For bridge fanatics, the Oregon Department of Transportation (ODOT) maintains a meticulous Web

site that features the engineering and historical details of our bridges: www.oregon.gov/odot/hwy/geoenvironmental/historic_bridges_Portland1.shtml. And for the rest of us, here are Portland's bridges, from north to south.

St. Johns Bridge (1931): The St. Johns Bridge is a beautiful, distinctive suspension bridge with 400-foot towers and Gothic arches. It links outer Northwest Portland with the North Portland community of St. Johns.

Fremont Bridge (1973): The Fremont Bridge is the newest bridge, but its beautiful arches have shaped the cityscape as profoundly as the older bridges on the Willamette. It's the longest bridge in Oregon and, at 902 feet, is the longest tied-arch bridge in the entire world. It carries traffic from Interstate 405 and U.S. Highway 30 to Interstate 5.

Broadway Bridge (1913): This drawbridge extends Broadway across the river from Northeast Portland to downtown, and it bears the distinction of being the largest rail bridge in the world—that means that its counterweights roll back and forth on bull wheels above the deck. But many Portlanders think of it as simply the "red bridge."

Steel Bridge (1912): Upon completion the Steel Bridge was immediately hailed as an exemplar of imaginative engineering. It is one of the only known dual-lift bridges in the world: The lower deck, accommodating Amtrak and freight trains, lifts independently from the upper deck, which carries light rail, trucks, and cars. The Steel Bridge River Walk allows bikes and pedestrians to cross the churning Willamette River just 30 feet below.

Burnside Bridge (1926): This bridge was designed by Joseph B. Straus, who also designed the Golden Gate Bridge. It is a drawbridge that provides good city views as well as subtle aesthetic details, such as the turrets on the operator's house.

Morrison Bridge (1887, 1905, 1958): When first built in 1887 by the Willamette Iron Bridge Co., the Morrison Bridge was the largest span west of the Mississippi. It was rebuilt in 1905 and again in 1958 as a drawbridge. The Morrison Bridge is between the Hawthorne and Burnside Bridges, and it provides entrances to and exits from I–5.

Leaving I–5 southbound at the City Center exit, which takes you to the Morrison Bridge, provides one of the loveliest views of downtown Portland, especially at night when the river, bridge, and city are illuminated.

Hawthorne Bridge (1910): The Hawthorne Bridge is the oldest bridge across the Willamette in Portland. It was finished in 1910 and remodeled in 1998–99; it now includes beautifully wide sidewalks and bike paths, making it a favorite for pedestrians and cyclists. The Hawthorne Bridge, lovely as it is, demands more patience than some bridges in town because it has a low clearance—53 feet at low water. In the spring, when the water is high, the Hawthorne Bridge raises even for small river traffic such as tourist steamer ships—and, joke residents, kayaks and canoes. Just so you know, on the east side of the river, the Hawthorne Bridge leads to Hawthorne Boulevard, but on the west side, Hawthorne turns into Main and Madison Streets.

Marquam Bridge (1966): A freeway bridge built in the 1960s to accommodate the city's increased traffic, the multilane, double-deck Marquam Bridge provides a panoramic view of the Willamette River, Tom McCall Waterfront Park, and downtown Portland that is unrivaled, but the bridge itself is no beauty. Connecting I–5 to Interstate 84 East on the east side and I–405 North on the west side, with major traffic arteries merging and dividing at both ends of it, it carries large volumes of busy traffic. But this traffic is often slowed by the balletic movements of entering, merging, and exiting drivers.

Ross Island Bridge (1926): The Ross Island Bridge sits high above the river. The bridge has pretty balustrades and an expansive view, but its aesthetic appeal is diminished by a high volume of speeding traffic. The Ross Island Bridge carries U.S. Highway 26 over the Willamette, connecting to Arthur Street on the west side and to Powell Boulevard on the east. Besides the volume of traffic, its other drawback is that the westside approach, which connects to Barbur Boulevard, Highway 43, and Arthur Street, is confusing and awkward.

Sellwood Bridge (1925): The Sellwood Bridge allows just two lanes of traffic to flow from Highway 43 on the west side to the Portland neighborhood of Sellwood on the east side. It is the busiest two-lane bridge in Oregon; because it is so high, the views (for passengers, anyway) are impressive. A good portion of the Sellwood Bridge is more than 100 years old; it includes sections of the original Burnside Bridge, torn down in 1925.

LAST IMPRESSIONS

Well, that's a sampler of the history, current sights, sounds, feel, and flavor of Stumptown, Puddletown, PDX, and the City of Roses—an overlay of four cities, a grid of four quadrants. Here, to polish off our profile, are a few more images:

At the hectic corner of Sandy Boulevard and 12th Avenue, the fresh smell of baked bread from Franz Bakery floats above the rush of traffic. It's Thursday morning, so garbage trucks creeping along side streets and tree-lined avenues, slow down for yellow bins filled with cans, bottles, and newspapers. We are serious about recycling here—the first place in the country to have a bottle bill. Just east of the Ross Island Bridge above a steady stream of traffic on Powell Boulevard, a bicyclist sheathed in Lycra stops on the bike bridge to gaze at sunrise-tinted glacial Wy'East in the native tongue, or Mount Hood as christened by Lewis and Clark. Out on the Willamette near the RiverPlace docks, a skiff with a multicolored Popsicle sail cruises by a dragonboat with an earnest crew practicing for races held during the Rose Festival. Farther downriver in a nest high in the girders of the Fremont Bridge, a peregrine falcon tends to her chicks, and far south on Ross Island, a pair of bald eagles soar above the sand and gravel quarry.

These raptors hang around here because it's a good place to live. We agree. We have some of the purest drinking water in the world, trickling down from Bull Run Reservoir high in the Cascade Mountains east of town. We are vigilantly keeping an eye on the purity of that water and the quality of our lifestyles all the while leaving as gentle a collective footprint as we can on the land beneath us. It is, as some would say, very Portland.

GETTING HERE, GETTING AROUND

Bordered by mountains, flanked by rivers, surrounded by fertile farmland, the Portland Metro area is well known for its beautiful setting. But don't let those high mountains fool you: Portland accommodates many modes of transportation and allows easy travel once you arrive. The territory is well served by trains, planes, and buses, and its public transportation system is comprehensive.

Portland International Airport, or PDX, is the regional airport for all of Oregon and much of southwestern Washington. From here, in addition to its national and international service, commercial air service provides flights to Eugene, Salem, and Medford. Feeder and regional airlines also serve Pendleton and Klamath Falls in eastern and southern Oregon, in addition to providing flights to Newport and North Bend on the Oregon coast. Flights to the airport in Redmond, Oregon, will take you to the popular resorts and natural attractions of Bend and the rest of central Oregon.

Portland's Amtrak station operates trains to and from Seattle, Los Angeles, and Chicago, as well as nearby towns such as Corvallis and Eugene. Greyhound buses provide ground transportation in all directions, and buses run regularly to and from Seattle, Tacoma, and Olympia; Boise; Denver; Salt Lake City; and major cities in California.

Two interstate highways intersect Portland. Interstate 84 runs east and west through the Columbia Gorge from Portland to Idaho and beyond, and Interstate 5 runs through Portland on its way from Canada to Mexico. Often you'll hear references to the I–5 Corridor, the stretch of I–5 that runs from Portland to Eugene.

From I–5, routes travel west across the Coastal Range to the Pacific Ocean and U.S. Highway 101 and east through several mountain passes, across the Cascade Mountains to central and eastern Oregon. During the winter some of the passes through the Cascades are closed. Those that remain open year-round may be subject to periodic closures due to weather. Traction devices (chains and studded tires) are often required for winter travel through the Cascades (and at times, through the Coastal Range). The Oregon State Police strictly enforce laws requiring motorists to carry traction devices.

NAVIGATING THE AREA

This is the Great American West, so travel distances are greater than in other parts of the country; for instance, Seattle, the closest large city, is three to four hours' drive north. But one of the most prized features of the Portland Metro area is its proximity to so many beautiful areas of recreation, nature, and culture. Year-round skiing at Timberline on Mount Hood is a 90-minute drive from the city center. A loop around Mount Hood to Hood River and then back down the Columbia Gorge is a pleasant way to spend the day, as is a trip to the Johnson Ridge Observatory at Mount St. Helens. The spectacular Oregon coast is less than two hours from Portland, and the heart of Oregon's wine country is no more than 45 minutes from downtown. (See Day Trips for more information on these outings.)

You will find that Portland is not difficult to navigate once you understand its idiosyncrasies. As we described in How to Use This Book, the city is divided into east and west by the Willamette River and north and south by Burnside Street. These serve as your orientation marks, and addresses and street numbers are organized around them. If you're on Southwest 5th Avenue downtown, you'll know that you're 5 blocks west of the Willamette River. Similarly, Burnside Street is the starting point for street addresses, and these rise in number the farther north or south that you travel from Burnside. So if your Southwest 5th Avenue address happens to be 423, you'll know that you're about 4 blocks south of Burnside.

GETTING HERE

By Air

PORTLAND INTERNATIONAL AIRPORT
7000 Northeast Airport Way
(503) 460-4234, (877) 739-4636
TDD (800) 815-4636
www.flypdx.com

Portland International Airport—which we call PDX (its aeronautical code)—is notably clean, light, and pleasant, with many comforts to serve the weary traveler. At times it feels more like an upscale shopping mall than an airport, and indeed, it has won top honors for its shopping and concessions from airport retailers across the nation—as well as accolades from the travelers who actually use them. *Conde Nast Traveller* has called PDX America's best airport for business travelers more than once—its easy access to downtown and its free wireless service being among the top reasons.

PDX is also safe. As elsewhere in the United States, travelers and their bags are now subjected to vigorous security checks, yet security lines and baggage screening are efficiently managed. There has not been a major civil airline crash at the airport since 1978, when a United Airlines DC-8 ran out of fuel and landed about a mile short of the runway. The airport's crews are experienced in responding to the Oregon winters, and the airport is rarely closed. But bad weather in other parts of the country, especially in Denver, Chicago, Los Angeles, and San Francisco, can cause delays in flights heading for Portland. At certain times of the year, particularly in the fall, early morning fog can wreak havoc with departure times at PDX, and some regional flights are affected by local weather at their intended destinations.

Arriving in Portland

Once you've arrived at PDX, you'll find a cadre of helpers to provide directions; they can point you to your connecting flight gate, the correct baggage carousel, or any other location within the airport complex. Airport service workers offer transportation to and from the passenger gates in electric carts. They can also point out the specially designated "meet and greet" areas: Unticketed persons are forbidden to go past security checkpoints, so if someone is meeting you, you will find them there.

Adults have their share of amusements too. Free wireless Internet access is available throughout most of the main terminal level of the airport. Besides the customary amenities—telephones, express package drop-offs, workstations with computer ports, fax machines, stamp machines, and ATMs—you can shop at some of the area's best stores. In the main terminal's Oregon Market, look for reading material at Powell's Books, sportswear at Norm Thompson's, woolen goods at Pendleton, athletic footwear and apparel at Nike, and souvenirs from our state at Made in Oregon. The restaurants at PDX tend to feature Pacific Northwest products and are nearly all locally owned. Thus the food options are quite decent (and fairly priced), and you'll be able to sample local and regional craft beers, delicious pastries, and other treats throughout the airport. Even better, shopping, food, restrooms, telephones, and other services are available on both sides of the security check, especially along Concourse C. Shops and restaurants are generally open from 6:00 a.m. to 9:00 p.m. daily. Coffee and espresso from Starbucks and Portland's Coffee People can be found throughout the airport—including a wee Starbucks bar by the escalators next to the baggage claim area.

Ground Transportation and Rental Cars

Transportation from the airport is available by light rail, taxi, and other ride services. You can, of course, also rent cars. Car rental agencies are on the terminal grounds, though several of them have only kiosks there.

Light Rail: The Red Line

Portland's light-rail system, MAX, is a convenient way to get downtown from the airport. The Red Line serves downtown and PDX: It takes about 40 minutes and costs $2.05, one-way. Trains are just outside the baggage claim area, and they are well marked with prominent signs. To take the Red Line into town, purchase your ticket prior to boarding the train at one of the vending machines inside the terminal, near the doors leading to the trains or outside near the track. You'll need to buy an all-zone ticket. The vending machines will accept $1 bills, change, and—for several tickets—credit cards. (You can buy tickets ahead of time online, if you are well organized; see http://trimet.org/store/index.htm.) Once you've bought your ticket, be sure to validate it in the machine prior to boarding, and hang onto this ticket for your entire ride—it acts as proof of payment. Cheerful TriMet transit authority employees are usually standing by to help you figure out tickets, destinations, and other problems. Trains to downtown leave about every 15 minutes at peak times and slightly less often at other times. See the TriMet entry later in this chapter for more information on the MAX line.

For other means of transport, you will find the Ground Transportation Center across the first roadway on the lower level of the airport, just across from the baggage claim area; that is, it is just east of the main terminal, in the direction of the parking garage. Posted signs will tell you whether you are in the right section for your chosen mode of transport; you can also ask the airport service personnel who are always in attendance to direct you.

Taxi service from the airport is permitted only by those companies licensed by the city of Portland. These companies are Broadway Cab (503) 227-1234, Green Cab (503) 252-4422, New Rose City Cab (503) 282-7707, Portland Taxi (503) 256-5400, and Radio Cab (503) 227-1212. Taxis to downtown Portland should cost $25 to $30; the trip downtown takes from 20 to 40 minutes. In addition, a number of hotels provide their own free shuttle services: DoubleTree Hotels offer shuttles every 30 minutes, and the Holiday Inn, every hour. Other hotels may also offer this service, and you can find out which ones by checking the Reservation Board in the baggage claim area. Some of these courtesy shuttles run regularly at scheduled times, while others must be summoned.

You will also find a number of other shuttle and towncar services in the Ground Transportation Center. The prices for these will vary depending on the number of passengers, the distance you will travel, and the luxuriousness of the vehicle. Shuttles and towncar services, unlike taxi service, are unregulated, so be sure to clarify the price before you begin your journey. Prices vary widely and depend on where you are

ℹ The best bargain for transportation from PDX is the light-rail MAX line—just $2.30 for a ride into town. If you're traveling with children, PDX offers several play areas to help distract them—these areas allow enough amusement to sustain children while waiting for their upcoming flights or to help release any leftover energy from having to sit still on the last one. (We sometimes visit this attraction on a rainy afternoon even when we have no other business at the airport.) If your flight arrives at a gate that attaches to Concourse C, you will find a good toy store, Creative KidStuff; and children can also occupy themselves with the sculptural "map" of Oregon's rivers embedded in the floor as well as with other diverting works of art.

going. Starting airport rates typically run from $15 to $35. Companies known to be reliable include Blue Star (503) 249-1837, Eagle Towncar (503) 222-2763, Pacific Executive (503) 234-2400, Willamette Express Shuttle (503) 280-9883, and Green Shuttle (503) 252-4422. PDX maintains a comprehensive Web site with links to all shuttle and towncar services to Portland and beyond, so ground transportation should be pain-free to find and easily arranged online or by phone.

Rental Cars

For car rentals at the airport, go to the parking garage's first floor. The agencies with offices in the garage include Avis Rent-A-Car (503) 249-4950, Budget Rent-A-Car (503) 249-4556, Dollar Rent-A-Car (503) 249-4793, Hertz Rent-A-Car (503) 249-8216, and Enterprise (503) 252-1500. Some car rental agencies have kiosks just outside the car rental center in the parking garage; these include Alamo/National (503) 249-4900. For more information see the section on renting a car, below.

Once you've left the airport, it should take 20 to 30 minutes to reach downtown, and there are clear directions to the freeways from the airport access roads. Airport traffic is funneled onto Interstate 205. To reach downtown, you will take I–205 South to the I–84 West exit. Follow I–84 to I–5, where you should follow the signs to City Center.

By Train

AMTRAK AT UNION STATION
800 Northwest 6th Avenue
(503) 273-4865 (station information)
(503) 273-4866 (daily arrival and
departure information)
(800) 872-7245 (reservations and
schedule information)
www.amtrakcascades.com
One of Portland's most charming postcard views is Union Station, with its brick clock tower that actually keeps good time. Our town's classic train depot, built in the 1890s, is one of the oldest

operating train terminals in the United States. Its appeal is evident in its high ceilings and marble floor, and its historic photographs add to the adventure of traveling by rail. This relic of the days before air travel also serves as what transportation planners call a "multimodal transportation center." This means you can, with relative ease, arrive in Portland by train or intercity bus and have immediate access to local bus and cab service (see Attractions for more information on this Portland landmark). In fact, because Union Station is part of the downtown Portland transit mall and falls within the Fareless Square boundaries, you can take a bus from the train station to downtown Portland for free.

Portland's Union Station is an important stop on several major rail routes. The Empire Builder, a passenger train that originates in Chicago, stops here, as does another classic train, the Coast Starlight, which runs daily from Los Angeles and to Seattle. Amtrak's Cascade route features the state-of-the-art, Spanish-built, high-speed Talgo, an ultramodern "tilt" train that runs from Eugene to Vancouver, British Columbia. If you're a train fan, consider a day trip north to Seattle or Olympia on the Talgo. If you tire of the scenery, you can plug in your laptop and settle in with one of the microbrews served on board.

By Interstate Bus

GREYHOUND LINES
550 Northwest 6th Avenue
(503) 243-2361, (800) 231-2222

613 Main Street
Vancouver, WA
(360) 696-0186
www.greyhound.com
Portland's Greyhound Lines bus station is a remarkably clean and modern terminal on the far northern end of the city's transit mall adjacent to Amtrak's Union Station, both of which are a short walk from downtown. The station has plenty of seating, a concession wall, and a small, pleasant cafe. Greyhound is the only transcontinental bus line serving Portland and Vancouver. The Greyhound terminal

is included in the public transportation system's Fareless Square, so once you've arrived, it is easy to connect with city buses.

By Car

As the Portland Metro region has grown, so has the amount of traffic and congestion. During rush hours, 7:00 to 9:00 a.m. and again from 3:30 to 6:00 p.m., car and bus traffic pours into downtown from all directions. Those going to high-tech jobs in Washington County have a reverse commute, but their numbers create rush-hour traffic in both directions on freeways, the region's main arterials, downtown streets, and often on secondary streets.

You will want to bear in mind a few things as you travel the city. The downtown area is laid on a grid of one-way streets, so look carefully before making a turn lest you find yourself heading straight into traffic. The major southbound street is Broadway; the major northbound street is 4th Avenue; 10th and 11th Avenues are also important north- and southbound streets. Naito Parkway (formerly called Front Avenue) runs along the Willamette River; it permits both north- and southbound traffic. Important eastbound streets are Market, Alder, and Columbia; westbound arterials include Clay, Washington, and Jefferson. Burnside allows both east- and westbound traffic, but the places where you are allowed to make a left turn off Burnside are rare in the downtown area.

Two major streets, 6th Avenue and 5th Avenue, are the arterials for the bus system downtown, making up a large component of the transit mall. These streets are also transformed into light-rail conduits. This is helpful to know if you are planning to ride the bus, but you also need to know it if you're driving downtown because you must be alert to the traffic markings. Some blocks along these streets are for mass transit only, some blocks allow cars, and some blocks funnel cars right into "turn only" lanes. Car drivers should also pay attention to the signs that warn you not to turn on red lights, because these signs prevent cars from being hit by MAX trains. Furthermore, you must allow buses the right-of-

way if you are driving behind them and they are signaling to pull into traffic. A flashing red yield sign on the bus will let you know if you are hogging the road illegally.

You should know a few other important streets and highways in the area. I-205, the freeway that takes you to the airport, will also take you south around the eastern edge of the city of Portland to communities such as Oregon City and West Linn before it reconnects with I-5 just south of Lake Oswego. To the north, I-205 takes you across the Columbia River into Washington State, hooking up with I-5 north of Vancouver. State Highways 99E and 99W are also critical roads. They are the eastern and western sides of Highway 99, the principal thoroughfare of Oregon before I-5 was built, which splits in two just north of Eugene. The directions "W" and "E" designate which side of the Willamette River you are on. South of Portland, Highway 99W is also called the West Pacific Highway, but in the city limits it has several names. In order, from south to north, they are Barbur Boulevard, Naito Parkway, and, when it finally crosses the Willamette again, North Interstate Avenue. Similarly, the East Pacific Highway, 99E, is also called McLoughlin Boulevard from Oregon City until just north of the Ross Island Bridge. At that point, Highway 99E splits into a northbound arterial called Grand Avenue, and a southbound arterial called Martin Luther King Jr. Boulevard (or MLK). These two rejoin north of Broadway to form Martin Luther King Jr. Boulevard. Both Highways 99W and 99E merge into I-5 immediately south of the Columbia River.

Driving east and west over the hills that divide the city from the western suburbs can present some difficulties. The main route, U.S. Highway 26, is responsible for some of the worst traffic in the city, just west of downtown, where it is called the Sunset Highway. This is the principal highway between downtown Portland and the west side of the metro region, and it gets backed up in the Sunset Tunnel, which takes cars under the west side of the hills, backed up again as it climbs the Sylvan Pass, and backed up yet again at the interchange with Highway 217. To travel east and west, you might try a couple of alternative routes. Burnside will take you over the hill into Beaverton from downtown; when it splits in two, follow Southwest Barnes Road to Highway 217. The Beaverton-Hillsdale Highway, or Highway 10, can be a good choice; you can also take I-5 south to Highway 99W or to Highway 217. But all these routes will present the driver with traffic, and they might take you well out of your way.

Another caveat: US 26 turns into a business route when it hits downtown Portland's west side. To follow it east through town, on your way to Mount Hood, for instance, you must be attentive to the signs that direct you toward the Ross Island Bridge, where the highway turns into Powell Boulevard for miles until it passes through the eastern Multnomah County town of Sandy and becomes a proper highway again.

Broadway can also be confusing because it extends from Northeast Portland (where it is called "Northeast Broadway") across the Broadway Bridge to downtown Portland, where it is technically named "Southwest Broadway." But nobody calls it that—downtowners call it just plain "Broadway." While Broadway passes through downtown, it takes the place of 7th Avenue, so you will find it between 6th and 8th Avenues. And after it passes through downtown, it turns into Broadway Drive. Look carefully at the street address of your destination.

Cars, buses, streetcars, light rail, bikes, pedestrians, and the occasional horse all share the streets of Portland. The freeways have additional factors to consider. Traffic not only consists of cars, motorcycles, vans, and the ubiquitous sport-utility vehicles, but also heavy trucks. It is not uncommon to find triple-trailers (legal on some Oregon freeways) and muddy, heavily loaded log trucks bumper to bumper with everyone else.

Driving on the freeways through the heavy Oregon mist requires particular attention. At higher speeds, hydroplaning on a sheet of water can occur, and stopping distances stretch when roads get wet. Spray from passing cars, buses, and trucks can muddy windshields, blocking a driver's vision before the windshield wipers can clear the water. Sudden entry into unseen pools of standing water, especially in the fall when leaves clog drains, can cause a driver to momentarily lose control. In winter, freezing rain and invisible black ice can make driving difficult for everyone, but especially for those who exceed speed limits.

Please don't drink and drive. Driving under the influence of intoxicating drinks or drugs is a serious offense in Oregon. If your trip calls for a visit to the wine country and a tasting of the vintages, take along a designated driver or limit your imbibing. It is also illegal to have an open container of an alcoholic beverage in your vehicle. Oregon's public safety officers are professionals who take their responsibilities seriously.

Distractions should also be kept to a minimum. Radar detectors are permitted, but it is illegal to have a television in a motor vehicle located in such a position where the driver can watch it. And be especially careful when you are talking on the phone!

Bicyclists have an equal legal right to the road, and drivers of motorized vehicles are required to stay out of marked bicycle lanes. Special blue pavement markings alert drivers to places where they must be particularly watchful of bicycle right-of-way; areas where bike lanes cross auto turn lanes are notorious for accidents, and the city is trying to make them safer for everyone. Also, you should know that it is legal for motorized wheelchairs to travel in bike lanes. And in downtown Portland you'll also find marked skateboard routes: You'll need to share the road with them too.

Some of Oregon's more traditional rules of the road follow:

- Moving violation fines can double in school and construction zones.
- At most intersections, and the exceptions are well marked, drivers can make a right turn through a red light after making a complete stop, as long as the turn does not cross other lanes of traffic.
- Car insurance is mandatory in Oregon, and drivers must carry proof of insurance.
- Oregon law requires the driver and all passengers to wear seat belts. Children four

and younger or weighing less than 40 pounds are required to ride in a secured car seat, and booster seats are required for children ages four to six or who weigh between 40 and 60 pounds. Failure to wear a seat belt is cause for a police officer to stop a vehicle and issue a warning or citation. The law applies to both Oregonians and out-of-state drivers. Motorcyclists, as well as their passengers, must wear helmets.

Speed limits are usually well posted. For cars, the speed limit is 55 mph on open highways, 65 mph on freeways outside metropolitan areas, 25 mph on residential streets, and 20 mph in business districts and school zones. Photo radar will occasionally enforce these limits, but signs will warn you if the area is patrolled by this system. Driving in Oregon is governed by the basic rule that a driver must always drive at a speed that is reasonable under existing conditions on all roadways at all times. To obey this basic rule, you may have to drive at a slower speed than the legal posted speed limit if conditions warrant it.

i **Oregon is one of two states in the country that prohibit self-serve gas stations. Don't try to fill your tank yourself, or you will be descended upon by irate attendants. Unfortunately, our laws do not mandate oil checks or cleaning of windshields; these you may have to do yourself.**

Getting to the Airport

To reach the airport, take the Airport Way West exit off I–205, which leads directly to the airport terminal, the car rental lots, and hotels on the airport's property (see our Accommodations chapter for those hotels near the airport). This exit will take you to the economy and other parking lots, to car rental agencies, and to the terminal.

Parking at the airport is not difficult. There are three main areas: the economy lot, the long-term lot, and the parking garage. If you plan to leave your car at the airport while you are gone, use the economy lot, which lies 2 miles east of the airport terminal. Rates are $8 per day, $3 per hour, with the seventh day free. Free PDX shuttles run from the lot to the terminal every seven minutes. (Be sure to remember whether you parked in the red or blue section.) Use the long-term lot for shorter stays exceeding four hours. Rates are $3 per hour and $14 per day maximum, and shuttles are available from this lot. (You can also walk to the airport through the garage tunnels, which are carpeted, well lit, and spacious.) The parking garage rate is also $3 per hour, but it will cost you $24 per day. There is also valet service for $10 per hour or $30 per day. For updated parking information, call (877) 739-4636 before leaving for the airport. In case you need it, the parking folks also provide free jump starts and flat-tire service. You can pay for parking with cash, debit cards, and major credit cards. You can check the airport's Web site to see how many parking places are available in the garage.

Once you arrive at the departing flight deck of the terminal, you can give your bags to the sky cap for many airlines or you can take them inside and check them there. All checked baggage is now screened, so allow for extra time if you are checking bags.

Passenger security has become efficient, flowing smoothly, with security personnel actively directing travelers through checkpoints. But you should nonetheless be prepared to wait in some long lines, especially during peak travel periods, as you and your luggage are thoroughly screened. Fortunately, after you have undergone your security check, the services available near the gates are good to excellent, so even if you have to arrive for your flight early, you still may have time for your croissant and coffee before you board the plane.

Airlines that serve PDX include the following:

Air Canada Jazz (888) 247-2262
Alaska Airlines (800) 252-7522
American Airlines (800) 433-7300
Continental (800) 523-3273
Delta Air Lines (800) 221-1212

Frontier (800) 432-1359
Hawaiian Air (800) 367-5320
Horizon Air (800) 547-9308
Jet Blue Airways (800) 538-2583
Lufthansa Airlines (800) 645-3880
Northwest Airlines (800) 225-2525
Southwest Airlines (800) 435-9792
United and United Express (800) 864-8331
US Airways (800) 428-4322

i If you have rented a car that must be returned at the airport, fill the gas tank before you leave for PDX. There are no gas stations on the airport's grounds. Once you are on I-205 or I–84 en route to the airport, you will need to leave the freeway to get gas.

Other Airfields

Besides PDX, the Port of Portland owns and operates three other airfields that are open for general aviation: Portland-Hillsboro, Portland-Mulino, and Portland-Troutdale Airports, all of which can be reached at (503) 944-7000 or through the Port of Portland, (800) 547-8411.

PEARSON FIELD
1115 East Reserve Street, Vancouver, WA
(360) 619-1295
www.cityofvancouver.us/pearson
Pearson Field, next to Fort Vancouver Historic Site and within walking distance of downtown Vancouver, has been operating since 1905, making it the longest-running airfield in the United States. Still open for general aviation, it has a 3,300-foot lighted runway and a Fixed Base Operator to help with refueling and other pilot needs. Antique aircraft and other memorabilia are on display on the grounds of the airfield at the Pearson Field Museum, (360) 694-7026 or www.pearsonairmuseum .org. Throughout the year the museum hosts several events, including Big Band dance concerts, fly-ins, and parachute jumps. (See the Attractions chapter for more information on Pearson Field.)

GETTING AROUND

Parking

Parking on downtown streets during business hours takes some patience, especially given downtown Portland's grid of one-way streets. Meters generally cost $1.25 per hour and allow parking for periods of time between 15 minutes and 5 hours. Don't try to stay past the time allotted: Cars are frequently monitored to make sure drivers don't overstay their welcome. Once a parking patrol member has started to write you a citation, it is yours.

If you do get a ticket, fines begin at $12 and go upward depending on the severity of your violation. Meters are enforced Monday through Saturday from 8:00 a.m. to 7:00 p.m. Parking after 7:00 p.m. is free in most areas, but in some—for example, near the Rose Quarter and at the Convention Center—metered hours extend to as late as 10:00 p.m. The meter will indicate the hours of operation. Sunday parking is free. Special parking zones for trucks, motorcycles, compact cars, theaters, hotels, churches, and carpools abound and are usually well marked with violations well enforced.

Portland has replaced its old coin-operated parking meters with SmartMeter stations. These central pay station machines work by issuing paper stubs that you adhere to your curbside window. The SmartMeters are convenient, taking change, debit or credit cards, and "smart cards." Smart cards are prepaid cards available from the Portland Office of Transportation, at 1120 Southwest 5th Avenue and at several vendors in town.

SmartMeters work like this: First, park your car and locate the closest pay station. You then deposit your fee in the machine. If you're using a debit or credit card, press the blue button to purchase increments of 15 minutes, or press the "maximum time" button, which buys you the full allotment of time in that meter zone. Your parking purchase must total at least $1.25 if you're using a debit or credit card. When you have indicated all the time you want, press the green button, and the pay station will print a receipt that states how much time you've purchased and when it expires. Be patient—sometimes the meters need to "think" for a minute or two while they are contacting your bank account. Tear off the smaller part of the receipt—keep this with you so you'll remember what time your meter is up. Peel the back off the larger part and use the sticky label to affix the larger part to the curbside window, so that the expiration time can be seen clearly from the outside. In other words, the sticky side faces the same way that the receipt does. The great thing about SmartMeters is that you can take the receipt with you and park at a different SmartMeter somewhere else.

Municipal and private parking garages are an alternative to on-street meters. There are six clearly marked Smart Park garages in downtown Portland, where parking is $1.25 an hour for the first four hours (after that, it's $3 per hour). On the weekend you can park at Smart Park for $2 for the whole evening when entering after 6:00 p.m. or all day on weekends for only $5. Many downtown merchants will validate your Smart Park ticket for two hours of free parking if you spend $25 or more in their stores. Private garages and parking lots charge anywhere from $2 to more than $10 an hour, depending on the time of day you arrive.

Construction and special events such as the Rose Festival Parade and the Portland Marathon affect on-street driving and parking, though the city's parking division makes a good effort to post warning signs about temporary restrictions. But if you ignore the signs and don't move your car, they will "move" it for you—right down to the city towing lot.

Outside of downtown Portland and popular shopping and eating districts such as Northwest 23rd Avenue and Northeast Broadway, parking is easier. At the large malls and shopping centers and popular attractions, such as the Oregon Zoo, you can expect the usual automobile anarchy.

Rental Cars

Most major rental car agencies are represented in Portland and Vancouver, and there are several local rental car providers as well. For car rentals at Portland International Airport, see the PDX entry. Downtown rental agencies are included in the following listings; they can lead you to branch offices throughout the city.

AVIS
330 Southwest Washington Street
(503) 227-0220, (800) 831-2847

BUDGET
2033 Southwest 4th Street
(503) 222-5241, (800) 527-7000

DOLLAR RENT-A-CAR
132 Northwest Broadway
(503) 228-3540

ENTERPRISE RENT-A-CAR
445 Southwest Pine Street
(503) 275-5359 (downtown)

1623 West Burnside Street
(503) 220-8200

HERTZ RENT-A-CAR
330 Southwest Pine Street
(503) 249-5727
(800) 654-1313

THRIFTY CAR RENTAL
632 Southwest Pine Street
(503) 227-6587-

Public Transportation

TRIMET
4012 Southeast 17th Avenue
(503) 238-RIDE (trip information)
www.trimet.org
TriMet is Portland's award-winning mass transit system. TriMet comprises the bus, light-rail, and streetcar systems, and it is noted for its efficiency, comprehensiveness, and accommodation—for example, it uses modernized low-level vehicles for easy boarding and unloading. Operating in three counties (Multnomah, Washington, and Clackamas), TriMet's buses are scheduled on 101

different routes that cover almost 600 square miles. The downtown transit mall extends all the way to Union Station for connections to Amtrak and to Greyhound bus service. Downtown Portland's Fareless Square, bordered by the Willamette River, Northwest Irving Street, and Interstate 405, provides free rides within its boundaries and along the transit mall, where riders can transfer to the light-rail service, MAX. MAX reaches from eastern Multnomah County west to Hillsboro in Washington County, with trains scheduled every 15 minutes during the day to all of downtown, Old Town, the Oregon Zoo, the Lloyd Center, the Rose Quarter, and the airport. MAX has three lines: the Blue Line, which runs east and west between Gresham and Hillsboro via downtown Portland; the Red Line, which runs from the Beaverton Transit Center through downtown to the airport; and the Yellow Line, which travels north and south between downtown and the Expo Center, along Interstate Avenue. Smaller conventional buses and vans now provide service on less-traveled suburban routes, and there is a wheelchair-accessible special service. In 2009, two MAX lines will serve riders traveling from Wilsonville to Beaverton and from Milwaukee to downtown Portland.

Fares—which apply equally to buses, light-rail trains, and streetcars—are based on a geographic zone system: $2.00 for one or two zones, and $2.30 for all zones. Fares are good for a one-way trip and are discounted for senior citizens and youth. Children six and younger ride for free. Bus drivers will not give you change, though dollar bills are accepted on the bus. A day ticket ($4.75) can be used on buses, streetcars, and light rail, traveling to all zones, and you can also get discounted fares if you buy weekly or monthly passes. These passes are widely available throughout the city at many drugstores, grocery stores, and bookstores. The TriMet Web site has a comprehensive list of outlets.

All TriMet tickets and transfers are good on any TriMet route. Passengers receive a time-sensitive transfer that also serves as a receipt. On the bus and streetcar, unless the rider has a pass

Portland accommodates many modes of transportation. RACHEL DRESBECK

or transfer, fares are paid upon boarding, but on MAX, they must be purchased and validated before boarding. MAX tickets are available from machines at every station. After you purchase your ticket but just before you get on the train, insert your ticket in the validator machines at the MAX stops. These machines stamp your ticket with the date and time. MAX tickets, streetcar tickets, and bus transfers can be used interchangeably; they are good for an hour or so past the time they are validated. Hold onto your ticket or transfer! TriMet inspectors can ask for proof of fare payment, and there is a hefty fine if you don't have proof that you are riding legally.

Bus routes vary in frequency and how early and how long each bus travels its route, but during peak times on the most traveled routes, buses run at least every 15 minutes if not more often, as do MAX trains. Schedules for individual bus lines and the light-rail lines are free and commonly available at banks, stores, post offices, bookstores, and dozens of other locations, or accessible on the Web at www.trimet.org.

All stops are marked by blue and white signs displaying the route numbers of the buses serving that line. Many are well lit, with covered bus shelters to protect you from the rain and wind, but not all stops are so well equipped. On the transit mall, there are more elaborate shelters with route maps and video screens displaying information and arrival times for the next bus. The system is divided into regions, designated by regional symbols; these symbols mark service to specific areas from the transit mall.

TriMet has an excellent safety record, but don't leave your common sense at home. After 8:00 p.m. you can ask the driver to let you off the bus any place that he or she can stop safely; many drivers will also stop at night if you wave the bus down between established stops. Be observant when boarding buses: Those marked with an "X" or "L" are express buses that most commonly run during commute hours. After leaving the transit mall, they will stop only at major stops until they reach a local transit center. Most drivers are very careful to announce that they are driving an express route. If in doubt, ask. TriMet's drivers, with rare exception, are courteous and knowledgeable and recognize the long-term value of being helpful to all riders.

i Say you're at your office one evening in the middle of winter. Say it's raining in that bone-chilling, soul-killing way that can characterize winter in Portland. Say you have to wait outside to catch your bus. Instead of taking a chance of dying of exposure, why not try Tri-Met's transit tracker? This incredibly useful service uses GPS to tell you when the bus is due to arrive at your stop—real time, not scheduled time. You can use Transit Tracker by phoning (503) 238-7433 or through Web-enabled cell phones (http://wap.trimet.org), or by logging on to your computer (www.trimet.org) or via your PDA (http://pda.trimet.org).

C-TRAN
2425 Northeast 65th Avenue
Vancouver, WA
(360) 695-0123, (503) 283-8054
www.c-tran.com

C-Tran is the bus service for Vancouver and Clark County, Washington. By arrangement with TriMet, C-Tran also offers service across the Columbia River to downtown Portland. To get from Vancouver to Portland, the ticket price is $2.35. C-Tran and TriMet honor one another's tickets, so an All-Zone ticket for TriMet can be used on C-Tran, except for the Portland Express.

Streetcars

For the first half of the 20th century, Portlanders used streetcars to get around town. Now Portland has brought them back in order to connect the major Westside business districts. Streetcars now travel a route that extends from the South Waterfront district on the Willamette, through Portland State University north to Good Samaritan Hospital (between Northwest Lovejoy and Northwest Northrup at Northwest 23rd), traveling through the Pearl District and along 10th and 11th Avenues. This means you can drive downtown for shopping, then hop on a streetcar to visit Powell's City of Books at 10th and Burnside before your lunch reservation in the Pearl District, all without having to move your car.

Like the bus, streetcars stop every 2 to 3 blocks, and they run from 5:30 a.m. to 11:00 p.m. Monday through Thursday and until 11:45 p.m. on Friday. Saturday hours are from 7:15 a.m. to 11:45 p.m. and Sunday from 7:15 a.m. to 10:30 p.m. They arrive every 12 to 15 minutes during peak hours and a bit less frequently at other times. Well-marked, glass-covered streetcar stops, however, are equipped with electronic screens that helpfully note when the next streetcar will arrive.

Fares follow the same schedule as the MAX and the bus, and their tickets and transfers are all interchangeable. To pay your fare, deposit exact change in the farebox when you board. Fareboxes take only $1 and $5 bills and coins. If you've

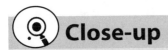# Close-up

Go by Tram

It's early morning, and quiet. The sun is stretching into the eastern sky, turning the clouds a rosy shade of pink. At the lower terminal of the Portland Aerial Tram, next to a large health-care center, a substantial number of people are already in line, ready to board. They are wearing white lab coats; they are wearing bike garb; they are wearing jeans; they are wearing suits. However they are dressed, they are waiting for one thing: for the silver oval tram car to settle into its dock so that they can board and take a three-minute ride to the top of Marquam Hill. There, they will go off to classes, jobs, or appointments at the main campus of Oregon Health and Science University (OHSU), a level-one trauma center and cutting-edge biomedical research hospital,which stands on a hillside above the city of Portland.

The Portland Aerial Tram opened for business in December 2006. At that time it began ferrying passengers from the top of the OHSU Marquam Hill campus to its beautiful outpatient facility, the OHSU Center for Heath and Healing, 3,300 feet (1 kilometer) away. OHSU was built on donated hillside land over many decades. It occupies a large cluster of buildings on the east side of Marquam Hill, part of the network of hills that stand guard over the west side of the Willamette River. As the university expanded over the years—adding clinics, improving its research capacity, attracting patients to its cutting-edge facilities—it ran out of room to grow. Eventually, the reclaimed South Waterfront district was proposed as the best place to expand, but physically connecting the two sites remained a challenge. The geography, as well as the Portland values of livability and proper city scale, made it impossible to simply build a new road from the river to the top of the hill.

Planners concluded that a tram, such as the kind that takes skiers up to the top of alpine terrain, would not only be a viable solution, but could be an interesting one. After all, it made sense: mountain trams transport passengers long distances over challenging terrain in extreme weather conditions. How complicated could it be to create one to transport employees, patients, and students 3,300 feet in less challenging terrain and less challenging weather? As a result, the second commuter tram in the United States—the first is on Roosevelt Island in New York—was built.

Of course, it was complicated. Those whose houses lay under the tram route worried about their privacy and objected to having two towers dominating their neighborhoods. And citizens grew concerned when the cost to build the tram turned out to be $57 million—almost four times the official estimate, mostly due to increased steel prices and corrections to the design. Letters to local papers took on a fevered tone, with many complaints about wasting the city's money. (Actually, the City of Portland paid for only 15 percent of the project. The bulk of the cost was footed by OHSU and South Waterfront property developers.) But after the tram opened, its distinctive imprint adding new variety to the skyline, most of the complaints quieted. People could not wait to ride it, to take the three-minute journey with its panoramic vista, its little swing as the cars pass the tram tower. Thousands more riders than were predicted flocked to the tram. The millionth passenger boarded months before the initial estimate.

The tram has two stations connected by a cable system that traverses an intermediate tower of 197 feet. The cars ride 175 feet above the ground at the highest point, and the gain in elevation from the lower dock to the higher is about 500 feet. The two cars operate in parallel, propelled by an engine at the lower terminal by the Center for Health and Healing. En route, the cars pass over the congested arterials of I-5, Barbur Boulevard, and Macadam Avenue. But most people aren't looking at the ground. They are looking at the spectacular view, with Mount St. Helens dominating the northern landscape and Mount Hood, directly east, reigning over all, with the carpet of the Willamette River, the skyline, and the hills of Portland stretched out before it. On a good day, you can see all the way to Mt. Rainier, but

The Portland Aerial Tram expands people's horizons.
PHOTO COURTESY OF OHSU

even rainy, gloomy days provide an interesting view, with the mists rising from the river and the streets glistening below.

The tram is designed to hold up under those gloomy days. The cabins are designed to withstand extreme weather conditions, as well as dangers such as earthquakes. There are multiple drive systems, as well as communications, safety, and monitoring systems. Before the tram was opened to the public, city rescue workers performed multiple rescue drills, famously featuring skeptical city council members who wanted to be sure that the tram was safe. Watching the council members being rappelled down from suspended tram cars was a sight to behold. But they needn't have feared: The cars were designed and manufactured by a Swiss company, Gangloff Cabins of Bern, Switzerland. The system itself was designed and built by Doppelmayr, another Swiss company—one that has been building and operating tram systems for more than 120 years and in 170 countries.

The tram cars, which weigh about 12 tons apiece, are hauled between the terminals on four 2-inch steel track ropes. In addition, a fifth cable of 7,000 feet, called the haul rope, operates on

continued

a bullwheel system to drive the cars. Each car can hold about 78 people plus the tram operator. A contest was held to name the cars, and the winning names were Walt and Jean. Walt Reyolds was the first African American to graduate from OHSU (when it was still called the University of Oregon Medical School); Jean Richardson was the first woman to graduate with a degree in engineering from Oregon State University.

The morning trip up is quiet, as visitors and OHSU staff, physicians, nurses, students, and patients mingle, chatting in hushed, pre-caffeinated tones or standing silently, contemplating the sunrise over Mount Hood and the Willamette River. An older rider tells a white-coated acquaintance that he knew Howard Vollum, the brilliant Portland-born physicist and founder of Tektronix, a leader in oscilloscope and other instrument manufacturing. Vollum and his wife, Jean, were great philanthropists and gave millions of dollars to OHSU for biomedical research and engineering. The pair of riders reminisce about the Vollums, Portland, and its history. Just as the tram docks at the upper terminal, the riders fall silent for a moment and observe the city below, the sun hitting Mount Hood, and the glorious morning. "The tram," one rider remarks, "is the best thing the city of Portland ever did."

To ride the Portland Aerial Tram: Tickets are purchased from a kiosk at the lower terminal at OHSU's Center for Health and Healing. (This outpatient facility also has an excellent cafe and coffee bar, just so you know.) Tickets cost $4, though children ages 6 and under ride for free, as do patients, visitors, and employees of OHSU (including Doernbecher Children's Hospital). The ticket kiosk takes coins and credit or debit cards, but not bills. Tickets are collected only on the way up, but all tickets are round-trip. If you are a patient or visitor, you will need to get a pass from your provider. If you have a monthly TriMet pass or annual streetcar pass, you can ride for free as well, but ordinary TriMet transfer passes are not accepted. The ride is quiet—there is virtually no noise from the tram itself. The cars are not climate controlled, which means they are cold in winter and stuffy in summer, but since the ride is so short, the lack of comfort is mostly an issue for the operators. The ride takes about three minutes, or a bit longer if it is windy.

The easiest way to get to the tram is to take the streetcar, which stops directly at the Center for Health and Healing on its southbound and northbound routes. It's also easily accessible by bicycle, and there is bike parking available; you can also take your bike on board. If you're driving, your best bet is street parking—metered spots are available on the blocks nearby.

The tram operates weekdays from 5:30 a.m. to 9:30 p.m., on Saturday from 9:00 a.m. to 5:00 p.m., and on Sunday from mid-May through mid-September from 1:00 to 5:00 p.m. It's closed on legal holidays. The tram departs about every 10 minutes. For the latest info, be sure to check the tram Web site, www.portlandtram.org. The Web site also provides maps and directions, as well as streetcar maps and schedules so you can plan your trip.

bought tickets elsewhere, simply validate the ticket once on board. (Riding within the Fareless Square is still free.) While the streetcar may be an old-fashioned form of transportation, these are thoroughly modern, with air conditioning, low-floor center sections, and full wheelchair access. They are clean and efficient.

Those with a nostalgic bent can still ride an old-fashioned streetcar. The Vintage Trolley, a trolley operation using replicas of the streetcars that once served the city, runs on Sunday from March through December. For more information check TriMet's useful Web site at www.trimet.org, which includes an itinerary of historic buildings that the trolley passes as it travels along. The Vintage Trolley charges no fare but welcomes donations.

Taxis

Portland, Oregon, isn't New York City or Washington, D.C., where taxis are a way of urban life. Good luck trying to flag one from the corner: They will rarely, if ever, stop. However, you can telephone for one. If you're walking around downtown, the best cab-finding solution is to head to a hotel and have the doorperson call a cab. If you're at a restaurant, the maitre d' will usually call one for you. If you know your plans for a specific trip or destination, phone ahead and schedule a cab. Fares start at $2.50 and go up $2.20 per mile—though that could increase as the price of oil increases. Cab fare from the airport to downtown for two passengers and their luggage should run about $30.00. Portland cab companies include the following; also see the Traveling by Air section for more information on taxi and towncar services:

BROADWAY CAB
1734 Northwest 15th Avenue
(503) 227-1234

GREEN CAB
10118 East Burnside Street
(503) 234-1414

PORTLAND TAXI
12624 Northeast Halsey Street
(503) 256-5400

RADIO CAB
1613 Northwest Kearney Street
(503) 227-1212

Sharing a Car

Portland is a great city for those who like to walk, bike, or use public transportation. Yet even if you have liberated yourself from car ownership, you may find yourself needing to use a car occasionally. That's where Zipcar comes in: It is a cooperative that allows its members access to cars across the city, distributing the cost and hassle of owning a car among all its members. Car sharing in Portland began with Flexcar, which was so successful here that it is spread to other urban areas in the United States and spawned other companies. In late 2007 Flexcar was bought by Massachussetts-based Zipcar, which operates on the same principles. Members are charged for the number of hours they use the cars and the number of miles they drive them, portioning the fees for insurance, gas, repair, and cleaning among everyone. Cars, trucks, minivans, and even cute Mini Coopers and other sports cars are available all day, every day, at specific locations around town. To use a car, you call ahead to make a reservation, pick up the car at the designated spot, and return it to the same location at the time you have arranged. For more information contact Zipcar at (503) 328-3539 or online at www.zipcar.com.

i Portland routinely receives accolades for its comprehensive approach to bicycling, and the city has put together an amazing Web guide for cyclists, whether you are new to town, visiting, or have been biking the city streets for years. This site offers information, maps, and ideas about how to incorporate biking into your life. Check it out at www.portlandonline.com/transportation.

Bicycling and Skateboarding

More and more people are riding their bikes in Portland, and many of these people are commuters. The city estimates that nearly 15,000 bicycles cross the Hawthorne Bridge each day, compared with 200 in 1975—representing almost 20 percent of all vehicles that cross the bridge. Cyclists are allowed on most of Portland's downtown bridges. The city—which has developed a comprehensive Bicycle Master Plan—has established nearly 200 miles of bikeways that include both off-street paths and bike lanes along streets. Special blue zones warn motorists that cyclists have the right-of-way in these lanes and that cars must yield to bikes when cars are attempting to turn a corner. Bright green boxes painted on the pavement at intersections tell drivers that bikes have

Portland is a great place to ride a bike. RACHEL DRESBECK

the right of way. Such attention to bicycle riding has earned Portland accolades across the nation, and it is routinely touted as an unusually bike-friendly big city, likely the most bicycle-friendly urban area in the country.

Portland has a vigorous city-sponsored bicycle office, which can be found at 1120 Southwest 5th Avenue, Room 800, (503) 823-7671. This office can provide maps and other information about bike routes, bike parking, and so on. The City of Portland Bicycle Program continues to expand and improve the region's network of bike paths, and they have posted signs all over town that tell cyclists how far, and in which direction, their destinations are. Bike storage lockers may be found in many parts of the city, and all TriMet's buses and MAX light-rail trains are equipped with bike racks.

Portland's reputation is in part due to the efforts of the Bicycle Transportation Alliance (BTA), founded in 1990. This award-winning advocacy outfit has been tireless in its efforts to establish

the infrastructure that allows Portland to be a capital of bike riding—advocating for more bike lanes, encouraging local developers to meet their legal requirements for bike and pedestrian access, providing safe storage lockers for bikes, and developing other initiatives to promote two-wheeled travel. They work with employers to promote bike commuting, which saves firms the steep cost of providing downtown parking. They initiated the campaign to allow bike access to the mass transit system and have been successful at creating bike access to most of the bridges that span the Willamette River—measures that have dramatically increased the number of bike commuters. Their insistence that streets should include people as well as cars has been great for the local economy: The successful redevelopment of the Northeast Broadway area around the Lloyd Center, with its bike lanes, wide sidewalks, and mellower traffic speeds, can be directly linked to the efforts of the BTA. And bicycles are at the heart of many new small businesses that capture Portland's independent spirit: Custom bike builders, athletic-wear designers, helmet innovators, and even transportation consultants are all making good livings thanks to early work by the BTA.

BTA organizes bike parking at festivals and other community events, carries out bicycle safety programs in the schools, and helps sponsor the annual Bridge Pedal (see our Festivals and Annual Events and Recreation chapters). Proceeds from the event not only benefit Providence Hospital but also help sponsor more bike programs. BTA may be reached at (503) 226-0676 or by visiting their informative Web site, www .bta4bikes.org.

Bicyclists aren't the only ones using human-powered wheels to get to work, school, and beyond. Skateboarders have joined them, having won a victory in 2001, when the city of Portland allowed them access to downtown and added their rights and responsibilities to the bicycle code. Now that skateboarding has become decriminalized, preferred skateboard routes have been designated, which you will find on green signs throughout the 200 blocks of downtown. Those who wish to ride their skateboards through town must follow a few strictly enforced rules: They must wear helmets if they are younger than 16, and they must wear lights at night, among other things. And tempting though it is, they must refrain from skating on the sidewalks. To learn more about biking and skateboarding in the Portland area, see the Recreation chapter.

Walking

Walking in Portland is one of its chief pleasures. Miles of paths line the waterfront, inviting pedestrians to ramble. Not only is the downtown area clean and well maintained, but the little village-like neighborhoods that make up the city encourage residents to walk to the store, the bank, the library, dinner, even work. The city has found that promoting foot traffic is a smart business move. And moving your legs to get to your business can also be a smart move; on any given morning, you will find pedestrians strolling across downtown bridges, taking advantage of their commute time to exercise their legs, minds, and souls as they prepare for their day. If you're thinking of relocating, you might consider the walking potential of any prospective neighborhoods. You might even find a great job in your own neighborhood and be able to walk to work. See the hiking section in the Recreation chapter and the Portland's Parks chapter for more excellent walks in the area.

HISTORY

But for the toss of a coin, you might be reading the *Insiders' Guide to Boston, Oregon*. Early settlers Asa Lovejoy and William Overton brought their canoe ashore at a clearing in the woods along the Willamette River. Both men agreed that it looked like a promising spot to site a town. But Overton, a drifter from Tennessee, lacked the 25 cents he needed to file a land claim. So he struck a deal with Lovejoy: They would share the 640-acre site if Lovejoy would put up the money. So the two partners filed a claim in 1842. But soon, Overton tired of the pioneer's life, and he sold his half of the claim to Francis Pettygrove. By 1845 the settlement in the clearing in the woods had grown enough so that the two owners knew they had to name their site. Pettygrove, a native of Maine, favored the name Portland, while Lovejoy, who came from Boston, wanted to name it after his fair city. The two men agreed to settle the matter by flipping a copper penny. Pettygrove won, and you can still see the "Portland Penny" on permanent display at the Oregon History Center.

EARLY HISTORY

Of course, the story of Portland and the surrounding area begins thousands of years before these 19th-century events, and well before Europeans ever touched Oregon's shores. The first migration to Oregon occurred during the Ice Age, when sea levels fell, exposing a narrow strip of land across the Bering Sea. The game animals that traveled across in search of warmer lands were followed by small bands of nomadic Asian hunters as early as 30,000 years ago. Historians believe that the first Native Americans, including the Klamath, Modoc, Bannock, Nez Perce, and Chinook tribes, came to Oregon between 10,000 and 12,000 years ago. The coastal tribes relied heavily on abundant salmon, shellfish, seals, and the occasional stranded whale. The tribes farther inland lived on game and altered the landscape as they burned forests and grasslands to attract their prey. This last group, the nomadic hunters and gatherers, were the ones to first greet the early European fur traders who reached the Oregon territory even before Lewis and Clark. At first they welcomed these strange visitors, and accepted their gifts, including guns, whiskey, trinkets, and tools.

The first European to see the Oregon coast was probably Juan Rodriguez Cabrillo, a Spanish sea captain who attempted to map the Pacific coast in 1543; however, he did not set foot on land. Sir Francis Drake is said to have had that honor in 1579 when he claimed the area for England in the name of Queen Elizabeth. That claim, however, was hollow, for it would be another 200 years before the next English vessel reached Oregon. Numerous European ships landed on the Oregon coast in the late 16th century and the early 17th century; however, those expeditions revealed little about the inland regions. By 1750 Russian trappers had worked their way down through Alaska and Canada to the Oregon shoreline in search of otter, but they did not establish a colony, choosing instead to build Fort Ross along the northern California coast in 1812. In fact, no less than four nations laid claim to Oregon—Spain, Russia, Britain, and the United States—but not one built a single settlement to signify a legal presence.

In 1788 John Meares blundered past the mouth of the Columbia River, and in 1792 Captain George Vancouver also missed it, leaving the second largest river in the United States to be discovered by Captain Robert Gray of Boston, who named it after his vessel, the *USS Columbia*.

In the early 1800s Oregon (and the American West in general) was still very much an uncharted place. Easterners heard tall tales about the western mountains and desert swarming with fierce savages, and about abundant resources, but very few had been there.

The Native Americans that lived in the area that would become Portland were anything but savages, however. The tribes that lived here—the Kalapuyas, the Clackamas, the Molalla, the Tualatin, the Chinook, the Multnomah, and the Wapato, among others—had sophisticated, multifaceted cultures well supported by the area's abundance. Many of the tribes were quite wealthy. Some of these groups were river tribes, who built large dwellings along the Willamette, Clackamas, Pudding, and other rivers. Other tribes—the Molalla, for instance—lived farther upland, in the foothills of the Cascades. The Molalla were a more nomadic hunting tribe, riding horses east and north toward the Columbia.

While there were occasional conflicts among these different groups, it was largely a peaceful region, with little war. Instead, these tribes had elaborate networks of trade, both within and among all the tribes in the region, as well as with the Eastern trappers who began to show up in the early 19th century. They had a lot to trade too. Though these tribes did not plant crops, many engaged in protoagricultural practices. For example, they burned the grassy fields to harvest grasshoppers, to flush out camas seed, and to ensure the health of the meadows. Division and specialization of labor was common, as were advanced systems for storing the roots, berries, nuts, elk, bear, and salmon that they gathered, hunted, and fished. And much legend and ritual were dedicated to thanksgiving and appreciation for all that the gods had given them in this beautiful place. Hundreds of thousands of people lived here for 10,000 years before Eastern settlers had ever heard of the place, dwelling in villages large and small, speaking a variety of languages, living out their own histories.

The Lewis and Clark Expedition

President Thomas Jefferson planned a secretive mission in 1803: to send a small party of men overland to the Pacific—a bold venture that no one before had even attempted. Congress covertly approved the trip, along with its budget of $2,500, because these explorers would be venturing outside U.S. jurisdiction onto British territory. Jefferson was looking for an expeditious water route to the Pacific via the Missouri River, its tributaries, and a legendary River of the West said to flow down from the Rockies to the Pacific, in hope that the distance between the east- and west-flowing rivers would be a one-day portage. It would be a simple route west for traders, emigrants, and adventurers. Aware of the opportunity, Jefferson also charged the group with collecting scientific information about the region's interior.

President Jefferson chose his neighbor, long-time friend, and personal secretary, Meriwether Lewis, to lead the contingent across the Louisiana Purchase and to the Pacific coast. Lewis, in turn, wisely selected frontiersman and mapmaker William Clark to be his coleader.

In the spring of 1804, Lewis and Clark, along with 31 men and the intrepid Newfoundland hound, Seaman, left St. Louis and started up the Missouri River heading west. Over the next two years the group—eventually christened the "Corps of Discovery"—would traverse present-day Missouri, Nebraska, the Dakotas, Montana, Wyoming, Washington, and Oregon. The journey took so long that the few insiders who knew about it feared that the members of the expedition had perished. But on December 5, 1805, Lewis and Clark reached the Pacific Ocean and Clark wrote in his diary, "We now discover that we have found the most practicable and navigable passage across the continent of North America." In reality, he couldn't have been further from the truth.

The route discovered by Lewis and Clark was far too difficult for others to follow. Indeed, no pioneer wagon ever did follow their trail. In fact, Lolo Pass, where their expedition crossed the treacherous Bitterroot Mountains in western

Montana, is a rough haul even today—two centuries later. But because their detailed maps and notes provided a wealth of scientific data, the West was no longer an uncharted mystery and their expedition was celebrated as a success. Although they examined only a small portion of the Northwest Coast and the Columbia River, they gathered much valuable and accurate information about the rest of the Northwest from friendly native peoples. Their reports stirred excitement in the East; their vivid descriptions of a land of bounty created an "Oregon fever" among fur traders who had previously trapped and traded in the Rocky Mountains.

The Fur Trade and Fort Vancouver

The second major westward expedition was not funded by a government but was backed by one of the world's richest men—John Jacob Astor, who whetted his appetite for adventure by reading about Lewis and Clark's great journey. By 1810 Astor saw an opportunity to make a new fortune: a fur-trading enterprise at the mouth of the Columbia River. But one dilemma stood in his way: How could he get his men safely across the uncharted American West? He had a couple of ideas and tried both a land and a sea route.

In 1811 he dispatched an overland party to follow the trail of the early explorers and to establish trading posts. He also sent another party there by sea, in a ship traveling around Cape Horn. The ship arrived safely but was destroyed afterward in a skirmish with Native Americans.

The land expedition also had problems. At a particularly dangerous spot on the Snake River, known as Caldron Linn, one of the canoes capsized, drowning at least one man and losing a large portion of much-needed supplies. Worse, the party soon discovered that the river did not become more placid downstream and that it was too treacherous to navigate. They came to the conclusion that there was no quick and easy route to the Pacific, an assessment that would stymie pioneers for the next hundred years.

Astor's overland party finally did make it to Oregon, but the enterprise was in deep trouble.

Their only hope was to send a few men back East to get help from Astor. Robert Stuart led the mission back to St. Louis—an arduous journey that took nearly a year. But Stuart made an incredible discovery along the way. In what is now the state of Wyoming, he found a 20-mile-wide gap in the Rocky Mountains where wagons could pass. Named South Pass, this route would unlock the door to western migration, and more than a half-million emigrants would eventually ride their Conestoga wagons through to the other side. Where Lewis and Clark had valiantly failed, Robert Stuart succeeded through a twist of fate.

Even before Robert Stuart's lucky discovery, adventurous entrepreneurs were at work in the western mountains. These "mountain men" were solitary fur trappers, and most had no home, no money, and no possessions—except what they wore and carried on their backs. They lived completely off the land, on a diet of buffalo, elk, and mountain goat. Many trappers roamed constantly in search of beaver pelts; many married Native American women and earned the respect and fondness of various tribes. Some were hired by the trading companies exploiting the area, while others remained freelancers; still others eventually settled down on land claims.

The companies that hired these men and bought their pelts played a crucial role in the shaping of Portland. John Jacob Astor's Pacific Fur Company did eventually establish a presence in the area, but it was not as great as that of its competitor: the Hudson's Bay Company, run by the British, who wished to control these fertile Northwest lands and secure for themselves the pelts and other riches that the territory promised. The Hudson's Bay Company, established in 1670, was an experienced operation. It had many outposts west of the Rocky Mountains from Alaska to Mexico. But supplying them was expensive and difficult (as Astor too discovered). Thus, the company decided to build a settlement that could sustain itself and perhaps produce enough surplus to furnish other outposts in the West, reducing the need for the costly ships that the company used to bring supplies to its people.

i Some historians believe that the name *Oregon* is derived from the French *ouragan,* meaning "storm" or "hurricane," because early French-Canadian trappers called the Columbia River the "River of Storms."

In 1825 the Hudson's Bay Company sent Dr. John McLoughlin to build a fortified settlement along the Columbia: Fort Vancouver, on the north side of the river. Its location was ideal—it was close enough to the sea that it could receive trading ships and send them back laden with pelts, and it was on a beautiful, richly soiled plain well out of the dangers of annual flooding.

Fort Vancouver became the administrative site and supply depot for the Columbia Department of the Hudson's Bay Company. Its goal was to make it impossible for Astor and the other fur companies to gain a foothold in the area, by establishing a huge network of trappers, traders, and Native Americans to harvest as many furs as possible, even if that meant eradicating an animal population in the area. To accomplish this, the fort became a self-sustaining community, with fields of grain and vegetables, dairies, and orchards. Mills were built for processing lumber and grain. Barrel-makers, bakers, and blacksmiths were hired and brought to the fort. Schools and churches were formed, and a hospital was built and maintained. By the time the first pioneers stumbled out of the mountains in 1842, Western civilization was well established.

McLoughlin was the chief administrator of Fort Vancouver for nearly 20 years, and without him, it is hard to say how the American pioneers would have fared. McLoughlin was a fascinating figure. He had good relations with the native peoples, and his principled administration was admired by many, though—like that of any good administrator—it was not without controversy. He enforced the company policy of protecting its interests while respecting the trade-friendly Native Americans and making no attempt to convert them into Europeans. But the American emigrants were a different story: They posed a direct threat to the comfortable monopoly that the Hudson's Bay Company enjoyed. McLoughlin was dismayed by them, yet he could not keep them out, since the legal claim of the British to the territory had not been established. At the same time, he felt compelled to help the pioneers as they arrived, sick and starving. His solution was to attempt to bring them into the fur trade, and to this end, he helped these emigrants establish themselves in the Willamette Valley, a difficult choice that was often in conflict with his duties to the Hudson's Bay Company.

In 1846 the British and American governments settled the territorial dispute, and Oregon became a territory of the United States. But under this treaty, British and other citizens could retain their rights to the land they had settled. McLoughlin established Oregon City as a hamlet for retired trappers from the Hudson's Bay Company and continued his work helping the pioneers, whose journey ended when they reached McLoughlin's new hometown.

AGE OF PIONEERS

Explorers who followed Lewis and Clark, such as John Frémont, were often so upbeat that they made the trip west seem easy and enjoyable, which it definitely was not. They were encouraged in their reports by the U.S. government, who wanted to make sure these resource-rich lands stayed out of the hands of the Russians and the British.

Oregon Trail

Driving this great movement was more than just positive reports. In 1843 the federal government allotted 640 acres of land to every adult homesteader and 160 acres to every child, with hopes of anchoring the United States' claims to the Northwest Territories. Most of those who came as far west as Oregon made the land trip. However, some came by water and did so even before a land route was established. The sea route never was a popular choice, though. The fare was prohibitive, and most westward-bound pioneers came from central states far from seaports. Also, the sea journey often took up to a full year compared with the wagon journey, which took five to eight months.

Those who did come by land took the route that came to be known as the Oregon Trail (although it actually forks in southern Idaho, with a lower extension ending in California). Legend enjoyed by Oregonians to this day has it that those who were greedy for gold headed south at the fork to California and those who wanted a better life headed north to the Oregon Territory. Nearly 2,000 miles long, the main route west stretched from Independence, Missouri, to Oregon City, Oregon. Portions of it followed the Platte River for 540 miles through Nebraska to Fort Laramie in present-day Wyoming. The trail wound along the North Platte and Sweetwater Rivers to South Pass in the Wind River Range of the Rocky Mountains. From there the main trail went south to Fort Bridger, Wyoming, before turning into the Bear River Valley and north to Fort Hall in present-day Idaho. The Oregon Trail followed the Snake River to Salmon Falls and then went north past Fort Boise. The route entered what is now Oregon, passed through the Grande Ronde River Valley, crossed the Blue Mountains, and followed the Umatilla River to the Columbia River. Shorter and more direct routes were developed along some parts of the trail, but they were often more difficult.

The first organized party of emigrants to actually reach the Oregon Territory came with the American pioneer physician Elijah White. Under the leadership of John Bidwell, an Ohio schoolteacher, this group loaded their wagons and left Missouri in 1841 and in 1842 reached Oregon. The terminus of their journey was the future site of Oregon City; later settlers would head for the verdant Willamette Valley. During the 1840s thousands of pioneers settled there, where wheat, fruits, and vegetables thrived. Others settled higher up, for gold prospecting and to harvest Oregon's bountiful supply of Douglas fir trees.

The Oregon Trail directed the flow of westward expansion and permitted the settlement and development of the Pacific Northwest. Before the completion of the first transcontinental railroad in 1870, an estimated 350,000 pioneers followed the Oregon Trail westward, more than all the other routes combined.

In Oregon, the trail's route has remained a principal course of east-west travel to the present day, though it lies buried beneath Interstate 84. The road crosses a diverse range of terrain—the rugged Blue Mountains in northeastern Oregon, the dry plateaus between Pendleton and The Dalles, the awesome Cascade Mountains and Columbia Gorge section, and even the geographic end of the trail in Oregon City, where the Willamette Valley settlements all began.

> **i** Of the estimated 350,000 settlers who migrated west on the Oregon Trail, at least 20,000 died en route. Cholera was the most common cause of death.

PORTLAND'S EARLY DAYS

As the Native American way of life was disappearing, the settlers were busy creating a new one. Gradually the Oregon Territory began to acquire the sheen of civilization. A dozen years after the first wagon trains arrived at the end of the Oregon Trail, the hamlets along the Willamette began sprouting business districts with general stores, blacksmith shops, tanneries, well-furnished hotels, and white-steepled churches. In Portland the crude log cabins of the frontiersmen were gradually giving way to tidy frame houses with glass windows, ornamental woodwork, and papered walls. A pristine tract of forestland in 1844, Portland boasted 821 residents by 1850, making it the region's most populous community. Mail arrived by steamship, which took the route around Cape Horn, and was distributed to the 40 post offices in the area. And thanks to the vision of New England sailor Captain John Couch, who chose Portland over Oregon City as a deepwater harbor for his shipping, the city soon became known as a port deserving its name.

As proper civilization took hold in Portland, the city also attracted a few lawless individuals who've served to provide color for our local

Oregon's pioneering spirit extends to many areas. Among other firsts, it was the first state to officially register all its voters, the first to directly elect U.S. senators, the first to create an initiative system—and in case none of the above worked out—the first to develop a system for recalling public officials.

history. One such person was Portland's "Sweet Mary," who created a floating brothel. Another was Joseph "Bunco" Kelly, a hotelier known for shanghaiing young men and selling them to ship captains short of crew members. Kelly carted them off when they were drunk. Upon waking, the young men had bigger problems than a hangover. Eventually, however, the wilder side of Portland, with its teeming saloons and shady houses of ill-repute, was tamed by an indignant citizenry. The prospering economy was turning Stumptown into a real city, complete with officials intent upon creating a structure of law and order. Rules of decorum came to Portland in the 1870s, when it became illegal to fire a pistol downtown or drive your carriage faster than 6 miles per hour. The town gained its most notable nickname in 1889 when local artist, writer, and bon vivant C. E. S. Woods called for an annual rose show. The Portland Rose Festival was launched that year in what would soon be known as the "City of Roses." Since the replacement of the downtown wharves in 1929 with a seawall stretching along most of the city's shoreline on the Willamette River, it has become a tradition to welcome a fleet of U.S. and Canadian warships to dock during this festival.

Part of the early economy was agriculture. In 1847 Henderson Lewelling brought the first apple, cherry, peach, plum, and pear saplings into the Willamette Valley, beginning a new agricultural venture. In 1849 the California gold rush created a huge demand for these crops and other staples, thus boosting Portland's economy. The first crop of 100 apples was sent to California mining camps, where there was such a scarcity of fresh fruit that scurvy (caused by a vitamin C

deficiency) was a leading cause of death. For a time the apples sold for the sum of $5 apiece, the going rate for a week's room and board. Other Oregon goods, ranging from lumber to eggs, remained in constant demand, which in turn fueled a new rush of men and women eager to farm in the Willamette Valley. In 1851 the city of Portland was officially incorporated. (For more details about Portland's early history, see the Relocation chapter, especially the Linnton and Oregon City sections, and the Area Overview chapter.)

In 1853 Washington split from the Oregon Territory, claiming land north of the Columbia River, which continues to form part of the interstate boundary. The next year, Oregon voters rejected statehood because they were split on whether to enter the United States as a slave state or as a free state. Although slavery was voted down, 7,277 to 2,645, only 1,081 men voted to let free Black men settle in Oregon compared with 8,640 who were opposed to their presence. Statehood initiatives were also rejected in 1855 and 1856. However, on Valentine's Day, 1859, Oregon became a state, with Oregon City, the largest city in the territory, becoming the capital and regional center for all the Oregon Territories.

Indian Treaties Ignored

In the 1860s prosperity continued for Portland's residents as the Oregon Steam Navigation Company secured a monopoly on all shipping on the Columbia River. By 1870 Portland boasted the largest population (9,565) in the Pacific Northwest until the Alaska gold rush of 1897 fueled Seattle's rise. In 1883 the transcontinental railroad arrived in Portland with President U. S. Grant on board. This linkage by rail enabled export of lumber, beef, salmon, and other goods to the major eastern cities, triggering the biggest economic and population growth spurt in the state's history.

Sadly, this led to the further subjugation and maltreatment of the state's indigenous peoples. Impatient settlers and loggers repeatedly trampled Indian treaties by taking land reserved for tribal peoples. Private property was a foreign concept to the Native Americans in the area, who believed the forests and fields were community properties for the general welfare of all. The friction intensified as miners stampeded into areas where silver or gold was found. Native Americans, who were neither taxpayers nor voters, protested the violations in vain. Battles and hostilities sporadically broke out throughout the West. In Oregon, Chief Joseph and the Nez Perce were routed from their homes in the Wallowas to eventually surrender in southern Canada. The Modoc tribe was forced off their land and herded across the California border where they held 1,500 troops at bay in the lava beds for six months. These conflicts were repeated around the western states until the last organized tribal resistance died out in the 1890s.

Logging

Logging was a cornerstone of the economy, and the timber industry was king in Oregon, pressuring Congress to repeal the Forest Preservation Act of 1891, opening up millions of acres of public land in Oregon and other northwestern states for huge clear-cuts. Theodore Roosevelt responded by setting aside large forest reserves where timber operations were prohibited. These reserves eventually grew into the USDA Forest Service, which later compromised his intent by allowing timber sales, a source of controversy that lingers today.

i When Portland's Esther Pohl Lovejoy was appointed to the Portland Board of Health in 1905, she became the first woman to lead the health bureau of a major American city. She put herself through medical school by working at the hosiery counter of the Lipman and Wolfe department store.

The Lewis and Clark Centennial Exposition

Lewis and Clark shaped Portland long after they departed the quiet native trails that lined the Columbia. Portland derives much of its appearance—even today—from the successful, extensive world's fair held here in 1905 to celebrate the 100-year anniversary of their expedition. The Lewis and Clark Exposition drew thousands of visitors to Portland and precipitated an economic boom, accompanied by a wave of building and development, especially in Northwest and Southwest Portland. Hotels and other civic buildings were constructed to capitalize on the wave of visitors. Few of the fair's actual structures remain—most of them were dismantled, and more than a few burned down. The fair's buildings were beautiful but not designed to last. Yet the hotels, department stores, and other pavilions that were built throughout the city remain today, furnishing the architectural bones of the city.

The Lewis and Clark Exposition also changed the appearance of the nation: It was here that plywood was introduced.

THE WAR YEARS

Wartime Workers and Population Growth

During World War I thousands of unskilled workers swarmed to Portland to work on Swan Island, a bustling center of shipbuilding and repair. But compared with World War II, the war to end all wars caused only a ripple in Oregon. It was World War II that forever altered the shape of the Portland area.

Henry J. Kaiser's Oregon Shipbuilding Corporation began building freighters of the famous Liberty Ship class when World War II was less than a month old. The first Kaiser shipyard in the Portland area was the St. Johns Yard. At the end of one year, it launched 36 ships. By war's end, the yard had built 141 vessels, including Liberty Ships and their successor, the Victory Ship.

During World War II the demand for wartime workers and the passage of tens of thousands of enlisted men and women through Oregon swelled the state's population from less than 1.1 million in 1940 to more than 1.5 million in 1950.

The city of Portland's 1940 population of 305,000 jumped to 374,000 residents in just three years.

> **i** Lone Fir Cemetery, on Southeast 20th between Morrison and Stark, holds the earthly remains of early Portlanders. These Oregonians—some with important historical names, some with ignominious ones—lie side by side, speaking eloquently of our common fate.

Minority Groups
The Rise and Fall of Vanport

Portland's new residents included large numbers of emigrants from the deep South: They arrived by the trainload, lured away from the poverty and oppression to work in the wartime shipyards of Henry Kaiser. Between 1940 and 1945 Portland's African-American population surged from 2,100 to 15,000.

The state was not always hospitable to minorities, and over the course of its history had created laws limiting the freedoms of everyone who wasn't white and Protestant. For example, Oregon's Ku Klux Klan once boasted a membership of 25,000 and even elected a leader, Grand Dragon Walter Pierce, as governor of the state. Pierce sponsored legislation in 1922 that barred all Catholic schools in the state in addition to attempting to deny African-American citizens their right to vote.

But the war efforts and the workers needed to sustain them created a dilemma. Henry Kaiser was busy building the Liberty Ships for the war effort, yet these new workers had nowhere to live. The sudden increase in population strained the city's ability to meet even the most basic needs of these war workers. The city authorities in Portland dragged their feet, not wanting to create housing for this influx of workers—who might then decide to stay. So Kaiser went around the city authorities and applied the same rapid building techniques to housing war workers as he did to making warships, assembling practically overnight the city of Vanport, just outside the city limits of Portland. It was built to sustain the workers, including providing for their families: It had schools, medical clinics, shops, even 24-hour day care, since many of Kaiser's employees were women with children. Nearly 70,000 workers and their families lived in this city. The major drawback was that it was built on a flat floodplain between the Willamette and Columbia Rivers.

Rapidly, Vanport became the state's second-largest city. Three years after the war, about 19,000 people still lived there. On Memorial Day, 1948, the rivers, swollen by rain and melting snow, broke the dikes protecting Vanport and swept the town away, killing 18 people. The city's entire population, then about one-fourth African American, became homeless.

Vanport was never rebuilt and today West Delta Park stands on the site of this former community.

Relocation Camps

African Americans were not the only minority group to suffer maltreatment. The Pearl Harbor bombing created widespread fear of espionage, sabotage, and an invasion aided by Japanese-American citizens. Under Executive Order 9066, issued in February 1942 by the federal government, Japanese-American citizens in certain sensitive areas were forced to relocate.

When the U.S. Army declared Oregon, California, and Washington "strategic areas," they forced more than 110,000 Japanese Americans into 10 relocation centers. More than 4,000 Oregonians of Japanese descent were moved to the Portland Assembly Center, formerly the Portland International Livestock Center. Between May and September of 1942, they lived in former animal stalls and barns, guarded by military police, while permanent relocation camps were built farther inland. Several years later, the Executive Order was rescinded, but the Japanese-American population lost their homes, businesses, and farms.

World War II in Portland

The war was closer to Portland than many people imagined. In June 1942 a submarine of the

Imperial Japanese Navy surfaced a few miles off the Oregon coast. Pointing her stern toward a suspected U.S. submarine base, the ship fired on Fort Stevens. In order to conceal the exact location of their coastal defense guns, the frustrated defenders were forbidden to return fire. Fort Stevens thus became the only military installation in the continental United States to come under direct enemy fire during the war. This was the first attack on the U.S. mainland since the War of 1812. But it was not to be the only Japanese attack here. Many ships were torpedoed off the Oregon coast. For years after the war, rusting mines drifted onto shore. Even today, fishing boats still pull up their nets and find a World War II–era bomb, torpedo, or mine.

Also, in September 1943, the Japanese launched a single-engine float plane that dropped phosphorus bombs in the Oregon forest northwest of Brookings and on other parts of the West Coast. These were the only bombs that fell on continental American soil during the war; their primary purpose was to start forest fires that would create fear and divert troops from the war effort. Of the hundreds of balloon bombs launched by the Japanese, 45 landed in Oregon. Fortunately, most of these fire starters fizzled in the Oregon rain. But one landed near Bly, a town of 750 people in southeastern Oregon, killing one adult and five children. These were the only civilian deaths from enemy action in the continental U.S. during the war.

One long-range target for these bombs may have been the U.S. Army base at Camp Pendleton. Here General Jimmy Doolittle trained B-17 bomber crews heading for England and for the famous attack on Tokyo. It was after Doolittle's highly symbolic raid that the bombs were dropped on our West Coast.

POSTWAR PROSPERITY

War's end brought more changes to Portland and Oregon. Returning veterans enrolled in large numbers at colleges, started families, and bought houses. During the postwar years, Portland prospered, like most of the nation. Wood products and fisheries filled the state's coffers in the postwar building boom, and Portland, as the major city in Oregon, benefited greatly. In the late 1960s and early 1970s, Republican governor Tom McCall, a true visionary, guided the state through a challenging phase by making controlled growth and environmental protection the top priorities of state government. One of his many important achievements was to lead a controversial but farsighted legislative effort to keep the coastline open to the public. As the economy was bolstered by the booming agriculture, timber, fishing, and tourism, many Oregonians enjoyed a period of economic growth and security. Then, in keeping with a national trend, residents and businesses began leaving the inner city in favor of the suburbs. Not all urban shops and homes were replaced with new ownership, and certain areas began to slide downhill. Gradually, islands of neglect began to appear in Portland's inner city. In the 1980s many huge projects of the Portland Development Commission focused on areas such as the riverfront and the downtown square area and neglected neighborhoods in Southeast, North, and Northeast Portland. A prime example is Pioneer Courthouse Square, a central plaza used for festivals, concerts, and lunches away from the office.

By the 1990s the timber industry, while still critical to Oregon's economy, was waning as old growth stands of trees were diminished by decades of overcutting and poor resource management. The fishing and salmon industries were, likewise, crippled by years of heavy gill netting and drift netting. Meanwhile, manufacturing was growing, fueled by telecommunications and computer technology industries in the Willamette Valley. From the late 1970s and mid-1980s, Portland's suburbs, particularly the Silicon Forest in Washington County, made huge strides, and manufacturing and high-technology companies began moving to the area, attracted by cheap water, utilities, space, and a high standard of living.

Oregon's position, between the states of Washington and California and connecting to the Pacific Rim nations, puts it in a large economic sphere that continues to generate growth. But the growth is not without controversy. As both Oregon and Portland continue to expand, arguments about how much to grow and where to grow have become more heated and intense. Mixed-use development, housing, apartments, and business continue to spring up along light rail lines and other innovations in transportation, such as the Portland Streetcar. The city's splashy megaprojects of the 1980s are now replaced by smaller, more community-driven developments in such places as Alberta Street in Northeast Portland. While the trend in the 1970s and 1980s was flight from the urban areas to the suburbs, since the 1990s people have returned to the city, starting businesses, fixing up old houses, and developing new properties. The results are increased jobs, housing, and livability for all Portlanders.

By focusing on developing the city, rather than allowing unregulated sprawl, Portland is better equipped than most cities to meet the challenges of the 21st century.

"The past is not dead. It isn't even past," observed William Faulkner. He was talking about the American South, but it's also true in Portland, even in ways that we may not notice. We drive down McLoughlin or Pettygrove, we visit the Multnomah or Clackamas County libraries, we rush by an old pioneer cemetery or restored farmhouse from the 19th century, but rarely do we give thought to the people who walked here before us—pioneer, fur trader, or Native American. Yet our lips echo with their names and our feet tread the same earth. Their spirits live on.

ACCOMMODATIONS

Visitors to Portland will find a variety of motel and hotel offerings, from the basic to the sublime. They range in style, in price, and in location, but no matter where you plan to stay, you should be able to find a place to lay your head and suit your needs. Portland's bed-and-breakfast inns offer visitors an alternative to hotel rooms, as well as a chance to explore the individual neighborhoods that make up the city. Staying in a bed-and-breakfast inn allows you the chance to see why people have chosen to live here and how the region's history, climate, geography, diversity, and growth have shaped their lives.

Price Code

The following price code for hotels, motels, and bed-and-breakfasts in this chapter is based on an average room rate for double occupancy during high season. While there is no sales tax in Oregon, there is a room tax of 12.5 percent.

$	$60 and less
$$	$61–$110
$$$	$111–$160
$$$$	$161 and above

Please note that many hotels and motels change their room rates at least twice a year, so the ranges we have quoted in this chapter are meant simply as a guide to point you in the right direction, not as the final word on the cost of your stay.

HOTELS AND MOTELS

You will find certain chains well represented throughout the Portland Metro area. For example, Marriott's Courtyard, Fairfield Inns, and Residence Inns, offering consistently clean and comfortable rooms, can be found in Beaverton, Southeast Portland, Hillsboro, Tigard, downtown, the Lloyd Center, North Portland, at the airport, and at other hubs. So can the Homewood Suites and the Garden Inns by the Hilton chain, Holiday Inn Express, Phoenix Inns, Ramada Inns, and many other well-known chains. We figure you know about these reliable places already, so in this guide we have concentrated on the standouts in the area, including some in these chains where appropriate. You should note that these chains may be your best bet in Southeast Portland, where independent hotels are few. In this guide we focus on the hotels in the center of town, but we've included some options for other parts of town, as well as for the outlying areas—and we've included some inexpensive choices for those weary travelers who just want a hot shower and a clean bed.

While the primary concentrations of lodgings are found downtown, at the Lloyd Center, the Oregon Convention Center, and near Portland International Airport, you will find accommodations throughout the city. A number of hotels are strung along Interstate 5 north and south of both Portland and Vancouver, in Gresham and Trout-dale along Interstate 84 east of the city proper, near U.S. Highway 26 as it heads through the city of Sandy, and up the Mount Hood Corridor. More accommodations can be found off Interstate 205, which serves as a regional ring road, allowing motorists to bypass Portland's center. Other popular locations for lodging include exits off Interstate 405 and near Highway 217 and US 26 south and west of Portland, where much of the Silicon Forest, Oregon's high-tech zone, is found. Across the Columbia River in Vancouver and Clark County are clusters of hotels and motels in the downtown area, north along I-5, and near the

Vancouver Mall just off I-205 after it crosses the river into Washington State.

If you are arriving at Portland International Airport, be sure to check the ground transportation reservations board. Some hotels offer free shuttle service. If you are staying downtown, the MAX light-rail line, in addition to the airport cabs, can take you there quickly and efficiently.

When you arrive, you will find that, as in most places, hotels offer smoke-free rooms and rooms for those who smoke, so guests can state their preference when making reservations. Likewise, some hotels accept pets. Others provide free lodging for children staying in the same room as their parents (or grandparents). Compliance with the Americans with Disabilities Act (ADA) means hotel rooms are easier to use for travelers with physical challenges and for older adults. All hotels are wheelchair-accessible unless otherwise noted. One more note: Many of the hotels listed here have excellent deals if you book them online, so be sure to look at their Web sites.

Not surprisingly, it is expensive to park your car downtown, where hotels charge about $30 per day. Some hotels do offer free parking for guests. Some provide valet parking at their own facilities or nearby garages; others offer their guests discounted parking at local garages.

i **With its renowned restaurants, proximity to the Willamette Valley wine country, and energetic cultural scene, Portland is becoming a vacation destination—and that means an emerging market for vacation rentals. Some good sources? Try Historic Hawthorne Rentals (www.historichawthornerentals.com/) for its stylish eastside locations. Old faithfuls Vaction Rentals By Owner (www.vrbo.com/vacation-rentals/usa/oregon) and Craigslist (www.portland.craigslist.org) are also reliable sources as well, though the former has more Portland-specific rentals.**

Southwest Portland

ACE HOTEL $$
1022 Southwest Stark Street
(503) 228-2277
www.acehotel.com

This Ace Hotel, though an offshoot of its Seattle brother, is very Portland, with an indie aesthetic and an attitude to match. It is indeed named after the card, which can be either high or low, and this theme is evident throughout. The 79 rooms vary widely in standards of luxury. The most expensive room costs about $250, while rooms with shared baths—or even those with bunk beds designed to house touring bands—run about $85. The hotel is furnished with locally designed things as well as salvaged ones, and many of the features from the residential hotel that existed there beginning at the turn of the century have been repurposed. That said, it is a very stylish hotel, and you might not know these things were old or recycled unless we told you. Local artists were hired to create murals throughout the hotel, but it's not just the artwork that is soulful. The lobby is very comfortable and attractive, with couches and free Wi-Fi (throughout the hotel, actually). Even the business center on the mezzanine radiates West-coast hip, providing MacBooks around a large table for you to check your Gmail, as well as a couch for work-induced narcolepsy.

The Ace Hotel is not for everyone. You should be forewarned that it is going for something other than the standard hotel experience, and adjust your expectations accordingly. For example, you will not find free coffee or newspapers, though delicious coffee is available right next door at the excellent Stumptown coffee shop. Soaps are handmade, but not overabundant, and you may be sharing a bathroom or using a glassed-in shower in your room. The hotel can also be noisy, given its location off Burnside and its ancient age. This hotel may not be the ideal choice for a romantic honeymoon or a tense business trip, but it could be ideal for a weekend getaway with friends, especially since its common spaces are so enticing and its location so central.

i Try the Portland Visitors Association Web site for deals on hotel rooms and help with planning your meeting: www .travelportland.com.

AVALON HOTEL AND SPA $$$
0455 Southwest Hamilton Court
(503) 802-5800, (888) 556-4802
www.avalonhotelandspa.com

The Avalon Hotel and Spa is a beautiful hotel with a special difference: It is the only hotel in the area dedicated to providing spa services as part of its mission and built—in an environmentally friendly way, no less—with these services in mind. And Portland residents, who don't usually stay in Portland hotels, believe this was a wise move. This hotel delights residents and visitors alike. Its commitment to old-fashioned luxury and service have made it an instant classic.

The Avalon is in an attractive building south of downtown on the Willamette River, in the South Waterfront district. It offers 99 rooms, 18 of them suites. They are decorated with cool grays and browns that complement the stone and wood interior accents, and they are warmed by vivid touches of red and green tones. Public spaces and rooms alike are outfitted with sleek but comfortable furnishings and plush rugs. Many rooms have balconies that look out on the Willamette, to Mount Hood, and beyond. Bathrooms, which feature marble, wood, and stone accents, are spacious. The concierge staff is outstanding. Room service is available from 6:00 a.m. to 11:00 p.m., and the full-service Rivers restaurant offers breakfast, lunch, and dinner. To keep things pristine, no smoking or pets are allowed.

Spa services are worth the extra cost. The slate-floored spa, which is downstairs, features an excellent array of services—including massages, facials, and pedicures—that promise restoration to tired bodies and souls. Body wraps of various concoctions of mud, antioxidants, and unguents are especially alluring. Don't miss the Raindance room, with its Vichy and Swiss showers.

THE BENSON HOTEL $$$$
309 Southwest Broadway
(503) 228-2000, (888) 523-6766
www.bensonhotel.com

A grand and historic Portland building, the Benson has been the hotel of choice for visiting U.S. presidents and other dignitaries since 1912, when it was built. Its builder, lumber baron Simon Benson, spared no expense, importing rare Circassian walnut paneling, Austrian crystal chandeliers, and Italian marble to adorn this beautiful hotel. This commitment to superior quality remains, and the Benson's simple but exquisite furnishings and legendary attention to detail in service offer a fine balance of warmth and elegance.

The 287 guest rooms and suites are spacious, amply furnished in a traditional style with pleasing modern touches. Neutral tones are complemented by pretty accents of color, and furniture is very well upholstered. Amenities include complimentary high-speed wireless, access to the fitness center, and umbrellas in every room. You can also request TempurPedic Sleep System mattresses. The Grand Suite features a baby grand piano, a fireplace, and a Jacuzzi, and penthouse suites offer delightful views of the city around you. Even the more modest guest rooms, however, exude a classic sense of understated luxury.

The Benson's London Grill restaurant has been a Portland favorite for generations. Its downtown location is convenient to galleries, theaters, restaurants, and shopping, and the convention center is a short MAX ride away. Even if you don't stay here, drop by the lobby bar for a drink.

i Traveling with Fido? The Governor Hotel, the Benson, and the Heathman, all downtown, are proud to accommodate your dog. The Hotel Vintage Plaza even has an honor bar just for your pooch. For a list of dog-friendly hotels in Oregon, visit Pets Allowed Hotels at www.pets-allowed-hotels .com/us/Oregon/PORTLAND/index.html.

EMBASSY SUITES PORTLAND DOWNTOWN $$$$

319 Southwest Pine Street
(503) 279-9000, (800) EMBASSY
www.embassysuites.com

The Embassy Suites, which occupies the site of the historic Multnomah Hotel, is a beautiful modern luxury hotel that retains the site's old-fashioned charm. This sophisticated hotel offers guests 276 two-room suites done in a pleasing and restful decor, with traditional furnishings in tasteful creams, beiges, and golds. The east-facing rooms afford views of Mount Hood, 60 miles distant. Amenities are good—they include 24-hour room service, a heated indoor pool, a sauna and whirlpool, and a well-equipped athletic center. A cooked-to-order breakfast and a nightly hosted manager's reception are included in the room rate. Guest rooms include voice-mail service, microwaves, refrigerators, wet bars, high-speed Internet access, 25-inch color televisions, and Nintendo systems, in addition to the coffeemakers, irons, hair dryers, and other expected conveniences. A day spa in the hotel, Salon Nyla, features Aveda products and offers pedicures, massages, and other wonderful treatments to help get rid of your jet lag. And conference suites with a combination of meeting and sleeping space make this hotel an excellent conference site. (It boasts 22,000 square feet of meeting and banquet space, including a lovely ballroom.)

The building has a colorful history. Not only has it hosted celebrities from Elvis Presley to Charles Lindbergh, it is the only hotel in Oregon to serve as an airport, however briefly. As part of the 1912 Rose Festival, Silas Christopherson flew his Curtiss pusher biplane off the hotel's roof. The *Oregonian* wrote that the flight would never be done again, but they were wrong. In September 1995 Tom Murphy, a pilot from Hood River, Oregon, with permission from more than two dozen government agencies, duplicated the flight during the building's remodeling.

THE GOVERNOR HOTEL $$$-$$$$

614 Southwest 11th Avenue
(503) 224-3400, (800) 554-3456
www.govhotel.com

The historic Governor Hotel is an inviting luxury hotel rooted in the past but offering every modern convenience. Early-20th-century murals depicting the travels of Lewis and Clark, as well as mahogany woodwork, deep leather chairs, and a fireplace make the lobby a comfortable retreat. The beautiful stained-glass dome in the adjacent restaurant captures the grandeur of the building, which is a National Historic Landmark. A well-executed historic restoration extends throughout the hotel, including the 100 guest rooms.

The Governor's rooms come in a variety of styles, from luxury suites to simpler guest rooms, but each is decorated in pretty, pale colors. Some rooms have fireplaces. All rooms come with the standard luxury hotel amenities such as coffee, room service, newspapers, voice mail, wireless Internet access, phones, irons, hair dryers, and robes. But you'll know you're in Portland by the recycling program and the windows that open to clean Northwest breezes.

You'll find a Starbucks in the lobby, and just outside the door is the Portland Streetcar line. The Governor is ideally situated close to downtown shops, galleries, and restaurants. Jake's Bar and Grill, a younger sibling of the original Jake's, one of Portland's oldest and most popular restaurants, is adjacent.

THE HEATHMAN HOTEL $$$$

1001 Southwest Broadway at
Southwest Salmon Street
(503) 241-4100, (800) 551-0011
www.heathmanhotel.com

This popular and elegant downtown hotel is in a superb location next to Portland's Performing Arts Center and within a few blocks of the Portland Art Museum and the Park Blocks. Known for its attention to detail and its outstanding restaurant, the Heathman Hotel is also distinguished for its collection of work by local and regional artists and by such contemporary American artists as Andy Warhol. The 150 rooms offer a complete array of luxury-hotel amenities. The Heathman offers a "sleep menu" featuring different types of beds, including TempurPedic mattress options. Suites range in size from 520 to 1,200 square feet, with the Symphony Suites providing an excellent value. Rooms are furnished in beautifully warm tones and offer high-definition televisions. All rooms have hard-wired secure Internet access, with free wireless access in the lobby areas. The minibars are stocked with snacks from Pacific Northwest companies.

The Heathman Restaurant has long been one of Portland's best; the adjacent Marble Bar is a beautiful place for an evening cocktail. Tea is served every afternoon (reservations strongly suggested) in the Tea Court Lounge. This lounge, with 25-foot ceilings, a handsome fireplace, and a grand staircase to the mezzanine, is an original part of the hotel, and it's a favorite spot to read, relax, or just people-watch. Evenings in the lounge feature light jazz or piano performances by some of the area's best musicians. There is 24-hour room service, and guests can arrange sessions with personal trainers in the fitness suite. The unique mezzanine library—where you can actually check out the books—offers signed editions by authors who have been guests at the hotel, including Tom Wolfe, John Updike, and Alice Walker. Finally, the Heathman has an outstanding multilingual concierge staff who will find you tickets to local shows, make your dinner reservations, hook you up with sightseeing tours, and fulfill other special requests. Perhaps this is why *Travel and Leisure* magazine has named it one of the top 500 hotels in the world.

THE HILTON–PORTLAND $$$$
921 Southwest 6th Avenue
(503) 226-1611, (800) 445-8667
www.hilton.com
In the center of Portland's vibrant downtown, the Portland Hilton features a well-lit, contemporary facility that boasts 782 guest rooms and 40,000 square feet of meeting space. The updated and airy rooms, some with views of Mount Hood and the Cascade Mountains, include computer dataports, personalized voice mail, and free cable television. The nicely furnished lobby features a two-story atrium, entrances on both Southwest Broadway and Southwest 6th Avenue, and well-defined spaces with couches, chairs, and tables providing privacy and quiet. There is an attractive display of works by regional artists, and just off the lobby there is a warm, dark-paneled bar and restaurant. The Portland Hilton Athletic Club includes a large indoor pool, a Jacuzzi, sauna and steam rooms, aerobic classes, and exercise equipment as well as the services of fitness trainers and a massage therapist. Serving an international clientele, the Hilton offers foreign currency exchange and a multilingual staff. Here too the concierge staff is remarkably attentive and knowledgeable; they will help you arrange your dinner and entertainment, as well as help you find your way around the city.

HOTEL DELUXE PORTLAND $$$-$$$$
729 Southwest 15th Avenue
(503) 219-2094, (866) 895-2094
www.hoteldeluxeportland.com
This stylish hotel lies just south of the Pearl District, west of downtown and off the MAX line very near PGE Park, so it is convenient to everything. The hotel's decor pays homage to the era of the classic studio films, with stills from memorable movie moments lining the corridors and coolly elegant rooms. But its amenities are strictly 21st century. Flat-screen HDTVs adorn each room, and each room also comes equipped with high-speed, wireless Internet access and an iPod station (as well as iPod menus, if yours isn't jiving with the ambience). You can have your choice of a variety of styles of pillow, and the Spiritual Menu and "Make It So" button will help you meet all the rest of your needs. Most important, the beds are supercomfy. The Hotel DeLuxe occupies the space of the late, lamented Mallory Hotel. We were sad to see the Mallory sold, but its offspring is an entirely worthy successor that has gained many accolades for its wonderful atmosphere. Be sure to check out the hotel bar, The Driftwood Room—a fine spot for a pre-dinner cocktail.

THE HOTEL LUCIA $$$-$$$$
400 Southwest Broadway
(503) 225-1717, (877) 225-1717
www.hotellucia.com

The comfortable, well-designed Lucia is well located at the northern edge of the heart of downtown, close to all the major business, tourist, and shopping districts.

This attractive little hotel features a polished, Pacific Rim aesthetic that is remarkably soothing after a tough meeting. The Lucia pays close attention to detail and thoughtfully provides pillowtop mattresses and plush robes, flat screen televisions, iPod docks, and high-speed wireless Internet access (for a daily fee) in its 128 rooms. Other nice touches include therapeutic Tazo teas, Torrefazione coffee, and Aveda bath products. Rooms feature a contemporary decor in soothing greens and earth tones and luxurious white linens. The hotel's restaurant features an outstanding Thai menu that is also available for room service.

The Hotel Lucia also features a permanent collection of the photographs of David Kennerly, the Pulitzer Prize–winning Oregonian and personal photographer to President Gerald Ford. His distillations of national life and international events are on display throughout the public rooms and in the guest rooms as well.

HOTEL MONACO $$$$
506 Southwest Washington Street
(503) 222-0001, (888) 207-2201
www.monaco-portland.com

Rooms at the Hotel Monaco are like French salons, decorated in creamy tones accented by beautiful modern fabrics in complementary orange, periwinkle, and deep browns, with eclectic furniture and opulent linens. There are 229 rooms, a number of them one-bedroom suites, but all rooms come with fine amenities that include state-of-the-art 32-inch plasma televisions, speaker phones and voice mail, Wi-Fi, and plenty of work space, as well as coffeemakers and complimentary Starbucks coffee to assist you through that really tough deadline. Meeting space is also available in the hotel.

The Hotel Monaco offers 24-hour room service and honor bars, and the restaurant downstairs, the Red Star Tavern and Roast House, is one of Portland's best (see our Restaurants chapter).

This hotel occupies a building listed in the National Registry of Historic Places. Guests are just a block from Pioneer Courthouse Square. Stations for the MAX going both east and west are also very close. The shops of Pioneer Place, as well as Macy's, Nordstrom, and Nike Town, are an easy 3-block walk from the hotel, and downtown theaters, museums, the Performing Arts Center, and a host of excellent restaurants are nearby. The hotel has its own art collection and a good relationship with the Portland Art Museum—you can arrange to have a curator give you a private tour. And if you get inspired, the staff provide blank canvas, brushes, and paint every evening during a hosted wine reception The hotel also offers free morning coffee, tea, juice, and newspapers. And don't miss the in-room spa services—not only are massages available, but indulgences such as facials and foot treatments are offered as well.

HOTEL VINTAGE PLAZA $$$-$$$$
422 Southwest Broadway
(503) 228-1212, (800) 263-2305
www.vintageplaza.com

Featuring a wine country theme that extends to the names of most rooms, to the interior color scheme, and to a nightly tasting of Oregon wines at the lobby fireplace, the romantic Hotel Vintage Plaza is an intimate downtown hotel with an atmosphere and style that cushion guests from the fatigue of travel, touring, or business. The Vintage Plaza has everything a guest would want. The rooms are private, warm, comfortable, and tasteful, and they include complimentary high-speed wireless Internet. All aspects of the hotel's service are personal and highly polished. There are "starlight rooms" with conservatory windows that let natural light flow into the room, and some two-story townhouse suites. Pazzo Ristorante occupies the ground floor; its Northern Italian cuisine touched by Northwest influences is popular with locals too. The hotel, on the north end of downtown, is close to major shopping, cultural, and business districts.

THE MARK SPENCER HOTEL $$–$$$
409 Southwest 11th Avenue
(503) 224-3293, (800) 548-3934
www.markspencer.com

The Mark Spencer is a particularly good choice for extended stays in Portland, and it has special packages for artists—especially actors, directors, and other performance-art personnel—who are making lengthy visits. The hotel's clientele also includes business travelers and new residents relocating to the area. Perhaps more modest and conservative than some of the newer and trendier downtown hotels, the Mark Spencer's location offers convenience and value in its 101 rooms and suites. Rooms come with fully equipped kitchens, spacious closets, both on-site laundry and valet service, access to an athletic club, cable television, voice mail, the *New York Times*, and wireless high-speed Internet service (fee-based). Afternoon tea is served daily in the lobby, as well as a light breakfast in the morning. In the same block as Portland's renowned Jake's Restaurant, the Mark Spencer is just across Burnside Street from Powell's City of Books and close to both the MAX and streetcar lines. The hotel also has a great value for out-of-town art lovers: special arts packages that include tickets to theater, museum, and other events in addition to accommodations.

i **Even if you're not staying in them, Portland's beautiful downtown hotels are good places to visit. The Marble Bar at the Heathman, the lounge at the Benson, and the bar at the Ace Hotel are but a few of the agreeable spots to while away an hour before dinner.**

THE MARRIOTT HOTEL–CITY CENTER $$$
520 Southwest Broadway
(503) 226-6300, (800) 228-9290
www.marriott.com/

The renowned Marriott service and the plentiful amenities you have come to expect are here presented in a boutique hotel setting. This hotel features nearly 250 rooms and 10 suites on 20 floors; it's got a cocktail lounge and a restaurant on the premises; it's in the heart of downtown but close to the Pearl District, the Chinese Garden, and the river. It's a good hotel for the business traveler: The rooms have high-speed Internet access (fee-based), and the hotel provides a generous amount of meeting space. The paneled lobby is quite lovely, with a big chandelier and a sweeping staircase just right for making a spectacular entrance.

THE MARRIOTT HOTEL $$$
Downtown Waterfront
1401 Southwest Naito Parkway
(503) 226-7600, (800) 228-9290
www.marriott.com/

Across Naito Parkway from the Willamette River and the Tom McCall Riverfront Park, the uppermost of the Marriott's 503 rooms perch 14 stories above street level, offeringfine views of Mount Hood. A popular choice for business travelers and meeting and convention attendees, the hotel also attracts its share of tourists. The Marriott includes two restaurants, two bars, an indoor pool, and a 24-hour athletic club. This is a full-service hotel in the broadest sense of the word, with some wheelchair-accessible rooms. The Marriott is convenient to Portland's financial district and government buildings and to all downtown attractions, as well as to recreation areas along the Willamette River. Champions, the hotel's sports bar, is a popular and lively lounge and casual restaurant. Champions, and the Marriott as a whole, is popular with NBA teams visiting Portland to take on the Trailblazers at the nearby Rose Garden, so diners may see a favorite basketball player coming in for a snack. The bar's high-tech television system lets it broadcast every NBA game simultaneously (unless the game is blacked out).

THE PARAMOUNT HOTEL $$$$
808 Southwest Taylor Street
(503) 223-9900, (800) 716-6199
www.portlandparamount.com

The Paramount Hotel opened in 2000 with 154 chic and comfortable rooms. This European-style hotel offers plenty of amenities for travelers, from same-day laundry services to video games. The rooms are lovely, bigger than what you'll find in most hotels, with added luxuries such as granite bathrooms. Some rooms come with terraces and jetted tubs, and two delightful suites are available—these have excellent views of the city, as well as fireplaces and whirlpools. All rooms come with dual-line phones and wireless Internet access; two large meeting rooms are also available. The stylish restaurant and bar, the Dragonfish Asian Cafe, also provides room service and catering for business functions. The downtown location could not be more central; the hotel is a heartbeat away from the Schnitzer, the Portland Art Museum, some of the best downtown shopping, and fabulous restaurants. The Paramount also offers a beautiful fitness center, if you haven't gotten enough exercise walking around downtown. The service, by the way, is excellent—friendly, helpful, and understated. Rates for U.S. government employees are available.

RESIDENCE INN PORTLAND–
DOWNTOWN/RIVERPLACE $$$
2115 Southwest River Parkway
(503) 552-9500
www.marriott.com
This Marriott-owned hotel is part of the familiar chain, but we include it here because of its stellar location on the Willamette River just south of downtown in the South Waterfront district. It is not only served by the Portland Streetcar line, but it is also within walking distance of downtown. You also have access to the beautiful paths, gardens, and parks along the river, as well as the restaurants and shops of RiverPlace—and the Portland Aerial Tram. The views from some rooms are wonderful, and the hotel itself is quite attractive. This Residence Inn features the usual amenities, but it also has an indoor pool and spa. Lobby areas have wireless Internet access, with wired access in the suites. All the rooms have fully equipped kitchens and that, along with its unsurpassed location, makes this hotel an outstanding value for families and other groups.

THE RIVERPLACE HOTEL $$$$
1510 Southwest Harbor Way
(503) 228-3233, (800) 227-1333
www.riverplacehotel.com
On the bank of the Willamette River, the RiverPlace Hotel offers rooms and suites facing the river or with a north view of the city's skyline. During the summer the hotel's patio is a good spot from which to view the frequent displays of fireworks, not to mention an unending, colorful stream of runners, in-line skaters, skateboarders, dog-walkers, cyclists, and people out for a stroll. The river hosts a 24-hour parade of tour boats, sailboats, personal watercraft, barges and log-tows, dragon-boats, yachts, kayaks, and the occasional sailboard.

Separated from the core of the downtown by busy Southwest Naito Parkway, guests can walk along the Tom McCall Waterfront Park to reach downtown's stores, galleries, and other attractions. There is also a small group of shops and stores along the esplanade, facing the river. The hotel is near the streetcar line and a short ride away from the Portland Aerial Tram.

The lobby is elegant, filled with large, artistic displays of fresh flowers, and the staff is well trained, polite, and attentive. Rooms are comfortable, with large baths and contemporary decor, featuring the usual amenities of a quality hotel—free Wi-Fi (in public areas), DVD and CD players, cushy robes, and luxurious bath products. Guests are given breakfast and have access to the adjacent RiverPlace Athletic Club, for a small fee. An excellent restaurant is on-site: Three Degrees, which offers regional specialties beautifully prepared.

THE WESTIN PORTLAND $$$$
750 Southwest Alder Street
(503) 294-9000
http://www.starwoodhotels.com/
One of the nicest downtown luxury hotels, the Westin imparts the feeling that its guests are the most important creatures in the world with the lushness of its surroundings and the attentiveness of its service. The rooms are elegant, with

cozy down duvets on the beds, and oversize, walk-in showers in the bathrooms. (The hotel also provides CD players and a CD library, which are useful because you might not want to leave the room.) Like all state-of-the-art hotels, the Westin's rooms come equipped with two-line phones and high-speed Internet access (fee-based). For events, the hotel has a number of different-size meeting rooms, as well as a ballroom. The Westin is able to make use of its corporate resources to provide desirable services like the Westin Kids Club and Business Office rooms, and the service is also remarkably thoughtful and charming. The Daily Grill restaurant serves attentively prepared American cuisine from 6:30 a.m. to 11:00 p.m. weekdays and Saturday and Sunday from 7:00 a.m. to midnight; 24-hour room service is also available.

Northwest Portland

INN AT NORTHRUP STATION $$$
2025 Northwest Northrup Street
(503) 224-0543, (800) 224-1180
www.northrupstation.com

The Inn at Northrup Station is a welcome addition to Northwest Portland, where there are few hotels. This stylish place features suites that balance a hip aesthetic with contemporary comforts. Its rooms are brightly colored and filled with modern furniture, with dramatic marble and granite in the bathrooms and kitchens. The hotel's large rooms also include the standard amenities, as well as little luxuries such as private decks and balconies and high-speed wireless Internet. The Inn at Northrup Station is well located between the lively shopping and restaurant districts on Northwest 21st and Northwest 23rd Avenues—and it's right on the streetcar line, offering easy access to the Pearl District and downtown Portland.

SILVER CLOUD INN $$$
2426 Northwest Vaughn Street
(503) 242-2400, (800) 205-6939
www.scinns.com

This Silver Cloud Inn is situated in Northwest

Portland, at the edge of an industrial area. Yet not only is it well placed for business travelers, it is also convenient for anyone wanting to explore Northwest Portland. The hotel is tidy, quiet, and within walking distance of good restaurants, an eclectic mix of small shops, a brewpub, and coffeehouses. Close to the intersection of the area's main freeways, the hotel is also near the trendy and chic shopping districts on Northwest 23rd and Northwest 21st Avenues.

The hotel offers covered parking, a fitness center and spa, a video library, a complimentary breakfast, cable TV, and high-speed Internet access in all the rooms. Pets are welcome. The hotel's location allows easy access to the highways following the Columbia River to the Oregon coast and to those leading east to Mount Hood and the Columbia Gorge.

Southeast Portland

BLUEBIRD GUESTHOUSE $
3517 Southeast Division Street
(503) 238-4333, (866) 717-4333
www.bluebirdguesthouse.com

Something beyond a hotel but not quite a bed-and-breakfast inn, the Bluebird Guesthouse brings much-needed and novel accommodations to Southeast Portland. The seven charming guest rooms and the public areas in this repurposed vintage Portland house are decorated with vivid colors and comfortable furniture. The Bluebird offers a light breakfast in the morning, but you may use the spacious kitchen to make any kind of meal you like—and if you don't feel like cooking, the Bluebird is within easy walking distance of a number of Portland's best restaurants, as well as coffeeshops, bars, retail, and other urban eye candy. It's also a 10-minute drive to downtown Portland, as well as convenient to public transportation. Two rooms have private bathrooms; the others share two and a half bathrooms (translation: no waiting). There are an ironing board and laundry facilities on site; towels, soap, shampoo, and so on are provided. Children ages 4 and older are welcome. One thing you should know: There are no televisions. However, there is a computer

The Jupiter Hotel is located near fun restaurants, galleries, and shops. RACHEL DRESBECK

that guests can use, and there's free Wi-Fi, too, for those who've brought their laptops.

JUPITER HOTEL $$
800 East Burnside Street
(503) 230-9200, (877) 800-0004
www.jupiterhotel.com

The Jupiter Hotel is at the center of the revival of "Lo-Bu"—Lower Burnside, on the east side of the Willamette River—and it has won accolades for its approach to hospitality since the minute it opened. The Jupiter is a restyled motel built in the 1960s, and the hotel evokes that era's Land-of-Tomorrow, modern sensibility. Its 80 rooms are divided into the "quiet" side and the "party" side, which is important information depending on how you view proximity to the adjacent Doug Fir Lounge (one of Portland's hottest night spots). The hotel offers the important amenities, as well as chalkboard doors for doodling, an outdoor fire pit, and Blu Dot furnishings. As the apotheosis of hip Portland, it's where the Beautiful People stay,

and you'll likely become more beautiful if you stay there too.

MONARCH HOTEL & CONFERENCE CENTER $$$
12566 Southeast 93rd Avenue
(503) 652-1515, (800) 492-8700
www.monarchhotel.cc

The Monarch Hotel & Conference Center in outer Southeast Portland is off I–205 with easy access to I–5 and I–84; it's close to Clackamas Town Center—one of Oregon's largest enclosed shopping malls. The Monarch, one of the nicest hotels in the area, offers free shuttle service to and from the airport and nearby shopping complexes. Most of the 20,000 square feet of meeting and convention space is situated around a lovely garden courtyard. The 192-room hotel accommodates groups from 10 to 1,000 and offers free parking.

Guests are invited to enjoy the open courtyard swimming pool (in season), which is adjoined by a year-round whirlpool spa and a nearby 20-mile jogging and biking path. Other amenities include Sam's Restaurant, which has built a good reputation, a multilevel lounge featuring live entertainment Wednesday through Saturday, and valet service.

North/Northeast Portland
Inner North/Northeast Portland

DOUBLETREE HOTEL LLOYD CENTER $$$
1000 Northeast Multnomah Street
(503) 281-6111, (800) 222-8733
www.doubletree.com
A local standard by virtue of its size (476 rooms) and location, this DoubleTree attracts business travelers and visitors, meetings, and conventions as well as dinners and ceremonies that bring out the black-tie and slinky-dress crowd. The lobby, restaurants, and parking garage bustle with swirls of activity, but this organized frenzy is easily left behind when you get to your room. Some of the rooms have views of the city skyline, the West Hills, and the Willamette River; others look out over Mount Hood. The hotel's location makes it a good choice for tourists. The Lloyd Center shopping mall is across the street; the Oregon Convention Center is just 3 blocks to the west. There is a light-rail stop nearby, and the hotel offers free parking. Guests can choose standard rooms or master suites complete with in-room spas. All rooms have a refrigerator and high-speed Internet access, with wireless access in the public areas of the hotel.

The hotel is served by the airport shuttle and has a swimming pool and a fitness center, covered parking, and a gift shop. Pets are welcome. One of the region's largest shopping centers, the Lloyd Center, with a Nordstrom, a Meier & Frank, and dozens of other stores, a food court, and a covered ice-skating rink, is a very short walk away. Two restaurants, the Multnomah Grille and Eduardo's, are on-site. The Executive Meeting Center, a full-service, state-of-the-art business meeting facility, is a major feature of this comfortable, well-situated hotel.

HOLIDAY INN–PORTLAND AT THE OREGON CONVENTION CENTER $$$
1441 Northeast 2nd Avenue
(503) 233-2401, (877) 777-2704
www.hiportland.com/about
This beautifully remodeled Holiday Inn is conveniently situated for business or pleasure: The Memorial Coliseum and Rose Quarter complex are 3 blocks to the west, the Oregon Convention Center is across the street, and the Lloyd Center shopping mall and cinema are just 3 blocks to the east. If you need to travel across town, Portland's MAX light-rail line stops across the street—and it's within the Fareless Square area. The 166 comfortably decorated, air-conditioned guest rooms (including master suites with spas) are each furnished with a mini-refrigerator, telephones, and free wireless Internet access. Free coffee and parking are provided to all guests. The service at this hotel also includes complimentary downtown parking and a staff that speaks Russian and Spanish (in addition to English).

MCMENAMINS KENNEDY SCHOOL $$
5736 Northeast 33rd Avenue
(503) 249-3983, (888) 249-3983
www.mcmenamins.com/Kennedy
The wonderful Kennedy School is one of our favorite recommendations for out-of-town guests. This unusual 35-room inn inhabits a pretty ex-school (now on the Historic Register), reclaiming classrooms and offices to provide comfortable and spacious rooms for guests. These rooms are charmingly decorated with rich colors and cozy, vintage furniture. Rooms include king- and queen-size beds, phones and modems, as well as private baths. Guests have access to free wireless Internet. A soaking pool invites guests to linger, and the restored gym is available for a game of pickup (as long as it's free of banqueters).

These are all good reasons to love the Kennedy School, but the inn is far more than a guest-house. This extensive campus is a destination for much of Portland—not only neighbors, but people from all over town frequent the excellent bars, restaurants, and theaters (for both movies and live music), drawn by the convivial ambience and the six-barrel brewery. The Kennedy School is very popular for meetings, reunion dinners, parties, and all manner of gatherings. It is an engine of neighborhood activity, helping to inspire the regeneration of surrounding blocks. This place is quintessential Portland.

Outer North/Northeast Portland (Near the Airport)

COURTYARD BY MARRIOTT– PORTLAND AIRPORT $$–$$$
11550 Northeast Airport Way
(503) 252-3200
http://www.marriott.com

Less than 3 miles east of the Portland International Airport, this facility offers plenty of user-friendly accommodations for business road warriors and leisure travelers alike and provides free, 24-hour airport transportation. The 140 rooms include free wireless Internet access, AM/FM clock radios, color televisions with cable, in-room coffee service, hair dryers, and irons and ironing boards. Each of the 10 suites has a microwave, mini-refrigerator, small bar sink, and two color televisions. There are also 10 wheelchair-accessible rooms. After dining in the Courtyard Cafe (or, if you prefer, enjoying a room service dinner), you may unwind in the cozy lounge watching the 32-inch television or soak your stresses away in the outdoor pool and whirlpool.

HOLIDAY INN PORTLAND AIRPORT $$$
8439 Northeast Columbia Boulevard
(503) 256-5000

Just minutes from the airport (yes, 24-hour free shuttle service is provided) and 15 minutes from downtown Portland, this thoroughly modernized hotel is attractive and comfortable. The 286 sparkling guest rooms feature keyless entry systems, new furniture, irons, hair dryers, and coffeemakers. Guests can take advantage of the on-site newsstand, gift shop, one-day laundry, and dry-cleaning services as well as car rental service and free parking. This inn offers an indoor swimming pool, saunas, a Jacuzzi, video games,

and exercise equipment. After you work up an appetite, your options include fine dining at the Northwest Grill and dancing and other nighttime fun at Flirts Lounge.

SHERATON PORTLAND AIRPORT HOTEL $$–$$$
8235 Northeast Airport Way
(503) 281-2500

A full-service hotel located on Portland International Airport grounds, this Sheraton is friendly as well as functional. All rooms feature a full-size working desk, lounge chair, two telephones, and a minibar. Guest services include a business center, an in-house travel agency, a gift shop, free wireless Internet access, an exercise facility, a heated pool, a therapy pool, saunas, and free parking. The Columbia Grille and Bar is open for breakfast, lunch, and dinner. The hotel offers 24-hour room service, as well as a lobby bar and espresso. This hotel is one minute from the terminal, so it's a great choice if you have an early morning flight.

Vancouver

THE HEATHMAN LODGE $$$
7801 Northeast Greenwood Drive
(360) 254-3100, (888) 475-3100
www.heathmanlodge.com

Known for its charming combination of Pacific Northwest lodge decor and modern conveniences, this hotel has a reputation for world-class service and attention. The lobby and other common areas are done in rustic pine, accented by the color and classic designs of Pendleton blankets and pillows; in fact, the 121 oversize guest rooms have Pendleton bedspreads. Most come with desks and fireplaces. All have free wireless Internet access, refrigerator, coffeemaker, and microwave, as well as an iron, ironing board, and hair dryer. Business travelers appreciate the two-line telephones, dataports, and voice mail. This hotel is equipped with an enclosed swimming pool, sauna and whirlpool, and complete fitness center. The 24-hour room service, laundry facilities, free parking, free morning newspaper, and delicious continental breakfast will also add to your comfort. The Heathman's restaurant, Hudson's Bar and Grill, offers excellent cuisine. Across from Vancouver Mall and a host of restaurants and other services, the Heathman Lodge is 15 minutes from the Portland Airport.

RED LION AT THE QUAY $$$
100 Columbia Street
(360) 694-8341, (800) 222-8733
On the banks of the Columbia River in downtown Vancouver, the Red Lion at the Quay is just off I–5 after it crosses the Columbia River. This wired hotel is a popular site for meetings, seminars, and banquets, and it offers both standard rooms (smoking and nonsmoking) and suites, some that include hot tubs. The Red Lion at the Quay is close to golf courses, maintains an outdoor pool, and is right off a 3K jogging path, if the fitness center isn't enough for you. The attached restaurant, the Pacific Grill and Chowder House, offers casual dining with a sweeping view of the Columbia River.

i The root word for *hotel* is "hostel" and in Portland we have two: in Northwest Portland at 1818 Northwest Glisan Street (503-241-2783) and in Southeast Portland at 3031 Southeast Hawthorne Boulevard (503-236-3380).

Outlying Areas
MCMENAMINS EDGEFIELD $–$$
2126 Southwest Halsey Street, Troutdale
(503) 669-8610, (800) 669-8610
www.mcmenamins.com/Edge
Like the Kennedy School (see Northeast Portland), McMenamins Edgefield is a reclaimed historic building. This inn was formerly the Multnomah County Poor Farm, and where the McMenamin brothers now grow grapes, the poor once labored to grow vegetables, raise pigs, and milk cows. The McMenamins are delightfully attuned to the echoes of the past and provide tours and books that detail the history of these grounds.

Edgefield is a big complex that includes a variety of operations besides hostelry. A large McMenamins' brewery is on the grounds, and it is also the home of the McMenamin brothers' winery. Edgefield holds many different events—conferences, concerts, weddings, and other large gatherings—and it has numerous facilities within its grounds to sustain these activities. In the main lodge is the Black Rabbit Restaurant and Bar, serving breakfast, lunch, and dinner daily. And you will also find the Power Station Pub and Theater, an English-style pub serving McMenamins' ales and showing feature films each night (kids are welcome at the first showing if their parents are with them). Other places include the Loading Dock Beer Garden and Grill (near the brewery), the Little Red Shed (a bar that serves the hard stuff and offers cigars), and the Ice House, which possesses the only television on the grounds, so that no one has to miss an important Blazers game.

Edgefield is a hotel in the European style, which is to say that most of its 100 rooms are served by bathrooms that serve the whole wing in which they are located. Several rooms with private baths are available, however. Rooms are spacious and handsome, decorated with old-fashioned furniture and in vibrant colors—and they are certainly luxurious by comparison to the standards of their past residents. Edgefield is regarded as a bit of a getaway, and rooms are free of phones and televisions, though business services are supplied if you are planning a meeting or business retreat. (To keep things in balance, an on-site masseuse is also available.) Room rates include the price of breakfast.

BED-AND-BREAKFAST INNS

Southwest Portland

THE FULTON HOUSE $$$$
7006 Southwest Virginia Avenue
(503) 892-5781
www.thefultonhouse.com
The Fulton House offers two well-appointed guest suites in a lovely 19th-century house near Willamette Park along the river, as well as near the

Portland Aerial Tram. While the house once served as a floating bordello, it has reformed its character and now provides nothing but the most respectable accommodations. Breakfasts are served buffet style, and treats are offered every afternoon. Both suites have private baths and sitting areas, as well as telephones, cable television, and wireless Internet access. The grounds of the Fulton House are lovely—lush green lawns and water features, beautiful flowers, and a wonderfully spacious porch and patio area. There, you will find a hot tub and an outdoor grill, both of which you may use. The Fulton House also has an extensive wine cellar, from which you may purchase something tasty to go with your grilling.

The Fulton neighborhood is one of Portland's oldest—indeed, it used to be a separate town—and it is filled with pretty houses and cute shops, as well as offering plentiful, free, and safe street parking. Its proximity to the Willamette greenway means that it is well situated for walking and biking along the river, but it is just a few minutes' drive from all the downtown attractions as well.

MACMASTER HOUSE $-$$$
1041 Southwest Vista Avenue
(503) 223-7362, (800) 774-9523
www.macmaster.com
MacMaster House is distinguished by its Greek columns, seven fireplaces, and leaded-glass windows. The house and guest rooms are decorated and furnished in a style that owner Cecilia Murphy calls "Parisian salon." Rooms typically have queen-size beds, luxurious linens and down comforters, fireplaces, cable TVs, VCRs, and a large film selection. Wireless Internet access is available. A few rooms have private baths, while others share a hallway bath. A nice feature of MacMaster House is the range of rooms, from a modest single to a capacious master suite. Local muralist Myrna Anderson has created a dreamlike atmosphere in several rooms that feature her work.

Guests gather in the dining room for a hearty breakfast that includes croissants, crepes, and omelets prepared by a creative kitchen staff. It is served on a staggered schedule. Breakfast is also offered on the patio and veranda June through October. Besides great food and conversation, guests are treated to views of the city's skyline, Mount Hood, and Mount St. Helens, which can be glimpsed through the trees outside the spacious rooms' windows. The MacMaster House sits in one of Portland's oldest and nicest neighborhoods, and the other large and immaculately kept homes in the neighborhood reflect a variety of architectural styles. The gallery of the Portland Society of Artists; Washington Park with its ponds, rose gardens, picnic areas, and tennis courts; the lively shopping district along 23rd Avenue; and Restaurant Row, along 21st Avenue, are all just a short walk away. There is convenient access to freeways as well as public transportation, including Westside MAX light-rail system.

i **The MacMaster House, in the King's Hill neighborhood, was built in 1895 by William MacMaster, a mover and shaker in the world of Portland business. MacMaster founded the Waverly Country Club and sent his daughters to school with the future Duchess of Windsor.**

TERWILLIGER VISTA
BED & BREAKFAST $$-$$$$
515 Southwest Westwood Drive
(503) 244-0602, (888) 244-0602
www.terwilligervista.com
Originally built for a prominent Portland family in 1941, the Terwilliger Vista is a large Georgian-style colonial house in the city's west hills. Large bay windows in the 6,000-square-foot home offer seasonal views of the city's skyline, Mount Hood, and the Willamette River, and, even on those darker days of winter, they fill the home with light. Located on a half-acre site colored by rose gardens, camellias, and rhododendrons, the bed-and-breakfast is minutes from downtown Portland but a world away from the usual urban irritants of traffic, noise, and crowds.

All five of Terwilliger's guest rooms are air-conditioned and offer either king- or queen-size beds, private baths, guest refrigerators, cable television, and fireplaces. A two-room suite is also available. Guests can enjoy a full breakfast from 7:30 to 9:30 a.m. in a spacious dining room. Breakfasts are served buffet style and feature healthy and delicious comfort food. A continental breakfast is available in the early morning for those whose schedules keep them from enjoying the full meal. Complimentary sodas, bottled water, port, and sherry are available in the library. The location is convenient to OHSU and the VA hospital, and the beautiful Olmsted-designed Terwilliger Boulevard is nearby, with wide pedestrian paths and city views. Terwilliger Vista is a gracious retreat from a day's activities, offering the convenience of close-in lodging with the privacy, quiet, and welcome comforts of a fine home. Children older than 10 are welcome. Call between 8:00 a.m. and 9:00 p.m., PST.

i The King's Hill neighborhood was the boyhood home of John Reed, the journalist who wrote *Ten Days That Shook the World*, a sympathetic account of the Bolshevik Revolution. Reed is the only American to be buried in the Kremlin Wall.

North/Northeast Portland

THE BLUE PLUM $$–$$$
2026 Northeast 15th Avenue
(503) 288-3848, (877) 288-3844
www.bluepluminn.com

This handsome inn in the Irvington district was built in 1900. It offers four rooms with private baths, some of which can be combined into suites. A major attraction of the Blue Plum, however, is the attentively prepared breakfasts that feature fresh Northwest ingredients. The same attention to delicious detail is found in their lovely afternoon tea. The dining room and living room are spacious and comfortable, with a carved fireplace as a notable feature. The vintage furnishings disguise the modern amentities such as wireless Internet access and convenient public transportation. The Blue Plum is in an excellent location—the beautiful neighborhood is a

pleasure for walking, and the inn is very close to the shops and restaurants of Broadway, as well as near the Lloyd Center shopping mall and the Oregon Convention Center. And it's just a short trip downtown.

GEORGIAN HOUSE BED & BREAKFAST $$
1828 Northeast Siskiyou Street
(503) 281-2250, (888) 282-2250
www.thegeorgianhouse.com

A stay here reveals why Portland prides itself as a city of distinct neighborhoods and one of the nation's most livable cities. A winding staircase, stained-glass windows, and antique furnishings create the mood at this urban bed-and-breakfast that quietly provides comfortable, air-conditioned lodging for visitors seeking relaxed accommodations. The surrounding neighborhood retains its residential character while being near public transit, shopping, and downtown. The Rose Quarter, with the Oregon Convention Center, and the covered Lloyd Center, with its mix of department stores, movie theaters, and restaurants, are also close by.

This classic, immaculately maintained Georgian colonial home was built in 1922 and has been featured in *Better Homes & Gardens*. The magazine noted that the bed-and-breakfast has created an atmosphere of an English country home. A breakfast of tea and pastries also reflects this charm.

Guest rooms have either a private or shared bath and are furnished with antiques. The lower-level spacious and very private Captain Irving Room includes a gas-log fireplace; the Victorian Eastlake Room overlooks the deck, gazebo, and English-style gardens, which feature roses and boxwoods and also provide a variety of berries, grapes, and kiwi for breakfast. The Lovejoy Suite, which has the feel of a bridal suite, has a queen-size brass canopy bed and a private bath with clawfoot tub. There is ample parking.

Children 12 and older are welcome in the Captain Irving Room. The inn has discounts for corporate travelers and for those on extended stays.

THE LION AND THE ROSE $$$–$$$$
1810 Northeast 15th Avenue
(503) 287-9245, (800) 955-1647
www.lionrose.com

This rambling but immaculately restored Victorian in the well-established Northeast Portland Irvington neighborhood could serve as a postcard image of a past era, offering guests a classic bed-and-breakfast experience. Convenient to all of Portland and the entire region, this inn is close to the popular shopping, restaurant, and latte district along Northeast Broadway. Lloyd Center, as well as the Oregon Convention Center, the Rose Garden, the Coliseum, and the Oregon Nature Information Center are also nearby. This inn is listed on the National Register of Historic Places, and its decor and atmosphere create a sense of relaxed elegance. Guests have the option of an early continental breakfast or, a bit later, the real thing. Guests are also served an afternoon dessert tea. The grounds include English-style gardens, a gazebo, fountains, and brick pathways. Smoking is permitted on the veranda.

All rooms have private baths, and the Rose Room features a queen-size bed and a Jacuzzi. Other rooms offer guests the chance to sleep in an antique Edwardian bed, a flat-top canopy bed, or a traditional four-poster bed. Children older than 12 are welcome. Occasionally this inn requires a two-night minimum, especially on weekends and holidays.

A PAINTED LADY INN $$$
1927 Northeast 16th Avenue
(503) 335-0700
www.apaintedladyinn.com

A Painted Lady Inn is a well-wrought little gem in the Irvington area, well situated to take advantage of shopping, restaurants, and entertainment, with easy access to downtown Portland as well. There are three guest rooms, and—a big plus—delicious, seasonal breakfasts served in your room (or the dining room if you wish). The guest rooms are airy and bright, and the common rooms filled with period furniture that complements this pretty house built in 1904. The grounds are lovely and include a back terrace for sunny morning coffee and newspaper-reading—as well as a porch swing.

PORTLAND'S WHITE HOUSE $$$
1914 Northeast 22nd Avenue
(503) 287-7131, (800) 272-7131
(503) 249-1641 (fax)
www.portlandswhitehouse.com

Completely restored to the grand splendor of 1911, Portland's White House was built of Honduran mahogany by early Portland timber magnate Robert Lyle. It has nine elegant guest rooms, all with private baths and featuring period furnishings and decor. The Garden Room sports a private terrace, and the Canopy Room has, of course, a canopied bed. With a circular drive, massive classic Greek columns, fountains, a carriage house, and Japanese maples, this inn bears some resemblance to its Washington, D.C., namesake. Guests can visit the parlor for sherry or board games. The inn is a local landmark, close to attractions on the city's East Side, and convenient to downtown. This remarkable inn serves a chef's breakfast by candlelight that includes their signature dish: salmon eggs Benedict with orange hollandaise. Children are welcome if you arrange it in advance.

i The beautiful Irvington district, home to many of Portland's bed-and-breakfast inns and more than 20 officially designated historic sites, was one of the first planned communities in the area. Its success was due partly to strict building codes and partly to the trolley that transported its banker and lawyer residents downtown.

Outlying Areas

BROETJE HOUSE $–$$
3101 Southeast Courtney Road
Milwaukie
(503) 659-8860
www.thebroetjehouse.com

On an acre of scenic grounds with century-old shrubs, flowers, and redwoods, this Queen

Anne–style inn, complete with four-story water tower, was built by noted Oregon horticulturist John F. Broetje in 1889. The building's history includes a role as a winery before its career as a bed-and-breakfast and a location for weddings, receptions, and other gatherings. This retreat is convenient to all the area's attractions and is 15 to 20 minutes from downtown Portland. Wireless Internet access is readily available. Guests are served a full country breakfast with signature dishes of oven pancakes topped with fresh fruit and coffee-cake muffins. After a night in one of three Victorian rooms furnished in Queen Anne style, guests can relax in the gazebo, the sitting room, or even in the inn's country kitchen. The hostess reports that the bridal suite with its private bath is their most popular selection.

RESTAURANTS

The Pacific Northwest has long been known for its regional abundance. The Kalapuya, Molalla, Clackamas, and other Native Americans who lived in the Willamette Valley ate remarkably well. And it wasn't just the sheer abundance of the game, camas roots, filberts, mushrooms, truffles, berries, and wild greens. It was also the clever way of cooking—for example, smoking salmon over open fires or roasting it on cedar planks. Their legends are notable for their gratitude over their good fortune.

Modern chefs in Portland are equally fortunate. They carry on that same tradition of using regional ingredients and preparing them in clever ways. While most chefs aren't serving camas roots—yet—they have a lot to work with. The Willamette Valley provides some of the most fruitful farmland in the nation, and we also have a mild climate with a decently long growing season. Like the rest of the nation, we are losing family farms. Yet a small but significant countertrend is also noticeable: The area has seen a revival of small, specialty farms in recent years, and local chefs make good use of these farms and the many farmers' markets in the area. The Portland chapter of the Chefs Collaborative, a national organization dedicated to serving Americans sustainably produced food that is local and seasonal, has instituted an innovative program called the Farmer-Chef Connection. This program brings farmers, fisheries, and other small purveyors together with Portland restaurants, a win-win situation for everyone: The chefs get the best and freshest produce imaginable, the farmers get to sell directly to the chef, and we customers get the best food. But the love of the local does not stop at produce. It also extends to the raising of specialty meats such as rabbit, to the crafting of perfect goat cheeses, to the baking of ideal loaves of crusty, chewy bread. And just as earlier inhabitants of the Willamette Valley migrated from Asia, Portland chefs also reflect our nomadic origins in their variety of culinary influences, from Alaska to Zanzibar. For a city of our size, we have an outsize reputation as a food mecca, a reputation that grows daily. As the *New York Times* recently noted, Portland is enjoying "a golden age of dining and drinking." Which raises the question of what you should drink with all this bounty. Our region is known especially for its excellent wine and beer, its fine coffee roasters and tea houses. We share the climate of the Burgundy region of France, and many of the varietal grapes that grow well there also grow well here. Hops—the ingredient that gives beer its piquancy—also grow well here. And while coffee and tea don't grow here, chilly, wet winters have given local roasters and tea brewers the necessary impetus to perfect those beverages.

OVERVIEW

This chapter divides restaurants into their geographic locations. Portland's destination restaurants are found all over the city. Talented chefs are working kitchens all over town, and many neighborhood places are also destinations for loyal followers and adventuresome people looking for something new. Unless noted, all the restaurants listed take the usual credit cards. By Oregon law restaurants have no-smoking policies, and as of January 2009, so do bars and taverns.

Price Code

Most restaurants have offerings at a range of

Oregon's bounty inspires Portland's chefs. CLEO BETHEL

prices. The price code here reflects the general cost of a single entree, excluding drinks, hors d'oeuvres, side dishes, and tips. As with other Portland purchases, there is no sales tax.

$	**$10 or less**
$$	**$11–$20**
$$$	**$21–$30**
$$$$	**More than $30**

SOUTHWEST PORTLAND

BIJOU CAFE $$
132 Southwest 3rd Avenue
(503) 222-3187
The Bijou's excellent breakfasts, lunches, and weekend brunches are a staple of the downtown crowd, and for atmosphere, there are few better places than this urbane and crowded spot. The entrees are attentively made using as many local and organic ingredients as possible. The Bijou makes some of the best French toast, pancakes, and egg dishes in Portland. The oatmeal is served with chopped filberts. The roast beef hash is delicious. And the oyster omelet with bacon and onions is definitely worth the wait you'll endure at the door.

BRAZIL GRILL $$$
1201 Southwest 12th Avenue
(503) 222-0002
This steak house serves churrasco-style grilled meats, a cuisine developed from the Brazilian cowboy habit of roasting meat over an open fire. Brazil Grill looks like a dentist's office on the outside, but upon entering the restaurant, you'll be transported a world away. The dining room is spacious, and the orange walls and dark floors are pleasing in their contrast, echoing the contrasts in the food. When you are seated at your table, your server will give you a red and green disk, for "stop" and "go." (When you're eating, turn the red side up; when you want more, turn it to the green side.) You'll start with side dishes that are served salad-bar style, inventive and delicious, and

that feature combinations such as curried sweet potato or green onions and pimentos with hearts of palm. When it's time for your meat course, you'll turn your disk over to green, and the servers will bring large skewers of grilled meats right to your table, and you choose from among the bounty. You'll find everything from sausages to skirt steak to pork loin to alligator, and, in between, you are served roasted pineapple as a palate cleanser. The wine list is small but intelligent, and the cocktails are very good as well. We don't know why anyone from a country as wonderful as warm and sunny Brazil would move to Portland, Oregon, but we are certainly glad that they have, and that they have opened Brazil Grill.

CARAFE $$
200 Southwest Market Street
(503) 248-0004
A favorite of the downtown crowd for both lunch and dinner, Carafe is the home of one of Portland's favorite chefs, Pascal Sauton. Sauton labored for many years as the corporate chef in restaurants at RiverPlace, but now he has the chance to flex his creative muscles, to the delight of Portland diners. This wonderful bistro is remarkably Parisian, with rows of outdoor chairs facing the street and an elegant but unfussy interior of dusky gold and reddish brown. Its prime location across the street from Keller Auditorium makes it a favorite before shows. But no matter what's playing, the true star will be the superbly prepared food—French classics such as *croque monsieur*, *frisée* salad with bacon, baked escargot, duck confit with olives, and bouillabaisse. We especially love the mussels cooked with shallots and cream, but even the lemonade here is impeccably French. The wine selection is full of excellent values, well chosen and in a range of styles and prices—including interesting *vins du table* available in (you guessed it) carafes. Carafe is open for lunch on weekdays and for dinner every day except Sunday. The service here is excellent and they will do anything for you, but it's best to call ahead if a show is playing at the Keller, for the place will be mobbed and you won't get a table without a reservation. Valet parking is available.

CASSIDY'S $$
1331 Southwest Washington Street
(503) 223-0054
Cassidy's reputation as a good late-night bar is so firm that we sometimes forget how good the food is. Premium-cut meats, steamed mussels in rich broths, creamy pastas—all these go beautifully with the local wines and microbrews that Cassidy's also features. The bar's dark paneling and old-fashioned wooden refrigerators remind us of Boston or New York, but the food and drinks are definitely Portland. It's close to PGE Park and the Crystal Ballroom, and it makes a fine after-event stop.

Rooms with a View

Feasting your eyes can be almost as satisfying as plain old feasting, and three places to do it are the Chart House, the Marina Fish House, and the Portland City Grill.

The Chart House (5700 Southwest Terwilliger Boulevard, 503–246–6963) is a beautiful spot to enjoy the visual feast of the city as it stretches to meet the foothills and Mount Hood in the eastern distance. The Marina Fish House (425 Southwest Montgomery Street, 503-227-3474) is special because of its location on the Willamette—the only floating restaurant with a 360-degree view of the city. The outdoor patio is a great spot to sip something cool and watch for great blue herons and other water-dwellers. And the Portland City Grill (111 Southwest 5th Avenue, 30th floor, 503-450-0030) sits atop the U.S. Bank Tower, where it hands out impressive views that stretch far afield and help you put things in perspective. It's perfect for a romantic drink before dinner.

CLYDE COMMON $$
1014 Southwest Stark Street
(503) 228-3333
The signature restaurant of the Ace Hotel, Clyde Common is a stylish space that attracts the beautiful people of Portland to its handsome zinc-topped bar and high-ceilinged dining room—a dining room that features communal tables, where you may find yourself sitting next to the beautiful people. Fortunately, the friendly staff makes sure there is also room for you. The scene, however, could be unbearable if the food weren't first-class. The bar on weekend nights is very festive, so if you need a quiet dinner, you might make another choice.

DAN AND LOUIS $$
208 Southwest Ankeny Street
(503) 227-5906
Dan and Louis is an old Portland tradition in a historic downtown building. They served only live oysters from their opening in 1907 until 1919, when they finally got a stove and could make oyster stew. They still serve both these dishes, but they also serve many oystery treats: oysters Rockefeller, barbecued oysters, and fried oysters, to begin with. Dan and Louis is unpretentious and simple; it is the oldest family-owned restaurant in town. Stick with the oyster dishes or fish and chips and you'll be content. Raw oysters are still their specialty.

EL GAUCHO $$$$
319 Southwest Broadway
(503) 227-8794
While many restaurants in Portland emphasize the local and regional, El Gaucho celebrates the exotic, with its Argentine steak, its ostrich filet with Madeira sauce, and its bananas Foster. The dining room is dusky and serene, with contemporary polished decor but nonetheless an ambience from another era. The service is impeccable—both friendly and understated, with a great deal of tableside attention. And the food is equally good. Starters include a good

crab cake, short ribs, and Wicked Shrimp—spicy shrimp with a piquant dipping sauce. The Caesar salad is outstanding. Steaks include the Gaucho (accompanied by lobster medallions and béarnaise sauce) and a rib steak stuffed with peppers, rosemary, and garlic. There's nothing like a waiter in black tie flambéing bananas Foster at your table to make you feel that civilization has not disappeared altogether.

HEATHMAN RESTAURANT $$$$
1001 Southwest Broadway
(503) 790-7752
www.heathmanhotel.com/heathman restaurant
The Heathman has maintained its stellar reputation as a premier Portland dining room. It uses the finest Northwest ingredients, prepared with rapt attention to detail. The menu varies seasonally, but you can expect standards such as Angus rib-eye steak, roast chicken, and crispy sweetbreads. The Heathman also offers less common dishes—for example, a buttery poached lobster finished at the grill and served with a nuanced sauce. The accompanying dishes—sautéed leeks, creamy whipped potatoes, fresh spring asparagus—are always designed to balance and complement the flavors and textures of the main ingredient. Over the years, the Heathman has featured guest chefs from all over the world to create special events and prix-fixe menus. These chefs have included Angelo "Balin" Silvestro, Michel Brunel, and André Soltner, among others. All this kitchen talent is aided by first-rate service and a simple, handsome decor that includes a collection of fine paintings. Because the Heathman Restaurant is part of the Heathman Hotel, it also serves breakfast and lunch, seven days a week. The breakfasts are exceptional, and if there are power lunches in Portland, you'll find them here.

HIGGINS RESTAURANT AND BAR $$$$
1239 Southwest Broadway
(503) 222-9070
The inventive ways in which chef Greg Higgins

uses seasonal, organic food from nearby farms, forests, and streams have won this handsome downtown restaurant the highest marks from critics—as well as from the customers that fill the restaurant every night. Higgins, who won the James Beard Award in 2002, is discerning and unpretentious in his combinations of textures and flavors, relying on traditional means of cooking adapted to contemporary eating habits. Because the menu is seasonal, it changes all the time; however, diners can always count on at least one vegan dish on the menu in addition to the beef, duck, fish, and other entrees. The bar menu carries some notable staples, among them an incredibly savory hamburger and a luscious pastrami sandwich (Greg Higgins makes the pastrami himself). Higgins has an excellent wine list that emphasizes Northwest wines, and a beer list that features about 150 different brews from the world over. A striking union of textures, colors, and light, the tri-level restaurant looks as good as the food does. The downstairs dining room, with its mahogany paneling and dark carpet, is both romantic and elegant; the middle dining room is vibrant with burnished floors and two-toned walls. And the bar, a local favorite, is at once comfortable and urbane. Higgins is open for lunch Monday through Friday and dinner daily.

HIROSHI SUSHI $$$
926 Northwest 10th Avenue
(503) 619-0580
Sushi master Hiroshi Ikegayai uses his connections to find the freshest, most delectable fish available in order to bring you some of the best sushi north of San Francisco. His mastery, however, is not in who he knows but what he does, bringing together deep experience in proper technique with innovation in his approach to flavors. Signature non-sushi dishes include sea scallops—he uses them in many unusual ways; for example, served stuffed with sea urchin and accompanied by a vinegar truffle sauce—as well as monkfish liver served with a miso–vinegar

combination. The sushi itself is perfect, whether you are ordering a single–fish dish such as the abalone or a fancy roll. Even the California roll is amazing, with actual crab and the accompanying cucumbers, avocado, and sesame prepared to maximize texture and flavor. You will also find good beer and sake. It's fun to sit at the sushi bar and see what the chefs themselves think is yummiest. Do this and you won't go wrong. Open for lunch and dinner Tuesday through Sunday.

HOT LIPS PIZZA $
1901 Southwest 6th Avenue
(503) 224-0311
www.hotlipspizza.com
Hot Lips Pizza is a special hybrid of New York style and Northwest ingredients (if it works for the Heathman and Higgins, why not Hot Lips?). Their pizza is consistently excellent. The crust is a good balance of crispy and chewy, and the flavors of the toppings are absolutely fresh and savory. Hot Lips also offers a Sicilian-style pizza and delicious warm pesto breadsticks.

HUBER'S $–$$
411 Southwest 3rd Avenue
(503) 228-5686
Self-described as Portland's oldest restaurant, Huber's opened its doors in 1879 as the Bureau Saloon. In 1884 the bartender, Frank Huber, became a partner and the rest is culinary history. One tale tells of the time during the flood of 1894 when chef Jim Louie stood in a rowboat behind the counter serving steamed clams and turkey sandwiches to customers who rowed in from the other side. Still known for its roast young tom turkey, Huber's attracts a steady clientele who also enjoy the Philippine mahogany paneling, stained-glass skylights, and a big brass cash register. A flaming Spanish Coffee at Huber's is a rite of passage for all would-be Portlanders. A happy hour (6:00 to 8:00 p.m.) features inexpensive appetizers with well drinks at the usual price.

JAKE'S FAMOUS CRAWFISH $$$
401 Southwest 12th Avenue
(503) 226-1419

JAKE'S GRILL $$$
611 Southwest 10th Avenue
(503) 220-1850
www.mccormickandschmicks.com

Even though Jake's is now owned by McCormick & Schmick's, which technically makes it a chain restaurant (a Portland chain), this restaurant retains its status as a landmark. Founded in 1892 by Jacob (Jake) Lewis Freiman, Jake's Famous Crawfish still has that turn-of-the-last-century ambience, with its maze of booths snug against brick walls, its antique oil paintings, deep wood paneling, beautiful bar, and crisp white linen. Jake's Grill, the house restaurant for the Governor Hotel, is also a favorite. Portlanders love these places, as much for the tradition of going as for the skillfully cooked steaks and seafood. Jake's Famous Crawfish specializes in high-quality seafood, and it's the custom in many families to take out-of-town guests here for the splendid oysters Rockefeller. Try the Stark Street Sturgeon with basil dijon, Goose Point oysters, or the half-pound king crab legs. Jake's Grill concentrates on comfort food, and favorites here include prime rib, pork chops, and pot roast. The bar at the Grill is also very good.

KARAM LEBANESE $$
316 Southwest Stark Street
(503) 223-0830

It's hard to know where to begin a description of this friendly and abundant place: Karam Lebanese not only has some of the most delicious Middle Eastern food in town, but some of the best service as well. The dining room is hospitable, and the menu well priced. You can tell a lot about a restaurant by how it does the simplest things, and in a Lebanese restaurant, you should first look at the pita. Here, it is indescribably warm and fresh, and if yours looks like it is getting cold, the servers whisk it away and replace it with a new basket. Even the drinks are special—both alcoholic and nonalcoholic drinks might be flavored with rose water or tamarind. The hummus is creamy, with just the right proportions of lemon and garlic, the falafel perfectly crisped, and even the tabbouleh is piquant and delicious.

But the main courses are what it's all about. Here, you will find a wonderful variety of dishes: a savory vegetable kabob served with delicate rice and tomato sauce, a chicken schawarma, or a "Meat Mezza," which offers small tastes of many dishes. Karam is especially known for its Goat Bil Tfeen, a stew in which goat is braised in red wine and garlic, and served with bulgur wheat, chickpeas, and potatoes. It is tender and delicious. Desserts are equally good, especially when you order a thick Turkish coffee with them. Favorites include the crispy baklava, as well as the less familiar knafe-B-kaak. This wonderful dish is composed of a mild cheese mixture that is blended with farina, baked, encrusted with pistachios, and served with a fragrant syrup. This dessert might be where ancient peoples got their ideas about the land of milk and honey, and it's yours for the ordering at Karam.

KENNY & ZUKE'S $$
1038 Southwest Stark Street
(503) 222-3354

This Jewish delicatessen fills a void in Portland, with stellar sandwiches. Signature dishes include the Reuben sandwich, as well as its variety of pastrami sandwiches on housemade rye bread. For example, the cheeseburger—while not exactly kosher—is the kind of thing you'll be craving after a long night of dancing and socializing. This beautifully grilled burger is topped with pastrami and melted Swiss. Pastrami sandwiches are also served with egg salad or chopped liver. All of these are delicious. Kenny & Zuke's is also open early and late, a bit of a mitzvah. You can eat their pastrami from 7:00 a.m. to midnight Tuesday through Thursday, until 3:00 a.m. on Friday and Saturday, and from 8:00 a.m. to 10:30 p.m. on Sunday.

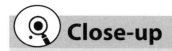 **Close-up**

Putting the Terroir on the Map

The Willamette Valley is known for its outstanding wines and unique *terroir*—a word that means earth or territory, one that winemakers use to denote the influence of the natural environment on the quality of the grape.

But if a grape can display terroir, so can other things—an apple, a pear, even lettuce—and the virtues of our terroir have been apparent throughout human history. Native tribes, pioneers, and all their descendants have extolled the abundance of the Willamette Valley and its rich soil, productive climate, and the resulting bounty.

Nevertheless, the idea that Portland is a food capital has only recently begun to emerge. This is in part because the existence of a genuine Pacific Northwest cuisine is debatable. While the ingredients have been there, the cooking traditions, with a few exceptions, have been slower to take root. This is understandable—after all, the written history of Oregon is short and the culture still evolving, while cooking traditions take generation after generation to blossom. Even in the early 1990s, there were few truly excellent restaurants in Portland. Now, however, Portland has become a restaurant destination, and one regularly reads in the pages of the *New York Times, Bon Appetit, Gourmet,* and other major publications of the world-class dining experiences so readily available here, down to the fast food—for instance, Burgerville, where you can get fresh strawberry milk shakes and hamburgers from organically fed cows—and grocery stores, such as New Seasons, which are reinventing the model of the supermarket (see our Shopping chapter).

A confluence of things has come together to create this nidus. The first is the arrival in the late 1980s and early 1990s of talented chefs such as Greg Higgins of first the Heathman and now Higgins Restaurant and Cory Schreiber, formerly of Wildwood. Higgins grew up foraging around his native upstate New York before he was trained in the kitchens of Alsace-Lorraine, and he knew good terroir when he saw it. Schreiber grew up here, so he was already familiar with Oregon's bounty. Both have been instrumental in creating a demand for local, artisanal food of excellent quality and have been tireless champions of the cause of using sustainable food that is in season and grown by local farmers, caught by local fishermen, or raised by local ranchers. It just tastes better.

Higgins has been an especially effective catalyst for this movement. Under his leadership, the Chefs Collaborative—an organization dedicated to seasonal and artisanal food—and other local groups established an annual conference called the Farmer-Chef Connection. This conference brings farmers and chefs together to talk about what to grow and how to get it to market. In this way, restaurants can serve the freshest food, direct from the source, and it has revolutionized the way food gets to the table in Oregon.

Award-winning chefs such as Higgins and Schreiber, along with such peers as Philippe Boulet, Vitaly Paley, Caprial Pence, and Dave Machado, laid the foundation for Portland's birth as a culinary capital. They were the early adaptors, establishing the economic conditions that made the transformation possible. They put Portland's restaurants on the national map. And once the system was in place, there was room for experimentation. New restaurants have opened all over town; restaurants that bring different cooking traditions—French provincial, Mexican, Peruvian, Spanish, Portuguese, Thai—to the palette of Oregon bounty.

There's an ongoing debate in the Portland food community about whether we really are a world-class capital for food. It's debatable whether we have any restaurants that merit three stars from Michelin, for example. Yet you could dine out every evening for a month at a different restaurant each time and have an excellent meal at every one of them. And when even cheap Thai food stands serve locally raised organic pork (see Pok Pok), you could argue that Portland is a contender for ranking among the great food cities. That's how you put the terroir on the map.

MCCORMICK & SCHMICK'S
HARBORSIDE AT THE MARINA $$$
309 Southwest Montgomery Street
(503) 220-1865

MCCORMICK & SCHMICK'S
SEAFOOD RESTAURANT $$$
235 Southwest 1st Avenue
(503) 224-7522
www.mccormickandschmicks.com

McCormick & Schmick's Seafood Restaurant has made its reputation by serving delicious seafood prepared creatively. And this reliable restaurant in a pretty, historic building is the mothership for the national chain. Good bets here are the seared ahi tuna, crab cakes, alder-smoked salmon, and shellfish—for example, simmered in a coconut, ginger, and lemongrass broth. Lunch is served Monday through Friday; dinner is served every evening. The Harborside McCormick and Schmicks, along the Willamette in the RiverPlace development, is a nice place for lunch and a cold beer on a hot summer day. Both have good happy-hour specials.

MOTHER'S BISTRO AND BAR $$
212 Southwest Stark Street
(503) 464-1122

Chef Lisa Schroeder wants us to eat the kind of homey dishes our mothers and grandmothers made—comfort food such as braised meats, roasts, stews, meat loaves, and other slow-cooked dishes. But these versions are prepared by an expertly trained chef, making them even better than you remember. Many of the recipes are from actual mothers that Schroeder knows. Both the bistro and the (full) bar are comfortable, and the bar, with its cushy velvet upholstery and gilded mirrors, is especially pretty. Schroeder changes her menu to reflect the seasons, but a typical menu might offer a Painted Hills beef burger or an Italian chopped salad, while dinner could bring chicken and dumplings, if you're lucky. Mother's also serves a weekend brunch that might include salmon hash or crunchy French toast dipped in corn flakes. Mother's is consistently excellent, and you should take your own mom there.

MURATA $$$$
200 Southwest Market Street
(503) 227-0080

Murata serves excellent sushi in a modest downtown building. But don't let appearances fool you: This is the real thing. The tasting menu, which is very expensive, is worth every penny and is the ideal showcase for Murata's talents. The tangy salads and savory noodle soups are as good as the sushi, but it's the latter that you'll be dreaming about later. Open for lunch and dinner Monday through Saturday.

ORIGINAL PANCAKE HOUSE $
8601 Southwest 24th Avenue
(503) 246-9007

This Portland classic has been serving fabulous pancakes, omelets, and other breakfast fare since 1953. This is the spot that launched the national chain, and it is justly famous for its apple pancake—an oven-baked confection with Granny Smith apples and a perfect cinnamon glaze; its puffy, lemony dutch baby; and its house-made corned beef hash. But anything you order here will be good: The restaurant pays detailed attention to the quality of its ingredients, using the best butter, eggs, and breakfast meats it can find. The restaurant has also won—along with Greg Higgins, Philippe Boulot, and other stars—a James Beard award. The Original Pancake House serves breakfast Wednesday through Sunday until 3:00 p.m.; no reservations. Cash or check only.

PAZZO RISTORANTE $$$
627 Southwest Washington Street
(503) 228-1515
www.vintageplaza.com/vpzdini

Serving breakfast, lunch, and dinner daily as the resident restaurant at the Hotel Vintage Plaza, Pazzo nicely balances elegance with informality. Pazzo offers a number of different dining spaces: the main dining room, the bar, and a kind of great private party room lined with bottles. Pazzo's cuisine is organized around the regions of Italy, and its pastas are outstanding; it also does a fine job with the accompanying grilled and sautéed meats, poultry, and fish. The bar selection is equally good: Not only is the list of Italian wines extensive, it is rounded out with fantastic grappas and vintage ports. The attractive bar also has a good selection of single malt scotches and small-batch bourbons. Because of its location within the Hotel Vintage Plaza and near so many hotels, Pazzo is also a good place to spot visiting celebrities.

RED STAR TAVERN & ROAST HOUSE $$–$$$
503 Southwest Washington Street
(503) 222–0005
www.redstartavern.com
Red Star has a bright atmosphere, a well-lit, comfortable dining room, and a diverse menu that is devoted to exploring American regional cuisine, from the South to New England to Texas to California. It includes, for example, wood-grilled baby back ribs, spit-roasted pork loin, oak-roasted vegetables with caramelized garlic, and sweet potato hash. Red Star draws inspiration from the methods of cooking from coast to coast, and they have a smoker, rotisseries, grills, and wood-fired ovens to experiment with. Red Star serves lunch and dinner daily—it is a great downtown lunch spot.

SOUTHPARK $$
901 Southwest Salmon Street
(503) 326-1300
Southpark is evocative of Casablanca—not only in its decor but also in its menu. We like the dining room, where they specialize in using Northwest ingredients—especially seafood—to showcase inventive Mediterranean-inspired dishes such as a bourride made from local seafood or almond-stuffed dates wrapped in delicate slices of Serrano ham. But we like the wine bar even more, with its murals, velvet drapes, and gleaming metallic bar. There, you can get the same menu or choose from the bar menu. The wine list is first class, and so is the service. Southpark is also good for cocktails and people-watching, not so much because it's a scene but because everyone,

including the servers, seems to be having such a nice time.

Another nice perk: Southpark will validate your ticket if you park at the garage next door to the restaurant after 5:00 p.m. Southpark is open for lunch and dinner daily.

THREE SQUARE GRILL $$
6320 Southwest Capitol Highway
(503) 244-4467
A beloved neighborhood spot, Three Square Grill is also a destination for Portlanders hankering for some roadhouse cooking Northwest style. Here you might find a beautiful salmon hash, hush puppies with jalapeño jelly, roasted chicken encrusted with herbs, or spicy garlic fries—we say "might" because it depends on what's in season. The chefs make as much as they can on-site, and that includes the desserts, the hamburger buns, "Bad Monkey" jalapeño sauce, and pickles—in fact, they are also the purveyors of Picklopolis pickles (www.picklopolis.com), the "Pickles of the Future." You can buy them at the restaurant or at the Hillsdale and Portland farmers' markets. Three Square Grill serves dinner every night.

VERITABLE QUANDARY $$$
1220 Southwest 1st Avenue
(503) 227-7342
The VQ has been a cocktail favorite for years, with its good location at the western edge of the Hawthorne Bridge and its pretty brick patio and its dark, old-fashioned bar. But it has a growing reputation as a destination for American cuisine inspired by Italy—and by the Pacific Northwest. First-rate signature dishes include osso bucco, as well as revolving fish specials (everything from ahi tuna with pineapple and avocado salsa to red snapper with kumquat). Appetizers are excellent—bacon-wrapped dates are a specialty. Also of note here are the remarkable and rare wines offered by the glass. The dining room has some nice views during the day and at night, depending on the table. The service, especially in the bar, is generally excellent. The VQ also offers an outstanding Sunday brunch.

NORTHWEST PORTLAND

ANDINA $$$
1314 Northwest Glisan Street
(503) 228-9535

This stylishly renovated warehouse in the Pearl District is a star in the Portland restaurant scene. Comprising a tapas bar, an aperitif bar, a wine shop, and the capacious dining room, Andina showcases the cuisine of Peru to great effect. It is a beautiful restaurant, both in the space itself and in the presentation of the food. One staple is the cooking of fish in lime juice, or cebiche, which is regarded by some as the national dish of Peru. Marinating fish in lime juice breaks down its proteins, just like cooking with heat, but it leaves the texture firm and fresh and it infuses the fish with wonderful citrusness. It is prepared here with onions, cilantro, spicy peppers, and salt, then served with corn and yams. Andina has a number of fish cebiches, but they also serve several vegetarian variations on this dish as well. The meat selections are also outstanding, from simple Peruvian rack of lamb with purple potatoes (the ancestor of all potatoes) to more complex dishes involving stir-fried beef and yucca. Andina also features delicious side dishes—for example, yucca leaves stuffed with cheese and peppers—and salads. The wine list is well-edited; the service at Andina is professional and the servers' knowledge is excellent, which is helpful if you are unfamiliar with Peruvian cuisine. Andina serves lunch Monday through Saturday and dinner every evening.

BESAW'S CAFE $
2301 Northwest Savier Street
(503) 228-2619

Besaw's is a neighborhood joint in northern Northwest, and while it serves very good lunches and dinners, we like it especially for breakfast, which is hearty and delicious. They feature all the staples, plus crispy bacon, apple sausages, succulent smoked salmon, and fluffy pancakes. Expect a wait on the weekends. Besaw's has been a restaurant since the Lewis and Clark Exposition in 1905, and its handsome bar dates from that period.

BEWON $$$
1203 Northwest 23rd Avenue
(503) 464-9222

BeWon offers first-rate Korean food in a sleek atmosphere, with attentive and expert service. Korean food is perhaps the least well known of the Asian cuisines, but BeWon is determined to change that. At this elegant little restaurant, you can order the fixed-price menu (about $25), which comes with eight traditional courses, or you can order a la carte. Offerings might include a pumpkin rice porridge, acorn jelly, a stir-fry of oyster and shitake mushrooms, a hand-rolled crepe. Main courses feature dishes such as salt-encrusted mackerel or traditional barbecued pork. But the adventure here is in the side dishes: Dried cod, kimchi, sugared seaweed, and other small tastings are served on tiny plates that can be refilled. The rice wine list at BeWon is also quite good.

BLUEHOUR $$$$
250 Northwest 13th Avenue
(503) 226-3394

Bluehour is routinely noted as the place to see and be seen in Portland, and it does provide a good backdrop for the beautiful people, with its dramatic curtains and low lighting. But don't overlook the food. It is always carefully prepared and well-balanced, and its cheese blights are outstanding. The dishes are inspired by France and Italy, everything from seared foie gras to osso buco. Bluehour is perhaps the slightest bit self-conscious of the role that it plays, and the menu reflects that—the starters are the star of this show. But everything is prepared handsomely, with a touch of adventure. Bluehour serves dinner every night, lunch Monday through Saturday, and brunch on the weekends.

DAILY CAFE $$
902 Northwest 13th Avenue
(503) 242-1916

The Daily Cafe, a stylish cafe in the Pearl District, serves breakfast, lunch, and dinner—as well as a standout Sunday brunch—and its attention to quality ingredients, seasonal menus, and friendly service has won hearts and minds all over town. The cafe serves breakfast and a bustling lunch, when crowds gather to sample tarragon chicken sandwiches and chewy panini. Daily specials are also offered, and they range from the soup du jour to special treats such as fried chicken. Dinners feature wonderfully roasted chicken, perfectly broiled rib eye, and other American-style cuisine creatively prepared. Desserts are always good. A word about the brunch: The Daily Cafe serves starters with brunch—for example, delicate little blintzes or rice puddings that just encourage your appetite for French toast, trout, and eggs—so go when you are hungry.

FENOUIL $$$$
900 Northwest 11th Avenue
(503) 525-2225
Fenouil is a large, attractive space off the "living room" of the Pearl District, Jamison Square. In fact, Jamison Square feels more like a Parisian "place" every day, so it's fitting that Fenouil should stand guard over it. The cuisine is French too: steak and fries, foie gras terrine, Alsatian salads, onion soup, and so on. The wine list is extensive, and it has a great selection of Spanish and French wines to pair with your nicely prepared rack of lamb. They offer regional dinners that feature the cuisine of various locales in France and other areas of the Mediterranean, accompanied by appropriate wines. These dinners are served at large communal tables, so they allow you to make some new friends as you discuss the virtues of your plate. Fenouil serves lunch Monday through Friday and dinner Monday through Saturday.

FRATELLI $$
1230 Northwest Hoyt Street
(503) 241-8800
Fratelli is a pretty restaurant in the Pearl District that features different regional Italian cuisines. It changes its menu frequently, but its high-quality, local, and seasonal ingredients, clever preparations, and poised and gracious servers have won it a devoted clientele. The entrees might include standouts such as salmon with pearl onions and

potatoes, linguine with mushrooms and pancetta, or seared free-range chicken wrapped in proscuitto. Antipasti are equally delightful, especially the bruschetta on house-made bread. The candlelit dining room lends a romantic atmosphere to your dinner, and unlike many contemporary restaurants, you can actually carry on a conversation.

FULLER'S RESTAURANT $
136 Northwest 9th Avenue
(503) 222-5608
Fuller's has been a Pearl District tradition since before it was the Pearl District, and it retains its working-class roots even as the city gentrifies around it. Of course, that's one of its attractions. Fuller's serves egg sandwiches, pancakes, and other traditional breakfast staples all day until 5:00 p.m on weekdays, 2:00 p.m. on Saturday. It has 28 stools. Don't be surprised to find yourself in conversation with the guy at the next stool; it's part of the routine. Bring cash—they don't take credit cards. Closed Sundays.

GIORGIO'S $$$
1131 Northwest Hoyt Street
(503) 221-1888
Giorgio's is a beautiful and authentic Italian restaurant in the Pearl serving lunch and dinner. Our favorites include the homemade pastas: the browned gnocchi, the delicate ravioli, the robust *pappardelle*. These are all served inventively, perhaps with braised wild boar or juicy spot prawns. Their other dishes—grilled meats, well-prepared seafood and fish, duck breast—are also good. The service is outstanding. During warm weather, you can sit on the patio and enjoy this feasting outdoors and people-watching, if you can look up from your dinner.

JUSTA PASTA $
1336 Northwest 19th Avenue
(503) 243-2249
Justa Pasta is the major pasta supplier to the region's top-tier restaurants, but it is also a great restaurant in its own right, serving dinner and lunch in its small (30-seat) venue—and one of the best bargains in town. Justa Pasta offers

several kinds of pasta and sauces at each meal, accompanied by bread from the Pearl Bakery and well-flavored salads. Some of our favorites include the butternut squash–hazelnut ravioli and the mushroom sauce. The pumpkin ravioli, the swiss chard ravioli, and the lasagna are excellent as well. But simpler dishes, such as bucatini in marinara sauce, are also truly satisfying. It is the perfect place for a cozy dinner. It can be difficult to find a seat, but in the summer a small patio creates more room.

PALEY'S PLACE $$$$
1204 Northwest 21st Avenue
(503) 243-2403

Paley's Place, run by an amiable couple in Northwest Portland, is justifiably one of Portland's favorite restaurants: Between chef Vitaly Paley's imagination and talent and Kimberly Paley's gregarious command of the dining rooms, Paley's Place offers one of the best meals in town. Here, the simplest ingredients are turned into Northwest-nuanced, French-inspired dishes prepared by a masterful chef. The menu is always changing, but you might find garlicky mussels prepared with hand-cut fries; a beautiful cut of Kobe beef; maple-glazed chicken with Granny Smith apples, sour cherries, and smoky bacon; halibut served with lentils, fennel, and fiddlehead ferns; or sautéed sweetbreads with leek potato gratin and pomegranate sauce. The restaurant, residing in a pretty, old house in Northwest Portland, has only 50 seats. Yet its two dining rooms, bar, and patio convey the feeling of a larger restaurant without losing any intimacy. Paley's is open seven nights a week for dinner only.

PAPA HAYDN $$
701 Northwest 23rd Avenue
(503) 228-7317

With the onslaught of excellent new patisseries and bakeries in Portland, it is easy to overlook the stalwarts. In Papa Haydn's case, this would be a mistake. It is still a charming place to go for fancy desserts in Portland, with an impressive array of elaborate gateaux, tortes, ice creams, tarts, and cheesecakes. Dishes such as lemon chiffon torte, marjolaine, peanut butter mousse torte, and black velvet cake draw folks with a sweet tooth from all over the city to the comfortable, polished dining room on Northwest 23rd Avenue. But don't overlook the dependably delicious pastas, salads, and grilled chicken and steak. Papa Haydn has another location in Southeast Portland.

PARK KITCHEN $$$
422 Northwest 8th Avenue
(503) 223-7275

On the shady and peaceful North Park blocks—just a few steps from the hurly-burly of Broadway—you will find Park Kitchen, a lovely little restaurant that offers an ever-changing menu of superlative tavern-style cooking. This restaurant is small, but the west wall opens up to the stately old trees that line the street, providing a wonderful continuity between indoors and out. The long, narrow bar is accented with mirrors and wood, and the fresh flowers add bright touches to the muted greens of the decor.

Chef Scott Dolisch is one of Portland's best, and everything here is tempting, beautifully prepared, and chosen with great care. Indeed, Dolisch was featured as one of America's 10 best new chefs by *Food & Wine* magazine in 2004. The menu changes often, but one of the charms of Park Kitchen is how much they make on-site, including hot dogs and potato chips. Breakfasts feature outstanding pastries, as well as comfort-food favorites such as corn bread pudding with bacon and cheddar cheese or house-made English muffins with bananas and peanut butter. Lunches offer an array of soups, salads, pastas, and *panini*. You might find, for example, tagliatelle with braised lamb and snap peas or mussels steamed with zinfandel. Dinners feature a range of both cold and hot small plates—salt cod fritters with malt vinegar, for instance, or leek and saffron tart—and provide the adventurous diner with many opportunities to experiment. The thoughtful entree choices are kept to a minimum but offer excellent variety nonetheless—grilled pork chops, spring lamb, risotto, and two kinds of fish were the stars of one recent menu. Dessert choices might include creamy butterscotch pudding in oatmeal shortbread, refreshing papaya-lime sorbet with coconut cakes, or an inventive s'more Napoleon pastry. Their attention to detail extends to the wine list, as well as the fine selection of bourbons and other liquors in the bar. Park Kitchen serves lunch and dinner. It's closed on Monday.

Portland Spirits

In addition to its microbreweries and purveyors of hand-roasted coffee, and artisanal wine, Portland is also home to a number of microdistilleries. These include Clear Creek (eau de vie and brandy), Rogue Spirits (gin and rum), and New Deal Distillery (vodka), and House Spirits (vodka, aquavit, and gin). But how can you tell whether these home-grown brews are better than, say, bathtub gin? To that end, the Wine & Spirit Archive offers classes in spirit appreciation, where you can train your palate to be more discerning: www.wineandspiritarchive.com/classes/certification/spirits.html. They offer the only such certification in the country.

PEARL BAKERY $
102 Northwest 9th Avenue
(503) 827-0910

Pearl Bakery is one of several excellent artisanal bakeries in town, featuring rustic Italian breads, as well as breakfast and dessert pastries. But Pearl Bakery also operates a tiny cafe in its retail operation on Northwest 9th. Here, you will find a wonderful array of *panini*, focaccia, and deli sandwiches. The sandwich fillings might include roasted eggplant and tomato pesto or fig and anise. They may offer a gorgonzola, pear, and arugula salad on walnut bread—an inventive variation on a classic fall salad. The breads are outstanding—traditional sourdoughs are favorites but so are country-style loaves such as levain with green or kalamata olives. Breakfast pastries include tempting specialties such as apple coffee cake and pear Danish. Pearl Bakery is a fine way to begin your morning or have an early lunch.

PIAZZA ITALIA $$
1129 Northwest Johnson Street
(503) 478-0619

This seductive little cafe serves authentic Italian dishes prepared by actual Italians. It is reminiscent of the cafes one finds on the back streets of Rome, with dishes lined up in the case, looking very modest until you bite into them. In this case, you may want to bite into the gnocchi with braised beef or the bucatini with pancetta, or both. Antipasti and salads are perfect as well. Piazza Italia serves lunch and dinner daily.

RINGSIDE $$$$
2165 West Burnside Street
(503) 223-1513

Step in to the RingSide and enter an old-world style where fine cuts of beef still reign supreme. The RingSide also has great ambience that recalls Frank Sinatra, James Bond, and nightcaps in dark and intimate bars. Over the last 50 years and three generations of owners, not much has changed at the RingSide. The prime and choice aged beef, fresh seafood, and excellent wine and service have helped RingSide garner more than 40 regional and national awards. If you're a rib connoisseur, try the 10-ounce RingSide Prime Rib served with au jus and creamed horseradish sauce. Also, don't leave without ordering the huge, luscious onion rings. The desserts, such as the chocolate raspberry torte (made locally by JaCiva's), an exquisite Swiss-chocolate layer cake with raspberry filling, are a terrific way to finish off your feast. RingSide is open weekdays for lunch and daily for dinner.

SERRATO $$$

2112 Northwest Kearney Street
(503) 221-1195

Serrato is dedicated to the proposition that eating is meant to be a pleasurable, unhurried event, and the pretty dining room, with its big windows and blond wood, does inspire a bit of lingering over the dessert wine. The Italian-inspired menu is varied, making good use of our region's abundance. Good choices for antipasti might include the tomato and mozzarella salad with olive oil and basil or the potato and spinach tart with arugula and truffle oil. The pastas and risotto are very good; we have had luck with the ravioli in particular, especially when it is stuffed with crab.

SILK BISTRO $$

1012 Northwest Glisan Street
(503) 248-2172

Silk, the showstopper bistro in the Pho Van dynasty, has its roots in a low-key Vietnamese restaurant in outer Southeast Portland that attracted a loyal following of customers seduced by its flavorful and fragrant noodle soups. Silk is the upscale incarnation of the original restaurant, where customers dine in a chic atmosphere permeated with pan-Pacific colors and lines and enjoy ingenious, haute Vietnamese cuisine. Here, you'll find fewer varieties of pho, but in compensation, you'll find outstanding salads, grilled chicken, and sweet-savory fish entrees. Stellar dishes include Goi Bap Chuoi, a salad composed of banana blossoms, chicken, grapefruit, and mint, and—of course—the pho: either a chicken with coriander or a beef made with round steak and lean brisket. The Chao Tom roll—minced chicken and shrimp wrapped around a small piece of sugar cane—is an intriguing appetizer. But the true stars of the menu are the fresh fish dishes, served steamed, grilled, lightly battered, and any other way the chefs at Silk devise.

WILDWOOD $$$$

1221 Northwest 21st Avenue
(503) 248-9663

Wildwood is a destination spot in Northwest Portland and it has developed a loyal following who come for the fine Northwest cuisine, expertly prepared. The decor is unfussy and contemporary, and many power lunches and dinners happen here, either in the dining room booths or in the busy bar. The seasonal menu offers the very best from our region.

SOUTHEAST PORTLAND

APIZZA SCHOLLS $$

4741 Southeast Hawthorne Boulevard
(503) 233-1286

Probably the most authentic New York–style pizza this side of the Hudson, Apizza Scholls is always busy. Luckily, since they don't take reservations, the pizza is worth the wait. Carefully crafted using a very hot oven, slow-rising dough, and local ingredients, these pizzas are so good that even New Yorkers like them. Open for dinner Tuesday through Saturday.

BAR AVIGNON $

2138 Southeast Division Street
(503) 517-0808
http://baravignon.com

Proprietors Randy Goodman and Nancy Hunt will tell you that Bar Avignon is just a bar, but don't believe them. This sleek and organic spot along Southeast Division offers a beautifully edited wine collection and wonderful spirits that frame an outstanding selection of small plates. These include silky cured meats, creamy cheeses served with honey and Marcona almonds, just-harvested salads, the ripest fruit, the crustiest bread from Little T American Baker up the street—in short, everything you need to make a complete meal for the entire family, provided they are all over 21. It's a lovely spot for a relaxed weeknight dinner. The service is attentive and the atmosphere is enlivening, full of attractive and convivial people who are all evidently enjoying themselves. You should join them.

BIWA $$

215 Southeast 9th Avenue
(503) 239-8830

For a city on the Pacific Rim, and considering

the number of Japanese language and cultural programs we have, Portland has surprisingly few authentic Japanese restaurants. Fortunately, Biwa has closed this gap. This restaurant is in the "small plates" style, emphasizing variety in taste and high-quality ingredients. Standout dishes include the vegetable salad, which features cabbage rolls, carrots, and daikon radish in a silky sesame dressing; a savory fried chicken; pork belly; *onigiri,* little stuffed rice and nori sandwiches; and offerings of two different noodle styles.—in particular, the pork ramen is stellar. Biwa is right next door to Simpatica, and chef Gabe Rosen is a close ally of theirs—which is reflected in all the meat dishes, but especially in the gorgeous beef tartare, marinated in sesame oil and garlic. Its dining room offers both booths and counter seats next to the open kitchen. Biwa also has a fine cocktail list, as well as an excellent selection of sake. Biwa is open Monday through Saturday.

CAPRIAL'S BISTRO AND WINE $$$
7015 Southeast Milwaukie Avenue
(503) 236-6457
www.caprial.com

Caprial Pence is Portland's favored culinary daughter, having won the James Beard award in 1991, opened her bistro in 1992, and starred in her own cooking show on PBS for years. In 1999 Caprial's Bistro and Wine transformed from a petite cafe with a chalk menu board into a lively and upscale bar and restaurant, with $9 cocktails and pale, overstuffed chairs. But Caprial's is still a good spot for unconventional bistro-style cooking. The restaurant pays homage to all the influences on our region, so diners will find many Asian-inspired dishes, especially of the sweet-and-sour variety—for example, a pork chop glazed in maple-infused stock. Other good bets include pan-fried oysters, pan-roasted sturgeon, and ravioli with feta cheese. Desserts here are especially good—and so is the thoughtful wine list. Caprial's is open for lunch and dinner. The noise level is high, but you'll feel like you're in the middle of things.

CASTAGNA $$$$
1752 Southeast Hawthorne Boulevard
(503) 231-7373

Castagna is a sophisticated and spare restaurant on the western end of Hawthorne, with a minimalist ambience that allows the food to take center stage. The presentation here is outstanding, and even simple dishes such as a butter lettuce salad, sea scallops, or french fries are beautifully arranged on large white plates. Castagna could not get away with this emphasis on appearance, however, if it did not back it up with some of the best food in the city. The seasonal menu—on which you might find grilled sea scallops with oyster mushrooms, little agnolotti pasta stuffed with duck confit, sautéed halibut with mussels and potatoes, or grilled rack of lamb—is Mediterranean influenced, with local ingredients providing the foundation. Everything from the white bean soup to the last crumb of bittersweet chocolate tartlet is impressive to both the eye and the palate. There is no place like Castagna in all of Portland. A less formal, and less expensive, cafe right next door, Café Castagna (1758 Southeast Hawthorne Boulevard; 503-231-9959), provides an excellent meal. Here, the ambience is low key, with its stone floor and wooden tables. You'll be happy in either place.

DELTA CAFE $$
4607 Southeast Woodstock Boulevard
(503) 771-3101

Southern food at its most gloriously soulful is the specialty at Delta Cafe. This inexpensive neighborhood place attracts its share of students from nearby Reed College, but it has a loyal following from all over, due to the generous portions of succulent ribs, hush puppies in brown gravy (aka "Pups in a Pond"), and fried chicken with all the trimmings. Funky music, odd furniture, and local art complete the atmosphere. Delta Cafe won't cost you much, but they accept only cash and checks. Open 5:00 to 10:00 p.m. daily; the bar is open until 1:00 a.m. on weekdays, 2:00 a.m. on weekends.

DETOUR CAFE $

3035 Southeast Division Street

(503) 234-7499

www.detourcafe.com

We love this little neighborhood breakfast and lunch cafe, open daily from 8:00 a.m. to 4:00 p.m. We love the modern DIY decor and the outstanding service. And we especially love the sandwiches, all of them. A flavorful BLT served on focaccia, for example—the focaccia is wonderfully chewy and fresh (made on-site), and the thick and crisp bacon is wonderfully complemented by creamy avocado. The Detour Cafe also makes excellent traditional breakfasts and serves great coffee. It's crowded on the weekends, when it serves a bustling brunch to bleary-eyed nightclubbers, so you might try a weekday lunch when it's slightly mellower.

EUGENIO'S $

3584 Southeast Division

(503) 233-3656

Eugenio's is a tiny, tiny Italian-style deli that serves some of the best espresso in town, as well as absolutely delicious sausage sandwiches (using the best Italian sausage anywhere, from local purveyor Fred Carlo) and thin-crust pizza. The sandwiches and salads are fresh, with novel combinations of high-quality ingredients—for example, the Draper Valley chicken that's used for the chicken salad. It also offers microbrews on tap and has a small but intelligently selected wine list. There are just a few seats, and sometimes half the space is taken up by musicians singing the praises of Eugenio, but if you are patient you will be justly rewarded with a fine, simple lunch or dinner.

GINO'S RESTAURANT AND BAR $$$

8051 Southeast 13th Avenue

(503) 233-4613

Gino's is an unpretentious trattoria that serves excellent Italian dishes. Other chefs come here when they go out to dinner. Down-to-earth classics include the wonderful clams steamed in white wine, chili, and butter; chicken Marsala; Grandma Jean's pasta (which comes with two pork ribs); and a tangy Caesar salad. In addition to the reliable favorites, you will find seasonal specials—rich stews of lamb, sautées of shrimp with red chilis, vegetable ragouts with polenta, for example. Seafoods are always fresh; the Painted Hills beef steaks are specially cut just for Gino's. Gino's serves dinner nightly.

J & M CAFE $

537 Southeast Ash Street

(503) 230-0463

On a quiet side street a few steps up from bustling Martin Luther King Jr. Boulevard is the J & M Cafe, one of the best places for breakfast and lunch in Portland. Wonderful food, an appealing low-key atmosphere, and reasonable prices make this restaurant an outstanding value. They handle the traditional breakfast dishes beautifully. First, the coffee is self-serve, which is a fine thing if you have to wait for your table. When it's time to order, you can't go wrong. The waffles are excellent—crispy on the outside, tender and flaky inside. The eggs are fluffy and savory, the scrambles imaginative—for example, a house-made chorizo with roasted red pepper, cheddar cheese, and sour cream. Their signature dish, the J & M plate, is their own variation on eggs Benedict: here, two basted eggs on an English muffin, topped with cheese in place of the hollandaise and thick, crispy bacon. The service here is first-rate. Cash only.

KEN'S ARTISAN PIZZA $$

304 Southeast 28th Avenue

(503) 517-9951

Ken's Artisan Pizza was born because owner Ken Forkish kept having to stay late at his bakery in Northwest Portland on Monday nights, when he first served pizza, because the lines were so long. Now he stays late in Southeast Portland, and the lines are even longer. Forkish uses a 700-degree oven, a perfect pizza technique, and keeps the menu simple, a combination that leads to incredibly satisfying dinners. The menu includes several salads, among them an excellent Caesar, as well as a seasonally changing prosciutto dish. Some kind of roasted vegetable dish is always available; this is dressed with something light and refreshing that plays up the flavors of the vegetables. Pizzas are also seasonal—in the fall you might find a squash pizza, while spring may bring roasted asparagus—but you can count on a Margherita, with tomato sauce, mozzarella, and basil or even arugula. Other regular toppings involve house-cured pancetta, anchovies, and Italian sausage. But it is the pizza dough that is the main event: perfectly crusty and chewy and balanced. The wood-burning pizza oven is also used to roast vegetables and cook dessert, which includes amazing cobblers, crisps, crostada, and other baked fruit desserts. Ice cream and other confections are also available. The interior is small but feels spacious because of the high ceilings and spare aesthetic. A well-edited selection of beer and wine is offered. Service is consistently professional, so even if you have to wait, the staff will see to it that your wait is pleasant. Ken's serves crusty pizza for dinner Tuesday through Saturday.

LAURO MEDITERRANEAN KITCHEN $$$
3377 Southeast Division Street
(503) 239-7000

It took almost no time for Lauro to gain a regional reputation when the neighborhood restaurant opened in 2004. Chef Dave Machado, the creative spirit behind Southpark for a number of years, brings his pan-Mediterranean sensibility to this stylish, friendly spot in Southeast Portland. He looks for the right combination of flavor and texture to update classics of bistro cooking, as well as regional specialties. Standout dishes include wonderfully sweet and savory stuffed plums, a fragrant chicken tagine, short ribs, and an amazing custard cooked with port. Wood-fired pizzas and outstanding burgers allow parents to bring children and eat in peace. Lauro also has an excellent selection of reasonably priced wines by the bottle and glass. Lauro's atmosphere is industrial chic—handsome combinations of wood, concrete, and glass—which pays homage to the building's former life as a warehouse yet sacrifices nothing in comfort. And the service is outstanding. Lauro serves dinner seven nights a week from 5:00 to 10:00 p.m. and lunches on weekdays.

LE PIGEON $$$
738 East Burnside Street
(503) 546-8796

Le Pigeon inhabits a small space on busy East Burnside Street, a space that is dominated by the open kitchen, a counter around the kitchen for diners, and a number of farmhouse tables. Le Pigeon does not take reservations, and they seat comparatively few people. It's decorated salvage style, with old chandeliers and repurposed chairs. In spite of these humble trappings, Le Pigeon is probably the most innovative restaurant in Portland today. Chef Gabriel Rucker trained in Napa, then established himself here to take advantage of the local ingredients and the atmosphere of possibility.

While he does use the typical local, seasonal approach, he does not fetishize it, and even more important, he uses these elements in completely novel ways. Menus change a lot, but there are some standout regulars—for example, the peanut butter and jelly sandwich with foie gras, served as an appetizer. Duck confit, crispy sweetbreads, and tongue make regular appearances, as do interesting sides such as pickled strawberries or gazpacho with melon. Desserts frequently incorporate foie gras or bacon to accent the silky sweetness of ice cream or the airiness of a profiterole.

But it would be a mistake to think that the push-the-envelope combinations, which have garnered remarkable local and national press, are what drive this restaurant. For when you get down to it, it is the perfectionist technique of Rucker that makes this place sing. Even simple dishes such as roast chicken display an authoritative touch, with crispy golden skin and perfect combinations of texture and flavor in the accompanying sides. When a chef can make the simple things as interesting as the star dishes, you know he is a master. Le Pigeon is open for dinner Wednesday through Sunday.

MICHAEL'S ITALIAN BEEF & SAUSAGE CO. $
1111 Southeast Sandy Boulevard
(503) 230-1899

Michael's serves wonderful Chicago-style meat

products: authentic meatball sandwiches, kosher hot dogs, and tasty beef sausages. Deep-dish Sicilian pizza is another house specialty. But Michael's beef sandwich is the most popular item and it's easy to see why—the top rounds are seasoned and roasted, thinly sliced, and marinated in a delicious secret house gravy, while the fresh rolls are stuffed with onions or peppers. Michael's is open Monday through Saturday from 10:30 a.m. until 9:00 p.m.

NICHOLAS RESTAURANT $
318 Southeast Grand Avenue
(503) 235-5123

Nicholas offers wonderful Lebanese and Mediterranean food at user-friendly prices. Nicholas Restaurant is a fun, casual place that serves giant pitas and heaping portions of ethnic food to the accompaniment of lusty music. We like everything about this place—the Mediterranean pizzas, the zesty calzones, and all the seafood dishes. The vegetarian mezza plate is a standout: It includes tabbouleh, two falafel balls, yogurt sauce, spinach pie, hummus, and all the fresh, hot pita bread you can eat. With a side dish it is more than enough for a couple. Nicholas is open Monday through Saturday from 10:00 a.m. until 9:00 p.m. and Sunday from 11:00 a.m. until 7:00 p.m. Nicholas does not serve alcohol, and only cash and checks are accepted. In spite of this, there are always lines out the door, so be prepared to wait a bit.

NOBLE ROT $$
2724 Southeast Ankeny Street
(503) 233-1999

Noble Rot is a wine bar by trade, but their dinners are wonderfully delicious and the atmosphere—especially during warm weather, when the garage door that composes its north wall is opened to the fresh air—is amiably stylish. The talented kitchen staff prepares some of the best entrees and appetizers in the city: Tangy, velvety macaroni and cheese, a chicken terrine, a salad of beet and smoked trout, a beautiful and simple butter lettuce salad, and an outstanding onion tart are some of our favorites, but the menu

changes seasonally, so you never know what delights await you. Equally compelling are the wines: Many pours available by the glass and good wine flight selections are fun to combine with your little snacks. And if one wine in particular calls to you, you can buy a bottle to take home. Closed Sunday.

NOHO'S HAWAIIAN CAFE $
2525 Southeast Clinton Street
(503) 233-5301

Noho's is a popular neighborhood cafe that offers tasty Hawaiian fare. The yakisoba noodles—served with veggies and a tangy sauce—are a favorite, but the menu offers a selection of exotic meals ranging from Korean short ribs to seafood entrees and yummy marinated chicken dishes. Everything is served with white rice and macaroni or green salad on the side and—for those who like to swap and share different foods—family-style meals are always available. Noho's is open Sunday through Thursday from 11:00 a.m. until 9:00 p.m., and on Friday and Saturday they stay open until 11:00 p.m. The cafe also offers catering services. Visit www.nohos.com for more details.

NOSTRANA $$
1401 Southeast Morrison Street
(503) 234-2427

Acclaimed as the *Oregonian*'s 2006 Restaurant of the Year, Nostrana has behind it a team from some of the best restaurants in a town of restaurants—specifically Genoa and Gino's and the Produce Row Cafe. Together they have built a spacious but warm restaurant that serves fantastic food at reasonable prices. And what should you order? Ask your server, but the Neapolitan-style pizza is outstanding, as are the antipasti and bruschetta. Pasta dishes feature house-made noodles and sauces inspired by Marcella Hazen. The grilled and rotisseried meats are perfectly done, sharing touches of Tuscany while being, at the same time, all Oregon. On the wine list you'll see a good selection of wines from Italy, though it also has some nice Oregon pinot noirs. Desserts are outstanding, and one in particular is deserving of mention: wood-oven-baked apple crisp with almond cream. This crisp is baked in the pizza oven—which means at about 700 degrees—and while it takes 20 minutes to prepare, its caramelized and creamy goodness is worth waiting for. Nostrana lives in an old grocery store. They have used the space well, placing tables far apart, but warming the restaurant by using cork floors, the pizza oven, and attractive lighting, elements that create an urbanized rustic feel to the place. Nostrana is open for lunch Monday through Friday from 11:30 a.m. to 2:00 p.m., and for dinner every night.

NUESTRA COCINA $$
2135 Southeast Division Street
(503) 232-2135

This remarkable restaurant in Southeast Portland serves Mexican food at its finest—not greasy rice and beans, but complex and savory dishes from Mexico's central regions. The service here is both expert and friendly, and the dining room is handsome, with mosaic tiles and accents of wood. But as pleasant as the service and dining room are, the food is what, rightly, should draw you. For one thing, the tortillas are *heche a mano*—made by hand using a tortilla press. The result is fragrant goodness that gets even better when you add a few drops of chipotle sauce. Salads and other appetizers are fresh and delicious. They offer a great Caesar salad (yes, it is a Mexican dish), ceviche, and savory little tacos made from shredded pork that are not just crowd pleasers but genuine haute cuisine. Entrees include succulent pork and lamb dishes, as well as truly excellent seafood dishes such as prawns cooked with garlic and spicy chiles, served with a perfectly complementary dish of black beans and plantains. Yum. For dessert, the cinnamon ice cream has no equal in town. One warning: The bar area is very, very small, so there are few options for waiting unless it's a summer night and you can chat outside on the sidewalk. But it is worth waiting for a table here. If you do get a seat at the bar, you should try one of the excellent margaritas; they are delicious. Nuestra Cocina is closed Sunday and Monday. However, they will serve you dinner Tuesday through Saturday, from 5:00 to 10:00 p.m.

OTTO'S SAUSAGE & MEAT MARKET $
4138 Southeast Woodstock Boulevard
(503) 771-6714

Otto's, a third-generation German butcher shop and deli, has the best smoked sausages around. This is the place to go for frankfurters, Swedish potato sausage, smoked German sausage, British bangers, bratwurst, ham hocks, and stuffed chicken breast. You will never get potato salad at a deli that even remotely compares with Otto's tasty concoction. As you would expect, dining is casual at Otto's—there are just eight small tables—but if you are a sausage connoisseur and love ethnic foods you will enjoy your stop here. Otto's is open every day except Sunday from 9:30 a.m. until 6:00 p.m.

PINE STATE BISCUITS
3640 Southeast Belmont Street
(503) 236-3346

Pine State Biscuits began as a stall in the Portland Farmers' Market, but after their lines snaked around the block and they kept running out of food, they opened this spot on Belmont. Here they serve fantastic breakfasts and lunch made with ingredients from their farmers' market friends. Specialties include amazingly delicious grits, as well as good sandwiches and hash browns. Biscuits are good too, but really, the star is the grits. If you never liked them before, you will now. Pine State Biscuits is open from 7:00 a.m. to 2:00 p.m. Tuesday through Sunday.

PIX PATISSERIE
3402 Southeast Division Street
(503) 232-4407
www.pixpatisserie.com

Pix specializes in pastry—cakes, tarts, tortes, petit-fours—and in chocolates. Here you will find a spectacular Carmen Miranda tart, with glossy fruit in artful balance. You'll find the award-winning Amelie, a chocolate mousse confection that embraces a well of orange vanilla crème brûlée. And you'll find traditional patisserie favorites, such as the Opera, a thin almond cake layered with chocolate ganache and coffee buttercream. Pix supplies many local shops and restaurants, as well as offering a charming retail shop that also serves as a petite cafe. Pix also has a large and sophisticated space at 3901 North Williams Street (503-282-6539), where classes and other events are located.

POK POK AND WHISKEY SODA LOUNGE $$
3226 Southeast Division Street
(503) 232-1387

Inhabiting a teeny hut and a vintage house on Southeast Division, Pok Pok's modest exterior belies its perfect and authentic Thai cooking. Pok Pok serves the cuisine of the northern part of Thailand, in particular the Chiang Mai valley. What does this mean for you? A mouthwatering balance of crispy and soft; of sweet, salty, and spicy; of yin and yang. Everything here is delicious, but the major draw is the roasted guinea hens, cooked on a special rotisserie that was imported just for this purpose. They have a gorgeous crispy golden skin, and the meat is juicy, infused with lemongrass, garlic, and smoke. Another wonderful dish is the Khao Man Som Tam, a dish of coconut rice, caramelized shredded pork, and fried shallots, but pretty much anything you get will be good. The Whiskey Soda Lounge takes Pok Pok's excellent dishes indoors, where they are expanded upon and can be accompanied by cocktails. In 2007 Pok Pok was named the *Oregonian*'s Restaurant of the Year, so getting seated can be challenging. They have an upstairs dining room that can take parties of five or more, and you can reserve tables for this purpose. Sitting outside on the porch or patio, however, is our favorite way to enjoy the deliciousness that is Pok Pok. Visit them Monday through Saturday. Lunch is served from 11:30 a.m. to 3:30 p.m.; dinner from 4:30 on.

THE PRESS CLUB $
2621 Southeast Clinton Street
(503) 233-5656

This little cafe in the Clinton Street area serves expertly prepared crepes, along with literary *panini* sandwiches and salads (that is, they are named after literary things), all of which are fresh and delicious. The Press Club also has an outstanding wine list, French press coffee, and a wide array of magazines—indeed, all press-related items. Serves breakfast, lunch, and dinner Tuesday through Sunday.

SABURO'S $
1667 Southeast Bybee Street
(503) 236-4237

Serving good sushi in Portland, Saburo's popularity is evident by the crowds who gather outside in the evening, awaiting beautiful slices of velvety, firm fish and magnificent, fresh rolls. The sake list is also good, as are the tempura, noodles, and other traditional dishes. We order these because we can't help it, and they are good, but the true attraction is the sushi. The lighting is bright and the tables are tiny and crowded. There are always long lines, so we have been known to write our names on the list and then sneak up to Caprial's for a cocktail.

SIMPATICA DINING HALL $$
838 Southeast Ash Street
(dining room entrance)
(503) 235-1600

Simpatica Dining Hall represents a national trend in dining—one that got a major boost from experimentation with the genre in Portland—the "Family Supper." Simpatica serves weekend dinners and brunches (since the chefs have day jobs as butchers and terrine-preparers for their other venture, Viande) to small numbers of people who know great food when they taste it and who are happy to commune with their fellow diners. Simpatica's preparations and service started out as experiments, but they have taken root because they really reflect the Portland ethos so well. The brunch features their wonderfully prepared meats, as well as traditional dishes such as waffles, biscuits and gravy, and crepes (albeit with inventive fillings such as squash and bacon). Dinners are typically served as a prix fixe menu with several choices. Vegetarians might be happier elsewhere, but for omnivores Simpatica is one of the best meals in town. Dinners are served Friday (starting at 7:30 p.m.) and Saturday nights (starting at 7:00 p.m.), brunches on Sunday from 9:00 a.m. to 2:00 p.m.

3 DOORS DOWN $$
1429 Southeast 37th Street
(503) 236-6886

3 Doors Down serves high-quality American-Mediterranean fare and pays attention to all the fine details that add to the enjoyment of a meal. The cozy and comfortable setting is a great place to enjoy the restaurant's wide range of house-made pastas. The risottos and Caesar salads are exceptional, as are the pastas and the entire range of appetizers. A signature, must-try dish is the bucatini pasta with meatballs, which is perfectly balanced and savory. The penne with vodka sauce is also a favorite. The bar is a lovely spot for a predinner aperitif. Closed Monday.

VICTORY $
3652 Southeast Division Street
(503) 236-8755

This charming spot in Southeast Portland is a favorite with the neighborhood and fans all over town, drawn by the handsome decor—green walls, tin ceilings, and unusual, handmade light fixtures—and by the sweet, sweet servers. In some respects, Victory is the ideal neighborhood restaurant—not because it is perfect, but because it indicates the benchmark quality that Portland restaurants regularly achieve. Here, they specialize in small plates, with a variety of excellent house-cured meats and a savory spaetzle in a delightful cheese sauce as signature dishes. But they also serve fine salads, mussels, a good cheese plate, and other cafe food. Victory has a well-edited wine list and a number of special cocktails that entice even people who don't live 4 blocks away. In fact, the owners of other Southeast Portland restaurants appear at their bar with a regularity that is telling. Victory is open for dinner nightly.

VINDALHO $$
2038 Southeast Clinton Street
(503) 467-4550

Serving exquisite food in the Indian tradition, Vindalho is unlike any other restaurant between Vancouver, British Columbia, and perhaps San Francisco. What Nuestra Cocina is to Mexican food, Vindalho is to Indian food: It displays a proper respect for the flavors and textures while at the same time taking advantage of the amazing basic ingredients the Pacific Northwest has to offer. Vindalho offers many traditional foods—aromatic naan bread, for instance, or lamb kofta (savory meatballs in a Pakistani curry sauce). You will also find beautiful and flavorful salads. For dinner, you may want to sample the curry, the pork, or any of the various preparations of chicken—including tandoori. The lamb is outstanding—grilled perfectly in the tandoori oven, it is succulent and juicy and nevertheless carries that beautiful smoky scent that is the hallmark of meat grilled outdoors. Whatever else you order, be sure to order the condiments—the sides of relishes and pickles that will bring your dishes together into a meal. Vindhalho is open Tuesday through Saturday, 5:00 to 10:00 p.m.

ZELL'S $
1300 Southeast Morrison Street
(503) 239-0196

Zell's is known particularly for its great German apple pancakes, authentic corned beef hash, and salmon eggs Benedict, but this breakfast-and-lunch spot is good at many other things too—specials such as eggs and paella, for example. Breakfasts are served with scones, toast, or English muffins, quick bread, or potatoes. Sandwiches, salads, and soups are also available, but breakfasts are served until closing. Zell's is open daily for breakfast and lunch.

NORTH/NORTHEAST PORTLAND

ACADIA $$$
1303 Northeast Fremont Street
(503) 249-5001

Located in a cute neighborhood, this handsome New Orleans–style bistro is packed with adventuresome diners who come in search of delicious Creole dishes, expertly prepared. Here you will find soft-shell crab, catfish taco, and jambalaya among the appetizers, as well as a delightful array of entrees such as Pork Chop Galatoire—a chop rubbed with ancho chili and honey, grilled, and served with crawfish, corn bread stuffing, and caramelized onion. During certain hours, they offer a nice fixed-price, three-course menu that features salad, a choice among three entrees, and either bread pudding or Cajun Velvet Pie for dessert. Acadia also has a full bar. They serve dinner Monday through Saturday and a special jazz brunch on Sunday.

ALBERTA OYSTER BAR AND GRILL $$
2926 Northeast Alberta Street
(503) 284-9600

The Alberta Oyster Bar and Grill serves wonderful oysters, of course, but doesn't stop there: You will also find melt-in-your-mouth sweetbreads or seared foie gras, crispy and succulent razor clams, halibut cheeks poached in a smoky broth, braised short ribs with gnocchi, maple-syrup-braised chicken, and other savory delights. Oysters can be had beautifully fresh, but they may also be served in other ways because the menu tends to change a lot. Chef Eric Bechard is quite creative, and so you may wish to try the "Chef's Whim," a prix-fixe menu composed of five courses. Putting yourself in the hands of a talented chef and expert servers is a fine way to open yourself to adventures in eating.

AUTÉNTICA $$$
5506 Northeast 30th Avenue
(503) 287-7555

Serving food in the style of the Acapulco region of Mexico, Auténtica may defy your expectations. There is a full bar, from which margaritas and other fine drinks flow. Meals begin with three kinds of salsa, and you will want to also order the outstanding guacamole. Seafood cocktails are a house specialty, and they range from a refreshing octopus salad to tangy ceviche. The soups are hearty, the flatiron steak is grilled perfectly, and the tostada is beautifully seasoned. The tamales are close to perfect. Because this restaurant is attempting to achieve authenticity, some things might surprise you, such as the saltine crackers served with the seafood cocktails. Just go with it. Dinner served Tuesday through Sunday.

BERNIE'S SOUTHERN BISTRO $$
2904 Northeast Alberta Street
(503) 282-9864

This fine bistro serves Southern dinners with nods to the Northwest in its use of some seasonal and local ingredients—though not only those ingredients, of course. But Bernie's cornmeal-crusted oysters are a nice twist on a local favorite, as are the green tomatoes (the Northwest gardener's yearly problem), here fried and served with smoked tomato coulis, hearty gumbo, fresh corn bread, and green-onion grits cakes. The catfish is plump, and the chicken-fried steak is savory. The appetizers are also notable, especially the hush puppies. Bernie's serves dinner Tuesday through Saturday.

CIAO VITO $$$
2293 Northeast Alberta Street
(503) 282-5522

Chef Vito DiLullo opened this attractive restaurant to serve his own neighborhood, on Alberta Street, but it has also become a destination dining spot since it opened in mid-2004. Ciao Vito serves honest food beautifully prepared at good value, and in this way, it feels more like Italy or France than Oregon. The focus of the menu is traditional Italian fare using Northwest ingredients, but there are always surprises. Even the simplest dishes—the antipasto, for example—are about 20 times better than anything you're likely to get west of Sicily. The calamari, served with aioli, is crispy, chewy, and delicious. The cured meats are a superb balance of fragrance, smokiness, and salt; the pickled vegetables taste fresh and tangy and are perfectly textured. The spaghetti carbonara is both creamy and earthy, complemented by the house-made pancetta. The chocolate *pots de creme* are worth savoring, no matter how full you are. The wine list is thoughtful, featuring Northwest and Italian wines at exceptionally reasonable prices. The service at Ciao Vito is professional and friendly. The word *handsome* has two meanings—good-looking and generous—and this affordable restaurant embodies both. Ciao Vito serves dinner Monday through Sunday from 5:00 to 10:00 p.m., except on Friday and Saturday, when dinner is served until 11:00 p.m.

FIFE $$$
4440 Northeast Fremont Street
(971) 222-3433

Fife is a beautiful restaurant in Northeast Portland, with an atmosphere that manages to be both sophisticated and warm. While primarily a neighborhood place, plenty of upscale followers from all over the city have beaten a path to the door to sample the American cuisine produced by chef Marco Shaw. The east side of Portland is home to a number of restaurants that are expanding the boundaries of local cuisine by bringing new sensibilities to the preparation of local, seasonable fare, and Shaw—who is also not afraid to use blue crab in his outstanding crab cake—is among the foremost. The menu stars less common meats such as quail, venison, rabbit, and buffalo, as well as silky pork shoulder and tender lamb. Starters have included a wondrous delicate squash soup, fragrant with cinnamon, in addition to the aforementioned signature crab cakes. A cheesecake featuring chèvre and pear creates an outstanding finale. Everything is prepared with skill and ingenuity, and the service is poised and professional.

i Oregon and Washington are among the vanguard of artisanal cheesemakers, and the Pacific Northwest Cheese Project is dedicated to making sure we know how blessed they are. Find them at http://pnwcheese.typepad.com.

LOVELY HULA HANDS $$$
4057 North Mississippi Avenue
(503) 445-9910

Chef Troy MacLarty trained at Chez Panisse, among other places, before he arrived in Portland, and this experience shows in the imaginative menu and inspired preparation of each dish at Lovely Hula Hands. The atmosphere is attractive and romantic, in a rehabilitated brick building that has beautifully contrasting wood accents and warm, tropical colors. You'll find a full bar with expertly prepared cocktails, among them their own signatures such

as Talulah's Bathwater, a sticky concoction of pomegranate molasses, tequila, fresh lime, and sugar, as well as the classics. The menu is haute Northwest cuisine, contrapuntal in textures and flavors. Salads are outstanding, often combining something savory, such as smoked fish or cheese, with something fruity, such as grapefruit, and something bitter, such as radicchio or fennel. Entrees are equally delicious; you may find, depending on the season, braised pork or fried chicken. Soufflés make frequent appearances on the menu and come highly recommended. Lovely Hula Hands does not take reservations, but you may want to call ahead if you have a larger group (more than 4 people). Open for dinner Tuesday through Sunday.

i For the most unvarnished restaurant reviews, news, and gossip, check out Food Dude's blog, An Exploration of Portland Food and Drink at www.portlandfoodanddrink.com. Food Dude started his blog as an antidote to reviews that sounded like advertising, in an effort to create a more reality-based picture of the Portland food and wine scene. He and his team review restaurants anonymously and multiple times, relating their experiences in great detail. As a result, he is irresistible reading for Portland foodies—including Portland chefs, who often lurk here. Sometimes they post too.

NAVARRE $$
10 Northeast 28th Avenue
(503) 232-3555

Navarre has been at the vanguard of a trend in Portland restaurants—small plates of wonderful food so you can have many different courses in one meal. The courses at this Spanish-inspired restaurant might include deliciously and simply prepared roasted meats, tangy braised greens, a beet terrine, pickled carrots, or house-cured meats, in addition to cheeses and desserts. Navarre also, like so, so many Portland restaurants, is market-based, meaning that they serve what is in season, even going so far as to have their own personal farmer. You can tell this by the preserves that adorn the shelves and serve as focal points for the decor. Navarre serves dinner every night.

ORIGINAL HALIBUT'S $
2525 Northeast Alberta Street
(503) 803-9600

A small restaurant in a great neighborhood, Original Halibut's serves wonderfully fresh fish and chips that are perfectly textured: crispy outside and tender inside. The chef varies the fish depending on the season and offers several battered delicacies each day. The clam chowder is also excellent.

PODNAH'S $$
1469 Northeast Prescott Street
(503) 281-3700

Podnah's serves excellent barbecue and its standard accompaniments in an unpretentious setting. It's one of the few places in town to get an iceberg wedge salad, but it's a salad that goes well with the sliced brisket, lamb spare ribs, and pulled pork. These and other smoky delights are made with local meats and served with refreshing slaws, beans, and other sides. Wine and beer are available, as are an impressive array of sodas. It's open for lunch and dinner Tuesday through Sunday.

SIAM SOCIETY $$
2703 Northeast Alberta Street
(503) 922-3675

Siam Society serves some of the best Thai food in town—well balanced, exquisitely fresh, and perfectly textured. Though the restaurant has a daily-changing menu, it tends to carry some items all the time, even if fillings or sauces might change. You will find a variety of salads and spring rolls based on what's in season; likewise for the soups. Entrees will not surprise you with their labels—fried rice, stir-fries, drunken noodles, curries, and so on—but the way they are prepared is unlike anything else in town in terms of attention to detail and balance. Service is excellent, and the setting is also striking. It occupies a renovated electrical substation and uses this to great effect. Soaring ceilings and tall windows make the restaurant feel spacious, and the patio is a lovely spot for a drink. Siam Society is open for dinner every night but Monday, and they have a killer happy hour from 4:00 to 6:00 p.m.

TORO BRAVO $$
120 Northeast Russell Street
(503) 281-4464

Toro Bravo carries the Spanish flag for Portland restaurants, as hospitable and friendly as the country, relaxed and sociable, but with outstanding food. It truly is a tapas "bar," and the best approach to take there is to order just a few dishes, hang onto the menu, and then order some more. Toro Bravo reflects the cuisine of many Spanish regions as interpreted by chef John Gorham, which means that it also reflects Oregon. The kebabs, the paellas, the tortillas: Each of these is prepared as a homage to the mother country but with decided Northwest accents. Local favorites include the coppa steak, prepared with spinach and golden raisins; bacon-wrapped dates; scallops; duck rillettes; and grilled chanterelle mushrooms. Plus there are enough dishes to please everyone from vegans to omnivores. You can order refreshing sangria, a number of house cocktails, and excellent wines. Toro Bravo is open for dinner nightly.

VANCOUVER

HUDSON'S $$$
Heathman Lodge
7801 Northeast Greenwood Drive
(360) 816-6100

The chefs who serve the dining room in this

comfortable hotel display its original take on the local and seasonal, with expertly prepared fish, fowl, and meat that is savory and succulent. The signature seafood cakes and flatbread are both amazingly delicious, and the wine list, featuring mostly West Coast wines, just right. Hudson's serves breakfast, lunch, and dinner every day.

ROOTS   **$$$**
19215 Southeast 34th Street
Camas, Washington
(360) 260-3001
Roots is a delicious spot for all the folks who are too tired to crawl back over the bridge for dinner, as well as those who never left. Why should Portland have all the fun? The menu is a beautiful concoction of whatever is fresh and seasonal—for example, Dungeness crab and line-caught salmon or wonderfully roasted chicken breast. The wine list is thoughtful, and the service friendly. For those of you in Portland, Roots is worth a trip across the river. Roots is open for lunch and dinner Monday through Saturday and for brunch on Sunday.

Did someone say . . . cake?

Then they might have been to Saint Cupcake (407 Northwest 17th Avenue; 503-473-8760) or Cupcake Jones (307 Northwest 10th Avenue; 503-222-4404) for cute and delicious cupcakes. Or they might have been to a festive occasion with a cake from Portland classics Helen Bernhard Bakery (1717 Northeast Broadway; 503–287–1251) or JaCiva's Chocolates & Pastries (4733 Southeast Hawthorne Boulevard; 503-234-8115). Or maybe it was Bakery Bar (1028 Southeast Water Avenue; 503-546-8110). Bakery Bar provides beautiful made-to-order cakes in its industrially chic spot near the Willamette River. They also offer wonderful pastries, cookies, scones, and sandwiches. But we bet you'll say cake.

BREWPUBS

Some anthropologists claim that beer, rather than bread, enticed human tribes to abandon the ways of the nomad and settle down to develop agriculture. It was a powerful inspiration. By 3000 B.C., the Sumerians were so devoted to the craft of brewing that it had a patron goddess: Ninkasi. If Ninkasi were looking for new recruits for her cult, she would have to look no further than Portland, where new disciples are born every day. Portland may have more microbreweries and brewpubs than any city in the nation—32 at last count—reflecting a climate hospitable to hops and a fanatic devotion to the homegrown. Our climate is excellent for growing hops (we grow at least 14 varieties) and barley, and beer brewing is a long tradition. Combine these resources with the do-it-yourself ethos left over from Oregon's hippie days, and you have a revolution in the making. All over the area, commercial brewers and backyard enthusiasts are creating microbrews, cask-conditioned ales, and other delights.

The most well known names in brewing legend here include Mike and Brian McMenamin, two brothers who have become not just brewers but real estate developers, hoteliers, and visionaries. They have more than 30 enterprises—including pubs, restaurants, hotels, inns, and theaters—throughout the city and beyond, stretching far south into the Willamette Valley and north to Washington. While their shadow has grown long enough that we have been known to call them the McMenamin Brothers, nonetheless, their pubs are wonderfully Oregon experiences. Most of them have splendid gardens and appealing interiors, and they all have good beer, from old standards such as Crystal, Ruby, Hammerhead, and Terminator Stout, to seasonal and other special beers.

Other important beer names are Fred Eckhardt, the beer writer whose most frequent label is "legendary," because his book *The Essentials of Beer Style* is regarded as the gospel by homebrewers and international beer judges; the Widmer Brothers, who made *hefewiezen* a household word (at least around here); and Henry Weinhard, the progenitor of beer production in the area. But many of the best beers in the area don't have well-known names or even their own pubs. Hair of the Dog—who named one of their special ales "Fred" after Fred Eckhardt—is one to keep your eye out for at taps throughout town.

Pubs and brewpubs have fast become a way of life for Oregonians, and many of them are very family-friendly, offering simple food and sometimes even craft-brewed root beer. As long as a pub is also a restaurant, most of them will allow children until 10:00 p.m. in designated areas. It is very common to see families in these pubs, so if you want to bring the little ones, don't be shy.

SOUTHWEST PORTLAND

FULL SAIL BREWING
307 Southwest Montgomery Street
(503) 222-5343
www.fullsailbrewing.com
Full Sail is a brewery that was established in Hood River, and this brewery is its Portland outpost. A small operation that makes light, easy-to-sip ales and lagers, Full Sail is next door to McCormick and Schmick's Harborside Restaurant and Pilsner Room. Sample one of Full Sail's brews as you gaze through a glass wall at brewers

making a new batch. Full Sail was one of the first microbreweries to figure out how to bottle their beer without losing any of its hoppy perfection, and this genius started a revolution in the hand-crafted beer world.

THE FULTON PUB
618 Southwest Nebraska Street
(503) 246-9530
www.mcmenamins.com
The Fulton Pub is a McMenamin operation, housed in a simple white building near Willamette Park off of Macadam. Here, you'll find Terminator, Hammerhead, Crystal Ale, Cascade Head, Ruby, and other brews. Many are brewed right there, while others are "imported" from other McMenamins breweries, which lie scattered throughout the city. Sometimes "guest" beers from other breweries are also available. The biggest attraction of the Fulton is the very nice garden on the west side of the pub—a lovely place to spend a summer Saturday afternoon.

RACCOON LODGE
7424 Southwest Beaverton-
Hillsdale Highway
(503) 296-0110
www.raclodge.com
On the western outskirts of town, you'll find the Raccoon Lodge, a large pub and brewery designed as a mountain lodge with high ceilings, ample dining space with wooden booths and Pendleton blanket cushions, wood trusses and wainscoting, and a monster stone fireplace surmounted by an elk's head and horns. In addition to its excellent beer, you'll find a variety of hand-cut french fries and dipping sauces, including Yukon gold, shoestring, tater tots, sweet potatoes, and ale-batter steak fries, all of which arrive in a big bucket. The dipping sauces include country gravy, Creole tomato, red chili barbecue, raspberry habañero, tartar, white cheddar sauce, and buttermilk ranch. More substantial fare is also available: jerked pork loin, fish and chips, vegetable pot pie, and chicken turned on a rotisserie after a lemon, garlic, and ale marinade. As for the brew, the Black Snout Stout is superb and

Ring Tail Pale and Bandit Amber are pleasant. If you order wine you have a choice of 10 reds or 10 whites, mostly from Oregon and California with an Australian chardonnay or cabernet tossed into the mix.

ROCK BOTTOM BREWERY & RESTAURANT
206 Southwest Morrison Avenue
(503) 796-2739
www.rockbottom.com
It seems like half of Portland's downtown workers cram into Rock Bottom at quitting time. Good choices include Cryin' Coyote Western Ale, White Pelican American Pale Ale, Falcon Red Ale, Big Horn Nut Brown Ale, and Black Seal Stout. The brew kettles are in a long hall upstairs next to the pool room with its eight tables, while downstairs a full bar, wooden tables, and booths are all friendly zones in the tradition of a village pub. Grub favorites are the hickory burger, alder-smoked salmon fish and chips, buffalo fajitas, and Mrs. Chow's Sizzling Shrimp Salad. Rock Bottom has several areas for private parties, and because children are allowed until 10:00 p.m., it's a low-key, friendly spot for family parties and other gatherings. Fans of this hot spot can take home T-shirts, sweatshirts, hats, glassware, and other kinds of souvenirs. As the brewmaster says, "You haven't hit Portland until you've hit Rock Bottom."

TUGBOAT BREWING CO.
711 Southwest Ankeny Street
(503) 226-2508
This charming little family-owned spot on a downtown side street is in the old tradition of cottage-style, handcrafted brewing—the kind of beer everyone used to drink and that you can only get on-site. The brewery is upstairs; downstairs is the book-lined pub, where you can curl up with a pint and spend a pleasant evening. Tugboat likes to make powerful British-style beers, and their offerings include a fantastic Extra Special Bitter, a hoppy India Pale Ale, a medium-bodied Hop Red, and a really special cask-conditioned stout. You may also wish to try their interesting Czech bitter brewed with imported Saaz hops. This is a wonderful pub, and there's nothing else like it

in the city. The owner also repairs watches—the brewery is housed in a historic watch- and clock-repair shop—in case yours has stopped.

NORTHWEST PORTLAND

BRIDGEPORT BREWPUB
1313 Northwest Marshall Street
(503) 241-3612
www.bridgeportbrew.com

The oldest of Portland's craft breweries, Bridge-port began in 1984 as the first microbrewery in town, producing 600 barrels per year. Now this groundbreaking, award-winning brewery produces more than 100,000 barrels each year.This picturesque brick-and-ivy brewpub is reminiscent of old German beer halls, especially the spacious upstairs, which is overflowing on the weekends. House standards such as Coho Pacific and Blue Heron are available, as well as cask-conditioned ales, which are naturally carbonated, unfiltered, and stored in kegs called firkins. Every Tuesday, brewers tap a firkin right on the bar for a fresh full-bodied taste direct from a gravity-fed spigot. Bridgeport offers a variety of British-style ales, including India Pale Ale, Extra Special Bitter, Black Strap Stout, and Porter conditioned in a bottle, keg, or firkin cask. The flagship ale is Blue Heron Amber Ale, brewed in honor of Portland's official city bird. Bridgeport also serves up a fine pizza, with dough made fresh daily from unfermented beer wort.

> **i** Why should wine have all the glory? Beer also complements food, so Higgins Restaurant (1239 Southwest Broadway, 503-222-9070) offers a comprehensive beer list, as well as advice about which beers will go best with your Northwest salmon.

DESCHUTES BREWERY & PUBLIC HOUSE
210 Northwest 11th Avenue
(503) 296-4906
www.deschutesbrewery.com

The Deschutes Brewery, originating in Bend, Oregon, is known for its outstanding brews such as

Mirror Pond Pale Ale, Obsidian Stout, Black Butte Porter, and the newest, Armory XPA (a pale ale). In this new site, Armory XPA is brewed in gorgeous copper vats made in Germany and calibrated with precision. In Portland style, the menu takes the normal pub fare up a notch, with local and organic meats and produce in the delicious burgers, pizzas, and fish and chips. Most of the food is made on site, including the cured meats, pickles, and tartar sauce. The pub is a beautiful space showcasing the virtues of salvage. The space itself was once an auto garage; the bar was carved from a single block of wood rescued from a demolished building; even the urinals, which were found abandoned in a warehouse in New York, are recycled. The interior is both spacious and cozy, with high ceilings, warm colors, and impressive carvings by J. Chester Armstrong, an Oregon artist, in the dining room. The good-natured servers will pour beer and serve you lunch or dinner from 11:00 a.m to midnight every day.

MACTARNAHAN'S TAPROOM
2730 Northwest 31st Avenue
(503) 228-5269
www.portlandbrew.com

This huge brewery in the Guild's Lake Industrial District at the edge of Northwest Portland shows off its 140-barrel copper brewing vessels by making them a part of its brewpub's interior design. The kettles are from the Sixenbrau Brewery, dating back to the 16th century in Bavaria. Added to this Teutonic touch are fancy steins and a menu of seafood, schnitzel, sausage, and other grilled meats cooked on an applewood rotisserie and grill. A covered patio is open for dining during the winter. As for the brew, the line includes a Bavarian-style Weizen and MacTarnahan's Scottish-Style Amber Ale, as well as the native-inspired Oregon Honey Beer, Black Watch Porter, and ZigZag Lager.

MCMENAMINS TAVERN
1716 Northwest 23rd Avenue
(503) 227-0929
www.mcmenamins.com

This original tavern in the chain is the only one

named after the "bros." It's a modest little spot a bit north of the cultural hubbub on 21st and 23rd Avenues. For a sense of history and a quiet brew, check it out. Try the Crystal Ale, an amber ale, or for a lighter taste, the Cascade Head Ale.

NEW OLD LOMPOC
1616 Northwest 23rd Avenue
(503) 225-1855

The place that started the Lompoc brewing empire, this pub is named after a bar in a movie with W. C. Fields and Mae West, *The Bank Dick.* Here you will find powerful beers brewed with great attention to balance. There are many seasonal brews, but the year-round varieties are also excellent. We recommend the rich Sockeye Cream Stout and the Proletariat Red, both strong beers that warrant total attention. But if you must be distracted by food, the menu has satisfying pub fare.

THE RAM'S HEAD
2282 Northwest Hoyt Street
(503) 221-0098
www.mcmenamins.com

With its comfy couches, easy chairs, booths, and long bar, the Ram's Head has the feel of a private club for the rest of us. The grub at the McMenamin brothers' pub is particularly good, especially the french fries—cut and cooked on the spot. Located on the street level of a four-story apartment building at the corner of Northwest Hoyt Street and 23rd Avenue, this classy beer joint is dead center in the heart of the Northwest scene. It's light and comfortable, and you can bring the kids until 10:00 p.m.

RINGLER'S
1332 West Burnside Street
(503) 225-0627
www.mcmenamins.com

Yet another McMenamins business, Ringler's brewpub is on the street level of a three-story operation including the Crystal Ballroom at the top and a brewery in the middle. A popular intermission zone for concerts and dance bands upstairs, Ringler's, with its madcap mosaics and

Byzantine carvings, a long bar, booths, and tables, also offers free pool on Tuesday and Sunday. If your thirst leans more toward the harder stuff than the brews trickling down from above, try McMenamins' Signature Margarita or the Crystal Ambush (Bushmill's Irish Whiskey, amaretto, and coffee topped with whipped cream). Enjoy the pizza, prime rib sandwich, or linguine with artichoke hearts. Those with a Brit heart might want to try the bangers and mash.

ROGUE ALES PUBLIC HOUSE
1339 Northwest Flanders Street
(503) 222-5910

This is Rogue's Portland outpost (they are based on the coast, in Newport), and it has taken advantage of its good Pearl District location to offer conference rooms and catering, as well as a Lego table (for those really tough meetings). This pub also offers the hard stuff, as well as its excellent beer. The beers served here include Rogue Red, Brutal Bitter, Buckwheat Ale, Porter, Stout, Rogue Smoke, and Maierbock; some of these are in pressurized kegs. They also usually offer a cask-conditioned beer.

SOUTHEAST PORTLAND

THE BAGDAD THEATER AND PUB
3702 Southeast Hawthorne Boulevard
(503) 236-9234
www.mcmenamins.com

This is a Southeast Portland landmark and a great place to uncoil. You can watch a first-rate movie for a couple of bucks or sit out on the picnic tables and survey the scene on bustling Hawthorne Boulevard. One of the McMenamins' five movie-house brewpubs, the Bagdad is a Hawthorne-area favorite. The movies are usually second-run features, and the lighting and sound quality are very good. The Bagdad carries the McMenamins brews that you'd expect: the fruity Ruby Ale; Hammerhead, a malty, hoppy, English-style ale; the dark and stout Terminator; a light and refreshing wheat ale; and a rich, smooth, chocolatey porter. Food choices in the pub next to the theater include nearly a dozen pizza options and everything from hot Thai noodles to black bean burritos. Most of the small pizzas, sandwiches, and specialties cost around $6.

THE BARLEY MILL
1629 Southeast Hawthorne Boulevard
(503) 231-1492
www.mcmenamins.com

This, the granddaddy of all the McMenamins brewpubs, opened in 1983, but the Barley Mill's roots reach back to 1934 when it operated as The Scuttlebutt the year after Prohibition was repealed. It's impossible to miss the cranky old barley mill stationed near the front door. Big picture windows shed light on this groovy place with loads of Grateful Dead paraphernalia and posters. You can choose between the large wooden picnic tables (inside and outside) or the cozy bar and smaller corner booths. The service is good—as at most McMenamins brewpubs—and there is a nice selection of ales. We like the Nebraska Bitter, the Hammerhead, and the India Pale Ale. Ask the bartender about the daily special, and if you feel adventurous, try the Brewery Taster, a sampler of six different microbrews. The Barley Mill also offers a basic selection of Edgefield Wines, including chardonnay, pinot gris, Riesling, and a few others. The Barley Mill offers plenty of good food, including hot and cold sandwiches and soups, salads, and pasta.

BRIDGEPORT ALE HOUSE
3632 Southeast Hawthorne Boulevard
(503) 233-6540
www.bridgeportbrew.com

Bridgeport Breweries is Oregon's oldest microbrewery, and this eastside outpost is one of our favorite spots. The quality of beverages and food is consistently high, and the stylish interior—with its neutral tones and mellow woods—is friendly and welcoming. This pub offers two cask-conditioned ales as well as six regular microbrews. Their most popular brew is the award-winning India Pale Ale, but we also love Bridgeport's flagship brew, Blue Heron Amber Ale. They also offer some very tasty seasonals, including the Summer Wheat Ale. Although there is no "happy hour" per se, on

Monday the India Pale Ale is served in 20-ounce imperial pints for cheap. The Ale House serves lunch seven days a week, and signature dishes include a wood-roasted oyster sandwich, a grilled eggplant sandwich, and the fire-grilled, seasoned ground-chuck Hawthorne Burger. The hand-tossed, 10-inch pizza pies are baked to perfection and complemented with unusual toppings such as grilled zucchini, smoked chicken, and cilantro. The Bridgeport Ale House is as popular with neighborhood families as it is with everyone else; you can feel like a grown-up again, sipping your beer in this attractive pub, even if junior is busy coloring in the high chair next to you.

> **i** You may find the urge to brew your own, if you stay in Portland long enough. For brewing supplies and expert advice, go to F. H. Steinbart, 234 Southeast 12th Avenue (503-232-8793), or Let's Brew, 9021 Northeast Killingsworth Street (503-256-0205), and they will help you get set up.

HEDGE HOUSE
3412 Southeast Division Street
(503) 235-2215

It's worth a trip across town to spend a summer evening at Hedge House, the latest offering from the expert brewers at Old Lompoc. The pub is in a cute yellow house on Division Street with cozy indoor spaces and a pretty patio. This pleasant atmosphere is underscored by great sandwiches, salads, and similar pub food—and of course, great beer. Our favorite brew is C-note, a wonderfully hoppy India pale ale, but when the weather is hot, few things are tastier than a cold Fool's Golden Ale. Cheap pints can be found on Tuesdays and weekends.

HOPWORKS URBAN BREWERY
2944 Southwest Powell Boulevard
(503) 232-4677
www.hopworksbeer.com

This busy pub brews organic, handcrafted beer and serves it in four beautiful spaces: an outdoor beer garden, an indoor family space that includes a play area, a mezzanine, and a bike-up bar. It's not just the beer that's organic. Every inch is devoted to sustainable restaurant practice, from the permeable pavers lining the beer garden to the rain barrels and composting system. But frankly, what you will notice is the excellence of the beer, which wins medals—including the 2008 World Beer Cup gold medal for its IPA and the silver for its bohemian-style lager. You can get sustainable New York–style pizza to go with it.

THE HORSE BRASS PUB
4534 Southeast Belmont Street
(503) 232-2202
www.horsebrass.com
No visit to Portland is complete without a stop at the Horse Brass for a pint of bitter and a game of darts. This gem of a place is a pub in the finest and truest sense of the word, offering plenty of atmosphere and 46 draughts of the finest microbrewed and imported beers, including Rogue YSB, the house beer for the Horse Brass Pub. Since 1976—more than a decade before most Portlanders had even heard of microbrews—the Horse Brass Pub has been a haven for crafted ales and authentic, home-style British fare. It is a noisy, gregarious place where folks have a smashing good time at the full bar or at one of the large round tables that bring friends and strangers together. The Horse Brass has been notorious for its smoky—very smoky—atmosphere, but in January 2009, an indoor smoking ban at all Oregon bars, clubs, and restaurants went into effect. While a crisis for some Horse Brass fans, this change is welcomed by others. Your frothy pint should taste just as refreshing, and you'll be able to see the dartboard more clearly.

LUCKY LABRADOR BREWING COMPANY
915 Southeast Hawthorne Boulevard
(503) 236-3555
www.luckylab.com
It's easy to miss the Lucky Labrador, which is located on the fringes of Southeast Portland's Industrial District. You don't want to do that because this is a big, sprawling, fun place with

tasty, handcrafted microbrews. It is a refurbished warehouse, and the atmosphere is open, spacious, and very casual. There is ample outside seating as well, with views of the surrounding industrial-area street scenes, while indoor scenes include a large mural that is a great takeoff on Andrew Wyeth's famous painting, *Christina's World*. People go here in groups to have fun together, so there aren't the usual barflies hanging around smoking and nursing drinks. The brews are good, especially the robust Black Lab Stout, a slightly malty Konigs Kolsch, and the crispy Top Dog Extra Pale. We also like Hawthorne's Best Bitter, which is an amber-hued, dry-hopped bitter, very characteristic of an English pint. The ales are served in 20-ounce pints and go for around $3. Plenty of cheap good food is available, including deli sandwiches, Bento (Japanese-style rice with vegetables, chicken, or other toppings), and a good selection of vegetarian dishes. There are two other Lucky Lab locations: the Lucky Labrador Public House (7675 Southwest Capitol Highway) and the Lucky Labrador Beer Hall (1945 Northwest Quimby).

i Most stores display beer beneath fluorescent lights and can stock only the stuff that flies off the shelves. But at Belmont Station (4500 Southeast Stark Street, 503-232-8538; www.belmont-station.com), the storage of beer is taken much more seriously. Single bottles are displayed on shelves out front, and the stuff actually for sale is kept in a darkened walk-in that has the demeanor of a bank vault. Stored this way, the beer lasts longer and tastes better. Belmont Station is open from noon to 10:00 p.m. Monday through Thursday and from noon to 11:00 p.m. on Friday and Saturday.

OAKS BOTTOM PUB
1621 Southeast Bybee Boulevard
(503) 232-1728
From the Lompoc beer empire, this friendly pub aspires to be a "third place"—a place that is not

work and not home but elsewhere, and thus one that allows for genuine relaxing and conviviality. To that end, they offer a great kids' menu in addition to their excellent beers, wines, and cocktails, so that everyone can sit down to enjoy themselves.

The food is carefully prepared and uses high-quality ingredients, in spite of its humble appearance. Look for the Tatchos: natchos made with tater tots. Trust us, they are great. The pulled pork sandwich is also delicious.

PHILADELPHIA'S STEAKS AND HOAGIES
6410 Southeast Milwaukie Avenue
(503) 239-8544
You've got two reasons to visit Oregon's smallest brewery: great ales and the most delicious Philadelphia cheese steak sandwiches this side of the Liberty Bell. The 10 handcrafted ales on tap range from the crisp and light Betsy Ross Golden Ale to the full-bodied Two-Street Stout. There's plenty of good food to choose from on the full menu, including beef and chicken cheese steaks and huge hoagies. The secluded back deck is a splendid place to kick back on a sunny day.

NORTH/NORTHEAST PORTLAND

ALAMEDA BREWING CO.
4765 Northeast Fremont Street
(503) 460-9025
Look for the huge copper hop in front of the Alameda brewpub—consider it a beacon for those seeking quality, hand-crafted ales. Alameda's head brewmaster Craig Nicholls is preparing some of the finest microbrews in town, especially the Black Bear Double Stout, which aficionados are calling one of the best nitro-pours anywhere. (Nitrogen causes all those tiny little bubbles that make the "cascading effect" and gives ales that delicious creamy head.) Alameda offers nine unique regular micros along with two or three seasonals and their popular homemade root beer. With well-priced 20-ounce pints, it's a great value. The food is excellent, affordable, and far more

ambitious than standard pub grub. Entrees range from whiskey baby-back ribs to artichoke linguini to smoked chicken ravioli. Sandwiches and burgers are standouts too. A children's menu is also available. The atmosphere—galvanized metal, acid-stained floor, and the white maple/stainless-steel hop-yard theme—works splendidly, as the brewery itself is located in the dining area.

CONCORDIA BREWERY
McMenamins Kennedy School
5736 Northeast 33rd Avenue
(503) 249-3983
www.mcmenamins.com/Kennedy
The McMenamins converted this beautiful old brick school into a wonderful neighborhood hub. The Kennedy School is an inn, a theater, a restaurant, and a brewpub—or rather, several pubs, for there are a number on-site. The Courtyard Restaurant occupies the center of the complex; the Detention Bar (which allows smoking) and the Honors Bar are on the periphery. There's also a wine bar—the Cypress Bar.

Beers include the usual McMenamin offerings, plus some guests. Much of the beer is brewed on-site. Food offerings are also standard—sandwiches, fries, salads, and other appetizery things, but with more variety in the entree department. For more information on the Kennedy School, see the Accommodations chapter.

THE LAURELWOOD
1728 Northeast 40th Avenue
(503) 282-0622
A friendly pub in the Hollywood neighborhood, the Laurelwood offers some of the best beer in the city. Brewmaster Christian Ettinger oversees this seven-barrel brewery and his attention to detail has paid off: The Mother Lode Golden Ale, their palest ale, won a gold medal at the World Beer Cup in 2002, as did their Piston Pale Ale. The Laurelwood also crafts a great line of organic beers. These include an India Pale Ale, a stout, and a great porter, along with seasonal beers. The menu is simple, with good beer food: onion rings, tacos, chicken strips, nachos, and savory

parmesan-garlic fries. The Laurelwood is spacious and warm, and it even has a play area for the kids. We expect to hear about many more medals in the future.

ST. JOHNS PUB
8203 North Ivanhoe Street, St. Johns
(503) 283-8520
www.mcmenamins.com
This historic building with its distinctive dome was part of the 1905 Lewis and Clark Exposition held in Northwest Portland. After the festivities commemorating the centennial of that famous journey, the structure was barged across the Multnomah Channel of the Willamette River to St. Johns, a small burg now tied to the mainland by a lovely bridge with cathedral arches. After a long history as a church, fraternal lodge, and a watering hole called Duffy's, the place was purchased by the McMenamin brothers, who turned it into a roadhouse with lots of old-time signs and enough horns on the wall to hang half the hats in the West. It has the usual drinks and menu loaded with the same tasty sandwiches and burgers found in the other historic theaters, schools, and hotels turned into emporiums of suds and grub by these omnipresent entrepreneurs. One of the most delightful beer gardens in town, it offers a charming and totally unique atmosphere, live music, and delicious microbrews (or wine). St. Johns is so different you have to go and experience it for yourself. With the long elegant wood bar, wood-burning stove, and a 7-foot-tall bird of paradise standing sentinel, it is truly like stepping into a time machine. St. Johns, like most of the McMenamin brothers' brainstorms, is full of treasures, including stained-glass windows, a bizarre assortment of hanging lights, Second Empire chairs, and an old-time piano that patrons sometimes play. There's extra seating upstairs. Although the brew is imported from the brewery at the Kennedy School in Northeast Portland, this nostalgia-drenched quaffing parlor is well worth inclusion in our list of brewpubs. (See also the entry in the Nightlife chapter.)

WIDMER BROTHERS GASTHAUS
929 North Russell Street
(503) 281-2437
www.widmer.com
The Gasthaus, in an old refurbished 1890s hotel adjacent to the Widmer's brewery, serves a complete menu, ranging from beer and appetizers to full dinners. There's plenty of exposed brick and wood lending character to this pub, which seats around 120. The Gasthous serves 12 of Widmer's microbrews; our favorite is the sublime Hop Jack Pale Ale, which is almost a bitter. Widmer Brothers Brewing Company is the top-selling craft brewer in the region and produces seven original European- and Pacific Northwest–style beers. Their flagship ale is America's Original Hefeweizen, a cloudy, golden-hued beer that's as easy to drink as it is to look at. Hefeweizen is bottled and kegged unfiltered and directly from the lagering tank, adding to its robust taste and unique appearance. There are a few outside picnic tables, which fill up fast in the summertime. The food ranges from gourmet burgers, to German specialties, to grilled swordfish. This place is popular with everyone from the Wall Street set to the shipyard workers on nearby Swan Island.

> **i** Beer aficionados in Portland still honor their patron goddess Ninkasi with a major festival: the Oregon Brewers Festival, held the last weekend of July. The lead-in for that festival takes place the weekend before with the the Portland International Beerfest, devoted to the part of the brewing world that isn't Oregon. Visit www.oregonbrewfest.com or see the Festivals and Annual Events chapter for more information.

VANCOUVER

SALMON CREEK BREWERY
108 West Evergreen Boulevard
(360) 993-1827
www.salmoncreekbrewpub.com
A delightful addition to downtown Vancouver, the Salmon Creek Brewery is a friendly, upscale

establishment that features a handsome bar meticulously hand-crafted from African hardwood and a ceiling of antiqued pressed tin. Accentuating the burnished atmosphere, the walls are decorated with old sepia photos recalling early Vancouver's heydays. Salmon Creek offers nine house brews, including Red Irish Ale, Golden Ale, Thunderbolt Porter, Nut Brown Ale, India Pale Ale, and the best-selling Scottish Ale. Although Salmon Creek offers almost any kind of sandwich you can think of, including a hefty and exceptionally tasty Reuben, the menu is more fine dining than pub fare, with an emphasis on traditional steaks, seafood, chicken, and pasta dishes. Outdoor patio dining is a pleasant option during summer months, with plenty of ivy, flowers, and plants.

COFFEEHOUSES

On a chilly Oregon morning, nothing is more enticing than the aroma of freshly brewed coffee. Portlanders have a well-established tradition of hanging out in coffeehouses that predates Starbucks, so you will find all throughout the city many different kinds of coffeehouse aesthetic, from the sleek urbane to the shabby chic. And the word *coffeehouse* may mean anything from a small espresso bar to a cafe to a combination of tavern and coffeehouse.

Whether you are a discriminating coffee connoisseur or an instant-coffee drinker beginning a new adventure, this chapter is created as a user's guide to start you on your quest for the perfect cup of coffee. Although we do talk about espressos, cappuccinos, and lattes, we also maintain an abiding respect for an honest, simple cup of good, fresh, coffee.

Below, we've listed some of the much-loved coffeehouses in the area. We also encourage you to explore for yourself to find your own favorites, because so many good coffeehouses are out there that we could never list them all. We've omitted Starbucks, since you'll find them everywhere, without even trying. You'll also find Peet's Coffee & Tea—Berkeley's riposte to Starbucks—which has made incursions into the Portland market. Peet's coffee has always been excellent, and even if Peet's, like Starbucks, is no longer a small, local business, these Portland shops are welcome variations in the coffee landscape. But our hearts are truly with our home-grown coffee shops.

SOUTHWEST PORTLAND

ANNIE'S COFFEEHOUSE
1728 Southwest Broadway
(503) 497-1016
This funky little coffeehouse on the Portland State University campus is a classic hangout for students cramming for midterms and office workers in nearby administrative towers stopping for a quick refuel. Along with a mismatched cluster of chairs and tables, this cheerful, low-key place features a cartoon mural along the back wall.

In the 1950s and 1960s, Portland's downtown coffeehouses were the incubators for bands such as Paul Revere and the Raiders and the Kingsmen—both of whom had a hit with "Louie, Louie."

MORNING STAR CAFE
510 Southwest 3rd Avenue
(503) 241-2401
www.morningstarcafe.com
This lively shoebox of a coffeehouse is on the ground floor of the historic old postal building in Old Town and attracts a menagerie of downtown types. We come here for the art on the walls as much as for the coffee. The sandwiches, however, are also excellent and can be delivered right to your office.

PAPACCINO'S
8421 Southwest Terwilliger Boulevard
(503) 452-8859
Papaccino's has two locations in Portland, one in Southeast and one in Southwest—and both within easy reach of college students needing a caffeine fix. Tucked away in a residential neighborhood near Lewis & Clark College, the light-

infused Terwilliger branch serves all your favorite drinks, expertly prepared.

STUMPTOWN COFFEE ROASTERS
128 Southwest 3rd Avenue
(503) 295-6144

Stumptown roasts better coffee than practically anyone, but even if they didn't, this great little cafe would be worth a visit. Part coffee shop, part tavern, part art gallery, and part newsstand, this bright and airy space invites you to spend an entire afternoon. Periodicals are available to read and buy, and the brick walls feature new works by local artists each month. This downtown coffee shop offers a wee bit more than its eastside partners: an imaginative selection of wine and beer. It's also open a wee bit later: 7:00 a.m. to 9:00 p.m. Monday through Saturday and 8:00 a.m. to 6:00 p.m. on Sunday.

NORTHWEST PORTLAND

ANNA BANNANAS
1214 Northwest 21st Avenue
(503) 274-2559

A Portland classic, Anna Bannanas lives in a beautiful old Victorian house and serves strong coffee drinks to the bleary-eyed. The atmosphere is funky and unpretentious, and the crowd therefore ranges from sleepy hipsters to purpose-driven professionals. It's a comfy place to settle in and read—they have a lot of good magazines and journals lying about—while you eat one of their wonderful muffins. Check out their milk shakes too.

COFFEEHOUSE NORTHWEST
1951 West Burnside
(503) 248-2133
www.coffeehousenorthwest.com

The star feature of this attractive space on West Burnside is the espresso. It's drawn from perfectly roasted Stumptown beans at the perfect time to grind (several days out of the roaster) and it's drawn *ristretto*-style, which means the first pulse out of the machine. This attention to quality has earned Coffeehouse Northwest loyal customers and many accolades. The location, on trafficky

Burnside, is challenging, but the focus on making perfect coffee has allowed them to overcome this challenge. They make amazing hot chocolate as well, and serve excellent pastries, but truly, this is a coffee geek's paradise.

KEN'S ARTISAN BAKERY
326 Northwest 21st Avenue
(503) 248-2202

So it's not strictly coffee, but this excellent French-style patisserie and bakery is one of the best places on the Westside to have coffee, or really one of the best places anywhere. Ken Forkish is one of the most important bakers in town, supplying many restaurants, and his pastries are outstanding—perfectly flaky and balanced but never heavy or greasy. Try to go in the morning, when they are freshest. You'll find a line, but the efficient people behind the counter will move you through quickly. The coffee is also very good, and there are many tables so you can read the paper and drink your coffee while you dissect your croissant.

KOBOS COMPANY
2355 Northwest Vaughn Street
(503) 222-2181
www.kobos.com

Kobos was a pioneer of coffee roasting, setting up retail roasting in 1973 and serving espresso beginning in 1981. This major roaster features specialty coffees, wonderful pastries, and a lot more. Teas, herbs and spices, chocolates and Torani syrups, and cooking utensils from around the world are temptingly displayed at their stores. They also sell gourmet kitchen utensils and supplies. And you can buy their delicious coffee online as well. Another Kobos outlet can be found at 200 Southwest Market Street.

THE NOB HILL PHARMACY CAFE
2100 Northwest Glisan Street
(503) 548-4049

The Nob Hill Pharmacy Cafe lives in the old Nob Hill Pharmacy, a classic institution that filled prescriptions and served malteds until 2005. While the original counter is missed, its latest incarnation has given Portland hope that civilization might survive, after all. It's not strictly a coffee-drinking spot—they serve good sandwiches, pastries, and even deviled eggs as well as their excellent espresso and coffee drinks. But the great thing about this cafe is that it's open 24 hours. In a row.

PEARL BAKERY
102 Northwest 9th Avenue
(503) 827-0910
Set on a busy street corner, this shop has two full windows lined with counters, stools, and small tables and chairs. The open atmosphere is great for those overcast days when we need every sunbeam we can get. Coffee and espresso or a good selection of fragrant teas are just the things to accompany the exceptional sandwiches, desserts, and breakfast pastries. See the Restaurant chapter for more information.

SOUTHEAST PORTLAND

CAFÉ PALLINO
3003 Southeast Division
(503) 232-0907
Café Pallino is a beautiful Italian-modern cafe that specializes in coffee, pastries, breakfasts, and *panini*—and gelato. The gelato is house-made and it is as good as anything you will find in Italy. The cafe is also excellent for groups—there are white leather couches and long, long tables, all designed for maximum conversation. But there are also nice smaller tables if you want to hunker down with your laptop and finish writing your blog post for the day. Which you can do, because there's also free Wi-Fi. A good hangout spot.

COMMON GROUNDS
4321 Southeast Hawthorne Boulevard
(503) 236-4835
This coffeehouse, on the eastern side of the Hawthorne shopping district, is both a neighborhood draw and a destination point, one of the best places in the city to read and write with your latte. Graduate students, artists, and writers flock to the place. They stock a good selection of periodicals, from the *New York Review of Books* to *Wired*, and the music is always good. Common

Grounds also serves wonderful food to help fire up the neurons. Great cookies, pastries, and other desserts are made right there, and the *panini* will keep you going.

FIRESIDE COFFEE LODGE
1223 Southeast Powell Boulevard
(503) 230-8987
The Fireside is not only open 24 hours, but it also makes free Wi-Fi available so you can put your caffeinated rush to good use on the Internet. The atmosphere is pine-lodge rustic, and they really do have a fireplace. They offer smoothies, sandwiches, and other treats in addition to their coffee.

HAVEN
3551 Southeast Division Street
(503) 236-6890
www.havencoffee.com
Haven is a serene coffeehouse in the morning and a lively scene at night. Art on the walls, handsome mission-style furniture, and tranquil sage-colored walls make Haven a supremely attractive place to work, dream, or chat. The espresso is drawn with meticulous attention. Their pastries are just right. This is a great spot as well for its ever-changing displays by local artists. It's open from 7:00 a.m. to 6:00 p.m. weekdays. On the weekend, everyone gets an extra half-hour of sleep, since they open at 7:30. One of our favorite hang-outs in Portland.

MUDDY WATERS
2908 Southeast Belmont Street
(503) 233-1923
www.muddywatersportland.com
A hip coffeehouse in the old style, Muddy Waters serves live music, spoken word, and visual art with its machiattos and shots in the dark. They open early (7:00 a.m.), but at night they really come alive. Their Web site has a busy, up-to-date events calendar. Muddy Waters also serves beer and wine, which can help with the open mike session you may be tempted to try.

THE PIED COW COFFEEHOUSE
3244 Southeast Belmont Street
(503) 230-4866

The Pied Cow is in an old Victorian home that looks like a cheerfully haunted house. Inside it is decorated with brass chandeliers and big comfortable sofas and pillows. It has an inviting porch and an outside dining area that is packed all year long, since it's heated. A specialty is the Ice Mocha Float—rich vanilla ice cream, espresso, chocolate, and whipped cream. The Pied Cow offers very inventive and tasty soups, appetizers, and desserts and on some evenings, live music. This coffeehouse has evolved from hippie to hipster, with the addition of a popular hookah bar, which draws avant-garde smokers from all over town. It's also open late. You can bring the children, but you may be spending a lot of time explaining things.

RIMSKY KORSAKOFFEE HOUSE
707 Southeast 12th Avenue
(503) 232-2640
One of the most unique stops in the city, Rimsky Korsakoffee House offers a wide range of specialty coffees, desserts, and live classical music. For a sinfully rich indulgence, feast on the Mocha Fudge Cake and the Rasputin's Vice—three scoops of coffee ice cream topped with raspberries. Another delight is the Tsar Sultan Suite—chocolate almond ice cream, almond syrup, and whipped cream. Open evenings only: 7:00 p.m. to midnight during the week and 7:00 p.m. to 1:00 a.m. on Friday and Saturday.

STUMPTOWN COFFEE ROASTERS
4525 Southeast Division Street
(503) 230-7702

3356 Southeast Belmont Street
(503) 232-8889
www.stumptowncoffee.com
Good coffee roasters frequently become victims of their own success around here, but thoughtful Stumptown may be an exception. This first-rate roaster, with six shops of its own as well as a wholesale and distribution outfit, is dedicated to sustainable business practices. That means they work in partnership with their coffee farmers and offer their employees health insurance. It means they have a separate roaster just for their organic coffee.

But the most sustainable business practice is offering an outstanding product, and that is where Stumptown is truly gifted. Their coffees are hand-roasted in small batches, which is the only way to ensure freshness and flavor. Their espresso drinks have a perfect frothy crema, and they are as beautiful to look at as they are to drink. Since they opened in 1999, they have gained a large and devoted following. And they supply much of the coffee to the other shops listed in this chapter, as well as to restaurants all over town.

Stumptown rates high on the hangout scale. All these shops exude a sort of post-millennial, photographer-Wolfgang-Tillmans aesthetic. The service is exceptionally friendly and competent. The Division shop closes about 6:00 p.m. most nights (unless there's an event), and the Belmont shop stays open later, until 9:00 p.m. Both open early—6:00 a.m. Any location is one of the best places you can find for coffee, in Portland or anywhere. Also see Southwest Portland. And two doors down from the Belmont shop, you can find the Stumptown Annex, where you can do a coffee tasting and compare these fairly traded, often organic varietals and roasts.

i **Coffee and doughnuts are a natural pair. For the best doughnuts in Portland, try Voodoo Doughnuts, which has made doughnuts into an actual art form. Besides the usual cakes and crullers, you'll find innovations such as the San Dimas—a doughnut with three kinds of chocolate on top—and the Arnold Palmer, one frosted with lemon and tea powder. These punk-rock alternatives to cupcakes can be found at 22 Southwest Third Avenue (503-241-4704) 24 hours every day. They are also licensed to perform legal marriages.**

TINY'S
1412 Southeast 12th Avenue
(503) 239-5859
Tiny's is a cool coffeehouse at the intersection of Southeast 12th Avenue and Hawthorne

Boulevard. It serves excellent coffee and VooDoo doughnuts to dunk in it, and it's the kind of old-school place where you can hang out for an hour or two. Tiny's serves delicious sandwiches and provides Internet access as well.

NORTH/NORTHEAST PORTLAND

ALBINA PRESS
4637 North Albina Avenue
(503) 282-5214
Albina Press is not only justly famous for their delicious coffee, but also for their barista expertise: they hire only the best, the kind that place highly in National Barista championships. The attention to the coffee combined with the capacious feeling of the space makes this an irresistible cafe for writing, reading, or just chatting for an hour or two or six.

ANNA BANNANAS
8716 North Lombard
(503) 286-2030
The North Portland outpost of this great coffeeshop offers a smoke-free environment, a lovely garden, and a play area for the children. There's also a meeting room, if you want to hold your crafting circle there. And of course, like the Northwest shop, you'll be served yummy pastries, muffins, sandwiches, and so on—not to mention coffee.

BEULAHLAND
118 Northeast 28th Avenue
(503) 235-2794
Beulahland is an ideal hangout spot, and it serves that perfect combination, coffee and beer, so you could stay there all day and well into the night. It's a good place to hang out because of the jukebox (with its great combination of '80s pop and punk), the pool table, and the pinball machine. At night, Beulahland has live music. They also serve simple but good coffeehouse fare (soups, sandwiches), and the beer selection is unboring.

FRESH POT
4001 North Mississippi Avenue
(503) 284-8928
www.thefreshpot.com
Portland does not lack small, locally owned coffeehouses, but there's always room for more of a good thing. The Fresh Pot occupies the historic Rexall Drug building in this renewing neighborhood, where it serves beautifully roasted coffee from Stumptown to neighbors and visitors. The Fresh Pot also runs the coffee bar in the Hawthorne Powell's. The Fresh Pot shops offers Wi-Fi to keep you connected.

> **i** The Fresh Pot had a starring role as a featured location in 2007's *Feast of Love,* starring Morgan Freeman and Greg Kinnear.

GRENDEL'S COFFEE HOUSE
729 East Burnside
(503) 595-9550
Grendel's serves good coffee and delicious bagels and pastries to the Lower Burnside folks. It's conveniently located across from the Jupiter Hotel. You can sit outside and watch the traffic pass, or you can go inside and borrow a computer to check your e-mail. The Wi-Fi is free, and the things you must pay for can be paid for with plastic.

RISTRETTO ROASTERS
3520 Northeast 42nd Avenue
(503) 284-6767
www.ristrettoroasters.com
Ristretto serves small-batch-roasted coffee for coffee purists, but even if you are not a purist, you will love this delicious coffee, attentively prepared on an old-fashioned Probat roaster. Good coffee stewards that they are, they will grind whatever kind of coffee bean you would like to try and make perfect, perfect drip coffee out of it. They also serve espresso, of course, and pastries, sandwiches, and other forms of carbohydrate. Free Wi-Fi, too. And you can buy their coffee online.

NIGHTLIFE

There is a kind of seasonal rhythm to nightlife in Portland. In the summer, when it stays light well into the evening, we spend our evenings outdoors—sitting in brewpub gardens, enjoying concerts at the Oregon Zoo or in the park, walking or biking along the Eastbank Esplanade, celebrating the festival du jour at Waterfront Park, cheering for the Beavers at PGE Park, or watching the sun slip along the Columbia River and below the horizon. In the winter, we get through the rainy months by amusing ourselves indoors—perhaps we go to dinner and a show. Perhaps we go to Powell's. Perhaps we just go bowling.

Whatever the season, Portland's nightlife is rich and varied. In this chapter, we cover fun for grown-ups: music, bars, dancing. Portland's scene is impossible to pigeonhole—we are not, for example, readily associated with a particular kind of music—but one thing is certain. We love parties. We love First Thursday and Last Thursday (see our Arts chapter); we love our many Waterfront Park festivals; we love those concerts at the zoo. We have a lot to celebrate.

You'll find nighttime things to do all over town, in every neighborhood—though, ironically, the heart of downtown has less street life and more cultural events in the evening. Throughout the area, however, you'll find clusters of people sitting at outside tables, happy and convivial, yet also behaving in a pretty civilized way. Look for beacons of nightlife along Southeast Division, Hawthorne, and Belmont; along North Mississippi and Northeast Broadway; along Northwest 23rd and 21st Avenues; and all throughout the Pearl District. The best sources of information on who's playing where are the local rags: the *Portland Mercury*; *Willamette Week*; the *Oregonian's* Arts and Entertainment section, which is published on Friday; and *Portland Monthly's* calendar (see our Media chapter). These papers will also tell you who is reading at Powell's, what's at the Portland Center Stage, and what's going on at Waterfront Park. Below are more ideas for when you are in the mood to go out.

NIGHTCLUBS, DANCING, AND LIVE MUSIC

Southwest Portland

BERBATI'S PAN
231 Southwest Ankeny Street
(503) 248-4579
www.berbatis.com

A big *L*-shaped dance club connected to a Greek restaurant that serves ethnic food in the bar section, this venerable venue has three hard liquor bars and a stage that hosts a variety of action, from alternative rock concerts to jazz gigs to open-mike comedy to swing dance lessons to

Songwriters in the Round. Cover charges range from $6 to $20.

BETTIE FORD LOUNGE
1135 Southwest Washington Street
(503) 445-8331

A sleek, modernist, downtown club, the Bettie Ford Lounge offers "Cocktail Therapy and Food Late"—as well as R & B, hip-hop, '80s music, and other funky beats to help you dance your troubles away. Join the scenesters and beautiful people at Bettie Ford's three bars, all of which serve tasty, tasty drinks. You can also reserve VIP rooms if you'd rather hang out than mingle. Cover varies.

CRYSTAL BALLROOM
1332 West Burnside Street
(503) 225-0047
www.danceonair.com
The Crystal Ballroom is a renovated dance hall with a floating floor on ball bearings and rockers. Back when it opened in 1914 as the Cotillion Hall, Portlanders could be arrested for dancing the tango. Since then it's witnessed the likes of Rudolph Valentino, Ike and Tina Turner, Jimi Hendrix, Marvin Gaye, the Family Dog, and the Grateful Dead. The dance hall closed in 1968 and sat empty for 30 years until the McMenamins tackled a major rehabilitation. Now Portlanders are once again enjoying this gracious space with its high-arched windows, curving balcony, rococo paintings, and, above all, that dance floor with a capacity for 1,500. Live bands play throughout the week, and Sunday brings ballroom dance lessons to the public. The dress code ranges from jeans and T-shirt to black cocktail dress or three-piece suit. There are a couple of bars serving microbrews and mixed drinks.

DANTE'S
1 Southwest 3rd Avenue
(503) 226-6630
www.danteslive.com
Dante's is one of the hottest scenes in downtown Portland—literally. Not only does it have a fiery oil drum to give the place a purgatorial glow, it also attracts a wildly diverse crowd. Could it be the exotic dancers? The expertly mixed cocktails? No—it's the great shows, from the American-Idol fantasists on Monday's karaoke night to the powerful duo Black Angel, who perform Thursday. Other nights are equally spectacular. Dante's is open Monday through Friday from 11:00 a.m. to 2:00 a.m., and on Saturday and Sunday from 7:00 p.m. to 2:00 a.m. The club offers a late-night Italian-American menu.

LOTUS CARDROOM AND CAFE
932 Southwest 3rd Avenue
(503) 227-6185
The Lotus is notorious for having been a bordello,

and something about the place encourages people to forget themselves once they are inside. But who can say whether it is the building's wicked past or the two floors for dancing and the stiff drinks at the bar? The Lotus attracts everyone from slumming college students to the beautiful people. Its interior is intact enough that Gus Van Sant used it as a set when he filmed *My Own Private Idaho*.

Northwest Portland
BARRACUDA
9 Northwest 2nd Avenue
(503) 228-6900
www.clubbarracuda.com
Barracuda features hip DJs, four bars, and a dance-party vibe. This gym-size dance floor is accented with the tropics: Large palm trees shade the dancers from the luminous glow of the VIP Havana and Cabana rooms on the second floor; drinks are served (for two or more) in fishbowls; the snacks are infused with coconut and Caribbean spiciness. The crowd tends to be under 30. Cover is charged after 10:00 p.m.

EMBERS
110 Northwest Broadway
(503) 222-3082
Embers is a gay dance club that practices tolerance by letting anyone in. With its three stages, it's a great place for dancing, and the music is a fun blend of retro, dance-party, and Top 40. Drag shows are a reliable feature of any night at the Embers. The bar alone is worth a visit.

OHM
31 Northwest 1st Avenue
(under the Burnside Bridge)
(503) 223-9919
Ohm is not just a dance club featuring electronica, it's the only dancing club featuring electronica that also has a meditation pool on the patio. Ohm also adds film, spoken word, and live music to its mix—it's an inventive place and a good night out.

When you want an old-fashioned cocktail, visit the Marble Bar at the Heathman Hotel to drink in the glamour of an earlier era. Wilf's, at Union Station, serves nightcaps with vintage charm. And the Space Room (4800 Southeast Hawthorne) is perfect when you're feeling more George Jetson than Cary Grant.

ROSELAND THEATRE AND GRILL
8 Northwest 6th Avenue
(503) 224-2038

The Roseland Theatre and Grill is a pleasant all-ages concert pavilion with a bar and roomy balcony upstairs for those over 21. The bill of fare is an eclectic mix of national music and comedy acts, local groups' CD release parties, and DJ dance boogies. A bonus is the emergence of the Roseland Grill downstairs. This narrow slot of a bar has a festive wall covered with posters from the long history of the Roseland.

TIGER BAR
317 Northwest Broadway
(503) 222-7297

With minimal signage and a mysteriously bland front door, Tiger Bar has the outward appearance of a private club. Inside it's an after-work, happening scene. For no cover charge you can join the artists, Bohemians, advertising execs, and other Pearl District habitués who come here to chat, sip an exotic cocktail like vodka-fueled Liquid Love or Damianas, and nibble on tiger prawns, pad Thai noodles, and other pan-Asian treats, all against the backdrop of a wall of electronic sound.

VAULT
226 Northwest 12th Avenue
(503) 224-4909
www.vault-martini.com

Signature habanero martinis and other frosty concoctions keep the well-clad patrons of this Pearl District hangout returning. Vault has millions of martinis (okay, 44) to choose from, as well as a long list of other cocktails. The ambience is upscale modern, with the work of local artists festooning the walls, a fireplace, and an 18-foot glass bar.

Southeast Portland

ACME
1305 Southeast 8th Street
(503) 230-9020
www.acme-pdx.com

Acme is a swell venue in Inner Southeast Portland that offers great music, comedy, and cabaret, as well as independent and DIY films. The booths are cozy, the bar is big, and the patio is even bigger. The bar food is fantastic and served from opening until closing, and it includes delicious house-cured meats among other things. Look on their Web site for upcoming events.

ALADDIN THEATER
3017 Southeast Milwaukie Avenue
(503) 233-1994
www.showman.com

This place lands all kinds of top-drawer acts from many different cultures in and outside of the United States. Aladdin's focus is eclectic: They feature everything from grunge to polka music to classical and neo-country. Once infamous for its record-breaking extended showing of the X-rated film *Deep Throat*, the Aladdin Theater is now famous for blurring the edges between musical genres and is the new darling of Portland's liberal-minded music scene. This place isn't just trendy, it's solid and innovative. Besides snagging some huge and widely respected talent, the Aladdin also books some terrific and often-overlooked artists. Tickets are available daily at the box office out front from 1:00 to 6:00 p.m. and just before the show.

BAR OF THE GODS
4801 Southeast Hawthorne Boulevard
(503) 232-2037

A unique selection of reasonably priced but heavenly tasting microbrews, free pool, and an outdoor patio await you at Bar of the Gods. On some evenings they show films beneath hanging bunches of plastic grapes.

BLUE MONK
3341 Southeast Belmont Street
(503) 595-0575
The Blue Monk is a modern venue for an old favorite: live jazz. They also show jazz movies. The food is Italian, but the atmosphere is decidedly American Urban. Upstairs is a fetching contemporary room with an open kitchen, where cooks are busy preparing steamed mussels, ravioli, or polenta. Downstairs, Portland's finest jazz musicians are jamming.

CRUSH
1412 Southeast Morrison Street
(503) 235-8150
This spacious and fun club draws Portland's most stylish with its brilliant rooms, great drinks, grooving DJs, and clever events. The lounge features comfortable couches and a wonderful chandelier made of liquor bottles, while the Blue Room is dedicated to a hopping dance floor. Crush's celebrated Vice Room, with its own bar, allows smokers to not have to stand outside in the rain. Look for all-day happy hour on Tuesday and "T-dances" on Sunday. Crush is an equal-opportunity employer of go-go dancers, as well, so have fun watching. A teeny cover is charged on Saturday night.

DOUG FIR
830 East Burnside Street
(503) 231-9663
The Doug Fir is the local epicenter of Portland nightlife. It looks like a mountain lodge that has been given a makeover by Danish modernists, and one reason it is popular is that the soft, indirect lighting makes everyone look as if they ought to be carded. The food is really good, and while some might claim that going to the Doug Fir for the food is like reading Playboy for the interviews, they might actually be telling the truth.

But the big draw is the club, which is downstairs. This space features some great bands from all over, and it's a great space to see them. It was designed and built specifically to showcase live music, with a fantastic sound system and stage. The Doug Fir is open seven nights. It's right by the Jupiter Hotel (see the Accommodations chapter), which has obvious benefits.

HOLOCENE
1001 Southeast Morrison Street
(503) 239-7639
www.holocene.org
Holocene is dedicated to the avant-garde of the Portland art and music scene, with an uber-modern interior, two large rooms, and a huge bar. Excellent dancing can be had here, as well as similar music experiences—secret shows by famous artists, up-and-coming bands that will be famous shortly, and other attractions keep hipsters crowding the place.

PRESS CLUB
2621 Southeast Clinton Street
(503) 233-5656
Along with its dinner menu and wine list, the Press Club serves up expertly prepared live and DJ'd music from local greats and beyond. The Press Club is small and intimate but feels wonderfully spacious, a combination that allows the musicians and the audience to bond. For more information see the listing in the Restaurants chapter.

PRODUCE ROW CAFE
204 Southeast Oak Street
(503) 232-8355
Produce Row is easy to miss, since it is hidden away in the bowels of Portland's Eastside. But it's worth the time to find it, with its excellent selection of beer and ales, genuine friendly service, and a variety of live music offerings ranging from jazz to bluegrass to folk. The vibe is very low-key and friendly, with lots of great local bands. (Don't try to have a conversation while they're playing; though; just relax and enjoy the show.)

North/Northeast Portland
BIDDY MCGRAW'S IRISH PUB
6000 Northeast Glisan Street
(503) 233-1178
www.biddymcgraws.com
This place is so authentic that it is cool without

even trying to be. This is a working people's bar, and the people who come here, many Irish of course, are as real and unpretentious as the four Guinness taps. Biddy's offers a lot more than stout ales and patrons oozing Celtic character. It serves up some of the best Irish food in the city, complemented with about 20 imports, microbrews, and hard liquor. Most evenings Biddy's offers live and authentic Irish music.

ℹ️ Two great bars for Celtic—and other—music are Kells, a handsome bar at 112 Southwest Second Avenue, and the Dublin Pub, a cozy place at 6821 Southwest Beaverton-Hillsdale Highway.

LAURELTHIRST PUBLIC HOUSE
2958 Northeast Glisan Street
(503) 232-1504

For the alternative folk music crowd, this is a premier nightspot. Laurelthirst is far more than a "flavor of the week." They've built a great place with a talented and creative kitchen, a variety of microbrews, and a good wine selection. They also draw some of Portland's most sought-after musicians. Laurelthirst also showcases some terrific and largely unknown talent during open-mike nights. The pub itself has great atmosphere: Brick walls and plenty of rough-hewn wood lend it character, and the postage stamp–size stage makes the music experience intimate.

MISSISSIPPI STUDIOS
3939 North Mississippi Avenue
(503) 753-4473
www.mississippistudios.com

Part recording studio, part concert venue, Mississippi Studios attracts artists from all over to their excellent space. Here, musicians such as Kristin Hersh, Rickie Lee Jones, John Gorka, and Freedy Johnston have all recorded or performed or both. It's a great place to see a show, with a beautiful outdoor garden, bistro, and bar adjacent (called Mississippi Station).

ST. JOHNS THEATERPUB
8203 North Ivanhoe Street
(503) 283-8520
www.mcmenamins.com

This renovated, circa-1906 church offers a charmingly different atmosphere for a casual evening out with friends. The St. Johns Theaterpub features one of the most delightful beer gardens in town, great live music, delicious microbrews, wines, and hard liquor to accompany your tasty sandwiches and burgers. The long, elegant wood bar and wood-burning stove make you feel as though you're stepping into a time warp. The pub—one of the McMenamin brothers' brainstorms—is full of treasures, including a 7-foot-tall carving of a big bird of paradise, stained-glass windows, a bizarre assortment of hanging lights, Second Empire chairs, and an old-time piano that patrons sometimes play.

WHITE EAGLE SALOON
836 North Russell Street
(503) 282-6810
www.mcmenamins.com

The White Eagle Saloon—which is now one of the McMenamin brothers' taverns—is indeed a raucous joint when the sun goes down, when people come to dance their blues away. It doesn't look like much from the outside, but don't let that fool you. The old brick building is narrow and long, so when you go inside the place, it seems like you're in an elongated basement except for the high ceiling. The crowded feeling can be claustrophobic, but that same closeness makes the enthusiasm more contagious when the bands turn up the heat. Plus, it helps protect

ℹ️ The Shanghai Tunnel, 211 Southwest Ankeny Street, takes its name from Portland's legendary 19th-century practice of "Shanghai-ing" unsuspecting bumpkins through tunnels that ran under the city. A friendly stranger would buy many drinks for a naive fellow, and the next thing the imbiber knew, he was far at sea with a big hangover and a stint as a forced laborer.

you against the ghosts that are thought to roam the well-storied building, which at one point was a stop on the "Shanghai tunnel network."

VENDETTA
4306 North Williams Avenue
(503) 288-1085
www.barvendetta.com
A bar with an old-fashioned sense of hospitality, Vendetta not only has a great happy hour and an attractive patio area, but it also has a cool shuffleboard table and live music. A fun neighborhood bar in a fun neighborhood.

POOL

RIALTO POOLROOM, BAR & CAFE
529 Southwest 4th Avenue
(503) 228-7605
Minnesota Fats would have felt at home in this downtown pool hall with its 15 full-size Brunswick tables, full bar, sumptuous menu, and downstairs off-track betting. In fact, a photo of Jackie Gleason portraying the legendary stick-man in *The Hustler* is prominently displayed in the bar. Open every day of the year, the Rialto offers a rack of balls and a long stretch of green for $5 an hour before 5:00 p.m. and $7 per hour afterward. If hoisting a cue for a couple of rounds stirs your appetite, try their potato skins with sour cream, bacon, and scallions or their grilled halibut dinner. If you're a vegetarian still yearning for something on a bun, try the gardenburger, one of Portland's hometown products that has spread to many of the nation's supermarkets.

SAM'S HOLLYWOOD BILLIARDS
1845 Northeast 41st Avenue
(503) 282-8266
This is an excellent place to shoot pool. Sam's has 13 gorgeous 8-foot pool tables and quality pool cues to match. The bar offers a dozen microbrews, and the kitchen prepares a variety of reasonably priced sandwiches and fried foods. It's clean, basically nonsmoky, and very friendly. The pool tables rent for $8 an hour.

TOUCHÉ
1425 Northwest Glisan Street
(503) 221-1150
touchepdx.com
Touché has a beautiful and competent restaurant downstairs and a fun, smaller pool room upstairs. It's popular, so you will probably wait, but the friendly bartenders will keep you happy as you do.

UPTOWN BILLIARDS CLUB
120 Northwest 23rd Avenue
(503) 226-6909
www.uptownbilliards.com
This is a great pool room with a no-smoking policy, so you won't regret your evening out when you get home. The vibe is mellow during the week, but it ramps up on weekends. In addition to its cocktails, Uptown has a great wine selection—plus an excellent happy hour Tuesday through Friday.

CABARET AND COMEDY

DARCELLE XV
208 Northwest 3rd Avenue
(503) 222-5338
Darcelle XV, Portland's hilarious female impersonator, and her/his Las Vegas–style cabaret revue strut their stuff Wednesday through Saturday. On Friday and Saturday, Men of Paradise, a Chippendale-style male strip show, takes over at midnight.

HARVEY'S COMEDY CLUB
436 Northwest 6th Avenue
(503) 241-0338
www.harveyscomedyclub.com
This is the longest-running comedy club in Portland. Locals sharpening their act, as well as well-known stand-up comics on national tours, crack up audiences with witty banter. Harvey's is a nonsmoking club with no drink minimums and no purchase required other than tickets to the show.

MISSION THEATRE & PUB
1624 Northwest Glisan Street
(503) 223-4527
www.mcmenamins.com

Looking for a sprawly, roomy place to watch a flick while downing a brew and slice of pizza? With its 300-seat capacity, the Mission Theatre & Pub is just the right spot for a relaxed evening. The movies cost $3 (except for the rare starred attraction), and once in a while a musical performer or group will take to the stage for an evening concert. While you're waiting for the show to begin, check out the large windows and ornate balcony facade—hints that the place has a long history. This well-preserved brick building originated as a Swedish Evangelical Mission in 1912, then became a longshoreman hiring hall. Now it's yet another renovation project initiated by the McMenamins, who have doubled as historical preservationists and brewmeisters. The Mission welcomes minors to Saturday and Sunday matinees with a parent or guardian.

SHOPPING

No sales tax in Oregon. What else do you need to know? All right, we'll tell you more. Portland is a great town for shopping. Here you will not only find the usual suspects—Gap, Pottery Barn, Banana Republic, and so on—but many interesting, chic, and homegrown shops. Portland's shopping is organized around its neighborhoods, and some of these neighborhoods have evolved into destination shopping districts; these composites of retail, business, and living spaces have blended in such a way as to create local shops that reflect and sustain the neighborhoods they inhabit. And Portland also has other unusual shopping opportunities. Portland Saturday Market, which takes place every weekend under the Burnside Bridge, proffers some of the most engrossing shopping in town; it's a carnival of commerce from March through December. For more information see the Festivals and Annual Events chapter or phone (503) 222-6072. Also see that chapter for information on the area's many fine farmers' markets.

Stores in Portland tend to open at 10:00 a.m., if not sooner. Closing hours vary—the smaller the store, the more likely it is to close by 6:00 p.m. The major downtown department stores stay open till 8:00 or 9:00 p.m. on some nights and close earlier on weekends. You'll find most of the larger stores and many of the small stores open six or seven days a week. Fred Meyer and the large grocery stores such as Safeway, Albertson's, Zupan's, and Thriftway are usually open at 7:00 a.m.; some are open 24 hours a day, seven days a week. Mall hours are generally 10:00 a.m. to 9:00 p.m.

We begin with an overview of the major shopping districts. Then we break the chapter into many categories, with shops listed alphabetically. (Since many shops have more than one location, we have deviated from organizing them by geography.) Here you'll find sections on Antiques, Books and Periodicals, Clothing, Food, Home Decor, Shoes, and ever so much more.

SHOPPING DISTRICTS

The soul of Portland shopping can be found in its shopping districts. Because the city organizes itself around its neighborhoods, the shopping and business districts play a vital role in creating neighborhood identity and atmosphere. It is possible to find neighborhood shopping so compelling and comprehensive that you won't want to leave your own turf. But that would be a mistake, because the variety of shopping districts gives insight into the character of Portland.

Shopping districts are clustered throughout the city, and we feature some of them here. In addition to those featured, you may want to explore the adorable shops on North Mississippi; the Hollywood District, with its epicenter

at Northeast Sandy and 41st; Beaumont Village, along Northeast Fremont between 40th and 50th; and the small collection of shops at Southeast 26th and Clinton. These little aggregates serve primarily the nearby residents, but they are worth prospecting. We encourage you to stroll whatever neighborhood you're in—unless you do a little fieldwork on your own, who knows what fine harvests are in store?

Northeast Portland
Alberta Street, Sabin Neighborhood, and Northeast Martin Luther King Jr. Boulevard

The north end of town along Martin Luther King Jr. Boulevard (locally known as "MLK") is the focus of a major city revitalization project that includes business development, transportation plans, and new housing. Community banks, city government, and neighborhood groups have converged to make this area one of the most vital places in the city. This gentrification is not without controversy, and not every citizen thinks that opening a new Starbucks counts as progress. The source of this renaissance is the distinctive homegrown businesses, ranging from restaurants and art galleries to clothing designers and gift shops. Northeast Alberta Street features much of the growth. There you'll find the marvelous **Tumbleweed**, 1804 Northeast Alberta, with clothes for women and children designed and made on-site; the convivial **Alberta Cooperative Grocery**, 1500 Northeast Alberta, which is the hub of neighborhood activity; **Bolt**, 2136 Northeast Alberta, with gorgeous fabric for the DIY set; and **Digs**, 1829

Northeast Alberta, featuring beautiful and innovative home and garden supplies, as well as a full design studio. **Grasshopper**, 1808 Northeast Alberta, will sell you fetching children's clothing, while **Office**, 2204 Northeast Alberta, has the most stylish products for your home office, as well as a great selection of stationery. You can explore them for yourself at **Last Thursday**, an artwalk held on Alberta Street the last Thursday of each month from 6:00 to 9:00 p.m. This monthly festival is something of a counterpoint to **First Thursday**, which takes place in the Pearl District. Both events will give you a picture of the spirit of these neighborhoods.

Nearby, you'll find the **Nike Outlet Store**, 2650 Northeast Martin Luther King Jr. Boulevard, as well as an **Adidas** retail store at 5020 Northeast Martin Luther King Jr. Boulevard.

Some of Portland's best shopping is in its neighborhoods—in this case, the Sabin area. RACHEL DRESBECK

Where Are the Malls?

Sometimes only a big shopping mall will do. The following are the major shopping malls in the area.

Southeast Portland
Clackamas Town Center
12000 Southeast 82nd Avenue
(503) 653-6913

Mall 205
9900 Southeast Washington Street
(503) 255-5805

North/Northeast Portland
Jantzen Beach Shopping Center
Interstate 5 at exit 308, Hayden Island
(503) 247-1327

Lloyd Center
2201 Lloyd Center
(503) 282-2511

Vancouver
Westfield Shoppingtown–Vancouver
8700 Northeast Vancouver Mall Drive
(on Washington Highway 500, between
Interstate 205 and I–5)
(360) 892-6255

Outlying Areas
Bridgeport Village
7455 Lower Boones Ferry Road, Tigard
(exit 290, I–5)
(503) 968-8940

Columbia Gorge Factory Stores
450 Northwest 257th Avenue
Troutdale
(503) 669-8060

Washington Square and Square Too
Highway 217 at Southwest Greenburg
Road, Tigard
(503) 639-8860

Woodburn Company Stores
1001 Arney Road, Woodburn
(exit 271, I–5)
(888) 664-SHOP

Broadway District

Northeast Broadway is a lively east-west stretch of shops, cafes, and offices; its bike-and-foot-friendly design has helped to make it one of the most enjoyable shopping districts in the city. Some—by no means all—of the major shopping attractions include **Oh Baby**, 1811 Northeast Broadway, for luscious lingerie; and **Halo**, 1425 Broadway, for the most stylish shoes. **Broadway Books**, 1714 Northeast Broadway, is an active, independent bookstore that carries a fine selection of history, local writers, and children's literature. **Dava Bead and Trade**, 1815 Northeast Broadway, will supply all your beads, findings, and other materials. **Emily Jane**, 1428 Northeast Broadway, carries beautiful handmade contemporary jewelry in a range of prices. **Kitchen Kaboodle**, at 1520 Northeast Broadway, has been purveying fine kitchenware and Northwest-casual furniture for more than 25 years; the **Goodnight Room**, 1517 Northeast Broadway, will outfit your child's room; and **Mimi & Lena**, 1914 Northeast Broadway, has high-end, cutting-edge clothes for women and their well-clad offspring. The anchor of all this glittery commerce is the **Lloyd Center,** Oregon's first indoor mall.

Southwest Portland
Downtown

Department stores, fashionable boutiques, and Pioneer Place, a pedestrian mall, are the highlights of downtown shopping. **Nordstrom**, 701 Southwest Broadway, needs no introduction; this downtown branch flanks the west side of Pioneer Courthouse Square and furnishes area residents with stylish clothes, shoes, and accessories. **Saks Fifth Avenue**, 850 Southwest 5th Avenue, carries beautiful clothing and accessories for men and women (and note—it's actually on 5th Avenue). On the north end of downtown, across Burnside from Powell's, you'll find cutting-edge bookstores, resale and vintage shops, and record stores. **Reading Frenzy**, 921 Southwest Oak, is especially striking—its collection of alternative periodicals is unparalleled. And on the other end of downtown, the **Oregon Historical Society**, 1200 Southwest Park, has an excellent museum store that provides artwork, books, jewelry, gifts, and other

Oregon-related items. **Johnny Sole**, 815 Southwest Alder, purveys Kenneth Cole shoes, Doc Martens, and other stylish footwear for damp Oregon weather. More downtown enticements include a large **Williams-Sonoma** at 5th and Morrison; **Kathleen's of Dublin**, 737 Southwest Salmon, for beautiful Celtic clothing, jewelry, china, and gifts; **Finnegan's**, 922 Southwest Yamhill, for toys and gifts; **Jane's Vanity**, 521 Southwest Broadway, for alluring underthings; and **Mercantile**, 735 Southwest Park, for upscale women's clothing. **Odessa**, 410 Southwest 13th Avenue carries chic clothes from Kerry Cassill and Mayle, while **Mario's**, 833 Southwest Broadway, equips male and female Portlanders with Prada, Armani, Helmut Lang, and other top designers. (Repeat after me: No sales tax in Oregon.)

PIONEER PLACE
Southwest Morrison Street, between 5th Avenue and 3rd Avenue
(503) 228-5800

Pioneer Place is the epicenter of shopping in downtown, with more than 80 different stores, including the only Saks Fifth Avenue in the Northwest, as well as Tiffany & Co. A huge atrium fills the building with light on even the darkest day and is frequently decorated with amazing hanging creations and designs reflecting the seasons. While shoppers are protected from the rain, Pioneer Place reminds them that they are still in Oregon with a series of fountains and tiny waterfalls that evoke the natural landscape. In the atrium, a fountain surrounded by flowers and plants draws children and their parents, who are praying that the little ones won't tumble in as they wish on their pennies. In the food court, a whole series of waterways provides soothing white noise for diners engrossed in conversation.

In the newest part of the mall, the rotunda, a large sculptural, floral fountain cascades water in controlled sheets; you're not supposed to touch it, but it is very difficult to obey this order. Escalators soar up the middle of the rotunda and the atrium all the way to the fourth floor (there are also elevators), providing fine vantage points for surveying the shopping landscape. A skybridge and an underground tunnel connect the rotunda and the atrium for those shoppers who wish to avoid the sidewalk route.

And what can you find here? Some of the most popular shops in the area, including **J.Crew, Eddie Bauer, Victoria's Secret**, various **Gap** stores, **Banana Republic, Ann Taylor, Talbots, J. Jill, Louis Vuitton, BCBG, Juicy Couture**, and a **Coach** store. Once you've figured out what to wear, **Twist** and **Gamekeeper** will provide presents for lucky people; and **Starbucks** and **Godiva Chocolate** will supply you sustenance. **Aveda** and **Origins** also have small shops here, for a little shopping aromatherapy.

Spas

Life can have its stressful moments even in beautiful Portland, and shopping can be hard on a person. When that happens, head to one of these day spas for a few hours.

Aequis Spa
419 Southwest 11th Avenue
Penthouse Suite
(503) 223-7847

Entering Aequis is like walking into a serene temple: It smells good, it's quiet, and acolytes pad about in bare feet ministering to your every need. Aequis provides expert massage—including couples massage—and aromatherapy and skin treatments. Your body is a temple, after all.

Avalon Hotel & Spa
0455 Southwest Hamilton Court
(503) 802-5800

Avalon offers a full range of spa services, from mud wraps to massages to makeovers. Favorite details from the Avalon Spa include the Raindance wet room and the Ayurvedic rituals that are incorporated into the skin-care routines.

Barefoot Sage
1844 Southeast Hawthorne Boulevard
(503) 239-7116
15325 Northwest Central Drive, No. 6
(503) 924-4711

Pampering for your feet, with the added benefit of naturopathic medical principles: The owner is a naturopathic physician, and the massage therapists are licensed.

Bellini's European Day Spa
2326 Northwest Irving Street
(503) 226-1526

Expert facial care in an urban oasis. You will look and feel much cuter after a few hours at Bellini's.

Common Ground Wellness Center
2927 Northeast Everett Street
(503) 238-1065

Portland's original day spa, Common Ground is a holistic healing and massage center set in a residential neighborhood in the Broadway area. It has been popular for many years for its serene atmosphere and soothing hot tubs and saunas. More Greenwich Village than Soho, Common Ground will not provide waxing or nail polish. But we love this place for its ethics, community service, and expert massages.

Nirvana Apothecary and Day Spa
736 Northwest 11th Avenue
(503) 546-8155

Wonderful facials, as well as waxing, pedicures, and other skin-care treatments are the specialty of this peaceful, Byzantine spa in the Pearl. They feature special services for men, as well. And they offer a good menu of massage.

Rejuvenation Day Spa
6333 Southwest Macadam Avenue
(503) 293-5699

Rejuvenation features the purest possible products, and they pay especially close attention to the air and water quality, with many filters to keep bad things out. One nice detail is the sanctuary, a quiet room for reading or resting between your massage and your wrap. Rejuvenation also offers yoga classes.

The food court, with a dozen or more vendors, fills the entire end of the lower level, and **Todai**, a popular Japanese restaurant, perches atop the rotunda. Two Smart Park garages flank the mall, so parking is easy, except during the holiday season. But Pioneer Place is also a MAX stop, so getting there without a car is not only easy but, during the busy season, advised.

Multnomah Village

Multnomah really does feel like a village—it is a tight-knit community in addition to its identity as a retail, coffee-shop, and hang-out mecca. Adding to the cohesive feel are the wonderful **Multnomah Arts Center,** 7688 Capitol Highway, a Portland Arts and Recreation facility offering classes in everything from acrylic painting to Zen flower arranging, and **Annie Bloom's Books**, 7834 Southwest Capitol Highway, an outstanding bookstore that draws people from all over the city. Other Village highlights include the two dozen shops of every variety. We especially like **Northwest Wools**, 3524 Southwest Troy, for beautiful yarns and other fibers; **Peggy Sunday's**, 7880 Southwest Capitol Highway, for upscale housewares; and **Birdie's Gift Shop**, 7847 Southwest Capitol Highway, for gifts, cards, and bath products.

Southeast Portland
Hawthorne District

The Hawthorne District is Portland's left-coast hip shopping area, where granola meets granita. **Powell's** on Hawthorne, 3723 Southeast Hawthorne, and **Powell's Books for Cooks**, 3747 Southeast Hawthorne, are the eastside siblings of the City of Books, and these are smaller and less overwhelming but still feature a fantastic selection and major literary events. If you've brought the little ones along, a stop at the toy store **Kids at Heart**, 3445 Southeast Hawthorne, is a must; then drag them to **Presents of Mind**, 3633 Southeast Hawthorne, to pick up a bijou for yourself—it has a play area for children so you can

concentrate on the jewelry, photo albums, cards, and other trinkets. Music lovers will find Hawthorne especially fruitful. **Crossroads Music**, 3130 Southeast Hawthorne, is a music seller's co-op, and the selection of recordings and equipment here is astonishing. **The CD/Game Exchange**, 1428 Southeast 36th, is a smaller venue with a great selection of used CDs. **Jackpot Records**, 3574 Southeast Hawthorne specializes in rare, independent, and avant-garde music, and carries new and used recordings. **Artichoke Music**, 3130 Southeast Hawthorne, will help you make music instead of merely listening to it; they carry musical instruments. Need something to wear? Try **Fyberworks,** 4300 Southeast Hawthorne, for casual, stretchy women's clothing. **Imelda's,** 3426 Southeast Hawthorne, is a destination shoe store for fashionistas all over town (it also carries shoes for men); **Red Light**, 3590 Southeast Hawthorne, brings the same crowd for vintage clothes. **American Apparel**, 3412 Southeast Hawthorne, will help you achieve a modernized '70s look. Hawthorne is the earthier alternative to the slick Northwest 23rd: You're more likely to get a whiff of patchouli than Chanel No. 5, although the **Perfume House**, 3328 Southeast Hawthorne, can supply either one.

LoBu

On the east side of the Willamette River, Lower Burnside, or "LoBu," has a number of terrific restaurants and shops. We love **Ivy Studio**, 800 East Burnside, which carries men's and women's clothing and accessories—as does **Hattie's Vintage**, 729 East Burnside. **Redux**, 811 East Burnside, carries a stunning collection of handmade jewelry, paintings, bags, and other gorgeously crafted trinkets. More stores are opening all the time here, since LoBu is the neighborhood of the moment, and after shopping you may not want to leave. If so, linger at the **Doug Fir Lounge**, 830 East Burnside, and if you want to linger even more, stay over at the incredibly hospitable **Jupiter Hotel**, 800 East Burnside; see our Accommodations chapter.

Sellwood District

Sellwood, one of Portland's most distinctive and historic neighborhoods, is brimming with charming antiques stores, particularly in the area along Southeast 13th Avenue, which is known as Antique Row. Because the shopping area is so condensed, you can park your car and then get around on foot. Laced in between the dozen blocks of antiques and collectibles stores, you'll find numerous delightful espresso shops and cafes.

Many shopkeepers hang signs on their buildings explaining their original use and date of construction, but our sources say that Sellwood has been known as Portland's antiques source since the 1950s. Since Sellwood was once a city in its own right (annexed in 1890), pride in the neighborhood runs deep. One could easily spend a day or two checking out the many stores, and if you do, keep an eye out for the **Sellwood Antique Collective**, 8027 Southeast 13th, for eclectic variety; the **Den of Antiquity**, 1408 Southeast Knapp for general antiques acquired with a loving eye; and **R. Spencer**, 8130 Southeast 13th, for a fine collection of furniture. (And while you're on that end of town, stop by the **Columbia Sportswear Outlet**, 1323 Southeast Tacoma, for great buys on last season's jackets.) The **Grand Central Bakery**, 7987 Southeast 13th, will refresh you with delicious soups and sandwiches before you head over to the Milwaukie Avenue section of Sellwood, which is actually called Westmoreland. There you will find **Stars**, a behemoth of antiques and collectibles. They are found at 7030 Southeast Milwaukie. For things that no one else has owned before, two good bets are the **Jealous Gardener**, 7011 Southeast Milwaukie, a cute garden and gift shop, and **Haggis McBaggis**, 6802 Southeast Milwaukie, for truly wonderful children's shoes and accessories. Haggis McBaggis is so family friendly that they encourage local parents to stop by and use the attractive bathroom if their kids need a diaper change. (See more about Haggis McBaggis in the Kidstuff chapter.) If you're not at the diaper-changing stage yet, but would like to be, **Tres Fabu**, on the corner of Milwaukie and Bybee, has fabulous wedding gowns and everything to go with them.

Northwest Portland
Northwest 23rd District

This upscale, trendy neighborhood includes a number of shops on 21st, but is known to Portlanders simply as Northwest 23rd. Filled with lovely Victorian homes and countless trees, this neighborhood is one of the prettier balances of the domestic and commercial in Portland, and it's a great walking neighborhood—the pedestrian traffic here is at times so uppity that it stops the automotive traffic. The foot traffic has created a democracy of fashion: The pierced hipsters sipping martinis at the Gypsy coexist comfortably with the bourgeois denizens dining at Wildwood, and that's because there is something for everyone. Chain representatives include the **Gap**, 2303 West Burnside; **Urban Outfitters**, 2320 Northwest Westover; **Restoration Hardware**, 315 Northwest 23rd; and the **Pottery Barn**, 310 Northwest 23rd. But the local hybrids are the real draw. For cool kitchen tools and accessories for the house, stop at **Kitchen Kaboodle**, Northwest 23rd and Flanders. For the culture hound, there is **Twenty Third Avenue Books**, at 1015 Northwest 23rd. If you're feeling underdressed, stop at Elizabeth Street, 635 Northwest 23rd (for women), or **Seaplane**, 827 Northwest 23rd, which carries beautiful dresses, many of them locally designed. **Urbino**, 638 Northwest 23rd, will help you make over your house with some of the most stylish furniture and housewares around. **What's Upstairs**, 736 Northwest 23rd, carries resale, cool jeans and locally designed jewels. **Girlfriends**, 904 Northwest 23rd, is the Portland branch of the hip San Francisco store that sells clothing and gifts for girls and their big sisters. On the edges of the district, **Ellington Leather Goods**, which sells its sleek handbags worldwide, has an outlet store at 1533 Northwest 24th.

i Many downtown merchants will validate your Smart Park parking slips if you spend $25 or more at their shops. It never hurts to ask.

Pearl District

Colonized by starving artists, then domesticated by hipsters, the Pearl District is now becoming the home of the haute bourgeoisie. Evidence of all three classes is readily apparent in the Soho of Portland. Not only are there dozens of art galleries (and a gallery walk the first Thursday night of each month) and an art school (the Pacific Northwest College of Art, 1241 Northwest Johnson), but the housewares, art supplies, furniture, clothing, hardware, and even light fixtures for sale in the area have a distinctly aesthetic quality to them. For clothing, try **Aubergine,** 1100 Northwest Glisan, for chic women's wear; **Nolita,** 923 Northwest 10th Avenue, for stylish denim for men and women, including Seven for All Mankind and Brochu Walker; and **Hanna Andersson**, 327 Northwest 10th, for colorful, comfortable clothes for children and their moms. **Richard Calhoun Old Town Florist**, 404 Northwest 10th, has elegant flowers. **Hunt and Gather**, 1302 Northwest Hoyt, has beautiful custom couches. Many gift and decorating shops pervade the area: Standouts include but are by no means limited to **Versailles in the Pearl**, 904 Northwest Hoyt; **Bella Casa,** 223 Northwest 9th; and **Cielo Home and Garden**, 528 Northwest 12th.

Oblation Papers, 516 Northwest 12th, sells handmade cards, invitations, and blank books. If all this walking around is making you hungry, stop at the excellent **Pearl Bakery**, 102 Northwest 9th, which supplies many restaurants in town, or **Piazza Italia**, 1129 Northwest Johnson, for a tiny bit of North Beach. **In Good Taste**, 231 Northwest 11th, can give you cooking supplies and lessons, if you'd rather go home to eat. **Patagonia**, 907 Northwest Irving, is in the Ecotrust Building, a century-old riverside warehouse undergoing "green" renovation. Brewery

Blocks north of Burnside between 11th and 12th contains a **Sur le Table** satellite and a shiny **Whole Foods** market. The Pearl covers a large amount of territory, so wear good walking shoes when you shop here. If you need to get them, you'll be in good shape, however, since several sporting apparel stores are clustered in the western end of the Pearl: **Lucy**, 1015 Northwest Couch, which sells women's (nonshoe) gear for yoga, biking, running, and other sports; **Adidas Heritage Store**, 1039 Northwest Couch, sells vintage-style and other fabulous-looking sportswear; **REI,** 1405 Northwest Johnson, carries serious sports equipment and clothing for men, women, and children who participate in actual athletic practices other than shopping; and so does **Title 9**, 1335 Northwest Kearney, only just for women.

ANTIQUES

Portland is the home of many, many antiques stores. Here is a sampling of them.

1874 HOUSE
8070 Southeast 13th Avenue
(503) 233-1874
This store, in Portland's historic Sellwood neighborhood, is jammed with a potpourri of old plumbing fixtures, stained glass, antique brass lighting fixtures, moldings, brass and copper hardware, and architectural items. Whether you need things for your doors, windows, or bathroom, this is the place to browse to your heart's content.

CLASSIC ANTIQUES
1805 Southeast Martin Luther King Jr. Boulevard
(503) 231-8689
Fine antiques from Europe and the United States, in addition to locally designed contemporary furniture, make this outpost a destination for citywide shoppers. Lighting and decor items are also good buys here.

HOLLYWOOD ANTIQUE SHOWCASE
1969 Northeast 42nd Avenue
(503) 288-1051

This fine collection of dealers has an excellent variety of furniture, art, collectibles, and table-ware. In particular, the variety of furniture is out-standing and of high quality—but much of it is also very affordable. Different dealers have differ-ent strengths, but you can usually find beautiful French antiques as well as mid-century modern. The owners are very smart and helpful.

LOUNGE LIZARD
1310 Southeast Hawthorne Boulevard
(503) 232-7575

Filled with retro furniture and home decor acces-sories, Lounge Lizard is just the spot for the newly antique. They aim to please—the prices are affordable and the service is friendly. Plus, they have a large selection of great, basic vintage furniture, as well as odd but wonderful other pieces. The lighting selection is excellent. If you never before thought of putting Eames knockoffs in your 1908 Craftsman, you might start thinking about it now.

RD STEEVES IMPORTS
140 West Main Street, Yamhill
(503) 662-3999

This place is a bit out of the way, but we're including it for two reasons: They carry an excep-tionally high-quality inventory of furniture and antiques and are such a draw that they supply more than 100 antiques dealers in five Western states. Located in the quaint town of Yamhill, RD Steeves offers imported (mostly from Europe) treasures, including English armoires, sideboards, bedroom suites, bureaus, china cabinets, stained-glass windows, and all sorts of unusual finds such as hand-cranked sewing machines, chimney pots, and paddles. RD Steeves, which is open Tuesday through Sunday, receives huge 40-foot containers of goods direct from overseas every few weeks—and when they do, it's a race to their front door because their markup is low for the general public and even lower for dealers.

THE SELLWOOD ANTIQUE MALL
7875 Southeast 13th Avenue
(503) 232-3755

The Sellwood Antique Mall is perfect for either the serious or frivolous collector. It has more than 100 different dealers, so the inventory changes constantly. The mall is one of the largest of its kind in the city, carrying a wide range of items from furniture to dishes to lighting fixtures. It also carries nostalgia items from the 1950s.

STARS
7030 Southeast Milwaukie Avenue
(503) 235-5990

Three hundred dealers and 30,000 square feet of antique and collectible furniture, linens, books, clothes, jewelry, dishes, and tchotchkes are here for the perusal of the antiques hunter. Because there are so many different dealers, the Stars empire cannot be comprehensively character-ized, but you're more likely to find a country primitive sideboard than a federal one, although you never know. The managers are very good about display—this is one of the most attractive antiques malls around.

BARGAINS AND THRIFT STORES

Did we mention there is no sales tax in Oregon? We recycle everything in Portland. For more sav-ings, check out the stores below.

CITY LIQUIDATORS
823 Southeast 3rd Avenue
(503) 238-1367

City Liquidators is a bargain-hunters' delight, packed to the rafters with low-priced stuff. Some of the hardware and tools are priced very low, as are carpets, planters, small pieces of furniture, and kitchen gadgets. The second floor is the fur-niture warehouse, and some of it is quite decent. We've seen many low prices on couches, arm-chairs, dining room and bedroom sets, futons, patio furniture, and much more. From pots and pans to entertainment centers and bookcases, City Liquidators offers everything you need to cheaply furnish a home or apartment. They also have a good selection of office furniture, equipment, and supplies. And they also have much that is just odd. The last time we were there, we overheard a man say to his father, "Do you see anything you can't live without?" "Or live with?" was the answer.

COLUMBIA SPORTSWEAR OUTLET STORE
1323 Southeast Tacoma Street, Sellwood
(503) 238-0118

3 Monroe Parkway, Lake Oswego
(503) 636-6593
It is worth the drive to Sellwood or Lake Oswego to pick up that parka, rain hat, or down vest you've been eyeing at the downtown store for 30 to 50 percent off the price. This nationally distributed sportswear line is Oregon's own; they supply L.L. Bean and other companies in addition to distributing their own gear. Their handsome flagship retail store can be found at 911 Southwest Broadway, downtown.

GOODWILL STORE
1943 Southeast 6th Avenue
(503) 238-6165
Goodwill in Portland is something of a phenomenon, a business model for all the other Goodwills in the nation because it is so successful. It became successful because it is clean and bright, with inventive advertising and a cheerful atmosphere. The selection of men's, women's, and children's clothes is extensive and reasonably priced. You won't waste time weeding out stained shirts and zipperless pants either. The books section is remarkably free of culls and very well organized. The turnover in just one day is fast. Besides clothes and books, there are plenty of domestic items—dishes, fabrics, odds and ends, wall decorations—and a music section with a ton of LPs. Prices are, however, climbing. You will no longer find Coach bags for $4.00 or vintage pottery for 99 cents. Bargains can be found, but you will have lots of competition, because everyone shops at Goodwill. Goodwill stores are found throughout the city and more are opening every day. Check out the downtown store at

838 Southwest 10th Avenue for the crème de la crème of fashion recycling.

HANNA ANDERSSON OUTLET STORE
7 Monroe Parkway, Lake Oswego
(503) 697-1953
The long johns, dresses, tights, clogs, and sportswear you and your children have come to know and love are here offered at a reduced price. Hanna Andersson is known for its high-quality, Swedish-style soft clothing in wonderful colors and patterns. (See the following Clothing section and the Kidstuff chapter for more information.)

NORDSTROM RACK
245 Southwest Morrison Street
(503) 299-1815

Clackamas Promenade
8930 Southeast Sunnyside Road
Clackamas
(503) 654-5415

Tanasbourne
18100 Northwest Evergreen Parkway
(503) 439-0900
Every savvy Portlander knows about "the Rack." This is the closest Portland comes to Filene's Basement, and while you probably won't see anyone disrobing in the aisles, there is no lack of competitive shopping. This store is filled with clearance merchandise from Nordstrom stores plus additional items made specifically for the store. You'll find men's and women's clothing and shoes, as well as a changing assortment of accessories, picture frames, and perfumes. Prices can be as much as 70 percent below the full retail price.

NORM THOMPSON OUTLET STORE
Oregon Mail Order Outlet Store
9 Monroe Parkway, Lake Oswego
(503) 697-2931
Next to the Columbia Sportswear Outlet Store, these stores are worth the extra effort to find. The Mail Order Outlet Store is a Norm Thompson spin-off, with an eclectic mix of clothes, accessories, gadgets, household goods, cleaning

solutions, cookware, outdoor clothes, and other things from Norm's lesser-known catalogs, Early Winters and Solutions.

PENDLETON WOOLEN MILL OUTLET STORE
2 17th Street, Washougal, WA
(360) 835-1118
www.pendleton-usa.com
This woolen mill, founded in 1912 and the leading producer of the Pendleton line of woolen clothing, is one of the most popular walking tours of the Portland-Vancouver area. The Washougal site offers the largest of the Pendleton Mill outlet stores and features great savings on new apparel, closeouts, and factory seconds. The tours, offered weekdays, afford an opportunity to see the looming of their extraordinary line of woolen blankets, which are collectibles and still sold in trading huts in the southwestern corner of the United States.

BOOKS AND PERIODICALS

Portland is a city of readers. We have the largest bookstore in the nation, Powell's City of Books, which is made even larger by the fact that it has a number of branches. However, Powell's can sometimes overshadow the other fine independent bookstores in the area, including interesting book selections at places like the Oregon Historical Society, Portland State University, or the Audubon Society of Portland. We also have the usual national chain bookstores here in town.

ANNIE BLOOM'S BOOKS
7834 Southwest Capitol Highway
(503) 246-0053
Tucked into the retail center of the Multnomah neighborhood, this store attracts loyal readers from throughout the area who appreciate the selection, the suggestions, and assistance of the well-read staff, as well as the cozy armchairs. The store is also well known beyond Portland proper for its Children's Corner, with books and a play area, and for its collection of titles on Judaism and Judaic culture and art. Annie Bloom's is frequently mentioned as a contender for Portland's favorite bookstore.

BROADWAY BOOKS
1714 Northeast Broadway
(503) 284-1726
If bigger, sprawling chain bookstores are a bit daunting, try Broadway Books. This charming shop in the Lloyd District has a thoughtful collection of diverse literaria. In addition to stocking a good selection of literary works, it sponsors poetry readings and author book-signing events. The owners and their employees are friendly, knowledgeable, and articulate, and the well-chosen selection here reflects their expertise; they have crafted one of the best bookstores in town.

CAMERON'S BOOKS AND MAGAZINES
336 Southwest 3rd Avenue
(503) 228-2391
Before there was Powell's—before there was any other bookstore in Portland—there was Cameron's. Tucked into a downtown storefront, Cameron's features windows filled with well-cared-for copies of *Life, Time, Look, Saturday Evening Post, Colliers,* and other publications from the era of the general-interest magazine. They also have back issues of *Sports Illustrated* and *Playboy* as well as a massive collection of comic books. Cameron's claims to have 100,000 magazines, mass-market paperbacks, and comics in stock and to be the home of the birthday magazine gift.

DAEDALUS BOOKS
2074 Northwest Flanders Street
(503) 274-7742
www.abebooks.com/home/daedalus/
Daedalus Books carries many kinds of books, but they specialize in the scholarly ones that are harder to find in other bookstores. For example, their philosophy inventory goes far beyond *Zen and the Art of Motorcycle Maintenance.* They are an exceptional resource for history and literature, as well as classics and linguistics. They carry both new and used books, and there is nothing quite like Daedalus in town.

GREAT NORTHWEST BOOKSTORES
3314 Southwest First Avenue
(503) 223-8098

With 150,000 or so books in stock, this is Portland's largest exclusively used bookstore. Some of the books here seem to have barely been opened, so "used" is somewhat of a misnomer. There is a good rare-book collection, a large selection of Western Americana and maps, old photographs, and what is called in the trade "ephemera"—booklets, menus, letters, handbills, and leaflets.

IN OTHER WORDS
8 Northeast Killingsworth Street
(503) 232-6003
Once inside this cheerful, cozy outlet for women's books and resources, you'll find a bounty of magazines, videos, cards, gifts, and new and used books. Open seven days a week, the store also sponsors readings and workshops.

LAUGHING HORSE BOOKS
12 Northeast 10th Avenue
(503) 236-2893
This unabashedly progressive and vibrant bookstore advertises itself as a resource for social change. Inside are new and used books devoted to political issues, a bulletin board listing meetings and workshops held by local political action groups, and a gathering space where poets and authors read from their works and actors perform.

THE LOOKING GLASS BOOKSTORE
7983 Southeast 13th Street
(503) 227-4760
In the more than 30 years that the Looking Glass Bookstore has been open, it has consistently offered a well-chosen selection of new books, both paperback and hardcover, and if it doesn't have what you want in stock, the staff can find it and get it to you. The store has an intriguing selection of magazines and journals and an excellent selection of note cards, including those by Oregon and other Northwest artists. For most of its history, The Looking Glass was downtown. The move to Sellwood has allowed it to refocus on four main areas: American and World history, political science, local poets, and contemporary literature. It also has an excellent children's selection—and

since the bookstore resides in a cute red caboose with lots of cozy corners for reading, the kids will be occupied while you are browsing.

MURDER BY THE BOOK
3210 Southeast Hawthorne Boulevard
(503) 232-9995
As the name implies, this bookstore is devoted to mysteries—hard-boiled, tea-cozy, police procedural—name your poison and you'll find it here. There are close-outs on sale at the door, shelves of used books, and the newest releases in both hardbound and paperback. Patrons of this unique shop get a newsletter announcing new releases and readings by mystery authors.

PERIODICALS AND BOOKS PARADISE
1928 Northeast 42nd Avenue
(503) 234-6003
This is a well-organized library/warehouse of vintage and new magazines and books. With a million issues in stock, it is said to be the largest collection on the West Coast. The prices on late-issue magazines are discounted about 75 percent from the regular retail price. We warn you, though—it's easy to lose track of time in this place, especially if you're a reader and love magazines.

POWELL'S CITY OF BOOKS
1005 West Burnside Street
(503) 228-4651
www.powells.com
Powell's is getting pretty close to an empire. (And yes, there is a Powell: Michael Powell is the mind and the will behind Powell's growth, positioning, and well-known civic involvement.) With more than a million books in a store covering several levels in a building filling an entire city block, Powell's is the largest bookstore in the country. It even has its own (small) parking garage. Powell's has become an attraction in its own right and really does deserve a visit . . . or two . . . or three. This is a maze of a store, so pick up a map as you enter. Sections are color-coded, and there are plenty of signs to direct you. The staff is helpful, courteous, and knowledgeable in case you have to ask directions.

You'll find both used and new books and a separate rare book room. There are books in other languages besides English, and not surprisingly, a small selection of reading glasses. Powell's also has an excellent children's section as well as a selection of cards, blank journals, and other papery things. The cafe, with its coffee, tea, and snacks, would be a good place to look through potential purchases if one weren't always getting distracted by the interesting people wandering in and out of the room. The frequent literary readings are a big draw. Powell's is open every day of the year and is usually busy, if not downright crowded; there are other sites at the airport and in Beaverton, 8725 Southwest Cascade, in addition to the other branches listed below. If you're looking for science- and technology-related items, visit the nearby Powell's Technical Bookstore, 33 Northwest Park. Powell's Books for Cooks and Gardeners, 3747 Southeast Hawthorne Boulevard, is devoted to cooking and gardening books, and they have a comprehensive selection of these, as well as tools, toys, and crafted artifacts. It's a great spot to track down a birthday or holiday gift for those who like to cook or garden, or practically anybody else. Powell's Bookstore on Hawthorne, 3723 Southeast Hawthorne Boulevard, is a general-interest bookstore; it is smaller and perhaps, based on its scale, more user-friendly. This branch also sponsors weekly readings by writers, poets, and performance artists.

Powell's online service is incredibly well organized and useful. Don't tell them, but a lot of people look up the books that interest them before they get to the store. It helps make the experience less overwhelming.

READING FRENZY
921 Southwest Oak Street
(503) 274-1449

Reading Frenzy, which specializes in publications by independent presses, sells things that you can't find anywhere else in Portland, and sometimes, anywhere else in the world. In addition to a fine selection of smart magazines, this shop carries locally and nationally published 'zines, literary quarterlies, and attractively published essays by academics such as Noam Chomksy. Reading Frenzy also serves as a meeting and distribution place for all kinds of alternative causes.

TITLE WAVE
216 Northeast Knott Street
(503) 988-5021

The bookstore for discards from the Multnomah County Library is so good that we don't even really want to tell you about it. Prices for paperbacks start at about $1 and go up from there. For hardbacks—which include both contemporary and older fiction, poetry, mysteries, cookbooks, and anything else you might want—look for prices to begin at $2. You will also find a great selection of books on tape and CD, music CDs, and LPs. Back copies of many magazines are also available, and the videos and DVDs are also worth perusing.

TWENTY-THIRD AVENUE BOOKS
1015 Northwest 23rd Avenue
(503) 224-5097

An excellent neighborhood shop for new books and periodicals such as the *New York Review of Books,* Twenty-third Avenue Books carries a general selection of books rather than specializing. However, it's a very good place to hear writers talk because the space is comfortable and intimate. It's much better to see Helen Schulman or David Sedaris here than on the stage at the Schnitz. And it is actually possible.

WALLACE BOOKS
7241 Southeast Milwaukie Boulevard
(503) 235-7350

Just a couple of blocks south of the Moreland business district antiques malls and small shops, Wallace Books is an old house with bookshelves in every room. It's fun to browse upstairs and down to find the words you want to snuggle with later as the day winds down. The store has the newest releases as well as lots of new and used genre paperbacks.

Other bookstores in Portland include:

BARNES & NOBLE
1317 Lloyd Center
(503) 249-0800

BORDERS BOOKS & MUSIC
708 Southwest 3rd Avenue
(503) 220-5911

CLOTHING

DUCHESS
2505 Southeast 11th Avenue
(503) 281-6648
www.duchessclothier.com

Duchess has evolved from a fun shop with Western-inspired clothes, reproductions of 20th-century classic silk slips, and petticoats to a purveyor of gorgeous custom men's suits in a range of historically inspired styles. The suits are also available in a range of prices. But these made-to-measure suits are all beautifully made, affordable, and will be well worth the effort.

ELIZABETH STREET
635 Northwest 23rd Avenue
(503) 243-2456

A stalwart of the Northwest 23rd shopping scene, Elizabeth Street features a beautifully edited collection of new and stylish women's clothing and accessories, both fancy and casual.

ELLINGTON LEATHER GOODS
1533 Northwest 24th Avenue
(503) 223-7457
www.ellingtonleather.com

Ellington makes Italian-inspired handbags, wallets, luggage, and other leather items, as well as a sophisticated line of microfiber bags. Their backpack purses are modern classics. Ellington also has a good Web store.

THE ENGLISH DEPT.
1124 Southwest Alder Avenue
(503) 224-0724

Co-owner Elizabeth Dye sells her own work here, as well as that of others. And what is this work? Why, beautiful and feminine clothes inspired by Jay Gatsby's yellow shirts and other literary fashions. Pretty dresses, jewelry, skirts, and tops.

FROCK
1439 Northeast Alberta Street
(503) 595-0379

This fun shop in Northeast Portland is terrific both for vintage and vintage-inspired clothing and for local designers. Current favorites include Mug Wump recycled handbags, cool men's shirts, and hand-dyed silk slips. Also look for pretty jewelry from local talent.

FYBERWORKS
4300 Southeast Hawthorne Boulevard
(503) 232-7659

Street clothes, beautiful accessories, and workout wear are the specialties here. We go for gorgeous hand-knit scarves, for silk shawls, for natural-fiber jackets, dresses, and tunics, and for the wonderful variety of locally made designs. Fyberworks often carries cute vintage and Portland-made home design objects in its friendly shop.

HANNA ANDERSSON
327 Northwest 10th Avenue
(503) 321-5275

Portland is headquarters for this nationally successful catalog shop featuring Swedish-style, high-quality clothing for kids and their moms. Designs are often, but not exclusively, made with cotton jersey. The underwear and pajamas are especially cozy and comfortable; and the clothes wear very well, through at least two children, and so are a good value. The store is clean, light, and wholesome. This civic-minded company passes along gently used Hannas to needy children—isn't that a good reason to shop here?

LANGLITZ LEATHERS
2443 Southeast Division Street
(503) 235-0959

Over the past 60 years, Langlitz Leathers has forged a worldwide reputation for crafting the highest-quality leather garments. Their shop is small—less than 3,000 square feet—and crowded. They have a total of 15 people working in an old, crusty building with hundreds of garments hanging around. Far from snobby, they welcome visitors and will be happy to show you every aspect of how they create custom leathers. Langlitz creates only about six garments per day. Half are custom built, and the others are built to stock pattern sizes for walk-in customers. Because their prices are relatively low for custom work (between $500 and $1,000 per garment), their services are in constant demand. They have different products, but the Columbia was the first jacket that store founder Ross Langlitz designed—in the mid-1940s—and it remains the flagship of the jacket line, reflecting the traditional look of motorcycling.

MARIO'S
833 Southwest Broadway
Men's Store:
(503) 227-3477
Women's Store:
(503) 241-8111
Mario's is the best source in town for urbane designer clothing, shoes, and accessories from Armani to Prada. Some readers may be familiar with the clean, spare luxury of the Mario's in Seattle, but this one is the original; it was one of the first residents of The Galleria and therefore may be regarded as a chief contributor to the beautification of downtown—and its residents. The store now inhabits a beautiful space in the Fox Tower.

MINK
3418 Southeast Hawthorne Boulevard
(503) 232-3500
Gorgeous dresses that will help you unleash your inner Daisy Miller: That is what Mink will provide you with—as well as great tees by Velvet and jeans by Joe's Jeans, and all the accessories to go with them. Mink also carries well-selected pieces from local designers. English majors and accountants alike will find something beautiful here.

MATISSE
1236 Northwest Flanders Street
(503) 287-5414
While Matisse does carry chic everyday clothes, many women shop here for the evening clothes, which are flowing things made out of gorgeous fabrics in flattering styles. Savvy Portlanders choose this shop for their Academy or National Book Awards dresses, and when they do, they can be confident that not only will their clothes be beautiful and stylish, but they won't look like everybody else either. Matisse also sells lovely shoes and jewelry, and they always have a little basket of markdowns right outside the door.

ODESSA
410 Southwest 13th Avenue
(503) 223-1998
Odessa sells fashionable clothes with a downtown feel; they have a good eye for singular pieces with distinctive lines. Most lines are from New York, London, and Los Angeles, and they include Eventide, VPL, and Jane Mayle. Odessa has beautiful evening clothes but also carries beguiling everyday clothes for the fashionista, such as Petite Bateau T-shirts, as well as beautiful home design fabrics from Kerry Cassill. You'll also find some shoes and handbags.

OLIO UNITED
1028 Southeast Water Street
(503) 542-5000
http://shop.oliounited.com
Housed in a reclaimed warehouse in the Central Eastside Industrial District, Olio United provides gorgeous clothes made of sustainably produced, recycled, and repurposed materials. They also offer home design products and gifts. The vibe is eco-modern, the look, delicious. Lines include, among many others, Preloved and Ivana Helsinki, and our favorite, beautiful recycled leather bags by Ashley Watson. Plus it's right next to the Bakery Bar, so you can reward yourself with cake for having made a local, sustainable, fabulous fashion choice.

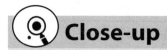

Close-up

Local Design

Portland has a history of supplying the nation with stylish, well-made clothing, and you've probably heard of Hanna Andersson, Jantzen, Columbia Sportswear, and Nike. You may have even seen local star Michelle DeCourcy's beautiful dresses featured on Oprah. But Portland's increasing urbanity is reflected in the growing number of successful local designers who have set up shop in the past few years, designers who are also receiving national attention. The following shops carry locally made and designed clothing by Portland's rising design stars.

Dragonlily
1740 Southeast Hawthorne Boulevard
(503) 234-LILY
www.dragonlily.org

Dragonlily is not simply a women's clothing boutique. It is a gallery dedicated to wearable art. Established by Jasmine Patten and Keri Roberts and featuring Portland designers, Dragonlily specializes in upscale women's clothing, jewelry, hats, and handbags, with attention to quality and detail that surpasses anything we have seen yet among local designers. Patten and Roberts feature their own lines (Ipseity and Dervish), as well as

generously apportioning space to other local, regional, and independent stars such as Suzabelle and Buddhaful. Everything in this shop has some wonderful surprise—an unusual collar, a stunning fabric, a well-placed tassel, for instance, or the beautifully embroidered motifs that adorn the clothes from Ipseity and Dervish's glamorous workout wear in animal patterns or a just-so embellishment that makes you feel beautiful as well as comfortable. You can stock most of your closet here, from pretty but edgy cocktail dresses to casual cords. The jewelry is also a standout—look for a wide range of items that include delicate, semiprecious earrings and necklaces at very reasonable prices and striking, one-of-a-kind enameled bracelets. Most of these designs are handmade right here in Portland, and we love the idea that we can have a friendly relationship with the women who dreamed up and executed these beautiful clothes.

Lena Medoyeff
724 Northwest 23rd Avenue
(503) 227-0011

Well-cut clothes in stunning fabrics—this is the hallmark of Lynn Solmonson, the designer behind the name Lena Medoyeff.

PIN ME APPAREL
3705 Northeast Mississippi Street
(503) 281-1572

Because everyone should have access to high fashion, Pin Me proffers lovely and affordable designer clothes in a wide range of sizes: 0 to 16, to be precise. They carry curve-friendly lines and organize clothes by color, so it's easy to put outfits together. And their accessories rock.

PORTLAND PENDLETON SHOP
Southwest 4th Avenue and Salmon Street
(503) 242-0037

On the east side of the Standard Insurance Building, this store offers the most complete collection of Pendleton clothing for men and women in all

of Oregon. Despite fashion's follies and foibles, Pendleton has always offered classic styles for men and women and excellent value. They've updated their clothing lines with a more contemporary look while retaining their well-known fabrics and colors. In addition to clothing, the store carries an excellent selection of blankets and pillows with dramatic designs and colors based on Western and Native American art and symbols.

RED LIGHT
3590 Southeast Hawthorne Boulevard
(503) 963-8888

Some of the best vintage clothing in Portland is found in this large, trendy shop, in addition to resale modern clothes from BCBG, Betsy Johnson,

These dresses, skirts, pants, and jackets for day or evening are truly alluring, and they'll make you so as well. You'll see a lot of embroidery, some of it by local artisans. Depending, of course, on the season, you may also see duponi silk, velvet, or lightweight wool, but whatever you see, it will be a simple design that allows the beauty of the fabric to stand out. These clothes are rather dressy, but for Portland, a Lena Medoyeff skirt with a T-shirt and flip-flops fit in just right.

Seaplane
827 Northwest 23rd Avenue
(503) 234-2409

Seaplane carries clothes that are a modern hybrid of Bond girl, Grace Jones, and Debbie Harry, with a little Marie Antoinette thrown in for good measure. Designers and proprietors Holly Stadler and Kathryn Towers feature beautifully sculpted dresses, sweaters, and skirts, and they share the love by showcasing other designers as well. With their amazing fashions and phenomenal events, this seminal design collective has been featured in the national and international press, putting Portland on the map as a fashion incubator.

Tumbleweed
1804 Northeast Alberta Street
(503) 335-3100
www.kara-line.com

Tumbleweed is the home base of designer Kara Larson and her Kara-Line brand of clothing. These urban cowgirl clothes are available throughout the city and the country. Her simple skirts and dresses are charming without being the least bit fussy; they are made of pretty prints in cottons and rayons. We also love the fact that you can talk to the woman who made them. They purvey an entire "rustic romantic" look, but the pieces blend well with things you already own and can really individualize a wardrobe. Dresses for little girls, vintage cowboy boots, pantaloons, sweaters, and other fabric delights (including a fun basket of remnants) round out the selection. They're on a personal mission to revive the dress—the store's motto is "Wear more dresses!" and after 15 minutes inside you can't help but think—all right, then! I will!

Urban Outfitters, and Bébé. The vintage selection is comprehensive and reasonably priced, with everything from slips to coats. Men and women alike will find wonderful old leather jackets, evening wear, sweaters, and, well, everything you could imagine.

SAVVY PLUS
3204 Southeast Hawthorne Boulevard
(503) 231-7116
www.savvyplus.com

Savvy Plus specializes in high-quality resale and new women's clothes size 12 and up. Most of the apparel is created using natural fibers and made in the good old U.S.A. They also carry some unusual jewelry that is handcrafted by local artisans. A great source for stylish and fabulous clothing in larger sizes. You can also consign your consumer-tested fashion items for other people to take home and love.

UNA
2802 Southeast Ankeny Street
(503) 235-2326

A tiny, beautiful shop in LoBu, Una is renowned for its well-edited collection of locally designed, cool clothes from New York and Los Angeles, and vintage offerings. Look for Portland designers such as Jess Beebe and Sarah Weick, as well as small labels from, well, all over. Una features accessories as well—including some home decor items, so you'll feel like you belong in your new outfit.

Portland Mercury columnist Marjorie Skinner dishes on the latest sales, trends, and other news in her weekly column Sold Out. Read it and you will never wonder what to wear again.

CRAFTS

BOLT
2136 Northeast Alberta Street
(503) 287-2658

Bolt is a beautiful fabric shop in the Alberta neighborhood with the feel of a boutique rather than a warehouse. The shop features luscious fabrics in contemporary designs, as well as the hippest patterns available. They also offer workshops and advice for the beginner, intermediate, and expert sewer.

COLLAGE ART MATERIALS AND WORKROOM
1639 Northeast Alberta Street
4429 Southeast Woodstock Boulevard
(503) 249-2190

These delightful spaces in the Alberta and Reed College neighborhoods carry an outstanding and thoughtful selection of craft supplies. They have an excellent selection of papers and bookbinding supplies, as well as great bonding agents, cutters, and other basics. The expert staff really knows their stuff and can make great recommendations for tricky crafting problems. In addition, they provide a great work space and classes. (See the DIY feature in the Arts chapter).

KNIT PURL
1101 Southwest Alder
(503) 227-2999

A beautiful downtown yarn shop, Knit Purl carries gorgeous yarns, aesthetically pleasing needles and other tools, and a wide, wide range of patterns and books. The staff is very wise and will help you read your confusing pattern in the nicest way possible. They also provide fabulous classes and open knitting circles—as well as knitting celebrity events.

YARN GARDEN
1413 Southeast Hawthorne Boulevard
(503) 239-7950

We should all honor our work by using the best materials available, and if knitting is your work, Yarn Garden is the place for the best tools. Luscious yarns in every weight, color, and texture; needles; patterns—all your knitting needs are served here. The staff is so knowledgeable and helpful for beginners and experienced knitters alike that you'll find half the afternoon has passed before you know it. They are open on Wednesday evening until 8:00 p.m.; that's when they hold knitting circles at which you can solicit and receive advice, trade ideas, or meet other knitters. Yarn Garden also has a good selection of books.

FLORISTS AND NURSERIES

PORTLAND NURSERY
5050 Southeast Stark Street
(503) 231-5050

9000 Southeast Division Street
(503) 788-9000

This is one of the highest quality nurseries in the area, with a fine, well-organized selection of trees, shrubs, plants, bulbs, seeds, and supplies in two Portland locations. On a sunny Saturday morning in April, you are sure to run into half the people you know, all doing what you are doing. The staff really knows their stuff, so if you don't have a green thumb, ask questions; they have information counters set up for this.

RICHARD CALHOUN OLD TOWN FLORIST
403 Northwest 9th Avenue
(503) 223-1646

1001 Southwest Broadway
(503) 224-0233

Before anybody was in the Pearl District, Richard Calhoun was—this urban pioneer was one of the first to appreciate the possibilities of the district. The shop is now owned by Wendi Day, who upholds the firm's outstanding reputation for high-design, Asian-inspired floral arrangements. Richard Calhoun Old Town supplies the flowers for many of the major spaces and events in the city, but they will also do flowers for your own house or event, so don't be shy about asking. The shop carries some handsome garden accessories and fountains in addition to its made-to-order arrangements.

i If you're planning to woo your sweetie with homemade cocktails in addition to flowers, note that Oregon's liquor stores are state-licensed. That means you have to shop at designated liquor stores, rather than the supermarket, for the hard stuff. They stay open until 7:00 p.m. and they're closed on Sunday. Be forewarned.

FOOD

Along with the usual chain supermarkets such as Albertsons, Safeway, Thriftway, and Fred Meyer, Portland is also home to a variety of Korean, Vietnamese, Japanese, Lebanese, Mexican, Russian, and German stores and delis. The national chains Wild Oats and Whole Foods specialize in organic and natural foods, with stores scattered throughout the city. Trader Joe's, the California-based chain, has four stores here: Look for them in Portland, 4715 Southeast 39th Avenue; in the Hollywood District at 4121 Northeast Halsey; in Beaverton, 11753 Southwest Beaverton-Hillsdale Highway; and in Lake Oswego, 15391 Southwest Bangy Road, next to the Ethan Allen Furniture Gallery. Zupan's Markets can be found in four locations: Belmont, Burnside, Macadam, and Raleigh Hills.

BOB'S RED MILL
5209 Southeast International Way
Milwaukie
(503) 654-3215
If you are into 100 percent stone-ground flours, Bob's Red Mill is an absolute must-stop. When their painstakingly restored, turn-of-the-20th-century gristmill burned in an arson fire, Bob Moore and his wife and business partner Charlee built up an amazing national business from the

once relatively small retail operation. But although Bob's Red Mill is now a giant, it still does things the old-fashioned way. The huge, 120-year-old millstones they salvaged from the fire still operate 24 hours a day, grinding out every grain under the sun—into flours, cereals, meals, farinas, and cracks. Bob's Red Mill is also a certified organic processor and carries a vast amount of organic whole-grain products. Their goods—which are free of chemicals, additives, and preservatives—are also kosher certified by the Rabbinical Council of America. The original plant is in a gorgeous, landscaped setting complete with a duck pond, with an attractive and well-organized on-site retail store for everything from rice, beans, nuts, seeds, milk powders, pastas, dried fruits, sweeteners, and other related products, in either bulk or small packages.

IN GOOD TASTE
231 Northwest 11th Avenue
(503) 248-2015
Gayle Jolley, who for years taught cooking classes at Sheridan (see below), opened this industrial-chic cooking arena in the Pearl District in 1999. Not only will you find the best, professional-quality cookware here, but you will also find specialty foods and a great wine selection. A bridal registry is available. But people come here for the cooking classes taught by excellent local chefs. In Good Taste also offers full-service catering and a lunchtime bistro to refresh those hungry Pearl District shoppers.

NEW SEASONS
1214 Southeast Tacoma Street
(503) 230-4949

7300 Southwest Beaverton-Hillsdale Highway
(503) 292-6838

5320 Northeast 33rd Avenue
(503) 288-3838

1954 Southeast Division Street
(503) 445-2888

6400 North Interstate Avenue
(503) 467-4777
www.newseasonsmarket.com

New Seasons is Portland's answer to Whole Foods. After the locally owned Nature's was sold and resold to big corporations, some of its former employees apparently missed having stores that were integral parts of neighborhood communities and driven by local interests. Thus, they founded New Seasons, which is designed to help bring back the local and seasonal to organic food. New Seasons is a full-service grocery store that features natural and organic foods, with exceptional produce and takeout in addition to traditional groceries, wine, and health and beauty aids. Moreover, the service is remarkably friendly and knowledgeable. Delivery service is also available.

PASTAWORKS
3735 Southeast Hawthorne Boulevard
(503) 232-1010

City Market
735 Northwest 21st Avenue
(503) 221-3002
www.pastaworks.com

Pastaworks makes fabulous fresh pasta and sauces right on-site, from light-as-air fettuccine to superbly flavorful ravioli. But Pastaworks is not only for pasta—it also sells everything you need to go with it, from the best produce to the most exquisite cheeses to the choicest organic meat. You'll find many local and imported specialty items here, including truffled olive oils from Italy and melt-in-your-mouth ginger cookies from Sweden. Wines are also a strong suit of the store; the Hawthorne branch offers tastings, as well as a fine selection of stemware, cookware, and cooking classes—as well as the best butcher and cheese counter in the city. In addition, there are a few tables outside where you can sit with coffee and rolls while you watch people shopping on Hawthorne. The City Market location is known for its wonderful fish and seafood collection, as well as its outstanding butchers.

SHERIDAN FRUIT CO.
408 Southeast 3rd Avenue
(503) 236-2113
www.sheridanfruit.com

Sheridan Fruit Co. is another Portland institution, offering many unusual herbs, exotic plants, and vegetables. It's a big, fun, bustling place to visit, and many people come to the Sheridan market from all around the Portland-Vancouver area. Sheridan's is known for its produce, but also carries an excellent selection of pasta, wine, meat, and cheese. Sheridan's also has a vast bulk section—and they make good espresso too. They are open Monday through Saturday from 6:00 a.m. to 8:00 p.m.

GIFTS

CHEEKY B
906 Northwest 14th Avenue
(503) 274-0229

This bright little shop in the Pearl District carries a wide selection of cool gifts, stationery, and home decor items, as well as jewelry for you and your canine friends. Shop here for jewels from Kimberly Baker, bags by Angela Adams, French Bull dishes, alarm clocks, lamps, journals, and so on. Well-edited collections and reasonable prices make this shop a standout.

KATHLEEN'S OF DUBLIN
737 Southwest Salmon Street
(503) 224-4869

This is a wonderful shop with a staff that is helpful and knowledgeable about their wares, which include Irish woolen sweaters and vests, linen shirts, and statues of St. Patrick. The shop is usually filled with the haunting sounds of Celtic music, ranging from the mournful wail of the pipes to IRA drinking songs and New Age melodies based on centuries-old music.

THE PAPER GARDEN
1713 Northeast 15th Avenue
(503) 249-0337

Beautiful writing papers, striking invitations, appealing journals, and glamorous gifts are the specialty of this delicious shop just off Northeast Broadway. The sleek sketchbooks will motivate your inner artist, and the fancy stationery will inspire you to get caught up on your thank-you

In Vino Veritas

Oregon is wine country and is justly famous for its pinots. Some passionate souls devoted to the blood of the Oregon soil have set up shop, making local wines available and bringing good international wines to the attention of Portland citizens. Each of the shops below likes to focus on boutique or hard-to-find wines; the ambience of each, their tasting events, and their prodigious variety of stock make them all worth visiting (perhaps not all on the same day). Many hold classes and other events, as well. The shop owners are as varied and fascinating as the wines they sell, so ask them about their passions.

E & R Wine Shop
6141 Southwest Macadam Avenue
(503) 246-6101
A wonderful wine shop with suburb service and smart owners, E & R has a nose for some of the best high-end wines available in the world. But they specialize in great wines from Italy. E & R also offers classes and tastings.

Great Wine Buys
1515 Northeast Broadway
(503) 287-2897
This friendly shop has friendly proprietors and a vast selection of wines from around the world.

Liner & Elsen
2222 Northwest Quimby Street
(503) 241-WINE
Liner & Elsen is regularly touted by the local and national press, and rightly so, for they offer outstanding service, selection, and stemware.

Mt. Tabor Fine Wines
4316 Southeast Hawthorne Boulevard
(503) 235-4444
This shop was named as one of the best wine shops in America four years running by *Food & Wine* magazine.

Portland Wine Merchants
Southeast 35th Avenue and Hawthorne Boulevard
(503) 234-4399
This shop is a favorite for Oregon wines and offers an excellent representation from the world over as well.

Urban Wineworks
407 Northwest 16th Avenue
(503) 226-9797
Urban Wineworks sells wine that other people make; they also are a winery themselves and purvey their own label. Stepping into their warehouse, you suddenly feel as if you're in Napa.

Vino
1226 Southeast Lexington Street
(503) 235-8545
Vino is a charming spot that features value-priced wines that would be difficult to find without the hard work of the owner, Bruce Bauer.

Three grocery stores also deserve mention for their superb wines: the **Pastaworks** at 3735 Southeast Hawthorne Boulevard; the **Fred Meyer** at Hawthorne Boulevard and Southeast 39th Avenue; and any **Zupan**'s (www.zupans.com).

notes. Also in stock: many perfect gifts for birthday girls, brides, and babies. Everything here is chosen with an eye for designs that are sophisticated but also warm, attractive, and colorful. The Paper Garden is the kind of shop that looks good and smells good and makes you feel good too.

THE REAL MOTHER GOOSE
901 Southwest Yamhill Street
(503) 223-9510

The Real Mother Goose is an eclectic cross of art gallery, potter's guild, and jewelry store. Here you'll find fine-crafted silver and gold jewelry, glass and pottery lamps, vases, dishes, and art objects as well as a small selection of handmade clothing. The furniture gallery in the downtown store features sophisticated, one-of-a-kind pieces done in fine and rare woods. The quality of design and construction are superb. If you would like something to carry home, look over the display of wooden boxes. There's a branch of this shop at Portland International Airport as well.

HOME DECOR

BERNADETTE BREU EXPERIENCE
1338 Southeast 6th Avenue
(503) 226-6565
www.bernadettebreuantiques.com

Bernadette Breu is Portland's maven for antiques and vintage home decoration, carrying everything from furniture to light fixtures to rugs to art—as well as providing top-notch design services. Her beautiful, light space just east of the Hawthorne Bridge will give you plenty of inspiration for decking out your home in the most sophisticated but comfortable way possible.

CARGO
380 Northwest 13th Avenue
(503) 209-8349

Those pictures in *Elle Decor* of lofts decorated with tansu chests and Indian saris have always looked appealing, but where do you get the saris and tansu chests to decorate with? In Portland, you get them at Cargo, which is a kind of upscale Cost Plus with many beautiful imports, mainly from India and Asia. High-quality silk pillows, baskets, wooden tea chests, bamboo blinds, and so on are all here, as well as sake sets and chopsticks. Cargo is also an excellent place for gifts.

HIPPO HARDWARE AND TRADING COMPANY
1040 East Burnside Street
(503) 231-1444

Hippo Hardware, a well-known Portland establishment for many years, carries a wonderfully eclectic assortment of plumbing fixtures, doors, lighting fixtures, and salvaged items for older homes. This place is far more entertaining than the average nuts-and-bolts hardware store and is full of functional curios and odd stuff that can be very useful if you know what to do with it (if you're like us and have no idea what it's supposed to do, just ask and someone will be glad to help you). It takes a long time to search through all the offerings, so plan accordingly. They will also custom build lighting fixtures. Don't forget to bring your old fixtures in here for a swap. It is a trading company, after all.

KITCHEN KABOODLE
Southwest 6th Avenue and Alder Street
(503) 464-9545

Northeast 16th Avenue and Broadway
(503) 288-1500

Clackamas Town Center
(503) 652-2567

Southwest Hall Boulevard and Scholls Ferry Road
(503) 643-5491

Northwest 23rd Avenue and Flanders Street
(503) 241-4040

Their motto is "We make your house a home," and they've been doing just that since 1975. Kitchen Kaboodle sells functional, unique house accoutrements, providing not only every possible gadget you might use someday, but the storage unit to put it in. This Portland institution has stores all over town; and whether you need an electric egg cooker, a potato ricer, an enameled French casserole, or a maple sideboard, you can find it here. The staff is very knowledgeable and friendly—make use of them. That's what they're paid for.

i The Central Eastside Industrial District is not just for container trucks full of vegetables and office supplies. There you will also find a range of the finest sources for house remodeling. In addition to Rejuvenation, 1100 Southeast Grand Avenue, lucky hunters will find exquisite antiques and decor at Bernadette Breu Experience, 1338 Southeast 6th Avenue, and classic marble at Oregon Tile and Marble, 1845 Southeast 3rd.

THE REBUILDING CENTER
3625 North Mississippi Avenue
(503) 331-1877
A nonprofit salvage outlet, the Rebuilding Center sells reclaimed hardware, windows, doors, plumbing fixtures, moldings, and lumber. This is the retail outlet of a firm that disassembles houses and other buildings; what is not immediately reused in other projects is sold here. For the recycling-conscious do-it-yourselfer, this place is heaven.

REJUVENATION
1100 Southeast Grand Avenue
(503) 238-1900
Another Portland landmark, Rejuvenation is well known nationally for its period lighting fixtures, but it also carries new and salvaged plumbing, doors, windows, moldings, and lumber. You'll also find handsome furniture and garden ornaments. This is a terrific resource center for home improvements; Rejuvenation has built a thriving business around helping people restore classic, turn-of-the-20th-century houses. A knowledgeable staff provides useful information and referral lists of competent home rehabilitation specialists. There's a tiny nook for children to play in while their parents browse; the Daily Cafe, inside the

store, is a good place for eating lunch while you figure out what to do with the salvaged staircase you've just bought.. Rejuvenation also sells their seconds, which can be a fine source for well-priced lighting fixtures and other things.

RELISH
433 Northwest 10th Avenue
(503) 227-3779
www.relishstyle.com
This sleek boutique stocks accessories and home and lifestyle objects with a modern aesthetic, many by local designers. The jewelry selection is outstanding—unusual in its materials and inspired in its lines.

SWEETWATER FARM
1400 Northwest Everett Street
(503) 227-4947
Richard Friedman sells furnishings that put the fun back in functional. This shop deals in colorful, funky furniture—everything from armoires to entertainment centers—and singular treasures made by artisans from all over the country. David Marsh and Shoestring Creations are two featured artists, but there are many more. In addition to the furniture, you'll find a striking array of jewelry, lighting, pillows, toys, and other surprises. Sweetwater Farm might be just the place to find the necessary touch of whimsy to go with the Eileen Gray daybed in your modern row house.

THE WHOLE 9 YARDS
1820 East Burnside Street
(503) 223-2880
Specializing in interior fabrics and trim, The Whole 9 Yards has developed a national reputation for its gorgeous fabrics, inventive combinations, and original style. Their chenilles, jacquards, and velvets are renowned, but they carry everything from duponi silk to cotton. They'll help you put together your drapes and upholstery, as well as providing you with general expertise, curtain rods and trim, and their own line of freshly designed, competitively priced furniture. The shop also offers brilliant classes in fashioning slipcovers, curtains, and pillows.

MUSIC

ARTICHOKE MUSIC
3130 Southeast Hawthorne Boulevard
(503) 232-8845

Don't settle for banging a gong; stop by this friendly music shop and strum an Autoharp or thump an Irish bodhran with a double drumstick. Here you will find guitars, banjos, mandolins, dulcimers, harps, accordions, and a fascinating assortment of unusual folk instruments. They also buy and sell all kinds of musical instruments and are extremely knowledgeable about the local music scene. Not only do they carry a wide selection of high-quality musical instruments, but they also feature live performances, music lessons, and cool events—among them open-mike sessions so you can show off your best bluegrass licks and a singing circle where you can sing your heart out and practice those harmonies.

JACKPOT RECORDS
209 Southwest 9th Avenue
(503) 222-0990

3574 Southeast Hawthorne
(503) 239-7561
www.jackpotrecords.com

In an iPod era, fabulous Jackpot Records is better than ever, with an outstanding catalog of new and used CDs and vinyl, as well as an online store and MySpace page. This great shop not only has excellent finds in indie music—as well as electronica, jazz, hip-hop, metal, blues, and more—but it also has amazing in-store events featuring bands such as the Decembrists, Sleater-Kinney, and Franz Ferdinand.

MUSIC MILLENNIUM/CLASSICAL MILLENNIUM
3158 East Burnside Street
(503) 231-8926

Music Millennium, a Portland institution since 1969, carries the latest releases from national, international, and local acts in every variety of music, from blues to spoken word and everything in between. The knowledgeable and friendly staff can help you find whatever you're looking for, as well as tell you about exciting in-store performances on the schedule. They also offer the widest selection of classical CDs in the entire city.

2ND AVENUE RECORDS
400 Southwest 2nd Avenue
(503) 222-3783

A voluminous outlet for all musical genres, 2nd Avenue has the biggest selection of hip-hop in town. You can also track down obscure performers on independent labels. Indie, metal, reggae, postpunk, and more are yours for the buying.

SHOES

Be sure to look in the Shopping Districts section for more great shoe stores.

BADDOLL SHOES/ODDBALL SHOES
1639 Northwest Marshall Street
(503) 525-2202, (503) 827-7800

These men's and women's shoes are some of the most cutting-edge shoes in Portland. And that's all you need to know.

HALO SHOES
1425 Northeast Broadway
(503) 331-0366

Halo features high-end shoes for fashionistas and their brothers. This cultured boutique specializes in beautiful and chic shoes from Corso Como, Fiorentini & Baker, CYDWOC, Costume National, and hard-to-find lines from around the world. Halo also carries sleek bags and other good accessories. Many of these beautiful shoes are handmade. An outstanding shoe shop, from service to selection.

IMELDA'S AND LOUIE'S SHOES
3426 Southeast Hawthorne Boulevard
(503) 233-7476

935 Northwest Everett Street
(503) 595-4970

Alluring shoes at reasonable prices—that's why stylish Portlanders seek out Imelda's and Louie's.

Kenneth Cole, Frye, Franco Sarto, Born, and Secs are some of the lines that Imelda's and Louie's carries; but also look for special handmade shoes from New York, groovy handbags, and really pretty jewelry. Everybody buys shoes here, because the collection is perfectly edited for Portland.

JOHNNY SOLE
815 Southwest Alder Street
(503) 225-1241

Johnny Sole can satisfy almost any shoe craving, from Seventh-Avenue high-fashion diva to Portland-style alternative-culture goth. Favorite lines include Diba, Giraudon, and Kenneth Cole. It's got a stand-out selection of cool yet weather-and-walking-appropriate boots. This light, spacious boutique in the heart of downtown features men's and women's lines.

NIKE TOWN
930 Southwest 6th Avenue
(503) 221-6453

If shopping were a secular religion, Portland's Nike Town, the progenitor of all other Nike Towns in the entire world, would be the Vatican. Nike Town is made of equal parts museum, gallery, temple, and store. Yes, you can buy shoes and other things here, but the real purpose of a visit is to honor the "swoosh" with generous offerings of currency and plastic. From the hip Nike-clad greeters to the spotlighted and enshrined sneakers, this is a cultural icon.

SHOEFLY SHOES
718 Northwest 11th Avenue
(503) 973-5555

This charming and attractive Pearl District store carries wonderful shoes for men and women from designers such as Cynthia Rowley, Cole Haan, and Charles David, as well as simple Keds. Plus, the staff is extra-helpful and nice.

ATTRACTIONS

Visitors come from all over to see what makes the Portland area different from other parts of the country and world. This chapter emphasizes the local and regional attractions—natural, historical, and contemporary—that define and characterize our area. Getting to these attractions is usually simple. Most are concentrated within the city center. Downtown Portland, which is encompassed in our Southwest Portland section, is agreeable for walking, and even if the weather is not entirely cooperative, the distances are relatively short. Fareless Square, a downtown zone along the bus mall (in which bus fare is free), invites visitors to join local residents on buses, MAX trains, and streetcars to get around downtown more easily. Visitors to attractions in outlying areas, such as Fort Vancouver, will depend more on cars. You can still take public transportation, but it requires more planning and commitment.

The entire Portland Metro area is an attraction, full of interesting things to watch, do, hear, and taste. During the spring and summer, expect the occasional parade, especially during the Rose Festival and on the Fourth of July, as well as street festivals, bike races, weekend runs, and even the occasional protest outside some government building. For more information about special happenings, see our Festivals and Annual Events chapter, and for other attractions, such as galleries and museums, see The Arts chapter. Additionally, if you're traveling with kids, you may want to check out the children's museums and amusement parks in the Kidstuff chapter. We have made every effort to report the most current and accurate hours and addresses. However, given the rate of change in the area, visitors are advised to call their destination beforehand to make sure the information is accurate.

Price Code

	Free
$	Less than $8
$$	$8–$16
$$$	More than $16

Prices reflect the cost of one adult admission. Most attractions have discounts for children, students, and seniors, so bring your ID.

SOUTHWEST PORTLAND

BERRY BOTANIC GARDEN $
11505 Southwest Summerville Avenue
(503) 636-4112
www.berrybot.org
Rae Selling Berry was by all accounts a legendary botanist, and her legacy lives on at the Berry Botanic Garden, the site of her estate. This garden

shouldn't be missed, especially during the spring and summer. The 6.5-acre estate features a collection of endangered plant species, the largest public rock garden on the West Coast, and major collections of lilies, native Northwest plants, and rhododendrons in settings that vary from a damp woodland to streamside plantings. The Berry Botanic Garden was the first seed bank in the nation to dedicate itself to the preservation of the flora of an entire region (the Pacific Northwest), and part of its mission is to sustain the botanical heritage of the area through an extensive research program. Classes and events are offered regularly. The garden is open by appointment every day from dawn until dusk. Because the garden is in a residential area, you'll need to call to make an appointment, but it's not difficult to get one. Also call for directions to the garden.

A recorded message will give them to you—be sure to have your pencil ready because they're delivered rapidly. Alternatively, you can look up directions on the useful Web site, which also has information about current classes and events.

HOYT ARBORETUM
4000 Southwest Fairview Boulevard
(503) 865-8733 (visitor center)
www.hoytarboretum.org

Hoyt Arboretum, which is part of Washington Park, not only provides more than 900 species of trees and shrubs to observe, but it also provides 183 acres and 10 miles of trails with striking views of the city, Mount Hood and Mount St. Helens, the Coast Range, and the rolling hills to the west, north, and east. Oaks, maples, cherry trees, Douglas fir, redwoods, blue spruce, Himalayan spruce, and bristlecone pine are but a few of the species that keep the arboretum fragrant in the spring, fresh and cool in the summer, and flushed with color during the fall. For those of us who weren't paying attention during Outdoor School, most species are labeled, and for those who want to learn more, tours are offered during the weekends from April through August. The trails do twist up and down the hills, so comfortable and sturdy footwear is suggested. A 1-mile section of the Bristlecone Trail is paved for wheelchair access and offers a good introduction to Washington Park. The grounds are open from 6:00 a.m. to 10:00 p.m. The lovely visitor center is open from 9:00 a.m. until 4:00 p.m. and until 3:00 p.m. on Saturday. It's closed on Sunday and major holidays. Admission is free.

INTERNATIONAL ROSE TEST GARDEN
400 Southwest Kingston in Washington Park
(503) 823-3636

For some residents and visitors, this park is what Portland is about. High above the city, offering an eastern view of the skyline, the Willamette River and its bridges, the snowcapped peaks of the Cascade Mountains (Mount Hood, Mount St. Helens, Mount Adams, and even Mount Rainier on some days), the Rose Test Garden is an almost obligatory stop for visitors. These appealing gardens beckon you to linger awhile, offering many summer concerts, plays, and other outdoor events in addition to lovely views. This site has been a public rose garden since 1917—it's the oldest public rose test garden in the nation. The five-acre gardens offer visitors the sight and scent of 8,000 plants representing some 500 varieties of roses, from those producing fragile miniatures to some with blossoms nearly 8 inches broad. The roses begin to bloom in May and usually reach their peak sometime in June, depending on the weather. But there will be flowers on the bushes until October, long after all but the most faithful rose fancier have gone home.

Visitors are free to wander through the gardens, admiring the flowers, inhaling the sweet fragrance, and capturing the colors on film. The rule here is simple: Look closely, breath in deeply the rose's aroma, admire, paint, photograph, and even envy the garden's bounty, but don't be tempted to pick a single stem, no matter how overcome by the passion for possession. There are no admission fees or formal operating hours, but there is a $500 fine for picking a flower. See the Portland's Parks chapter for information on other public rose gardens in Portland.

IRA KELLER MEMORIAL FOUNTAIN
Southwest 3rd Avenue and Southwest Clay Street

Named after Ira C. Keller, a self-made millionaire with a well-developed social conscience, this water sculpture with misty falls and rectilinear pools is across from the Keller Auditorium in downtown Portland. In spring and summer, downtown workers eat lunch, nap, talk with friends, read, and sun themselves to the soothing sounds of water cascading down the structure's various levels. Children splash in the cooling waters and delight in the fountain's different waterfalls, pools, concrete and metal islands and terraces, and the design's overall human scale.

Ada Louise Huxtable, the New York Times's respected architecture critic, described the fountain as "perhaps the greatest open space since the Renaissance"—no faint praise for a work of public art, especially in a city with many public spaces. There is no admission charge.

JAPANESE GARDENS $
611 Southwest Kingston Avenue
(503) 223-1321
(503) 223-9233 (for tours)
www.japanesegarden.com
A Japanese ambassador to the United States once commented that this site in Washington Park is the most beautiful and authentic Japanese garden outside of Japan. Established in 1963, the Japanese Gardens was designed by Professor Takuma Tono, a distinguished landscape and garden designer, and his achievement is remarkable, compressing five different garden spaces—the Flat Garden, the Strolling Pond Garden, a Tea Garden with a *chashitsu* (a ceremonial tea house), the Natural Garden, and the Zen-inspired Sand and Stone Garden—into little more than five acres. The trees and plants, water, and rocks here change with the season, offering visitors different perspectives of color, texture, shape, shadow, and sound throughout the year. In spring, azaleas and flowering cherry trees illuminate the garden. During the summer, flowering shrubs and annuals create dramatic spots of color contrasting with differing tones and shades of green. The varieties of graceful irises provide accents of purple to the garden's green.

In fall the garden is aflame with color as the delicate leaves of the Japanese maples turn and brilliantly burst into heated reds and oranges, yellows, and golds. Though the winter months are less flamboyant, these gardens can be restorative to your soul even during the long weeks of gray, damp days. At least once a year, a covering of snow creates an ethereal but short-lived monochromatic landscape that equals in its own right the beauty of the other seasons.

Managed by the nonprofit Japanese Garden Society of Oregon, the gardens are open daily, except on Thanksgiving, Christmas Day, and New Year's Day. Hours vary according to the season, but visitors can be assured of admission between 10:00 a.m. and 4:00 p.m. except on Mondays,

when the garden opens at 12:00 p.m. In summer the last visitors are admitted at 6:30 p.m., with the gates closing at 7:00 p.m. Guided tours are available, as well as special annual events, including a moon viewing in September, a bonsai exhibition in October, and an excellent art and gift exhibit and sale in December. A fine gift shop lists a wide range of books on Japanese art, culture, and gardens among its offerings. The Japanese Gardens, save for a few areas, is wheelchair accessible.

i The Equitable Life building, designed by renowned Portland architect Pietro Belluschi and completed in 1948, was one of the first modern glass towers, and it was a major trendsetter. It was the first building to be clad in aluminum, the first to use double-glazed windows—and the first to be completely air-conditioned. You can find it at the intersection of Southwest Stark and Southwest Washington Streets.

MULTNOMAH COUNTY LIBRARY
Central Branch
801 Southwest 10th Avenue
(503) 988-5123
www.multcolib.org
Each day of the week, thousands of citizens stream through the handsome doors of the Central Branch of the Multnomah County Library. While the library's holdings are extensive, it is no mere warehouse for books: It's a major component in the cultural life of the city. The Central Branch is an exemplary balance of intimate and public space, of cool marble and warm wood, of airy reading rooms and snug alcoves, of formal exhibits and cafe conversation. Its popularity attests to the success of this balance.

The library has dozens of programs, workshops, groups, and events that draw in visitors from all over the area. These range from lectures and roundtable discussions with regional writers to Saturday afternoon concerts to brownbag forums on stress relief to printmaking workshops. The Central Branch is dedicated to the principle of lifelong learning, and therefore offers classes, tutoring, and other resources for every age group, from senior-focused lectures and computer workshops to story times, art projects, and other child-focused events to delight small patrons. Its flourishing programs prompted Portland writer Sallie Tisdale to wonder whether the Central Branch wasn't getting too noisy. Fortunately, the Sterling Room for Writers, available by application only, can provide writers with some peace and quiet.

The Multnomah County Library is the oldest public library building west of the Mississippi. Some, but only some, of the highlights include the Beverly Cleary Children's Library (see the Kidstuff chapter), with both cozy reading nooks and high-tech media capabilities. This enchanting room recruits thousands of small new book lovers each year, sustaining their devotion as they get older with good research facilities for school reports and with splendid books, videos, and CDs to entertain them. The Henry Failing Art and Music Library contains one of the most significant sheet music collections in the nation, along with robust collections in the history of painting, photography, and handicrafts. The Meyer Memorial Trust libraries for science and business and for government documents are among the most-used collections in the library. The Grants Information Center provides the necessary data for those who would like to find financial resources for their worthy projects. The John Wilson Room houses rare books and paper-type artifacts, such as the *Nuremburg Chronicle* (dating from 1493). John Wilson was an Irishman who arrived in Oregon in 1849, and his library was the foundation for this collection devoted to, among other things, Pacific Northwest history, Native American books, children's literature, and the history of the book.

The library is open every day: Monday through Saturday, from 10:00 a.m. to 6:00 p.m., except on Tuesday and Wednesday, when it's open until 8:00 p.m.; Sunday, the library is open from noon until 5:00 p.m. Portland citizens don't like to be far from coffee, so Starbucks operates a small store, and the coffee scenting the air on the main floor adds a piquant Portland touch.

OREGON HISTORICAL SOCIETY MUSEUM $$
1200 Southwest Park Avenue
www.ohs.org

The Oregon Historical Society Museum is a fine place to begin a visit to Portland; it covers the history of Oregon from the earliest Indian civilizations through the saga of the Oregon Trail right up to the issues surrounding Portland's light rail. Before you even enter the building, the two eight-story-high trompe l'oeil murals by Richard Haas present dramatic views and symbols of Oregon's past. The West Mural, at Southwest Park Avenue and Madison Street, captures in larger-than-life scale the key members of the Lewis and Clark Expedition including Sacagawea, and her child, Baptiste; Clark's slave, York; and Seaman, the dog. The other mural, visible from Broadway and Jefferson Streets, symbolically depicts early Oregon characters, among them Native Americans, trappers, and settlers.

The Oregon Historical Society Museum, completely renovated in 2003, is neither dusty nor staid. Part museum, part research facility, it's a leading and influential force in the city and state, sponsoring seminars, workshops, festivals, and celebrations, in addition to its extensive library and its own publications. The center holds a fine collection of historical photos, documents, and artifacts. An afternoon spent here will illuminate Pacific Northwest history in surprising and engaging ways.

The museum store offers a well-chosen selection of books on Oregon and Northwest history, attractions, and personalities, many of which are written by Oregonians and other regional authors, and some of which are published by the OHS's respected press. The shop also has maps, trinkets, and jewelry, as well as an excellent selection of postcards, note cards, and prints, many produced by local artists and photographers. The Oregon Historical Society Museum is open Tuesday through Saturday from 10:00 a.m. to 5:00 p.m. On Sunday, the museum is open from noon to 5:00 p.m. The research library is open Wednesday through Saturday from 1:00 to 5:00 p.m (Tuesday, it is open to members only). There is no cost for children younger than five.

OREGON MARITIME CENTER AND
MUSEUM $
On the waterfront at the foot of Southwest
Pine Street between the Morrison and
Burnside Bridges
(503) 224-7724
www.oregonmaritimemuseum.org
This small museum, housed in a charming old stern-wheeler tug, is a treasure chest filled with artifacts, models, historic paintings, and a collection of navigational instruments recounting Oregon's seagoing history. One room details the regional shipbuilding industry during World War II, and many of the exhibits feature military craft launched in Oregon's waters. The museum includes a small gift shop with a selection of nautical items and books. The museum's hours are 11:00 a.m. to 4:00 p.m., Wednesday through Sunday.

THE OREGON ZOO $$
4001 Southwest Canyon Road
(503) 226-1561
www.oregonzoo.com
The Oregon Zoo is the newest name for a zoo originally established in 1887 with the gift to the city of an animal collection from a wealthy and idiosyncratic Portland pharmacist, Richard Knight. The Oregon Zoo has evolved from a hodgepodge of animals kept at the back of a pharmacy into a world-class research facility, offering a constantly changing mix of exhibits and other amusements. It's an internationally recognized and respected center for breeding Asian elephants, and it features an imaginative re-creation of the African rain forest. It's undergone a significant overhaul and renewal in the past few years, including a major new commitment to educating visitors about the animals of the Pacific Northwest.

The Oregon Zoo continues to make a serious effort to improve the animal habitats. As if in response to a homier atmosphere, the zoo's animal population is remarkably fertile, and the nursery is one of the most popular exhibits with adults, children, and the Portland media.

This well-liked attraction, second only to Multnomah Falls in the number of visitors it receives each year, offers a variety of other diversions that do not focus on animals. The Zoo Railway is a narrow-gauge railroad running two trains, including a replica of the 1960s streamlined Aerostar, along a route through part of the zoo, into Washington Park and the Rose Gardens. The zoo railroad has the only surviving railway post office in the country and you can amuse your friends back home by sending them mail with its unusual postmark. During Halloween and the Christmas season, the Oregon Zoo hosts many special events in which the train plays a role, such as a festival of lights, which is best seen from the train (see the Festivals and Annual Events chapter).

As you might predict, the zoo has a terrific gift shop and several restaurants and refreshment stands, including the AfriCafe, a restaurant that suggests huts found in a traditional African village.

During the summer the zoo hosts a series of concerts on a stage surrounded by terraced lawns. Many of these concerts are free with zoo admission; others cost more. The mild evenings, popular artists, and availability of catered food, regional wines and beer, and coffee combine to make these concerts into events that express the very essence of Portland. Many people bring a picnic (you can bring anything edible except alcohol into the zoo) and sprawl on blankets in the late afternoon sunshine before the music begins. Spontaneous outbursts of dancing will occur in front of the stage. It's a fine thing to see people of all ages and ways of life come together at these events; everyone loves to sit on the big lawns listening to great music under the lovely skies at twilight with friends and families.

The Oregon Zoo is open every day except Christmas Day. Gates are open from 9:00 a.m. until 6:00 p.m. from April 15 through September 15 and 9:00 a.m. to 5:00 p.m. from September 16 through April 14. There is a $1 fee for parking. The zoo stays open for an hour after the gates close, unless you're attending a special event or concert, when you can stay longer. Admission is $2.00 for everyone (except children 2 and under, who are always admitted free of charge) on the second Tuesday of each month. The zoo also features an ever-changing thrill ride for $3.00. The Zoo Railway has a separate charge of $3.00

to $4.00 for adults and $2.50 to $3.25 for kids and for seniors 65 and older, depending on the loop. By car, the zoo is best reached by a well-marked exit from westbound U.S. Highway 26 as it leaves downtown Portland. There is a light-rail station at the zoo, and ART the Cultural Bus also stops at the zoo. On summer weekends and during many concerts, parking can be particularly scarce, so light rail may be the least frustrating way to get here–plus you get $1.00 off your admission (See the Portland's Parks chapter for more information on the zoo.)

PIONEER COURTHOUSE
555 Southwest Yamhill Street
Pioneer Courthouse, the second-oldest federal building west of the Mississippi, was Portland's first restoration project back in the 1970s. Built in the late 1860s of beautiful Bellingham sandstone, the Italianate building survived ill-considered plans that would have had it demolished for a mundane office building in the 1930s, for a parking lot in the 1940s, and for a new federal office building in the 1960s. Most of the city's residents don't know it, but you can climb to the cupola of Pioneer Courthouse for a rarely seen view of the city. This is a free trip back to 1877. Hanging between the cupola's eight windows is a series of restored photos of the city in that year by a local photographer, A. H. Wulzen. Many of the photos were taken from the cupola and offer the viewer a most unusual "before and after" scene. To reach the cupola, enter the courthouse (not the Post Office on Southwest 6th Avenue) from Southwest Yamhill Street. There is a stairway to the cupola, though you may have to pass through a metal detector, the times being what they are. Admission is free.

PIONEER COURTHOUSE SQUARE
Between Broadway and Southwest 6th Avenue at Southwest Yamhill and Southwest Morrison Streets
www.pioneercourthousesquare.org
Pioneer Courthouse Square has been many things during its long life. The site was home to the city's first public schoolhouse; then home to the Portland Hotel, a massive and impressive building that was torn down, to much local dismay, to make way for a parking lot. Now, however, this wonderful piece of real estate is known as "Portland's living room" for its warm blend of red brick, park benches, flowers, sculpture, and coffee. Look at the bricks in the square's open spaces, and you'll see the inscribed names of more than 64,000 Portland residents, companies, and other Oregonians who paid $25 each to buy the bricks: The citizens of Portland rallied to install this project against some local ill will. (You can still buy a brick, but in these inflationary times, the price has gone up to $100.)

By the early 1970s, downtown Portland was choking on its own traffic, and stores and other businesses were fleeing to the suburbs where parking was easier and the surroundings less threatening, if more bland. Instead of prolonged municipal hand-wringing, Portland ripped up a freeway, tore up almost the entire downtown, and invited pedestrians back into the city's core with a transit mall and free bus rides, wider sidewalks, trees, flower-filled planters, public art, and a squad of uniformed workers paid to keep the streets and sidewalks clean, give directions to visitors, and prevent crime by simply being visible and pleasant. The result has been one of the most honored urban renaissance projects in the nation, and Pioneer Courthouse Square is its epicenter. Food vendors, a flower stand, a Starbucks, and public restrooms add to the charm, and the city's light-rail system runs on two sides of the square, making it accessible to everyone. The Portland Oregon Visitor Association and TriMet both have major offices here, along with maintaining rooms for meetings and other occurrences, and a new facility, Ticket Central, allows people to buy tickets for events around town.

One thing about the decor of Portland's living room: It can surprise you. The square attracts diverse crowds that tolerate and even amuse each other and who, with very rare exception, get along quite well, illustrating the city's acceptance of individuality. Expect to see street musicians, jugglers, pierced and tattooed teenagers, and street people with their studded leather jackets, army surplus camouflage, and assortments of pet dogs, snakes, kittens, and birds—in addition, of course, to tourists, students, and city office workers strolling about. The Weather Machine, a piece of whimsical but functional sculpture, informs passersby of the weather: A blue heron means mist and drizzle, a golden sun goddess predicts clear skies, and a copper dragon warns of approaching storms, heavy rain, and winds. The square is open to all at no charge.

Pioneer Square hosts an unending series of special events (see the Festivals and Annual Events chapter), including contests, cultural festivals, a giant civic Christmas tree, a yuletide tuba concert, a sand castle contest, officially sanctioned skateboarding competitions, and anything else residents can get approved.

PITTOCK MANSION $
3229 Southwest Pittock Drive
(503) 823-3624
www.pittockmansion.com
Henry Pittock, founder of the *Oregonian*, the city's daily newspaper and the largest paper in the state, built himself a château 1,000 feet above the city. The mansion stayed in the family for 50 years, until 1964, when it was sold to the city of Portland. This 22-room, 16,000-square-foot, antiques- and art-filled house is now open to the public. Guided tours of the house are offered each afternoon, and visitors can wander through the gardens of roses, azaleas, and rhododendrons. In spring, flowering cherry trees add their color to the grounds. The view is spectacular. The adjoining Pittock Acres offer hiking and walking trails and are part of the Audubon Society's Wildlife Preserve.

The mansion's gatehouse, which once was the gardener's cottage, is now the Gate Lodge, and it is part of the museum complex. The Pittock Mansion is open for public viewing seven days a week from 11:00 a.m. to 4:00 p.m., except in July and August, when it opens at 10:00 a.m. The mansion is closed on major holidays, for a few days in late November when holiday decorations are being put up, and during January for annual maintenance. The Pittock Mansion is often rented by businesses, private groups, and families for dinners, receptions, meetings, and weddings, but these events are limited to evening hours.

POLICE HISTORICAL MUSEUM JUSTICE CENTER
1111 Southwest 2nd Avenue
(503) 823-0019
www.portlandpolicemuseum.com
You may not want to know the motives of some of the other people visiting here with you, but don't miss this small museum, which highlights the fascinating history of crime and punishment.

The museum displays a retired police motorcycle, a working traffic signal, a collection of badges, uniforms, weapons, handcuffs, and other tools of the trade representing both sides of the cops-and-robbers paradigm. There is also a great collection of historical photos. Current and retired Portland police officers make up the volunteer staff, so mind your manners. Entry to the museum is free, though donations are welcome. The museum is open Tuesday through Friday, from 10:00 a.m. to 3:00 p.m. There's also a gift shop. If you're over 18 you'll need some photo ID since it is, actually, in the building that houses the city jail.

PORTLAND ART MUSEUM $$
1219 Southwest Park Avenue
(503) 226-2811
www.pam.org
The Portland Art Museum, the oldest museum in the Pacific Northwest, has become an attraction with new dimensions, an attraction that extends beyond the allure of the Pietro Belluschi–designed building and the art within it. The museum has gained much attention for its major exhibitions and even more major fund-raising capabilities. The results have been impressive: After an extensive expansion, the museum now has the space for new galleries, educational facilities, a multimedia room, an appealing public sculpture garden, and a cafe. This new wealth of space has allowed the museum to better feature its important collections in Northwest and Native American art and in European painting,

as well as creating space for recent acquisitions. (In 2000 the museum procured the collection of the distinguished New York art critic Clement Greenberg.) But the museum has also become a lively force in the cultural life of the city, enlisting young patrons in its philanthropic drives, arranging family programs, sponsoring lectures and evening events, and generally making a big splash. Hours are Tuesday, Wednesday, and Saturday, 10:00 a.m. to 5:00 p.m.; Sunday from noon to 5:00 p.m.; Thursday and Friday the museum is open until 8:00 p.m. Reduced ticket prices are available for children and seniors. For more information see The Arts chapter.

PORTLAND BUILDING
1120 Southwest 5th Avenue

Completed in 1984, this wonderful, controversial, 15-story building still evokes potent reactions from local, regional, and national architects, designers, critics, local politicians making some point about public spending and public art, and almost everyone who views it. Designed by Michael Graves as the first public building in a postmodern style in the United States, the colorful Portland Building houses an administrative wing of Portland city government, next door to Portland City Hall, so between 8:00 a.m. and 5:00 p.m. you can walk around the lobby and other public areas where local artists' works are on display. On the second floor there is a display detailing the building's design and construction as well as information about the equally controversial but now-beloved statue of *Portlandia*, looming over the street from a three-story ledge.

Portlandia was installed in 1985 after being barged up the Willamette River and trucked through downtown. This large, hammered-copper statue, which is second in size only to the more traditional *Statue of Liberty*, represents a modern mythological incarnation or descendant of Lady Commerce, the classic female figure on the city of Portland's official seal. With strong, 9-foot-long thighs and a plunging bronze decolletage, *Portlandia* has been called heroic, revealing, X-rated, and even "statuesque." While some still dissatisfied citizens want her relocated to

a more (or less) visible location, the statue was designed for this location. She will remain where she is. There is no admission charge.

i Portland has a comparatively large requirement for public art (2 percent of publically funded projects). The Portland Building is a great place to begin to see it; there you'll find a short exhibit on the public art program, as well as a map with a walking tour. The map is also available from the Regional Arts & Culture Council (www .racc.org/publicart).

PORTLAND CITY HALL
1221 Southwest 4th Avenue

Portland City Hall, built in 1895, underwent extensive renovation during the late 1990s. This ambitious project not only restored this Italianate building's original floor plan and reestablished its original look and feel but also preserved one of the most historically important buildings in the city. While the building retains much of its traditional appearance on the outside, its infrastructure is modern and energy-efficient. The building has also been made more accessible to the public, and a number of very Portland touches have been added, including a coffee bar, a secured bicycle parking shelter, and a rose garden that replaced a small, inefficient parking lot. The renovation has also restored natural light, air, and color to the interior of the building by uncovering the original skylights, by refurbishing the beautiful woodwork and floor tiles, and by ripping out walls that had enclosed the stairwells, exposing the decorative copper plating that had once adorned them.

City Hall displays a number of artworks commissioned for the building, adding to the city's growing inventory of public art. On the northwest side of the first floor, you will find the "Evolution of a City," a television screen display of photos taken over the past 100 years of all parts of the city. Created and produced by two local artists, the installation presents a series of high-resolution digital images of the archival photographs. In addition to the photographs, works from the city's special collection, the "Visual Chronicle of Portland," are displayed in the lobby on the first floor. This collection of works on paper was established in 1985 and is continually updated; each work renders the artist's view of the distinctive characteristics of Portland. As you wander through the building, you will find other works of art, permanently or temporarily displayed, and if you are there on the first Thursday of each month, you will find the opening of a new exhibit featuring a local artist from 5.00 to 7:00 p.m. The friendly folks at the Information Desk can help you find out about all the art. City Hall is open from 6:00 a.m. to 7:00 p.m. Monday through Friday. Admission is free.

i For a wackier side of Portland art, visit Velveteria. This small museum features highlights from a collection of more than 1,000 velvet paintings featuring Elvis, tropical cuties, clowns, and other staples of the genre. Find them at 2448 East Burnside Avenue (503-233-5100 or www.velveteria.com). They are open Friday through Sunday from noon to 5:00 p.m. Admission is $5. It's very Portland.

PORTLAND VINTAGE TROLLEY
Lloyd Center/Downtown Transit Mall
Portland's Vintage Trolley uses four oak-paneled replicas of the city's now discarded Council Crest Streetcars. You can catch the trolley on any MAX stop from the Galleria to Lloyd Center or along the Portland Streetcar routes. The trolley's schedule of operations varies with the season, but in general, trolleys run on Sunday from March through December, from noon to 6:30 p.m. The ride is free, donations welcome. (See the Getting Here, Getting Around chapter for more information.)

TOM MCCALL WATERFRONT PARK
Bordering Naito Parkway and the
Willamette River from Broadway Bridge
south to River Place
If Pioneer Courthouse Square is Portland's living room, then the Tom McCall Waterfront Park is the city's front yard. The park starts at the Broadway Bridge, stretches south for about 2 miles and then converts into a portion of the Greenway, a path continuing south to Willamette Park, a total distance of 3.25 miles. Once an ugly freeway cut off the downtown from the Willamette River. Led by Governor Tom McCall, planners came up with the Downtown Plan of 1972, which included the removal of the freeway and the creation of open space that would again reunite the city and river. This space would eventually be named Tom McCall Waterfront Park for the Oregon governor who was instrumental in restoring the space to the public. Portlanders have adopted the park with such fervor that it is in danger of being loved to death by an unending series of events, including the Rose Festival Fun Center, the Bite, Brewers' Festival, Cinco de Mayo, Blues Festival, Fourth of July fireworks, and the Race for the Cure (see the Portland's Parks chapter for more on this park and the Festivals and Annual Events chapter for more on these special outings). The city installed hardier sod, improved drainage, and made other changes to help the park bear the wear and tear of all these festivities.

Center stage for Waterfront Park is the Salmon Street Springs Fountain at the foot of Southwest Salmon Street. In hot weather, this fountain, with its spurting jets of water, attracts crowds of adults and children who play and splash in the streams of water and the shallow pool. The dock for the *Portland Spirit*, an excursion boat offering cruises on the Willamette, is also nearby.

The Waterfront Story Garden, a lighthearted cobblestone and granite monument to storytellers, is one of a small number of memorials. Another is the Japanese American Historical Plaza, sometimes referred to as the Garden of Stones. This solemn memorial is best walked from south to north. Along the memorial's formal plaza are stones, some broken, some cut, some shattered, to represent the disrupted lives of 110,000 Japanese Americans interned in camps throughout the western United States during World War II. The stones are carved with inscriptions in English (quotations from Oregonians of Japanese ancestry who were interned) and in Japanese (often written in Japan's unique poetry, haiku). Farther north, near the Steel Bridge, is the Friendship Circle. This sculpture emits the sounds of a Japanese flute and drum and honors the Sister City relationship between Portland and Sapporo, Japan.

Across from the Oregon Maritime Museum is the battleship *USS Oregon* monument. The *Oregon,* known as "McKinley's Bull-dog" because of its role in the Spanish-American War, was a turn-of-the-20th-century battleship launched in 1893. Between the two world wars, the *Oregon* was tied up along the sea wall at the foot of Southwest Jefferson Street as a memorial and museum, but in 1942, as a patriotic gesture, the ship was returned to the U.S. Navy. One of the ship's masts was removed before she was reclaimed by the navy, and it is that battleship-gray mast from which the American and Oregon flags fly along the river.

The final monument along Waterfront Park is, unfortunately, little noted. In a tribute to the staff of the Canadian Embassy in Tehran, Iran, who helped a number of American diplomats and their families escape during the yearlong Iran Hostage Crisis, a small group of Portlanders commissioned a plaque honoring their bravery. The monument is often overlooked and at times is not well maintained, but it is a heartfelt tribute to the quiet bravery of the Canadian diplomatic corps and the Canadian nation.

VIETNAM VETERANS MEMORIAL
World Forestry Center
4033 Southwest Canyon Road
Oregon's tribute to its Vietnam veterans sits on 11 acres of land in the southwest corner of Hoyt Arboretum, above the World Forestry Center. The Vietnam Veterans Memorial honors the 57,000 Oregonians who served in Southeast Asia, listing by name and date of death the state's nearly 800 known dead and still missing. The memorial puts those deaths in a historical context by including references to state, national, and international events occurring at the same time. The site is reverent, graceful, and solemn, and often the only sounds are those of quiet footsteps, the wind,

and the hum of distant traffic. As at the national memorial in Washington, D.C., visitors often find personal remembrances—military insignia, campaign ribbons and medals, faded pictures, flowers, toys, candles, photos of sons and daughters, grandsons and granddaughters—left near a name. Each Memorial Day, an honor guard of ROTC cadets from the University of Portland stands a silent 24-hour guard at the memorial. The ceremony and vigil ends with all the names of the dead being read aloud, to show they are not forgotten, and with the haunting sounds of taps echoing through the trees and hills. The monument is open for viewing during daylight hours. No admission is charged.

WASHINGTON PARK
Southwest Park Place at Southwest Vista Avenue
(503) 823-7529
Washington Park is set on 546 acres on the city's West Hills, where it overlooks downtown Portland and east beyond into the mountains. It is the home of the Oregon Zoo, the World Forestry Center, the Japanese Garden, the Children's Museum, and the Rose Gardens. All these attractions are within walking distance of one another, if you're a sturdy walker. The Zoo, Forestry Center, and Children's Museum are right off the MAX stop, and the Japanese and Rose Gardens are about a mile away along the roads or trails of Washington Park. You can also take the zoo train, which has a station at the Rose Gardens, or the TriMet #63 buses that traverse the park and back to town. (You can also take ART the Cultural Bus. ART is a propane-powered bus painted by Henk Pander, one of Portland's best-known artists.)

The simplest way to the park is a clearly marked exit from westbound US 26 as it leaves downtown Portland and climbs over the West Hills toward Beaverton (follow the exit signs that say OREGON ZOO and WORLD FORESTRY CENTER). This highway is easily accessible (and well marked) from Interstate 5 via Interstate 405. Visitors coming from Portland's Eastside can use either the Fremont Bridge or the Marquam Bridge. If you're downtown already, the two easiest ways to enter Washington Park Place are via Southwest Vista Avenue above PGE Park or close to the intersection of Burnside Street and Northwest 23rd Avenue, at the Uptown Shopping Center. This entrance is the most convenient from Northwest Portland.

This is one of Portland's most popular parks. On summer weekends, especially during the Rose Festival, and during any special event or concert in the park, traffic can be vicious and parking all but impossible. Seriously consider light rail, bus, or even a cab or town car as an alternative to driving. See the listing in the Portland's Parks chapter for more information.

WILLAMETTE SHORE TROLLEY $$
Southwest Bancroft and Moody
(just west of the Old Spaghetti Factory) and
State Street Terminal
311 State Street, Lake Oswego
(503) 697-7436
www.trainweb.org/oerhs/wst.htm
A ride on the Willamette Shore Trolley between Portland and Lake Oswego or the reverse offers a different perspective on the river and several Portland neighborhoods. The trolley runs on a once-abandoned track between Macadam Avenue and the river; it provides riders with close-up views of close-in east-bank neighborhoods, river traffic, residential and commercial development at Johns Landing in Southwest Portland, and some nice riverfront homes in Lake Oswego.

You may notice that the trolley pulls or pushes a small vehicle, called a donkey, which generates power for the electric motor: There are no wires along the route, so the trolley has to create its own power. The Lake Oswego station is downtown, in a section with galleries, shops, restaurants, and coffee shops within walking distance. The actual streetcar used for the trip may vary: In the past, the trip has used an Australian streetcar; a double-decker Blackpool tram from the United Kingdom is now on the tracks. During December the trolley makes some evening runs for riders to view the Parade of Boats, Portland's annual display of decorated and illuminated boats. During the spring and summer, the trolley runs from Lake Oswego at 10:00 a.m., noon,

2:00 p.m., and 4:00 p.m., and from Portland at 11:00 a.m. and 1:00, 3:00, and 5:00 p.m., Thursday through Sunday. On Friday and Saturday there is an extra run from Lake Oswego at 6:00 p.m. and from Portland—a one-way trip—at 7:00 p.m.

WORLD FORESTRY CENTER MUSEUM $
4033 Southwest Canyon Road
(503) 228-1367
www.worldforestry.org
Before Oregon's Silicon Forest, there were real forests where giant trees were felled by handsaws and axes, hauled or floated to mills, and then cut and finished to build the nation's houses and factories. Built by a consortium of timber and related industries, the World Forestry Center Museum offers information and hands-on exhibits emphasizing the forests of the Pacific Northwest and beyond. There are exhibits of petrified wood and a sculpture of a tiger carved from a 1,000-year-old tree for the 1988 Olympics. An intriguing 70-foot talking Douglas fir tree is designed to interest children as it explains to them how it grows. There are also adventure rides—a white-water "rafting" trip and a 45-foot lift up into the tree canopy (these carry small extra charges beyond the price of admission).

The Forestry Center also hosts a range of special activities, including an annual show featuring Oregon woodworkers and carvers and an exhibit of wooden toys. A gallery features rotating exhibits of photography and other art. The Forest Store, the center's gift shop, offers wooden gifts and other items in keeping with the forest theme. The World Forestry Center Museum is open daily from 9:00 a.m. to 5:00 p.m. Parking will set you back $1 per car.

NORTHWEST PORTLAND

OREGON JEWISH MUSEUM $
310 Northwest Davis Street
(503) 226-3600
www.ojm.org
The Oregon Jewish Museum lives at Montgomery Park, once the huge warehouse for Montgomery Ward but now remodeled for office

space. The museum, which is the only institution in the Pacific Northwest devoted to Jewish history and culture, features an archival library with papers and oral histories about the history of Jews in Oregon, permanent exhibits, and changing exhibits of Jewish history both in Oregon and throughout the world. Call for more information or to make an appointment to visit the museum. The museum is open Tuesday through Friday from 10:30 a.m. to 3:00 p.m., and on Sunday from 1:00 to 4:00 p.m.

PORTLAND AUDUBON SOCIETY SANCTUARY
5151 Northwest Cornell Road
(503) 292-6855
www.audubonportland.org
The Portland Audubon Society, a nonprofit group with a long and established concern about Oregon's ecology and wildlife, has worked closely with government agencies to further protect Oregon's natural beauty. A leading example is the Audubon Sanctuary, a 160-acre tract surrounded by Forest Park, a 5,000-acre municipal park, and linked to that park's Wildwood and Macleary Trails. Most visitors arrive by car not only to walk the trails and spot birds, but also to visit the Wildlife Care Center. Here injured owls, hawks, herons, cranes, and other birds and waterfowl are cared for until they can be returned to the wild.

Audubon House includes one of the best selections of books on natural history and wildlife. There is also an interpretive center, a nature store, and a viewing window overlooking the feeding platforms for resident songbirds. Hours for the sanctuary and gift shop are 10:00 a.m. to 6:00 p.m. Monday through Saturday and 10:00 a.m. to 5:00 p.m. on Sunday. There is no admission charge to visit the sanctuary.

PORTLAND CLASSICAL CHINESE GARDEN $
Northwest 3rd Avenue and Everett Street
(503) 228-8131
www.portlandchinesegarden.org
The exquisite Portland Classical Chinese Garden, more formally known as the "Garden of Awakening Orchids," is a double-walled oasis built in a traditional Chinese style with extensive help from Portland's Chinese sister city Suzhou. It inhabits a city block at the north end of Chinatown and serves as a retreat from the chaos of urban life. But it's more than a retreat. The garden integrates the elements of water, stone, light, shadow, color, texture, and fragrance to form an enclosed small world that mysteriously feels as though it unfurls the entire universe within its walls.

Mysteries are at the soul of this place, but its physical existence is due to attentive design and careful building. Clever planning makes good use of views and space; you would never know from the outside that the garden holds a lake of 8,000 square feet, and from the inside, it's hard to remember that the sidewalk is 12 feet away. You enter through a series of courtyards designed to help you make the transition from the outer world of hurry and work and wander along paths, over bridges, beside water, and through rooms with enticing names like "Celestial House of Permeating Fragrance" or "Reflections in Clear Ripples." Similarly, pavilions are named after the meditations they are meant to inspire—"Flowers Bathing in Spring Rain" or "Painted Boat in Misty Rain." The Tower of Cosmic Reflections is a tea house run by Portland's Tao of Tea (traditional Chinese tea and snacks).

Within each discrete space is a carefully arranged display of stones, trees, shrubs, flowers, or other components. Classical Chinese gardens, unlike the gardens of the emperor, were built by gentlemen scholars for their own use, so their scale is small, focusing on the well-wrought detail. No pebble is insignificant. Latticed windows give sunshine a template to decorate the elaborate mosaic floors. Banana plants live underneath the rain gutters to allow a beautiful sound to permeate the garden when it rains and the water splashes onto them. Rocks left in Suzhou streams 60 years ago by grandparents to be naturally sculpted by the water have been harvested by grandchildren and placed with delicate care. All five senses are honored in the feel of the stones, the fragrant blossoms, the sound of water, the taste of tea in the tea house, and the sight of, well, everything.

The deliberate re-creation of nature's spontaneous workings—the Chinese garden is meant to inspire you to think about this paradox and others like it. For the scholars who possessed them—scholars who today would be bureaucrats or businessmen—gardens were places of freedom from the pressure and constraints of official life, where their owners could meditate upon the paradoxes of the freedom found in duty or the nature found in culture. One reason the Chinese Garden is powerful is that such paradoxes are not foreign to us moderns. We buy cars and houses in order to be free but then must slave away to pay for the houses and cars.

It is easy to enjoy the garden on your own, but if you want to learn more about its history, traditions, and symbolism, we strongly recommend taking one of the tours. The garden is open daily, from 10:00 a.m. to 5:00 p.m., November through March, and from 9:00 a.m. to 6:00 p.m., April through September. Public tours are offered at noon and 1:00 p.m., and private tours can be arranged. The garden is wheelchair accessible.

UNION STATION
800 Northwest 6th Avenue
(503) 273-4865

The neon GO BY TRAIN sign on the tower of Portland's Union Station harkens back to an earlier era of travel, but this large brick building still plays a key role in the city's transportation network. Amtrak trains on long-distance journeys stop at Union Station, heading for Seattle, Chicago, San Francisco, and Los Angeles, and there are daily, super-modern trains to Seattle that contrast with the old-fashioned setting of the station itself. A visit to Union Station is an exercise in nostalgia, with its massive, dark ticket counter, its echoing marble floors and walls, and its majestically high ceilings. There is a small snack shop in the station offering microwave meals, soft drinks, sandwiches, postcards, trinket souvenirs, and T-shirts; outside the snack shop are quaint paintings of railway scenes. Next to the waiting area is Wilfs, a long-established restaurant and lounge. With its Victorian red-flocked walls and terrific piano bar, it has drawn an eclectic crowd for lunch, dinner,

and evening drinks for most of this century. On a damp, rainy Portland night, an Irish coffee at Wilfs, savored while listening to the pianist, is good for the soul.

SOUTHEAST PORTLAND

CRYSTAL SPRINGS RHODODENDRON GARDEN $
Southeast 28th Avenue
(1 block north of Woodstock Boulevard)
(503) 823-3640

Long periods of gray days create a great appreciation for color in many Oregonians. You can see this in the well-tended public and private gardens that celebrate the coming of spring and summer with tulips, lilacs, daffodils, azaleas, magnolias, roses, and rhododendrons. Beginning in April Oregonians flock to the seven-acre Crystal Springs Rhododendron Garden to savor the brilliant colors of the garden's 2,500 rhododendrons, azaleas, and other plants. While spring is prime time here, the gardens are a delight at any time of the year. In the fall, the Japanese maples and sourwood trees burst into flame, a defiant gesture against the coming monotones of winter. A spring-fed lake attracts a permanent colony of ducks and other waterfowl, not to mention the area's population of birders. Even when the seasons' colors have peaked, the garden attracts visitors looking for solitude and a temporary respite from urban life.

From the first of March through Labor Day, on Tuesday and Wednesday admission fees are waived. Adult admission is $3 the rest of the time. Children are always free. The park is open from dawn to dusk. (For further information see the Portland's Parks chapter.)

KIDD'S TOY MUSEUM
1301 Southeast Grand Avenue
(at Main Street)
(503) 233-7807

The bumper sticker proclaiming "whoever dies with the most toys wins" may have been inspired by Kidd's Toy Museum. This world-class collection of toys, particularly toy cars and other transportation vehicles, originated as one person's hobby gone wild for more than 25 years. The collection also includes toy trains and planes, railroad items, police badges, and a range of mechanical banks. To preserve the collection, the owner created a museum that is open to the public free of charge. The Kidd's Toy Museum is closed on Sunday and open Monday through Friday from 9:00 a.m. until 5:30 p.m. and from 9:00 a.m. until 1:00 p.m. on Saturday.

LEACH BOTANICAL GARDEN
6704 Southeast 122nd Avenue
(503) 823-9503
www.leachgarden.org
Beginning in the 1930s, Lila and John Leach, two amateur botanists, started their five-acre garden along Southeast Portland's Johnson Creek. Credited with discovering 11 new species of Northwest plants, the Leaches eventually grew their garden to include some 14 acres. More than 1,500 species of native ferns, wildflowers, shrubs, and irises contentedly grow in the garden. Rock gardens, bog gardens, and an experimental recycling and composting center have recently been added. The garden is open Sunday from 1:00 until 4:00 p.m. and Tuesday through Saturday from 9:00 a.m. until 4:00 p.m. Admission is free. (Also see the entry in the Portland's Parks chapter.)

OAKS AMUSEMENT PARK $$
Southeast Spokane Street at the east end of the Sellwood Bridge on the Willamette River
(503) 233-5777
www.oakspark.com
Oaks Park is a throwback to the days when streetcar companies built amusement parks to stimulate ridership. Originally opened in 1905, Oaks Park has survived the demise of the streetcars (and may yet witness their rebirth), the introduction of television and video games, and several floods to amuse and entertain yet another generation of Portlanders. This isn't Disneyland and it isn't high-tech. Nevertheless, the old-fashioned rides such as the Screaming Eagle and the Tilt-a-Whirl, as well as gentler teacups and merry-go-rounds, are still irresistible.

Besides the games of skill and chance, Oaks Park offers a sedately scary tunnel of love, a giant slide, and a small roller coaster. New rides are in the works, as well as the remodeling of some of the creaky buildings. Picnic tables and fireplaces are available for family use, and there are no rules prohibiting bringing in your own food. The usual amusement park menu of cotton candy and deep-fried "food-on-a-stick" refreshments are also offered. The park's roller-skating rink clearly harkens back to a different era of entertainment, but it is still very popular. It is one of the oldest continuously operating roller rinks in the country and the only one with a live Wurlitzer organ. (Skate rentals are available.) The park is open throughout the year, but its high season is clearly during the summer. It also sponsors Fourth of July fireworks, weather permitting. For more information, refer to the Kidstuff chapter. Gate admission is free, but rides, games, and roller-skating carry fees.

OREGON MUSEUM OF SCIENCE AND INDUSTRY (OMSI) $$
1945 Southeast Water Avenue
(503) 797-6674
www.omsi.edu
One of the most popular attractions in Oregon and one of the five largest science museums in the nation, the Oregon Museum of Science and Industry is really a series of very different exhibits and elements. OMSI is a hands-on museum where visitors, especially children, are encouraged to touch things, try experiments, and question why things happen.

Adults and children alike will enjoy the presentations in the large-screen OMNIMAX theater and the variety of programs in the Murdock Sky Theater, a domed theater for programs on astronomy. The core of the museum is a series of specialized exhibit halls, each with a different emphasis and exhibits. The Earth Science Hall shakes things up with its realistic Earthquake Room. In addition to its permanent exhibits, OMSI offers an exciting array of temporary exhibits— among them was Body Worlds 3, a fascinating exhibit in which plastinated human and mammalian bodies were displayed to show their inner workings. Other exhibits present information about natural phenomena and allow visitors to discover the complex interrelationships of the earth's seemingly unrelated elements. The Life Science Hall focuses on human growth in the fullest sense of the term and includes a house and an office illustrating designs for accessible living and assisting technology. At the Information Science Hall, visitors can beam a personal message into the vastness of space and receive information on the knowledge and skills that created technology as we know it and that constantly expand it.

While there is a separate admission charge for *USS Blueback,* the U.S. Navy's last diesel-powered submarine, visitors should not miss a tour of this vessel. The *Blueback* tour lasts 40 minutes, and visitors should carefully read the "Tips for *USS Blueback* Visitors" brochure before buying a ticket. This is a real submarine, with confined spaces, no windows, and no onboard restrooms; access is by ladders instead of stairs. Children must be at least four years old and 36 inches tall to tour the submarine.

OMSI is closed Monday except when a public school holiday falls on a Monday. During the school year it is open Tuesday through Sunday 9:30 a.m. until 5:30 p.m., except for Sunday, when it is open from 9:30 a.m. until 7:00 p.m. Summer hours are Monday through Sunday 9:30 a.m. to 7:00 p.m. During the year, OMSI offers a variety of camps, classes, field trips, and special programs for students, adults, and families. The facility has an ATM, a cafe, and vending machines. Not surprisingly, there is a large, well-stocked gift shop with a wide range of science-oriented objects, toys, T-shirts, games, and books. There is also an OMSI Science Store in the Washington Square Shopping Center in Beaverton. Parking is free.

NORTH/NORTHEAST PORTLAND

THE GROTTO $
Northeast 85th Avenue and Sandy Boulevard
(503) 254-7371
www.thegrotto.org

This long-established, 62-acre Catholic sanctuary is an oasis in Portland's urban cityscape. The Grotto is both a religious shrine and a garden. Staffed by the Servites, or the Order of the Servants of Mary, the grounds include lush groves of towering fir trees, ferns, rhododendrons, and other native plants. Our Lady's Grotto, a rock cave carved into the base of a 110-foot-high granite cliff sheltering a marble replica of Michelangelo's Pieta, is the central attraction. The Grotto's upper level contains well-tended gardens, streams, and ponds while offering incredible views of the Columbia River Gorge, Mount St. Helens, and the Cascades. The Meditation Chapel features a floor-to-ceiling glass wall with a panoramic view of the Columbia River, and on a clear day, Mount St. Helens and Mount Adams. A Servite Monastery, a Peace Garden, and an interesting collection of wood sculpture are also within the Grotto's boundaries. Parking is free. During Christmas, the Grotto takes on a seasonal air, and crowds come to see the story of the nativity told with cleverly arranged lights. A small fee is charged for admission to this "Festival of Lights." The Grotto is open seven days a week from 9:00 a.m. until 8:00 p.m., and in the winter from 9:00 a.m. until 5:30 p.m.

VANCOUVER

Vancouver's diverse attractions range from the restoration of original Fort Vancouver and Officers Row to the Ridgefield Wildlife Refuge. While Vancouver shares the Columbia River with Portland, the city is historic and vibrant in its own right. The area code for all attractions in Vancouver and Southwest Washington is 360, and it's always a long-distance call from Portland.

CLARK COUNTY HISTORICAL MUSEUM $
1511 Main Street
(360) 993-5679
www.cchmuseum.org
A good starting place for a visit to Vancouver, the museum displays a range of historical artifacts relating to the founding and growth of the area. Additional displays and exhibits document the original Native American residents of the region.

There is also an exhibit detailing how the expansion of the railroads across the country and along the Pacific Coast changed the area's economy, population, and contact with the rest of the nation. The museum is open all year (except on major holidays) Tuesday through Saturday from 11:00 a.m. until 4:00 p.m.

HENRY J. KAISER SHIPYARD MEMORIAL
In Marine Park on Boat Launch Road at the end of Marine Drive
(360) 619-1111
During World War II, the Henry J. Kaiser Shipyards in Vancouver and Portland turned out 140 Liberty ships, T-2 Tankers, and escort carriers ("baby flat-tops") for the war effort. The city of Vanport, north of Portland, was built to house the 38,000 workers who migrated to the region from throughout the country to build the ships. The workforce included a large number of African Americans who were recruited in the South and brought to Oregon and Washington by the trainload. The descendants of these workers who stayed after the war formed the core of the area's African-American population, which added to the region's cultural diversity.

The shipyards closed shortly after the end of the war and Vanport was destroyed in a postwar flood. Now, only faint traces of the shipyard's wooden ways remain along the river. The three-story Henry J. Kaiser Shipyard Memorial and Interpretive Center recognizes and honors the contributions of these workers not only to the Allied victory in World War II, but also for their continuing contributions to the region's culture and economy. Admission is free. (For more on Vanport and shipbuilding during the war years, see the History chapter.)

ESTHER SHORT PARK
6th Street and Columbia Drive
(360) 619-1111
This five-acre site is the state's oldest public square and includes the Victorian Rose Gardens and the 1867 Slocum House, an Italianate structure that is one of the few remaining buildings from Vancouver's earliest residential neighborhoods.

Moved from its original site during an urban renewal project, the Slocum House now serves as a theater. With downtown Vancouver experiencing a period of renaissance and revitalization, this park, with its gardens and Victorian-era benches, fountains, and lights, serves as an anchor to the city's past.

FORT VANCOUVER NATIONAL HISTORIC SITE $
1501 East Evergreen Boulevard
(360) 696-7655, ext. 10
www.nps.gov/fova
Fort Vancouver was originally built by the British not only as a fur-trading center, but also as an attempt to solidify Britain's claim to the entire Northwest Territory. One of 34 such forts the Hudson's Bay Company built, Fort Vancouver became an American outpost in 1846 when a treaty between the United States and Britain established the 49th parallel as Canada's southern border. Now restored and administered by the National Park Service, Fort Vancouver offers a look at frontier life through a range of restored buildings, exhibits and displays, and re-creations.

Adjacent to Fort Vancouver National Historic Site sits Vancouver Barracks, the first military post in the Oregon Territory. From this base, Americans explored Alaska, fought the Indian Wars, provided security to settlers, and developed an early network of roads, dams, and locks. From May 1849 to the present, Vancouver Barracks has been an active military post. To the north of the Fort Vancouver National Historic Site and just across a vast parklike green is Officers Row, an immaculately restored and rare collection of 21 Victorian-era homes built between 1850 and 1906 by the federal government. The houses were the residences for the military officers and other government officials and their families assigned to Fort Vancouver, Vancouver Barracks, and the army's Department of the Columbia. Homes such as these were once common on American military bases, but this is the only entire Officers Row preserved in the nation. Among the army officers who lived on Officers Row were Generals Phillip Sheridan, Benjamin

Bonneville, and Omar Bradley. Guests at Officers Row included three U.S. presidents: Ulysses S. Grant, Rutherford B. Hayes, and Franklin Delano Roosevelt. This site is open from 9:00 a.m. to 4:00 p.m. daily during winter and 9:00 a.m. to 5:00 p.m. during summer.

THE GEORGE C. MARSHALL HOUSE
1301 Officers Row
(360) 693-3103

This Officers Row house, now called the George C. Marshall House, was the home for the commanding officer of Vancouver Barracks. Originally built in 1886 and now completely restored and furnished with antiques from the 1880s, the house is home to the local office of Washington's governor. General Marshall, who was awarded the Nobel Peace Prize in 1953, served as Vancouver Barracks' commanding officer from 1936 to 1938 and lived in the house during that period. In 1937 Marshall opened his home to the three Russian fliers who landed at Pearson Airfield after their transpolar flight. The building was later renamed to honor his service to the nation as the U.S. Army's Chief of Staff during World War II and later as Secretary of Defense and Secretary of State. The George C. Marshall House is open seven days a week, except for major holidays, from 9:00 a.m. to 5:00 p.m. There is no charge.

THE GRANT HOUSE
1101 Officers Row
(360) 693-1727

The Grant House is the oldest building on Officers Row and was named after Ulysses S. Grant. Prior to his work winning the Civil War and serving as a U.S. president, Grant was the base quartermaster. In 1879 he returned for a visit and to reminisce over his time at Fort Vancouver—which did not include staying in this house, since it was built after he served here. Nevertheless, it is an interesting building.. The Grant House, which is open Monday through Saturday from 11:00 a.m. to 5:00 p.m. and Sunday 10:00 a.m. to 2:00 p.m., now sees action as the Grant House Folk Art Center. In addition to exhibits of American and Northwestern folk art, there is a gift gallery featuring work of regional artists, and Sheldon's Cafe. There is no admission fee to the Grant House, but donations are accepted.

PEARSON AIR MUSEUM AT
PEARSON AIRFIELD $
1115 East 5th Street
(360) 694-7026
www.pearsonairmuseum.org

At the east end of the Fort Vancouver National Historic Site, this newly expanded aviation museum captures the achievements and excitement of the Golden Age of Aviation in the 1920s and '30s. As part of Vancouver Barracks, Pearson Airfield was established in 1905 as a dirigible base. The early, unwieldy lighter-than-air ships displaced the officers' polo ponies, as the airfield is built on a former polo field.

Having welcomed its first airplane in 1911, Pearson Airfield is the oldest operating airport in the nation. The museum's recently expanded facilities include an airplane hangar dating from the 1920s as well as a new theater, computerized flight simulators, and a working aircraft restoration center. While there are some contemporary aircraft on display, the heart of the museum's aircraft collection and related exhibits reflect earlier eras, concentrating on civilian aviation developments during the two decades before World War II.

Pearson Airfield played an important role in the development of airmail service as a center of early commercial aviation and as an early army aviation base. Tex Rankin and Charles Lindbergh flew from this field, and in 1937 the Russian aircraft making the first nonstop transpolar flight landed here. The Soviet Transpolar Monument, displayed outside the museum, commemorates the accomplishments of the three Soviet aviators who made that historic flight. After unexpectedly landing at Vancouver (they were trying to reach California), the aircrew was greeted by General George C. Marshall, then the officer commanding Vancouver Barracks.

The museum also has a well-stocked gift shop and hosts a variety of lectures and presentations on aviation history and several aviation-themed

The Pearson Air Museum commemorates the longest-running airport in the United States. REBECCA PALMER

special events throughout the year, including flights of vintage aircraft. If you want to break for a sack lunch, there are a few picnic tables in a very nice open green space directly across from the museum. On Father's Day, all dads are admitted free and get a chance to win a ride in an antique aircraft. The museum is open Wednesday through Saturday from 10:00 a.m. until 5:00 p.m.

OUTLYING AREAS

BONNEVILLE DAM
Off Interstate 84 (exit 40),
Cascade Locks
(541) 374-8820
www.nwp.usace.army.mil/op/b/
A half-hour of scenic driving through the Columbia River Gorge will take you to the Bonneville Dam, which has an attractive visitor center with interactive exhibits, short films, and displays that illustrate the history and culture of local and

regional Native American tribes. You can watch steelhead and Chinook salmon climbing the fish ladders and boats passing through the locks. There are no restaurants here, but this is a popular picnic stop for schoolchildren on field trips or families exploring nearby trails, so there are lots of picnic tables, some of them covered. Admission is free. Hours are 9:00 a.m. to 5:00 p.m. for the visitor center; other areas may be open later.

END OF THE OREGON TRAIL
INTERPRETIVE CENTER $$
1726 Washington Street, Oregon City
(503) 657-9336
www.endoftheoregontrail.org
The End of the Oregon Trail Interpretive Center is in Oregon City and officially designated as the true end of the Oregon Trail. On Abernethy Green, just off Interstate 205, the center has created a local landmark with its three stylized 50-foot-tall

covered wagon–shaped buildings. While everyone in Oregon talked about the sesquicentennial (150th anniversary) of the Oregon Trail, and there were all sorts of events during the yearlong celebration in 1993, these people went out and did something, telling not only the settlers' stories but the effect this large migration—300,000 people over the course of 30 years—had on the indigenous peoples and the land. Just as important, the center's organizers had the courage and determination to make something new, a trait they share with the people they honor.

The first years of the center were difficult: The year after the center opened, the site was flooded in one of the worst winters in recent Oregon history. The next year, high winds ripped apart the canvas coverings on the huge wagons. Undaunted, organizers recovered. Costumed trail guides lead visitors through a tour of the center that includes a multimedia dramatization of three representative journeys across 2,000 miles of frontier. The tour also uses live presentations, demonstrations, and well-researched and well-prepared exhibits of artifacts and heirlooms to retell the pioneers' epic stories.

The shows are scheduled for specific times, so this is not a self-guided museum. Visitors spend an average of 90 minutes at the center. On summer (May through September) weekdays and Saturdays, there are eight scheduled presentations. On summer Sundays, there are seven. The winter schedule (September through May) allows five daily presentations. During the summer, the center hosts a locally written presentation called the *Oregon Trail Pageant*, which mixes music (some of which is performed on authentic and reproduction instruments of the era), dance, and drama to tell the story of the Oregon Trail. Not unexpectedly, there is a gift shop, the George Abernethy & Co. Merchandise museum store, featuring the usual variety of souvenirs, called heritage items, and Northwest handicrafts. Hours are Monday through Saturday 9:00 a.m. to 5:00 p.m. and Sunday 10:00 a.m. to 5:00 p.m. during the summer schedule.

HULDA KLAGER LILAC GARDENS $
115 South Pekin Road, Woodland, WA
(360) 225-8996
www.lilacgardens.com

Well worth the drive, the Hulda Klager Lilac Gardens are easy to find. Just take I-5 north of Vancouver, look for exit 21, and follow the signs. It's a lovely garden, especially during the annual Lilac Festival held during April and May each year, when dozens of varieties of lilacs are in full bloom. The lilacs truly flourish and flower on these well-kept and fertile grounds. The house is listed on the National Register of Historic Places and features a large collection of antique dolls and period furniture and artifacts. There is also a small gift shop. The Lilac Gardens are open year-round, but are most popular, and most crowded, when the blossoms are in flower in late spring or early summer. Gardeners from throughout Washington and Oregon come to buy cuttings and seedlings to plant in their own gardens. The Mager House is open for tours during the Lilac Festival (see the Annual Events chapter). Hours are 10:00 a.m. to 4:00 p.m. daily.

OREGON MILITARY MUSEUM AT CAMP WITHYCOMBE
Highway 212, Clackamas
(503) 557-5359
www.swiftview.com/~ormilmuseum

The Oregon Military Museum is housed in a Quonset Hut on an Oregon Army National Guard facility. To get here, take I-205 to Highway 212, which heads toward Estacada. After 1/8 mile, turn left on Southeast 102nd and follow to the main-gate entrance of the camp. Its displays and exhibits emphasize the history and accomplishments of the Oregon Army, Oregon Air National Guard, and Oregon veterans. With limited space and resources, the museum's collection includes uniforms, artifacts, models, paintings, a small but impressive library and archives, and, perhaps most important, a knowledgeable and helpful staff. The museum also has a significant collection of restored and functional wheeled and tracked military vehicles and artillery pieces.

The view west from Crown Point to the river below and Portland beyond. RACHEL DRESBECK

When visiting, ask to see what was called on national television the "Oh, My God Room." This is actually a very large vault containing the museum's significant collection of handheld weapons. Admission is free although donations are welcomed. The Oregon Military Museum is open on Saturday and Sunday from 9:00 a.m. to 5:00 p.m. or by appointment. The staff is very cooperative in arranging private tours. Freedom isn't free, but visiting this museum is—there is no charge.

VISTA HOUSE AT CROWN POINT
40700 East Columbia River Historic Highway
www.vistahouse.com
Officially Crown Point State Park, Vista House was conceived as a monument to Oregon pioneers and to the completion of the Columbia River Highway from Portland to Hood River in 1916 (see the Day Trips chapter's section on the Mount Hood–Columbia Gorge Loop). Two years later, the building was completed. The view from Vista House, which is 733 feet above the Columbia River, is one of the state's most popular, dramatic, and beautiful sights. It can be reached by taking the Historic Columbia River Highway (Highway

30) off I–84 at Corbett (exit 22), 15 miles east of Portland.

Designated a Natural Landmark of national significance, Vista House is also listed on the National Register of Historic Places. Visitors will not only be impressed by the sweeping views of the Columbia River, the Cascades, and the Columbia Gorge, but also by the endurance of the cyclists who pedal their way up the winding hills to Vista House. Sunsets and sunrises are spectacular. If you plan on photographing the evening or morning colors, bring a tripod, because the winds can cause a handheld camera to vibrate. In fact, you should be prepared for windy times in general. There is a small gift shop inside the building, but the real attraction is the view. Standing on the edge of the viewing area, often facing into the east wind, the sheer magnitude of the meeting of the mountains and river is dramatic. Admission is free. The Vista House is open spring through fall from 9:00 a.m. to 6:00 p.m. daily, and on winter weekends from 10:00 a.m. to 4:00 p.m., weather permitting.

KIDSTUFF

If a place has a reputation as being great for children," one of our friends once observed, "it's probably no good for adults." Fortunately, he wasn't referring to his native city. Portland is a great place both for children and for the adults who live with them. Many of the area's major attractions—Washington Park, the Chinese Garden, the Oregon History Center—interest persons both small and large, and many of the attractions designed just for children hold a kind of giddy appeal for their guardians. Here, then, are some of our favorite places to go with children in the Portland Metro area and a little beyond.

Price Code

	Free
$	Less than $7
$$	$7–$15
$$$	More than $15

ATTRACTIONS AND MUSEUMS

Portland

ALPENROSE DAIRY
6149 Southwest Shattuck Road
(503) 244-1133
(503) 244-9492 for BMX information
(503) 246-0330 for Velodrome information
(503) 246-2826 for Portland Quarter-Midget
Racing information
www.alpenrose.com

We love Alpenrose Dairy, a rich blend of past and present. The dairy has been in operation since 1891 and still produces cream, milk, ice cream, cottage cheese, and sour cream (though the cows have moved west and south to other Willamette Valley farms). As the city encroached on the pastureland in the 1950s, the dairy's far-sighted owners, the Cadonau family, began to incorporate entertainment into their business. Now the dairy includes a wide range of family activities. Dairyville, a little frontier town, faithfully reproduces the pioneer atmosphere through its displays of shops and other buildings (including an old-fashioned ice-cream parlor!). Nearby displays also feature vintage autos and antique music players—everything from music boxes to Victrolas to a calliope. An opera house that seats 600 is the home of a 4,000-pipe organ that used to reside in the old Portland Civic Auditorium.

Alpenrose is not just for antiques buffs, however. It also features the Alpenrose Stadium, dating from 1956, which still hosts Little League games, including the Little League World Series. And there are several racing arenas: a quarter-midget track, a BMX track, and a beautiful Olympic-style velodrome. All these arenas are humming with activity. The quarter-midget races feature miniature race cars powered by gas or alcohol and driven by kids. The velodrome, one of only 20 in the United States, holds fast races on bikes with no brakes as well as gentler pre-event races for kids.

Alpenrose also hosts several popular seasonal events. At Christmastime, Dairyville is transformed into Storybook Lane, with the farm's animals—aided by the benefits of good set decoration—in starring roles such as Peter Rabbit and the Three Little Pigs. Each spring, a fairy festival is held, as well as a large Easter egg hunt that delights hundreds of children every year. Each summer, Alpenrose holds a rodeo for the city set.

Other events occur throughout the year. The quarter-midget races, bike races, and Little League events are free, with varying schedules. (Little League spectators are encouraged to buy from the concessions, the proceeds of which support the teams, but you may bring in food. No concessions are available for the bike races.) For information on the bike races at the velodrome, check the Oregon Bicycle Racing Association's Web page: www.obra.org/track.

JEFF MORRIS FIRE MUSEUM
Belmont Firehouse
900 Southeast 35th Avenue
(503) 823-3615
www.jeffmorrisfoundation.org/fire
museum.php
This museum occupies a historic firehouse, and here you will find a collection of antique fire equipment that helps children learn about the history of fire fighting. Predecessors of the modern era include an 1863 hand-pumper, an 1870 hand-drawn ladder truck, and an 1870 steam-pumper engine, as well as lots of fire-fighting paraphernalia. There's also a modern fire engine that helps you learn what it's like to fight fires today. Plus, you can slide down the fire pole. This little museum is the legacy of Jeff Morris, a firefighter who established the safety-education program at the Portland Fire Bureau and who died of cancer in the 1970s. Admission is free. Hours vary, so call before you go.

PORTLAND CHILDREN'S MUSEUM $
Washington Park across from the
Oregon Zoo
4015 Southwest Canyon Road
(503) 223-6500
www.portlandcm.org
The Portland Children's Museum, which dates from 1949, was wonderfully renovated in 2001 and became an instant hit with local children. It's especially popular with preschoolers, who adore the high-quality, innovative, and varied play spaces, which range from a child-size grocery store and restaurant to the ingenious waterworks room, where children turn cranks and wind pulleys to rush water through pipes and pools (plastic aprons are provided). Other spaces are devoted to dressing up, to music, and to art. The clay room allows children to pound, roll, and shape real clay. Next door is a small room that features a variety

of papery workshops—everything from painting with watercolor crayons to sewing little books. (Older children especially like the art workshops, which include pottery painting and the "Garage," a studio for making art out of recycled materials.) All these activities are supervised by friendly, knowledgeable staff. The museum also offers amusements just for babies, various organized events, special activities for the holidays, and spaces for birthday parties, as well as facilities for field trips and group tours. The museum is open Monday through Saturday from 9:00 a.m. to 5:00 p.m., and Sunday from 11:00 a.m. to 5:00 p.m. (though hours may vary seasonally, so call first). On the first Friday of the month, the museums stays open late and admission is free from 5:00 to 8:00 p.m. Admission is free to members and children younger than one. Parking costs $1. TriMet Bus #63 serves the museum, and the MAX line makes its Washington Park stop just across the parking lot. The museum is also the home of the Opal School, an arts-based charter school (see the Child Care and Education chapter).

OAKS AMUSEMENT PARK $$
Southeast Spokane Street at the
east end of Sellwood Bridge
(503) 236-5722
www.oakspark.com
An appealing and old-fashioned amusement park, Oaks Park dates back to the Lewis and Clark Exposition in 1905 and has entertained generations of Portland families. Oaks Park inhabits 44 acres on the Willamette and features rides, games, and a roller-skating rink. (It's also the home of the Multnomah County Fair.) The park offers more than two dozen rides, including a Ferris wheel, a carousel, a miniature train, and bumper cars for smaller children and the Teacups, the Frog Hopper, and the Screamin' Eagle for their big sisters and brothers. Go-karts and miniature golf are popular draws, as is the roller-skating. Not surprisingly, Oaks Park is an irresistible birthday party venue. Concessions are available, but picnics are welcome. Parts of the park are closed during the winter, but the roller rink stays open all year-round. Admission into the park is free,

except during the county fair and on the Fourth of July; rides, activities, and roller-skating will cost you, though. Ride bracelets are the best value. Games, go-karts, and golf are priced separately. The Oaks Park Web site has good directions and more information about hours and prices; you can also call, of course. (See the Attractions chapter for more information.)

OREGON MUSEUM OF SCIENCE AND INDUSTRY (OMSI) $$
1945 Southeast Water Avenue
(503) 797-4000
www.omsi.edu

OMSI (pronounced Ahm-zee) is nestled on the banks of the Willamette River and is home to the state's biggest science exhibitions and laser light shows. It is a preferred destination for wiggly preschoolers on rainy afternoons, as well as for older children on field trips. OMSI has the gift of making science and technology interesting without reducing it to mindless entertainment, and children really love this place. The museum has standout permanent and temporary features. For example, OMSI has featured Grossology, devoted to explaining the yucky side of the human body. No one who saw Grossology will ever forget being inside the giant nose or seeing—and smelling—how human gas is manufactured. Similarly, OMSI was the site of Body Worlds 3, co-sponsored by Oregon Health and Science University. This remarkable exhibit focused on the full range of anatomy, featuring plastinated human figures that revealed the mysteries of the body, complemented with exhibits and activities from the region's only academic health center. Among the permanent exhibits, you'll find a fascinating display on fetal development as well as a computer station that allows you to see what your face will look like in the coming decades. Wonderful exhibits cover the geology and weather of the region—and should you want to prepare yourself for the Big One, you will find an earthquake simulator. For children younger than seven, the Discovery Space, with its sand, water, slime, magnets, levers, and other intriguing features, will provide hours of entertainment.

Richard Scarry's Busytown is a frequent visitor, much to the delight of the preschool set.

Children also love other parts of OMSI: the *USS Blueback* (a diesel-powered submarine now permanently moored on the banks of the Willamette), the planetarium, and the OMNIMAX theater with its million-dollar projector and five-story screen. Snacks are welcome; concessions are available too. Expect to pay a separate fee for the OMNIMAX theater, laser shows, the submarine, and the planetarium. OMSI also has a great education program and camp. If you think you'll go a lot, you should buy a membership. (For more details, see the Attractions chapter.)

THE OREGON ZOO $$
Washington Park
4001 Southwest Canyon Road
(503) 226-1561
www.oregonzoo.org

The Oregon Zoo is a well-visited attraction, but it has a number of features beyond the extensive and naturally compelling animal exhibits that make it a great place for families. First, children love to see how wild animals live in their habitats: Many of the exhibits attempt to faithfully re-create how the animals would live in the wild. Second, there is a lot for children to do: animals to pet, things to climb on, trails for skipping, benches for resting. Many exhibits allow you surprising proximity to the zoo's creatures; there's nothing quite like the feeling of being mistaken by a butterfly for a flower or having to stop in the aviary to let an exotic hen herd her little chicks across the path or being separated by a mere inch or so of glass from a fierce, hungry-looking Amur leopard. Third, the zoo has a great train. Fourth, the zoo is dedicated to saving animals and teaching people about them. For example, the Oregon Zoo has the most successful elephant management program in the country, and more than two dozen baby elephants have been born here since 1962, when Packy was the first elephant born in the United States in 44 years. Packy still lives here and celebrates his birthday every April.

The zoo also has many special events, programs just for home-schooled kids, and well-run, popular day camps during school breaks. During the winter, Zoo Lights—light displays shaped like animals—draw large holiday-season crowds, even on rainy and chilly winter nights. The zoo train is the best way to see them, but lines are long, so dress warmly. During the summer, concerts that feature jazz, folk, world, and many other kinds of music (many of which are free with zoo admission) entice families to spend the late afternoon at the zoo and then sit down with a picnic dinner. They feast on the amphitheater lawn, swaying to the music and honoring the end of the beautiful summer's day. Sometimes the elephants wander out and sway along with the crowd. These concerts are one of the best things about a Portland summer.

The Oregon Zoo is open every day, except Christmas Day, from 9:00 a.m. until 6:00 p.m., except from October 1 to March 31, when it is open from 9:00 a.m. until 4:00 p.m. The zoo stays open for an hour after the gates close, unless you're attending a special event or concert, when you can stay longer. The Zoo Railway has a separate fee. By car, the zoo is best reached by a well-marked exit from westbound U.S. Highway 26 as it leaves downtown Portland. Parking is $1 per car. The zoo is also accessible via TriMet Bus #63 and the Washington Park MAX stop. On summer weekends and during many concerts, parking can be particularly scarce, so light rail may be the least frustrating way to get here. Admission is $2 on the second Tuesday of each month, and the zoo is very crowded then, as well. If you think you'll go to the zoo often, a family membership is a must. (See the Attractions chapter for more information on the zoo.)

PORTLAND ART MUSEUM $$
1219 Southwest Park Avenue
(503) 226-2811
www.portlandartmuseum.org
The Portland Art Museum has a number of programs designed to educate—and entertain—children and their families. Museum Family Sundays (MFS) are held occasionally throughout the year in conjunction with major exhibitions. These programs help children explore the artistic process, inspired by the displays in the museum. Families can make their own works of art—their own Giacomettis, Calders, Klimts, and Monets—as well as learn about the originals through discussions, lectures, and performances. MFS are not regularly scheduled; you should call or check the Web site to find out when they will be held. Family days are scheduled once a month; they feature special tours, story times, and art-making activities. And the museum also offers art classes for ages three and older (including adults) on weekend evenings, weekends, and during school breaks. A family membership is highly recommended if you plan to go more than once a year. You'll have access to great programs, and you'll save money. Hours are Tuesday through Saturday 10:00 a.m. to 5:00 p.m., except on Thursday and Friday, when the museum is open 10:00 a.m. to 8:00 p.m.; Sunday from noon to 5:00 p.m. Family programs can fill up fast, so plan ahead. (For more information see the Attractions chapter.)

WORLD FORESTRY CENTER $
4033 Southwest Canyon Road
(503) 228-1367
www.worldforestry.org
The World Forestry Center makes a quiet change from the zoo and offers a cool respite from a hot summer day. This museum is dedicated to educating us about the roles that forests have played in culture and in nature. Its permanent collections feature a number of interesting exhibitions, including one on the history of tropical rain forests. These life-size dioramas were developed in collaboration with the Smithsonian, and they tell the story of three different forest families and their struggles in the changing tropical woods. The 70-foot talking Douglas fir tree that stands at the center of the museum is also a draw—as are two adventure rides, one featuring a white-water rafting experience and the other, the Canopy Lift, a chance to view the forest from a bird's eye by rising 45 feet into the air. (There are small separate charges for the rides.)

The Forestry Center also features the Forest Discovery Lab for children, which offers hands-on activities such as puppet shows, stories, and building forests. The Center hosts a range of special activities, including an annual show featuring Oregon woodworkers and carvers and an exhibit of wooden toys. A gallery features rotating exhibits of photography and other art. The World Forestry Center Museum is open daily from 10:00 a.m. to 5:00 p.m. Memberships are offered for free to K–12 teachers.

Outlying Areas

A. C. GILBERT MUSEUM $
116 Marion Street NE, Salem
(503) 371-3631, (800) 208-9514
www.acgilbert.org
Pretending you are a Maasai herder, a 19th-century explorer, or a modern astronaut are just a few of the compelling activities available at the A. C. Gilbert Museum in Salem—a truly worthy excursion from Portland. This museum complex, made up of three Victorian houses on the Willamette, is filled with interactive exhibitions that are so interesting you might forget they are supposed to be good for you. It's hard to say which you'll like best. Is it the Frozen Shadow room, which captures your shadow on the wall? Is it the bubble room, where you can inhabit a giant bubble? Perhaps it's the Earth's Fury room, which allows you to build buildings and towns and then wipe them out with floods and earthquakes. You will also find many other diversions, including a room devoted to puzzles, a toy-inventors' workshop, a toddler room, and wonderful temporary exhibitions, educational programs, and special events. A. C. Gilbert, a Salem native, was a toy inventor who gave us, among other things, the Erector Set and American Flyer trains. This museum is a fitting tribute to his contribution to American childhood. Hours are Monday through Saturday 10:00 a.m. to 5:00 p.m. and Sunday from noon to 5:00 p.m.

BONNEVILLE DAM AND FISH HATCHERY
Off Interstate 84 (exit 40)
Cascade Locks
(541) 374-8820
www.nwp.usace.army.mil/op/b/

Children and their parents will love the beautiful half-hour drive from Portland through the Columbia River Gorge to the Bonneville Dam and its next-door neighbor, the Bonneville Fish Hatchery. The dam's attractive and informative visitor center is brimming with interactive exhibits, short films, and displays that illustrate the history and culture of local and regional Native American tribes. Watching the big boats pass through the locks is truly compelling, as are the dam's huge generators inside the powerhouse. Little ones are entranced by the sight of steelhead trout and Chinook, coho, and sockeye salmon stubbornly climbing the fish ladders, though sometimes older siblings grumble about dam breaching and salmon policy. Summer is the best time to go—that's when the fish are most active. At the fish hatchery, watch the trout and sturgeon that you can feed (25 cents per handful). No restaurants are nearby, so you may want to bring food—there are numerous picnic tables (some covered). On the return trip, take a hike along one of the many trails at or near Multnomah Falls, one of the area's premier attractions any time of year. The Army Corps of Engineers, which operates the dam, suggests that you call before your visit. First, many events for children are held, so you might want to plan for them. And second, increased security measures have made the schedule less predictable. You'll want to make sure it's open before you set out. Admission is free.

ENCHANTED FOREST $$
8462 Enchanted Way SE, Turner
(503) 371-4242
www.enchantedforest.com
We were grateful to finally have children so that we could have an excuse to visit the Enchanted Forest, just south of Salem and a little bit less than an hour's drive south from Portland. This amusement park features imaginative rides, displays, and activities for children of all ages (though some rides have height requirements). One of the nicest things about this place is the balance between thrilling rides and gentler activities. A half-timbered English Village and a replicated Old West town are fun to poke around, while a bobsled-

inspired roller coaster and a scary haunted house provide more adrenaline-inducing entertainment. And the Big Timber Log Ride is a fun, splashy way to cool off on a hot summer day. The fountain features a light show coordinated to its cascading jets. Children also love exploring the storybook-theme displays, including the rabbit hole from *Alice in Wonderland*, the cottage of the Seven Dwarfs, and the home of the Old Woman Who Lived in a Shoe. In addition, you'll find bumper boats, a Ferris wheel, and trails to explore.

The price of admission will allow you into most activities, but a number of the most popular features—including the haunted house, the log ride, and the bumper boats—require an additional fee. Ride bracelets that also cover the cost of admission are probably the best deal. Concessions are available, but picnics are welcome. Children two and younger are admitted at no charge. The park is easily accessed from the freeway. Take Interstate 5 south from Portland to exit 248 (Sunnyside-Turner) to get there. It's open from 9:30 a.m. to 5:00 p.m. during the week and until 6:00 or 7:00 p.m. on the weekends.

THRILL-VILLE USA $$$
8372 Enchanted Way SE, Turner
(503) 363-9376
www.thrillvilleusa.homestead.com
Thrill-Ville USA is the California Adventure to the Enchanted Forest's Disneyland. The big draw is the enormous water slide, where people whoosh down four stories of cascading water to be deposited in the pool. This amusement park also features classic rides such as the Tilt-a-Whirl and the Octopus; its roller coaster, the Ripper, is Oregon's largest. The brave can try a 100-foot free-fall SCAD dive. Bumper boats, miniature golf, and go-karts are also popular. For the wee ones, you'll find the Little Ripper (a much smaller roller coaster) and a pretty carousel in addition to the standard calmer children's rides. Thrill-Ville USA is open daily from 11:00 a.m. to 6:00 p.m. from June through Labor Day. Take I–5 south from Portland to exit 248 (Sunnyside-Turner). You can purchase discounted tickets online.

FARMS

It is a habit of many Portland children to mark the seasons by what's going on at area farms. Summer is berry- and peach-picking season, fall means it's time for the pumpkin patch, winter brings Christmas trees, and spring means tulips. Many local farms have made the most of their naturally interesting happenings and have become attractions in their own right. For a complete guide to local farms, seasonal bounty, and agriculture activities for kids, check Oregon Agri-Business's consumer Web site: www.oregonfresh .net. In the meantime, here are some of our favorites.

FIR POINT FARMS
14601 Arndt Road, Aurora
(503) 678-2455
www.firpointfarms.com
About a half an hour's drive from downtown Portland, Fir Point Farms offers flowers, fresh produce, tours (by reservation), a deli, gift shop, and Tillamook ice cream. In the fall, Fir Point Farms is the host to swarms of pumpkin-picking schoolchildren, and weekends in October feel more like a farm exhibit in Central Park than a farm in Oregon, but between the excellent homemade doughnuts and the hay-wagon rides, it's not easy to resist the charm of Fir Point Farms, even with the crowds. A big, slippery slide that dumps you into a pile of hay is a popular entertainment. Other allurements include a spooky hay maze, pony rides, and the chickens, turkeys, cows, horses, and goats. You can feed most of the animals, and the owners have capitalized on the attraction of this activity for city folks by charging 25 cents for a handful of chow. The greedy goats are the most fun to watch as they storm unwary visitors. In addition to their large, wooded pen, the goats have a tree house for their amusement, where they scamper along platforms 12 feet in the air, peering down at gawking parents and children. You can send food up to the goats by means of buckets on pulleys. That alone is worth the trip. Fir Point Farms is open from 9:00 a.m. to 6:00 p.m. every day but Monday, April through December. Fall weekends have the

most activities. There is no charge for admission, but rides and games will cost you.

ℹ️ If you watch The Learning Channel's *Little People, Big World*, you might know that the family it features, the Roloffs, have a working farm near Hillsboro. Area residents have been purchasing their Halloween pumpkins from the Roloffs for years, and you can too. Their farm is open daily during pumpkin season, and they offer hayrides in addition to golden squashy wonders. Find directions to the farm and harvest-season hours at www .mattroloff.com/thefarm.

FLOWER FARMER $
2512 North Holly Road, Canby
(503) 266-3581
www.flowerfarmer.com
www.phoenixandholly.com

When you visit the Flower Farmer, south and east of Portland in Canby, you will find yourself with plenty of company—and not all children. The main draw is the train, and in particular Sparky and Fred. Sparky is a pint-size, 30-horsepower diesel engine that pulls the Phoenix and Holly Railroad's 15-inch narrow-gauge train through flowerbeds and fields on a winding half-mile circuit of tracks. The bright red caboose is named Fred. Together they attract daily crowds of preschoolers, schoolchildren, seniors, and anybody else with a love of narrow-gauge trains. The train makes its circular journey through tunnels and past fun displays, making a stop at a petting zoo with chickens, turkeys, and a miniature donkey. Another stop brings you to a pumpkin patch, with a colossal hay pyramid that kids love and parents hate. The final stop is the gift shop, with ice cream and other treats, as well as a good selection of dried flowers, fresh flowers, and seasonal produce. The Flower Farmer is open from May through December from 11:00 a.m. to 6:00 p.m. on weekends, but the hours may vary, so be sure to call ahead. Many events are scheduled throughout the year, especially at Halloween and Christmas.

THE PUMPKIN PATCH $
16511 Northwest Gillihan Road,
Sauvie Island
(503) 621-3874
www.thepumpkinpatch.com

The Pumpkin Patch on beautiful Sauvie Island swarms with schoolchildren on field trips in the fall, but it's open as early as June. Its classic red barn is home to rabbits, pigs, and other animals. The u-pick fields are filled with luscious berries (for example, strawberries, raspberries, blueberries) as well as apricots, nectarines, tomatoes, flowers, and, of course, pumpkins. During the harvest festival, wagon and pony rides keep the little ones busy. An elaborate, scary, dark, and beloved corn maze (or "corn maize" as they like to call it) attracts older kids and adults, especially on crisp fall nights. (Be forewarned: It is very muddy, even when the weather is dry, and it gets cold.) To get to the Pumpkin Patch, take U.S. Highway 30 west to Sauvie Island and circle left under the bridge. This will place you on Gillihan Road, and you'll find the farm after about 2 miles—watch for the signs.

RASMUSSEN FRUIT AND FLOWER FARM
3020 Thomsen Road, Hood River
(541) 386-4622, (800) 548-2243
www.rasmussenfarms.com

Rasmussen Farms—an hour's drive from Portland in the scenic Hood River area—is a destination throughout the year because of its varied harvests of cherries (July), pears and apples (September), and pumpkins (October). Rasmussen's Halloween celebrations make it one of the most popular pumpkin patches around. At the foot of Mount Hood, the beautiful setting of this farm would be enticing with or without the pumpkins. Rasmussen is open from April until just before Thanksgiving, 9:00 a.m. to 6:00 p.m. daily. (Rasmussen also has a good online store).

SLEIGHBELLS
23870 Southwest 195th Place, Sherwood
(503) 625-6052, (866) 857-0975
www.sbells.com

A visit to the Sauvie Island Pumpkin Patch is a rite of passage for schoolchildren. TOM BETHEL

Oregon produces more Christmas trees than any other state in the union, and during December, you can't drive 2 miles in the countryside without running into three tree farms. Many families begin their holiday season with a trip to Sleighbells on the weekend after Thanksgiving, where they pick out their tree and sip hot cocoa. Sleighbells is more than a tree farm, however; it's a holiday extravaganza. The gift shop features a variety of collectible ornaments from Christopher Radko, Polanaise, Slavic Treasures, Chase, Snowbabies, and Department 56 among other lines (that is to say, breakable things). Wreaths and garlands are available during the season, and gifts and crafts are available year-round. Of note are the strolling peacocks that lend an exotic air. You can choose between precut trees or hacking one down yourself. Sleighbells also offers a variety of different activities throughout the year. It's open from 10:00 a.m. to 6:00 p.m. daily.

PLANES, TRAINS, AND AUTOMOBILES

CANBY FERRY $

South end of Mountain Road, Wilsonville
North end of Holly Street, Canby
(503) 650-3030
www.co.clackamas.or.us/transportation/
transit/ferry.htm
The charming Canby Ferry is an echo of the past, when the Willamette was not festooned with bridges. If you follow Holly Road north from the Flower Farmer (see separate entry in this chapter) to the end, you'll reach the ferry, in operation since 1914 and one of the few remaining river ferries in the area. The friendly operator will take you and your car across the river on a platform ferry that holds nine vehicles and takes about five minutes. The ferry tracks peacefully along a cable in the river. After you cross, you can take Mountain Road north; it will turn into Stafford Road and take you to Interstate 205. (From the other direction, take I–205 to Stafford Road and proceed south, following Mountain Road.) This little journey is one of the favorite details of our

trips to the Flower Farmer and Fir Point Farms. Everyone used to cross the Willamette this way, and it's both a welcome respite from modern hurry and a reminder of what we take for granted. There is a small charge for cars; bikes and pedestrians ride free. The Canby Ferry runs from 6:45 a.m. to 9:15 p.m. daily.

COLUMBIA GORGE STERNWHEELER $$$

Cascade Locks
(503) 224-3900, (800) 224-3901
www.sternwheeler.com
Sternwheelers were once common along the Columbia and Willamette, though now they are a means to a pleasant afternoon or evening rather than a means of transportation. The Columbia Gorge Sternwheeler, as it chugs down and back through part of the Columbia Gorge National Scenic Area, is a fine way to learn about Lewis and Clark, the Oregon Trail, Bridge of the Gods, and the river routes that were the area's first freeways. Boarding begins at Marine Park in Cascade Locks (take I–84 east from Portland to exit 44, which takes about 45 minutes). The cruise takes about two hours. Summer is the best time to go, for you can sit out on the deck and watch the windsurfers race you. The Columbia Gorge also offers a sunset dinner cruise and a champagne brunch cruise on the weekends, but the scenery is enough of a feast. They also offer special events that coincide with the Fourth of July and other holidays as well as dances and many other fun events. The schedule is limited from October through May. During December the Columbia Gorge Sternwheeler cruises the Willamette, boarding from downtown Portland at Waterfront Park and allowing good views of the holiday-illumined city.

CONCOURS D'ELEGANCE $$

Pacific University
2043 College Way, Forest Grove
(503) 357-2300
www.forestgroveconcours.org
This classic and vintage car event, held in July, features 40 different classes of automobiles that have been lovingly restored and preserved. It's

also a fund-raiser put on by the Rotary Club of Forest Grove, which passes along the proceeds to local community service and scholarship funds. The beautiful Corvettes, Cadillacs, and Model Ts are so different from today's minivans and SUVs that kids can spend a couple hours wandering through the 300-car exhibition. For kids who like cars, this is a fun event and a nice day trip.

MALIBU GRAND PRIX $$$
9405 Southwest Cascade Avenue
Beaverton
(503) 641-8122
www.maliburaceway.com

The Portland version of the Malibu Grand Prix has lots of entertainment for the pre-license crowd, from whizzing round the track in an F-50 to the latest video games to batting cages. The Grand Prix has two racetracks and three go-kart models, and some of them go quite fast (helmets and harnesses are required). The F-50s require a height of 4 feet 6 inches and an age of at least eight, and if you'll be chauffering your children, they must be at least 3 feet 6 inches. The Malibu Grand Prix is a popular site for birthday parties. Hours are Monday through Thursday, 11:00 a.m. to 9:00 p.m.; Friday and Saturday, 11:00 a.m. to 11:00 p.m.; Sunday, 11:00 a.m. to 8:00 p.m. You'll get a better deal if you buy laps in bulk.

PEARSON AIR MUSEUM
1115 East 5th Avenue, Vancouver, WA
(360) 694-7026
www.pearsonairmuseum.org

The Pearson Museum, part of the Vancouver Historic Reserve, is committed to preserving the nation's oldest operating airstrip. Its family activities include interactive exhibits at the Children's Hands-on Activity Center, which teaches kids about the science of flight through various stations. These allow kids to experiment with airflow and air resistance, propeller speed, and other interesting things that you've always wondered about. The museum is open Wednesday through Saturday, 10:00 a.m. to 5:00 p.m. (See the Attractions chapter for more information.)

PHOENIX AND HOLLY RAILROAD $
2512 North Holly Road, Canby
(503) 266-3581
www.flowerfarmer.com
www.phoenixandholly.com

This little 15-inch, narrow-gauge train pulls hordes of schoolchildren through the fields of the Flower Farmer. If your children are fans of trains, they will love this one. (See the entry for the Flower Farmer in this chapter.)

SHADY DELL PACIFIC RAILROAD
Pacific Northwest Live Steamers
31083 South Shady Dell Drive, Molalla
(503) 829-6866
www.pnls.org

Something about the Molalla area inspires train building. Pacific Northwest Live Steamers, which dates from the 1960s, was one of the first hobby trains in the area. This beautiful, four-acre private park is devoted to a small-scale railroad featuring handcrafted steam-, electric-, and gas-powered locomotives that wend their way around a 3,800-foot, 7.5-inch-gauge track. The park is open from May to October on Sundays and holidays from noon to 5:00 p.m. Admission is free, but (tax-deductible) donations are welcome.

THE SPRUCE GOOSE $$
Evergreen Aviation Museum
Highway 18, 1 mile east of McMinnville
(503) 434-4180
www.sprucegoose.org

This museum is not only the home of the giant Spruce Goose—the Hughes Air H-4 Hercules, which is actually made out of birch—but it also houses myriad aircraft from U.S. aviation history in its 121,000-square-foot facility, including the Apollo Lunar Module. The museum, which is set in the midst of verdant fields in the middle of wine country, features a replica of the Wright brothers' original 1903 craft as well as fighter jets, commercial planes, and, in the spirit of those aviation pioneers, home-built aircraft from the 1990s. It also features an IMAX theater. The museum is open daily from 9:00 a.m. to 5:00 p.m.

except Thanksgiving, Christmas, and New Year's, with tours at 11:00 a.m. and 1.30 p.m. Children five and younger are admitted free of charge, and special discounts are available for students, seniors, and military folk, past and present.

**THE WESTERN ANTIQUE AEROPLANE &
AUTOMOBILE MUSEUM**
Ken Jernstedt Airfield 4S2
1600 Air Museum Road, Hood River
(541) 308-1600
www.waaamuseum.org
The Western Antique Aeroplane & Automobile Museum, in beautiful Hood River, features not only beautifully restored old planes and cars, but also planes and cars that actually still work. Here you will find Model T's and Studebakers, as well as a very large collection of operating antique planes—among them a rare Curtiss Jenny. The museum also has an extensive restoration program, and they hold numerous events throughout the year where they take the planes up in an inspiring homage to human endeavor.

SPORTS

Portland is a city full of outdoor enthusiasts, and they seem pretty much born that way, but their inclinations are abetted by facilities all over the city. Words can hardly do justice to the extensive, well-run, and popular programs run by the Portland Parks and Recreation Department. They offer the greatest variety of sports and other athletic activities in the city, including dancing, swimming, even snowshoeing. They offer class sessions continually and also sponsor team sports such as soccer and basketball. Call them at (503) 823-PLAY. You can also find out about organized team sports by contacting your child's school.

In general, Portland's parks, sports programs, and trails are filled with children. The city has many parks with excellent playground equipment, and much of that equipment has undergone a renaissance in the past few years. Exceptional playgrounds include Washington Park, where the substantial, bright red, blue, and yellow equipment near the Rose Garden

is designed to keep preschoolers and their big brothers and sisters occupied for hours; Laurelhurst Park, which has a series of bridges that are good for playing tag; Gabriel Park, with its bright green grassy hills that look like they're straight out of *Teletubbies;* Sellwood Park and its wonderful tall fir trees; and Mount Tabor Park, which has views of Mount St. Helens in addition to its climbing structure and swings. Many school grounds are adjacent to parks and have good equipment, as well. Places that inspire bursts of running in children include Waterfront Park, Pioneer Courthouse Square, the Eastbank Esplanade, the plaza in front of OMSI, and the big lawn at the Oregon Zoo. The Hoyt Arboretum draws families who love to hike, and Powell Butte, just east of town, offers a network of easy trails so that children can explore the vestiges of the old farm it once was. (More information about the parks and their programs in the area may be found in the Portland's Parks chapter, and more information about sports may be found in the Recreation chapter.)

Bowling

Bowling is a fun, inexpensive, rainy-day activity in the Portland Metro area, and many of the area's bowling alleys offer family specials, foolproof bumper bowling, glow-in-the-dark cosmic bowling, and other enticements. Birthday parties are often held at bowling alleys, and many lanes have good deals on packages. Shoes are available at all the places listed below. (For more information see the Recreation chapter.)

Portland

AMF CASCADE LANES $
2700 Northeast 82nd Avenue
(503) 255-2635

AMF PRO-300 LANES $
3031 Southeast Powell Boulevard
(503) 234-0237

AMF 20TH CENTURY LANES $
3550 Southeast 92nd Avenue
(503) 774-8805

GRAND CENTRAL LANES $
808 Southeast Morrison Street
(503) 236-2695

HOLLYWOOD BOWL $
4030 Northeast Halsey Street
(503) 288-9237

INTERSTATE LANES $
6049 North Interstate Avenue
(503) 285-9881

Outlying Areas

AMF TIMBER LANES $
2306 Andresen Road, Vancouver, WA
(360) 694-8404

KELLOGG BOWL $
1306 Southeast Main Street, Milwaukie
(503) 659-1737

SUNSET LANES $
12770 Southwest Walker Road, Beaverton
(503) 646-1116

VALLEY LANES $
9300 Southeast Beaverton-Hillsdale
Highway, Beaverton
(503) 292-3523

Ice-Skating

THE ICE CHALET $$
953 Lloyd Center
(503) 288-6073

This popular ice-skating rink, at the Lloyd Center shopping mall, brings people of all ages to scoot, slip, and skate their way around the ice. Shoppers stand about, sipping coffee, watching beginners lurch past orange cones and pairs of ice dancers whoosh elegantly by. Besides offering ice-skating and hockey lessons, this is a favorite place for birthday parties and all sorts of festive occasions. The Ice Chalet also offers a summer camp for youngsters who are serious about wanting to learn to skate. Ice skates are available to rent.

MOUNTAIN VIEW ICE ARENA $$
14313 Southeast Mill Plain Boulevard
Vancouver, WA
(360) 896-8700
www.mtviewice.com

Whether you are looking for hockey, lessons, birthday parties, or just a place to wear out the children, the Mountain View Ice Arena is there for you. Public skating times are Monday through Friday, 10:00 a.m. to noon and 2:00 to 5:15 p.m. and Saturday from 1:00 to 4:00 p.m. You can also skate Sunday, Tuesday, and Thursday evenings from 7:30 to 9:30 p.m. Skates are available to rent.

Miniature Golf

Miniature golf is the ideal way to keep those grade-schoolers busy when summer starts to get boring. Miniature golf can be found at the Family Fun Center (listed under Games in this chapter) and the Mount Hood Summer Action Park (listed under Summer Activities in this chapter), and the Oaks Amusement Park (listed under Attractions and Museums in this chapter). We also like Tualatin Island Greens (20400 Southwest Cipole Road, Tualatin; 503-691-8400 or www.tualatinisland greens.com). The putting course on this public range consists of 18 famous golf holes reduced to scale, so it will be extra fun for anyone with a serious interest in golf. For the not-so-serious golfers, try Glowing Greens (509 Southwest Taylor Street; 503-222-5554), which features glow-in-the-dark pirate miniature golf. They are open on Friday and Saturday from noon to midnight and on Sunday from noon to 10:00 p.m. It's a change from the usual birthday party juggernaut.

Rock Climbing

PORTLAND ROCK GYM
21 Northeast 12th Avenue
(503) 232-8310
www.portlandrockgym.com

Are your kids climbing the walls? Why not let them do it in a place with a 38-foot rope and bouldering courses? This fun climbing gym also has lots of classes and camps for children—and is a popular spot for birthday parties. The instructors are patient and friendly. The Portland Rock Gym is open Monday, Wednesday, and Friday from 11:00 a.m. to 11:00 p.m.; Tuesday and Thursday from 7:00 a.m. to 11:00 p.m.; Saturday from 9:00 a.m. to 7:00 p.m.; and Sunday from 9:00 a.m. to 6:00 p.m. (See the entry in the Recreation chapter.)

Roller-Skating

Roller-skating is available at several rinks throughout the area. You can rent skates or bring your own provided they don't have black brakes. Oaks Park (listed under Attractions and Museums in this chapter) is one of the largest and best rinks in the area, and it has a Wurlitzer theater organ besides. The Mount Scott Community Center (5530 Southeast 72nd Avenue; 503-823-3183) is the cheapest, a great place for birthday parties. Skate World (1220 Northeast Kelly, Gresham, 503-667-6543; and in Hillsboro, at 4395 Southeast Witch Hazel Road, 503-640-1333) has some good family programs that allow parents in street shoes to help their beskated preschoolers around the rink.

Skateboarding

Portland is a skateboard mecca. It even has designated skateboard paths downtown. Resources for skateboarders include Cal's Pharmacy Skateboards and Snowboards (15 Northeast Hancock Street; 503-233-1237), where they will charmingly and attentively help even clueless parents; they also run the Department of Skateboarding, an indoor skate park right next door to the shop. Cal Skate Skateboards (210 Northwest 6th; 503-248-0495) also has a fantastic selection. An essential resource is the Web site www.skateoregon.com, which features a comprehensive guide to all the skate parks in Oregon. And because there are nearly 100, there's probably one near you.

BURNSIDE SKATEPARK
Under the Burnside Bridge on the east side of the Willamette River
This legendary skate park was built by hand by ambitious skateboarders—illegally. But then the city realized that public concrete everywhere would be better served by allowing a place for skateboarders to go, and they sanctioned it. And thus a revolution was born, for the builders of the Burnside Skatepark inspired a national movement. It's still one of the best. There are no fees and few rules here, but if your kids are inexperienced, try to go at off-peak times (early in the day).

CHEHALEM SKATEPARK
1210 Blaine Street, Newberg
(503) 538-7454
This landmark facility is worth a special trip. *Skate Oregon* calls this the best skatepark on Earth, with 29,000 square feet of skatable surface. It was designed and executed with the help of actual skateboarders. There's also a BMX track at the same site, so BMXers are not competing for space. Chehalem Skatepark is free; helmets are required.

Games

ELECTRIC CASTLES WUNDERLAND $
3451 Southeast Belmont Street
(503) 238-1617

10306 Northeast Halsey Street
(503) 255-7333

11011 Southeast Main Street, Milwaukie
(503) 653-2222

4070 Cedar Hills Boulevard, Beaverton
(503) 626-1665
www.wunderlandgames.com
Your kids will finally have something to do with the nickels they collect for bottle deposits. Wunderland carries all the hottest video and pinball games, including test games. New games arrive all the time. If you're a pinball wizard, some of the payoffs from video and pinball games can be redeemed for prizes. Wunderland is also a very popular spot for birthday parties.

FAMILY FUN CENTER AND BULLWINKLE'S RESTAURANT $$$

29111 Southwest Town Center Loop
W Wilsonville
(503) 685-5000
www.fun-center.com/wilsonville

The Family Fun Center offers a double-story game arcade, batting cages, go-karts, and bumper boats. Miniature golf helps them work on their hand-eye coordination, while a flight simulator provides some high-tech fun. Laser tag is featured as well. The restaurant, Bullwinkle's, specializes in kid-friendly cuisine such as pizza and burgers.

ULTRAZONE $

Holly Farm Shopping Center
16074 Southeast McLoughlin Boulevard
Milwaukie
(503) 652-1122
www.ultrazoneportland.com

The big attraction here: high-tech interactive, laser-tag games. The futuristic atmosphere, with mazes, strobe lights, and special sound effects, adds to the enjoyment. Ultrazone is recommended for kids older than five. Adults like to play too, and corporations will sometimes sponsor team-building events here, so don't be surprised if you spy Joe from accounting.

The Arts

Children have many opportunities to both participate in and watch the performing arts in Portland. In addition to the annual *Nutcracker* performances by the Oregon Ballet Theater and the summer concerts at the Oregon Zoo, you'll find a variety of child-centered theater programs. The puppet theater, Tears of Joy Theater, (503) 284-0557, and the Oregon Children's Theatre Company, (503) 228-9571, perform seasonally for children and adults; the Ladybug Theater, (503) 232-2346, has ongoing performances for small and big children. Many of these organizations offer wonderful summer camp experiences.

CHILDREN'S LIBRARY AT CENTRAL MULTNOMAH COUNTY LIBRARY

801 Southwest 10th Avenue
(503) 988-5340

Once you enter the Central Library, take a right turn and discover the Children's Library. As you enter this brightly illuminated treasure trove of books, videos, and artwork for kids, a bronze tree catches your eye. This arboreal fantasy has a hollow trunk for play and storytelling inside. The library has one activity that should keep kids busy during the summer: the summer reading program, which is theme-based and offers prizes. It also offers story times. While you're there, pick up a copy of *InfoLines,* the library's newsletter, which gives information about other library programs and events.

METRO ARTS KIDS CAMP AT PORTLAND CENTER FOR PERFORMING ARTS

9333 Southeast Pine Street
(503) 408-0604
www.pdxmetroarts.org

Professional educators, visual artists, and performers from the Oregon Symphony, Oregon Ballet Theatre, and various theater companies help students create their own works of art, sing, play instruments, paint, dance, and act in live performances.

NORTHWEST CHILDREN'S THEATER AND SCHOOL

1819 Northwest Everett Street
(503) 222-4480
www.nwcts.org

An outstanding operation, Northwest Children's Theater produces frequent and imaginative shows with children in starring roles. Their classes and camps are first-rate, and they have been responsible for many budding Portland stars. Shows range from interpretations of classic fairy tales such as *Sleeping Beauty* to adaptations of works such as *The Devil and Daniel Webster* to musicals such as *Honk!* to *Hamlet* to original works, all performed with incredible professionalism.

OREGON CHILDREN'S THEATRE
600 Southwest 10th Avenue
(503) 228-9571
www.octc.org
This professional theater company takes props, makeup, and sets to Portland-area schools to ignite the magic of drama in classroom workshops and assemblies. And then, at Keller Auditorium, this marvelous outfit turns it around by bringing local kids onstage to help present plays and musicals. They adapt great children's classics such as *James and the Giant Peach, Tales of a Fourth Grade Nothing,* and *Lily's Purple Plastic Purse* into accessible and exciting theater.

RUN FOR THE ARTS
(503) 225-5900
Every year Portland children do their part to raise moral and financial support for the arts in their schools by running laps for bucks. The run, which is sponsored by Young Audiences, a nonprofit arts group, is organized around pledges made and then fulfilled when these youthful track stars chug around their playgrounds throughout October or April. Each school schedules its own run during one or both of these months and decides how to use the funds that are raised, which go to a variety of arts-related activities and instruction. Among the projects funded by the Run for the Arts have been presentations by a touring African-American ballet troupe, a quilt-making workshop, musical and play productions, and mosaic sculptures decorating the front steps of one of the schools. More than 100 schools from Vancouver to Beaverton participate in this annual run.

SUMMER ACTIVITIES

Portland has so many parks and playgrounds and is so close to both the mountains and the ocean that summer is never boring. The chapters on Recreation and Spectator Sports and on Portland's Parks give comprehensive and plentiful accounts of the Parks and Rec activities and programs. The Festivals and Annual Events chapter surveys the best of the seasonal events. There are also lots of summer camps in the area, with focuses in equestrian pursuits, sports (golf, baseball, soccer, basketball, and roller hockey), arts, theater, science, African arts, music, computers, cooking, fashion design, eco-awareness, politics—all in addition, of course, to plain old sleep-away camps with singing around the campfire. (Nostalgic parents don't have to be left out, either: Camp Westwind, on the Oregon coast, organizes a few sessions each summer for parents and children.) OMSI and the Oregon Zoo both offer popular summer camps. The free monthly papers *Metro Parent* and *Portland Family* provide comprehensive lists of camps each year. You can pick them up at any local library, most schools, and many children's stores. The Oregonian also publishes a special section every spring that lists camps in the Portland area. Financial aid for camps is often available; your camp can provide information.

SAND IN THE CITY BEACH PARTY
Pioneer Courthouse Square
(503) 238-4445
Held in early July, this benefit for the Kids on the Block Awareness Program transforms Portland's festive downtown patio into an ocean beach when more than 250 tons of sand are shaped, slapped, and molded into sand castles, dragons, and other wild critters by teams of local businesspeople. In addition to this jovial competition, master sand sculptors give demonstrations, and children can create their own works of art in a kids' sandbox. Food and craft booths are plentiful, too, as well as live music, clowns, and puppet shows. For further information on Sand in the City, see the Festivals and Annual Events chapter.

SUMMER ACTION PARK $
Mount Hood Ski Bowl on US 26
(503) 222-2695
Think the only action on the slopes is in the winter? Think again. The clever people at Mount Hood Ski Bowl maintain the Summer Action Park,

which offers more than 25 attractions, including the Northwest's only Alpine slide, as well as Indy Karts, bungee jumping, adventure river rides, kiddy jeeps, batting cages, and horse and pony rides. Visit on the way to or from Ski Bowl at Camp Creek, Tollgate Campground, or one of the many gorgeous campsites in lush Mount Hood National Forest just off US 26. Prepare a picnic basket or stop at the Dairy Queen in the nearby village of Rhododendron. Mount Hood is an hour's drive east of Portland on US 26. (For more information see the Day Trips and Recreation chapters.) All-day passes include unlimited rides down the half-mile Alpine slide.

SPECIAL PARK PROGRAMS

CHILDREN'S PROGRAMS
Metro Regional Parks and Greenspaces
(503) 797-1850
www.metro-region.org
Metro Regional Parks and Greenspaces Department runs many engaging activities and programs at their various sites throughout the metro area. Especially for Kids, an eight-week outdoor series, takes place at popular Blue Lake Park (8 miles east of downtown Portland off Marine Drive in Gresham). Four- to 10-year-olds enjoy the fun programs, which focus on interactive entertainment emphasizing the performing arts, cultural awareness, and nature themes. Outdoor performances, which are free with park admission, are held on Wednesday, rain or sunshine, from June through the middle of August at Blue Lake Park. Call for more information about the summer schedule of performances, which include everything from comedy and jugglers to live rain forest animals and folk music. Blue Lake is also the site of summer day camps, as well as interesting crafts instruction in things such as pioneer candlemaking and animal-track casting.

Oxbow Adventures, held at Oxbow Park, is perfect for curious kids—and parents—who would like to learn about plant identification, bird and animal habits and habitats, and other useful stuff. Wetland Explorers teaches children about the wetland habitat and the birds, bugs, turtles, and other creatures that live in it; these workshops are held at different wetland areas in the region. Call the phone number provided or visit Metro, Portland's regional government, on the Web at www.metro-region.org/parks/ green scene/greenkids.html for further information on kids' activities in the parks, and see the Portland's Parks chapter for more general information on these parks.

i Part of the challenge with having children is that they get in the way of your yoga practice. Don't let it happen to you: Yoga Shala offers child care for some of its classes, so you can put the *chi* back in children. And they offer kids' classes too. See a schedule at www.yogashalapdx.com.

SWIMMING POOLS AND WATER PARKS

Portland

THE CITY OF PORTLAND PARKS AND RECREATION DEPARTMENT
(503) 823-7529
The City of Portland offers a host of fun, healthy, year-round activities. In the summer the aquatics programs are exceptionally popular; the swimming lessons are a cherished summertime ritual. The department offers swimming lessons for kids from toddlers on up (adults too!). Young swimmers can get advanced lifeguard certification, take diving lessons, or just come to splash at open swim time. Classes are offered at every pool listed here. Most of the swimming pools are open from early in the morning until late at night, and many offer amusing activities. The pools at the Southwest Community Center and at Mount Scott have been beautifully refurbished with water toys, water slides, current channels, and other enticements. Call the park nearest you for specific information and rates. (See the Portland's Parks chapter for more information.)

Indoor Pools

BUCKMAN SWIMMING POOL $
320 Southeast 16th Avenue
(503) 823-3668

COLUMBIA SWIMMING POOL $
7701 North Chautauqua Boulevard
(503) 823-3669

MATT DISHMAN POOL $
77 Northeast Knott Street
(503) 823-3673

MLC POOL $
2033 Northwest Glisan Street
(503) 823-3671

MOUNT SCOTT SWIMMING POOL $
5530 Southeast 72nd Avenue
(503) 823-3813

SOUTHWEST COMMUNITY CENTER $
6820 Southwest 45th Avenue
(503) 823-2840

Outdoor Pools

CRESTON SWIMMING POOL $
4454 Southeast Powell Boulevard
(503) 823-3672

GRANT SWIMMING POOL $
2300 Northeast 33rd Avenue
(503) 823-3674

MONTAVILLA SWIMMING POOL $
8219 Northeast Glisan Street
(503) 823-4101

PENINSULA PARK SWIMMING POOL $
700 North Rosa Parks Way
(503) 823-3677

PIER SWIMMING POOL $
9341 North St. Johns Street
(503) 823-3678

SELLWOOD SWIMMING POOL $
7951 Southeast 7th Avenue
(503) 823-3679

WILSON POOL $
1151 Southwest Vermont Street
(503) 823-3680

Outlying Areas

NORTH CLACKAMAS AQUATIC PARK $
7300 Southeast Harmony Road, Milwaukie
(503) 794-8080
www.co.clackamas.us/ncprd/aquatic
This Disneyland-ish water world is a wonderfully wet place for the kids to cool off during the long hot days of July and August. With wave pools, wading pools, diving pools, three water slides, and a whirlpool, you can bet the little ones will return home all tuckered out. Adults pay a little more. (See the Recreation chapter for more information.)

RESTAURANTS

OLD WIVES' TALES
1300 East Burnside Street
(503) 238-0470
This restaurant is popular with kids—and has built up loyalty with their parents too—for providing a large, well-stocked playroom in addition to the good children's menu and savory sandwiches, soups, and other light fare. Sit in a booth by the window and watch the street theater of Burnside. Old Wives' Tales also serves beer and wine and is open for breakfast, lunch, and dinner, seven days a week

i Saturday matinees at the McMenamin pub theaters—the Kennedy School, the Bagdad, and the Mission—are perfect for inexpensive family movies.

SIP N KRANTZ
901 Northwest 10th Avenue
(503) 336-1335
This family-friendly, sleek coffeeshop on Jamison Square in the Pearl attracts parents with wee ones from all over the city. It's got a great menu for children and adults, but even better, it has a whole room outfitted with soft furnishings, toys, books, and DVDs where parents can let the little ones loose while they sip their four-shot lattes. Plus, it's in the Pearl District, so you can remind yourself there is life beyond toddlerhood.

SKYLINE RESTAURANT
1313 Northwest Skyline Boulevard
(503) 292-6727
This is a child-friendly, old-fashioned, locally owned drive-in (though no one drives in any more) that has been serving delicious grill food for more than 50 years. Kids' meals include plain hamburgers without all the scary sauces and condiments that frighten children. You'll like your condiment-laden cheeseburger too.

SHOPPING FOR TOYS, BOOKS, AND MORE

SATURDAY MARKET
Underneath the Burnside Bridge between Southwest 1st Avenue and Southwest Ankeny Street
(503) 222-6072
www.portlandsaturdaymarket.com
The Portland Saturday Market, which also runs on Sunday, is a characteristic Portland experience that children love. In addition to the vendors of tie-dye, candles, jewelry, pottery, and stained glass, you'll find lively entertainment of every variety (especially music). The food is delicious, and the eye candy is even better. Saturday Market takes place from the first weekend in March to Christmas Eve. On Saturday the market opens at 10:00 a.m. and closes at 5:00 p.m.; Sunday hours are 11:00 a.m. to 4:30 p.m.

Books

BARNES & NOBLE BOOKSTORE
Lloyd Center
1317 Lloyd Avenue
(503) 249-0800

18300 Northwest Evergreen Parkway
Beaverton
(503) 645-3046
These Barnes & Noble bookstores not only offer books but also have story times for preschoolers. At the Lloyd Center, stories are read on Tuesday mornings; at Beaverton, on Saturday mornings. Maybe you'll get to browse a little too.

BORDERS BOOKS
708 Southwest 3rd Avenue
(503) 220-5911

2605 Southwest Cedar Hills Boulevard, Beaverton
(503) 644-6164

16920 Southwest 72nd Avenue, Tigard
(503) 968-7576
Borders' book events, signings, crafts, and story readings are held at different times depending on the location, so in theory, you could hear a story practically every day. Downtown, events are held at 2:00 p.m. on Saturdays. At Beaverton they are held on Tuesday mornings, and at the Tigard store they are held on Friday mornings.

A CHILDREN'S PLACE
4807 Northeast Fremont Street
(503) 284-8294
A Children's Place has books galore—more than 30,000 titles geared for younger readers—and a large music selection for kids, but that's just for starters. You can also buy a wide variety of educational toys and puzzles here, as well as games to stimulate those fertile imaginations, a good stock of art supplies, and musical instruments. A Children's Place hosts book fairs as well as Thursday-morning readings.

COSMIC MONKEY COMICS

5335 Northeast Sandy Boulevard

(503) 517-9050

A fine, large comic store with a wall of Manga and every variety of comic books. Cosmic Monkey is open Wednesday through Saturday, from noon to 6:00 or 7:00 p.m.; call to check closing time.

EXCALIBUR COMICS

2444 Southeast Hawthorne Boulevard

(503) 231-7351

A premier outlet for comics in the Portland area, Excalibur carries collector's items, books, and alternative comics in addition to their mainstream offerings. Not everything is G-rated, but they do have an impressive selection of children's comics, as well as good service. And you can rent anime flicks and other DVDs from Excalibur.

POWELL'S CITY OF BOOKS

1005 West Burnside Street

(503) 228-4651

www.powells.com

While Powell's City of Books is fully covered in the Shopping chapter, it is worth noting that the children's resources at Powell's are phenomenal. Not only do they carry current favorites, but they have vast holdings of used books, classics, collector's items, and, most important, a knowledgeable staff to help you find the perfect book for your child. Furthermore, they carry excellent educational materials; whether you are a homeschooling parent, a teacher, or simply an interested adult, you will be astonished at the wealth here. Visiting the store is a fine way to spend a day—while Powell's wants parents to watch their little ones and to refrain them from terrorizing the place, they also want to cultivate future readers, so exploring the wares is encouraged. The Hawthorne branch also has a good, though smaller, children's section

Toys

CHILD'S PLAY

907 Northwest 23rd Avenue

(503) 224-5586

A fine neighborhood shop in the Northwest Portland district, Child's Play features well-made, inventive toys. You'll find a decent selection of seasonal toys and dress-up clothes as well as lines like Playmobil, Lego, and Brio. The wide array of Breyer horses and accoutrements is another big draw. The store also carries books. It's useful to note that the shop has a parking lot (a rarity in the area) and is conveniently located next to a place that carries wrapping paper and party supplies.

FINNEGAN'S

922 Yamhill Street

(503) 221-0306

At Finnegan's you'll find whole cities of dolls, lots of building blocks, sidewalk chalk, ant farms, flower presses, boomerangs, dump trucks—in short, every kind of toy a child could imagine. Though it is large, it never has that frantic feeling that so many of the big chain toy stores cultivate; even during the holidays when it's really busy, Finnegan's manages to exude serenity. It could be the well-organized and competent staff, or perhaps it's the high-quality toys. They carry a vast selection of Brio, Plan, and Playmobil toys, lovely Ravensburger puzzles, great craft kits, plush toys, books, and more. And you'll find a lot of cool toys for party bags—bubbles, tops, creatures, chalk. The Hello Kitty Photo Sticker Machine, which will turn your image into stickers, is worth a stop even if you don't have any kids. Finnegan's also offers online gift certificates, which is incredibly convenient.

KIDS AT HEART

3435 Southeast Hawthorne Boulevard

(503) 231-2954

www.kidsathearttoys.com

Kids at Heart is a sweet neighborhood store in the Hawthorne shopping district; it keeps area residents supplied with birthday presents, art supplies, Playmobil sets, and Brio trains, but it's worth a trip for nonresidents too. Kids at Heart has a fine collection of dress-up clothes, games, and science-oriented toys—kits turning children into spies and explorers have been recent hits at parties. You won't find Barbie, but you will find Madeline dolls and Groovy Girls in addition to a whole wall of trains and building toys. They also carry many clever and ingenious baby toys.

Clothes

GENERATIONS
4029 Southeast Hawthorne Boulevard
(503) 233-8130
Beautiful natural-fiber clothing for children and their mothers (their pregnant and nursing mothers, that is), as well as a fine selection of baby accessories and some toys, draws people from all over town to this cozy shop on Hawthorne. The clothing and accessories for pregnant and nursing women is excellent, and the children's clothing is adorable. You will also find some consumer-tested clothing and shoes for resale.

GRASSHOPPER
1816 Northeast Alberta Street
(503) 335-3131
www.grasshopperstore.com
Grasshopper offers wonderful clothes for children, many of them handmade right there (or down the street at the "mother" store, Tumbleweed). Brands include the store's own Wild Carrots, Kate Quinn Organics, and Picaflor, among many others. There is also a large selection of well-made, lead-free toys. The beautiful space is a pleasure to shop in, and your children will also enjoy themselves, possibly almost as much as you. Grasshopper is open daily from 10:00 a.m. to 6:00 p.m. (5:00 p.m. on Sunday and Monday).

HAGGIS MCBAGGIS
6802 Southeast Milwaukie Avenue
(503) 234-0849
Finally, a store that understands the parental shopper: We are buying things for our children that secretly we want to wear ourselves. So the fancy shoes, wonderful tights, jewels, and very imaginative accessories that also come in adult sizes are a few reasons to shop in this colorful, attractive store. Another reason is the beautiful, clean, and spacious bathroom that stocks disposable diapers for emergencies. And still another: the kids' toys. Yet one more is the big cookie jar. Did we mention the adult sizes?

HANNA ANDERSSON
327 Northwest 10th Avenue
(503) 321-5275
Beautiful, well-made cotton clothes that look good and feel good are the specialty of this amazing Portland store, and it has acquired an international following through its catalog sales since its founding here in 1983. These clothes last a long time—even the tights. The clothes are meant to last for more than one child, so the company has a program to pass on gently used Hannas to needy children. Hanna Andersson is open Monday through Friday 10:00 a.m. to 6:00 p.m. and on Saturday from 10:00 a.m. to 5:00 p.m. (See the Shopping chapter for more details.)

HENNY PENNY
405 Northwest 10th Avenue
(503) 222-7676
This light-filled shop is great for baby and young children's clothes with a sophisticated twist. Expect beautifully designed natural-fiber sweaters, dresses, pants, and shirts in cool neutrals and bright colors. Gifts, accessories, and books complete the inventory.

NIKE TOWN
930 Southwest 6th Avenue
(503) 221-6454
Nike Town is the high-tech, ultramodern retail outlet for shoes, shirts, caps, and other sports apparel with that famous swoosh logo. The corner store is easy to spot with its life-size metallic silhouette of His Airness, Michael Jordan, on the south wall. Inside are plaques celebrating other noted athletes, interactive displays, multimedia delights, and video theatrics. (See the Shopping chapter for more information.)

POLLIWOG
2900 Southeast Belmont Street
(503) 236-3903
www.polliwogportland.com
Beautiful, beautiful children's clothes for new-borns and their siblings up to age six are the specialty of this pretty store in Southeast Portland—though they also sell diaper bags, gifts, wooden toys, and accessories as well. Shoes from See Kai Run are best-sellers, as well as wonderful baby T-shirts by Glug. Polliwog also carries dresses by Mister Judy, handmade in Portland.

i What better way to spend a summer evening than watching a movie with the family at the drive-in? The 99W Drive-In is happy to oblige every weekend spring through fall. You can find it at Highway 99W and Springbrook Road in Newberg (503-538-2738; www.99w.com).

FESTIVALS AND ANNUAL EVENTS

Almost everything, from the sacred to the mundane, seems to have its own festival or event in our area: We love to find reasons to celebrate. In this chapter, which is organized chronologically, we cover a wide range of festivals of all types and sizes in Portland and the metro area, the more-rural surrounding Oregon counties, and in Vancouver and Clark County, Washington. In a culture of mass marketing, mass media, and mass consumption, these celebrations help define and distinguish a particular area, preserving an awareness of local identity and history. Most important, they preserve a sense of place.

Some of the largest events in the area include athletic contests such as the Portland Marathon and the Hood-to-Coast Relay. Other draws feature Waterfront Park: In the summer, Portland's Tom McCall Waterfront Park hosts the Oregon Brewers Festival, the Rose Festival Fun Center, and the Waterfront Blues Festival. The area also has a chance to showcase its increasing number of farmers' markets during the summer. There you will find specialty and organic food products, flowers and nursery stock, not to mention the area's agricultural bounty (see the Close-up on the Portland Farmers' Market in this chapter). Portland's Old Town hosts the Saturday Market, an open-air craft and food event held each weekend from March until Christmas. Downtown's Pioneer Square is another popular site for performances of all sorts and smaller ethnic, art, food, and other festivals. The Mount Hood Jazz Festival, held in early August at Gresham Main City Park, just east of Portland, attracts noted musicians such as Bruce Hornsby, David Sanborn, and Mose Allison, and an audience from throughout the western United States and Canada. But there are many other festivals, and you can find something happening every weekend, somewhere.

Local newspapers are the best source of what is going on when you are visiting. The *Oregonian's* Friday A&E section and Homes & Gardens of the Northwest insert all carry detailed listings and calendars of a wide assortment of events in the entire region. *Portland Monthly* magazine also maintains an excellent calendar, and the smaller community and weekly papers will also carry this information. The Portland Oregon Visitors Association (POVA), at (503) 275-9750 or (800) 962-3700, keeps an online events calendar: www.travelportland.com.

Finally, this is Oregon and we are used to the weather. Outside events are rarely canceled because of weather, though it may occasionally cause changes in schedules and performances. In general, though, the show goes on. Dress accordingly.

JANUARY

REEL MUSIC
Northwest Film Center
1219 Southwest Park Avenue
(503) 221-1156
www.nwfilm.org
The annual celebration of music on film is one of two popular winter events sponsored by the Northwest Film Center. It's held at the Whitsell Auditorium in the Portland Art Museum, and the event features film showings, concerts, and speakers. Admission fees vary, so call ahead.

ROSE CITY CLASSIC ALL BREED DOG SHOW
Portland Expo Center,
2060 North Marine Drive
www.rosecityclassic.org

Portlanders love their dogs, and this event allows owners from throughout Oregon and southwest Washington to show off their pets (or vice versa). Breeders bring their offspring, and vendors peddle everything dogs, or their masters, might need.

FEBRUARY

CHINESE NEW YEAR
Various locations
Lucky money, fireworks, and feasting—what's not to love about Chinese New Year? This 15-day festival offers parades, parties, and other events to bring in the new year with style. Dancers dressed in traditional lion costumes scare off the evil spirits and bring good luck to Chinatown—an area of town that once housed immigrants from the Kwangtung province of Canton. You can celebrate Chinese New Year at various venues across town, in particular at the Portland Classical Chinese Garden (503-228-8131; see our Attractions chapter).

GREATER PORTLAND INTERNATIONAL AUTO SHOW
Oregon Convention Center
777 Northeast Martin Luther King Jr. Boulevard
(503) 235-7575, (800) 251-1563
New cars, old cars, minivans with more cup holders than wheels and spark plugs, tricked-up pickup trucks, and concept cars that will never dirty their tires on a real city street are all polished up and sparkle and gleam for this annual paean to our love affair with the automobile.

PACIFIC NORTHWEST SPORTSMEN'S SHOW
Portland Expo Center
2060 North Marine Drive
(503) 246-8291
The region's oldest and largest show of its type, this adult toy show is for those who fish, camp, hunt, and hike. There are hundreds of new products and services along with free seminars, exhibitions, and hands-on demonstrations.

PORTLAND INTERNATIONAL FILM FESTIVAL
Various locations
Northwest Film Center
1219 Southwest Park Avenue
(503) 276-4310-
www.nwfilm.org
Whether you're the type who goes to movies or critically views a cinema, you can sit in the dark for hours and hours looking at professional, experimental, traditional, and avant-garde film during this well-attended event sponsored by the Northwest Film Center. Admission fees vary, but in general, the more movies you attend, the lower the cost per viewing, if you buy a pass or block of tickets. Movies (as many as 80) are shown in local theaters over a three-week period. The opening and closing nights feature the Portland premiers of new major movies. Matinee tickets are available.

MARCH

ANTIQUE & COLLECTIBLE SALE
Portland Expo Center
2060 North Marine Drive
(503) 282-0877
www.palmerwirfs.com
Billed as "America's Largest Antique and Collectible Sale," this extravaganza will have something for everyone. Admission is $7, but there is an additional parking fee that doubles the cost of this show that has 1,800 booths filling the Expo Center with intriguing items from the past. They'll appraise your old stuff for $5 per item, too. They repeat this event in July and October.

PORTLAND SATURDAY MARKET
under the Burnside Bridge on
Southwest 1st Avenue
(503) 222-6072
www.saturdaymarket.org
Since 1974 Saturday Market (it is open on Sunday too) has been another "must see" for visitors. You can enjoy street theater (some intentional, some not), sample from a range of food booths, and buy everything from candles, macramé, pottery,

stained glass, clothing, hemp products, local produce and handmade housewares, furniture and toys, and tools and trinkets. Not as countercultural as they once were, vendors may dress like Deadheads but in reality are small business owners, and there is a fair amount of gray hair and middle-aged spread under the embroidered denim and sandals. Everything is made by hand. The market runs until Christmas. During the holiday-shopping madness, it is as packed as any department store or mall.

REED ARTS WEEKEND (RAW)
Reed College, 3203 Southeast
Woodstock Boulevard
(503) 771-1112
www.reed.edu/raw
This four-day gala of dance, poetry and prose readings, exhibits and musical performances includes the work of Reed students and that of important artists from Portland and beyond. There are performances and master classes, and everything is intellectually and aesthetically stimulating and challenging. And the college's Southeast Portland campus is beautiful, with a small but excellent art gallery, a superb performing arts center, and a great bookstore.

ST. PATRICK'S DAY
Various locations
For some inexplicable reason, Portland has turned St. Patrick's Day into a multiday party. Kells Irish Restaurant and Pub hosts a street fair, live Celtic and Irish music, and demonstrations of Irish crafts. They also serve beer (Harp and Guinness flow freely), and you can ward off the damp chill with an Irish coffee or some Irish whiskey. Other shops, restaurants, pubs, and bars flaunt their Irish heritage or make it up for a day as they join in the celebration. You can get ready for St. Patrick's Day at Kathleen's of Dublin, 860 Southwest Broadway, (503) 224-4869, one of the best shops for Irish (and Scottish) merchandise, including clothing, tapes, and CDs; Celtic-inspired jewelry; and teacups and teapots. Celtic Corner, 4142 Northeast Sandy Boulevard, (503) 287-3009, is another good

source of St. Patrick's Day supplies. If you should be at a loss for how to properly celebrate this occasion, call the All Ireland Cultural Society, (503) 286-4812.

SHAMROCK RUN
Tom McCall Waterfront Park, between
the bank of the Willamette River and
Bill Naito Parkway
www.shamrockrunportland.com
One of Portland's most popular running events, the Shamrock Run is a fund-raiser for Doernbecher Children's Hospital Foundation, one of the state's most popular and successful charities. The event includes a Leprechaun Lap, a 1-kilometer run, walk, or jog; the Shamrock Stride, a 4-mile walk; and an 8-kilometer race. The entry fee varies with the runner's age and selected event but includes a souvenir T-shirt. There is usually a variety of freebies for runners, walkers, and their supporters, including food items and beverages.

APRIL

AGFEST
State Fairgrounds, Salem
(503) 581-4325, (800) 874-7012
www.oragfest.com
The Agfest is a celebration of the industry that plays a large role in all our lives: agriculture. Here you will find representatives of everyone from angora rabbit breeders to grass seed farmers to orchard growers, who gather here to teach people about their work. The Agfest winds throughout most of the fairgrounds, with many activities and events. Crafts, puppet shows, country dancing, and music are featured, along with farm animals of many varieties. Particular favorites include the horse shows, the llamas, the miniature horses, the sheep shearing, and the petting zoo. You can also take a ride in a wagon pulled by horses or by tractors. Children love to follow the elaborate scavenger hunt in the Ag Country display: Not only do they get to sample Oregon products such as pears, cherries, and shrimp; collect seeds to plant at home; and gather up

pencils, candy, and other paraphernalia, but they also learn a remarkable amount. Before you head home, be sure to tour the booths in the main exhibition hall and pick up starter plants for excellent prices, as well as wares from local artisans. This fun event is a favorite with families in the Willamette Valley, and more Portlanders should attend. Admission is low; adults pay $6, and children 12 and under are admitted for no charge. To get to the Agfest, follow Interstate 5 to exit 256 (Market Street), and then follow Market west. Turn right (north) onto 17th Street, which takes you directly to the fairgrounds. Be prepared to pay a few bucks for parking.

CRYSTAL SPRINGS
Early Rhododendron Show
Crystal Springs Rhododendron Garden
Southeast 28th Avenue and Woodstock
(503) 771-8386
The beautiful Crystal Springs Rhododendron Garden hosts two celebrations of this native flowering shrub, one on the first Saturday in April and the other during Mother's Day weekend in May. The April show features hundreds of early blooms and these signs of spring are the perfect way to remind yourself that the rains will eventually taper off. (See the Portland's Parks chapter for more information about this wonderful public park.)

LILAC FESTIVAL
Hulda Klager Lilac Gardens
Woodland, WA
(360) 225-8996
www.lilacgardens.com
If your visit coincides with the spring blossoming of lilacs, the 30-minute trip north from Portland to Woodland is worth it. Set on 5.5 acres near the Columbia River, the Hulda Klager Lilac Gardens holds the promise of spring when the fragrant bushes burst into color. This is a popular event for color-starved Pacific Northwesterners who spend hours wandering the grounds admiring the hues and smelling the fragrance of both rare and more common varieties of the plant. Bouquets and

cuttings are also available for purchase. There is a small gift shop in the farmhouse, and refreshments are available. Donations are welcomed at this National Historic Site.

Blossom Time

The Hood River Valley, east of Portland, is prime orchard country, and during late March and all through April, it is blanketed in pink and white blossoms. A drive to see the peach, apple, pear, and cherry blossoms makes a perfect half-day trip, and whether you take the long route over Mount Hood on U.S. Highway 26 or the shorter way (east along the Columbia Gorge via Interstate 84), your drive will be spectacular. Call the Hood River Chamber of Commerce, and they'll send you a blossom-time brochure: (800) 366-3530.

TRILLIUM FESTIVAL
Tryon Creek State Park, 11321 Southwest Terwilliger Boulevard, Lake Oswego
(503) 636-4398
www.tryonfriends.org
The Trillium Festival celebrates our native Oregon plant at this quiet 635-acre park, tucked away between Lewis & Clark College and Lake Oswego, less than 10 minutes from the busy concrete ribbon of I-5. The free event features a variety of nature-related and craft activities for children at the visitor/learning center. Visitors can purchase plants, trees, and shrubs to help support the park's educational programs and maintenance. There are easy walks along the park's rolling trails and streams and food and music for the body and soul.

TUALATIN VALLEY RHODODENDRON SHOW
Jenkins Estate, 8005 Southwest
Grabhorn Road, Aloha
(503) 629-6355

Slightly off the usual visitor's path in the suburban hills, the Jenkins Estate at any time is worth a visit, but during early spring, the estate's 2.5-acre rhododendron garden is ablaze with blossoms. The gardens are also filled with daffodils, Japanese and other plum and cherry trees, camellias, and azaleas. Best of all, next to the sheer beauty of the blossoms, the event is free and visitors can stroll the well-kept grounds and visit the big house from Portland's past.

WOODBURN TULIP FESTIVAL
Woodburn
(503) 634-2243, (800) 711-2006
www.woodenshoe.com

Emerging from the gray Oregon winter, hundreds of thousands of tulip bulbs burst into color each spring at several nurseries in this small town just south of Portland. Oregonians flock to the varied colored fields, rejoicing at this welcome sign that they survived another winter. Entry is free, and visitors can purchase cut flowers, order bulbs, snack on local foods, and be tempted by the nurseries' bounty and gift shops. The actual dates vary slightly in response to the severity of the winter, but this event, like spring, is worth the wait. During the festival weeks there is a $5 vehicle charge on Saturday and Sunday; Monday through Friday it's free.

MAY

CERAMIC SHOWCASE
Oregon Convention Center, 777 Northeast
Martin Luther King Jr. Boulevard
(503) 222-0533
www.ceramicshowcase.com

If you want to know what Oregonians do when it can rain from October to May, visit this annual event sponsored by the Oregon Potters Association. The show, which is the largest event of its kind in the United States, fills several huge rooms with pottery and ceramics by dozens of potters from throughout Oregon and Washington. Admission is free. If you buy something, these people know how to pack it so it gets to your home unbroken.

CINCO DE MAYO
Tom McCall Waterfront Park between
the bank of the Willamette River and
Bill Naito Parkway
www.cincodemayo.org

Portland is a Sister City to several cities throughout the world, including Guadalajara. This is a huge waterfront event celebrating the country's holiday, one of the largest such events in North America. It features Mexican and Latino food, crafts, art, music, and dancing, as well as carnival rides and other festive touches. The entry fee is $8 for those 12 and older and $2 for kids 4 to 11.

CRYSTAL SPRINGS RHODODENDRON
Mother's Day Show
Crystal Springs Rhododendron Garden
Southeast 28th Avenue and Woodstock
(503) 771-8386

May brings out the full glory of our indigenous rhododendron, and what better way to honor your mom than by walking with her down the lovely, winding paths of the Crystal Springs Rhododendron Garden? The Garden features thousands of blooming rhododendrons, azaleas, and other plantings all during Mother's Day weekend in May—a spectacular sight. (See the Portland's Parks chapter for more information about Crystal Springs Rhododendron Garden.)

DOGGIE DASH
Tom McCall Waterfront Park
between the bank of the Willamette
River and Bill Naito Parkway
(503) 323-6656
www.oregonhumane.org/doggiedash/

Most races don't allow Fido, but this one encourages dogs of all kinds, since it's a fundraiser for the Oregon Humane Society. Sponsored by a local radio station, the Doggie Dash is a 2-mile run/walk/trot for canines and their owners. The entry fee includes a T-shirt (for the runner) and doggie treats (for the dogs). Costumed runners, both canine and human, are not uncommon.

MEMORIAL DAY WEEKEND IN THE WINE COUNTRY
Willamette Valley Wineries Association
(503) 646-2985
www.willamettewines.com

This is an increasingly popular self-guided tour of more than 100 vineyards and wineries, including some not open at any other time of the year. The event features wine and food matches from some of the region's best chefs and vintners. Advice, maps, lists of participating vineyards and wineries, and other details (telephone numbers, open hours, etc.) are available on the Web site above. This festive weekend draws thousands into the fertile valley to taste the region's pinot noirs, syrahs, and other notable wines. This is a unique opportunity to try barrel tastings, reserves, and the special vintages that the winemakers like to hold back. The wineries are open for the festival from 11:00 a.m. to 5:00 p.m. on Saturday and Sunday. (For a feel for the region, see the Northern Willamette Valley's Wine Country section in the Day Trips chapter.)

JUNE

CHAMBER MUSIC NORTHWEST
Reed College
3203 Southeast Woodstock Avenue

Catlin Gabel School
8825 Southwest Barnes Road
(503) 223-3202, (503) 294-6400
www.cmnw.org

Brilliant, challenging, soothing, and *inspiring* are all words to describe this series of 25 performances and concerts held throughout June and July. Director David Shifrin, a renowned clarinetist and Avery Fisher Prize recipient, brings the world's best musicians to this wonderful festival. Preconcert picnics feature gourmet foods, wines, coffees, and desserts. The admission fee is reasonable and series tickets are available, but order in advance for the best seats. On Fridays adults can bring children ages 7 to 18 for free.

FESTIVAL OF FLOWERS
Pioneer Courthouse Square, between
6th Avenue and Broadway,
Morrison and Yamhill Streets

This event mixes a fair amount of flat, open space and the talent and imagination of an artist, hundreds of volunteers, and 15,000 or so potted annuals. The volunteers turn the flowers into a work of art that honors Portland's beautiful public gardens. After a few days, when thousands of onlookers have admired the piece, the flowers are sold to the public at wholesale prices.

LAKE OSWEGO FESTIVAL OF THE ARTS
George Rogers Park, Lake Oswego
368 South State Street
(503) 636-1060
www.lakewood-center.org

A small, free, family-oriented event in this upscale suburb, the festival includes arts and crafts booths, a juried art competition, food booths, and activities for children and families. Somewhat low-key, it is a good example of a community event that retains its human scale while drawing a good crowd and some excellent artists.

NATIVE AMERICAN POWWOW
Delta Park, North Denver Avenue and
Martin Luther King Jr. Boulevard
www.powwowtime.com

The largest regularly scheduled gathering of Native Americans in Portland, this festival includes members of various tribes who share their dances, ceremonies, crafts, music, and indigenous foods with guests. The event turns this urban park into a large encampment that attracts residents and visitors from throughout the region.

PORTLAND ROSE FESTIVAL
Portland Rose Festival Association
Various venues citywide
(503) 227-2681
www.rosefestival.org

Besides the selection and crowning of the Rose Queen, there are more than 100 different official Rose Festival events, including three parades, dragon boat races, a carnival-like fun center on the waterfront, several art exhibits, tours of ships from the U.S. and Canadian Navy and Coast Guard, an air show, a ski race, a hot-air balloon race, the CART (Championship Auto Racing Teams) races, and a world-class rose show. This event draws thousands and thousands of visitors every year, and it marks the beginning of the summer season—no matter what the weather is doing.

PRIDE NORTHWEST
Various locations
(503) 295-9788
www.pridenw.org
Pride Northwest is Portland's annual gay, lesbian, bi, and trans celebration that includes music, events, a fun run, a pet parade, and the great Pride Parade, which is held on Sunday. The Pride Parade, a splendid event, draws more than 50,000 people and is Portland's third largest annual parade. There is also a festival of food, crafts, and booths by gay/lesbian–friendly organizations and services.

JULY

A NORTHWEST FOURTH OF JULY
As in other parts of the country, the Fourth of July celebrates not only the national birthday, but the full-fledged arrival of summer. Local celebrations of this holiday reflect a sense of national and local identity, and picnics, block parties, barbecues, concerts, parades, and fireworks are favorite ways to celebrate. Local weather lore indicates that summer in Oregon begins on July 5. Moist, low clouds can sometimes affect fireworks displays, and chilly temperatures can keep residents bundled up.

There are dozens of neighborhood celebrations and festivals as well as several large displays of fireworks along the Willamette and Columbia Rivers. Oaks Park and Waterfront Park along the Willamette have the two most central displays,

and if you position yourself just right along the river, you can see both of them at once. Other venues, such as the Portland International Speedway and PGE Park have also displayed fireworks in the past. All over town, you'll find live outdoor music (especially at the Waterfront Blues Festival, below), barbecues, picnics, block parties, and festivity. Two special regional traditions are listed below, one at Fort Vancouver and one in the little town of St. Paul, south of Portland.

CONCERTS IN THE PARKS
Citywide, various locations
(503) 823-PLAY
Summer in the city: Early evening light softens but still gleams off the river; the current laps gently at the river's banks, a counterpoint to the fading, distant hum of traffic; and music soothes and stimulates the quiet crowd that has gathered at Waterfront Park to hear the Oregon Symphony. Or perhaps the crowd is on its feet and dancing the rhumba at Mount Tabor. Whatever the music and wherever the park, these free concerts are held during July (and often into August) throughout the city. You'll find a free concert of one kind or another just about every night of the week. Information about these concerts is available at all Portland Parks and Recreation facilities, as well as libraries throughout the city. You can also find concert schedules and locations at the Portland Parks Web site: www.portlandonline.com/parks.

CONCOURS D'ELEGANCE
Pacific University, 2043 College Way
Forest Grove
(503) 357-3006
www.forestgroveconcours.org
Concours D'Elegance is the largest event of its type in the Pacific Northwest. Organized by the Forest Grove Rotary Club, the event is held on the pastoral campus of Pacific University and features more than 350 classic, vintage, and antique touring and sports cars from virtually every era of automotive history. This is a one-day event, usually held on a Sunday in mid-July. Admission for adults is $15, and for children 6 through 16,

$7. (Some discounts are available if you buy your tickets ahead of time.) In addition to the display of cars as art and investments, there is a range of musical entertainment and assorted refreshments. If you go, plan on spending a full day in Forest Grove. This is a neat little town where, in typical Oregon fashion, loggers and mill workers share neighborhoods with college students and professors and those who commute to downtown Portland. There are a growing number of small retail establishments, antiques stores, restaurants, and coffee shops. Don't miss the gallery operated by the Valley Art Association.

DA VINCI DAYS
Oregon State University–Corvallis
760 Southwest Madison, Suite 200
Corvallis
(541) 757-6363
www.davinci-days.org
This wonderful event, inspired by Leonardo da Vinci, brings together art, science, and technology—with the idea that they should never have been separated in the first place. The festival exhibits show you why. It's a three-day celebration that includes everything from a regional art show to performances of original dance. There are skateboard and teen band competitions, a film and video festival, jazz performances, a children's parade, Ultimate Frisbee, and street theater. A range of demonstrations and hands-on activities related to the yearly theme is also scheduled. This is an ideal event for adults and children. You can buy tickets just for the day ($10 if you're 13 or older and $5 if you're between 6 and 12), or for the whole weekend ($15 and $10 respectively).

INTERNATIONAL PINOT NOIR CELEBRATION
Linfield College
900 Southeast Baker Street
McMinnville
(503) 472-8964, (800) 775-4762
www.ipnc.org
This celebration draws oenophiles and wine experts from throughout the country to this small college for three days of tastings, talks and tours, eating, and entertainment. Half of the 60 pinots are from right here in Oregon, and the other half arrive from the world over. The event encourages you to mingle by dividing participants into two groups for activities, which makes for very interesting conversations, especially as the afternoon proceeds. Advance reservations are mandatory— fewer than 400 tickets are sold for this event, and tickets sell out quickly, despite the price tag of $975. (Tickets are sold on a first-come-first-served basis, starting in February.) The Passport to Pinot Noir is a separate mini-festival held on Sunday afternoon. The $125 admission allows you tastes of more than 60 pinot noirs, food from local chefs, a great lecture, and a Reidel glass to keep.

MOLALLA BUCKEROO
The Buckeroo Grounds, Berkeley
Avenue, off Highway 211, Molalla
(503) 829-8388
www.molallabuckeroo.com
Since 1913, professional riders, ropers, and other persons skilled in the arts of the Western ranch have been coming to the Molalla Buckeroo (that's Oregon-speak for rodeo). Admission prices vary from about $13 to $15, depending on how old you are and where you sit. Matinee prices are discounted. This event includes dances, barbecues, trail rides, parades, and, of course, three days of professional rodeo, all during the Fourth of July holiday.

MOUNT ANGEL ABBEY BACH FESTIVAL
Mount Angel Abbey, One Mt. Angel Drive,
Mount Angel
(503) 845-3321
www.mtangel.edu/bach/
While the state's largest celebration of Bach is held in Eugene, this event is an opportunity to hear some of the master's music superbly performed in an unusual setting. Each night of the festival opens with a vespers service and then a recital, after which the entire audience gathers outside in groups of four for picnic suppers before heading in for the evening's featured performance. Held on the final Wednesday, Thursday,

and Friday in July, the festival's 500 nightly seats are sold out months in advance and available only by mail. If you want to attend, call or e-mail well ahead and get your name on the mailing list (503-845-8272 or bach@mtangel.edu).

Mount Angel is best known for its annual Oktoberfest (see the September section), an event that has been called the state's largest party. On the other hand, the town is worth visiting at other times of the year, even if you don't have tickets to the Bach Festival. The drive down, especially on the back roads, takes you through some of the richest farmland in the world. The century-old Benedictine abbey and seminary sit on a 300-foot-high hill overlooking the town of Mount Angel and the area's fertile valley. The abbey has a small, eclectic museum and gift shop, and tours are available by prior arrangement.

In downtown Mount Angel, St. Mary's Church, 575 East College Street, (503) 845-2296, is an inspiring and historic example of neogothic architecture. Originally built in 1912 to serve the religious needs of the German Catholics who settled in the area, the church was severely damaged in 1993's Spring Break Earthquake. The restoration was daunting, but the results are incredible. The Mount Angel Brewing Company, 210 Monroe Street, Mount Angel, (503) 845-9624, a locally owned brewpub and restaurant, also makes a nice stop.

MT. HOOD OREGON TRAIL QUILT SHOW AND OLD-TIME FIDDLER'S JAMBOREE
73370 East Bugsy Trail, Rhododendron
(888) 622-4822
www.mthoodterritory.com/events
This two-day free event is held in Rhododendron, a small town at the base of Mount Hood, 45 miles from Portland. The festival includes a display of antique quilts dating back 150 years to the era of the Oregon Trail, contemporary quilts, other quilted items, and quilting supplies. The music is also outstanding.

OREGON BREWERS FESTIVAL
Tom McCall Waterfront Park, between
Naito Parkway and the Willamette River
(503) 778-5917
www.oregonbrewfest.com
Oregon has a reputation for making fine brews, and so it's not surprising that this popular festival draws more than 50,000 people who come to Portland's waterfront to taste our region's excellent local beers and ales as well as those from elsewhere. The festival invites 72 brewers from across the continent to show off their craft, and about a third of these brewers are from right here in town. You can expect to find more than a dozen styles of beer and ale, ranging from stouts to wheat beers and porters (but only one product from each brewery is allowed). And craft-brewed root beer and cream soda, lemonade, cider, and coffees are also available. A selection of locally prepared specialty foods, most of which may be eaten without utensils, is also available. Local musicians, including some of the area's best performers, offer entertainment. Moderation as well as the use of mass transit, taxis, and designated drivers are all seriously encouraged. While clearly not a family event for those with underage offspring—though children are allowed—the festival encourages enjoyment, beer tasting, and a little bit of education about the brewer's art and product. There is zero tolerance for any type of boisterous, unruly, or other antisocial behavior. All local laws are well enforced by Portland's blue-clad finest, and the event is monitored by the sponsoring association and the Oregon Liquor Control Commission. Admission is free, but visitors must purchase a $5 mug for tasting and purchase tokens in advance in order to fill it (tokens and mugs are sold at the same site). Tokens are $1 each; a full glass of beer is $4, while a seven-ounce taste is two tokens. All of this must be paid for with cash; an ATM is available on-site. No credit cards are accepted. The festival runs Thursday through Sunday of the last full weekend in July.

Completely Fair

With their farm animals, 4-H kids, crafts exhibits, carnival rides, and country music, county fairs provide some of the best summer entertainment around. In July look for the Hood River County Fair, (541) 354-2865, and the Washington County Fair and Rodeo, (503) 646-1416. In August try the Yamhill County Fair, (503) 434-7524; the Clackamas County Fair (503) 266-1136; and the Clark County (Washington) Fair, across the river, (360) 397-6180. In late September Multnomah County holds its fair right here in Portland, (503) 761-7577. For information about all the fairs in Oregon, visit www.oregonfairs.org.

OREGON COUNTRY FAIR
13 miles west of Eugene on
Highway 126, near Veneta
(541) 343-4298
www.oregoncountryfair.org
The Oregon Country Fair is a wondrous alloy of beautiful handicrafts, displays of alternative energy sources, acoustic music, funky vaudeville acts, excellent food, arts displays, and much more. If you have the time (Veneta, near Eugene, is a good two-hour drive from Portland), the Country Fair is worth the trip. It's a cultural experience unique to Oregon. The Fair is the event in which Oregon reveals its inner hippie. Musicians, mimes, and magicians; crafters and cooks; all will entertain, even amaze you with their skill. Be sure to call the above number for directions and order advance tickets through Ticketswest (www.ticketswest.com)—none will be sold at the site. Friday, the fair's first day, offers the complete experience with fewer visitors. Some child care is available on-site. This event is extremely popular,

so parking and traffic may give you a lot of headaches. You might instead take one of the buses that Lane County Transit thoughtfully sends out to the fair site. If you do park at the fair, be sure to respect the residents who live near the grounds.

No dogs, video cameras, glass containers, or alcoholic beverages are allowed at this event.

PORTLAND SCOTTISH HIGHLAND GAMES
Mt. Hood Community College
Northeast 257th Avenue, Gresham
(503) 293-8501
www.phga.org
This celebration of all things Scottish features bagpipe bands and soloists, Highland dancers, fiddlers, and those unusual and muscle-straining Scottish athletic competitions. Visitors can enjoy ethnic Scottish foods and beverages and browse a range of imported clothes, jewelry, and other items. Admission is in the $10 to $20 range.

THE ST. PAUL RODEO
St. Paul
(503) 633-2011, (800) 237-5920
www.stpaulrodeo.com
St. Paul, a small rural Willamette Valley town south of Portland off of I-5, holds a rodeo that's one of the best in the country, with riders competing for prizes in several categories. Even the big city folks get out their jeans, Western shirts, and cowboy boots to join the fun. There are food and beverage booths, a carnival with rides and games of chance and skill, Western dancing for grown-ups, lots of music, a traditional small-town Fourth of July parade, and, of course, fireworks. This is a real slice of Americana. If you are in town and without other plans over the Fourth, this is worth the short ride. To see the rodeo, you'll need a ticket; these run from about $12 to $18, depending on the luxuriousness of the seat. And it's best to order them ahead. Parking is free.

SALEM ART FAIR & FESTIVAL
Bush's Pasture Park, Salem
(503) 581-2228
www.salemart.org/fair/
This event is worth the drive down I-5 to Salem

from Portland or Vancouver. Approximately 200 artists and craftspeople from throughout the entire West display (and gladly sell) their works. Children and adults will enjoy the range of entertainment, concerts, demonstrations, and puppet shows. The event is also an opportunity to walk through and admire a superb rose garden, a Victorian home, and an excellent community gallery. Admission, parking, and a shuttle service are free. Leave Fido home, though.

SAND IN THE CITY
Pioneer Courthouse Square, between
6th Avenue and Broadway, Morrison
and Yamhill Streets
(503) 238-4445
Now you can get even with your parents for all the times they told you "don't bring the whole beach home with you." It's not the whole beach (Oregon has some 300 miles of coastline) but it's enough—270 tons—to allow 18 teams of architects and others to design and build sand castles and other structures in the center of downtown. Amused and intrigued onlookers are allowed to provide unsolicited advice during this three-day fund-raising event for Kids on the Block, an organization that uses puppetry and drama to teach kids about healthy living. The event also includes puppet shows, music, and a children's sandbox. Sand in the City is sponsored by Yoshida, and it's free, with a suggested donation of $3.

STATE GAMES OF OREGON
Venues vary
(503) 520-1319
www.stategamesoforegon.org
The State Games involve more than three dozen "grassroots" sports, ranging from arm wrestling and badminton to footbag (hackey-sack) and pickleball, indoor soccer, and water polo, most with at least two or three categories of competition. More than 16,000 people from throughout Oregon and neighboring states will participate at sites throughout the metro area. The State Games of Oregon are a statewide, multisport, Olympic-style competition (individual and team

sports) created by the Oregon Amateur Sports Foundation and supported by proceeds from the Oregon Lottery. With some exceptions, only Oregon residents can compete. Admission for spectators is free. Registration fees vary; call for information.

WATERFRONT BLUES FESTIVAL
Tom McCall Waterfront Park
between the bank of the Willamette
River and Naito Parkway
(503) 973-FEST
www.waterfrontbluesfest.com
There may be some irony about a four-day blues festival held over the Fourth of July weekend in one of the most livable cities in the nation. The blues are perhaps the American musical genre, rooted in hard times and forged with heartache. If you've been down so long that it looks like up to you, then you may not notice that the festival is held on the green sloping banks of a river with a snowcapped mountain bathed in evening light as a backdrop. Nor would you notice the free fireworks that end the Fourth of July concert or the fact that the festival brings some of the nation's, and the Northwest's, finest blues artists to the city. One of Portland's premier events, the Waterfront Blues Festival has been packing them in by land and sea (boaters anchor off the seawall to listen to the music sans admission charge) for more than 15 years. If you don't mind not seeing the performers, spread a blanket on the grass beyond the festival area, close your eyes, and listen with all your heart. Admission is $10 and two cans of food for the Oregon Food Bank—all proceeds go to support the Oregon Food Bank.

AUGUST

THE BITE OF OREGON
Tom McCall Waterfront Park, between
Naito Parkway and the Willamette River
(503) 248-0600
www.biteoforegon.com
Portlanders do love their summer festivals—It must have something to do with being able to

get outdoors without layers of Gore-Tex and a rain hat. The Bite is another local celebration of food, eating, and conspicuous food consumption, and it draws people from all over to eat their way from one end of Waterfront Park to the other. Restaurants from all over the state ply their wares, top chefs show off for one another in a local *Iron Chef*–style competition, and local breweries and winemakers offer their tempting concoctions. The admission charge of $7 supports the Oregon Special Olympics. Three stages of music and dancing are also featured. Fireworks end the event—another beloved staple of Portland's summer festivals.

CELEBRATION OF CULTURES
Vance Park, Gresham
Downtown Gresham
(503) 618-2866
Once a quiet, distant city of farms and fields, Gresham is now the fourth-largest city in Oregon, welcoming light rail and building new neighborhoods and restoring the downtown. For a long time people felt, to quote Gertrude Stein, that "there was no there, there." That's not true anymore. This free event is sponsored by the Gresham Sister City Association to honor its three overseas sister cities: Ebetsu, Japan; Sok-Cho, Korea; and Owerri, Nigeria, and the city's own increasingly diverse population and identity. The event includes foods from different countries and cultures, a splendid parade, blessings from local Native Americans, folk dancing, arts demonstrations, and many kinds of music.

FESTA ITALIANA
Pioneer Courthouse Square, between
6th Avenue and Broadway,
Morrison and Yamhill Streets
www.festa-italiana.org
For a few days in August, Pioneer Courthouse Square turns into a proper Italian piazza. The Festa Italiana is full of strolling musicians, art displays, and the culinary arts of a dozen or so Italian restaurants offering pizza, pastas, and other fare. All this and a wine garden draw an afternoon and early-evening crowd from the suburbs and downtown offices. A bocce ball tournament is a prominent feature, but the biggest draw is the wine-making—including the chance for you to get in on the action by stomping grapes.

FIESTA MEXICANA
Legion Park, Woodburn
(503) 981-3365
www.woodburnchamber.org
Just down the freeway (south on I–5) from Portland, Woodburn is a growing city in its own right, not a true suburb. A growing Hispanic population in the Willamette Valley adds diversity, color, and a continuing cultural influence to Oregon. Less commercial and flashy than Portland's Cinco de Mayo celebration, this event reflects the real lives, food, art, music, and traditions of Hispanic Americans. Admission is free, and the event is well worth the short drive.

HOOD TO COAST RELAY
Starting at Timberline Lodge
Timberline access road off US 26
just off Government Camp
(503) 292-4626
www.hoodtocoast.com
Since 1982, teams have gathered at Government Camp, on Mount Hood, to run a 195-mile relay race all the way to Seaside at the Oregon coast. Twelve people are on each team. The race, which is billed as the largest relay race in the world, attracts more than 16,000 people—runners, walkers, spectators—from all over. Walking events are offered in addition to running events, and some of the racewalkers are impossibly fast. This race is very exhilarating and therefore popular; many teams are made up of people who wouldn't ordinarily find themselves in any kind of race whatsoever. Because of its popularity, the organizers have a strict registration policy and expect you to register well in advance. But even if you're not racing, the event is fun to follow, whether you're watching the runners speed through Portland or joining them in celebration at Seaside.

INDIA FESTIVAL
**Pioneer Courthouse Square, between
6th Avenue and Broadway,
Morrison and Yamhill Streets
(503) 645-7902
www.icaportland.org**

The India Festival draws Oregonians whose families originated on the Indian subcontinent, as well as everyone in town who loves Indian food, spices, art, jewelry, arts and crafts, music, and dance. It's a sensory carnival, with colors, music, and aromas blending intriguingly. There's no admission charge for this Pioneer Square event.

MT. HOOD HUCKLEBERRY FESTIVAL & BARLOW TRAIL DAYS
**65000 East US 26, Mt. Hood Village
(503) 622-4798**

Events like these are important for the area's suburban and urban populations because they help maintain awareness of the state's agricultural heritage and bounty. While Oregon is currently known for high-tech products, expensive athletic shoes, and tourism, agriculture remains one of the three largest industries. This free event emphasizes the region's history, for it takes place on part of the Oregon Trail, and the state's natural wealth—in this case, berries. You can buy jams, pies, sauces, tarts, and syrups; enjoy a salmon bake; and take tours of the historic Barlow Trail, which led pioneers around Mount Hood and down into the Willamette Valley. There's also lots of great information about Native American history and that of the Oregon Trail.

MT. HOOD JAZZ FESTIVAL
**Gresham Main City Park
Powell Boulevard and Main Avenue
(503) 661-2700
www.mthoodjazz.com**

The Mount Hood Jazz Festival is one of Portland's biggest musical events. Advance tickets start at about $20 for the Friday main-stage show, and $25 for the Saturday main-stage show—well worth the cost, for the open-air festival attracts some of the biggest and most respected names in jazz. Ray Charles, Madeleine Peyroux, David

Sanborn, and Oregon native Chris Botti have been headliners, but the depth of talent and skill of the other 20 or so performers—soloists, singers, and groups from a trio on up in size—are equally as impressive. The largest jazz festival in the state, this is a popular event inspiring both patrons and performers to return year after year. The festival recognizes that having fun is as important as the music and manages to balance those concerns very well. Parking is free in downtown Gresham.

OBT EXPOSED
**South Park Blocks, between Salmon
and Main Streets
(503) 227-0977**

Much more than just very limber and graceful men and women in black tights, this open-air studio with no admission charge brings viewers "backstage" to see how much work, practice, and skill is involved in the dance world of Oregon Ballet Theater. A fascinating marketing and awareness-building effort, this event features ballet members who spend two weeks practicing in tents as part of their preparation for the new season. Much more than a publicity ploy, it's a traffic-stopping effort to bring art into the light.

OBONFEST
**Oregon Buddhist Temple
3720 Southeast 34th Avenue
(503) 254-9456
www.pdx-obon.org**

Set in a residential neighborhood, this is a Japanese-American Buddhist Festival of the Ancestors, which offers another perspective on multicultural life in Portland. The free festival is also an opportunity to learn about the long and not terribly comfortable history of Oregon's Japanese-American community. More cultural than strictly religious, the fest includes Japanese and other Asian foods, crafts, music, and dancing.

STREET OF DREAMS
**Location and specific times vary
(503) 684-1880
www.streetofdreamspdx.com**

To showcase their talents each year, between

seven and ten local builders create a custom-designed, -decorated, and -landscaped house in a selected enclave. These are clearly not starter, or even average, homes: Prices begin at more than $2 million. *Extravagance* is the word here. But for a comparatively modest admission fee, it is a pleasant way to spend an afternoon seeing how and where the affluent plan to live. The event, a fund-raiser for local nonprofit organizations, opens with a black-tie tour. Hors d'oeuvres and liquid refreshments are included. (See the Relocation chapter for additional information.)

TUALATIN CRAWFISH FESTIVAL
Tualatin Commons and Community Park
8535 Southwest Tualatin Road, Tualatin
(503) 692-0780
www.tualatincrawfishfestival.com
As this once-rural suburb grows into a city, it continues to celebrate a tradition dating from 1957. The event is split between the Commons in downtown Tualatin and the Community Park just a short stroll away. This popular event features parades, a 5K race, remote-control boat racing, a pancake breakfast, and many, many booths. You'll find lots of crawfish dishes, including a crawfish cookoff. Many activities are designed just for the children, and there's plenty of entertainment—music, dancing—for adults as well.

SEPTEMBER

ALBERTA STREET FAIR
between 18th Avenue and 30th Avenue
along Alberta Street
www.albertastreetfair.com
This blossoming mercantile strip in Northeast Portland celebrates its hipness with a multicultural neighborhood celebration featuring artwork, music, food, children's activities, and a free trolley. If you miss this event, you can enjoy the art galleries, restaurants, and boutiques that are popping up along this busy street by attending Last Thursday Walks every month. (See The Arts chapter for more information on Last Thursday Walks.)

ART IN THE PEARL
Northwest Park Blocks, between West
Burnside and Northwest Glisan at
Northwest 8th Avenue
(503) 722-9017
www.artinthepearl.com
More than 100 artists gather here each Labor Day weekend for a lively three days of culture and commerce. In addition to artists and high-end crafters selling their wares, musicians and theater groups perform on a central stage. And you can try out artistic pursuits for yourself in the Education Pavilion, which has activities for children and their grown-up friends. And, naturally, you'll find the usual festival food booths.

MT. ANGEL OKTOBERFEST
throughout downtown Mt. Angel
www.mtangel.org
Despite a long history of German settlers, Mount Angel didn't make Oktoberfest a commercial activity until 1965. Now the free event lasts four days, beginning with the traditional Webentanz, or May Pole dance, and it's become the largest folk festival in the state. There are four stages with nearly continuous live music, demonstrations of traditional Bavarian folk dancing, and street dances on Friday and Saturday nights. Visitors will also find food booths (German and other) and craft booths. In addition to the traditional Biergarten and Wiengarten, there is now a Microgarten with locally brewed beers. For younger visitors there is a Kindergarten with rides and other entertainment geared for youngsters.

OREGON STATE FAIR
Oregon State Fairgrounds, Salem
(503) 947-3247
www.oregonstatefair.org
The Oregon State Fair is an updated American tradition, held the last week before Labor Day (which means it sometimes falls in August). The fair still has strong roots, and support, in the state's rural areas and agricultural and ranching communities and industries, but in a larger sense, the fair celebrates and honors Oregon's

past, acknowledges the present, and recognizes the future. The fair offers 4-H and Future Farmers of America displays, animals, and products along with a carnival, horse racing, and booth after booth of food and other products. The fair draws visitors from throughout the state and region. Tickets at the gate are $8 for adults, $6 for seniors, and $5 for children ages 6 to 12. Parking is free, but lots fill early. There is also a shuttle from nearby Chemeketa Community College, where you can also park for free.

PICA TIME-BASED ART FESTIVAL
224 Northwest 13th Avenue, Suite 305
(503) 242-1419
www.pica.org/tba
The Time-Based Art Festival is a fun, avant-garde 10 days of performance, hosted by PICA (see The Arts chapter) and dedicated to celebrating the aesthetics and art practices of the moment. What does that mean for you? Ten days of lectures, workshops, salons, shows, happenings, exhibitions, films, and parties. Because the festival is dedicated to cultivating the new, the forms these events take resist labels. You might find films by cutting-edge artists such as Zoe Beloff or Guy Maddin. You might find a discussion of what Homeland Security means for artists. You might find performances by the Headlong Theater, Wally Cardona Quartet, Antony and the Johnsons, Tracey and the Plastics, Lone Twin, Reggie Watts, or the Lifesavas. You might find events at toney downtown hotels or under gritty urban bridges. You just never know what you might find, so check it out. You can buy tickets to individual events, or you can buy passes ($75 and up) to see lots of events. Art professionals receive special discounts. See www.pica.org/tba for updated event and price information.

SAUERKRAUT FESTIVAL
Downtown Scappoose
off U.S. Highway 30
(503) 543-2010
www.scappoosecommunity.org
About 30 minutes outside of Portland along the Columbia River, Scappoose is home to those crispy Steinfeld's Pickles and an annual outdoor Sauerkraut Festival. There are also craft booths and entertainment, a Volkswalk, and, of course, food booths with lots of sauerkraut. Admission is free.

SWAN ISLAND DAHLIA CONFERENCE SHOW
Clackamas County Fairgrounds, Canby
(503) 226-7711
www.dahlias.com
Nursery stock—everything from grass seed to irises, tulips, and ornamental bushes—is a huge industry in northwest Oregon. Large fields of dahlias and other flowers flourish in the fertile soil around Portland, and this free event offers information for both professionals and enthusiasts. The fairgrounds are 30 miles south of Portland on Highway 99 East.

OCTOBER

GREEK FESTIVAL
Holy Trinity Greek Orthodox Church
3131 Northeast Glisan Street
(503) 234-0468
This is a very popular event drawing visitors from throughout northwest Oregon and southwest Washington who come to enjoy Greek music and dancing, arts and crafts displays, and, of course, lots of food. At the gate, you'll trade your dollars for Greek *talents*, which you'll spend on food, icons, and other wonderful things. Visitors are invited to participate in the dancing, and there are tours of the beautiful Holy Trinity Church.

HALLOWEEN PUMPKIN FEST
Fir Point Farms, 14601 Arndt Road
Aurora
(503) 678-2455
www.firpointfarms.com
Fir Point Farms is a real, working farm producing flowers and nursery stock, pumpkins, hay, and a variety of fruits and vegetables. It is also a roadside fruit and vegetable stand where you can buy locally grown produce and flowers. They

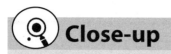

Close-up

Portland's Farmers' Market

From the 1850s to 1941, Portland had a thriving public market. As late as the 1930s, the Yamhill Public Market, in what is now Old Town Portland, was a 5-block spread of booths, stalls, tables, and baskets all loaded with fresh produce, meat, and poultry brought into town daily by farmers and ranchers. The city rented these curbside stalls for 16 cents a day.

Today the tradition continues, with the Portland Farmers' Market held in the Park Blocks on April through November weekends at Southwest Broadway and Montgomery Street near Portland State University, and June through September on Wednesday at Southwest Park and Salmon.

Founded in 1992, the market has dozens of vendors selling farm-fresh produce, cut flowers and bedding plants, vegetable and herb starts, locally raised organic meat and poultry, smoked and fresh seafood, and artisan breads and cheeses. Much, but not all, of the produce is organically grown. In addition, there are many vendors with delicious prepared food featuring local fare.

Open-air markets have been the heartbeat of villages for thousands of years and can still be found around the globe by travelers searching for the real feel of a land and its people. Here in Portland that feel includes the image of mounds of green lettuce heads or a huge tub full of sugar-fried popcorn, the sounds of a fiddle player bowing a jump tune next to a farmer from the Coast Range town of Alsea bagging up a half-pound of goat cheese. You'll find cinnamon twists, croissants, and pastry here, as well as shitake mushrooms and organically grown tomatoes. Gardeners can take home honeysuckle starts and dahlia tubers among many other plants.

As well as the wealth of good food at great prices, the market offers a series of events throughout its season. Chefs-in-the-Market cooking demonstrations let you watch some of the best chefs in Portland cooking with farmers' market produce on Saturday at 10:00 a.m., June through October. Monthly celebrations are an important feature of the market because they underscore the seasonal nature of food, from the height-of-summer Berry Festival to the Summer Loaf Bread festival held in August, which brings more than 20 area bakeries to the market, along with a wood-burning demonstration oven, featured bread-baking speakers, and amateur and professional baking contests. In September more than 50 peak-season tomato varieties are sliced and placed on paper plates with name tags along a row of tables. It's your tough assignment to taste them and write down your comments. A Harvest Festival, held in late October, celebrates the season with a pumpkin pie contest, jack-o'-lantern carving, and other fall traditions.

The Portland Farmers' Market—and all the farmers' markets in the area—give Portland citizens the chance to connect with the important people who sustain us, a chance that we don't have very often. It may be the Age of Information, but we still have to eat food that someone grows. And what better way to appreciate your food than to meet the person who grew it?

Portland Farmers' Market
Portland State University
1800 Southwest Broadway at Montgomery
(503) 241-0032
www.portlandfarmersmarket.org

April through November, Saturday, 8:00 a.m. to 1:00 p.m.

REGIONAL FARMERS' MARKETS

The Portland Farmers' Market is only one of many in the region. Here's a partial list of others in Portland and in outlying areas, each with its own character. The Oregon Department of Agriculture will also send you a pamphlet with all of the farmers' markets in Oregon. Contact them at (503) 525-1035 or online: www.oregonfarmersmarkets.org.

PORTLAND

Hillsdale Farmers' Market
Wilson High School-Rieke Elementary
Parking Lot
1407 Southwest Vermont Street
www.hillsdalefarmersmarket.com

May through October, Sunday, 10:00 a.m. to
2:00 p.m.; November through March, every
other Sunday, 10:00 a.m. to 2:00 p.m.

Hollywood Farmers' Market
Northeast Hancock, between 44th and
45th Streets
(503) 709-7403
www.hollywoodfarmersmarket.org

May through October, Saturday, 8:00 a.m.
to 1:00 p.m.

Interstate Farmers' Market
Overlook Park, North Fremont Street and
Interstate Avenue
www.interstatefarmersmarket.org

Mid-May through September, Wednesday,
3:00 to 7:00 p.m.

People's All Organic Farmers' Market
3029 Southeast 21st Avenue
(503) 232-9051
www.peoples.coop

Year-round, Wednesday, 2:00 to 7:00 p.m.

Portland Farmers' Market
Eastbank
www.portlandfarmersmarket.org
Southeast 20th Avenue, between
Hawthorne Boulevard and Belmont Street
on Salmon Street

June through September, Thursday, 3:30 to
7:30 p.m.

OUTLYING AREAS

Beaverton Farmers' Market
Hall Boulevard, between 3rd and 5th
Avenues
(503) 643-5345
www.beavertonfarmersmarket.com

May through October, Saturday, 8:00 a.m.

to 1:30 p.m. June through August, a second
day is added: Wednesday, 4:00 to 7:00 p.m.

Gresham Farmers' Market
Miller Street between 2nd and 3rd
(503) 341-4135
www.greshamfarmersmarket.com

May through October, Saturday, 8:30 a.m.
to 2:00 p.m.

Hillsboro Farmers' Market
(503) 844-6685
www.hillsboromarkets.org
There are three Hillsboro Farmers' Markets:
2nd and East Main on Courthouse Square

May through October, Saturday, 8:00 a.m.
to 1:00 p.m.
1st and 3rd on Main Street, Courthouse
Square

June through August, Tuesday, 5:30 to 8:30
p.m.
Orenco Station

May through October, Sunday, 10:00 a.m. to
2:00 p.m.

Lake Oswego Farmers' Market
Millennium Plaza Park at 1st and
Evergreen Streets
(360) 737-8298
www.ci.oswego.or.us/farmersmarket

May through October, 8:30 a.m. to 1:30 p.m.

Milwaukie Farmers' Market
Main Street, between Harrison and Jackson
(503) 407-0956
www.milwaukiefarmersmarket.com

May through October, Sunday, 9:30 a.m. to
2:00 p.m.

Vancouver Farmers' Market
Downtown Vancouver
next to Esther Short Park
(360) 737-8298
www.vancouverfarmersmarket.com

April through October, Saturday, 9:00 a.m. to
3:00 p.m.; Sunday, 10:00 a.m. to 3:00 p.m.

The Portland Farmers' Market rewards you with delicious produce lasting long beyond the harvest season.
CLEO BETHEL

have an excellent selection of locally made baked goods (like strawberry-rhubarb pie), dried fruits, mustards, jams and jellies, and fruit butters. There is a shop full of all sorts of country merchandise. A couple of times a year, the owners attract good crowds of city dwellers, visitors, and locals for a series of holiday events.

At Halloween, Fir Point Farms hosts a hay maze and wagon rides. The grounds are filled with carved and decorated pumpkins, and there are pony rides, face painting, and entertainments for children, as well as a giant pumpkin weigh-off.

Rabbits, chickens, and turkeys are on hand for petting and watching, and the farm's goats climb a series of ramps and tree branches to get an aerial perch on the activities. For a quarter you can buy a handful of goat food and winch it up to a platform where the goats are waiting for their reward.

No admission is charged, although there are small fees for rides. While picnics are welcome,

refreshments are available for modest prices. This is great fun not only for children but for adults too. The farm is a few minutes off I-5 at the Aurora/Canby exit, and there are lots of signs pointing you in the right direction. (See the Kidstuff chapter for more on Fir Point Farms and other pumpkin patches.)

HOWL-A-WEEN
The Oregon Zoo, 4001 Southwest Canyon Road in Washington Park (503) 226-1561
www.oregonzoo.com
The Oregon Zoo holds many seasonal events, and Howl-a-Ween is one of the favorites. This event lets kids trick-or-treat in a safe environment—and learn more about the zoo animals as they go. A scavenger hunt sends them to different places around the zoo, where they answer questions and complete activities. All kids who finish the hunt are given bags of candy and prizes when

they leave. Howl-a-Ween is usually held on the weekend closest to Halloween. This event is free with regular zoo admission.

OKTOBERFEST
**Oaks Park, at the east end of the
Sellwood Bridge
www.oakspark.com**
This Oktoberfest at Oaks Park on the banks of the Willamette River features delicious German sausages and other treats, a sausage-eating contest, oompah bands, polka, and other Germania. For the younger set, a *kinderplatz* (children's place) complete with Radio Disney is a big draw. Visitors will find traditional German foods, beers, and wines supplemented with local favorites, as well. Admission is $5 for adults, $2 for kids, and $3 for those 62 and older.

PORTLAND MARATHON
**(503) 226-1111
www.portlandmarathon.org**
While the 26.2-mile run is the logical centerpiece of this event, this well-organized open marathon, now in its fourth decade, includes a 5-mile run, a 10-kilometer (6.2-mile) run, a 10-kilometer Mayor's Walk, a noncompetitive 2-mile kids' run, and a 2-mile Special Olympics run. It is very friendly to walkers. For those who haven't entered the marathon, there is also a sports medicine and fitness fair. The Portland Marathon has a reputation as a true people's race, where anyone can enter. It is, however, a qualifier for the Boston Marathon. (For information on other running events, see the Recreation chapter.)

SALMON FESTIVAL
**Oxbow Regional Park, Sandy
(503) 797-1850**
A regional icon, the native and wild salmon is nearly an endangered species. This festival is a chance to see the Chinook swim upstream to spawn, learn about their habitat, and understand that we all are involved in their ultimate fate. Among other activities are a salmon bake (it's still okay to eat them) and displays by various

organizations committed to the environment and the restoration and health of the salmon habitat. Admission prices run about $8 per car. To get to the park, drive 6 miles east of Gresham on Division Street. Fido should stay home.

NOVEMBER

CHRISTMAS AT THE PITTOCK MANSION
**3229 Northwest Pittock Drive
(503) 823-3624
www.pittockmansion.org**
Perched 1,000 feet above Portland's downtown, the Pittock Mansion (see the Attractions chapter) is the grandest of all Portland's mansions. As such it is appropriately decorated and lighted for Christmas. The usual admission fee applies, but there are often performances of choral and other musical works requiring additional admission during this time of year, so call ahead in order to know what to expect.

PIONEER COURTHOUSE SQUARE HOLIDAY HAPPENINGS
**Pioneer Courthouse Square, between
6th Avenue and Broadway,
Morrison and Yamhill Streets
(503) 223-1613
www.pioneercourthousesquare.org**
The one Portland tradition visitors must hear (and see) to believe is the annual Tuba Concert. With 100 or more tuba players ranging from symphony members to enthusiastic novices risking badly chilled lips and fingers, the downtown echoes (and echoes) with unique renditions of favorite holiday songs and carols. At times you can almost hear the carolers making a good-faith effort to match the tuba sounds. Don't miss it. The city's Christmas tree is displayed here too, delivered from a local tree farm by a log truck, an event guaranteed to tie up traffic, but only the real Scrooges get upset. The tree-lighting ceremony happens right after Thanksgiving, and it is a sight to behold. The city's official menorah is lit nearby when Hanukkah begins.

WINE COUNTRY THANKSGIVING
Willamette Valley Wineries Association
(503) 646-2985
www.willamettewines.com
This popular tour is held the fourth weekend in November, following Thanksgiving Day. Sponsored by the Willamette Valley Wineries Association, the event highlights dozens of wineries and vineyards with new vintages, winery tours, sale prices, and lots of food, crafts, and music.

WORDSTOCK
Various locations
(503) 546-1012
www.wordstockfestival.com
Portland is a city of readers, and Wordstock is our annual festival of the book. This gala event brings writers and readers together for three days of workshops, dinners, music, readings by best-selling authors and rising stars, a book fair, a special Children's Festival, and other fabulous events. Past Wordstocks have featured writers such as Ira Glass, Dave Eggers, Gore Vidal, R. L. Stine, Ariel Gore, Ursula LeGuin, Carl Hiaasen, and Donald Hall. Admission to Wordstock is about $5, depending on your age, and about $25 to hear the keynote speakers.

DECEMBER

FESTIVAL OF THE TREES
Oregon Convention Center, 777 Northeast
Martin Luther King Jr. Boulevard
(503) 557-8733
To benefit the Providence Medical Foundation, local designers and celebrities decorate 45 8-foot trees. The trees are auctioned off during opening night, with bids beginning at $500. There are also gingerbread and other displays, holiday entertainment, and demonstrations of arts and crafts. Admission is $5 for adults and $4 for seniors; children 3 to 12 are admitted for $3.

HOLIDAY LIGHTS DISPLAYS
Various locations throughout the city, including:

FESTIVAL OF LIGHTS AT THE GROTTO
Sandy Boulevard and Northeast
85th Avenue
(503) 254-7371
www.thegrotto.org

ZOOLIGHTS FESTIVAL AT THE OREGON ZOO
4001 Northwest Canyon Road
in Washington Park
(503) 226-1561
The darkness of winter nights is charmingly dispelled by these glimmering displays of holiday lights in various neighborhoods and at the Grotto and the zoo. Admission is charged at both the Oregon Zoo and the Grotto. The Grotto hosts the largest choral festival in the Pacific Northwest, with singers from 130 or more school, church, and civic choral groups performing in a 600-seat chapel. The chapel's acoustics are cathedral quality, enhancing the practiced voices of the choirs. The nativity story is told in lighted dioramas, and there is a petting zoo for children. Suitable refreshments—hot chocolate, cider, and the like—are available here. Admission is $7 for adults and $3 for those ages 3 to 12.

The Oregon Zoo hosts a month-long display with thousands of lights on trees and buildings and holiday lights arranged into animal silhouettes that raise and lower their heads or perform other animated gestures. The zoo stays open late, and evenings feature local choirs performing holiday music and adult-size elves bearing treats. The additional charge to ride the Zoo Train is worth it to see the displays from a different perspective. ZooLights can get very crowded, so be prepared for a wait for the Zoo Train and dress warmly!

Various neighborhoods compete with each other for the most lavish displays, though the traditional winner is Peacock Lane. A must-visit street for many years, residents on Peacock Lane have now enlisted computers and fiber optics to enhance their displays. The lights and displays draw visitors like moths to electric flames. Some visitors prefer to drive down the 2 blocks or so, but the traffic backs up fast. Others park nearby, bundle up, and walk up and down the street to admire the displays. Hot chocolate is sold from a little booth to warm those who choose to see the lights on foot.

THE *NUTCRACKER*
Oregon Ballet Theater, Keller Auditorium
Southwest 3rd Avenue and Clay Street
(503) 227-0977
www.obt.org
Oregon Ballet Theater has revived the George Balanchine version of Tchaikovsky's ballet. This holiday classic sells out every year—though tickets are usually available because they give many performances—and has been a tradition among some Portland families for generations. Reservations are mandatory, but the ticket price range is reasonable.

PARADE OF CHRISTMAS SHIPS
Willamette and Columbia Rivers
www.christmasships.org
Local boat owners decorate their crafts, then form a floating convoy and sail up and down the Columbia and Willamette Rivers each night for several weeks in December. Owners have an informal competition among themselves for the most colorful display and some boats broadcast

Christmas carols. All in all, nearly 60 craft participate. If the weather is bad, find a riverside restaurant or bar, order an Irish coffee or a local stout, and enjoy the floating spectacle snug and warm. If the weather is tolerable, try standing on the Hawthorne or Sellwood Bridges over the Willamette south of Portland as the twinkling fleet sails under the bridge upstream and back. Park in East Sellwood and then stroll out onto the bridge. Dress for chilly winds.

SINGING CHRISTMAS TREE
Keller Auditorium
222 Southwest Clay Street
(503) 557-8733
www.singingchristmastree.org
The Singing Christmas Tree is a long-standing, glorious singing event involving 300 singers. There is an actual "tree" involving about half of the singers, and the rest are strategically placed to act out scenes from cherished Christmas tales, both secular and religious. The pageant also features beloved musical performers from Portland and beyond. It's right up there with *The Nutcracker* as a ritual for Portlanders at holiday time.

THE ARTS

Portland has always taken a playful approach to art, starting in the 1970s when our mayor, Bud Clark, was photographed by Michael Ryerson at the bus mall, facing a statue by Norman J. Taylor. The statue is entitled *Kvinneakt*, or in Norwegian, "nude woman." But Clark was not just looking: He was wearing an overcoat (and not much else else) and flashing the statue. The poster that was subsequently created was called "Expose Yourself to Art," and it was a bestseller that helped set the tone for the arts scene in Portland.

This playful legacy has remained as Portland evolves from a sleepy provincial town to a more sophisticated city. We have the second-oldest museum building on the West Coast, but the spirit of Portland's art is not constrained by history. Thus, the arts are alive here—both the classical disciplines and the experimental counterparts that invigorate and refresh. Because it is comparatively simple and pleasant to live here—one doesn't need a car, for example—the city attracts people who want to make art and who want to start arts-related businesses. These have flourished over the past 10 years and have made important contributions to the economy and overall livability of Portland.

Portland has major strengths in the literary arts, as well as in music, visual arts, and performance. To find the where, what, who, and perhaps why of most of the above, here's a selection of the most intriguing, vital, happening arts outfits in the Portland area. The listing includes performance and cultural centers, arts organizations, dance assemblies, literary venues and groups, a profile of the Portland Art Museum, musical ensembles, arts schools, theatrical troupes, and visual arts opportunities.

CULTURAL CENTERS AND ARTS ORGANIZATIONS

COMMUNITY MUSIC CENTER
3350 Southeast Francis Street
(503) 823-3177
www.portlandonline.com/parks
Community Music Center was built in 1912 and served the neighborhood as a fire station until it was abandoned mid-century. Now beautifully renovated, it's a training center for hundreds of music students in the Portland area who present their recitals at the center. Most of those school-age musicians who train at the center are learning to play stringed instruments, including violin, viola, cello, and bass. Many students go on to play with the Metropolitan Youth Symphony and Portland Youth Philharmonic. The center, a member of the National Guild of Community Schools of the Arts, is also a recipient of Chamber Music Program grants from the Amateur Chamber Music Players Foundation. The Community Music Center also hosts concerts in its acoustically sophisticated performance space.

INTERSTATE FIREHOUSE CULTURAL CENTER
5340 North Interstate Avenue
(503) 823-4322
www.ifcc-arts.org
This community-based theater/art gallery is a cultural mecca with an emphasis on art, music, drama, and social issues. Its offerings are diverse, focusing on the local and the unusual, from Vietnamese classical guitarists to visual artists from the Gullah Islands. In the theater, patrons

Confluence Project

Lewis and Clark's expedition in 1804 heralded many changes for the people who lived in the Pacific Northwest. As the bicentennial of that journey was celebrated, local Native American tribes and civic groups asked artist Maya Lin, who designed the Vietnam Veterans Memorial in Washington, D.C., to help them commemorate this anniversary. The result is the Confluence Project, a series of seven installations along the Columbia River, designed and shepherded by Lin with the participation of everyone from schoolchildren to respected community elders—including artists, architects, city planners, and even state departments of transportation. The sites are in varying stages of completion, but they include a stunning land bridge at Fort Vancouver, where the Klikitat meets the Columbia River, an installation at the Sandy River delta, and a large, completed project at Cape Disappointment, where the Columbia meets the Pacific Ocean. For more information, directions, and events concerning this remarkable project, visit the project's Web site: www.confluenceproject.org.

can watch new plays from local and and national playwrights. Facility hours are Monday through Saturday 10:00 a.m. to 5:00 p.m., and gallery hours are noon to 5:00 p.m. This dynamic organization works closely with local high school and college students, and together they produce some of the most exciting visual and performance art in town.

MULTNOMAH ARTS CENTER
7688 Southwest Capitol Highway
(503) 823-2787
www.portlandonline.com/parks
This former middle school on the northern edge of Multnomah Village is now a learning center for artists, musicians, and craftspeople from all over the Portland Metro region. MAC offers a full menu of tai chi, yoga, and art classes for everyone, from toddlers dabbling with mom and dad to preteens learning cartooning, to serious graphic artists using the right side of their brains. There are burgeoning theater, music, and dance departments as well as classroom and hall rentals. It is also home to the Basketry Guild and Portland Handweavers Guild. All this is reasonably affordable, with fees ranging from $20 to $170. A catalog, available at the center or through Portland Parks and Recreation, describes this bounty of opportunities along with a credo that says MAC "empowers the people in Portland to live life artfully."

OREGON POTTERS ASSOCIATION
(503) 222-0533
www.oregonpotters.org
The nonprofit Oregon Potters Association presents a large exhibit of works by more than 400 Oregon and southwest Washington clay artists every year at the Oregon Convention Center, 777 Northeast Martin Luther King Jr. Boulevard. Admission is free to the exhibit, which features clay art including dinner and functional ware, jewelry, sculpture, outdoor garden sculpture, tile work, fountains, and vessels. Throughout each day artists will demonstrate their individual techniques. Attendees can learn how to make a vessel with a potter's wheel or be entertained with a bit of pioneer history while watching artists throw pots on an old wagon wheel.

THE PORTLAND CENTER FOR THE PERFORMING ARTS
1111 Southwest Broadway
(503) 248-4335
(503) 796-9293 (events)
www.pcpa.com

Looming as the centerpiece of the city's cultural district, the Portland Center for the Performing Arts hosts more than 900 events, entertaining more than one million ticketholders. The center comprises more than three main buildings:

The Keller Auditorium on Southwest 3rd Avenue between Market and Clay Streets, (503) 274-6560, is a big box of a place with a capacity of 3,000 seats. It's where audiences watch Broadway musicals and operas and enjoy concerts by out-of-town performers. Built in 1917, it was renovated in 1968. The on-site box office is open on show days only, but tickets can be purchased at other times at the Portland Center for the Performing Arts ticket office located in the lobby of the New Theatre Building. Hours are Monday through Saturday, 10:00 a.m. to 6:00 p.m.

The Arlene Schnitzer Concert Hall, Southwest Broadway at Main Street, (503) 274-6564, is the grande dame of the performance halls. A building with a grand past, it's currently the home of the Oregon Symphony and host to several traveling theater productions, lectures, and other entertainment.

Just south of the Schnitzer is a complex with two theaters: the Newmark Theatre and the Dolores Winningstad Theatre. Adjoining both is an award-winning lobby area with a stunning rotunda topped by a glittering dome. The Dolores Winningstad Theatre is an Elizabethan or "black-box" theater with 292 seats; the Newmark Theatre is a 916-seat room designed to emulate the Edwardian-style theaters of Europe.

PORTLAND INSTITUTE FOR CONTEMPORARY ART
224 Northwest 13th Avenue
(503) 242-1419
www.pica.org
Dedicated to bringing innovative and relevant contemporary art, music, and theater to Portland, this advocacy group and gallery is also known for its former Dada Ball where even the most staid bureaucrats astonished the crowd with their outrageous costumes. PICA has also staged many other memorable events, such as *Monsters of Grace,* a multimedia opera by Robert Wilson

and Philip Glass, and the work of performance artist Karen Finley. PICA provides residence and other forms of sustenance to artists, as well as education, exhibition, and performance programs. Its Time-Based Art festival (see our Festival and Annual Events chapter) is the culminating event of Portland's summer season. This lively avant-garde gala, modeled on the Edinburgh Festival in Scotland, celebrates every kind of performance art. PICA has become a major cultural force in Portland, attracting the loyalty of artists and patrons alike. There is a resource room with hundreds of exhibition catalogues, periodicals, DVDs, and books on contemporary art, as well as an archive of all past PICA productions. Hours are Monday through Friday, 10:00 a.m. to 5:00 p.m. It's open to the public with a modest $2 fee.

DANCE

OREGON BALLET THEATRE
818 Southeast 6th Avenue
(503) 222-5538 (tickets), (503) 227-0977 (administration)
www.obt.org
Leaping, pirouetting, and gliding since 1989, the Oregon Ballet Theatre not only presents classics such as *Giselle* and *The Nutcracker* but also stretches its collective creativity through showcasing the work of new choreographers. Artistic director Christopher Stowell, known for his own precise technique as a dancer in the San Francisco City Ballet, brings that same athletic precision to his work with the Oregon Ballet Theatre corps—but goes beyond that to really make use of dance as a means of expression. He is also committed to live music, which makes the experience of watching the Oregon Ballet Theatre even more exciting. Although most of the performances are at the Keller Auditorium and the Newmark Theatre (see the Portland Center for the Performing Arts for more information), Oregon Ballet Theatre also takes to smaller stages such as Lincoln Hall at Portland State University as well as touring engagements throughout the United States. Oregon Ballet Theatre also has an outstanding classical ballet school.

WHITE BIRD DANCE
5620 Southwest Edgemont Place
(503) 245-1600
www.whitebird.org
White Bird Dance brings exciting dance performances to Portland with most shows staged at the Arlene Schnitzer Concert Hall, but a few performances require more intimate venues. White Bird Dance has sponsored the Paul Taylor Dance Company; Ballet Hispanico, the nation's leading Hispanic-American dance company; and the Diavolo Dance Company, a group that leaps, spins, and flies through the air. White Bird also collaborates with local dancers to create innovative choreography and sponsors education and outreach programs for the Portland Public Schools and other groups.

FILM

CINEMA 21
616 Northwest 21st Avenue
(503) 223-4515
www.cinema21.com
Cinema 21 is easily the front-runner in the small contingent of art and foreign film houses in town. With its single screen, loose-sprung seats, less than impeccable sound, and vaguely shabby lobby, this comfy parlor is an aging neighborhood movie house redefining itself as the place to catch a cult favorite, the big hit at Cannes, a black-and-white B-flick, or a martial arts marathon just in from Taiwan. Their quarterly program calendars on a newsprint poster look great on the fridge. Tickets are $8, $7 for students, and $5 for children and seniors. Cash and checks only.

CINEMAGIC
2021 Southeast Hawthorne Boulevard
(503) 231-7919
This little blue box is a classic with a jukebox in the lobby and a steady parade of classic films and contemporary ones—sometimes second-runs, but often not, especially for international and independent films. Plus, the old-fashioned movie theater atmosphere is alluring. Tickets are $4 before 6:00 p.m. and $6 for adults and $4 for

children and seniors after 6:00 p.m. All tickets are $4 on Mondays. Cash and checks only.

CLINTON STREET THEATER
2522 Southeast Clinton Street
(503) 238-8899
www.clintonsttheater.com
Once exclusively a film theater, this multipurpose rumpus room offers poetry readings, performance art pieces, concerts, and movies of various genres, including science fiction, foreign, classic, and art films, most of which are decidedly not mainstream. Tickets are $6; matinees are $4; and on Tuesday, all shows are $4. The *Rocky Horror Picture Show* is a regular feature, showing every Saturday night at midnight—since April 1978, in what is undoubtedly the longest run of the cult favorite. All shows after 7:00 p.m. are for those 21 and over (except *Rocky Horror*). Catch their blog at www.clintonsttheater.com/blog/, which proves they are not stuck in 1978. Cash only.

HOLLYWOOD THEATRE
4122 Northeast Sandy Boulevard
(503) 281-4215
www.hollywoodtheatre.org
Open since 1926 this grand movie parlor is not only a splendid place to see a movie, but it's also a cultural center with classes, events, and workshops. This theater has been restored to its original glory, and it offers one of the few screens in town devoted to art and foreign films, as well as Hollywood classics, old and new. Tickets are $6.50, $4.50 for seniors and children 4 to 12. All shows on Monday night are $4.00.

LAURELHURST THEATER AND PUB
2735 East Burnside Street
(503) 232-5511
www.laurelhursttheater.com
This classic neighborhood movie house offers pizza, wine, and microbrew beer with second-run films, independent films, and classics at $3 per show for adults 21 and older. On weekend afternoons, children accompanied by an adult can see the matinee shows; children's tickets are $1. (All shows after 3:00 p.m. are for ages 21 and

older.) Check it out for its neon swirl out front and along the ceiling.

NORTHWEST FILM CENTER
1219 Southwest Park Avenue
(503) 221-1156
www.nwfilm.org
An adjunct of the Portland Art Museum, the Northwest Film Center is an educational facility with a broad curriculum of filmmaking, screenwriting, and similar classes that can lead to a certificate of film study. The film center also houses a media arts resource center, and happily for the rest of us, it is also a terrific conduit of current and classic art and foreign films. Costs for classes vary depending on length and topic. Call the center for more information on tuition. Every year the center sponsors three major festivals: an international film festival that brings dozens of award-winning movies from all over the globe; the Northwest Film and Video Festival featuring work by regional filmmakers, animators, and cinematographers; and Young People's Film and Video Festival. Films are screened at the museum's Whitsell Auditorium, Southwest Park and Madison; the Guild Theatre, Southwest 9th Avenue; and local Regal Cinemas.

The Portland International Film Festival is the biggest film event in Oregon. It is two weeks of screen madness, with nearly 100 films from 30 countries shown at theaters all over town. The Northwest Film and Video Festival, while not so large, is in some ways more interesting. It not only showcases local talent, but it brings in important independent filmmakers, such as Todd Haynes, Gus Van Sant, and Matt Groening. The institute also sponsors a cool festival devoted to sound and vision: the Reel Music Festival.

LITERARY ARTS

The literary arts are where Portland truly shines. With Powell's—the biggest bookstore in the country—as a foundation, Portland has one of the most well-read citizenries around, and writers like to visit Portland because people actually attend their book signings and are likely to read the books. The three major branches of Powell's (Burnside, Hawthorne, and Beaverton) have author events almost daily. Another lively literary place is the downtown Borders (708 Southwest 3rd; 503-220-5911)—this store has signings, discussions, and performances in its bright little cafe. But many of the bookstores in town have author-related events (see the Shopping chapter for these stores), and sometimes these smaller venues provide more personal interaction with the writers. Local colleges—especially PSU, Reed, and Lewis & Clark—also sponsor author events and discussions. The *Oregonian, Willamette Week,* the *Mercury,* and the stores themselves are all good places to check to see who is in town.

Another important literary event is Literary Arts Inc.'s Portland Arts and Lectures series, which features writers with national and international reputations—such as David Sedaris, Ira Glass, Annie Dillard, Adrienne Rich, and Seamus Heaney—who speak at the Arlene Schnitzer Concert Hall to sell-out crowds. This is perhaps the biggest literary happening on the West Coast.

"I LOVE MONDAY!" READINGS AT BORDERS
708 Southwest 3rd Avenue
(503) 220-5911
Each Monday in the cozy tea nook of this bookstore, rambunctious poet and emcee Dan Raphael hosts readings by visiting writers and locals signed up for open-mike night. He also uses one of the Mondays to present a forum on various literary subjects. The get-togethers are free and usually start at 7:00 p.m.

IN OTHER WORDS
8 Northeast Killingsworth Street
(503) 232-6003
www.inotherwords.org
In Other Words sponsors a number of events that encompass literature and music by women. Readings by noted writers such as Ariel Gore and Annie Dawid, children's story hours, and open mikes for poets and other local talents are regular features. The Luna music series on the last Friday of each month features live music by women artists, and "Girl" movies are shown on the third

Friday. In Other Words also sponsors writing workshops and other classes. Their Web site is a treasure trove of information, books for sale, and a good calendar.

LITERARY ARTS, INC.
224 Northwest 13th Avenue, #306
(503) 227-2583
www.literary-arts.org
In addition to the Portland Arts and Lectures Series, this busy bunch sponsors Oregon Literary Fellowships, Writers in the Schools, and the Poetry in Motion project. Portland was the first city on the West Coast to launch a Poetry in Motion program, and ours also includes poetry from local schoolchildren. Literary Arts also sponsors the Oregon Book Awards at which writers and their friends gather every year to watch as book awards are presented for poetry, fiction, literary nonfiction, drama, and work aimed at young readers.

MOUNTAIN WRITERS CENTER
2804 Southeast 27th Avenue, #2
(503) 232-4517
www.mountainwriters.org
Since 1973 Mountain Writers has been sponsoring readings, lectures, and classes for writers. Its invited speakers have included Nobel Prize–winning writers as well as brand-new voices, from all over the world and from the Portland Metro area. Programs include readings at local colleges and universities, outreach to high school students, residencies in Portland for visiting writers, and sponsorship of visits by writers to rural

i Portland is the home of the literary journal *Tin House*, which also publishes books and sponsors an excellent writing workshop each summer at Reed College. Faculty have included luminaries such as Charles D'Ambrosio, Anthony Doerr, Denis Johnson, Walter Kirn, and Abigail Thomas. The workshop also gives writers opportunities to meet with editors and agents. Find out more at www.tinhouse.org.

areas. But it is most well known for its eight-week workshops and short-term master classes. These are open to emerging writers.

POWELL'S CITY OF BOOKS
1005 West Burnside Street
(503) 228-4651

3747 Southeast Hawthorne Boulevard
(503) 235-3802
8725 Southwest Cascade Avenue

Beaverton
(503) 643-3131
www.powells.com
The preeminent venues for literary readings in the Portland area are arguably the three Powell's bookstores: the Mothership on Burnside, the Eastside store on Hawthorne, and the newest store in Beaverton. All three have authors' readings in the evenings throughout the week. Expect everything from writers who are on the top-10 list to those who are just starting their careers or causing a hubbub with offbeat books. Schedules are available at all stores and advertised in local newspapers and magazines. Often, while the novelist, poet, or journalist is signing books after the reading, you can have a chat with these intriguing scribes.

WORDSTOCK
Various locations and the Oregon
Convention Center
(503) 546-1012
www.wordstockfestival.com
This wonderful event is devoted to all things book-related. It involves readings, lectures, teachers' workshops, music, a children's fair, and a giant book sale, mostly all taking place at the Oregon Convention Center. Founded by journalist, novelist, and ex-professional-baseball player Larry Colton, this event has grown over the years and now involves more than 200 writers who speak at the fair, as well as more than 100 exhibitors and thousands of attendees. Wordstock also invites star-quality writers such as Gore Vidal, Dave Eggers, R. L. Stine, Ursula LeGuin, and Joyce Carol Oates to speak and mingle with their readers.

Best of all, this awe-inspiring event is all for a worthy cause: All proceeds go to the Community of Writers, a nonprofit organization whose mission is to work with teachers to improve student writing. For more details, see our Festivals and Annual Events chapter.

MUSIC

CHAMBER MUSIC NORTHWEST
522 Southwest 5th Avenue, Suite 725
(503) 294-6400 (tickets)
Chamber Music Northwest, under the inspired direction of artistic director David Shifrin, promotes the diversity and exquisite beauty of chamber music, old and new. This organization, housed at Reed College, brings renowned soloists and ensembles for a year-round program of music, lectures, films, symposia, master classes, and other events. Their season is divided into a summer concert festival and a fall-winter-spring series, and they are often organized thematically. Guest artists have included such stars as Bill T. Jones, the Orion Quartet, and Anne-Marie McDermott. Chamber Music Northwest also collaborates frequently with other groups in town—White Bird Dance, PICA, the Oregon Symphony, for example, as well as making good use of the Reed College faculty. Many events include intelligent lectures and discussion about the music, its history, and its context. Their concerts are usually held at Reed College and Catlin Gabel School, but some events occur elsewhere. Wherever they are, however, you should make the effort to see this outstanding series.

OREGON REPERTORY SINGERS
909 Southwest Washington Street
(503) 230-0652
www.oregonrepsingers.org
The 65 voices of the Oregon Repertory Singers present neglected classics as well as contemporary pieces to international acclaim. Directed by versatile conductor Gilbert Seeley, the group often joins the Portland Baroque Orchestra to reinterpret work by Handel, Mozart, and Bach.

They also have an extremely well-run youth choir program, with 170 children in 6 choirs.

OREGON SYMPHONY
923 Southwest Washington Street
(503) 228-1353
www.oregonsymphony.org
Perhaps the most telling aspect of the Oregon Symphony is its exuberant refusal to fit the stereotype of a bunch of stuffed shirts playing dull music for other stuffed shirts. Rather, this ensemble of world-class performers and a lustrous list of conductors and musicians stopping by combine to offer a remarkable package of series for all ears. PSO features two main programs, the Classical Series and the Pops. The Classical Series features a breathtaking array of music from the masters, including the usual stars such as Beethoven, Bernstein, and Schubert, and also those composers who deserve a little more recognition. The Pops series, whose conductor is Portland favorite Jeff Tyzik, is devoted to more contemporary music, incorporating themes from movie music, jazz, Latin music, popular songs, and other favorites. The Pops series is especially well liked for its inclusion of big stars such as Roberta Flack or Oregon native Chris Botti. Youth-focused programs are designed to further classical music for the next generation, and these popular programs feature music set to stories, music from *Star Wars,* and other contemporary classics. The symphony also devotes a month to performing Mozart. All of these programs are available in a variety of different packages, though you can, of course, purchase just one ticket at a time.

The sensitive and exciting principal conductor of the Oregon Symphony is the European-trained Carlos Kalmar, who also serves at the helm of Chicago's Grant Park Music Festival. He has won the hearts and ears of Oregonians.

PORTLAND BAROQUE ORCHESTRA
1020 Southwest Taylor Avenue
(503) 222-6000
www.pbo.org
The Portland Baroque Orchestra is devoted to

the performance of classical and baroque music on original instruments (or replicas) to provide an authentic experience of the great composers. It is worth attending a concert to hear them play music written between 1600 and the mid-19th century on these instruments. To enhance this time travel, visiting soloists on violin, cello, and harpsichord join the orchestra to render historical versions of Handel, Haydn, and Mozart.

PORTLAND YOUTH PHILHARMONIC
421 Southwest Hall Street
(503) 223-5939
www.portlandyouthphil.org
Portland Youth Philharmonic has a long and lustrous history as the country's first youth orchestra. In 1912 Oregon's first children's orchestra was christened as the Sagebrush Symphony. This group turned into the Portland Junior Symphony in 1924 and then in 1930 it settled into its current title. Over the past 80 years, this assembly of young musicians has performed at the Arlene Schnitzer Concert Hall, recorded CDs, performed in Washington, D.C., and New York City, and toured overseas, including three weeks in Australia, to the delight of music lovers worldwide. Examples of the sort of music this talented group presents are Tchaikovsky's *Violin Concerto,* Schubert's *Unfinished Symphony,* and Gershwin's *Rhapsody in Blue.* The Youth Philharmonic has two full symphony orchestras, as well as a strong orchestra for younger students.

SCHOOLS

OREGON BALLET THEATRE AND SCHOOL
816 Southeast 6th Avenue
(503) 227-0977
This ballet school provides dance instruction to nearly 300 children and adults each year. Students perform with the professional company in selected performances and in the school's annual performance each spring. One of the highlights of this school is its Summer Dance Program with a curriculum that includes studying with guest instructors in classical ballet technique, pointe work, Spanish classical, flamenco, modern dance,

and Russian character dance. Students also get a chance to attend other summer dance programs throughout the nation through scholarships awarded in the spring.

OREGON COLLEGE OF ART & CRAFT
8245 Southwest Barnes Road
(503) 297-5544
www.ocac.edu
Located on a nine-acre wooded knoll, the Oregon College of Art & Craft was founded in 1907 as part of the Arts and Crafts Movement that emerged as a response to the Industrial Revolution. The emphasis of this movement was on beautifully crafted, handmade objects rather than those created via the assembly line. Almost a century later, OCAC continues this tradition with classes in painting, drawing, printmaking, book arts, ceramics, photography, and woodworking. The school also offers "Art Adventures," a kids' summer camp with classes in metalsmithing, watercolor, photography, printmaking, and other opportunities to create arts and crafts.

PACIFIC NORTHWEST COLLEGE OF ART
1241 Northwest Johnson Street
(503) 226-4391
www.pnca.edu
Pacific Northwest College of Art has been providing visual arts education for more than 90 years by offering a bachelor of fine arts degree as well as continuing education and community outreach programs. Founded in 1909 as the School of the Portland Art Association, the school was part of the Portland Art Museum complex on Southwest Park in a five-floor facility designed by Pietro Belluschi, retired dean of the School of Architecture at M.I.T. who was a student at the Museum Art School. In 1981 the school changed its name to the Pacific Northwest College of Art; in 1994 the college became institutionally separate from the museum, and in 1998 the college moved to its present location, a former warehouse. An intriguing feature of this space is the Swigert Common, a 26-foot-high space where student, regional, and national artistic talent is exhibited.

THEATER

ARTISTS REPERTORY THEATRE

1515 Southwest Morrison Street

(503) 241-1278

www.artistsrep.org

A charming black-box theater is home to this company, known for taut performances of new plays and classics. A good example is *Metamorphoses*, by Mary Zimmerman—a recipient of the MacArthur "genius" fellowship. ART's beautiful space has two separate theaters; both are intimate and actor-focused—the ideal environment for its cutting edge performances that include many West Coast and world premieres.

DO JUMP!

Echo Theater

1515 Southeast 37th Avenue

(503) 231-1232

www.dojump.org

This one-of-a-kind physical theater and dance troupe has been celebrated since its beginning in 1977 for its distinctive choreography, which also features aerial acrobatics and live music. Do Jump! now regularly performs at the downtown Newmark Theater and tours the nation, but its home is still the unpretentious Echo Theater just off Hawthorne Boulevard. That's also the home of its wonderful camps and classes that teach stilt walking, trapeze flying, aerobatics, and other gravity-defying tricks to children and adults. Do Jump! has become a classic Portland experience.

IMAGO THEATRE

17 Southeast 8th Avenue

(503) 231-9581

www.imagotheatre.com

Imago Theater blends physical comedy, acrobatics, and pathos, and somehow brings all of these characteristics together to perform award-winning shows that have traveled as far as Broadway. This boundary-blurring company performs new works as well as adaptations of classics. They are best known for their comedy Portland's most avant-garde theater ensemble, Imago tackles edgy drama and comedy that slice across theatrical history from Japanese Noh to Sartre's *No Exit* to contemporary works by emerging playwrights. When Imago is not touring the globe, Portlanders line up to see their newest, strangely captivating performances.

MIRACLE THEATRE GROUP

425 Southeast 6th Avenue

(503) 236-7253

www.milagro.org

Comprising Miracle Mainstage, Teatro Milagro, and Milagro Bailadores, this Portland-based operation is the largest Hispanic arts and cultural organization in the Pacific Northwest. Since it started in 1985, Miracle Theatre has offered Hispanic theater, arts, and cultural experiences throughout the region, particularly to low- and moderate-income Spanish-speaking audiences and those in rural settings who often don't get to see quality drama. Mainstage presents four English-language plays by Hispanic playwrights and two festivals each season on the Portland stage. Teatro Milagro is the group's touring theatrical company that journeys to rural communities in Oregon, Idaho, Montana, Washington, and Wyoming, where it invites local amateur actors and youth-at-risk to join the troupers onstage. Milagro Bailadores, a touring dance company, travels to schools throughout the western United States, where it entertains as well as informs audiences about Latin American dance and music.

PORTLAND CENTER STAGE

128 Northwest 11th Avenue

(503) 445-3700

www.pcs.org

Portland Center Stage, our city's only fully professional resident theater company, presents its dramas and comedies in the new Gerding Theatre in a beautiful LEED-certified (Leadership in Energy and Environmental Design) building in the Pearl District. Recent productions have included *West Side Story*, the *Fantasticks*, and a wonderful adaptation of Ken Kesey's novel *Sometimes a Great Notion*. PCS also shows compelling Christmas shows such as *The Santaland Diaries* and *A Christmas Carol*. Tickets prices depend on seating and day of the week. In addition, PCS sponsors an intensive playwrights' festival each summer.

PORTLAND OPERA
211 Southeast Carruthers Street
(503) 241-1802
www.portlandopera.org
Since the early '60s, the Portland Opera has been presenting operas that have earned the group a ranking in the top 15 opera companies in the United States. It was also the second company in the United States to use supertitles (English translation projected above the stage). This will come as good news to those who find it difficult to follow the plot through aria after aria, though not all opera fans are pleased. As well as presenting classic operas such as *Aida, Carmina Burana,* and *The Mikado,* Portland Opera became the first opera company in the world to sponsor a subscription series to national touring Broadway musicals. This "Best of Broadway Series" has brought *The Sound of Music, Sunset Boulevard, Les Miserables, The Wizard of Oz,* and many more crowd-pleasers to the Keller Auditorium.

SOWELU
4319 Southeast Hawthorne Boulevard
(503) 230-2090
www.sowelutheater.org
Dubbed Sowelu (So-way-loo) after a lightning-bolt Nordic rune meaning "life process," this award-winning ensemble company is performing new and original work in Southeast Portland. Sowelu performs original works created with an ensemble approach, works that are inevitably profound to experience and compelling to look at. The company is also dedicated to sustainability for artists, and so they come together not only to create and perform theater but also to share resources, provide workshops and classes for young artists and teens, and support works in progress.

TEARS OF JOY THEATRE
700 Northeast 136th Avenue
Vancouver, WA
(503) 248-0557, (360) 695-3050
www.tojt.com

A puppeteer ensemble that has grown far beyond the days of Punch and Judy, Tears of Joy Theatre, based in Vancouver, Washington, has been delighting kids and adults for years with its mythologically driven dramas, life-size puppets, and wondrous costumes. As well as touring through the United States, Tears of Joy also performs at the Winningstad Theatre in Portland. Tears of Joy also has a Puppet Camp where children ages 7 to 12 get to join the puppeteers in creating their own puppet plays. Kids build puppets and masks and learn performance skills. These camps, usually during summer, are funded by the city of Vancouver.

i **The Regional Arts & Culture Council is an important source for arts education, advocacy, and stewardship in the Portland metro area. And it's also the best place to find out about about Portland's substantial public art program. Visit them on the Web at www.racc.org.**

VISUAL ARTS
The two major events in the Portland visual arts scene are First Thursday and its reverse image, Last Thursday. On the first Thursday of each month, galleries, shops, and museums are open into the evening in the Old Town, Pearl, and downtown districts. Even on rainy nights, these are festive and crowded events, with street musicians, performing artists, and exhibitionist art students lending a carnival air to the evening. First Thursdays are usually the evenings that new exhibitions are opened. It is great fun, but parking in the Pearl can be maddening. Like us, you can park in a downtown garage and take the streetcar to the Pearl.

Last Thursdays are a kind of Bohemian retort to First Thursdays. This event is held on Northeast Alberta Street, and it includes the galleries that are sprouting thickly in this area of urban renewal. On Alberta pay special attention to the exhibitions and receptions at Guardino Gallery, Onda, Talisman, and everywhere else along this vibrant little strip. Here too you will find the carnivalesque. The Interstate Firehouse Cultural Center (5340 North Interstate Avenue) is another important visual-arts venue in this area.

THE ART GYM
Marylhurst University
17600 Pacific Highway
(503) 699-6243
www.marylhurst.edu
Unlike many college art museums and galleries that, for better or worse, only reflect work undertaken by faculty and students, The Art Gym at Marylhurst is a consistently exciting venue for contemporary artists in and out of school, often out on the cutting edge. Once the gymnasium for this private school, the 3,000-square-foot gallery is large enough to hold sizable sculptures and large installations. The Art Gym is open Tuesday through Sunday noon to 4:00 p.m.

AUGEN GALLERY
817 Southwest 2nd Avenue
(503) 224-8182
www.augengallery.com
A venerable institution in Portland's art world, the Augen Gallery sustains its reputation for eclectic fine art with a large collection featuring not only local artists but internationally renowned masters such as Stella, Hockney, Motherwell, and Warhol as well. Put this gallery on your itinerary when you begin your sampling of art during your First Thursday stroll.

BLACKFISH GALLERY
420 Northwest 9th Avenue
(503) 224-2634
www.blackfish.com
Look for the sign of the wooden fish to swim with or against the tide of art lovers moving in and out of this popular gallery. Here the artwork of the nation's oldest artists' cooperative is displayed during monthly exhibits. Examples of this widely varied effort include abstracts, weavings, and sculpture. The gallery is open Tuesday through Saturday 11:00 a.m. to 5:00 p.m.

BLUE SKY GALLERY AND NINE GALLERY
1231 Northwest Hoyt Street
(503) 225-0210
www.blueskygallery.org
These two galleries are the quintessential Pearl District art scene. Blue Sky, around since 1975, offers a tasty blend of contemporary, international, and historical photographs, while its neighbor is a lively venue for a group of local artists who have fun dreaming up the next show. The galleries are open Tuesday through Saturday noon to 5:00 p.m.

ELIZABETH LEACH GALLERY
417 Northwest 9th Avenue
(503) 224-0521
www.elizabethleach.com
One of Portland's premier art scenes, Elizabeth Leach Gallery, located in the spacious Hazeltine Building in the heart of Old Town, represents both Northwest and national artists in monthly exhibitions. This gallery features cutting-edge work, and attendance on First Thursday is practically required. Hours are Tuesday through Saturday, 10:30 a.m. to 5:30 p.m.

GUARDINO GALLERY
2939 Northeast Alberta Street
(503) 281-9048
www.guardinogallery.com
This epicenter of a vital rebirth of culture along Northeast Alberta Street is making a small tsunami in the Portland art world with high-quality exhibits of local painters, printmakers, and sculptors. When you stop by the string of galleries, studios, and shops on Alberta that celebrate Last Thursday, be sure to visit Guardino Gallery. Chat with the Guardinos, who are happy to share their thoughts on the artists on display as well as their own ongoing creative work. Or you can stop by any time Tuesday through Saturday from 11:00 a.m. to 6:00 p.m., or Sunday from 11:00 a.m. to 4:00 p.m.

LAURA RUSSO GALLERY
805 Northwest 21st Avenue
(503) 226-2754
www.laurarusso.com

One of Portland's largest and most prestigious galleries, Laura Russo Gallery offers classical and controversial artwork by the Northwest's finest artists as well as young talent in a setting that is itself a work of serene art. The gallery is open Tuesday through Friday, 11:00 a.m. to 5:30 p.m. and Saturday, 11:00 a.m. to 5:00 p.m.

MUSEUM OF CONTEMPORARY CRAFT
724 Northwest Davis Street
(503) 223-2654
www.museumofcontemporarycraft.org
The Museum of Contemporary Craft is dedicated to promoting the beauty of handmade arts in Oregon, sponsoring permanent and traveling collections of exquisite ceramic, glass, metal, and fiber art. Its permanent collections feature regional stars such as Don Sprague and international artists such as Vladimir Tsivin and Gail Nichols, but you will also find much space devoted to emerging artists. The gallery has always been devoted to providing craftspersons with a way to sell their work at a fair price, and the sales gallery here is outstanding, offering expert help for the novice and the seasoned collector. The gallery was founded in 1937, built in part with Works Progress Administration funds, and it is the oldest nonprofit gallery in the country. In 2008 it moved to a handsomely renovated space in the Pearl District, with help from a large grant from investor and philanthropist Paul Allen, and was able to massively expand its offerings. The museum offers family programs on Sunday, as well as lectures, discussions, and classes throughout the week. Crafts have long been considered fine art in Portland, and this museum displays the highest form of these ideals.

NEWSPACE CENTER FOR PHOTOGRAPHY
1632 Southeast 10th Avenue
(503) 963-1935
www.newspacephoto.org
This center is devoted to the photographic image, providing resources for students, artists, teachers, and professionals. It has a wonderful gallery space that shows the work of new and established photographers, but it also offers classes, darkroom space (for those who have not converted solely to digital), and help with access to lighting. They also help out artists by reviewing portfolios and teaching workshops on how to market your wares.

QUINTANA GALLERIES
120 Northwest 9th Avenue
(503) 223-1729
www.quintanagalleries.com
A popular stopping spot in downtown Portland since it opened in 1972, Quintana has a bounty of American Indian and Hispanic art. Walking by its windows is a show in itself with a sumptuous display of Northwest tribal masks and totems as well as pueblo pottery, fetishes, and other crafts from the Southwest. The gallery also has a good collection of photographs by Edward Curtis as well as collector-quality antiques.

i For the latest announcements, reviews, and news about the Portland arts scene, check out PORT at www.portlandart.net. This site, sponsored by the movers and shakers of the Portland art world, features outstanding writing about what's being shown around town and what to think of it.

PORTLAND ART MUSEUM
1219 Southwest Park Avenue
(503) 226-2811
www.portlandartmuseum.org
The Portland Art Museum is architecturally and artistically our city's pride and joy even if we quarrel about what exhibits are inside. The second oldest fine arts museum in the Pacific Northwest, it was established in 1892 when business and cultural leaders created the Portland Art Association and ponied up dough to collect a group of 100 plaster casts of Greek and Roman sculpture. It was a start. In 1905 the museum found a physical location at Southwest 5th Avenue and Taylor Street, and in the 1930s it ended up in its current building designed by the noted architect, Pietro Belluschi. In fall 2000 the museum reopened

 **Close-up**

DIY Portland

AMANDA HORTON—ALLIUM DESIGNS

One evening in New York, jewelry designer Amanda Horton was out on a first date. Prospects didn't look good. For one thing, they were at a bar that specialized in whiskey, and her date had just ordered a pomegranate martini. The cocktail waitress narrowed her eyes. Then she noticed Horton's earrings—and was delighted to find out Horton had made them herself. Recently, Horton had had time on her hands. New York is expensive, even if you have a decent job. Thus, to fill her evenings, she had returned to an old hobby, jewelry making. But it was about to become more than a hobby. It turned out that the cocktail waitress was starting a showroom for local designers. She wanted to include Horton's jewelry.

Horton was brought up in Albany, Oregon, and lived in Portland after graduating from the University of Oregon. Straining at the lovely but somewhat limited horizons of her native state, she moved to New York, writing grants for local schools. The whiskey-bar conversation was a catalyst. Soon, Horton was making and selling a lot of jewelry. She returned to Portland in 2006, propelled by the hope that it would be easier and less expensive to set up her jewelry business in Portland than it was in New York.

Portland has a nationally noted culture of do-it-yourselfers, crafters, and artists. The reasons for this phenomenon are not entirely clear. While Portland has a vibrant visual-arts scene and interesting museums and so on, it's not, well, New York. It's not even Zurich, which has one of the best small museums in the world. It's a provincial capital—with all the drawbacks and benefits. The main drawback is that it's not a world stage, but the main benefit is that there's room. It's comparatively cheap to live here, and there are enough like-minded compatriots that you can feel sustained in a community. Portlanders are in love with their city and wild about anything locally produced, from music to wine and beer, from food to design and craft. It is part of the ethos of the place. So there are structures in place to help a new designer succeed.

Upon Horton's return to Portland, everything fell together. Almost immediately, she found an ideal spot: a holiday sale hosted at the Egg Collective and Launch Pad gallery in Southeast Portland. This creative space is an incubator for numerous area designers, and here she met many like-minded craftspersons. Horton notes that, once you are linked to the DIY network, you find out everything that's going on. Soon she was selling her pieces at shows around the area, including the popular Crafty Wonderland event, an extravaganza of local artists and designers held each month at the Doug Fir Lounge. At one of these shows, she met the proprietor of DIY Lounge@Collage, the excellent craft supply store and workspace, who was looking for people to teach classes. Since teaching is something that Horton has an abiding interest in, she agreed—for her, part of the satisfaction in creating is in teaching others how to create.

Horton's pieces are simple and clean, her aesthetic an organic one. She wants to design for people who don't have $10,000 to spend but who want to have versatile and beautiful ornaments that they can wear every day—and still pass on to the grandchildren one day. Her current favorite materials are quartz and other semiprecious minerals; she eschews manmade

after an extensive renovation in the Hoffman Wing: three floors devoted to Native American art and new exhibit space for European, regional, contemporary, and graphic art. There is also a gift shop, outside sculpture garden, and the Whitsell Auditorium used for ceremonies and films. Now one of the 25 largest museums in the United States, the Portland Art Museum has a collection of more than 32,000 works of art from American Indian artifacts to Monet's *Waterlilies* to stones. Quartz, she says, is a very versatile stone, one that can look elegant in a formal setting but look just as beautiful with a T-shirt. It also has tactile properties that attract Horton. "I can't buy my supplies online," she says. "I have to touch them and look at them." She is an expert metalsmith as well, hand-forging gold, brass, and silver into lovely, simple links. Metalsmithing was a skill she learned in high school. Being a craftsman in that profound sense, she says—not just knowing how to use a hot glue gun or a butane torch but actually knowing how to weld and solder, how to transform metal from one state into another, and understanding the inherent properties of the material—is immensely satisfying. Likewise, she prefers oldschool approaches—for example, using silk thread to bead and knot and even making her own needles. This attention to detail is time-consuming but it's precisely this approach that makes pieces special and long-lasting. "You can buy a cute necklace from Target," she observes, "but you won't have it for the rest of your life."

Like many fine crafters, Horton is hesitant to call herself an artist, defining art as being motivated by the desire to communicate. "Art," she says, "is channeling something through yourself to speak to others." Design sometimes reaches those heights, she notes, but it's not the primary purpose. Craft, in contrast, is more about the product per se—not necessarily about reaching people. Design provides the middle ground: an aesthetic experience of the everyday, one achieved through working with matter. For Horton, the links in a necklace or the beading of an earring are designed through the process of creating. The Swiss painter Paul Klee observed that you must adapt yourself to the contents of the paint box—the materials you use control you; you don't control them. Horton does not subscribe to a grand vision of jewelry design, but, like Klee, she is inspired by the actual properties of the material, which tell her what to do as she manipulates it. "For me, design is part of the process. I have to work with something before I know what it will be."

DO IT YOURSELF

Want to check out the DIY landscape for yourself? Here are some tips.

DIY Alert (www.diyalert.com) is a fantastic resource for Portland crafters, with an e-mail alert system, a calendar, resources, and a blog that has excellent interviews with creative people from all over the area. It's run by master crafter and the queen of DIY in Portland: Diane Gilleland, aka Sister Diane.

Collage Art Materials & Workroom is at 1639 Northeast Alberta Street and 4429 Southeast Woodstock Boulevard, (503) 249-2190. (Also see the Shopping chapter for more information). Class and workshop schedules can be found at www.diylounge.com.

Crafty Wonderland is held the second Sunday of each month from 11:00 a.m. to 4:00 p.m. in the Doug Fir Lounge, 830 East Burnside (all ages welcome). Admission is free.

The Egg Collective, featuring the Launch Pad Gallery, can be found at 534 Southeast Oak Street, (971) 227-0072, or www.launchpad.org.

Amanda Horton sells her jewelry at www.alliumdesigns.com. If, like her, you need to see and touch what you're buying first, you can find her designs at Union Rose, 2023 Northeast Martin Luther King Jr. Boulevard, (503) 287-4242, or Presents of Mind, 3633 Southeast Hawthorne Boulevard, (503) 230-7740. Register for her classes at www.diylounge.com.

an impressive assembly of Asian art. To display the large collection of Asian paintings, ceramics, prints, and sculptures, three permanent Asian art galleries have been added to the museum's exhibit space. After strolling past a changing gallery that reflects the flavor of the permanent displays, visitors can view art in the Japanese, Chinese, and Korean galleries.

In the fall of 2005, the museum opened its new gallery in the beautifully renovated Mark

Building, an old Masonic temple immediately adjacent to the museum. This renovated space provides 141,000 square feet for the new Jubitz Center for Modern and Contemporary Art, as well as two ballrooms, a library, and offices.

The museum frequently stages extravagant touring exhibits featuring art from the ancient to the modern. These have included important collections of artifacts from China and Egypt, as well as the late paintings of Monet and other French masters. The Portland Art Museum was one of the few sites chosen to display "From Fra Angelica to Bonnard: Masterpieces from the Rau Collection," a significant private collection from Europe. The museum also featured "Edward Weston: A Photographer's Love of Life," displaying the work of the influential American photographer. The late Dr. Gordon Gilkey, curator of prints and drawings at the museum, organized this stunningly comprehensive display of contemporary prints from 74 countries. The museum also embraces edgy modern art and has an ideal space to show it in the Jubitz Center.

The Portland Art Museum also sponsors numerous events and classes, many of which are family-friendly. The museum is open Tuesday, Wednesday, and Saturday from 10:00 a.m. to 5:00 p.m.; Thursday and Friday from 10:00 a.m. to 8:00 p.m.; and Sunday from noon to 5:00 p.m. Admission is free to museum members; nonmember prices are $10 for adults. For information on shows and programs, call (503) 226-2811.

RECREATION AND SPECTATOR SPORTS

Oregonians have their share of skyscrapers, computer chip plants, and BMW dealerships, but we also have forests, snow-topped mountains, phenomenal river gorges, a 300-mile coastline, one of the most fertile valleys in the world, a lacy network of creeks and rivers, and an extensive system of parks and wilderness areas. Though the great expanse of our state may be crisscrossed with highways, while even our trails may be crowded with exuberant hikers, there is still a wild, true outback here where a soul can find solitude, clean air to breathe, and a vision of unspoiled land, river, or seacoast. The Portland area in particular is home to or close to some of our best outdoor attractions. So Portlanders love to get out and about—to bike, hike, paddle, putt, shoot, set the hook, and slide down our slippery snowy slopes. In this chapter we've listed some of our favorite spots, so you can try out your outdoor or indoor recreational skills in our beautiful Portland setting. We've included a few organizations and commercial operations that can help you on your way.

As for spectator sports, the biggest game in Portland is the National Basketball Association's Trailblazers, but there are lots of other seats to cheer from, including those at minor league baseball games with the Portland Beavers (who season young players on behalf of the San Diego Padres), ice hockey with the Winter Hawks, and soccer matches with the Portland Timbers. PGE Park, a downtown stadium, is the home of the Timbers and the Beavers, while the Blazers play at the even fancier Rose Garden. But there are many other contests to watch in the Portland area. Later in this chapter, we give you the lowdown on these athletic showdowns.

RECREATION

NATURE OF THE NORTHWEST INFORMATION CENTER
800 Northeast Oregon Street
(503) 872-2752
www.naturenw.org

Near the Convention Center and Lloyd Center, this information center is open from 10:00 a.m. to 5:00 p.m., Monday through Friday. Outdoor recreationists come here to examine books and pamphlets about geology and other natural history features of Oregon. Topographic maps, brochures, and books are also on sale. You can also obtain from them a free publication list from the Oregon Department of Geology—as well as the information-packed Web site, which has the lowdown on passes, hikes, and other crucial information.

Biking

Bicycling magazine has repeatedly proclaimed Portland the most bike-friendly city in the United States. People ride their bikes to work, to school, for fun, or for sport—no matter how steep the hill or how dreary the weather. TriMet provides help for this popular form of transportation with racks on its buses and light rail. You can store your bike on the front of the bus or train and ride to your neighborhood or out into the country for a recreational spin. There are also many bike repair shops where you can chat with bike mechanics or do the work yourself for a small fee. In short, if you've got skinny or fat tires, a rusty, beloved Schwinn or a shiny new Yeti, this is a great town for biking.

A fine resource for any Oregon cyclist is *Oregon Cycling Magazine*, which is actually a free newspaper published 10 times a year. This informative medium is sponsored by the Eugene-based Center for Appropriate Transport, and in it you'll not only find calendars, racing schedules, and lists of bike shops and co-ops, but you'll also find essays devoted to every aspect of cycling. It's widely available at bike shops, or for $20, you can have it delivered to your mailbox for a year. Write them at 455 West First Avenue, Eugene, Oregon 97401 or visit www.oregoncycling.org.

i The most comprehensive source of bike information in town is *BikePortland* (www.bikeportland.org), an online daily bulletin of bike news, policy, and analysis. It also provides an incredibly useful registry of stolen bikes and advice about how to get them back.

Biking Organizations

BICYCLE TRANSPORTATION ALLIANCE (BTA)
233 Northwest 5th Avenue
(503) 226-0676
www.bta4bikes.org
With nearly 5,000 members statewide, the mission of the Bicycle Transportation Alliance is to get more people out of cars and on bicycles for the commute to and from work. BTA coordinates its efforts with the Bike Gallery chain and Cycle Oregon to promote cycling as a fun, healthy, and environmentally friendly mode of transport. If you want to work to get more bike lanes and biker-friendly legislation, this is an outfit that will appreciate your help.

Portland is filled with cyclists. RACHEL DRESBECK

PORTLAND UNITED MOUNTAIN PEDALERS (PUMP)
818 Southwest 3rd Avenue, Suite 228
www.pumpclub.org
Dedicated to active, responsible mountain biking, Portland United Mountain Pedalers arranges rides, maintains trails, puts out a newsletter, and keeps Portland mountain bikers organized. You don't need to be a member to participate in events, which include everything from weekend rides to weeknight clinics. Rides may be as "simple" as a night jaunt through Forest Park or as involved as a bike camping trip in the Cascades. (If you're a nonmember planning to join a ride, you should call first so the group doesn't leave without you.) The newsletter, the *Mountain Pedaler*, is widely available at bike shops. PUMP doesn't keep an organization phone, but it does have an active Web site with useful information.

PORTLAND WHEELMEN TOURING CLUB
(503) 257-7982 (ride hotline),
(503) 666-5796 (information)
www.pwtc.com
The Portland Wheelmen Touring Club, founded in 1971, promotes cycling via a social organization for cyclists with more than 1,100 members. The primary focus of the club is recreational riding. It sponsors up to two dozen rides on a weekly basis, including rides every day of the year and many evenings. You don't have to be a member to go on a ride, but if you are one, they'll keep your stats for you. The outings are listed in their monthly newsletter, *Riders Digest,* available at most Portland area bicycle shops and in the *Oregonian's* arts and entertainment section every Friday.

Popular Rides

PORTLAND BRIDGE PEDAL
Bike Transportation Alliance
(503) 226-0676
For information on this trek, call its sponsors. Held every August, this third-largest urban bike ride in the country brings together a very long string of more than 10,000 participants who bike and hike over bridges crossing the Willamette River. The city closes nine of these spans to auto traffic so that the noncompetitive bikers can claim the bridges as their own. During their 28-mile trek, these pedalers can gaze down at a bustling cityscape, freighters getting loads of wheat at huge grain elevators, and other bikers struggling up the on-ramp. At the end of the ride, a festive get-together celebrates biking with T-shirts, certificates of accomplishment, and vendors selling cold drinks and spicy grub.

i Every year, 2,000 cyclists take to the road for seven days, cruising through hundreds of miles of Oregon's most beautiful scenery to raise money for Oregon community development and preservation. Cycle Oregon is a fully supported tour—and that means hot showers, excellent meals, massages, folks to carry your gear, and every other detail considered—so you can relax and enjoy the scenery while you pedal. For more information visit the Cycle Oregon Web site, www.cycleoregon.com.

WORST DAY OF THE YEAR RIDE
www.worstdayride.com
This festive event, sponsored by the Community Cycling Center, celebrates the hideous winter biking weather that Portlanders endure with a 2,000-cyclist ride. You can choose between two loops—an 18-mile urban one or a 40-mile course that takes you out to Hillsboro. Both start at the Lucky Labrador Brew Pub (915 Southeast Hawthorne). Riders show up in costumes but ready for any kind of weather. Proceeds benefit the Community Cycling Center, which uses the funds to give bikes to low-income kids and for other worthy things.

Mountain Biking

The controversy over where mountain bikers can take their rugged rigs and still help protect the environment has settled down here in the Portland area. Most local mountain bikers are sensitive enough to stay on marked trails. Maps of those trails are available from the Outdoor Recreation Program at Portland Parks and Recreation, 1120 Southwest 5th Avenue, Room 1302, (503) 823-5132. Portland United Mountain Pedalers (PUMP; see their individual listing in this chapter) is another good resource. Let them know you want to be on their mailing list for a newsletter that publishes information on weekend rides. A third spot to get the lowdown on climbing high

---

Portland Bike Shops

These shops can help you find a bike, the tools to repair it, all the gear you'll need for soggy commutes, and information about where to ride on the weekend. Some of them will also rent bikes. Others sell custom bikes—a burgeoning industry in Portland. BikePortland (www.BikePortland.org) also has comprehensive information on custom bikes.

Beckwith Bicycles
4235 Southeast Woodstock Boulevard
(503) 774-3531

Bicycle Repair Collective
Southeast 45th Avenue and Belmont Street
(503) 233-0564

Bike Central Co-op
732 Southwest 1st Avenue
(503) 227-4439

Bike Gallery (six stores)
5329 Northeast Sandy Boulevard
(503) 281-9800

1001 Southwest Salmon Street
(503) 222-3821

4235 Southeast Woodstock Boulevard
(503) 774-3531

3645 Southwest Hall Boulevard, Beaverton
(503) 641-2580

200 B Avenue, Lake Oswego
(503) 636-1600

10950 Southeast Division Street
(503) 254-2663
www.bikegallery.com

Citybikes Worker's Cooperative
734 Southeast Ankeny Street
(503) 239-6951, (503) 239-0553 for repair shop

Fat Tire Farm
2714 Northwest Thurman Street
(503) 222-3276
www.fattirefarm.com

REI
1405 Northwest Johnson Street
(503) 221-1938, (360) 693-0209

7410 Southwest Bridgeport Road
Tualatin
(503) 624-8600

2235 Northwest Allie Avenue
Hillsboro
(503) 617-6072
www.rei.com

River City Bicycles
706 Southeast Martin Luther King Jr. Boulevard
(503) 233-5973
www.rivercitybicycles.com

Veloce Bicycles
3202 Southeast Hawthorne Avenue
(503) 234-8400

into the hills is the Fat Tire Farm, 2714 Northwest Thurman Street, (503) 222-3276. This bike shop not only fixes and rents mountain bikes but also sponsors the annual Fat Tire Cross Crusade, a cyclocross event held in winter that takes mountain bikers along a course that changes from paved road to gravel to mud.

LEIF ERIKSON DRIVE

Start at the end of Northwest Thurman Road in Northwest Portland. This 6-mile ride takes you along the paved, gravel, and dirt roads that loop along the ridge that defines Forest Park, the largest tree zone within a U.S. city. It's a wild trek down steep slopes. You may have to dodge boulders and hikers, but once on top you'll get a spectacular view of the city to the east.

POWELL BUTTE NATURE PARK TRAIL SYSTEM

Start in the parking lot of Powell Butte Nature Park at the end of Southeast 162nd Avenue. This network of 9 miles of biking, hiking, and horseback riding trails is perhaps the most popular mountain bike trail in the metro area. This 570-acre park is home to old orchards, meadows, cattle pastures, and lots of hawks, deer, coyotes, and other wildlife. The trails are sometimes closed during winter months.

Boating

A city at the confluence of two major waterways and surrounded by myriad ponds and lakes, Portland has a lot of boats parked in driveways, moored at docks, and afloat as homesteads. All through summer the Willamette River swarms with nautical traffic, water-skiers zooming the more tranquil waters below Ross Island, and sailboats wending between downtown bridges. And during the winter holidays, volunteer boaters decorate their crafts and line up for the Parade of Christmas Ships as they take a week of chilly nights to entertain Portlanders with their imaginative use of lights shining on dark water.

The Willamette's major launch sites, both operated by Portland Parks and Recreation, (503) 823-7529, are at Willamette Park and Sellwood

Riverfront Park. Others are RiverPlace, an elegant moorage close to downtown on the Willamette, (503) 241-8283, and Chinook Landing Marine Park, (503) 665-4995, which has six launch lanes on the Columbia River. The Oregon State Marine Board has an amazingly helpful online guide that details boat ramp information, regulations, route planning, cautions, fishing, and more (www.boatoregon.com). Wherever you launch, be sure to put the children in life jackets: It is required by law. And you'd better put on one yourself too.

i Bike riding can be a great form of exercise for city children. But parents rightly worry about safety: Dogs, cars, and other cyclists can make riding hazardous. The Community Cycling Center is dedicated to teaching children about bicycle safety, riding, and repair. Contact them at 2407 Northeast Alberta Street, (503) 546-8864; www.communitycyclingcenter.org.

Rentals

BLUE LAKE PARK
20500 Northeast
Marine Drive, Fairview
(503) 661-6087
From Memorial Day to Labor Day, from 11:00 a.m. to late afternoon, you can rent a canoe or paddleboat from the Blue Lake dock for less than the price of a matinee. Note: It also costs $4 per car to enter the park.

ISLAND SAILING CENTER
515 Northeast Tomahawk Island Drive
(800) 303-2470
www.islandsailingclub.com
If you're into sailing, you'll want to check out the Island Sailing Club. Here you can rent a 20-foot Santana for $150 for a half day or $180 for a full day or a 23-foot Santana for $190 for a half day and $225 for a full day on the Columbia. For a more ambitious adventure, the club will rent a charter sailboat for up to a week out

of a moorage in DesMoines, Washington, near Seattle. You don't have to take one of these large, sleek beauties out for the whole week. For the uncertain, captains can also be rented—$100 for a half day, twice that for a full day.

SPORTCRAFT MARINA
1701 Clackamette Drive, Oregon City
(503) 656-6484
www.sportcraftmarina.com
This is a good rental operation for those who want to boat on the Willamette River. Open year-round Tuesday through Saturday from 9:00 a.m. to 4:00 p.m., they rent, with a $50 deposit, solo canoes and kayaks for $15 for the first half hour and $5 for each additional hour; tandem canoes go for $20 for the first half hour and $5 for each additional hour. If you want to rent a craft on Sunday or Monday, call for special arrangements.

WILLAMETTE SAILING CLUB
6336 Southwest Beaver Avenue
(503) 246-5345
www.willamettesailingclub.com
If you're going to be here a while, you might consider joining this member-run group dedicated to small sailboats, which moors its craft near Willamette Park. If you're a member you can rent a dinghy here. The club holds meetings and classes and invites members to crew with each other.

i Portland sometimes has the feeling of a provincial European capital. Is it the skyline? The river wall and bridges? Or is it the bocce ball and pétanque players in the city parks? For a little bit of France, join the pétanque players on Saturdays at Portland's own Place de Vosges, Jamison Square (visit www.laboulerose.com for a calendar and other information). If you're the bocce type, the Portland Bocce League (www.port landbocce.com) plays tournaments during July and August in the public courts found on the North Park Blocks, Northwest Glisan Street and Park Avenue.

Bowling
Bowling never seems to lose its appeal, even with electronic scorekeeping. Below are a couple of favorite lanes. For a longer list, see the Kidstuff chapter.

INTERSTATE LANES
6049 North Interstate Avenue
(503) 285-9881
This bowling alley not only features cosmic bowling—where black lights turn the pins a spooky white, and lasers flash through the air to the beat of cosmic tunes—but it also is completely non-smoking. They do birthdays and corporate events as well. They serve beer, wine, and pizza. Cosmic bowling happens between 10:30 p.m. and 1:30 a.m. on Friday and Saturday night.

VALLEY LANES
9300 Southwest Beaverton-Hillsdale Highway, Beaverton
(503) 292-3523
www.valleylanes.com
Home of glow-in-the-dark laser lanes, Valley Lanes also offers bumper bowling for kids. It has 32 lanes open from 9:00 a.m. to midnight, seven days a week. Fees are $2.95 per game from 9:00 a.m. to 5:00 p.m. Monday through Friday and $3.95 per game at other times. Shoe rentals are $3.00 per pair. Valley Lanes also has all-you-can-bowl cosmic bowling—as well as a full-service restaurant and lounge.

Camping
In a region renowned for a vast menu of camping sites, it's hard to pick just a few to recommend, but here are some nearby sites that are at the top of the list. Note that some state parks require a $3 day-use fee; you can also purchase an annual pass for $25. Camping fees depend on the park, the time of year, and the luxuriousness of the facility. For state park information call (503) 986-0707 or (800) 551-6949. If you want to make a reservation (a good idea), call (800) 452-5687. You can register online at www.oregonstateparks.org.

MILO MCIVER STATE PARK

South side of Clackamas River off Spring-water Road, 4 miles northwest of Estacada

(503) 986-0707, (800) 452-5687 (reservations)

This spot is an excellent stop for RVs with its 44 electrical hookups and 4 primitive tent sites. Lots of trailheads lead into riverside forests, and plenty of meadows invite roaming about. Open as a park all year, it is available for camping March through November. To get there take Interstate 205 to Highway 212. Make a lazy right turn off Highway 212 onto Highway 224, which leads to Estacada. From here backtrack down the river on Springwater Road to the park.

MOUNT HOOD RECREATIONAL AREA

Mount Hood Information Center

65000 East U.S. Highway 26, Welches

(503) 622-4822, (888) 622-4822

(877) 444-6777 (campsite reservations)

www.mthood.info, www.reserveamerica.com

Zigzag Ranger District

70220 US 26

(503) 622-3191

You'll find plenty of gorgeous spots in the Mount Hood Wilderness only 60 miles east of Portland. To get there, take I–205 to Southeast Powell Boulevard, which morphs into US 26, the trail up the hill to all the fun.

Backpackers can take one of many trails leading from Timberline Lodge, a National Historic Monument with huge beams and logs for posts and lintels. This justly famous hotel, built in 1937, offers rustic luxury—if such a thing is possible— in its rooms, but campers might be more interested in the wonderful restaurant.

For those who want to stay down in the trees, there are plenty of campsites and picnic areas. With 15 sites on the Salmon River Road, Green Canyon is a charming stop close to a store for stocking up on all that gooey stuff that goes into s'mores.

To get there, take US 26 to Zigzag, then drive 4 miles northeast on the Salmon River Road (2618) to the campground. One of the

prettiest campsites in this wilderness area is Toll-gate, on the banks of the Zigzag River 1 mile east of the tiny town of Rhododendron. Another good campground, Camp Creek, with 30 sites, lies on Camp Creek Road a short distance beyond the Tollgate turnoff.

One of the largest and most popular campsites in the Mount Hood National Forest is Timothy Lake, acclaimed as one of the 10 best camping spots in the West by *Sunset* magazine. This scenic lake with its postcard view of Mount Hood is easily accessible from Portland. Take US 26 beyond the junction with Highway 35 and turn south on Skyline Road and east on Forest Road 57, both of which are marked with signs to Timothy Lake. Once at this huge lake, which is ringed by fir, hemlock, and pine trees, pick a spot at one of its three main campsites, or simply hike or canoe to a more secluded camp. To make a reservation at Oak Fork, Gone Creek, or Hoodview, call (877) 444-6777, the number for ReserveAmerica. For more information on camping in the Mount Hood Recreational Area, call the Zigzag Ranger District at the number above or write to them at 70220 East Highway 26, Zigzag, Oregon 97049. A day-use pass will set you back $5; an annual pass is $30.

OXBOW REGIONAL PARK

6 miles east of Gresham on Division Street

(503) 663-4708

Oxbow Regional Park is a close-in site for tent camping that's open all year and operated by Metro, the regional governing body that runs the zoo, TriMet, and other public services. Six miles east of Gresham on Division Street, this site has 45 tent and RV campsites with no hookups. The cost is $15 per night and a $4 vehicle entry fee. Firewood is $4 per bundle. As in all Metro parks, no dogs are allowed.

Canoeing, Kayaking, and Rafting

Paddlers looking for water deep enough for their canoes, kayaks, or rafts can find a launch spot within minutes anywhere in the Portland area. Here, where the Clackamas, Sandy, Willamette, and Columbia Rivers amble together west toward the Pacific Ocean, are stretches of flat calm, cataracts of white fury, and fast water rippling over dappled round boulders. And for those who want to just ease along, there are also a few boat-friendly lakes and ponds. Here's a sampling of aqua-jaunts available close to town.

BLUE LAKE
8 miles east of Portland in the town of Fairview along Interstate 84
Blue Lake Regional Park, at the gateway to the Columbia Gorge, is just 20 minutes east of downtown Portland. Although it gets crowded, it is worth a visit for its accessibility and amenities. Chinook Landing Marine Park, adjacent to Blue Lake Regional Park, is a sizable boating facility with a six-lane launch ramp and picnic area. There are also trails through nearby wetlands for opportunities to view wildlife.

MULTNOMAH CHANNEL
Multnomah Channel is a backdoor watercourse that starts at the southeast tip of Sauvie Island and winds northwest through a lacy wild of sloughs, swamps, and grassy pastures to the little lumbertown of St. Helens and a confluence with the Columbia River. If you want to meander up or down a stretch of the channel, a good spot to launch your canoe or rowboat is the Sauvie Island Boat Ramp at the junction of the Burlington Ferry and Sauvie Island Road, just north of the intersection with Reeder Road. (See the entry on Sauvie Island in the Portland's Parks chapter.) You'll find picnic tables, toilets, and plenty of parking nearby.

ROSS ISLAND
A loop around Ross Island is a great two-to three-hour canoe or kayak trip that will get those kinks out of your arms and back. The put-in spot is Willamette Park in Portland's southwest side. Once in the river cross over to Ross Island, hang a right around its northern tip, and go down the Holgate Channel to the entrance to the lagoon. After you visit this tranquil pond—where you may spy a Swainson's thrush, black-headed grosbeak, or spotted sandpiper—paddle down the channel, around the southern edge of the island, and back downriver to Willamette Park.

SMITH AND BYBEE LAKES
In North Portland, 2.5 miles west on Marine Drive off I–5
Smith and Bybee Lakes are the liquid portions of a 2,000-acre wildlife area across the mouth of the Willamette River from Sauvie Island. Here at the confluence of the Columbia and Willamette Rivers is a huge intersection of waterfowl flight paths where federal, state, and regional agencies have established refuges for birds wintering or just passing through. Canoeists and kayakers can paddle quietly among thousands of mallards and Canada geese as well as great blue herons nesting along the shoreline. Osprey are common in the summer, and bald eagles take over their fishing spots in wintertime. Nesting great horned owls have also been sighted. You can reach these lakes by taking I–5 north of Portland to the Marine Drive West exit. Drive west 2.5 miles to the parking lot on the south side of Marine Drive or continue to the Kelley Point Boat Launch farther west on Marine Drive. From the launch it's a short cruise down a slough to the southwest edge of Bybee Lake. Once you arrive at the lakes, if the sun is cooperating, it will be easy to spot lots of Northwest painted turtles basking on logs.

TUALATIN RIVER PADDLE TRIP
Tualatin Riverkeepers
12360 Southwest Main Street
Tigard
(503) 620-7507
www.tualatinriverkeepers.org
A canoe paddle down the Tualatin River is a terrific family outing on a placid stream that starts near Hillsboro west of Portland and wanders quietly through 16 hamlets before it joins the Willamette River just south of Oregon City. Tualatin Riverkeepers is a nonprofit group dedicated to protecting this fragile watercourse. Every year Riverkeepers sponsors a number of guided paddle trips for the general public through a seldom-seen stretch of this pristine watercourse.

Rentals and Resources

ALDER CREEK KAYAK & CANOE
250 Northeast Tomahawk Island Drive
Jantzen Beach
(503) 285-0464

1515 Southeast Water Street
(503) 285-1819

BROWN'S FERRY
5855 Southwest Nyberg Lane
Tualatin
(503) 691-2405
www.aldercreek.com

Alder Creek is a good place to rent a canoe or kayak on Tomahawk Island, a close neighbor of Hayden Island, where I–5 crosses the Columbia. This full-service outfit offers a complete line of gear for white-water enthusiasts, as well as low-key paddlers. Alder Creek also has outlets in Bend and Hood River, should the desire to kayak overtake you when you are visiting there.

PORTLAND RIVER COMPANY
RiverPlace Marina and
6342 Southwest Macadam Avenue, next to Willamette Park
(503) 459-4050
www.portlandrivercompany.com

Portland River Company, with two locations, provides everything you will need to paddle a single or double sea kayak. It also offers guided tours. The Ross Island 2.5-hour tour costs $45. First-time kayakers and experienced paddlers alike will enjoy this marine view of Portland. The adventure starts at RiverPlace Marina; crosses over to the historic USS Blueback, a submarine docked at Oregon's Museum of Science and Industry; and continues upriver, circling Ross Island, where you may catch sight of great blue herons, osprey, and bald eagles.

Climbing

A glance to the east or north will suggest that Portlanders have plenty of mountains and cliffs to climb when they get the urge. At roughly 11,235 feet, Mount Hood or Wy'east, as this gorgeous peak is still known, looms above the Cascade ridges. When spring chases the snow up this glacier (the season lasts from May to July), technical climbers grab ice axes and crampons for various ascents suited for novices to masters. It is a relative easy climb until the last 1,500 feet. Due to cagey weather fronts and unstable snow, this last stretch is far more difficult: Rescue units are often plucking unlucky climbers off the steep slope. Other sites that will challenge the crampon crowd are Horsethief Butte, 2 miles east of the Dalles Bridge on Highway 14, and Broughton's Bluff at Lewis and Clark State Park east of Troutdale on I–84. Just 30 minutes from town, Broughton's Bluff offers a number of tough climbs.

i Climbers and other recreators on a budget will appreciate Next Adventure, which carries—in addition to new equipment—a wide variety of used, consigned, closed-out, and traded climbing gear, as well as equipment for lots of other recreational activities. Find them at 426 Southeast Grand Avenue, (503) 233-0706 or www.nextadventure.net.

MAZAMAS
909 Northwest 19th Avenue
(503) 227-2345
www.mazamas.org

This 3,000-member mountaineering group is named after Mount Mazama, a huge mountain that blew itself apart to create Crater Lake in southern Oregon. Founded in 1894 when 193 climbers ascended to the summit of Mount Hood, the Mazamas are legendary for all the mountains they've climbed and the resources they provide for their members. To join all you have to do is climb a mountain with a living glacier.

OREGON MOUNTAIN COMMUNITY
2975 Northeast Sandy Boulevard
(503) 227-1038
www.e-omc.com

Oregon Mountain Community—or known fondly

as OMC—carries everything for the serious climber and mountaineer, including climbing and backpacking gear, from crampons, axes, and ropes to get you up the mountain to probes, beacons, and shovels in case it falls down on top of you. They also host classes and lectures, run a repair shop, and offer rentals of every kind of ski, snowshoe, and other winter sports gear.

PORTLAND ROCK GYM
21 Northeast 12th Avenue
(503) 232-8310
www.portlandrockgym.com
The Portland Rock Gym was an urban pioneer, seeing possibility in the Lower Burnside neighborhood when no one else did. They can help you do something similar with your climbing skills. When the weather is keeping you off the rocks, or when you want to fine-tune your ascension skills, stop by Portland Rock Gym for some indoor climbing on a 40-foot wall. The Portland Rock Gym has 8,000 square feet of climbing space and offers classes and equipment rentals, as well as yoga classes, camps, and activities for kids after school. The gym is open Monday, Wednesday, and Friday from 11:00 a.m. to 11:00 p.m., Tuesday and Thursday from 7:00 a.m. to 11:00 p.m., on Saturday from 9:00 a.m. to 7:00 p.m., and on Sunday from 9:00 a.m. to 6:00 p.m.

STONEWORKS CLIMBING GYM
6775 Southwest 111th Avenue, Beaverton
(503) 644-3517
www.belay.com
While Stoneworks has the usual features of a rock gym, and rents gear, holds classes, and sponsors competitions, it is really renowned for its bouldering area, which is more than 2,000 square feet and has drawn national accolades. For a monthly fee you can take advantage of the intriguing overhang bouldering and a large number of different holds. Stoneworks is open Monday through Thursday from 4:00 to 10:00 p.m., Friday from 4:00 to 8:00 p.m., and on weekends from noon to 8:00 p.m.

Fishing and Fly-Fishing

Anglers who live in the Portland area can wet their lines all year long. Spring chinook salmon and summer and winter steelhead spawn up the Clackamas and Sandy Rivers, and rainbow trout can be hooked in those streams as well as the Willamette River and in Blue Lake, a popular fishing hole and recreational site. A good spot to land a steelhead is at the confluence of the Clackamas and Willamette Rivers near Milwaukie. The Oregon Department of Fish and Wildlife (ODFW) keeps a minimum of spawning salmon en route to their upstream beds by issuing quotas in Portland-area water. But as long as the season is open, go for it. To find out where they're biting and where it's legal to hook them, call ODFW's 24-hour automated number, (503) 947-6000 or (800) 720-6339, or visit them online at www.dfw.state.or.us/resources/fishing. Fisherfolk can also catch bass and crappies in the Willamette and sturgeon and shad in the Columbia and Willamette as well as in sloughs and bays feeding into those streams. ODFW has a free pamphlet, "Guide to Warmwater Fishing in the Portland Metropolitan Area," which will guide fishers to piers, pilings, and ponds where those lunkers lay about.

Sporting Goods Stores and Marinas

FISHERMAN'S MARINE & OUTDOOR
1120 North Hayden Meadows Drive
(503) 283-0044
www.fishermans-marine.com
This huge, locally owned store has anything you'd ever want, from bait to spinners to outboard motors, and you might be able to coax the location of a hot fishing hole out of the friendly clerk. They are wise in the ways of the fish that live in Oregon and Washington.

KAUFMANN'S STREAMBORN
11960 Southwest Pacific Highway
(503) 639-7004
www.kaufmannsstreamborn.com
Kaufmann's provides fly-fishing equipment, workshops, and worldwide bookings for piscatory

Close-up

The Rajeff Fly Fishing School

Tim Rajeff and Katherine Hart, the delightful people who run the Rajeff Fly Fishing School, hold local classes for private clients and groups in both casting and fly fishing. They also hold workshops across the country. The school provides comprehensive insight into this mystical sport; they concentrate on casting, since that's the hardest part of fly fishing, but they also have sessions in which they teach students about fish feeding habits, how to use flies that match fish food, and how to read the water, tie knots, and make the best use of your equipment. And they give classes for women only.

A one-day comprehensive fly fishing school in the Portland area costs $225 per person, with a four-person minimum. If you want to spend the weekend working on your casting, two-day schools can be arranged. They will also take the "school" just about anywhere and have held classes everywhere from Mongolia to the Bahamas to Oregon's Deschutes River; contact them if you want them to run a workshop in your area.

Private lessons in the basic techniques of fly casting for one person run about $125 per hour, with a two-hour minimum. For two to four persons, the cost is $200 per hour. For the one-day casting school, the cost is $250, with a minimum of four persons. They will also develop custom classes just for you or your group. These classes might cover distance, accuracy, saltwater fishing, or fishing with two hands.

All the members of the Rajeff Fly Fishing School suffer from incurable wanderlust and would love to take you with them when they travel to Alaska, the Bahamas, Russia, Mongolia, or wherever else they happen to be searching for fish. Contact them to find out more information about the trips they have planned and how you might join them.

You can reach the Rajeff Fly Fishing School at (360) 694-2900 or by e-mailing kathh@rajeff sports.com.

---

outings abroad. This beautiful store has evolved from the days when the Kaufmann brothers tied flies in their parents' garage. Kauffmann's offers classes in spey casting and trips down the Deschutes River, among other things.

Hiking

A visitor to Portland may glance about at all the folks with backpacks, cargo shorts, and bandanas striding about the urban landscape and guess that most of us are heading for a hike. Maybe so—or maybe it's just the fashion here. Either way, an abundance of nearby trails await hikers of all levels, from those wanting a mellow stroll, such as the 2-mile nature path through Marquam Park, to those dedicated enthusiasts who might enjoy the 27-mile Wildwood Trail along the crest of Forest Park. Portand Hikers (www.portlandhikers

.org) has up-to-date information about trail conditions and a comprehensive searchable database of Oregon (and some Washington) hikes. Here are a few close-in hikes among this wide range of possibilities.

COLUMBIA GORGE
Rooster Rock State Park, I–84, exit 25
(503) 695-2261
www.oregonstateparks.org

COLUMBIA RIVER GORGE NATIONAL SCENIC AREA
902 Wasco Avenue, Suite 200
Hood River
(541) 308-1700
www.fs.fed.us/r6/columbia/forest
Sweltering Portlanders and Vancouverites have a couple of choices for relief from hot summer

days. They either head for the coast or the Columbia Gorge. If they choose the latter, they can stretch their legs on lots of shady trails up and down high, heavily forested basalt promontories. If they decide on a hike to the summit, they get an eye-popping view of one of the largest, most scenic river valleys on the planet. This 300,000-acre wilderness encompasses 22 state parks and is crisscrossed with 167 miles of well-maintained to rough trails. From 15-minute walks to 20-mile days, there are hikes for all ages and abilities.

From bluffs above, hundreds of creeks cataract down steep wooded ridges, and waterfalls hide mossy caves. And alongside the creeks are pathways of varying difficulty: Mount Defiance Trail, Wahkeena Loop with Devil's Rest Option,

Bridal Veil Falls and Overlook Loop Trail, and Starvation Ridge Trail. To get to all these trails, take I–84 east along the Columbia Gorge to the Corbett exit (number 22). From there you take the Columbia River Scenic Highway, which travels along the top of the southern bluff to Vista Point and then down the cliff to a stretch of magic with all the above hikes and viewpoints easily accessible. Just watch for signs. If you want to plan an excursion to any of these shady glens and sparkling waterfalls, call the number listed here. You can also find out all you need to know by stopping by the Multnomah Falls Information Center in the Multnomah Falls Lodge, a centrally located facility with restrooms, a restaurant, and on-duty rangers. Public spaces in the gorge are

Multnomah Falls. JAMES THOMAS

overseen by either of the two agencies listed above. There is also more information about the Columbia Gorge in the Day Trips chapter.

DOG MOUNTAIN
Washington State Highway 14, milepost 53
Columbia River Gorge
Located about 12 miles east of the Bridge of the Gods, Dog Mountain is a popular hike for a reason: spectacular views of the Gorge, the Cascades, and the amazing wildflowers along the way. It's a bit strenuous, with a 700-foot climb in the first half-mile. Then you have the choice to take a steep, direct route to the top of the mountain or a longer but gentler trail. The east trail (the longer trail) has the most impressive views. Both end up on top of Dog Mountain, a summit of 2,984 feet. You can bring your dog to Dog Mountain, but you both must watch out for poison oak. To get there, take I–205 north to Washington State Highway 14 and park at the trailhead, milepost 53, on the north side of the highway.

THE MARQUAM PARK TRAIL
Southwest Marquam Street just off
Southwest Sam Jackson Road
(503) 823-5122
A guide with references to stops along the way is available at a nature shelter at the beginning of the hike. The climb leads through leafy bowers until it arrives at Council Crest Park, the highest point within the city limits, at 1,070 feet above sea level.

OAKS BOTTOM WILDLIFE REFUGE
(503) 823-5122
This stretch of wild along the east side of the Willamette is a treat for city dwellers who want to get into the woods in a hurry. To get here from downtown Portland, take the Ross Island Bridge to Powell Boulevard. Turn south on Milwaukie Avenue and just after crossing Holgate Boulevard, look for the parking lot on the west side of the street in the 5000 block. From this trailhead you angle down the hill into the refuge. Another approach is the trail that begins at the north end of Sellwood Park at Southwest 7th Avenue. To get to this starting point, you can take the Sellwood

Bridge and bear left after crossing the Willamette. Along with beavers and muskrats, this wetland along the river is home to woodpeckers, warblers, orioles, and great blue and green herons. It can be muddy, so wear appropriate footgear.

OVERLOOK TRAIL
Washington Park
(503) 823-7529
This wheelchair-accessible trail is 0.25 mile of hardened gravel surface connecting the MAX Zoo Station with Hoyt Arboretum. There are also links with the Wildwood Trail (see separate entry in this chapter). The 10-foot-wide path makes frequent switchbacks as it ascends a gentle grade to the top of the hill and the arboretum's outdoor living museum of trees.

You can catch the beginning of the trail across the street from the MAX station at the north end of the World Forestry Center. If you are driving instead of taking MAX, park at the zoo.

TRYON CREEK STATE PARK
11321 Southwest Terwilliger Boulevard
(503) 636-9886
www.oregonstateparks.org
Just south of the Lewis & Clark College campus, Tryon Creek trickles through a deep ravine, the last free-flowing stream in the metro area and one of the few urban streams that still has a steelhead run. Bike paths and wide, paved, woodsy boulevards invite visitors from all over the area to explore the more than 600 acres of woodland. One trail in particular, Trillium Trail, is beautifully and fully wheelchair accessible. At the bottom of the ravine, an interpretive center with nature displays explains the plants, animals, and other features of the park. This site is a happy memory for thousands of kids who've come here on field trips. There is no fee to use this state park.

THE WILDWOOD TRAIL
Near Vietnam Veterans Memorial
in Washington Park
(503) 823-7529
Easily accessible from the MAX Zoo Station, this trail goes over hill and woody dale through Forest

Park. At 4,900 acres, this is the largest park within a U.S. metropolis. Free maps of the trail are available at the Hoyt Arboretum Visitor Center at 4000 Southwest Fairview Boulevard, which is also on the trail itself.

Ice-Skating

THE ICE CHALET
953 Lloyd Center
(503) 288-6073
www.lloydcenterice.com

While this shopping-mall ice rink offers lessons for young Olympics hopefuls, it is also popular with teens and adults, who swoosh about the ice oblivious to shopping spectators. This rink provides the gamut of lessons, parties, summer camps, broomball, and other icy activities. Admission is $6, with discounts for scouts, mall employees, seniors, and folks in the military. You can rent ice skates for $3.. (Also see the listing in the Kidstuff chapter.)

Motorcycling

ROSE CITY MOTORCYCLE CLUB
www.rose-city-mc.org

Tracing its origins back to 1911, Rose City Motorcycle Club is Oregon's oldest AMA Chartered Road Club. Its 250-plus members ride a wide variety of motorcycles, including touring, cruising, and sport bikes. In addition to its internal activities, such as monthly Saturday breakfasts and rides, the club annually hosts the 250-mile Annual Rose City Oregon Tour, which benefits the Oregon Kidney Association. These motorcyclists also join others in a remarkable visit to kids in the Doernbecher Children's Hospital right around Christmas. The sight of all these leather-clad bikers bearing presents and wearing Santa costumes is definitely memorable.

Roller-Skating

OAKS AMUSEMENT PARK
Southeast Spokane Street north of
Sellwood Bridge
(503) 233-5777
www.oakspark.com

Open year-round as part of a surrounding carnival, this large roller-skating rink is vintage Americana, with a huge Wurlitzer pipe organ playing Tuesday through Thursday nights and Sunday. A live DJ is on duty Saturday night. It's a great chance to join everyone as they "skate backwards" to the driving beat of oldies and goldies. Fees are $5.75, $6.75 on Friday and Saturday night. (For more information on roller-skating, see the Kidstuff and Attractions chapters.)

Running

Portland—with its miles of trails and mild weather—is a great running town. For one thing, it's in Oregon, where Nike was born. Heroes such as University of Oregon coach Bill Bowerman, along with Phil Knight of Nike, invented the waffle-soled running shoe, and legendary runner Steve Prefontaine brought thrills to the solitary sport. And for another, we have many running events throughout the year. Major races include the Portland Marathon, the Cascade Runoff, the Hood to Coast Run, the Race for the Cure, and the Shamrock Run, but these are just the most well known. A running event seems to happen almost every weekend somewhere within 100 miles of the city. Important resources for Portland runners include several Web sites: www.xdevents.com, for extreme running events is one, and Team Oregon, www.teamoregon.com, is another really useful Web site that coordinates running resources in the area, providing links to the Portland Marathon and hosting a calendar of area running events and races. It also sponsors marathon clinics and scheduled practice runs, as well as good running coaches; Team Oregon's coaching programs are very reasonably priced. The Portland Marathon's number is (503) 226-1111. Runners should also visit Running Outfitters, 2337 Southwest 6th, (503) 248-9820, and Pacesetter Athletic, 4306 Southeast Woodstock, (503) 777-3214, for good gear and information about clubs, races, and other events. Popular running trails include Mount Tabor Park and the Wildwood Trail in the Hoyt Arboretum (unpaved) and Terwilliger Boulevard and both sides of the Willamette River (paved).

ℹ️ You might think you're tough and can run a marathon or schuss down those black diamond runs and barely break a sweat. But until you've tried Studio X's boot camp and power classes, you won't know what tough is. The trainers and classes at Studio X specialize in the science of human movement, and they will revolutionize your approach to moving through space. Find them at 2839 Southeast Stark Street, 503-236-7114 or www.studioxfitness.com.

Skiing and Snowboarding

MOUNT HOOD WILDERNESS

Looming above the valley like a white-robed monarch, 11,239-foot Mount Hood is the state's largest peak. During the winter months, the flanks of the mountain draw thousands to Mount Hood Meadows, Timberline, and other popular resorts for Alpine and Nordic skiing, snowmobiling, and snowshoeing. Also, the area abounds in cross-country ski trails for those who want to get away from it all.

Downhill

COOPER SPUR

Highway 35, 23 miles south of Hood River
(503) 352-7803
www.cooperspur.com
Cooper Spur, on the north face of Mount Hood, is a 50-acre resort with 10 ski runs and 2 tubing runs. It's a fine place to learn to ski—most of the runs are beginner or intermediate grade, and the classes are organized around stations so that you can work on the areas you need to improve. Lessons are short so that you can get a lot of practice on the slopes, with instructors available to help you all day long.

MOUNT HOOD MEADOWS

FR 3555, 6 miles north of the junction of
Highway 35 and US 26
(503) 337-2222, (800) SKI-HOOD
www.skihood.com

This day-ski area is located on the sunny, wind-protected east side of Mount Hood. For 30 years Mount Hood Meadows has enticed skiers and snowboarders to Oregon's most challenging terrain. Currently 10 chair lifts, including 3 high-speed quads, provide access to 82 trails over 2,150 acres. Mount Hood Meadows offers several easy slopes down the mountain and one double black diamond. This is a good place to go if you are a beginner or very advanced.

MOUNT HOOD SKIBOWL

87000 East US 26 at Government Camp
(503) 272-3206
(503) 222-2695 (info line)
www.skibowl.com

This popular ski bowl is the closest action to Portland, 52 miles east of town. It has a top elevation of 5,056 feet, a vertical drop of 1,500 feet, four double chairs and five surface tows, and 960 acres to play upon. Skiers and snowboarders have 65 day runs and 34 night runs, with the longest run, Skyline Trail, measuring 3 miles. The season generally lasts from mid-November to mid-April. On the main slope there is the option of going on a separate trail, which includes many jumps, rails, and a half-pipe. Ski Bowl also offers the longest night skiing in America. This resort is an excellent place for first-timers; many great lessons and deals are offered, and the staff are very inviting.

SUMMIT SKI AND SNOW PLAY AREA

US 26 at the east end of Government Camp
(503) 272-0256
www.summitskiarea.com
Summit Ski and Snow Play Area has been open since 1927. It's the second-oldest resort in the United States, with a vertical slope of 306 feet. The slopes at Summit are not steep, so this is a good place to bring beginners. Still, it is also just as great to go there as an intermediate skier. Summit attracts many families, not only for the skiing but also because of the fantastic tubing hills.

TIMBERLINE LODGE AND SKI AREA
6 miles north of Government Camp, off
Forest Road 50
(503) 622-7979
(503) 222-2211 (ski report)
www.timberlinelodge.com

To get to this resort built in the '30s, turn north from US 26 at the eastern edge of the town of Government Camp and go 6 miles up FR 50. Boasting the longest ski season in North America, Timberline has more than 1,000 acres of snowfields for skiers and snowboarders. Thanks to the Palmer chairlift, skiers have access to 300 acres situated between 7,500 and 8,500 feet in elevation, not to mention some of the most scenic views in Oregon. Because of its terrain, Timberline is a good choice for beginners and intermediate skiers. Overnight lodging is available, but it fills up fast. To book one of the lodge's 59 rooms, call (800) 547-1406. For information regarding snow conditions, call the lodge's snow phone at (503) 222-2211 or (877) 754-6734.

Cross-Country

BERGFREUNDE SKI CLUB
10175 Southwest Barbur Boulevard
(503) 245-8543
www.bergfreunde.org

As the local branch of an international club with more than 2,500 members, the Bergfreunde Ski Club organizes activities that go beyond the winter season. They offer year-round entertainment for active adults, including organized rafting, golf, dance, and theater outings as well as cross-country skiing. Bergfreunde, or "friends of mountains," is a socially lively club for men and women 21 and older. They meet on the first Wednesday of each month at the Governor Hotel, 614 Southwest 11th Avenue.

MOUNT HOOD MEADOWS
Forest Road 3555, 2 miles north
of Highway 35
(503) 337-2222

This resort offers a full-service Nordic center and 15 kilometers of trails on Mount Hood.

Wildflowers frame the beautiful Timberline Lodge and the misty mountains beyond. JAMES THOMAS

i Snow removal on roads leading to ski areas is costly. To help pay for this service, Sno-Park permits ($15 per year, $7 for three days, or $3 for one day) are required to park legally in winter recreation areas from November through April. Sno-Park permits can be purchased at ski areas, outdoor stores, or DMV offices. Don't leave home without one!

OREGON DEPARTMENT OF TRANSPORTATION SKI AREAS
(503) 986-4000
www.tripcheck.com/winter/snoparks
There are 16 Sno-parks in the Mount Hood region operated by the Oregon Department of Transportation. Popular spots are Bennett Pass, Glacier View, Snow Bunny, Frog Lake, and Trillium Lake.

OREGON NORDIC CLUB PORTLAND CHAPTER
(503) 649-9612
www.onc.org/pdx.html
Organized in 1968 by Nordic ski enthusiasts interested in cross-country skiing on public land, the Oregon Nordic Club now has more than 400 members. Activities are usually day and overnight trips, most of which are held on weekends. The Portland chapter of the Oregon Nordic Club also sponsors ski-related special events, including a yearly ski sale, a ski instruction and demonstration day at Teacup Lake, and sanctioned competition. On the first Tuesday of each month, a general membership meeting is held at the Multnomah Art Center, 7688 Southwest Capitol Highway, with potluck beginning at 6:30 p.m. The Web site listed above get you information on the week's events.

Swimming
NORTH CLACKAMAS AQUATIC PARK
7300 Southeast Harmony Road
Milwaukie
(503) 557-7873, (503) 794-8080
www.co.clackamas.or.us/ncap
This popular swimming pool has three water slides and a 4-foot wave pool. The park is open Monday

through Friday from 4:00 to 8:00 p.m., and Saturday and Sunday from 11:00 a.m. to 3:00 p.m. and 4:00 to 8:00 p.m. Admission fees are $4.99 for children ages 3 to 8; $6.99 for those ages 9 to 18 and seniors 62 and older; and $9.99 for all others. Families can get a discount on Sunday and Friday. Please don't bring in any outside food or drinks.

TUALATIN HILLS AQUATIC CENTER
Howard M. Terpenning Recreation Complex, 15707 Southwest Walker Road
Beaverton
(503) 645-7454
This aquatics center is located in the Terpenning Recreation Complex, a sprawling 90-acre park in the Tualatin Hills southwest of Portland. A close competitor to the North Clackamas Aquatic Park, it draws folks from all over the region on those muggy days when it's great to take the plunge. Call for drop-in hours. Children who live within the boundaries of the Tualatin Hills Parks and Recreation District pay $1.50 with residency cards; nonresident children pay $3.00. Adult residents pay $2.00, while nonresident adults pay $4.00.

i If you have special needs or disabilities that have kept you from fully enjoying the great outdoors, try Adventures Without Limits, (503) 359-2568 or www.awloutdoors.com. This outfit sponsors hikes, cross-country ski trips, snowshoeing, indoor rock climbing, and canoe adventures. Fees are charged, but scholarships for day trips and overnighters are available.

YMCA OF COLUMBIA-WILLAMETTE
Metro Family
2831 Southwest Barbur Boulevard
(503) 294-3366

Northeast Community Center
1630 Northeast 38th Avenue
(503) 284-3377
www.ymca-portland.org
In the great tradition of Ys everywhere, these Portland YMCAs have good-size pools for the

general public as well as their members. Non-members pay a day-use fee, which also allows for use of other facilities at the Y.

Portland City Pools

Portland Parks and Recreation has six indoor and six outdoor pools at its various parks and centers throughout the metropolitan area. To find the pool nearest your location, see the list below. The outdoor pools are open only during the summer. Pool hours vary, but most are open from 6:00 a.m. to 9:00 p.m. daily, opening a little later on the weekends. Most of the time, there are lanes devoted to adult lap swim, but these may be taken over during swim team practices or other events. Admission to Portland Parks and Recreation pools varies, but will run about $3 to $4 for adults, about $2 for those 3 to 17, and free for kids 2 and younger. The information line for aquatics is (503) 823-7946. For further information call the numbers below.

INDOOR FACILITIES
BUCKMAN SWIMMING POOL
320 Southeast 16th Avenue
(503) 823-3668

COLUMBIA SWIMMING POOL
7701 North Chautauqua Boulevard
(503) 823-3669

MATT DISHMAN POOL
77 Northeast Knott Street
(503) 823-3673

MLC POOL
2033 Northwest Glisan Street
(503) 823-3671

MT. SCOTT SWIMMING POOL
5530 Southeast 72nd Avenue
(503) 823-3183

SOUTHWEST COMMUNITY CENTER
6820 Southwest 45th Avenue
(503) 823-2840

OUTDOOR FACILITIES
CRESTON SWIMMING POOL
4454 Southeast Powell Boulevard
(503) 823-3672

GRANT SWIMMING POOL
2300 Northeast 33rd Avenue
(503) 823-3674

MONTAVILLA SWIMMING POOL
8219 Northeast Glisan Street
(503) 823-3101

PENINSULA SWIMMING POOL
700 North Rosa Parks Way
(503) 823-3620

PIER SWIMMING POOL
9341 North St. Johns Street
(503) 823-3678

SELLWOOD SWIMMING POOL
7951 Southeast 7th Avenue
(503) 823-3679

Tennis

The Portland Parks and Recreation Department has close to 100 tennis courts in the metro region. Here's a short list of some of the best ones in town.

CRESTON PARK
4454 Southeast Powell Boulevard
These two courts are rarely used, so you're almost guaranteed immediate access. Advantages include high metal walls that save errant balls. The downside is that Creston Park is down in a woodsy swale where it might seem gloomy. The courts are not lighted.

IRVING PARK
Northeast 7th Avenue and Fremont Street
These courts are well-lit and popular with folks on the inner east side of town.

LAURELHURST PARK
Southeast 39th Avenue and Stark Street

With its tranquil duck pond, huge fir and cedar trees, and sloping lawns, Laurelhurst Park is one of the loveliest and most peaceful spots in town. The two tennis courts here are old relics that are often busy, but it's worth the wait. Plan on playing during the day, for there is no lighting.

MOUNT TABOR PARK WESTSIDE
Entrance near Southeast 62nd Avenue and Main Street

Three courts are tucked against the base of a living volcano and near one of the city's drinking-water reservoirs. They are also along a trail leading up to the top of Mount Tabor and its terrific view of the downtown skyline. Play a few sets under the lights then stroll around the reservoir and up to the summit to catch a spectacular view of the glittering city across the river.

TENNIS CENTER
324 Northeast 12th Avenue
(503) 823-3189
www.pdx10s.com

These four indoor and eight outdoor courts make this one of Portland's most popular facilities. To play you need to make a reservation and pay a fee of $20 per set of 1 hour and 15 minutes for the indoor courts. Open court reservations are available from 6:45 a.m. to 9:10 p.m. Monday through Friday and from 6:45 a.m. to 10:00 p.m. on weekends. Outdoor courts are available on a first-come, first-served basis. There is plenty of good lighting, lots of easy parking, showers, and restrooms.

WASHINGTON PARK
400 Southwest Kingston Avenue

This is a popular spot for tennis players who also like to stop and smell the roses at the nearby rose garden. The courts are not in perfect condition, but you'll have the pleasure of playing in a beautiful location close to the zoo, the Japanese Garden, and lots of places for postgame hikes.

Outlying Areas

LAKE OSWEGO INDOOR TENNIS CENTER
2900 Southwest Diane Drive
Lake Oswego
(503) 635-5550

This court is convenient for those living south of Portland. The center is open every day from 6:00 a.m. to 10:00 p.m. This friendly court welcomes everyone for games and private lessons; it offers senior discounts. General rates are $13 per court per hour.

Windsurfing

On a bright and windy day in the Columbia Gorge, motorists cruising along I–84 on the Oregon side or down-winding Washington Highway 14, are entertained by the multicolored confetti of windsurfers' sails sprinkled on the broad Columbia River. Ask any group of windsurfers, and they'll enthusiastically regale you with the wonders of this world-class stretch where the wind blows hard against the sail and boards whip up and down the river.

Hood River is booming with windsurfing shops, manufacturing plants, and windsurfing schools as well as cafes, saloons, motels, and other services aimed at the thousands of visitors with those easily recognizable poles and canvas on top of their rigs. Retail shops in Hood River include Hood River Windsurfing, 101 Oak Street, (541) 386-5787 or (800) 211-8207; Big Winds, 503 Cascade, (541) 386-6086 (these two shops also offer windsurfing schools); and Windance, 207 Front Street, (541) 386-2131. Check the bulletin boards in these shops for events, classes, and more arcane info appealing to those who scoot around on the water on a surfboat with a sail.

The best spots to launch are the Hook and Event Center at exit 63, off I–84, and the Hatchery and Swell City, a couple of miles west of the Hood River Bridge on the Washington side of Hood River's Sailpark at exit 64.

Yoga

Yoga is very popular in Portland—and has been for years. You will find all varieties of yoga instruction here, from straightforward hatha to more philosophical kundalini. Finding the right yoga studio or teacher is a personal thing, like finding the right therapist, so you may want to try different classes with different teachers until you find one who can challenge you in the right ways. Portland has many yoga studios, but here are several that we have found offer a wide variety of classes and have excellent reputations for outstanding teachers. Expect to pay between $8 and $16 per class. Most studios offer significant discounts if you buy in bulk.

THE BHAKTISHOP
2500 Southeast 26th Avenue
(503) 244-0108
http://thebhaktishop.com/

DIANE WILSON YOGA STUDIO
1017 Southwest Morrison Street, #508
(503) 227-1726
www.dianewilsonyoga.com

HOLIDAY'S YOGA CENTER
3942 Southeast Hawthorne Boulevard
(503) 224-8611
www.holidaysyogacenter.com

JULIE LAWRENCE YOGA CENTER
1020 Southwest Taylor Street
(503) 227-5524
www.jlyc.com

MOVEMENT CENTER
1025 Northeast 33rd Avenue
(503) 231-0994
www.mcyoga.com

PRANANDA YOGA AND ARTS CENTER
1920 North Kilpatrick Street
(503) 249-3903
www.prananda.com

SUNSET YOGA CENTER
10200 Southwest Eastridge Street
(503) 626-6245
www.sunsetyoga.com

YOGA IN THE PEARL
925 Northwest Davis Street
(503) 525-9642
www.yogainthepearl.com

YOGA SHALA
1812 Northeast Alberta Street
(503) 281-4452

3249 Southeast Division Street
(503) 963-9642
www.yogashalapdx.com

YOGA UNION
2043 Southeast 50th Avenue
(503) 235-9642
www.yogaunioncwc.com

SPECTATOR SPORTS

Auto Racing

This is the American West, so the national love affair with the internal combustion engine, painted and polished sheet metal, and the excessive consumption of imported fossil fuels is in full bloom. Auto racing has everything we love: speed, noise, big and powerful cars, gasoline, beer, fried food, and an absence of cops and dress codes.

PORTLAND INTERNATIONAL RACEWAY
West Delta Park
1940 North Victory Boulevard
(503) 823-7223
www.portlandraceway.com
Portland International Raceway is situated in a big park at the north end of the city, with Mount Hood providing an appropriate background to the drama on the field. The racetrack is to the west of I–5 at exit 306-B. This is where sports cars and motorcycles do their stuff. The raceway also

hosts bicycle races, motocross, and other less revved competitions. Admission fees and starting times vary according to the event. The season at PIR is July through November, with most races held on weekend nights.

WOODBURN DRAGSTRIP
7730 Highway 219 (I–5 exit 271)
(503) 982-4461
www.woodburndragstrip.com
Half an hour's drive south of town, the Woodburn Dragstrip showcases motorcycle, dragster, and funny car events from May through September. Classes include pro stock cars, alcohol-run dragsters and funny cars, jet cars, sport compacts, and street-legal drags with mandatory mufflers. Woodburn also sponsors events for junior racers (8 to 17 years). They even have track-side camping spaces available for those folks who don't want to miss a thing. Admission fees and starting times vary according to the event.

Baseball
THE PORTLAND BEAVERS
PGE Park, 1844 Southwest
Morrison Street
(503) 553-5400 (information)
(503) 553-5555 (tickets)
www.pgepark.com
Every few years, Portlanders bring up the subject of major league baseball—which teams we could seduce into playing here, where to build a stadium, how we will pay for it. . . . But while the dreamy talk of MLB goes on, in the stadium—walking the talk—are the Portland Beavers. We've had several minor league teams throughout the years, but this is our first AAA team, and an evening ball game cheering them on at PGE Park is one of summer's chief pleasures. The park, refurbished in 2000, is a perfect setting for these games: Its wrought-iron fence and friendly appearance convey the old-fashioned atmosphere that fans love about minor league ball. You'll find the stadium just west of downtown, on 18th and Morrison; the MAX line stops right in front. It's within walking distance of many restaurants, hotels, bars, brewpubs, and coffee shops, and in the park you'll find a good bar and grill run by the Widmer Brothers that offers seating right on the edge of the field. The ticket prices are still a good value—bargain tickets can be as low as $2.99, single seats are about $9.00, and even the "luxury" seats are only about $15.00. The Beavers play day and night games from mid-June through early September. For you cynics, surprisingly few games are rained out. A word to the wise: It is next to impossible to park near the stadium. Do yourself a favor and take the MAX train. All Beavers tickets enable you to use TriMet for free on game day.

i If you're attending a game at PGE Park, your ticket is more valuable than its seat price: It also serves as a TriMet pass on the day of the event. You can use it to ride to and from PGE Park on any bus or MAX train. So buy your ticket in advance! And take advantage of this service, because there is no parking near the stadium.

Basketball
THE PORTLAND TRAILBLAZERS
The Rose Garden, 1 Center Court
(503) 234-9291
(503) 321-3211 (events hotline)
www.nba.com/blazers
The Portland Trailblazers—who play in the Western Division of the National Basketball Association—are beloved by Portlanders: They get us through the long rainy months of winter and give us plenty of thrills and lots of misery. The team is now owned by Paul Allen, who cofounded Microsoft with Bill Gates. The Blazers are almost always playoff contenders, though they haven't won the NBA title since 1977, when they were led by Bill Walton and coach Jack Ramsey. Still, hope springs eternal, and each new season we think, "This year, for sure!"

The Rose Garden, with seats going from $20 (bring your own oxygen) to more than $145, is one of the best places to be a spectator. It's a great show, with the BlazerDancers swooshing about and many events for the audience. The Rose Garden's 32 public restrooms do have piped-in radio for play-by-play updates, and there are 700 television monitors so you can watch the game while waiting in line for your gardenburger and local brew.

There's a certain cachet about having season tickets or, even better, a corporate luxury box, but these may be hard to get. However, ordinary tickets are usually available even on game day, depending on the opponent. You can often find refreshments-plus-tickets deals and other promotions too. Tickets are available from the Rose Garden box office and from Ticketmaster, (503) 224-4400, which is also partially owned by Paul Allen. The Blazers' season begins in October; when it ends depends on their skill, luck, opponents, and other playoff-related criteria.

If you go to a game, be prepared to pay a lot for parking. Consider parking and riding: MAX runs to within 100 yards of the Rose Garden and TriMet may eventually figure out, as BART did in San Francisco and Oakland, that they should put on extra trains the nights the Blazers play.

Golf

JELD-WEN TRADITION
Peter Jacobsen Productions
(503) 526-9331
www.jeld-wentradition.com

The Tradition, one of four major tournaments played on the PGA Champions Tour, formerly known as the Senior Tour, has a new home in Oregon and a purse of more than $2 million. The tournament is held at the gorgeous Crosswater golf course in Sunriver, one of the state's finest but about a three-hour drive from Portland.

Until 2002 the Tradition was played on a Jack Nicklaus–designed course in Scottsdale, Arizona. As in the past, it is sure to feature the big stars of the Champions Tour, such as Hale Irwin, Tom Watson, Craig Stadler, and the luminaries of champion PGA golf. This tournament is accompanied by all the bells and whistles

you would expect for an important PGA event, including prime-time live coverage on the East Coast. Tickets are available at the gate or online at www.jeld-wen tradition.com. They may also be purchased over the phone, (503) 672-8159. Ticket prices start at $20 for single-day tickets that are prepurchased to $50 for tickets with clubhouse privileges.

To some extent, the JELD-WEN Tradition replaces the Fred Meyer Challenge, which was established by Oregon native and PGA Tour champ Peter Jacobsen in 1985 to raise money for children's charities in Oregon. Jacobsen enticed famous golfers from Arnold Palmer to Greg Norman to John Daly to play best-ball golf in 12 two-man teams and raised millions of dollars for worthy causes. After Fred Meyer pulled its sponsorship, Peter Jacobsen and his company sought new sponsorship for the original event. Then JELD-WEN—a Klamath Falls, Oregon, company and the largest manufacturer of windows and doors in the nation—stepped up to the tee, providing a great opportunity for Oregon golf.

SAFEWAY CLASSIC TOURNAMENT GOLF
(503) 626-2711
(503) 287-LPGA (ticket sales)
http://safewayclassic.com

The Safeway Classic, now held at the Pumpkin Ridge golf course (see the Golf chapter), is tied for second-oldest event on the LPGA (Ladies' Professional Golf Association) tour. Portland has been hosting it since its inception in 1972, and each year the tournament grows in status, with a purse that is now almost $2 million. Even more impressive, the tournament has raised more than $7 million for local charities. It draws more than 50,000 people over the week of the tournament. Weekly tickets are $25; daily tickets are $10; but check for promotional deals, especially if you shop at Safeway.

Hockey

PORTLAND WINTER HAWKS
Western Hockey League
Portland Memorial Coliseum &
Rose Garden, 1 Center Court
(503) 238-6366
www.winterhawks.com

The Hawks, as they are locally known, are another Portland treasure; they've been favorites since they started playing here in 1976. This is a strong, fast-playing team that is a perennial contender for their league's championship. Success on the ice in Portland means a trip to the "big show," the National Hockey League (NHL), for players. The team consistently draws a good crowd, and there are lots of special fan events. While there are no $1-million free-throws from center court, at least once a year the Hawks freeze a good load of silver dollars on the surface of the ice and then let a small number of lucky fans scramble, slide, and slip (sans skates) as they attempt to gather up the coins. The Hawks fly over the ice from late September through March; games start at 7:00 p.m., except on Sunday, when they start at 5:00 p.m. Tickets to a game range from about $15 to $25. Season tickets range from about $500 for a season at rinkside to about $200 for students or seniors on the third tier.

Horseracing

PORTLAND MEADOWS
1001 North Schmeer Road
(off I-5 at exit 306-B)
(503) 285-9144
www.portlandmeadows.com

Portland Meadows features horses galloping nose to nose. Racehorses have been bred and raced in Portland for nearly a century, though Portland Meadows has only been around since 1946. There are the usual snack bars and restaurants at the track, but you can also sit in the stands with your binoculars, lucky charms, and wallet to watch your favorite race around the oval. Neon light aficionados will appreciate the large-scale animated racehorses adorning the track's

entrance, which are visible from I-5. Admission is free and so is parking; some areas of the park may charge a few bucks for prime viewing. The season is from October to April.

Lacrosse

LUMBERJAX
Rose Garden, 1 Center Court
(503) 797-9739
www.portlandjax.com

Professional lacrosse is new to Portland—kind of surprising, because in some ways it's a very Portland sport. For one thing, it can be played indoors, out of the rain, and for another, it's a little bit iconoclastic. The 2005–2006 season saw the debut of Portland's professional lacrosse team, the LumberJax, who shook things up not only by being only one of three expansion teams to make the playoffs but also by winning the West Division title—something no lacrosse expansion team had ever done. They also ended their season sharing, with Buffalo, the best record, at 11 and 5. The LumberJax play for love, almost, since most of them have day jobs, but this just seems to make them all the more dedicated. And the fans know it, which is why they love the LumberJax too.

Soccer

PORTLAND TIMBERS
PGE Park
1844 Southwest Morrison Street
(503) 553-5400 (information)
(503) 553-5555 (tickets)
www.pgepark.com

The sports landscape in Portland has endured some seismic shaking in the past few years, with many teams falling apart, then re-collecting themselves. But one thing that never changes is Portland's love for soccer. The revived Portland Timbers, our men's A-League team, began playing in PGE Park in 2001, with coach Bobby Howe, to immediate success, making the playoffs their first and second seasons. Besides being a great player and one of the most respected coaches in the world, Howe, who left the team in 2005, was an experienced ambassador for youth soccer—he was the head coach of the Washington State Youth Soccer Association. Since millions of school-age boys and girls now play soccer, the Timbers have a big following among Portland's younger set and their parents, and everyone is watching to see how coach Chris Agnello will do. Equally important, mom or dad can take the kids to see the Timbers without having to take out a home equity loan. General admission starts at $15, but you can get special family tickets from Fred Meyer and other sponsors. The Timbers play from April through September.

Other Spectator Sports

Most of the area's colleges and universities—Portland State University, University of Portland, Lewis & Clark College, and Reed College, among others—have sports programs that may include football, basketball, soccer, and baseball teams. The University of Portland has consistently produced decent men's and women's basketball teams, as well as championship women's soccer teams. Tiffeny Millbrett, who scored the winning goal in the historic 1996 Olympic gold-medal match against China, was a University of Portland star (and a Portland native). PSU's Vikings play football at PGE Park, and their men's and women's basketball teams are fun to watch (some years are more fun than others). PSU's women's softball team, which competes in the Pacific Coast Softball Conference, offers free admission. They play at Erv Lind Stadium (Northeast 57th, 2 blocks south of Halsey). The smaller schools, such as Reed and Lewis & Clark, may not have men's and women's teams that are contenders in all sports, but they play good college ball and attract some excellent track-and-field athletes, rowers, and lacrosse players. And local high school teams are always fun to watch in any sport. There is also a range of amateur teams and leagues playing everything from rugby and soccer to Ultimate Frisbee, lacrosse, and nighttime softball.

Coed kickball for grown-ups is a major deal in Portland, and there are at least three leagues—complete with interleague rivalries—that organize games and run tournaments: Underdog Sports (www.underdogportland.com/), Northwest Kickball (www.nwkickball.com/), and Oregon Kickball Club (www.oregonkickball.com/flash.html). It's just like recess. Good times.

PORTLAND'S PARKS

The Portland Metro area offers an amazing amount and variety of park space, from Forest Park, which, at 4,900 acres, is the largest urban forest in the nation, to Mills End Park, which, at 452 square inches, may be the smallest park in the nation. Portlanders like to weave green spaces, no matter how tiny, into their urban landscape, so that wherever you go in this city, you are never far from a park. Moreover, the parks here serve diverse functions: Many are community gardens, many are educational centers, some are attached to schools and are used for playgrounds, some are golf courses, some are left alone and preserved as wildlife habitats. And some are just old-fashioned parks with benches, swings, and duck ponds.

Whatever their nature, Portland's parks really do offer something for everyone, and they are so much a part of Portland life that we probably take them as a given. Through our parks, countless citizens of all ages have learned to swim, dance, knit, speak Spanish, use computers, paint with oils, identify native plants, and climb mountains.

OVERVIEW

Portland Parks and Recreation manages most parks within the city boundaries; their resources are extensive, and it is easy to get information from them about their many offerings, the breadth and depth of which are astonishing. They put out a useful catalog each season that gives the details of the tennis lessons, swimming lessons, arts and dance classes, and the innumerable other programs; call (503) 823-7529 to request one, or browse online for a downloadable catalog and to register for classes: www.portlandonline.com/parks. The department also runs a compelling Outdoor Recreation Program whose offerings change seasonally but will include things like sea kayaking, sailing trips to the San Juan Islands, classes in fly-fishing, and tours with historical themes. The Outdoor Recreation Program can be reached at (503) 823-5132. For those of you who like your parks raw, the city maintains more than 7,600 acres of space devoted to wildlife, including Smith and Bybee Lakes, Powell Butte, Elk Rock Island, Marquam Nature Park, Oaks Bottom Wildlife Refuge, and

Forest Park. In addition, a regional trail system called the 40 Mile Loop, together with the Willamette Greenway Trail, links 140 miles of paths throughout the area, forming a circle through and around the city. Maps of this system, which was originally inspired by the Olmsted Brothers, are available from Portland Parks and Recreation for about $2. You can read more about some of these parks and programs in the Attractions, Kidstuff, and Recreation chapters.

The city of Portland is not the only organization that maintains wonderful parks in the area. Metro, our regional government, in addition to establishing growth boundaries, keeping up the zoo, and running the mass transit system, is also responsible for a number of parks and grids of open spaces. You can find out more about Metro's parks by visiting them online at www.metro-region.org/parks. And the State of Oregon has a fine Web site that gives a comprehensive look at the parks in the state system: http://www.oregon.gov/OPRD/PARKS. But no matter who is running the parks, we love them. Here, then, are some of our favorites.

CITY PARKS

Southwest Portland

COUNCIL CREST PARK
Southwest Council Crest Drive
(503) 823-7529
High in the Southwest Hills—perhaps higher than anywhere else in the city—rests verdant Council Crest Park. This 42-acre site used to host an amusement park, but the traces of that history have vanished, and now it's a quiet neighborhood park with a large water tower. You'll also find trails, natural areas, restrooms, and picnic tables, and a spot for weddings. But the major draw is the view—from here you can see five major peaks of the Cascade mountains: Mount Hood, Mount St. Helens, Mount Jefferson, Mount Adams, and, on a good day, Mount Rainier. It's an excellent spot to regain perspective.

GABRIEL PARK
Southwest 45th Avenue and Vermont Street
(503) 823-7529, (503) 823-2840
(Southwest Community Center)
A large, multifaceted park, Gabriel Park draws enthusiasts from all over the city. Within the 90 acres of the park, you'll find tennis courts, picnic tables, trails, community gardens, sports fields, and a dog off-leash area. In addition, the splendid Southwest Community Center, which has spotless gyms and pristine swimming pools, gives it that country-club feel. The community center holds the usual breathtaking array of classes and programs; call them for their latest catalog.

HOYT ARBORETUM
Washington Park
4000 Southwest Fairview Boulevard
(503) 823-7529, (503) 865-8733
www.hoytarboretum.org
Hoyt Arboretum lies within the boundaries of Washington Park. Its 214 forested acres offer unsurpassed arboreal beauty as well as beautiful views of the city, and it's large enough that you can get into some backwoods areas where you aren't bumping into other hikers every time you round a bend in the trail—though it's popular with trail runners, so be careful when rounding those blind corners. Hoyt Arboretum features a collection of conifers, 10 miles of trails, the vestiges of our rural past, and some striking views of the city and the Cascades. We love to take the Fir Trail all the way to the Pittock Mansion. It only takes about 45 minutes, and the view is stunning. (See the Attractions chapter for more information.)

JAPANESE AMERICAN HISTORICAL PLAZA
Southwest Naito Parkway near the
Burnside Bridge
(503) 823-7529
This poignant site along the Willamette River in Waterfront Park just north of the Burnside Bridge memorializes the Japanese-American citizens who were banished to internment camps during World War II. Cherry trees border the plaza. "Talking stones," sculptures, and other artwork beautifully relate the story of this sad part of our history in the hope that it might not be repeated.

i The Web site for Portland Parks and Recreation allows convenient online registration for classes. Visit www.portlandparks.org.

JAPANESE GARDENS
Southwest Kingston Road and
Washington Park Drive
(503) 223-1321
(503) 223-9233 (for tours)
www.japanesegarden.com
The Japanese Gardens comprise five different gardens within 5.5 acres and have received, in their nearly 40 years of existence, many accolades for their beauty and fidelity to Japanese traditions. Tours are available. The admission cost is $8.00 for adults and $5.25 for students older than six; college students and seniors pay $6.25. (See the Attractions chapter for a full account.)

PLAZA BLOCKS
(Chapman and Lownsdale Squares)
Southwest 4th Avenue and Main Street
(503) 823-7529

This tiny (1.84 acres) but well-loved park consists of two adjacent city squares and is also known as Lownsdale Park. In 1974 the squares were designated Historic Landmarks; they have been public spaces for about 150 years. Chapman Square, the southern square, was donated to the city by early Portland attorney William Chapman, while Lownsdale Square was contributed by Daniel Lownsdale, who arrived in Portland in 1845. The squares were originally popular sites for public oratory and other gatherings. And they have a quaint history—at one time, the idea was that women would gather at Chapman Square, while the men would have Lownsdale to themselves. Lownsdale Square is the home of a military monument, the Soldiers' Monument, built in 1906, a granite pillar supporting the likeness of an infantryman. This soldier represents Oregon's contribution to the first major force of American troops dispatched overseas, the Second Oregon United States Volunteer Infantry. And two small cannons at the base of the monument are from Fort Sumter; they honor the Northern and Southern soldiers killed during the Civil War. A large bronze elk stands alert right in the middle of Main Street, between the two squares, reminding us of the wildlife that used to graze freely there. It's actually a fountain, built in 1900 at the behest of then-mayor David Thompson. It's hard for modern residents to imagine that the fountain, which has a special drinking trough for horses and dogs, was initially regarded as monstrous by some local residents (notably the Exalted Order of Elks). Later residents objected to its placement in the middle of the road, but it appears that, unlike its natural predecessors, the bronze elk is here to stay.

WASHINGTON PARK
Western end of Southwest Park Place
(503) 823-7529

The crown jewel of the city's park system, 145-acre Washington Park is one of the oldest, best-loved, and well-used parks in Portland, offering beautiful

i Your dog needs to run, but you live in the city. Where can Fido get plenty of exercise? Portland has nearly 30 parks with off-leash areas devoted exclusively to dog exercising all day, year-round. Wherever the park, you must clean up after your dog or face fines from the city and the ire of your neighbors. Dogs also should be properly vaccinated, licensed, obedient to voice command, and in other ways model citizens. With so many parks now featuring off-leash areas, there is bound to be one near you. These areas are well-marked, so look for the signs or visit www.portland online.com/parks and click on the "Activities" menu.

scenery; summer concerts; statuary; playgrounds; water reservoirs; fantastic views of Mount Hood, its foothills, and the Willamette Valley; and some of the region's premiere attractions. This is the home of the famed International Rose Test Garden with more than 400 varieties of roses, the Japanese Gardens, the Children's Museum, and the Oregon Zoo (see the Attractions chapter). Besides these world-renowned sites, and the lush trees, shrubs, flowers, and ferns, the park is a treasure trove of history and a tribute to prescient urban planning. Washington Park has been a city property since 1871, when 40 acres were purchased for the development of a park—at a time when most of the city was still wilderness. Early residents thought the city was crazy.

By the turn of the 20th century, however, Portland was glad to have the park, and never more so when they hired the distinguished Olmsted brothers, the landscape architects who designed New York's Central Park, to advise them on their own park system. The Olmsteds envisioned a series of parks that would be linked together with greenways all across the city. But they also made some specific suggestions for Washington Park, including the preservation of the natural habitat in addition to formal plantings.

While the major attractions of Washington Park are obvious, some of the minor ones are just as interesting. The first public statue of a woman is here—it's the bronze *Sacagawea*, the intrepid Shoshone who made it possible for Lewis and Clark to navigate the West, which was commissioned for the Lewis and Clark Exposition in 1905. Women all over the nation contributed money to pay for this statue. The park is also home to an arresting Lewis and Clark memorial, consisting of a granite shaft with the seals of the states of Oregon, Washington, Montana, and Idaho at its base; the foundation stone for this memorial was laid in 1903 by Theodore Roosevelt himself.

Washington Park's attractions also include the World Forestry Center, the Oregon Vietnam Veterans Living Memorial, and the Hoyt Arboretum with its miles of nature trails. And you will find many facilities for recreators of all ages: An archery range, group picnic facilities, stage, covered picnic areas, a soccer field, and tennis courts are all here. And if you have children, don't miss the fanciful play structure just south of the Rose Garden. This bright and inventive gem has slides, bridges, swings, sand, musical toys, ropes, and anything else your children never knew a playground ought to have until now.

WATERFRONT PARK
(Gov. Tom McCall Waterfront Park)
Southwest Naito Parkway from Southwest
Clay Street to Northwest Glisan Street
(503) 823-7529
This 36-acre city park, which stretches into Northwest Portland, showcases the Willamette River and hums with activity on sunny days. Hugging the west bank of the river, Waterfront Park extends from Southwest Clay Street to the Steel Bridge, 22 blocks in all; it's the site of many Portland events from the Rose Festival to the Brewer's Festival to the Blues Festival (for more information, see the Festivals and Annual Events chapter). It seems as if something is always going on there, but often it's not an organized event, just throngs of joggers, bikers, and those out for leisurely lunchtime strolls along the pleasant waterside pathway. There are basketball courts, fountains, statuary, and opportunities to sightsee, both for people

watchers and those more interested in the scenic views of barges and cruise ships passing under the bridges.

You may want to see the Battleship *Oregon* Memorial, erected in 1956 to honor the late-19th-century *USS Oregon*. Also, the benches near the Salmon Street Springs are a great place to hang out on a warm day: You can watch people frolic in a large, beautiful fountain controlled by an underground computer that changes the pattern of the fountain's water jets. If you are an early bird, the morning sunrises as viewed from Waterfront Park are incredibly gorgeous sights, with clear views of majestic Mount Hood and several of the smaller mountains on the east side.

WILLAMETTE PARK
Southwest Macadam Avenue and
Nebraska Street
(503) 823-7529
Nestled along the banks of the Willamette River and just a few miles south of downtown, Willamette Park is undoubtedly one of Portland's busiest and most popular parks. This is a fine place for boating, picnicking, watching the Fourth of July fireworks celebrations, or just hanging around. The parking lot fills up fast, especially in the summertime and on weekends, and some areas of the park itself can get a little crowded. But with more than 30 acres, including a boat ramp, soccer field, tennis court, playground, and hiking and bicycling trails, there's room to spread out. If it's raining and you have an outdoor party or barbecue planned, Willamette Park has covered group picnic facilities.

i If you're interested in exploring more deeply the city wildernesses of Portland, have a look at *Wild in the City: A Guide to Portland's Natural Areas.* This collection of essays is a fine, comprehensive, and detailed guide to the green spaces in our city, published by the Oregon Historical Society and edited by Michael C. Houck and M. J. Cody.

Northwest Portland

COUCH PARK
**Northwest 19th Avenue and
Glisan Street
(503) 823-7529**

First thing: It's pronounced "kooch." But however you say it, this little neighborhood park, with lovely trees and a playground, is a draw for residents and for the students next door at the Metropolitan Learning Center. And it is a true neighborhood park, even down to its design and execution, which was largely the work of students and neighbors. Its namesake, Captain John Heard Couch, was responsible for the alphabetized street names of this sector of town, which he developed. The park site was originally the estate of one of Captain Couch's daughters and her family.

FOREST PARK
**West Hills, Northwest Skyline Road
to the city of St. Helens
(503) 823-7529**

Forest Park is remarkable for many things, one of which is its size. At 4,900 acres, it is thought to be the largest urban forest in America. The city bought the property at the end of the 19th century; they had thought about turning it into a park ever since the Olmsted brothers suggested it would be a good use of the property, and the park, after much debate, was finally established in 1948. Today Forest Park gives Portland residents more than 60 miles of trails for running, walking, and biking. It is a haven for more than 110 species of birds and more than 50 species of mammals, including the human visitors who love to hike and picnic under its lush forest canopy. You'll find Forest Park on the eastern side of the Northwest Hills, once called the Tualatin Mountains, and when you get there, you'll be hiking along some of the same trails—some of which are now paved—that farmers used as shipping routes. Visit the Portland Parks and Recreation Web site at www.portlandparks.org for a detailed map of Forest Park. Forest Park is also part of the 40 Mile Loop, the regional trail system that winds through the city.

WALLACE PARK
**Northwest 25th Avenue
and Raleigh Street
(503) 823-7529**

Wallace Park is constantly busy with community activities, in part because it is right next to Chapman School and in part because of its namesake, Hugh Wallace. He was the city councilman responsible for this park, and the buzz of activity within it is a fitting tribute. The four-acre park contains basketball and tennis courts, softball and soccer fields, places to picnic and play horseshoes, and a playground. A major feature of this park is the flock of Vaux's Swifts that makes an annual stop on its migration south for the winter. In late August they begin to gather every evening near sunset. As more swifts arrive, they begin to circle a large chimney at Chapman school, which they have adopted as a roost site. All at once, they dive into the chimney, and the sight of 10,000 swifts funneling themselves into their chambers is one to behold. This nightly ritual draws people all through September; they spread out on the lawn with picnic dinners and observe the ritual. The local red-tailed hawks and other raptors have also noticed this, making for high nightly drama. Watching the swifts and the hawks raises many questions—where are the swifts during the day? How do they decide it's time to swirl into the chimney? How do the hawks know it's time to drop by? Luckily, the Audubon Society will often visit the park during the peak of swift-watching season (mid-September) to provide answers to these and other burning questions. *NOTE:* Wallace Park does not have a parking lot, and the available parking in this neighborhood is limited. The streetcar stops nearby—we recommend that or bus line 15 or 17.

Southeast Portland

CRESTON PARK
**Southeast 44th Avenue and Powell Boulevard
(503) 823-7529**

This green, tree-filled oasis bordering bustling Powell Boulevard is a great place for a summer birthday party or even a quiet, shady lunch. Less than 15 acres, it offers an outdoor swimming pool, lighted tennis court, well-equipped playground, group picnic facilities, and restrooms. While the pool gets very crowded on warm days and is a favorite for summertime swimming lessons, the park grounds are usually quiet and serene on weekdays. Weekends are a different story; many reunions and parties are held here.

CRYSTAL SPRINGS RHODODENDRON GARDEN
Southeast 28th Avenue and
Woodstock Boulevard
(503) 823-7529, (503) 771-8386

Crystal Springs offers the tranquility of a peaceful refuge away from the hurried pace of urban living. In the early spring and summer, its gardens explode in a riot of colors with every size and shade of rhododendron and azalea imaginable. A host of birds and waterfowl also thrives in the sprawling ponds, where children of all ages enjoy feeding the ducks. Crystal Springs also holds annual shows (see the Festivals and Annual Events chapter), at which visitors can see unusual rhododendrons and azaleas not normally found in this area. From Labor Day through February, admission is free. From March through Labor Day, admission is $3 for those older than 12 if you visit between 10:00 a.m. and 6:00 p.m. Thursday through Monday. Duck food is sold separately.

LAURELHURST PARK
Southeast 39th Avenue between
Stark Street and Burnside Street
(503) 823-7529
(503) 823-4101 for dance class information

The Olmsted-inspired Laurelhurst is among the most popular parks in the city for picnics, cookouts, or summer fun. Its 34-plus-acres offer a huge variety of trees, shrubs, and flowers as well as a 3-acre pond with a small island as a centerpiece and many ducks as residents. A paved path circles the pond and the entire outer edge of the park and is well used by early-morning runners and walkers. Laurelhurst is a terrific location for larger get-togethers; there's something for

everyone to do here, including basketball and tennis courts, a large horseshoe pit, and an excellent play structure. The Laurelhurst Studio is here; it's the Eastside conduit for ballet, tap, and other dance programs in the Parks and Recreation system. The park is gorgeously landscaped; it was once judged as the most beautiful park on the West Coast.

LEACH BOTANICAL GARDEN
6704 Southeast 122nd Avenue
(503) 823-9503

The Leaches were a couple devoted to plants: John Leach was a pharmacist and his wife Lilla was a botanist. Together they collected more than 2,000 species, some of which they discovered. The Leach Botanical Garden was their estate; its nine acres have been given over to preserving and studying plant life and maintaining a seed bank, as well as preserving the legacy of the couple who made this lovely, botanically diverse sanctuary possible. The grounds include the garden, the manor house, and natural areas. Garden and guided tours are free, and special tours are given by appointment. (For more information see the Attractions chapter.) There's a gift shop and library; classes are offered for adults and children. It's closed on Monday.

MT. SCOTT PARK
Southeast 72nd Avenue and Harold Street
(503) 823-7529
(503) 823-3183 (Community Center)

Harvey W. Scott was the editor of the *Oregonian* from 1865 to 1910 and by all accounts was a force to be reckoned with (you can see him in statue form, pointing west, at the top of Mt. Tabor). Mt. Scott Park is named for him. The park encompasses 12 arboreal acres with a playground, softball field, and tennis courts as well as picnic benches. The Mt. Scott Community Center, on the grounds of the park, offers one of the nicest pools you'll find anywhere. Did we say one pool? Make that two—a beautiful lap pool and a fun leisure pool with a great water slide, current channel, and imaginative built-in water toys as

The Leach Botanical Garden is devoted to native plants. RACHEL DRESBECK

well as a separate spa. The facility also has meeting rooms, gyms, classes, an auditorium, and a roller-skating rink. Call for times and fees (which are low—about $3.75 for adults).

MT. TABOR PARK
Southeast 60th Avenue and Salmon Street
(503) 823-7529
This park affords some of the best views in the city of rugged and stately Mount Hood and Mount St. Helens on the one side and Portland's West Hills on the other. This park is truly a wonderful place for picnics or for walking on wooded trails. Mt. Tabor has a number of reservoirs for Bull Run water, the city's water source; these are contained in whimsical crenellated tanks that are nonetheless heavily watched. (Don't try to throw anything in!) The 196-acre park also offers basketball courts, a stage for theater or music, lighted tennis courts, group picnic facilities, covered picnic areas, volleyball courts, trails, and public restrooms. The play structure is a big draw for families—they've situated it to take advantage of the sunshine, though the big fir trees still provide plenty of shelter.

Mt. Tabor sits on top of an extinct volcano; this volcano distinguishes Portland as one of two U.S. cities to have an extinct volcano within city limits (the other city is Bend). Many paths, some paved and some not, wind through the park and offer entirely different vistas. Sometimes you feel as though you're in the woods, but right around the bend you may be reminded of an orchard. The hilly terrain makes the park a favorite with runners, dog walkers, mountain bikers, disc golfers, go-karters, and just about anyone who likes a good view and a vigorous climb. Birders may be spotted early in the morning. In fact, the birders are on to something—a sunrise at Mt. Tabor is spectacular and worth the struggle out of bed in the morning.

OAKS BOTTOM WILDLIFE REFUGE
Portland Parks and Recreation
(503) 823-6131
Great blue heron are the star attraction here, but you can also view 139 other species of birds in this 160-acre refuge. The trail is easy and only 1 mile long, thus it's good for small children. The park is on a floodplain of the Willamette, so the trail can get quite muddy. This park is not wheelchair accessible. (See the Recreation chapter for more information.)

POWELL BUTTE NATURE PARK
Southeast 162nd Avenue and
Powell Boulevard
(503) 823-1616
We love big Powell Butte Nature Park, the site of a long-ago farm—its vestiges there to remind us of our history. Its entrance is unprepossessing, but a walk along the trails is more than rewarding, for soon you will find large meadows that encourage birds of prey as well as raccoons, foxes, and coyotes; shady old orchards; ripe blackberries if you're lucky; and amazing views. It's possible to see a number of peaks from this volcanic mound. Powell Butte attracts mountain bikers, joggers, and a lot of equestrian activity over its 9 miles of trails and 608 acres. There's also a 0.5-mile, wheelchair-friendly trail. You really have to get out and walk or bike around to enjoy this area, which stretches all the way down to Beggar's Tick Wildlife Refuge, a large marshy wetland busy with birds and wildlife.

SELLWOOD PARK
Southeast 7th Avenue and Miller Street
(503) 823-7529
Tall, well-spaced trees distinguish this pretty park, which is a crowd pleaser for its sports fields, excellent playground, and wonderful round swimming pool. The park has both sunny, grassy, open spaces and shady, cool refuges. On the bluff above Oaks Bottom and the Willamette River, you'll get pretty river views as you peer between the trees. Trails link Sellwood Park to Oaks Bottom and Oaks Park. The pool is outdoors, so it's

open only during the summer, but it is popular. An abundance of picnic tables encourage large groups—it's a favorite spot for reunions and company parties.

SPRINGWATER CORRIDOR
Southeast Ivon Street to Boring, OR
Springwater Corridor is a 20-mile rails-to-trails route comprising the southeast part of the 40-Mile Loop. It begins at Southeast Ivon Street near the Willamette River in Southeast Portland and ends in the town of Boring, a wide spot on the road to Mount Hood a few miles south of Gresham. The route is a popular trek for walkers, in-line skaters, and those in wheelchairs, on bikes, and astride horses. It's mostly blacktop or chip-sealed surface, with a thin gravel surface on the last 4 miles. The trail takes you through neighborhoods in Portland, eventually spilling you into farmland, wetlands, and nature reserves. There aren't any steep hills or dangerous dips, so even those in need of gentle trails can enjoy this charmingly rural bike path. One of the trail's delights is a sense of local history that is soon evident as you discover remnants of the old Bellrose rail line and read historical markers that tell how farmers used this very route to take produce west to Sellwood residents and their families and to nearby Oaks Park.

Flanking the route are huge clumps of blackberry vines, lots of sweet peas, long-stemmed blue chicory, Queen Anne's lace, 5-foot-tall mullein, spirea with its fluffy pink cones, dark brown Indian tobacco, and magenta poppies. You will also see a great variety of birds, including hawks, herons, and kingfishers, and you'll see mammals—perhaps even a coyote.

Along the way to Boring, you'll pass the Beggars-Tick Wildlife Refuge, a postage-stamp-size wilderness in the heart of the farm belt. The trail eventually takes you alongside Gresham's city park, with its grassy knolls, nature walks, and recreational facilities. Beyond the park, the corridor passes by the Columbia Brickworks, founded in 1906 and still in business as the oldest brick kiln in Oregon. It's fun to try to spot mossy brick stacks hiding in the bushes along the trail.

After the brickworks, the trail fades into a gravel path angling southeast to Boring. Unless you're the sort that insists on completing every trail to say you have done so, turn around here at the beginning of the gravel and head back to Portland.

WESTMORELAND PARK
**Southeast McLoughlin Boulevard
and Bybee Street
(503) 823-7529**

Expansive, 47-acre Westmoreland Park brings folks from all over town to play baseball—the fields are lighted, and on summer nights they seem to illuminate the whole neighborhood. But Westmoreland also has casting ponds, soccer fields, tennis courts, and a terrific playground to interest people. In addition, the duck ponds lure many kinds of waterfowl, and interesting things happen when the water-birds mingle with the toddlers.

North/Northeast Portland

ARBOR LODGE PARK
**North Bryant Street and Delaware Avenue
(503) 823-7529**

Portland has many little parks like Arbor Lodge. This small neighborhood park adjoins Chief Joseph School and offers some nice trees, softball and soccer fields, a tennis court and playground, restrooms, a wading pool, and horseshoe pit. On a sunny day this is a wonderful spot to bring a picnic basket and spread a blanket. You can enjoy a magazine while the kids romp on the playground.

CATHEDRAL PARK
**North Edison Street and Pittsburgh Avenue
(503) 823-7529**

This park—situated on the banks of the Willamette River and one of Portland's most scenic spots—is named after the tall gothic arches that support the St. Johns Bridge, towering above the park and inspiring that sense of awe that you're bound to have in a cathedral. The park, which has a stage, is home to popular summertime concerts; it also includes soccer fields, a boat ramp and docking facilities, and trails. Cathedral Park is often peaceful, belying its lively history—not only is it the site of the very first plat for the village of St. John's, but it is also suspected to have been a favorite fishing site for the Native Americans who lived here before.

COLUMBIA PARK
**North Lombard Avenue and Woolsey Street
(503) 823-7529**

Healthy competition is a good thing, and when the old city of Albina saw that Portland was developing Washington Park, they were not going to be outdone. They purchased 30 acres on Lombard Street in 1891. Soon after, however, Albina was annexed to Portland. But it took many years before Columbia Park, which was eventually patterned after a park in Berlin, became the handsome, wooded place it is today. In addition to the grounds, the park offers fields for soccer, baseball, and softball, lighted tennis courts, volleyball courts, and a swimming pool.

GRANT PARK
**Northeast 33rd Avenue and
Ulysses S. Grant Place
(503) 823-7529**

President Grant visited Portland three times, but this park, named in his honor, is now more famous for its Beverly Cleary Children's Sculpture Garden, in which Ramona Quimby, Henry Huggins, and his pooch Ribsy, all born of Cleary's lively imagination, are fixed in bronze. (A few blocks away is the actual Klikitat Street, where Ramona "lived," and the neighborhood where author Cleary herself grew up, attending Grant High School in the 1930s.) The sculptures sit atop a fountain, and in the summer, children play there all day long. At Grant Park you'll also find nice sports fields, tennis courts, and a swimming pool.

KELLEY POINT PARK
**North Kelley Point Park Road
and Marine Drive
(503) 823-7529**

This quiet and out-of-the-way 96-acre park is one of our favorite places in the entire Portland Metro area, offering a large sandy beach and views of the Willamette and Columbia Rivers as well as Mount Hood and Mount St. Helens. Picnic tables are scattered all over this park—some are even on the beach—and there is a wide variety of conifers and deciduous trees. The park is named for Oregon advocate Hall J. Kelley, who was a great friend to the state. He wanted to found a city at the convergence of the Willamette and the Columbia, but with 20/20 historical hindsight, it's a good thing he was overruled. Still, the park named in his honor is a wonderful spot, and it provides the anchor for the 40 Mile Loop—a fine legacy, in any case.

PENINSULA PARK AND ROSE GARDENS
North Albina Street and Rosa Parks Way
(503) 823-7529
Portland emerged as a city at a historically astute moment from the perspective of a park lover, and Peninsula Park demonstrates why. Its formal design was characteristic of its early-20th-century era; it is most known for its rose garden, but its striking gazebo bandstand is also historically important (it's a Portland Historic Landmark and a National Heritage Historical Structure). And its playground, as well as the community center (a city first), made Peninsula Park quite novel when it was finally finished in 1913. (It was also an early example of urban renewal. Previously the site had been home to a roadhouse and a racetrack.) The rose garden is still important, with two acres of roses—almost 9,000 plantings of them. The park, in the Piedmont neighborhood, also includes a softball and soccer field, swimming pool, basketball court, tables for picnics, a fountain, and lawn bowling.

WILSHIRE PARK
Northeast 33rd Avenue and Skidmore Street
Acquired by the city of Portland in 1940, pretty Wilshire Park in the Beaumont-Wilshire neighborhood is popular with softball players and families. Besides the ball field, the 15-acre community park offers some very nice trees, group picnic facilities, a jogging track, a good playground, and ample tables for birthday parties.

Vancouver and Outlying Areas
BLUE LAKE REGIONAL PARK
Northeast 223rd Avenue between
Marine Drive and Sandy Boulevard
(503) 797-1850
www.metro-region.org
Sweltering Portlanders are fond of natural Blue Lake, which is maintained as a regional park by Metro and is just 8 miles east of downtown Portland, making it easily accessible on summer days. The 64-acre lake has 400 feet of swimming beach and—especially fun for the little ones—a special children's play area in the water. But there's lots for everyone here—a fishing dock and boat rentals, basketball and volleyball courts, playgrounds, baseball fields, and picnic shelters. A food concession stand will supplement your picnic. The Lake House provides facilities for events such as weddings or retreats. Trails wind their way through the park; these are especially nice for cyclists, and you can rent bikes on-site. The park also hosts numerous programs and events, many of which are geared toward children (see our Kidstuff chapter for more information). You'll need to pay an entrance fee of $4 per car.

ELK ROCK ISLAND
Willamette River, near Southeast 19th
Avenue and Sparrow Street, Milwaukie
Elk Rock Island is actually part of the Portland Parks system; it's one of the designated natural areas, given to the city as a preserve for natural beauty that would restore the spirits of the citizens. This big volcanic rock, perhaps the oldest in the Portland area, is an excellent spot for bird-watching and offers some of the most diverse terrain around. Prized spots include herons, hawks, kingfishers, and egrets. This park also includes a hiking trail.

FRENCHMAN'S BAR COUNTY PARK
Lower River Road, off Fourth Plain
Boulevard, Vancouver, WA

This park offers a lot on its mile-long stretch of sandy beach along the eastern shore of the Columbia River. Activities you can enjoy here include bird-watching, sunbathing, fishing, boating, picnicking, and watching the huge container ships, tankers, and freighters that sail up the waters of the Pacific Northwest's mightiest river. There are plenty of walking trails too, plus eight sand volleyball courts, a grassy amphitheater, and some playground equipment for the little ones. This spot also affords a terrific view of Mount Hood.

RIDGEFIELD NATIONAL WILDLIFE REFUGE
Northwest 269th Street (Washington Highway 501) at Interstate 5, exit 14
(360) 887-4106
www.fws.gov/ridgefieldrefuges/complex/
Between Vancouver and Woodland, Washington, this 5,150-acre refuge features pasture, woodlands, and marshland. Much of the wildlife that sustained the area's Native American population and the later European settlers is still found here. The refuge's population includes deer, coyotes, nutria, foxes, rabbits, beavers, and otters. The population swells as 200,000 or more migratory birds and waterfowl travel the Pacific Flyway (depending on the season) and either stop and rest in the preserved wetlands or decide to spend the winter there. The refuge's permanent waterfowl and avian population includes herons, cranes, swans, geese, and eagles. There is a well-marked 1.9-mile loop trail that is an easy, if sometimes muddy, walk, even for children. This is a day-use-only area. Though hiking and fishing are allowed, fires and off-road vehicles are not permitted. Binoculars, spotting scopes, and cameras with tripods and long lenses may make viewing and wildlife photography easier. A footbridge over a set of busy railroad tracks is an added attraction, allowing an unusual perspective on the Amtrak trains and the hardworking freight trains running up and down the Pacific Coast. The Ridgefield Refuge Office, 301 North 3rd Street, is open weekdays from 7:30 a.m. to 4:00 p.m., and it has dozens of informative brochures and a useful map to the refuge. Open from dawn to dusk all year long, the refuge is free

to all ages, but leave Fido at home. (Bicycling, horseback riding, and ATVs are also not allowed.) There is a $3 day-use fee.

SAUVIE ISLAND
U.S. Highway 30, about 10 miles west of downtown Portland
www.sauvieisland.org/what-to-see-and-do/
Sauvie Island, a beautiful island of fertile alluvial soil northwest of the city at the confluence of the Willamette and Columbia Rivers, is not, strictly speaking, a park. It is hardworking farm country. But the roads are so pretty, and the u-pick farms, river beaches, parks, and wildlife areas are so enticing, that the entire island seems like a park to many Portland residents who converge there on Saturday morning to pick blueberries or ride their bicycles. This is a mixed blessing. It's good, on the one hand, that we can see the farms that grow our food and that the farms are supported by local dollars. On the other hand, its bucolic nature encourages people to visit, thus increasing traffic and busyness, diminishing the bucolic nature of the place.

In an effort to preserve that nature, some of the island has been set aside in wildlife preserves and parks. The Sauvie Island Wildlife Viewing Area, maintained by the Oregon Fish and Wildlife Department, is an excellent spot for bird-watching. There you will see the ubiquitous ducks and Canada geese, but you may also spy swans, bald eagles, sandhill cranes, herons, and rare species of gull. Winter is an especially good time to look for these birds because many species stop here on the way to warmer places, and some reside here all season, but be aware that some parts of the refuge are closed in the winter. You'll need a day permit to park at the wildlife area—these may be obtained at the Cracker Barrel Grocery, at the north end of the Sauvie Island Bridge. (You can't miss it—it's the only building right off the bridge on the island side.) The wildlife area is also north of the bridge. For more information about the wildlife area, you may contact Oregon Fish and Wildlife at (503) 621-3488.

More wildlife, as well as human relationships to it, can be seen at Howell Territorial Park, which is part museum and part natural area. This 93-acre park comprises the James F. Bybee House, the Agricultural Museum, old orchards and pastures, and sizable natural areas, including a lake and wetlands. You can see an incredible variety of birds and mammals in the natural areas, while the museums permit a glimpse into the days of the early pioneer settlers, with a fine collection of historical artifacts.

The museums are open during the weekend from the first week of June through Labor Day. The hours are noon to 5:00 p.m. Guided tours are offered on the half-hour. (You may also reserve the park for special events; the number for that service is 503-797-1850.) To find the park, take US 30 to the Sauvie Island Bridge. Once you've crossed the bridge, follow Sauvie Island Road north for 1 mile, then turn right on Howell Park Road, where you'll immediately see the parking lot on your left.

Sauvie Island Road, by the way, wraps around the whole island. The island is crisscrossed by other roads that wind through farms, orchards, and fields, and following any of them will eventually lead you to something interesting. The u-pick farms that are all over the island are as big an attraction as the parks, and during harvest season—May through October—you will find many people picking berries, flowers, peaches, pumpkins, corn, and everything else that grows well here. Farm stands sell produce for those folks who'd rather not get dusty. During October the Pumpkin Patch draws thousands of schoolchildren for hayrides and pumpkin picking; it's a rare Portland child who hasn't chosen a jack-o'-lantern here. You can find this institution by circling under the Sauvie Island Bridge and following the road south. Whichever direction you drive, be respectful of the residents, the cyclists, the chickens, the schoolchildren, and everyone else sharing the road with you. In short, drive carefully!

STATE PARKS NEAR PORTLAND

General information about all state parks is available at (800) 551-6949. To reserve campsites call (800) 452-5687. You can also look up these parks online at www.oregon.gov/OPRD/PARKS/.

BALD PEAK STATE PARK
9 miles from Newberg along Bald Peak Road, 5 miles northwest of Highway 219 North (Hillsboro-Silverton Highway)

If you're the kind of person who hasn't lost interest in Sunday driving, you might like Bald Peak. A pretty state park near Hillsboro, but high above the Willamette Valley, Bald Peak is still close enough to town to be an alluring spot for a spontaneous picnic on a sunny afternoon (no water, though, so pack your own). Bald Peak offers lovely views of the valley and a number of Cascade peaks in Washington and Oregon, including Mt. Rainier if the visibility is good.

BATTLE GROUND LAKE STATE PARK
Northeast 249th Street
Battle Ground, WA
(888) 226-7688 (reservations)
www.parks.wa.gov

One of the biggest attractions in southwest Washington, Battle Ground Lake State Park tempts recreators from all over the area who are drawn by 280 acres of swimming, fishing, horseback riding, boating, and hiking as well as 50 campsites. The park is 21 miles northeast of Vancouver; it has a splendid lake in the center of an extinct volcano. The park is open from 6:30 a.m. until dusk from April to September and from 8:00 a.m. until dusk the remainder of the year. Summer camping is a breeze with the available kitchen shelters and showers—but remember, this park fills up fast. Kitchens with electricity may also be rented for large groups (20 to 150 people); fees depend on the number of people.

CHAMPOEG STATE PARK
Directly off Highway 99 West,
7 miles east of Newberg
(503) 678-1251, ext. 221

Pronounced "sham-POO-ey," Champoeg State Park is a place where Portlanders flock for the concerts and other events in the pretty amphitheater, but the park has even more to offer. First, there are the trails that cross the 615 acres; these curl through woods, meadows, and wetlands and are wonderful for bicycling or hiking. Then there's the historical interest: The park is on the grounds of the first settlers' government, and two museums and many educational programs and tours help to bring that early history alive. The park is regularly visited by school buses full of children eager to learn what life was like during pioneer days. There is a $3 daily day-use fee, but a $25 annual permit grants access to all day-use areas in state parks across Oregon, including this one.

MILO MCIVER STATE PARK
Springwater Road, 4 miles west of Estacada
(503) 630-7150
Milo McIver State Park is a quiet park less than an hour's drive from downtown—the perfect place to go camping after work. The Clackamas River shoots through here, so you can use the park as home base for kayaking or rafting days. The park also rents horses; its trails and fields are fine country to explore this way. Another attraction is the disc golf course (18 holes). In the summer a variety of recreational and educational programs are offered, including a Civil War reenactment. All these interesting activities are in addition to the sweet, simple pleasures of camping: The park has

more than 50 sites of various levels of sophistication. Like many other state parks in Oregon, a $3 daily day-use fee is required (unless you want to spring for the annual pass at $25); overnight camping fees depend on the site.

TRYON CREEK STATE PARK
Off I–5 (exit 297)
Terwilliger Boulevard
Southwest Portland
(503) 636-9886
Lucky schoolchildren have fond memories of this pristine state park that's just a few minutes from downtown, the closest state park to the Portland Metro area. Actually it's within the metro area, which is the reason so many field trips are held here—that, and the fact that so much native wildlife can be found here. One of the few streams in the city that steelhead use for spawning is found here, and the native trillium plant grows abundantly. Tryon Creek State Park has shady trails perfect for biking and walking, and lots of signs tell you about what you're seeing. Much of the park is wheelchair accessible. Day camps are a staple of summer life at Tryon Creek, and guided tours are available as well as a gift shop. These last things are run by the Friends of Tryon Creek State Park; call them at (503) 636-4398. There is no fee to use Tryon Creek.

GOLF

Golf enthusiasts will be happy to discover that their sport has flourished all around the state of Oregon. From courses situated in fertile valleys below the snowcapped Cascades to the high-desert links with fairways framed by lava rock outcroppings, peppery sagebrush, and twisted junipers, this is a golfer's paradise. Many superior golf courses have sprung up in coastal regions, in southern Oregon, and around Bend, the gateway to central Oregon.

Oregon offers an amazing diversity of golf courses, and the Portland Metro area courses are some of the most interesting, challenging, and attractive in the state. With dozens of both public and private courses to choose from, you're sure to find the links to suit you, whether you're a seasoned professional or a neophyte.

Professionals and amateurs alike have found Portland to be a friendly host for tournament play. Portland is home to several major golf tournaments—the LPGA Safeway Classic and the JELD-WEN Tradition have been regular events (also see the Recreation and Spectator Sports chapter for more information). The U.S. Amateur Open has been played in Oregon from time to time, most notably at Pumpkin Ridge in 1996, when Tiger Woods won it.

OVERVIEW

It's easy to see why the area has an outstanding reputation for golf. In Portland, and in the numerous courses a few minutes just outside the city, the golf courses are beautifully laid out and meticulously cared for. Small lakes and streams do a good job of defending par, and in the summertime, the greens throughout the region are quite fast. While the terrain is impressive, even for well-traveled golfers, and the facilities are superb, golf in Oregon is an affordable luxury. In Portland, greens fees fall mostly in the $25 to $45 range and sometimes lower. Discounts are available for weekday and off-season play, and afternoon and twilight rates are also common. Factor in relatively low costs for meals (and accommodations, if necessary), and golf here can be a downright thrifty habit—and a healthy one too. Walking is not only permitted at most of the courses, but here in fitness-oriented Portland, it's also encouraged.

Most Portland-area courses are open year-round, but May to September is prime golfing time. The off-season may be a good time for you to visit a familiar course or to try a new one, because then the courses are quieter and less crowded. In the Portland area alone, about 30 golf courses are open to the public and all rent clubs and carts. The city's four municipal golf courses offer some outstanding golf and lower-than-average greens fees. You can make tee times six days to one hour in advance for the municipal courses—Eastmoreland, Heron Lakes, Red Tail, Rose City, as well as the Metro-run Glendoveer—by phoning one central number, (503) 823-4653. Also, many area courses offer discounted greens fees for juniors, seniors, or both. Senior players may need a discount card—call Portland Parks and Recreation at (503) 823-4328 for more information. Whatever your age or level of play, you are sure to love Oregon golf as much as we do.

This chapter is devoted to the 18-hole courses in the area that we like to play the most, but many more are out there: Colwood (503-254-5515), Gresham Golf Course (503-665-3352), Meriwether National Golf Course in Hillsboro (503-648-4143), Oregon City Golf Course (503-518-2846), Camas Meadows Golf Club (800-750-6511 or 360-833-

2000), Orenco Woods (503-648-1836), and Three Rivers (360-423-4653 or 800-286-7765) are fine local courses. And that's only a few of them. You will also find lots of 9-hole gems, such as St. Helens Golf Course (503-397-0358) and McKay Creek (503-693-7612). Complete listings of Oregon golf courses are available at information kiosks at the POVA information center, the airport, the zoo, and other tourist gathering places. *NOTE:* Non-metal spikes are the only kind allowed on most Portland golf courses.

Price Code

For one 18-hole round of summer weekend golf. Cart prices are not included. Rates may change for senior and junior golfers, during the week, and winter months.

$	$25 or less
$$	$26–$50
$$$	$51–$75

PORTLAND

BROADMOOR GOLF COURSE $$
3509 Northeast Columbia Boulevard
(503) 281-1337
This is one of the friendliest, cheapest, and most popular golfing locations in Portland proper. Broadmoor was built in 1931, and since then it has been a favorite of Portland golfers, whatever their ability. The 18-hole, par-72 course unfolds over 220 acres, dodging water hazards and trees; the billowing fairways flanked by the Broadmoor Lake and Slough add aesthetic interest to the technical challenge of maintaining a low score. In addition, Broadmoor offers a well-equipped golf shop and full-service clubhouse. Carts are optional; reservations are recommended 13 days in advance.

EASTMORELAND GOLF COURSE $$
2425 Southeast Bybee Boulevard
(503) 775-2900
(503) 823-4653 (tee times)
Rated one of the top 25 public golf courses in the United States by *Golf Digest,* Eastmoreland is Portland's oldest and one of its most beloved greens. Eastmoreland has an endless variety of

i Wednesday is Golf Day for the *Oregonian.* Check the sports section for the latest news, events, and convenient discount coupons for local golf courses.

trees and shrubs on its 6,529 yards and is bordered by Crystal Springs Lake, the Rhododendron Gardens, and Johnson Creek. The course, which is the site of the annual city championship, also offers a pro shop, restaurant, snack bar, reception and meeting rooms, and a double-deck covered and lighted driving range. The greens fees are among the best values of all the local courses. Rates may vary according to the season. Junior and senior rates are available. Carts are optional. Call six days in advance for reservations or to inquire about lessons.

GLENDOVEER GOLF COURSE $$
14015 Northeast Glisan Street
(503) 253-7507
(503) 823-4653 (tee times)
This par-73 course is an excellent place to golf, and it is usually quite busy. Glendoveer, with 36 regulation holes spread out over 280 acres of hills, trees, and water hazards, offers junior and senior rates on the weekdays. This place features a golf shop, driving range, and a great clubhouse with big-screen sports TV and outdoor seating for special events. Regular visitors know this course has a split personality. That's because most of the course swells with hills, except for the front 9 holes of the west course, which are as flat as paper. The east course spans 6,296 yards, while the west course runs 5,922 yards. Glendoveer also offers a pro shop and indoor tennis and racquetball courts; the restaurant and lounge, the Ringside, is a Portland steakhouse favorite and worth a trip even if you're not a golfer. Reservations should be made six days in advance; lessons are available.

HERON LAKES GOLF COURSE $$
3500 North Victory Boulevard
(503) 289-1818
(503) 823-4653 (tee times)

Offering two splendid golf courses designed to try every skill level, Heron Lakes combines a blend of bunkers and water hazards, the latter adding an aesthetic appeal to the technical challenge. The two courses, the Greenback (6,621 yards) and the Great Blue (6,916 yards), which is the flagship of Portland's golf program, were designed by world-renowned golf architect Robert Trent Jones II. Listed by Golf Digest as one of America's top 75 public golf courses, Heron Lakes has hosted numerous important golf events. Many birds, including bald eagles, Canada geese, and great blue herons, add to its beauty and make life interesting for golfers. Facilities include a pro shop, snack bar, and natural-turf driving range. Holiday fees may be higher. Call in your reservations six days in advance—they go fast.

RED TAIL GOLF COURSE $$
8200 Southwest Scholls Ferry Road
(503) 646-5166
(503) 823-4653 (tee times)
This 7,100-yard championship 18-hole public golf course in Southwest Portland is a redesigned course on the site that was formerly known as Progress Downs. Red Tail has incorporated significant advances in drainage systems—always a problem for Oregon golf—and even during the winter, the ball rolls and springs instead of sinking into muddy grass. The PGA golf pro, Mark Bolton, heads a staff that is renowned for its teaching ability, and they have state-of-the-art instruction facilities to help you perfect your game. Red Tail is run by Portland Parks and Recreation, so its lush greens and beautiful driving range are available at very reasonable prices—about $35 for 18 holes.

ROSE CITY GOLF COURSE $$
2200 Northeast 71st Avenue
(503) 253-4744
(503) 823-4653 (tee times)
One of the oldest golf courses in the entire state, Rose City is a challenging course in a beautiful setting. The long par fours and tree-lined, narrow fairways on the 18 regulation holes demand concentration and will test your technical skills. With plenty of hills, sand and water hazards, and trees

spread over 6,520 yards, this course plays long and affords excellent scenery. Rose City also has two of the hardest finishing holes in all of Portland public golf. Facilities include a pro shop and a full-service snack bar. Reservations are recommended and are taken only six days in advance. Lessons can be scheduled with a pro.

WILDWOOD GOLF COURSE $$
21881 Northwest St. Helens Road
(503) 621-3402
Beautiful Wildwood on the outskirts of Northwest Portland offers 18 regulation holes on one of the most gorgeous courses in the area. No fewer than three creeks run through the 5,756 yards of hilly greens. You can spend a whole day here, practicing your swing in the driving range, browsing in the pro shop, and celebrating your birdies in the full-bar clubhouse. Lessons are available and reservations should be made a week in advance, but Wildwood can probably squeeze in one or two golfers on short notice. Note that the driving range allows irons only.

OUTLYING AREAS

CHARBONNEAU GOLF CLUB $$
32020 Southwest Charbonneau Drive,
Wilsonville
(503) 694-1246
It's no exaggeration to say that this executive course is unique, not only to the area but to the world. Lakes and trees are abundant on the three finely manicured 9-hole courses, which test the skills of beginners and professionals alike. This lush course is a mix of par fours and long and short par threes. The grass driving range is in a bucolic setting with well-tended turf. The practice area is the equal of any PGA Tour site. When you call a week in advance for reservations, you may also inquire about the junior and senior rates.

FOREST HILLS GOLF COURSE $$
36260 Southwest Tongue Lane, Cornelius
(503) 357-3347
West of downtown Portland off U.S. Highway 26,

Make golf a family event by taking the kids to the Children's Golf Course, a pretty par-9 executive course along the Willamette. It features lessons, clinics, and tournaments for young golfers, but grown-ups are welcome too. You'll find it at 19825 River Road, Gladstone, (503) 722-1530.

this high-quality facility is equally suitable for the lone golfer or the big tournament. The 18 regulation holes are scattered across 6,173 yards of a hilly, well-groomed course that is adorned with magnificent trees and water hazards that look easier than they play. Forest Hills offers a golf shop with a reputation for outstanding service, as well as a driving range, full-service clubhouse and restaurant, and three practice greens. Lessons are offered. Make reservations a week in advance.

LAKE OSWEGO GOLF COURSE $
17525 Southwest Stafford Road
Lake Oswego
(503) 636-8228
With an abundance of trees, water, and hills, this splendid 18-hole executive course is both challenging and lovely. Local golfers find the topography the perfect place to practice their short game, and though it's an executive course, Lake Oswego Golf Course has the reputation of being a real challenge. The pro shop carries great equipment and the 19th Green Cafe & Grill offers an extensive menu as well. With just 2,693 yards, there are no golf carts here, but lessons are available.

LANGDON FARMS GOLF CLUB $$$
24377 Northeast Airport Road, Aurora
(503) 678-4653
Just off Interstate 5 about 20 minutes south of Portland, Langdon Farms is popular with Portland golfers. This par-71, 18-hole course laid out over 6,935 yards is notable for its unusual contoured terrain. There are few shade trees, so golfers should wear a hat and apply sunscreen when playing on a hot or sunny day. Lessons are available as well as a driving range. Greens fees include cart rental. Rates vary widely—prime-

time summer fees are at the high end, but afternoon rates throughout the year offer good value. Several special rates are available at Langdon, among them the one for early birds. Call for more information, and make your reservations two months in advance. The clubhouse resembles a turn-of-the-20th-century farmhouse, reminding golfers that they're playing in some of the most fertile farmland in the nation.

LEWIS RIVER GOLF COURSE $$
3209 Lewis River Road, Woodland, WA
(800) 341-9426
Just a half-hour's drive north from Portland, this picturesque public golf course offers gorgeous scenery along the winding Lewis River. The 6,352-yard course is graced with many trees and lakes. Lessons are available. This well-established golf course can handle large groups and tournaments. Besides the driving range and putting green, Lewis River offers a pro shop, restaurant, banquet rooms, and patio dining.

MOUNTAIN VIEW $$
27195 Southeast Kelso Road, Boring
(503) 663-4869
Exactly one-half of the way between downtown Portland and Mount Hood, this is a dandy place for 18 regulation holes of golf. Mountain View offers plenty of hazards and hills throughout its 5,926 yards and affords a terrific view of Mount Hood. Be sure to ask about hole number 12; with an 18-story drop from the T-box to the green, it is a huge attraction—one of the most unusual holes in the state. Lessons are available. Make reservations seven days in advance.

PERSIMMON COUNTRY CLUB $$$
500 Southeast Butler Road, Gresham
(503) 661-1800
There's a lot to like about this sprawling 6,445-yard golf oasis located in the east side suburbs: gently rolling hills, sculpted, manicured greens and fairways, and a friendly staff that makes you feel at home. Persimmon is a semiprivate club, which means that members have first crack at tee times. There's everything you need for a fun day

of golf, including a clubhouse, golf shop, driving range, two putting greens, a chipping green, and the Persimmon Grill, which offers an extensive menu. Nonmembers may reserve tee times three days in advance. Lessons are available. Greens fees include carts.

ℹ️ For the most encyclopedic Internet review of golf in Oregon and southwest Washington, visit the truly excellent Web site www.oregongolf.com. This fine resource gives exhaustive details on each course and links you to the maps to get you there.

PUMPKIN RIDGE $$$
12930 Old Pumpkin Ridge Road
North Plains
(503) 647-4747, (888) 594-GOLF
Pumpkin Ridge comprises two first-rate courses, a public course, Ghost Creek, and a private course, Witch Hollow. Ghost Creek stretches over 6,839 beautiful yards, and it is one of the premier golf facilities open to the public on the entire West Coast. Tiger Woods won the U.S. Amateur Open here in 1996.

Witch Hollow is the home of the private Pumpkin Ridge Golf Club. Both courses have bentgrass tees, greens, and fairways. Both are nearly unrivaled in the Pacific Northwest. Amenities include an 18,000-square-foot clubhouse with golf shop, meeting facilities, teaching center, and restaurant. Practice facilities include bunkers, putting and chipping greens, and an expansive driving range. Package deals are available for corporate or tournament outings. Top professional golfers are available for lessons. Fees change with the season, so inquire when you make your reservations 60 days in advance. If you plan to golf at Pumpkin Ridge a lot, take advantage of their Ghost Card, which offers a discounted rate for frequent players.

QUAIL VALLEY $$
12565 Northwest Aerts Road, Banks
(503) 324-4444
A drive of 30 minutes west on US 26 will take you to the superb Quail Valley Golf Course, which is surprisingly difficult for a course that looks so flat. The difficulty is due to the abundance of water hazards and other environmentally sensitive areas that challenge players in all the right ways. This 6,603-yard course is a favorite for winter play, because it is very well drained.

RESERVE VINEYARDS GOLF CLUB $$$
4805 Southwest 229th Avenue, Aloha
(503) 649-8191
One of the area's newest golf courses, the Reserve Vineyards offers two 18-hole courses in the heart of Willamette Valley wine country. The par-72 courses were designed by John Fought and Bob Cupp, and together these courses offer some of the best golf in the state. The mansionlike, 40,000-square-foot clubhouse includes four dining areas and a deli, a pro shop, a wine-tasting area (there are vineyards on and near the course), locker rooms, a trophy room, and a 2,000-square-foot deck. The club is a popular location for corporate golf tournaments as well as weddings, banquets, and social events, but its claim to national fame is that it has been the home of the Fred Meyer Challenge and the Jeld-Wen Tradition (see the Recreation and Spectator Sports chapter for more information). Make reservations 14 days in advance.

SKAMANIA LODGE GOLF COURSE $$$
1131 Skamania Lodge Way
Stevenson, WA
(800) 293-0418
Don't let this very short par 70 fool you: This course is tough. It is hilly. The rough is brutal. The trees are thick. The extremely tight fairways should encourage you to leave your driver in the trunk. And bunkers lie in wait for you on the green side on several holes. But these challenges—along with the spectacular setting and views—make this one of the most beloved courses in the area. Skamania Lodge Golf Course is about an hour's drive east from Portland through the Columbia Gorge, and it's attached to Skamania Lodge, on the north bank of the Columbia. The impressive views of the Columbia are reason enough to visit. Many Skamania regulars advise you to rent a cart

because of the hills. It's also recommended that you call two weeks in advance for tee times, but if you're staying in the lodge, you don't have to call so far in advance. To get there follow Interstate 84 east to the Bridge of the Gods. This toll bridge ($1) will take you across the river, and from there, simply follow the signs.

STONE CREEK GOLF CLUB $$
14603 Stoneridge Drive, Oregon City
(503) 518-4653

This beautiful par-72 municipal course, designed by Oregon's own Peter Jacobsen, is situated on 165 diverse acres in Oregon City. The front 9 inhabit a pastoral meadow, and the back 9, wooded wetlands. In fact, water hazards are everywhere—three lakes, four wetlands, and Stone Creek itself. You'll also find views of Mount Hood—and 41 bunkers. This course was designed expressly to challenge and delight players at every level of golf, from the novice to the pro, with rewards for risky shots. The hardest hole is number 5, with its narrow frame of tall fir trees and uphill slope. The 13th hole is also notable; there, your blind tee shot goes over a hill and lands out of view, then you play uphill to a green encircled by majestic firs. Stone Creek provides an all-grass driving range that stretches over 6.5 acres, with six target greens and facilities to practice bunker shots. Club amenities include a pro shop, a full-service deli with three brews on tap, and a clubhouse suitable for parties.

TRI MOUNTAIN $$
1701 Northwest 299th Street
Ridgefield, WA
(360) 887-3004, (888) 874-6686

Tri Mountain is close to downtown Portland and even closer to downtown Vancouver; its reputation for sogginess has been improved with drainage systems, and golfers agree that this fun course is well maintained. Sand bunkers are numerous, and 11 lakes that come into play over most of the course's holes keep golfers on their toes. The yardage of this par-72 course is 6,580, and every yard is interesting. Carts are available, as is a full-service clubhouse and an aquatic driving range.

GOLF SPECIALTY STORES

Looking for some new golf shoes or perhaps a nice set of new titanium woods? No problem. If golf is your game, you will find plenty of Portland-area shops that carry the latest and best equipment and supplies. Many stores do repair work and offer extensive selections of new and used clubs, bags, putters, and apparel. Here are several specialized stores in the area you may want to visit.

FIDDLER'S GREEN
91292 Highway 99E, Eugene
(541) 689-8464, (800) 548-5500
www.fiddlersgreen.com

All right, so it's not in Portland. Still, Fiddler's Green is worth a visit if you are in the Eugene area—they are the largest golf pro shop in the country. Attached to an 18-hole executive course, Fiddler's Green is an ideal place to stock up on gloves, shoes, balls, clothes, and clubs. The driving range provides a good try-out area. This family-run business has numerous fitting experts to help you select the proper clubs. They also will repair your clubs, even regripping them while you wait. Fiddler's Green advertises itself as "the golfer's candy store," and we see no reason to argue. Call them for a catalog.

i Fiddler's Green, the golf superstore in Eugene, publishes a colorful, free map of all the golf courses in Oregon and Washington. It's widely available at places where tourists are likely to congregate: at the airport, car rental kiosks, and attractions such as the Oregon Zoo.

GOLFSMITH
10263 Northeast Cascades Parkway,
Cascade Station
(near Portland International Airport)
(503) 287-0196
www.golfsmith.com

This large, spacious store—one of a national chain—carries the latest gear and clothing and the old reliables as well. In addition to supplying you with shoes, balls, and clubs, they also offer repair services, customizing, lessons—and even workshops on making golf clubs, a service sure to take a few strokes off your game. Tennis gear is also available. The staff is extremely friendly and helpful. Golfsmith is usefully open until 9:00 p.m. It's near IKEA at the Cascade Station shopping center.

LADY GOLF CLASSICS
5123 Southwest Macadam Avenue
(503) 223-9100
Lady Golf specializes in golf apparel and equipment, including clubs, shoes, and accessories for women. Their apparel ranges from size 2 to size 22.

NORTH WOODS GOLF
7410 Southwest Macadam Avenue
(503) 245-1910, (800) 666-1910
North Woods Golf focuses on the creation of custom-fit woods and irons made right there in the shop, especially ones that feature graphite shafts. However, they are also distinguished by their experts in repair and run the largest repair shop in town.

GOLF EVENTS

Oregon has hosted two regular tournaments, the LPGA Safeway Classic and the Fred Meyer Challenge, which PGA notable Peter Jacobsen founded as a fund-raiser for local charities. But in 2002, Fred Meyer ended its sponsorship of that great charity event. No worries: We now have one of the PGA Champions Tour major events to replace it. In addition to these events, roving tournaments of many kinds will alight here, including the U.S. Amateur Open and the U.S.G.A. National Amateur Public Links Championship. Oregon also has its own regiment of local tournaments: The Oregon Golf Association is the best source of information on these. They may be reached at (503) 981-GOLF or online at www.orgolf.org.

ℹ The Oregon Golf Association, the local liaison to the USGA, will help you establish your handicap, find out about regional tournaments, and answer your questions about golf courses. Contact them at (503) 981-GOLF.

THE JELD-WEN TRADITION
(A PGA Champions Tour Event)
Peter Jacobsen Productions
(503) 672-8159 (tickets)
www.jeld-wentradition.com
With a purse of well over $2 million and major PGA Champions Tour stars (think Tom Watson, Hale Irwin, and Fuzzy Zoeller), the Jeld-Wen Tradition brings worldwide attention to Oregon golf. This tournament is played on the beautiful Crosswater golf course in Sunriver, about three hours away from Portland but worth the drive. You can purchase tickets by the day, by the event, or by the practice round. The Tradition has replaced the former Fred Meyer Challenge as the signature PGA event in Oregon; from 2003-2008, it was held at the Peter-Jacobsen-designed Reserve Vineyards Golf Club. (For more on this event, see the Recreation and Spectator Sports chapter.)

SAFEWAY CLASSIC TOURNAMENT GOLF
(503) 626-2711
(503) 287-LPGA (ticket sales)
http://safewayclassic.com
The LPGA Safeway Classic has a purse of almost $2 million; it raises millions for children's charities and is one of the most popular events in Portland golf. Tickets run about $10 per day, $25 for the week, but Safeway shoppers can receive significant discounts—and kids under 17 are free when accompanied by an adult. It's held at some of the Portland area's showcase golf courses: Starting in 2009, you can find it at Pumpkin Ridge. (See the Recreation and Spectator Sports chapter for more information on this great golf event.)

DAY TRIPS

A chief pleasure of living in or visiting Portland is its proximity to so many other beautiful places. A two hours' drive west of Portland will take you to the magnificent Oregon coast with its forests, huge rock formations, and unsullied beaches. An easy hour's drive east leads to the awe-inspiring Columbia Gorge and its stunning waterfalls and, by another route, the majestic Mount Hood. If you drive south, in an hour you'll reach the largest and one of the loveliest state parks in Oregon, Silver Falls State Park, a hiker's and horseback rider's paradise. So pack your picnic basket, a thermos of coffee or tea, a good map and, of course, your *Insiders' Guide,* and go discover Oregon firsthand.

SILVER FALLS STATE PARK

SILVER FALLS STATE PARK
20024 Silver Falls Highway SE
Sublimity
(800) 551-6949 (information)
(800) 452-5687 (reservations)

In the lower elevations of Oregon's Cascade Mountains, just 26 miles east of Salem, lies Silver Falls State Park. Here, one of the most beautiful trails in Oregon, Canyon Trail (also known as the Trail of 10 Falls) descends to a forest floor covered with ferns, mosses, and wildflowers amid stands of Douglas fir, hemlock, and cedar and the rushing waters of Silver Creek. Silver Falls has one of the highest concentrations of waterfalls in the country, and five of them fall more than 100 feet. This park also has beautiful meadows and excellent facilities, and it's a fine place to spend a day or two. If you aren't in a hurry, the drive to Silver Falls can be part of the fun. Take either Highway 99E or Interstate 205 from Portland to Oregon City. Then just follow Highway 99E along the Willamette River to Woodburn and then turn onto Highway 214, which cuts through the picturesque towns of Mt. Angel and Silverton on the way to Silver Falls. A faster route is to take I–5 South. Just past Salem, take Highway 22 east to Highway 214 and head east for 25 miles. From Portland the drive takes about an hour and 15 to 20 minutes.

At the park all the main attractions are easy to find. The well-maintained Canyon Trail winds along the banks of the north and south forks of Silver Creek leading to 11 majestic waterfalls. These range from the grand South Falls (177 feet) to the delicate Drake Falls (27 feet). Four of these falls have an amphitheaterlike surrounding, allowing one to walk behind the falls and enjoy the cool and misty spray.

Canyon Trail (which does not allow pets and is open to hikers only) joins with the Canyon Rim Trail to complete a 7-mile loop. The trail runs behind several of the taller falls and along the brink of others, providing an exciting excursion for hikers of all ages and levels of endurance.

South Falls, one of the most spectacular sights, is an easy walk from the main parking area and the gorgeous Silver Falls Lodge. The trail descends to the bottom of the canyon and follows the South Fork of Silver Creek 1 mile to Lower South Falls. A quarter mile farther, the trail turns east and follows the North Fork of Silver Creek upstream past at least six more waterfalls.

If you want to see some lush scenery and waterfalls, but don't want to walk too far, follow Highway 214 a mile or so past the main entrance and you will come to a trailhead that's within a few hundred yards of Winter Falls, North Falls, and Upper North Falls. The distance from South Falls to North Falls is approximately 4.5 miles.

To hike the entire circuit requires a good three to four hours and more if you stop for lunch. For most people who enjoy the canyon at a leisurely pace, the hike is an all-day adventure. Of course you need not hike the entire trail. Shorter trips may be made by returning via the Ridge Trail or the Winter Falls Trail. Some hikers prefer leaving a second car at the North Falls parking lot to avoid the 2-mile return hike.

To preserve its primitive nature, there are no shelters, picnic tables, or restrooms along the Silver Creek Canyon Trail, but benches and bridges across the many smaller streams are pleasant spots for a picnic. For safety's sake remember the bicycle trails are also used by hikers and the horse trails are open to bicycles and hikers alike.

At Silver Falls you will find RV, cabin, and tent camping in the overnight campground. Additional cabin rentals and complete group accommodations can be found at Silver Falls Conference Center, (503) 873-8875.

Some state parks in Oregon charge a nominal day-use fee to cover maintenance costs, and Silver Falls is one of them. You'll need to purchase either a $3 day-use pass or—if you plan to visit a lot of parks—a $25 annual pass that buys access to all state park day-use areas for one year.

i Silver Falls State Park offers 14 miles of trails for horseback riders, 4 miles of paved bicycle paths, and dozens of miles of hiking trails.

MOUNT ST. HELENS

MOUNT ST. HELENS NATIONAL VOLCANIC MONUMENT
Spirit Lake Highway
Washington Highway 504
www.fs.fed.us/gpnf/mshnvm/
Mount St. Helens was once known as "the Mount Fuji of America" because its symmetrical beauty was reminiscent of the famous Japanese volcano. But on May 18, 1980, after nearly two months of smaller earthquakes and steam eruptions, Mount St. Helens began a series of massive, explosive eruptions after an earthquake with a magnitude of 5.1 struck at 8:32 a.m. Within seconds, the volcano's unstable and bulging north flank slid away in the largest landslide in recorded history, triggering a destructive blast of lethal hot gas, steam, and rock debris that swept across the landscape at 684 mph. Temperatures reached as high as 572 degrees Celsius, melting snow and ice on the volcano and forming torrents of water and rock debris that gushed down river valleys leading from the mountain. Within minutes, a massive plume of ash thrust nearly 12 1/2 miles into the sky, where the wind carried about 490 tons of ash across more than 22,000 square miles of the western United States and, in trace amounts, around the world.

The lateral blast, which lasted only the first few minutes of a nine-hour continuous eruption, devastated 250 square miles of forest and recreation area, killed thousands of animals, and left 57 people dead. The eruptions and huge avalanche removed about 4 billion cubic yards of the mountain, including about 170 million cubic yards of glacial snow and ice. The eruption also caused mudflows so severe that they blocked the shipping channel of the Columbia River 70 river miles away.

The volcano periodically spewed steam and ash for several years, eventually settling down enough for the region to rebuild. In 1982 President Ronald Reagan designated 110,000 acres around the volcano as Mount St. Helens National Volcanic Monument. Trails, campgrounds, and visitor centers were established to accommodate the thousands who visited each year.

Now Mount St. Helens is one of the most popular day-trip destinations in the Pacific Northwest. It is an easy, scenic two-and-a-half-hour drive from Portland. There is a lot to do and see on this trip, so start early in the morning and pack some ice and refreshments in the cooler. Take I–5 to exit 49 (the Toutle/Castle Rock exit), which will lead you onto Washington Highway 504 (Spirit Lake Memorial Highway). The first stop, just 5 miles east, is the Mount St. Helens Volcanic Monument Visitor Center (360-274-0962) on the shore of Silver Lake. Don't miss the scaled-down, walk-in replica of the volcano: It really helps kids (and grown-ups, too) understand what's behind all the blasting. A short and easy trail just outside the center leads to a viewpoint overlooking Silver Lake and Mount St. Helens. This facility is operated by Washington State Parks; there is a $3 fee per adult for visiting, but it is worth it.

Continue driving east past some of the most striking scenery in the Northwest, from the washed-out stretches of the Toutle River to the white carcasses of the fir trees that laid themselves down before the awesome power of the volcanic blast. Highway 504 winds around the north fork of the Toutle River, and overlooks along the road offer views of the crater, Castle Lake, Coldwater Lake, and the mountain's northwest lava dome.

Hoffstadt Bluffs Rest Area offers a spectacular view of the landslide that preceded the blast. Elk Rock Viewpoint offers another stunning view into the still sediment-choked Toutle River Valley.

Just 5 miles farther up the road from Coldwater Ridge, Highway 504 ends at Johnston Ridge Observatory (milepost 52; 360-274-2140). Only 4 miles from the volcano's crater, this wheelchair-accessible-site affords views of the inside of the crater and its dome. It was named in honor of brave geologist David Johnston, who was keeping watch over the mountain for the U.S. Geological Survey and whose final words warned the world of what was to come. This magnificent center is a fitting tribute. The center also offers an incredibly high-quality movie about the eruption, along with many fascinating, interactive displays and kiosks.

There is much to do on the mountain, so you'll have some decisions to make. Ask for a map of Mount St. Helens at a visitor center—it will help you understand your options. One great adventure is to circle the entire mountain by following improved forest roads. It is possible to do this from June until the first snowfall—usually in November or December.

Other monument highlights include Windy Ridge and Spirit Lake, which rose 70 yards as a result of the blast. Consult with visitor center staff about selecting the best route.

Finally, although it is several hours away (by way of the Woodland exit and off Forest Road 83), Ape Cave is worthy of mention. The largest lava tube in the Western Hemisphere, this 12,810-foot tunnel wasn't explored until 1946. The Ape Cave Information Center is open daily, and guided tours of the caves are available during summer months.

You will need a pass to visit the tourist centers at the monument. These can be purchased at any of the three visitor centers, and we recommend the multiuse pass, which gives you access to the Mount St. Helens and Johnston Ridge Observatory centers and to Ape Cave. Adult multiuse passes are $8; children 15 and under are free. Discounts for seniors are also available. The monument is open year-round, though Johnston Ridge and some of the viewpoints and trails are closed by snow from October through May. (Cross-country skiers and snowmobilers will find Sno-Parks at Marble Mountain, Cougar, and Wakepish, but you'll need a Sno-Park permit. See the Recreation and Spectator Sports chapter for more information.) The visitor centers may be on limited schedules during the winter. If the volcano is active, it may be closed to climbers, though barring a major eruption, the other monument sites tend to remain open.

Pets are welcome at some parts of the monument, but dogs must be leashed where they are permitted. Some areas with especially delicate ecosystems prohibit pets altogether. Take notice of signs.

Excellent picnic and day-use areas are plentiful, but there are few places to purchase food. No overnight accommodations are available on the grounds of the monument, but nearby towns offer lodging, camping, and supplies.

For the most spectacular views of the crater, try to go on a sunny, summer day. But do remember that it is the Northwest, and even sunny days can bring clouds to the mountaintops.

On October 1, 2004, the volcano awoke from its slumber, emitting steam and erupting ash to signal a new phase of geological activity, which is ongoing, rebuilding the dome of the mountain. A volcanic eruption puts daily cares in perspective like nothing else, and despite the potential danger, residents have been enthralled by the reminder that Mount St. Helens has a mind of its own.

i You might hear Oregonians refer to distances in hours instead of miles. Don't be confused—it's just our way of talking. To translate, use an average 50-miles-per-hour figure to account for traffic, stops, and winding roads. So how far from Portland is the Oregon Coast? In distance, about 100 miles. In Oregon-speak, about two hours.

MOUNT HOOD–COLUMBIA GORGE LOOP

When friends visit from out of town and ask what they should do, we send them to the Columbia Gorge. The Gorge showcases our region beautifully, with its dramatic cliffs, tumbling falls, and the mighty Columbia rolling along despite the obstacles we have put in its way. Extending the tour by adding the rich farmland of Hood River and the drive over the archetypical Mount Hood deepens that sense of place, so precious to Oregonians. Here, we recommend an optimal tour of the region, one that you could drive in a day or that you could lengthen with an overnight stay. You can also reverse the drive or easily cut it short. The total length of the journey will be something between 100 and 160 miles, depending on where you stop, where you linger, and where you detour.

These days, cars and trucks whiz down Interstate 84 at great speed. But before the freeway, drivers had to rely on the road that is now the Columbia Gorge Scenic Highway. This narrow, winding road, with its many moss-covered bridges, was dedicated in 1916 by President Woodrow Wilson. One can only imagine the harrowing journey it must have been when it was the principal route east from Portland. Now it is

The Columbia River is still a mighty and mysterious river. JAMES THOMAS

quieter and less crowded, though on summer days you can still find yourself crawling through the shady forest behind an ambitious RV.

To reach the Gorge along this route, begin by taking I-84 east to Troutdale to exit 17 and follow the signs designating the Scenic Highway. The road takes you through Troutdale, along the swift Sandy River, until you turn up and onto the rural bluffs that overlook the Columbia. Just past the little town of Corbett, you will find the **Portland Women's Forum**, a pretty wayside that provides a spectacular view east of the Columbia Gorge, particularly Crown Point, Rooster Rock, and Beacon Rock, and north into the Washington Cascades.

Just east of the Portland Women's Forum is the road to Larch Mountain, a 29-mile detour (round-trip) that leads to some of the most breathtaking views of the Cascades in the entire area. The road winds through fields and forests until you get to a large parking lot, where an easy, paved trail takes you to a special viewing area that tells you which peaks you are seeing—on a clear day, this can mean a view north all the way to Mount Rainier. Closer in you'll see Mount St. Helens, Mount Adams, Mount Hood, and Mount Jefferson, as well as the verdant, rolling foothills of the Cascades. Larch Mountain also provides picnic areas and other hiking trails, and it's a popular place to watch the Perseid meteor shower in August. (The road may be closed in winter—its final elevation is 4,050 feet.) A note of caution: The Larch Mountain detour is slow going, so it may not be for everyone. And don't bother if the cloud cover is thick. But the payoff is worth it if you have the time and if the weather is cooperative.

Returning to the highway, turn right to continue down the Scenic Highway. After a number of hairpin turns, you will find yourself at **Crown Point Vista House**, a pretty stone building that affords views west and east of the river and the Gorge. Crown Point is especially popular at sunset, when the river washes west into a red and orange sky underlined by the lights of the city and the view east fades into soft purple twilight as the cliffs grow dim. (See the Attractions chapter for more on Crown Point Vista.) East of

Crown Point Vista, the highway turns into the forest and provides access to—and views of—the dozens of waterfalls that trickle and gush from the cliffs above on their urgent errand to meet the Columbia below. Many of the biggest falls have waysides, trails, and parks that invite you to explore and linger. Latourell Falls, easily accessible via a paved, 150-yard trail, plummets from a basalt outcropping 250 feet above. Bridal Veil and Wahkeena Falls are next, and then you will arrive at **Multnomah Falls**. Multnomah Falls—at 620 feet, the second-highest waterfall in the United States—is a premier attraction in the state (and indeed warrants a special exit from I-84, in addition to being accessible via the Columbia Gorge Highway). Most visitors are content to view the falls from the viewing area behind the **Multnomah Lodge** (503-695-2376; www.multnomah fallslodge.com), a beautiful historic building that houses a restaurant, gift shop, and information center. For the information center, call the U.S. Forest Service at 503-695-2372. Some visitors venture a bit farther, taking the paved path first to the bridge beneath the falls and then to the top of the falls (1 mile, uphill).

But if you want to make the effort to hike the entire 3.25-mile loop, you will be rewarded with a cool, sylvan walk that takes you along the ridge just west of the falls and past Upper Wahkeenah Falls, before dropping back down to the parking lot. To follow this loop, from the paved overlook spur, you'll continue along the unpaved trail, across the stone bridge, until you reach the junction for the Perdition Trail. Bear right along this trail along the ridge for 1.2 miles. The trail has a number of stone staircases, and just past the steepest and longest set, you will meet the Wahkeenah Trail. Take this, staying to the right and passing Upper Wahkeenah Falls. You'll meet with pavement again about half a mile before Wahkeenah Falls; then stay on the path above the highway for another half mile, until you reach the Multnomah Falls parking lot.

Resuming your trip, the next stop on the Columbia Gorge Highway is **Oneonta Gorge**. Here the reward of the trail, should you choose to take it, is a walk behind the falls. Horsetail Falls is next, before the highway connects back to I–84 at milepost 35.

Once you are back on the freeway, the next destination is the **Bonneville Dam** (541-374-8820), the oldest Army Corps of Engineers project along the Columbia River. It's fun to watch the salmon struggle up the fish ladder along the dam or to throw chow at the fry in the nearby Bonneville Hatchery. (See the Attractions and Kidstuff chapters for more information on the Bonneville Dam and Fish Hatchery.)

i For maps, trails, and other information on the Columbia Gorge, call the Columbia Gorge National Scenic Area offices at (541) 308-1700 or visit www.fs.fed.us/r6/columbia/forest.

About 2 miles past the Bonneville Dam is the town of Cascades Locks, as well as the Bridge of the Gods, an impressive steel toll bridge that takes you across the Columbia into Washington and to the **Columbia Gorge Interpretive Center** (990 Southwest Rock Creek Drive, Stevenson, WA; 509-427-8211; www.columbiagorge.org). This museum, designed to resemble a sawmill, offers an absorbing thematic history of the Gorge based on who lived here and what they did. It is a good complement to the **Cascade Locks Museum**, back on the Oregon side (1 Northwest Portage Road; open daily May through September, noon to 5:00 p.m.; 541-374-8535). This little museum was formerly the home of a lockman. It dates from 1905 and features many fascinating artifacts and photos from life along the river 100 years ago. In front stands the Oregon Pony, the first steam locomotive on the Pacific coast and the first west of the Missouri. Cascade Locks was built around the site of the navigational pass that allowed boats around a series of Columbia River rapids. Since the building of the dam, of course, these rapids have been submerged, but Cascade Locks is a great stop because of its historic museums, its park, its summer stern-wheeler tours (see the Kidstuff chapter), and its two restaurants:

Charburger (714 Wanapa Street; 541-374-8477), which offers cooked-to-order burgers, home-baked pies and cookies, and striking views of the Columbia; and its neighbor, the **East Wind** (541-374-8380), an old-fashioned drive-in with excellent soft-serve ice cream.

Back on I–84, your next stop will be Hood River. Just west of town, at exit 62, is the historic and luxurious **Columbia Gorge Hotel** (4000 West Cliff Drive; 541-386-5566; www.columbiagorgehotel.com), famous for its dining room views and its lavish five-course farm breakfast. The pretty grounds sit atop a waterfall that plunges 208 feet.

Hood River is known for two things: windsurfing and orchards. For a span of 70 miles east and west of Hood River, windsurfers swoop and glide through the chilly Columbia waters, taking advantage of the wind that gusts persistently through the Gorge. Hood River is a pleasant little town, with many charming shops, art galleries, and restaurants. For information about windsurfing see the Recreation and Spectator Sports chapter, but also feel free to ask in any of the plentiful surf shops in town. Other stops might include the **Hood River Hotel** (102 Oak Avenue; 541-386-1900 or 800-386-1859; www.hoodriverhotel.com), an appealing 1913 vintage building that houses a good restaurant. Also try the **Full Sail Brewery**, home to some of the finest beer in Oregon (or anywhere). Guided tours are available daily on the hour from noon until 5:00 p.m. for those older than 13. And all ages are welcome at the pub if they are eating. Pub hours are noon to 8:00 p.m. daily. The brewery is found at 506 Columbia Street (541-386-2247).

Hood River is a good place to turn around and head back to Portland along I–84. But if you decide to explore further, your efforts will be rewarded.

Follow the main street of Hood River as it angles southeast on Highway 35 into the lovely Hood River Valley, home to thousands of acres of orchards and farms. Less than a mile from town, as the highway clings to the hillside, turn up the road marked by the sign designating a panorama point. This will take you to a vista point, with much of this beautiful valley laid before you. Two terrific times to visit the Hood River Valley are during the Hood River Blossom Festival, held in mid-April, and the Hood River Harvest Festival in mid-October. But at any time the trip through this pocket of traditional farmland is a journey beyond life in the city.

After leaving the valley Highway 35 starts to curve around the eastern slope of Mount Hood. Soon you begin to catch close-up glimpses of Mount Hood's glacial cap, and if you use your imagination, you can sense the wonder felt by pioneers who opted to take a path around the mountain instead of rafting down the dangerous Columbia. Just before the confluence of Highway 35 and U.S. Highway 26, a historical marker announces that you are crossing Barlow Pass, named for Sam Barlow, a trailblazer who found a way down the mountain and set up a toll road. Barlow charged $5 per wagon and 10 cents per head of cattle for those hearty and brave enough to slide and rope their wagons down the muddy slopes and treacherous canyons that are now traversed by US 26. Another historical marker shortly after the Barlow Road marker is a poignant reminder of the cost of this detour. The **Pioneer Woman's Gravesite** is a short distance from the road; there you can also view intact wagon ruts near the gravesite.

Once on US 26 heading west, there are a number of spots of interest. One is **Trillium Lake,** a picnic site and fishing hole stocked with rainbow trout. To get there take Forest Road 2656 a couple of miles before reaching Government Camp. If it's ski season, you can go to Timberline, Summit Ski area, or Mount Hood Ski Bowl (see the Recreation and Spectator Sports chapter) for some world-class downhill action. Or if you are simply thirsty and hungry, stop at **Mt. Hood Brewing Company** (503-622-0724), at the west end of Government Camp for microbrews and great sandwiches. **Timberline Lodge** (503-622-7979; www.timberlinelodge.com) is worth a visit whether or not you ski and even if no snow is on the ground. This attractive lodge, made of hand-hewn logs and great stones, is a National

Historic Landmark built in 1937 as part of the Works Progress Administration (WPA). It stands as a monument to the talents of its builders and to its era. The lodge also features an outstanding restaurant, as well as several cafes and other eating areas. (If you are taking two days, it would make an excellent halfway stop.)

After descending from the ski zone, you'll come to Welches, a mountain town with lodging, shopping, dining, and even golf. **The Resort at the Mountain** (503-622-3101; www.theresort .com) not only offers gracious accommodations but the Three Nines golf course. You might also want to stop here at the Mount Hood Information Center for information on just about everything going on around the mountain.

One last site to see is the **Philip Foster Farm and Homestead** at 29912 Southeast Oregon Highway 211 (503-637-6324). To get there take Highway 211 at its juncture with US 26 in Sandy, and go south for 6 miles to the little hamlet of Eagle Creek. This farm was the site of a much-welcomed rest stop along the Oregon Trail, and as many as 10,000 emigrants ate their 50-cent dinners of steak, potatoes, coleslaw, and biscuits. Foster was an entrepreneurial fellow as well as a restaurateur, and he anticipated and met the needs of weary pioneers. Here they could stock up on fruit, grain, and other supplies and their livestock could partake of the Foster family's hay, before proceeding west and south into the Willamette Valley. Today you'll find a working farm complete with house, barn, garden, orchard, and blacksmith shop. Visitors are invited to help with chores. There is also a picnic spot and a general store. Hours are Friday through Sunday 11:00 a.m. to 4:00 p.m. June through August and just Saturday and Sunday during September.

MARYHILL MUSEUM

You don't have to travel all the way to England to see Stonehenge. You can drive less than two hours to the Maryhill Museum, in Goldendale, Washington, across from Biggs, Oregon. Maryhill is in a chateau built in 1914 by Sam Hill, the famous developer of the Columbia River Gorge Scenic Highway. (Hill, a Quaker and pacifist as well as an entrepreneur, also built the handsome Peace Arch on the border between Canada and the United States at Blaine, Washington.) Sam Hill named the house for his daughter Mary, building it atop the windy bluffs at a breathtaking spot where you can see the transition in the landscape from the green west to the dry and golden east. The house was never a home, however, and Hill was persuaded by his friend Loie Fuller, a pioneer of French modern dance, to transform it into a museum. She was also able to help him acquire a good collection of Rodin sculptures to display in it.

Indeed, despite its remote location, the museum boasts an impressive collection of European art as well as Native American artifacts, art, and jewelry. Hill had a number of other influential friends, among them Queen Marie of Romania and Alma Spreckles (of the San Francisco sugar family). Through them, Hill was able to secure many fine paintings and objets d'art. Maryhill is also an official site along the Lewis and Clark Trail, and since 2003 the museum has featured a number of remarkable exhibitions and programs devoted to the bicentennial of their voyage.

Maryhill's grounds are equally lovely. They cover 26 acres, with formal gardens, a sculpture garden, roaming peacocks, and stunning views of the Gorge. The museum (509-773-3733; www .maryhillmuseum.org) is open March 15 through November 15 from 9:00 a.m. to 5:00 p.m. daily. Cost is $7 for adults ($6 for seniors) and $2 for children 6 through 16. The grounds are free. You will find a cafe and gift shop at the museum.

Maryhill's full-size replica of Stonehenge is 4 miles east of the museum. Sam Hill built it as a monument for the war dead of World War I, and subsequently, the museum has added memorials to Klikitat County soldiers who died in World War II, Korea, and Vietnam. No admission is charged to visit Stonehenge.

To get to Maryhill, take I–84 to the Biggs Junction exit. Take U.S. Highway 97 north to Washington Highway 14, traveling west 3 miles to Maryhill, at 35 Maryhill Museum Drive.

NORTHERN WILLAMETTE VALLEY'S WINE COUNTRY

In the 1960s Oregon wine pioneer David Lett started planting grapes, and everyone thought he was crazy. But he had observed something important. Roughly in the same latitude as Burgundy, the great wine-producing province in France, Oregon's northern Willamette Valley has a cool marine climate, rich soil on the southern slopes of rolling hills, and a long, gentle season with ample sunny days. Now, decades later, Oregon wines hold their own against the best wines in the world.

But don't take our word for it. Taste these remarkable varieties yourself by taking a tour of northwestern Oregon's wine region. It's a delightful drive through some of the state's most bucolic countryside. Many of the wineries are open to visitors; and some are near fine restaurants and inns along one of the most popular tourist loops on the West Coast.

First, plan for a journey that starts in the morning and loops out into the wine country and back to Portland by evening. Second, stop by the **Oregon Winegrowers' Association**, 1200 Northwest Naito Parkway, Suite 400, (503) 228-8403, and pick up *Vintage Oregon*, a comprehensive guide with maps, addresses, phone numbers, examples of wine labels, and descriptions of wineries in the Willamette Valley. Or download it here: http://oregonwine.org/. We cannot emphasize enough how essential this guide is. It will tell you which tasting rooms are open to the public, the hours that tasting rooms are open, and other important information for your trip. It even has a space for note-taking. (This guide is also available at some of the better restaurants in town, and if you are staying in a downtown hotel, chances are good that the concierge has a few copies.) Give yourself time to plan a good route and to designate a driver. It will make your trip much better.

Once the planning is out of the way, you can get on the road. If you don't mind missing the **Ponzi Vineyards,** take Highway 99 southwest of Portland. Look for blue-and-white signs

A beautiful old oak tree in the midst of Oregon wine country. JAMES THOMAS

directing travelers to tasting rooms, vineyards, and wineries.

If you opt to visit Ponzi Vineyards, take I–5 to Highway 217 and on to Highway 210 for 4.5 miles to Vandermost Road. Turn left and head south, following signs to 14665 Southwest Winery Lane. Here, with the exception of January and holidays, visitors are welcome to sample the wines of the pioneering Ponzi family, who have been instrumental to the establishment of Oregon's wine industry and to its continued success.

Heading west from Ponzi or Portland, you near Newberg, one of the larger communities in Yamhill County. As you glide down a ridge into Newberg, you'll come upon two wineries across the highway from each other. **Rex Hill Vineyards**, north of the highway, has a showcase winery, an elegant tasting room with a fireplace and antiques, and some of the oldest vines in the county.

West of Newberg, as Highway 99 passes through Dundee and beyond, there is a cluster of wineries and vineyards that could take up most of your day. A worthy stop is **Erath Winery** up on Worden Hill above Dundee, where pioneering wine-maker Dick Erath produces his award-winning pinot noir. The tasting room has a terrace that is a great spot for picnicking while gazing across the Willamette Valley.

Right on Highway 99W in downtown Dundee is **Argyle**, which is housed in a former hazelnut processing plant while its tasting room is in a restored Victorian house. Dundee is also the home of two excellent restaurants: **Tina's** (760 Highway 99W, 503-538-8880), which is a highly rated place that specializes in local, seasonal dishes; and the **Dundee Bistro**, next to the Ponzi Wine Bar (Highway 99 and 7th Street; 503-554-1650).

Sokol Blosser Winery, a short drive up Sokol Blosser Lane, 3 miles west of Dundee, has a walk-through showcase vineyard—the only one of its kind in Oregon. One of the state's oldest and largest wineries, it has a tasting room open all year long, picnic grounds, and a gift shop. Many events are held here.

Continuing south, you will eventually reach the small city of McMinnville. This pretty college town is the home of the International Pinot Noir Festival (see the Festivals and Annual Events chapter) and has several tasting rooms and wine bars. If these prompt a request from your designated driver to have the evening off, you can stay at the Hotel Oregon, a McMenamin brothers operation. McMinnville is also the home of the Spruce Goose (see the Kidstuff chapter).

From here you can retrace your route a few miles north until you reach Highway 47, which takes you north past **Chateau Benoît, Hamacher,** and **Elk Cove Wineries**. Continue on until you reach Highway 10, which returns you to Portland via Beaverton.

But if you are really adventurous, there is an alternative to driving through the Oregon Wine Country. **Vista Balloon Adventures** (800-622-2309) in Newberg offers aerial tours in hot-air balloons for around $200. This is a lovely way to see wine country—though a little far from the tasting rooms.

THE OREGON COAST

About 100 miles west of Portland, you will find some of the most spectacular coastline in the world. The Oregon coast is a favorite destination for Portlanders, offering a complete range of experiences from resorts to rustic. To get there, take US 26 west, following the signs that direct you toward the ocean beaches. Once past town, this road winds through picturesque farmland before it climbs the Coast Range mountains.

When you reach U.S. Highway 101, turn north toward Astoria if you want to visit Fort Clatsop, the site of Lewis and Clark's winter encampment. This historical re-creation is as entertaining as it is educational. Or turn south on US 101 for Cannon Beach. By now you're probably ready for lunch,

and Cannon Beach, a lively beach town, has many shops and restaurants, as well as beautiful hotels and spas. Cannon Beach is the home of the famous **Haystack Rock** (at 235 feet high, the third-tallest coastal monolith in the world).

A bit farther south, you'll encounter **Neah-kahnie Mountain**, with a trail leading to its summit and a view that is breathtaking for its scope up and down the coast and back into the Nehalem Valley. Neahkahnie is an excellent viewing area for whales in the spring and fall.

Continuing south, you'll pass through the charming towns of Manzanita, Nehalem, and Wheeler. Manzanita, which lies just west of US 101, has especially good beaches, and all three towns are filled with charming shops. Next you'll reach the fishing villages of Garibaldi and Bayside and on to Tillamook. Just to the west of this friendly blue-collar burg is the **Three Capes Loop**, a 35-mile byway off US 101 between Tillamook and Neskowin. As you cruise through gentle, misty dairy country that has a time-out-of-mind feel, you'll get far enough west to check out Cape Meares to the north, Cape Lookout midway, and Cape Kiwanda at the end of the loop. This last cape is right next to Pacific City, where dory anglers compete each year in a contest to see who can launch their fishing boat into the surf, row around yet another Haystack Rock, and return with a real fish.

Just a short way down the coast is Neskowin, a sweet little town with a pretty beach in the shadow of Cascade Head, a looming monolithic outcrop favored by hikers seeking solace in a genuine rain forest. After hiking or playing on another beach for a while (who would ever get tired of beachcombing, sifting sand for shiny agates, whirling bull kelp whips, and poking at puckery sea anemones?) drive a few more miles south to the junction of US 101 and Highway 18.

Here you have a choice of directions. You can continue south along the coast, past Lincoln City on to Newport with its fascinating Oregon Coast Aquarium, Hatfield Marine Science Center, historic Nye Beach, and scenic Yaquina Head lighthouse and bird-watching station. It's an easy, if long, journey back to Portland from Newport either by backtracking to Highway 18 or heading east on U.S. Highway 20 to Corvallis and then on to I–5 and north. But it will make for a long day, so you may want to plan for a stay-over in one of the many hotels and motels along US 101.

Or you can choose to take Highway 18 and angle back to Portland, stopping for some great grub at the **Otis Cafe** at Otis Junction, 2 miles east of US 101 (541-994-2813). Just past Otis you'll enter the Van Duzer Corridor, a stretch of ancient firs that frame the road with their verdant grandeur. Beyond the forest, and past the Spirit Mountain Casino and a broad valley dotted with barns and farmhouses, you'll cruise through Yamhill County and on to Portland. Once home, after dumping sand out of your sneakers, you'll start planning another trek to Oregon's wondrous coastline to revisit favorite spots and discover a few more.

RELOCATION

Portland is repeatedly honored across the nation as being one of the best places to live. Its setting among mountains, farmland, and rivers contributes to its desirability, and so does its solid economy and unfrenzied style of life. Yet above all, we are a city of neighborhoods. And this may be the true secret of Portland's charm, the source of its community feeling. Government agencies such as Metro, nonprofit organizations such as the Coalition for a Liveable Future, neighborhood associations, far-sighted real estate developers, and plain old unaffiliated citizens keep the neighborhood spirit alive and provide a foundation for its strength to grow. After you've had a look at some of our neighborhoods, we'll turn to the topic of real estate and let you know about ways to find your own place in our beautiful metropolitan area. And we'll tell you other important facts about moving to the area.

NEIGHBORHOODS

Researchers predict that the Portland Metro area will increase to 2.5 million people in the next 50 years, an increase of about 1.5 percent each year. All these new people will have to live somewhere, but we also need to protect forests to clean the air and water (and the spirit), and we need to preserve the farmland to feed all these new residents. That's where Metro comes in. Metro planner Malu Wilkinson says that the role of the Metro government, which comprises Washington, Clackamas, and Multnomah Counties, is "to coordinate the land use policies across the region so that we grow in the direction that the citizens want." This unusual tri-county government helps to protect open spaces, to allow for coordinated transportation management, and to stabilize development by encouraging population density instead of suburban sprawl.

Metro and the kind of planning it embodies is not without its critics from both sides of the political spectrum. Developers rankle under the land-use plans, while environmentalists worry that the urban growth boundary actually encourages growth by requiring a certain amount of urban space to be dedicated to development. The best hope is that the competing interests will work in fertile tension with each other. For

example, Metro's encouragement of affordable housing and mass transportation have sparked some of the most innovative developments in the nation. Orenco Station, which was built in Hillsboro specifically to take advantage of the light-rail line, has been dubbed "America's Best Master Planned Community" by the National Association of Home Builders. This assemblage of cottages, craftsman retros, and row houses reverberates with an old village way of life. Similarly, highly accoladed projects such as the Belmont Dairy, Irvington Place, and Albina Corner, which reclaimed underused urban space and now provide attractive, mixed-use facilities and affordable housing for lower- and middle-class residents, might never have happened without the productive constraints of land-use planning.

Once again, however, the neighborhoods are key to these kinds of developments. Since neighborhood associations and other groups have much community involvement and representation, they influence deeply the nature of the planning and development that takes place around them. Some, but not all, of the Outlying Areas make use of the neighborhood spirit to encourage smart development. Newer developments may lack the strong identity that the city neighborhoods possess. And they may be less likely to acquire it, since they are often built in a way that does not foster community interaction. However, there are notable exceptions: Fairview Village, to the east of the city, is renowned for its incorporation of public, commercial, and green spaces, in addition to its pretty houses. Fairview Village also has a school and day-care facilities. Similarly, Canyon Creek in Wilsonville, built by former Metro Council member and developer Don Morrisette, is a planned community of 117 houses designed to be within walking distance of the major employers in Wilsonville. Canyon Creek Meadows also incorporates greenways, leaving unbuilt, for example, at least three acres of forested space. These new developments may mark a trend in the creation of neighborhoods, a trend that profits not just the developers, but the souls of the residents who live in them.

Old or new, upscale or downhome, Portland's neighborhoods embody the genius loci of the city. From the friendly, front-porch lifestyles of St. Johns to the funky old Victorian houses of inner Southeast Portland to the stately manors of the Dunthorpe district, Portland is home to a healthy array of diverse and distinct communities. We have 94 formally recognized neighborhoods in the city of Portland alone. This chapter is meant to serve as an overview of Portland Metro area neighborhoods. In the first section of this chapter we try to give you a feel for Portland's four distinct areas—Southwest, Northwest, Southeast, and North/Northeast—and also to introduce you to Vancouver and at least some of the communities outside Portland's formal borders.

Southwest Portland

The heart of Southwest Portland is the downtown area. Not only is it the home of many businesses, cultural organizations, government agencies, and public spaces, it is also the home of many residents, who like the urbane atmosphere and the proximity to work and nightlife. Portland's downtown is a mecca for shoppers, with department stores such as Nordstrom, Macy's, and Saks Fifth Avenue, as well as the Pioneer Place shopping center, all within several blocks. Pioneer Courthouse Square

is a popular meeting place and offers a wide range of free, live entertainment during the noon hour. But despite the tempting stores, the impressive statues, and the well-designed business towers, nothing defines downtown Portland as well as the Willamette River.

In the early 1970s the city underwent a huge renewal project, ripping apart a four-lane highway along the west bank of the Willamette and transforming it into beautiful Tom McCall Waterfront Park. It is the site of numerous concerts, festivals, and celebrations as well as a showplace for community events. Eight blocks west, Park Blocks, a 25-block boulevard of trees, grass, flowers, fountains, and statues, offers another urban refuge for workers, shoppers, and students. Nearby are many of the city's most important cultural and recreational facilities, including the Portland Art Museum, the Oregon Historical Society, the Performing Arts Center, and the Arlene Schnitzer Concert Hall. Just outside the inner city is Washington Park, home to the Metro Washington Park Zoo, the tranquil Japanese Gardens, the World Forestry Center, and Hoyt Arboretum.

Beyond the park's boundaries to the south and west are several of the most established, picturesque, and tree-lined of all the city's neighborhoods. Collectively referred to as the "West Hills," each of these neighborhoods nonetheless has distinctive features. For example, Arlington Heights, one of Portland's most scenic neighborhoods, just west of downtown above the city center, gives residents easy access to the spectacular Portland Rose Test Gardens and all of Washington Park. The houses here tend to be older, and the architecture diverse—one house is a miniature replica of Canterbury Castle in England. Arlington Heights's neighbor, Portland Heights, also displays diverse architectural styles. Ranging from Victorian cottages to the latest contemporary dwellings, these houses are noted for their lovely gardens and spectacular views. Nestled amid the Southwest Hills, Council Crest affords extraordinary views of both the city and the western valleys. Farther west, on the other side of the hills, you'll find Multnomah Village, named by *Money* magazine as one of Portland's best neighborhoods. This charming neighborhood offers the grace of older houses and the vitality of the newer ones; but all houses are tempered by a hint of the rural past—it wasn't formally annexed until 1954, and some of the most desirable houses yet repose on unpaved roads. Multnomah Village itself is a notable shopping and business district that offers a congenial center to village life. (See the Shopping chapter.) The newest neighborhood is the South Waterfront district. This glass high-rise village across from Ross Island, reminiscent of Pacific Rim cities such as Vancouver, British Columbia, is defining itself as the leading edge of Portland development. Built on landfill along the Willamette on a parcel that was once used for building ships, the South Waterfront district is anchored by Oregon Health and Science University's Center for Health and Healing and the Portland Aerial Tram. The luxury condominiums and stellar apartments have new shops and restaurants on the ground floors, and along the banks of the river, greenway trails are under construction. The residents, however, are already defining themselves with a strong community voice; they are deeply involved in shaping the character of the neighborhood.

More Southwest Neighborhoods

CORBETT-TERWILLIGER AND LAIR HILL

On a 4-mile-long ribbon of land along the west bank—one of the most scenic segments of the Willamette River—you'll find the Corbett-Terwilliger and Lair Hill neighborhoods, directly south of downtown Portland. Residents here are indirectly responsible for preserving the character of our city. Years ago, when urban renewal crept its way to the north end of these older neighborhoods, a backlash resulted in establishment of the South Portland–Lair Hill Historic Conservation District, the first protected historic district in Portland. This was an appropriate gesture, given that Portland's very first building, a cabin constructed by William Johnson in 1842, was built in what became this neighborhood, near Southwest Gibbs and Interstate 5.

Not all preservation is good, however, and not all renewal bad. A section of the area's riverfront is in the process of converting from heavy industry to upscale residential and business development.

HILLSDALE NEIGHBORHOOD

Hillsdale is just 3 miles from downtown Portland, but its location atop the Southwest Hills gives it an almost rural feel. Hillsdale's commercial district evolved in the 1940s along old dairy-cow pastures, and after the war, as suburban-style houses were built in the area, the virtues of things such as sidewalks were forgotten. Now Hillsdale residents are guiding developments to foster accessibility and community. Southwest Terwilliger Boulevard, one of Portland's favorite scenic routes for bikers, pedestrians, and cars—and the product of community planning efforts—is a hallmark feature along with Oregon Health and Science University, one of the major employers in the state.

HAYHURST NEIGHBORHOOD

A unique feature of the Hayhurst neighborhood area is the Alpenrose Dairy, which continues to operate as a dairy, as well as serving as a community center offering sports fields, picnic facilities, entertainment, and bicycle racing. In a sense, Portland's most familiar dairy symbolizes the wholesomeness of this middle-class area, which is made up mostly of single-family houses and is creating ways to accommodate growth while preserving its distinctive neighborhood character and livability. Hayhurst School and its nature learning garden and Pendleton Park with its neighborhood planting projects are some of the community-friendly features of this neighborhood.

GOOSE HOLLOW

Goose Hollow's name goes back to the 1870s when women who lived there raised flocks of geese. Early residents of the district were the barons who guided the destiny of the region from its raw pioneer days through the prosperity of the 1890s and the following war years. But while Portland boomed between 1970 and 1990, Goose Hollow slumbered. However, since 1991, Westside light rail and high-density planning have spurred unprecedented developments, pumping more than $50 million in improvements into the 3.2-square-mile district. Bordered by downtown, Washington Park, the University District, and Burnside Street, the western end of the district is hilly and residential, while the eastern portion is flat and commercial.

Northwest Portland

Across Burnside Street, Northwest Portland (one of the area's most popular places to live) offers panoramic views of the mountains, the Willamette River, and the city. Northwest Portland is a delightful blend of old and new and of classic and Bohemian, and community interaction is extremely high in this area as residents and neighbors strive to create a secure and friendly living environment. Northwest Portlanders find boutique shopping, art galleries, coffee, and culture within easy walking distance. Well-built and beautifully reconditioned Victorian houses, huge fir trees, and lush parks and gardens provide an old-world feel. Though many of its three-story Victorian estates have been converted into condominiums, Northwest Portland has retained its elegance and appeal. The numerous shops on Northwest 21st and 23rd Avenues offer unusual and distinctive wares, though chain stores like Pottery Barn and Gap are slowly encroaching. Still, this is one of the toniest areas of the city—also one of the most densely populated.

Excellent hospital facilities, fine schools, many banks, good grocery stores, and a highly efficient public transit system that includes the new streetcar system add to the desirability of Northwest Portland. Possessing a wide range of socioeconomic diversity, the area supports an impressive variety of employment, volunteer, and recreation opportunities. And it's moments away from Washington and Forest Parks as well as downtown.

More Northwest Neighborhoods

PEARL DISTRICT

Money magazine designated the Pearl District as one of the best places to live in the best city to live in. This comes as a surprise to some old-timers. Not long ago the area was a grimy, downtown postindustrial wasteland. Today it is one of the most fashionable locations in the close-in city. Extensive renovations and adaptive use of historical and other structures have led to lofts, row houses, new restaurants, theaters, art galleries, and new retail activity. Also, a flurry of important new urban creative-commerce entrepreneurs, ranging from small Internet service providers to internationally known advertising and multimedia companies, are staking out territory here.

In addition, the Pacific Northwest College of Art, PICA, and other arts organizations have chosen the Pearl as their home. Well-clad entrepreneurs sip coffee next to spiky-haired students; art supply stores and antiques shops vie for attention; cool lofts with cityscape views perch above truck-loading ramps. The atmosphere in the Pearl is a heady brew of past and future productively engaging. Important retail and residential developments include the Brewery Blocks (on the site of the old Henry Weinhard Brewery), between Burnside and Northwest Davis, as well as an innovative restoration project by Ecotrust. The latter, the Jean Vollum Natural Capital Center, 907 Northwest Irving, holds a major Patagonia retail shop in addition to other shops and offices. This restored brick building is constructed with eco-friendly timber and energy-efficient spaces. Its roof is planted with native vegetation that keeps the building cool and filters rainwater.

The Pearl District draws urbanites young and old, and more recently, families with children. Many of the newest shops and cafes are taking advantage of this new demographic trend. The work in progress here should give hope to cities everywhere.

LINNTON

The great documenter of Oregon, Ralph Friedman,

writes that the cofounder of Linnton, Peter Burnett, foretold that Linnton would one day "be the great commercial town of the territory." Peter Burnett went on to be elected the first governor not of Oregon but California, which is telling. Linnton was platted in 1843; at the time, its location near forest and river seemed preferable to the flooding swamp of Portland. By the time it incorporated, in 1910, the bustling town had its own train service, two newspapers, and a jail. In 1921 the plywood mills employed more than 1,000 workers, but that prosperity came to a halt during the Depression and then was killed beyond recovery during the 1940s, when fires burned down the mills. Things got worse as the century crept along, when trucks began to replace railroads as the favored means of transportation, and, in a concomitant development, Linnton's business district was demolished to make way for a larger road.

Today, however, Linnton is being rediscovered and its property is among the newly desirable. New houses are being built on the hillside and younger families are moving in. The neighborhood association has embarked on a master plan to guide the developments along the river and the highway.

OLD TOWN–CHINATOWN NEIGHBORHOOD

As its name implies, Old Town–Chinatown is one of the pioneer neighborhoods of Portland. Besides serving as the Chinese District, the city's early docks and railroad station were teeming with sailors on shore leave and loggers from the nearby woods, creating colorful—if rowdy—city scenes.

This neighborhood, which lies just east of the Pearl District, serves as a gateway to downtown Portland. Art, music, culture, great ethnic food, unique architecture, small businesses, major corporations, and residents of all income levels thrive here. Numerous social service agencies harmoniously coexist with for-profit businesses. The diversity of the residential population is reflected in the housing, which ranges from single-resident hotels to upper-end apartments and lofts. The Chinese and Japanese cultural roots of the area are manifested in old buildings as well

as new developments, particularly in the Classical Chinese Garden on Northwest 3rd and Everett.

i Want to know more about Portland's neighborhoods? Check out the useful Web site sponsored by the Office of Neighborhood Involvement Programs and Services: www.portlandonline.com/oni.

Southeast Portland

The east side of Portland has seen a renaissance during the last decade. Expansive renovation, busy commercial activity, and general vigor have ignited the return to the city of many former suburbanites and the reclamation of the city by confirmed urbanites who always understood the virtues of established neighborhoods with beautiful parks, good schools, and appealing architecture, especially in the close-in neighborhoods. These neighborhoods offer a reduced commute time and greater access to cultural life than the suburbs. The Hawthorne and nearby Belmont Districts, which are subdivided into many distinctive neighborhoods such as Richmond, Sunnyside, and Buckman, are filled with single-family houses and mixed-use apartment buildings. Bakeries, coffeehouses, boutiques, music shops and bookstores, pubs, and restaurants are within walking distance of many houses, buses run frequently, and street life is abundant. Historic Sellwood is known for its Antique Row, composed of more than 50 antiques stores tucked into the neighborhood of Victorian houses and turn-of-the-20th-century architecture. Where Sellwood meets the river, you'll find Oaks Bottom, home to the Oaks Bottom Wildlife Sanctuary, a refuge for herons, beavers, ducks, and other marsh animals and birds. Here, the neighborhood floats in houseboats along the river's edge. Sellwood is also renowned for its strong community spirit. Westmoreland is graced with one of the city's most beautiful parks, while Eastmoreland's residential neighborhood, across McLoughlin Avenue, is quiet and tranquil, bordered by the lush Eastmoreland Golf Course, Reed College, Crystal Springs

Lake, and the Crystal Springs Rhododendron Gardens. Eastmoreland claims on city surveys to be the happiest neighborhood in all of Portland.

Surprisingly—given its proximity to downtown—inner Southeast Portland has taken longer than other neighborhoods to complete its revival. It might be because its early renewal efforts lost momentum, or it might be because much of it is industrial, but for whatever reason, its renovation seemed to stall. It remained purely industrial.

That is now changing, and there are signs of mixed development. The Eastbank Esplanade opened up the east side of the river to pedestrians and cyclists, and they love the subtle promise of the west views of the Willamette and the city skyline. By connecting all the bridges from the Steel Bridge to the Sellwood Bridge, the Esplanade seems to have shaken things up and people are looking at this chicly industrial area once again. For example, more influential restaurants opened in the past several years in inner Southeast Portland than in any other neighborhood—the chef behind nationally acclaimed Le Pigeon chose a renovated storefront in Southeast Portland for his restaurant, and chef Dave Machado opened up not just one but two major restaurants in the area (Lauro and Vindalho). New restaurants seem to open weekly along Southeast Division, and Southeast Belmont is is a mecca for coffeehouses—Stumptown Coffee has two of them there. Southeast Portland is more affordable than almost any other place in Portland for both business and houses; if you factor out the high prices of Eastmoreland, the houses in Southeast Portland are probably the best value for the money in town right now.

The trendiest neighborhood in town is "LoBu"—Lower Burnside—home of the Doug Fir Lounge, the Jupiter Hotel, and Simpatica supper club. The enterprising folks who have started businesses there took advantage of the fact that the area had been stuck in a time warp and used it to their advantage, since everything comes around again eventually. Technically, LoBu straddles both Southeast and Northeast Portland, but in terms of spirit and aesthetic, it is Southeast all the way.

More Southeast Neighborhoods

ARDENWALD–JOHNSON CREEK NEIGHBORHOODS

Overlooking the Willamette and bounded by several creeks, the scenic Ardenwald–Johnson Creek neighborhood lies between Portland and the pioneer river town of Milwaukie and is a part of Clackamas and Multnomah Counties. The neighborhood sits on a bluff and most houses are modest post–World War II structures, but the area was originally settled on land donation claims in the 1800s.

The Johnson family, among the earliest settlers and for whom Johnson Creek is named, is still active in efforts to maintain the creek, which is known for its untamed rampages in the springtime.

The Springwater Corridor Trail, one of the area's greatest natural amenities, the Tideman Johnson Park, and the Milwaukie riverfront are a few of the noteworthy features that lend character to these neighborhoods. Housing in this area is available in a wide range of styles and prices.

HOSFORD-ABERNETHY

Also called Ladd's Addition, this neighborhood was settled in the mid-1800s. In the southeast sector, Hosford-Abernethy is one of Portland's oldest neighborhoods. The Ladd tract—one of the nation's first planned communities, with sidewalks, paved streets, electricity, and a streetcar line—began developing early in 1900. After World War II many of the residents abandoned the neighborhood in favor of the suburbs, and the area declined. Beginning in the 1970s hundreds of historic houses have been restored, bringing back its sense of neighborhood, and now it might be considered an exemplar of good planning. One hundred years later, this neighborhood has some of the most valuable property in the city.

Retail storefronts, schools, parks, churches, community gardens, movie houses, live theater, restaurants, and coffee shops are within easy walking distance, but the centerpiece is still Ladd Circle's beautiful garden and the little shops that surround it, which provide the neighborhood with a meeting place and a focus.

ℹ️ Each April *Portland Monthly* magazine (www.portlandmonthlymag .com) devotes itself to describing the climate of real estate and emerging trends— and gives their stamp of approval to the 20 top neighborhoods and why they consider them such, including statistics on commute times, crime rates, and other information of interest. This popularity contest—of great interest to homeowners all over town—is not available online, but you can buy back issues from the Web site.

HAWTHORNE BOULEVARD

Southeast Portland's hip Hawthorne Boulevard supports a thriving district. Here, high-density housing meshes with retail activity, fashioning one of the city's premier shopping and living districts. Pedestrian-friendly and lined with gift stores, period clothing shops, and distinctive restaurants, this district is bordered by the Central Eastside Industrial District, home to the Oregon Museum of Science and Industry and industrial plants that provide 20,000 jobs.

Hawthorne Boulevard ends at the base of Mount Tabor, an extinct volcano and one of the city's most beloved parks. The four Mount Tabor reservoirs hold a large portion of Portland's drinking water, piped straight from the pristine Bull Run Reservoir. The park is blessed with an abundance of picnic tables, trails, bike paths, and stands of old growth Douglas firs and other trees. Its panoramic view of downtown and the West Hills should not be missed, especially at sunset.

North/Northeast Portland

Many Oregonians regard this section of Portland as an area of tremendous opportunity. Here, Portlanders are rightfully proud of their old, well-established neighborhoods featuring lovely houses and elegant, historic mansions. And that pride has been refreshed, since many intense

redevelopment activities are pumping new life and vitality into this section of the city, making it a more exciting and appealing place to live, work, and visit.

Beautiful older houses line the tree-shaded streets in the Northeast neighborhoods of Laurelhurst, Irvington, and Alameda. Some of the houses in the Alameda neighborhood, especially those along the periphery of the ridge, afford good views of the Willamette River and the downtown skyline. Alameda and Irvington share schools and shopping districts, and both are among the most highly-prized neighborhoods in town.

Attractive shopping areas draw people from around the region, and so does Portland's Convention Center, between the Lloyd District and the river. The MAX train stops outside the center's north entrance and also serves the adjacent Rose Quarter, a 43-acre complex featuring the Memorial Coliseum arena, the Rose Garden arena, the One Center Court entertainment complex, and four parking garages. The Rose Quarter hosts a variety of sports events, including the Portland Trailblazers, the Portland Winter Hawks, college basketball, and indoor soccer. Around Lloyd Center, the Northeast Broadway Business District is blossoming, and just east, the delightful Hollywood District offers a wonderful blend of affordable housing and great small shops. Grant Park is another popular neighborhood. With the eponymous park at its center, this tree-lined area of pretty single-family houses, many of which were built in the 1920s and 1930s, has great schools, an incredibly convenient location, and a superfriendly vibe.

Other neighborhoods farther north, such as Hayden Island, St. Johns, and Kenton, offer their own distinctive charms. These areas, rich in character and history, are blessed with many well-tended parks and green spaces.

More North Portland Neighborhoods

OVERLOOK NEIGHBORHOOD

Nestled along a high bluff above the Swan Island industrial area and Willamette River Overlook in North Portland, the Overlook neighborhood was once the home of many shipyard workers. Today it has drawn a diverse ethnic population, reflected in an elementary school population among whom 22 percent study English as a second language.

This historically rich district is home to Kaiser Town Hall, a cherished neighborhood meeting place; popular Overlook Park; Saint Stanislaus Church and Polish Hall, the site of a yearly festival and repository of cultural heritage; the Interstate Firehouse Cultural Center, a recycled firehouse used for a wide variety of community activities; and the Overlook Community Center. With its beautiful older homes, it is undergoing a major gentrification boom.

BRIDGETON

The first bridges over the Columbia River crossed here, giving Bridgeton its name. Local anglers once moored their boats in little floating shanties that later gentrified into Bridgeton's delightful floating houses. The Columbia River outpost is now rebuilding itself as a dense urban community as houses built in the 1920s along a streetcar line for local meat-packing plant workers are being replaced with townhouses, hotels, condos, and commercial buildings. The old-timers are working together with their new neighbors to create a healthy living environment and to keep the waterways a refuge for wildlife and native plants as well as people. Bridgeton is working to accommodate higher density development slated for this area, using zoning tools such as design review to maximum advantage.

ST. JOHNS–CATHEDRAL PARK NEIGHBORHOOD

At the tip of the North Portland peninsula near the confluence of the Columbia and Willamette Rivers lies Cathedral Park and adjacent St. Johns, one of Portland's oldest communities. Once an independent village, it still has the feel of a small community, especially in its bustling retail district. The industrial area surrounding St. Johns is a source of employment for residents but also a point of conflict as the community struggles to protect its

livability and adjacent natural resources. The St. Johns Bridge, the jewel of Portland's bridges, is the area's most visible landmark, and the graceful arches of its base give Cathedral Park its name. The popular park represents a 10-year effort by the locals to preserve some of the riverfront for public use. The area is also home to Smith and Bybee Lakes, both unique natural and recreational resources.

More Northeast Portland Neighborhoods

CENTRAL NORTHEAST NEIGHBORHOODS

The Central Northeast area holds nine sprawling neighborhoods, three distinct business districts, and the 50,000 people who live and work there. This colorful section of the city includes a contrasting blend of semirural areas and intensely urban ones and a diverse and multicultural population.

A few of the highlights include the Southeast Asian Vicariate, the cultural hub of the area's Southeast Asian population; the historic and wonderfully refurbished Hollywood Theatre, namesake of its neighborhood and a community restoration project; the Villa de Clara Vista, a housing project for the Latino population; and East Columbia, a farming community on the Columbia River. Also, the Grotto, a religious retreat and a place of quiet beauty and solitude, is an important attraction.

PIEDMONT NEIGHBORHOOD

Piedmont was originally developed as Portland's first suburban community—and a bit of a snooty one at that. Renters were discouraged, and no commercial activity was allowed in the district. Lovely Edwardian houses are a feature of the neighborhood.

Piedmont's character changed during World War II, as Kaiser began to employ shipbuilders, who flocked to the pretty, nearby houses in Piedmont and either bought them or rented them. Although this solid neighborhood was once a popular choice for starter houses, its stability was disrupted by the recession of the 1980s and a wave of crime problems. Thankfully the area is enjoying an unprecedented rejuvenation as a wide range of community development projects are under way. These include foot patrols, landlord training seminars, concerts in Peninsula Park, a first-time homebuyer's club, and other projects that promote property improvements.

2008 Average House Prices by Area

Portland

North	$268,000
Northeast	$312,000
Southeast	$284,000
West	$503,000

Outlying Areas

Gresham/Troutdale	$254,000
Milwaukie/Clackamas	$371,000
Oregon City/Canby	$306,000
Lake Oswego/West Linn	$577,000
Northwest Washington County	$394,000
Beaverton/Aloha	$280,000
Tigard/Wilsonville	$378,000
Forest Grove/Hillsboro	$293,000

(Figures are from the Realtors Multiple Listing Service and reflect first-quote averages for the period ending February 2008. "West" includes both Northwest and Southwest Portland.)

CONCORDIA NEIGHBORHOOD

A large, northeast Portland neighborhood dating back to the turn of the century, Concordia was once considered a suburb. Now indisputably urban, this neighborhood is an exemplar of urban renewal. Thanks to the efforts of the neighborhood association and enterprising entrepreneurs, the commercial spine of this area, Alberta Street, is a vital, thriving artery. Concordia University, for which the neighborhood was named, is just 3 miles from downtown and continues to play an important role in the area's positive changes.

A showcase of these positive developments is the old Kennedy School, a neighborhood landmark since 1915. Declared surplus decades ago by the school district, the building slowly deteriorated over the years as competing interests wondered what to do with it. Portland's McMenamin brothers solved the problem by converting it into a huge attraction, complete with pubs, a bed-and-breakfast inn, and a movie house. (See our Brewpubs and Accommodations chapters.) The beneficial effects of the Kennedy School development have helped to revive the real estate market in the area and have spilled over into nearby neighborhoods.

SABIN NEIGHBORHOOD

Sabin is another highly diverse residential neighborhood comprising mostly older houses that has gentrified mightily since 2000. In recent years the nonprofit Sabin Community Development Corp. has developed more than 100 units of housing for very-low-income families in the area.

In other endeavors, Sabin hosted Portland's first multicultural festival and stages an annual Alberta Street Festival on the revitalized Alberta Corridor. Tree plantings and murals add to the friendliness and attractiveness of the area. Retail activity is starting to take off, and urban pioneers are buying their first houses in this area, where handsome old houses may still be reasonably priced.

ELIOT NEIGHBORHOOD

Formerly the city of Albina, which was established in 1872 and annexed to Portland in 1891, the Eliot neighborhood in inner Northeast Portland started out as a community of European immigrants. Today it is one of the foremost residential and cultural centers of the African-American community.

From 1960 to 1990 the area lost more than half its housing to urban renewal projects,

Community gardens are thriving in Portland's neighborhoods—including this one in the Sabin neighborhood.
RACHEL DRESBECK

conversion to business and institutional use, and neglect, but the Albina Community Plan is helping it to rebound. The Eliot neighborhood is increasing its density and restoring its population, and it also received a commitment from the city to end conversion of housing land to other uses.

HAZELWOOD/GATEWAY NEIGHBORHOOD

Saddled atop the old Barlow Trail, one of the earliest pioneer routes across the Cascade Mountains into Portland, is Hazelwood. This neighborhood stretches throughout eastern Portland on both sides of Burnside, and most of the area's housing was built during the post–World War II development boom of 1946 to 1960. Some of these developments include high-quality projects such as Cherry Blossom Park. Hazelwood, like most of the outer east area, remained unincorporated until it was annexed to Portland in the 1980s.

This has been a combined blessing and curse. It allowed the community to acquire new urban services but also forced it to adapt to a new political system and absorb new development at a fast pace. Other distinctive features of Hazelwood include the new East Portland Police Precinct, Midland Branch Library, the Gateway Apartments mixed-use project, Midland Park with plantings by local students, and the blossoming Gateway business area.

NORTH MISSISSIPPI AVENUE

Both historic and innovative, North Mississippi Avenue is undergoing a renaissance. This neighborhood was a vibrant hub in the early 20th century, complete with its own streetcar line. But history passed it by and left it with vacant lots and buildings, crime, and deterioration. After suffering generations of neglect, North Mississippi

Avenue is now filled with young entrepreneurs who are bringing the deserted storefronts to life and filling the vacant lots with gardens and new buildings. Cafes, art galleries, bakeries, flower nurseries, antiques stores, and other mom-and-pop enterprises are revitalizing the street, and many of these urban pioneers make their homes here as well, living above or next to their businesses. Unlike many neighborhood improvement projects, this one has been specifically designed to protect its longtime residents from the unintended consequences of gentrification, and residents see it as a model for future urban renewal. Its present reputation, however, is that it's one of the hippest neighborhoods in Portland.

i Community newspapers are the glue that holds the neighborhoods together. Neighborhood association meetings, traffic plans, and discussions with local legislators and officials combine with personal essays, advertisements, and advice columns to provide community spirit and critical information for residents. Look for papers locally in stores, coffee shops, and kiosks—and see the Media chapter for more information.

Vancouver

In the blink of an eye, Vancouver increased in size from 26 square miles to more than 44 square miles and nearly doubled its population from 68,000 residents to 128,000. At the stroke of midnight on January 1, 1997, with the Eastside annexation, Vancouver, which sits across the Columbia River directly north of Portland, became the fourth-largest city in the state of Washington and the second-largest city in the Portland Metropolitan region.

The seat of Clark County, Vancouver is one of the fastest-growing regions in the United States. This burgeoning high-tech port and city, with a current population of more than 160,000, was established as a fur-trading center by the Hudson's Bay Company in 1825. The trading post and historic Fort Vancouver, surrounded by a fertile plain, soon became the commercial center for the Pacific Northwest. Although neighboring Portland's superior port facilities made it the leading city of the area, Vancouver's role remained essential to the economy and character of the region.

Outlying Areas

West of Portland

BEAVERTON

Midway between Mount Hood and the Oregon coast, Beaverton is 7 miles west of downtown Portland in Washington County at the crossroads of U.S. Highway 26 and Highway 217. With a population of more than 80,000, and its status as the largest city in Washington County (total population of more than 500,000), this suburb of Portland is coming into its own as a mini-metropolis.

Spread over 15 square miles, the town features many shopping areas, including Beaverton Mall, Beaverton Town Square, and Washington Square. Tree-lined streets highlight the clean neighborhoods, while a 25-mile network of bike paths and trails connect its well-groomed playgrounds and green spaces. Building activity is vigorous.

In the city itself there are 100 parks—one within a half-mile of every house—encompassing 1,000 acres and offering 30 miles of hiking trails. Beaverton is relatively prosperous and its school district is one of the most esteemed in the state. However, the major traffic artery leading to Beaverton, US 26, or the Sunset Highway, becomes quite congested, particularly during peak traffic hours.

HILLSBORO

Incorporated in 1876, the city of Hillsboro has grown from a tiny farming community into a modern city of nearly 90,000 residents. Originally called Hillsborough, the city was named for David Hill, one of the pioneers who crossed the Oregon Trail and became one of the state's original legislators.

About 20 minutes due west of Portland, Hillsboro is spread out over 19 square miles in the heart of the Tualatin Valley. Today, as the seat of Washington County in the heart of one of Oregon's booming high-tech communities, Hillsboro lies within the 9,000-acre Sunset Corridor, Oregon's fastest-growing economic development region. Many impressive facilities have sprung up in Hillsboro, including one of the highest-quality corporate parks in the United States: 319-acre Dawson Creek Park, which contains seven lakes, fountains, promenades, and more than 5 miles of pedestrian and bicycle trails.

TIGARD AND TUALATIN

Tigard and Tualatin are the southwest outposts of the metro area, both characterized by major new commercial, industrial, high-tech, and residential development. About 45,000 residents live in Tigard; many commute to Portland, but others work in nearby electronics or computer firms. It's a young town—a third of its residents fall in the 20 to 44 age demographic. Tualatin had 750 residents in 1970. It now has 25,000, the great majority of whom arrived between 1990 and 1999, when the city grew by more than 45 percent. Its gazillion new housing developments are big hits with families—there are more children than 20- to 44-year-old adults here. As with Tigard, many people find work close to home in business services, manufacturing, and other modern forms of employment; there also remains a great deal of agricultural work in the area.

East of Portland

FAIRVIEW

Incorporated in 1908, this scenic, east-county town is just off the Columbia River and near Sandy Boulevard and Interstate 84. Landmarks of this charming village include Fairview Lake and popular Blue Lake State Park (see the Kidstuff chapter for children's activities in the park). The planned housing community of Fairview Village—a showcase of single-family houses, row houses, and duplexes—is inside city limits, as is a vintage Grange Hall. The 9,700 residents have their own grade school and post office as well as a city hall and other important civic buildings. Fairview, wedged between the city limits of both Portland and Gresham, has a distinct flavor of its own, accentuated by the river, lakes, and forests.

GRESHAM

Once a land of berry fields and farmland, Gresham has blossomed into a bustling city of 100,000 residents while still retaining its small-town appeal. Now the state's fourth-largest city, Gresham sits at the east end of the MAX light-rail system, providing its residents with cheap, efficient transportation into downtown Portland. Situated in eastern Multnomah County and encompassing 22.5 square miles, Gresham is the gateway to the Columbia Gorge and Oregon's year-round playground, Mount Hood National Forest. Its downtown area is particularly appealing and easy to navigate. Colorful, pedestrian-friendly, and well-designed, it offers a wide variety of restaurants, retail shops, and services in a concentrated area. Gresham also maintains an excellent educational system. Every August, Gresham hosts the famous Mount Hood Festival of Jazz, which has showcased such renowned performers as Ella Fitzgerald, The Manhattan Transfer, and Anita Baker (see the Festivals and Annual Events chapter).

South of Portland

LAKE OSWEGO AND WEST LINN

These two riverside residential cities are pretty and quiet, with reputations for fine schools and well-to-do inhabitants. Lake Oswego, with a population of more than 36,000, is known for its older English cottage- and Tudor-style houses built in the first half of the 20th century, but today most people live in contemporary houses, many of which are in developments. However, you can find the vestiges of its sleepy rural history evident in the properties that still boast horse pastures and chicken coops. The neighborhood associations are busy and active. Lake Oswego is alluring to many people, but there's only so much of it to go around, so its neighbor West Linn has seen much growth in the past decade. In fact it's grown about 40 percent since 1970—but its residents still number only about 24,000 people. Both towns are a short commute from downtown Portland, traffic permitting.

Oregon City

This historic city 10 miles south of Portland was founded in 1844. Oregon City was the first incorporated city west of the Rocky Mountains, and when the city of San Francisco was originally platted, its papers had to be filed at the federal courthouse in Oregon City. Because the town awaited at the end of the Oregon Trail, and because Oregon City was the place where pioneers refreshed and restocked before traveling to their new farms south in the Willamette Valley, it became known as Pioneer City.

For decades the city thrived as a mill town, but today its economy is becoming much more diversified, and its population is nearly 30,000—and growing. Housing developments seem to be springing up in its outlying areas almost overnight. The downtown area, nestled on the banks of the Willamette River, is still a beehive of commercial, retail, and community activity.

Milwaukie-Gladstone

Small-town charm, life on the waterfront, easy access to big city amenities—all these describe Milwaukie, the City of Dogwoods. Situated between Oregon City and Portland on Highways 99 East and 224 in Clackamas County, Milwaukie, a city with more than 20,000 residents, has been named as one of the 50 best places in the nation to raise a family. Milwaukie and neighboring Gladstone (population 12,000) provide clean environments, good transportation, excellent schools and health care, and many cultural and recreational opportunities. Many shopping centers, industries, and commercial businesses flourish near this modest-to-upscale area.

North of Portland

Camas

Established in 1883 when a mill, surrounded by towering Douglas fir trees, was built on the banks of the Columbia River, Camas lies just east of Vancouver in Washington. Now better known for its explosive growth than for its reputation as a mill town, this city was named for the camas lily, a staple in the diet of the native tribes. Although

it remained a small and peaceful river town for a century, the explosive growth of the Portland-Vancouver Metro area is leading Camas and its 20 neighborhood associations to rapid changes.

REAL ESTATE

If you are new to Oregon and looking to buy a house in the Portland area, you may be in for sticker shock. People really like living in this area, and houses in the Portland Metro area are priced significantly higher than the national average. It is becoming increasingly difficult to find a decent single-family house in the city for less than $200,000—even as the market begins to reflect national trends of price declines.

This trend of high-priced real estate isn't exactly new to Portland. The cost of housing in the metro area increased by 50 percent between 1991 and 1995, and the median price (meaning as many houses were sold above that price as below it) of a house in the Portland area increased to $290,000 in early 2007, from $97,000 in 1992. The housing market's appreciation rate in 2005 ranged from 14 percent to 20 percent, depending on the area. In 2008, however, these rates dropped substantially. The average appreciation in the Metro area was 5.8 percent. No area had double-digit appreciation from March 2007 to March 2008; the highest rate was in North Portland, where houses appreciated by 8.2 percent. By the end of 2008, Portland real estate values were, like most areas in the nation, experiencing declines—about 10 percent down from the peak prices in 2007. That said, this area is better protected than many. Oregonians took out fewer adjustable-rate mortgages than Californians, among other things.

Mortgage rates are still comparatively low, making more houses affordable. While this is good news for buyers, don't look for the bottom to fall out of Portland's housing market any time soon, even in a soft market. All things considered, Portland's housing picture is a good, if expensive, one, affording shelter in price ranges to accommodate most styles of life. An abundance of small, older houses is on the market, and new house, apartment, and condo construction is under way almost everywhere you look. The cost of energy makes houses close to downtown and other centers of employment very attractive, and prices may remain more stable in these areas.

Southwest Portland

With city center as its hub, the Southwest area features every different kind of housing opportunity you could imagine. Downtown has single-family residences, duplexes, and triplex housing, and all kinds of condominiums; many have glorious views and all the amenities you could ask for. You will not find anything for less than $300,000, and prices run into the millions of dollars. Outside of downtown, the inner Southwest area in general features woodsier settings than the east side, with lots that tend to be larger than those found across the river. The west side is also more expensive—average prices here are about $474,000. Perhaps the most prestigious area is Portland Heights, featuring large, older houses with spectacular views starting at well over $500,000. Council Crest, which borders Portland Heights, is another upscale, established neighborhood with fantastic views.

The Southwest Hills, Raleigh Hills, Bridlemile, Burlingame, and Multnomah Village areas are some of the other Southwest options, each with a wide variety of old and new construction offering an array of choices for home owners. You can find small starter houses or condos for about $200,000. Goose Hollow, Lair Hill, and the Johns Landing area feature an eclectic mix of older houses with architectural charm as well as an explosion of condominiums, row houses, and town houses, many with views of the Willamette River. The prices of houses here reflect their architectural diversity.

Other Southwest Portland possibilities include the Corbett-Terwilliger and Lair Hill neighborhoods, where fine bungalows and Victorian houses sell at prices that averaged about $411,000 in 2007, though sometimes you can find them for less. Or more—some hilltop houses in the southern end of this area afford magnificent views of the Willamette River. Hillsdale and Hayhurst, like much of the area, have many fine houses on big lots with an average price of about $342,000; these neighborhoods have a slightly suburban feel to them.

Northwest Portland

No area in the city has seen higher appreciating values than the Northwest District. An urban treasure of wonderful older architecture abounds here—including Old Portland, Victorian, Georgian, colonial, and bungalow styles—but most of the single-family residences average more than $800,000. There is also a wide choice of condominiums and row houses available, some newly built, as well as older houses radiating charm and character that have been subdivided into smaller units.

The Northwest neighborhoods also include tony Forest Heights and Kings Heights with expensive new houses, most of them in developments with "custom" floor plans and other prepackaged features. In general the West Hills have most of the seven-digit gated communities. Trees are being felled daily to make room for their mini-mansions, and the forests are toppling like dominos all the way out to the Coast Range. However, the deforestation makes for spectacular views in all directions.

Perhaps the hottest area currently is the Pearl District (see the Neighborhoods section for greater detail), with many older industrial sites converted into high-end residential and combined residential-occupational loft spaces.

Southeast Portland

Southeast Portland features many established neighborhoods with a strong sense of community and average sales prices of $269,000. And a lot of people want to live there: The market is busy, with houses remaining on the market for just days or even hours for a well-priced property, even in this challenging market.

Richmond, Belmont, and Sunnyside are some of the neighborhoods along or near Hawthorne (see the Neighborhoods section); the market here is hot, the houses for sale are scarce, and when they do come up for sale, they sell in three hours. The desirable Mt. Tabor area has a wider variety of houses in price and style, and at its heart is Mt. Tabor Park, which sits on an old dormant volcano and has splendid views of Mount Hood as well as downtown. The architecturally consistent Eastmoreland has, perhaps, the most luxurious houses. Home to a lush golf course, Eastmoreland borders the stately brick and ivy Reed College and showcases older, magnificent houses, many on large lots that are priced in the $600,000 range and up. Its large canopy of trees and distinctive street layout add to its appeal. *Money* magazine designated Sellwood, the south border of the city, as a top neighborhood in Portland. You will find a mix of housing styles, ranging from modern row houses to pioneer homesteads and stately houses that overlook the river. Prices vary, of course, but you can still find good values.

The Buckman area, South Tabor, Woodstock, Brooklyn, Montavilla, and Mall 205 neighborhoods feature more modest houses with smaller price tags. These areas are near good schools and plenty of shopping areas and are a great option for those on a budget or seeking starter houses. Also, older houses in the Hosford-Abernethy area tend to be below Portland's overall median price (though its immediately adjacent neighbor Ladd's Addition features houses far beyond the median price).

North/Northeast Portland

The Northeast section, where average house prices were $337,000 in early 2008, is famous for its older, established neighborhoods of friendly, involved communities. Many lavish and expensive houses preserve the features of days gone by. Alameda, Laurelhurst, and Irvington are all just minutes from downtown and near the flourishing Lloyd Mall Shopping Center; here you will find some of the most beautiful houses in town, with prices that reflect their desirability. Alameda and Irvington not only have some of the best real estate, but they also have thriving commercial districts—particularly along the prosperous

Northeast Broadway Corridor—that add character to the neighborhood. You can find some of the city's finest shops and restaurants here; the schools tend to be very good, and the residents cosmopolitan (see the separate listings for more information on these neighborhoods). Laurelhurst is more residential but bordered by great commercial avenues—Belmont and Hawthorne to the south, Northeast Broadway to the north—and has as its centerpiece lush Laurelhurst Park. Laurelhurst, Alameda, and Irvington tend to be more expensive than other Eastside neighborhoods, but within each area you will find a variety of houses, and there are still deals for those handy with a paintbrush and wood stripper.

Bargains are getting scarcer in North and Northeast Portland. North Portland's appreciation rate was more than 20 percent from 2005 to 2006, and from 2007 to 2008 it was still more than 8 percent—the area with the fastest appreciation rates in the city.

You'll most likely find houses at less than $300,000 in Irvington Heights, the popular Boise and Sabin areas, Beaumont and Wilshire, and Parkrose. Rose City, surrounding one of the area's most popular golf courses, has seen housing costs skyrocket in the last couple of years, but it still has reasonable prices for its many charming postwar bungalows. Many great houses in all price ranges surround Glendoveer, another Northeast golf course.

Eliot has seen significant new housing development, positive new retail ventures, and the refurbishing of its historic older housing stock. In this area it is not unusual to see two or more vintage houses on the same block undergoing a restoration. The Hollywood District is a particularly appealing area characterized by an exceptionally wide range of ethnic restaurants, small businesses, and eclectic housing styles. Hollywood has been the focus of major urban renewal projects in recent years.

North Portland is still an affordable part of Portland—the average sales price in early 2008 was $283,000. North Portland is receiving much attention these days as the next neighborhood due for a major renaissance. A number of neighborhoods, such as Overlook and Arbor Lodge, have wonderful older houses at very reasonable prices, and walking-friendly, tree-lined streets. Housing in Bridgeton offers interesting possibilities and is also among the city's most affordable. North Portland is the home of the University of Portland, and the university area is considered the North's prime neighborhood, with elegant houses and panoramic views of the Willamette River and Swan Island. St. Johns, long a steadfast, unpretentious working-class neighborhood, has seen a rising popularity, particularly for new house owners.

i **For the most comprehensive picture of Oregon communities, check out the Web site of the Oregon Department of Community and Economic Development, www .econ.oregon.gov. You will find an amazingly detailed breakdown of life in Oregon, community by community, in handy pdf files.**

Vancouver and Outlying Areas

North of Portland, across the Columbia River, Vancouver is reinventing itself for a new century. Vancouver has 64 neighborhoods, and the housing prices in this oldest city in Washington state are generally lower than in Portland. But the market is booming, with tract houses and mini-mansions bursting forth from the earth seemingly overnight. During noncommute times, Vancouver is about 20 minutes from downtown Portland; Camas, its suburb to the east, just a few minutes more. The whole of Clark County is ripe with big new houses, some with acreage. Your money will definitely go far here, comparatively speaking.

South of Portland are many other livable communities. Dunthorpe is an unincorporated bit of Valhalla along the west bank of the Willamette. The large trees, lovely views, top-rated schools, and fine estates draw some of Oregon's most influential residents, among them former governors, senators, and ball players. The housing prices here belong in the "if you have to ask, you can't afford it" category.

Just to the south, and long considered the home of many of the finer neighborhoods in the entire metro area, Lake Oswego boasts a quick and scenic commute to downtown Portland as well as many lovely and grand houses. A good number of those houses—especially those commanding the highest price tags—are sprawling lakeside mansions or large, elegant houses with lake views. This postcard-like city is clean and quiet and its school district is considered top-notch. In Lake Oswego, median house prices are the most expensive in the metro area. While some properties are available for about $400,000, the view, lakeside, and country club properties cost millions of dollars. The area also boasts a multitude of condominiums, particularly in the Mountain Park area, with one-bedroom condos going for more than $100,000.

Like many of the newly developing "hot spot" communities in and around Portland, West Linn essentially started as an old farming and ranching community and, for a long time, was considered Lake Oswego's poorer cousin. In more recent years the area has seen an explosion of new construction, taking advantage of the wonderfully lush countryside, and many houses are situated on oversize lots. No longer anyone's poor relation, real estate prices in West Linn have been steadily rising; they are similarly priced to Lake Oswego's.

The second-largest community outside of Portland's city limits, Beaverton features a wide array of housing, from small houses to lavish mansions, as well as many condominiums. An average house in Beaverton sold for around $313,000 in 2007. The western edge of Beaverton, as with all the outer Southwest communities, is undergoing a development boom, with thousands of condominiums and single-family dwellings—and the Home Depots, Targets, and Olive Gardens to support them—erected in the blink of an eye where yesterday the horses were pastured and the strawberries grew.

Situated around Intel and the many newer high-tech industrial parks, Aloha and Hillsboro are also booming with new construction, and many older, established neighborhoods in these cities are loaded with cute, affordable houses. In the Hillsboro area, an average-price house sold for $285,000 in early 2008. Tigard, Tualatin, and Wilsonville are experiencing similar breathtaking development of entire villages of houses with three-car garages. The average price in these communities is higher, running to about $347,000. Although not far from Portland proper, the commute from all these towns can be a grind, especially if it in anyway involves the Sunset Highway (US 26). Enough development is happening, however, that you might be able to find a job on the west side and obviate the commute problem.

East of Portland, Gresham is the largest area outside Portland's city limits, and the once working-class and farm neighborhood has—like everywhere—seen an amazing amount of growth, while still retaining some of its wide-open appeal. Gresham provides a good blend of old and newer housing (average price is $269,000), with many affordable houses. Beyond Gresham are the rural and scenic towns of Boring and Sandy, with many houses on big spreads, for those looking to start their own "Bonanza." Many of the newer houses are priced around the $250,000 range, but there's acreage to be had for a good price.

The Clackamas area, home of the still-thriving Clackamas Town Center shopping area, is also buzzing with new construction activity, and subdivisions, featuring the typical "three-bedroom, two-bath, double-car garage" family-oriented houses, are sprouting up overnight here as well. Average prices in this area are about $335,000. Nearby Gladstone and Milwaukie have similar markets.

The real estate scene in Oregon City, Canby, and Damascus is affected by the steady growth of the Portland area. These and other surrounding communities are enjoying strong housing markets with new subdivisions popping up wherever the developers can find vacant land. The increase in growth and activity has also made historic houses in towns such as Oregon City a very hot commodity, with prices going up rapidly.

Houses—New or Used?

During the urban flight of the 1970s, many Portland families abandoned city living to flock to new houses in the suburbs. Now a revival is sweeping through the metro area as home owners are rushing back to the older houses in close-in neighborhoods.

People want to buy a piece of the past and are getting back to front-porch living and knowing their neighbors, according to Ron Rogers, a Realtor with more than 20 years' experience specializing in older houses on both sides of Portland. "The old houses have real personality and are well crafted. Plus it's great to be close to work and to walk to a movie or cafe." Although the boom started on the west side, Rogers and other experts say the east side, where properties are more available, is still torrid.

But if you are buying a vintage house and gearing up for some major improvements, don't be surprised to find a few problems lurking behind the solid wood siding and hardwood floors. Plumbing and wiring problems scare a lot of people off, but if the house has a good foundation and "solid bones," those things can be fixed. Before jumping in, get to know your house's strengths and weaknesses. (For more information about home improvement resources, see our Shopping chapter.)

The competition between house remodeling and new house construction is a pendulum that swings back and forth, but several factors in Portland are tilting the scales in favor of the fixer-uppers. With the spiraling costs of land and building materials, the expense of constructing a new house has doubled in the last decade. The increased focus on achieving higher urban population densities and maintaining the urban growth boundaries are other important factors. "A lot of people who would have bought new houses 10 years ago are now buying older houses, remodeling, and building additions," says Tom Kelly, owner of Portland's premiere remodeling company, Neil Kelly Co. "Portland is extremely eclectic so there are sizes and styles of houses for every taste and budget."

We couldn't agree more. But if you are looking for a fixer-upper, plan on doing some research before making any financial commitments. Check out several neighborhoods and talk to a few different Realtors about promising residential areas. Compare schools, property values, and the quality of the nearby roads. If you like a place in the daytime, go back at night and look around. Problems and noise often come out after respectable people pull their shades. For great inside information, check with long-time residents; they often provide a wealth of information and are good sources because they have no vested interest in a property transaction. Ask lots of questions, never assume anything, and don't be satisfied with a single opinion. The main challenge may be to find a house with no major structural problems, but you'll also want to live in a safe, clean area with decent neighbors. Remember, even if you fall in love with a house, never sign anything binding until the property is checked out by a qualified inspector.

Older Portland Houses

Older sections in many of the charming inner-city neighborhoods feature Victorian, English Tudor, bungalow, or old Portland houses along streets lined with 100-year-old trees. Here we give a description of these typical Portland houses.

CLASSICAL VICTORIANS

These are the "beautiful painted ladies," featuring solid wood trim, hardwood floors, and ornate cedar shingle siding and roofs. The ornate two- or three-story houses, built mostly between 1875 and 1910, are found all around the Portland Metro area, especially in the inner Northwest and Southeast neighborhoods. The charming and cozy Victorians can present challenges everywhere from their stone foundations to the hand pattern-cut roofs, and complications in these unique houses also frequently arise in plumbing, heating, and electrical upgrades. In addition, many Victorians are framed with 20-foot-long 2x4s so additional studs and fireblocking must be added.

CRAFTSMAN BUNGALOWS

Stone or brick foundations and large porches with battered columns are hallmarks of these houses, which were built from the turn of the 20th century to just before World War II. Low-pitched roofs, wide, overhanging eaves, and exposed roof rafters are distinctive features of these high-quality and sturdy houses. A mix of wood and brick exterior and wood shingle or composition roofs, these structures seldom present serious problems. Still, basement seepage often occurs—it is Oregon, after all—and electrical and plumbing upgrades are commonly required.

PORTLAND FOUR-SQUARE

These two-story, one roofline structures, known as "Old Portland–style" houses, were mostly built between 1910 and 1935. They may retain their original lighting fixtures, molding, and built-in cabinetry, though many of them went through unfortunate "modernization" in the 1970s and 1980s. Usually sitting on a hand-poured concrete foundation, these solid houses feature huge front porches. Though crafted with the best timber money can buy, such houses often require major kitchen renovations, insulation, and weatherization. Check to make sure the electrical system is up to date.

COLONIAL REVIVAL

Elegance and classic lines define Portland's colonial revival houses, built between 1910 and 1955. Concrete foundations, wood frames, and full basements, along with temple entry, stately pillars or columns, and a gabled roof, are their hallmarks. These two-story, wood-frame houses—often located in the city's finer neighborhoods—are also rich with moldings and trim, cornices, and elegant, small, paneled windows. Beware of lead plumbing that must be replaced with copper. Also, the colonial revival house often needs weatherizing, and because of their symmetry, additions are problematic.

WESTERN RANCH

Footings or slab foundations, all-wood frames, and composition roofs are characteristic of this type of sprawling one-level house. Of course, these popular houses are still being built, but their real heyday was between 1950 and 1960. Overall, the ranch houses present few problems; still, windows and roofs often need repairs, and interestingly, basement conversions are a popular improvement. The most flexible of all housing styles, ranches pose few limitations for vertical or horizontal additions.

NORTHWEST CONTEMPORARY

Solid concrete foundations, wood frames, and oversize two- or three-car garages typify these houses, built from the 1960s to the present. Vaulted ceilings, "great rooms," dramatically pitched roofs, heavy beams and timbers, and lots of glass lend character to these versatile two-story structures some critics refer to as "McMansions." Generally, the Northwest-style houses have fewer complications with electrical and plumbing upgrades, but be on the lookout for shoddy construction and materials, especially when it comes to siding. Windows with blown seals are a common headache, and inferior craftsmanship and construction materials can result in warped walls, squeaky floors, and worse. Also, most of these houses have little interior architectural detail; that you'll have to do yourself.

New Portland Houses

If you are interested in building a new house, choose your builder carefully and get plenty of information. You can start by calling the Home Builders Association at (503) 684-1880, or visit their really useful and well-linked Web site, www.homebuildersportland.com. Talk to your pickiest neighbors to see who they liked. Ask for written bids, get every detail of the project in writing, and have a lawyer take a look at any contract (and keep the original contract!). Don't make large down payments, and wait until after the inspection to make your final payment. Make sure contracting licenses are up-to-date and contractors are insured. Ask for references, call them, and if possible, have a look at the work itself. And remember, you get what you pay for. Look really carefully at low bids—they might be fine, but they also might reflect a misunderstanding about the work or a lack of experience with your kind of project.

NEIL KELLY CO.
804 North Alberta Street
(503) 288-7461

15573 Southwest Bangy Road
www.neilkelly.com

This top remodeling firm is worth a special mention because of its ability to combine profitable business practices with good ecological thinking and loyal ties to its North Portland neighborhood. The founder, Neil Kelly, had an eighth-grade education and rode the rails during the Depression, but he created a true Horatio Alger story with this company in the heart of North Portland. Today, his son, Tom, is carrying on the family legacy. Their business practices are efficient and responsible and dedicated to accountability. The company is committed to using sustainable woods and other components designed to promote responsible resource consumption. House repair "teams," consisting of a carpenter, sales estimator, and general contractor, run many projects but may be a single person wearing all hats—with one person handling everything, there is less overhead and no one else to blame for delays, cost overruns, and mistakes. Neil Kelly Co. and its employees have received many awards for community involvement and industry leadership, among them the designation as a "Founder of a New Northwest" by the Sustainable Northwest organization, and the Better Business Bureau's 1998 Business Integrity Award. And its philosophy and high-quality work have paid off: Neil Kelly is one of the most successful contracting companies in the Northwest. Neil Kelly offers free seminars that help people understand how to best remodel their houses—down to cooking demonstrations that feature the latest appliances. They also have an entire division devoted to assessing and improving your house from a "systems" perspective—light, heat, air, and so on. One of the few all-union general contractors in the area, for the past several years Neil Kelley has been named one of the best 100 companies to work for by *Oregon Business* magazine. (For more information on Neil Kelly Kitchens, see the Shopping chapter.)

STREET OF DREAMS
Home Builders Association of
Metropolitan Portland
15555 Southwest Bangy Road
(503) 684-1880
www.homebuildersportland.com
Builders showcases have proliferated across the land, but ours was the first! The Street of Dreams started in 1976; each year a new development is built to spotlight the latest, most mouthwatering trends in home design. The popular Street of Dreams is the place where home owners learn that two dishwashers are ever so much more convenient than one or that granite floors are not just attractive but absolutely critical. We're waiting for the houses run entirely by fuel cell, and until then, we'll take the yearly tour with covetous pleasure. And we're not alone—the summertime exhibit draws more than 80,000 people. Moreover, the Street of Dreams is a fund-raiser for Doernbecher's Children's Hospital. For several years the particularly generous firm of Wallace Custom Homes has donated time, materials, and labor to create the Miracle House, the proceeds of which benefit the hospital. Who said nothing good ever came from envy?

i If you don't know what your tenant rights are, or if you have questions in general, call the Renter's Rights Hotline at (503) 288-0130. They have experts who can help you with advice as well as information and referrals.

Condominiums and Row Houses

Portland also offers a wide variety of condominiums and row houses. While conventional houses in most desirable locations are going for well over $200,000, many buyers are turning to condominiums, which can be purchased for less. Although condo living isn't for everyone, many people who can't afford their dream house can still get into a very nice condo for much less and make a great investment. Key assets include what many condo dwellers call easy living: quick access to city shopping and employment, low maintenance, and no grass to mow, trees to prune, or snow to shovel.

In some aspects the whole city benefits from the condominium phenomenon, which promotes the concept of the Urban Growth Boundary and higher population density in the city, particularly along the main transportation corridors. Condos increase the number of owner-occupied houses, which many neighborhoods assume is a big plus because they bring stability, so in the long run, condos can increase property values for all.

Some condominiums are older, converted apartment complexes, while others are modern, upscale developments featuring recreation facilities and health clubs. Many complexes have professional landscaping reminiscent of wooded estates with hiking trails and babbling brooks.

Interiors of the modern condominiums offer features similar to what you'd find in a single-family house: designer colors, tile floors, fireplaces, and wall-to-wall carpeting. Some feature private terraces and vaulted ceilings. In downtown areas such as Goose Hollow and the Pearl District, many of the old warehouses are being converted into light, airy, and very stylish lofts.

Apartments

The Portland Metropolitan area offers a wide variety of apartments in diverse areas, designs, and price ranges. Residents can choose large apartment complexes offering security and health clubs or tiny efficiency apartments. Finding the right apartment can be challenging, especially if you are on a tight budget, but there truly is something for everyone. Apartment seekers may find downtown or the Northwest area highly competitive. However, if you are able to live in different areas such as St. Johns or outer Southeast, you increase your options immensely. Move-in expenses for a single person, including rent and damage deposits, can easily total $1,000. On the east side, a simple studio may range in cost from $500 to $700, and a two-bedroom apartment may cost anywhere from $550 to $1,500. On the west side, a similar studio ranges from $600 to $800, and a two-bedroom apartment, from $650 to $2,000.

The Sunday *Oregonian* is a good place to start an apartment search because the information is so current. *Willamette Week,* which is published every Wednesday, also has a very good rental section. *For Rent* magazine is another resource; it's available for free at many local supermarkets and in little kiosks in urban neighborhoods. Even just thumbing through the pages will help you get a feel for what is available in the Portland area, but be forewarned—most of the listings are really advertisements taken out by developers, so if you rely too heavily on this publication, you will not get a complete picture of the rental scene. Still, it can be useful for comparison purposes, and you may find a perfectly lovely apartment. But your best bet is to search Craig's List (www .portland.craigslist.org) and buy a copy of the *Oregonian.* You can also walk around in neighborhoods you'd like to live in and look for for rent signs and moving vans.

Apartment-Finding Help

If you don't want to go apartment hunting alone, a few businesses specialize in helping people find the right match. Some of these places are busy and less than efficient at returning messages; if you call on weekends, you are likely to end up talking to an answering machine. Still, these services help hundreds of people each month, and if you are new in town and without friends or relatives, or if you are trying to find a place from a distance, they can be a godsend.

Several services offer information about apartment housing over the telephone: -the Apartment Guide (503-525-0636) and NW Rental Service (503-228-5201) may be worth a telephone call.

AMERICAN PROPERTY MANAGEMENT
2154 Northeast Broadway
(503) 281-7779
This agency offers free apartment information and has more than 300 complexes to choose from. They cover a wide range of neighborhoods in the metro area and are a good place to start a search.

Other Kinds of Housing

Alternative Housing

In addition to conventional housing, the Portland scene has several communities of houseboats nestled along the Willamette and Columbia Rivers. These floating houses, for rent and for sale, are ideal for avid water enthusiasts. You can even fish out of, and tie your boat to, your front door. And best of all you may never have to worry about mowing the lawn again! The metropolitan area also has several spacious mobile home communities with large areas for double- and triple-wide houses. These often feature recreation centers, swimming pools, and tasteful landscaping. Ask your Realtor about alternative housing.

Temporary Housing

Temporary housing facilities vary from elegant suites to family units with kitchens to bed-and-breakfasts in historic mansions to bare-but-clean motel rooms. For those with travel trailers, there are a good number of RV parks surrounding the area available on weekly and monthly rents. For help in locating temporary lodging, call either the Oregon Lodging Association, (503) 255-5135, or the Portland Oregon Visitors Association, (503) 222-2223. Of course, if you are already in contact with a real estate agent, the firm's relocation department may be able to provide a list of temporary lodging facilities.

Student Housing

The state's largest college, Portland Community College, offers no student housing. Portland State University, the University of Portland, Marylhurst College, Reed College, and Lewis & Clark College all encourage full-time students to take advantage of dormitories. The student housing tends to fill up fast, and if you are planning to attend college in Portland, you should get on the housing list as soon as possible. In most cases you must register for classes first. The housing, for the most part, is first come, first serve, and the nicer accommodations go fast. There is a tremendous amount of development activity around Portland State University's blossoming University District, so more housing is available. Some students who prefer to live off campus team up with their peers and share two- or three-bedroom apartments or houses. Many families or property owners who rent out rooms or efficiency apartment to students advertise on bulletin boards near the student unions or other popular meeting places. Wherever you decide to live, keep in mind that automobile parking is a huge hassle for students, so bicycles, buses, and light rail are popular options.

Buying a House

Help for First-Time Buyers

PORTLAND HOUSING CENTER
3233 Northeast Sandy Boulevard
(503) 282-7744
www.portlandhousingcenter.org
Buying a house is the biggest, most important investment that most people make in their lives, and jumping through all those hoops can be a complicated and frustrating process. If you are a first-time house buyer, you may be eligible for help. Through the combined efforts of the federal government, Multnomah County, and the city of Portland, the Portland Housing Center offers counseling and first-time-buyer programs that can help you overcome such barriers as financing and credit problems. This program also offers classes in first-time house buying, and as many as 600 individuals each year benefit from the services. If you qualify financially, it doesn't matter whether you are new to the area or have lived here all your life. Give the Portland Housing

Center a call. Their well-trained, informed, and courteous staff can often do a preliminary screening over the telephone, and they also offer comprehensive information and referral services.

Realtors

For people relocating to a new area, one of the first and most important contacts is their real estate agent. Most of the larger real estate companies have relocation departments dedicated to making your move easier. These specialists have a good working knowledge of the area, neighborhoods, schools, and commute routes. It is important that you get along with your agent and establish a good working relationship. Be sure to ask about his or her experience with the kind of house you are looking for—and especially with the neighborhood you are interested in. Agents tend to specialize in neighborhoods, so look for an agent with the right expertise. Be prepared to answer lots of questions about your lifestyle, the type and size of house you want, and your price range. Armed with the right information, these professional house and apartment finders can start the hunt for you before you arrive and can sometimes help arrange temporary housing. You can also ask them to help you get preapproved financing, but you may be better off seeking an independent source. For more information on selecting a real estate agent, contact the Portland Board of Realtors at (503) 228-6595. Listed below are some of the area's agencies; many of them have offices citywide, in addition to the branches we have included here.

SOUTHWEST PORTLAND
THE HASSON COMPANY
10960 Southwest Barnes Road
(503) 643-9898
www.hasson.com

JOHN L. SCOTT REALTY
5457 Southwest Canyon Court
West Hills
(503) 291-1900

OREGON REALTY
8552 Southwest Apple Way
(503) 297-2523

RE/MAX—EQUITY GROUP
8555 Southwest Apple Way, Suite 330
(503) 680-1221

8405 Southwest Nimbus Avenue, Suite C
(503) 670-3000
www.equitygroup.com

WINDERMERE CRONIN & CAPLAN REALTY
2424 Southwest Vista Avenue
Portland Heights
(503) 227-5500

6443 Southwest Beaverton–Hillsdale
Highway (Raleigh Hills)
(503) 297-1033

NORTHWEST PORTLAND
COLDWELL BANKER BARBARA SUE SEAL
2275 West Burnside Street
(503) 224-7325

GREATER PORTLAND REAL ESTATE
1925 Northwest Overton Street
(503) 227-5570

HASSON
25 Northwest 23rd Place
(503) 228-9801
www.hasson.com

HOYT STREET REALTY
1130 Northwest 10th Avenue
(503) 227-2000
www.hoytstreetrealty.com

REALTY TRUST
1220 Northwest Lovejoy Street, Suite 130
(503) 294-1101

WINDERMERE CRONIN & CAPLAN REALTY
636 Northwest 21st Avenue
(503) 222-9701

733 Northwest 20th Avenue
(503) 220-1144
www.windermere.com

SOUTHEAST PORTLAND
CENTURY 21, RICKARD REALTY
12046 Southeast Sunnyside Road
Clackamas
(503) 698-7653

HANNA REALTY
6432 Southeast Foster Road
(503) 774-8893
www.hannarealty.net

JOHN L. SCOTT REAL ESTATE
4111 Southeast Woodstock Boulevard
(503) 775-4699

MT. TABOR REALTY
6838 Southeast Belmont Street
(503) 252-9653

PORTLAND'S ALTERNATIVE REALTORS
3144 Southeast Belmont Street
(503) 238-7617
www.climbatree.com

REALTY TRUST
5015 Southeast Hawthorne Boulevard
(503) 232-4763
www.realtytrust.com

SOCOLOFSKY/GMAC
3828 Southeast Division Street
(503) 234-1502

WINDERMERE REAL ESTATE, MORELAND
1610 Southeast Bybee Boulevard
(503) 233-7777

NORTH/NORTHEAST PORTLAND
CENTURY 21 REALTY, PENINSULA
6110 North Lombard Street
(503) 286-5826

ERA FREEMAN & ASSOCIATES REALTORS
1122 Northeast 122nd Street
(503) 256-0220

FARRELL & ASSOCIATES REALTORS
4772 North Lombard Street
(503) 283-1900

LAURELHURST REALTY
3046 Northeast Glisan Street
(503) 232-6750

REALTY TRUST
3902 Northeast Sandy Boulevard
(503) 416-2000

RE/MAX—EQUITY GROUP
2100 Northeast Broadway
(503) 287-8989
www.equitygroup.com

TOWNSHIP PROPERTIES INC.
4122 Northeast Broadway
(503) 281-8891

WINDERMERE CRONIN AND CAPLAN REALTY
825 Northeast Multnomah Boulevard
(503) 284-7755
www.windermere.com

VANCOUVER AND OUTLYING AREAS

COLDWELL BANKER
12000 Southeast Mill Plain Boulevard
Vancouver, WA
(360) 892-8200

14201 Northeast 20th Avenue
Vancouver, WA
(360) 574-4600

8101 Northeast Parkway, Vancouver, WA
(360) 892-7325

HASSON
15400 Southwest Boones Ferry Road
Lake Oswego
(503) 635-9801

OREGON REALTY
10205 Southeast Sunnyside Road
Clackamas
(503) 652-2260

1124 Northeast Burnside Street, Gresham
(503) 661-7344

PRUDENTIAL NORTHWEST PROPERTIES
5 Centerpointe Drive, Suite 150
Lake Oswego
(503) 624-9660

7720 Northeast Vancouver Mall Drive,
Suite 120, Vancouver, WA
(360) 256-1120

532 Northeast 3rd Avenue, Camas
(360) 834-1041

VANCOUVER REALTY
8515-B Hazel Dell Avenue
Vancouver, WA
(503) 285-1248 (from Portland)

WESTLAKE PROPERTIES
21420 Willamette Drive, West Linn
(503) 656-0323

WINDERMERE RELOCATION
Centerpointe Drive, Lake Oswego
(503) 598-0800
www.windermere.com

CHILD CARE AND EDUCATION

Portland's solid sense of community, reinforced by consistently high marks for its quality of life, makes it a fine place to raise a family. But even here, child care can be difficult to find, especially for infants and toddlers, and choosing a school causes much soul-searching among parents of future kindergarteners and of families moving into the area. Parents are often bewildered by the number of decisions they must make in choosing the nature and scope of their children's care and education. To make those decisions easier, we survey the territory for you. And you may also be interested in other local resources. Two free publications, *Portland Parent* and *Portland Family,* offer regular updates on child-care facilities in the area and on local schools. Another good source is *Portland Monthly,* which compiles extensive data from the state on local public and private schools. And informal networks through community centers, libraries, religious organizations, and word of mouth can put parents in touch with good care-givers and schools.

CHILD CARE

State Programs and Initiatives

The Oregon Commission for Child Care; OCCC; www.oregon.gov/employ/ccc, an advisory board to the governor, studies the issues concerning the development of accessible, affordable, and high-quality child care and makes legislative recommendations based on its findings. The OCCC has become a major player on these issues since its inception in 1985, and one of its major successes has been the creation of a program for child-care resource and referral, the Child Care Division of the Oregon Employment Department. This division certifies child-care centers through criminal history checks and inspections of facili-ties. It also registers family child-care businesses, though it does not inspect them. (Family child-care providers are still required to undergo crimi-nal background checks and a certain amount of training.) The division sponsors mentoring and training programs for providers, working closely with the Center for Career Development in Childhood Care and Education at Portland State University.

Child Care Resource and Referral Network

The Child Care Division of the Oregon Employ-ment Department has also developed the Child Care Resource and Referral (CCR&R) agencies (www.oregonchildcare.org). These community-based agencies strive to provide all parents with as much information and as many options for quality child care as possible. The CCR&R agencies direct parents toward resources for child-care screening as well as to other com-munity resources, including child-care provider support groups. Although the CCR&R programs are extremely busy, and you must leave a mes-sage on a recording, they generally return calls within a reasonable amount of time and are quite helpful. CCR&R staff are knowledgeable and will answer questions about a wide range of topics and dispense information about child-care accreditation, local workshops for providers, and information about scholarships to help cover training and accreditation fees. Your local CCR&R representative can also meet with you and pro-vide a personal consultation to address concerns about your child-care situation, health and safety matters, child development issues, activities for children, and even technical information regarding business development, taxes, and zoning. CCR&R resources are considerable, including a lending library of videos, books, toys, and equipment, so don't be afraid to ask for help or advice. Check the Web site to find the one nearest you.

Work and school may help you with your child-care needs. Since Oregon gives employers good tax breaks when they subsidize child care, many employers keep their workers happy by offering this benefit. For example, Hanna Andersson offers a child-care subsidy; and Nike maintains child-care, preschool, and kindergarten facilities for some of its workers. If you're still working on your degree, Portland Community College campuses have lovely, though limited, child-care programs for students and staff. Call the Sylvania Campus at (503) 977-4424 for information about cost, hours, and availability. The Rock Creek Campus also provides evening child care Monday through Thursday from 5:00 to 10:00 p.m. for older children (4 to 12). Call (503) 614-7511 to find out more. Portland State University also has an excellent facility: the Helen Gordon Child Development Center (503-725-3092; www.hgcdc.pdx.edu). The workers here are students well trained in child development.

Child-care Providers

Finding someone to care for your child can be remarkably stressful, but surveying the territory will make things a little easier. Regardless of what option seems to best suit your needs, you should start your search for child care early. A range of care is available, but a lot of other parents are looking for qualified help for their child-care needs, and waiting lists are not unusual. It takes time to find the right person or center for your child and your family.

Doulas and Early Care

Child care begins early for some of us. Many Portland parents find the transition to their new roles goes more smoothly with the help of a doula, a professional family helper who provides nonmedical assistance to new parents at home. Doulas may show anxious parents how to hold, bathe, dress, and feed the new little one; they may take care of the house or older siblings; they may aid with nursing; in general, they help to keep things peaceful and calm. Since hospital stays for postpartum women are notoriously abbreviated, a doula could be just the person to ease you through the surprise of new parenthood. You can find doulas in a variety of places. Your ob-gyn may have some contacts, and midwives are very good sources; often midwifery practices include them on staff.

Sometimes all you need is the support of other parents. Hospitals and health-care organizations will often run programs for new parents and their infants. Hosted by nurses or other health-care professionals, these free or low-cost forums allow you to ask questions about breastfeeding, child development, and other issues. Just hanging out with the other parents is comforting, especially when you find out they all feel the same way that you do. Check with your hospital or HMO to see whether they offer such programs, and on the Web look in the Craig's List community section under Child Care, where parent support groups may be listed as well as discussion forums for parents (http://portland.craigslist.org/). And don't forget the power of the spoken word: Most of the people we know found their groups informally, through their childbirth education classes, friends of friends, story time at the library, the baby swings at the park, the Baby Gap store at the mall, or interesting conversations about baby acne at the local Starbucks. Later, when the babies get bigger, these groups are invaluable resources for setting up casual babysitting co-ops.

i Nursing your little one can be challenging. For support and advice, try the Nursing Mothers Counsel of Oregon, (503) 282-3338 or www.nursingmothers counsel.org.

Nannies

If you read the *New York Times,* you might worry that hiring a nanny will require you to sign away not just your first-born child but his or her entire inheritance. However, this is still Oregon, and while nannies are expensive, they are still affordable for many families. In fact, nanny care is growing in popularity, for it may be the least disruptive to the family. Nannies can be full- or part-time; they can live in your house or in their own; they can be temporary or long-term. The salary of your nanny can range from $400 to $800 or higher per week for a nanny who lives out to $300 to $650 or higher per week for one who lives with you. Part-time nannies may earn up to $17 per hour—$14 per hour is a standard rate for the area. It all depends on what you want them to do: Nannies have widely varying responsibilities and duties, such as housework, meal preparation, and picking the children up from school and driving them to sports or extracurricular functions. You should make it clear what duties the job entails and spell them out in a contract.

Two good sources for nannies are Northwest Nannies and Care Givers Placement Agency. Contact Northwest Nannies at (503) 245-5288 or www.nwnanny.com. You can reach Care Givers Placement Agency at (503) 244-6370 or online at www.cgpa.com. Both agencies can find you temporary or permanent full- or part-time help. Care Givers will also help you find temporary emergency child care; contact them in advance, if you think you might be subject to emergencies, to see how their system works. While the nannies we have known have been trustworthy, reliable, and resourceful, nannies are not licensed in Oregon; going through an agency may afford you some protection since the agency screens the applicants and expects them to have some training. If you want to take on the job of performing background checks yourself, however, Craig's List (www.portland.craigslist.org) can be a fantastic resource for finding child-care help.

Day-Care Centers and Family Care

Day-care centers are open 52 weeks a year, are licensed by the state, and are usually staffed with a number of teachers who are supervised by a director. They can charge up to several thousand dollars per month for full-time care, depending on the scope and number of children you enroll. Caregiver–child ratios are strict and vary with the age of the child. Day-care centers are becoming increasingly specialized and are more competitive than ever. These centers, which according to state law must provide at least 35 square feet of space per child, can be quite large and usually offer lots of recreational and educational activities to help children acquire new skills as they burn off their seemingly endless supply of energy. There are hundreds of day-care facilities in the area. Many families choose one close to either home or work, but wherever you live and work, you'll have to sort through the facilities to find one that coheres with your outlook on things. As you might expect, the kind of care and theory behind it varies widely; we have pretty much everything here, from Waldorf-based philosophies to Montessori philosophies to Piaget's philosophies, and everything in between. Many day cares incorporate religious themes. Some of the nationally known chains that operate in Portland are the Learning Tree, Kindercare, La Petite Academy, and Children's World, but there are many locally grown centers for you to probe.

i **Saturday Academy (503-725-2330; www.saturdayacademy.pdx.edu) is an award-winning, innovative enrichment program for kids in grades 4 through 12. Area professionals share their labs, equipment, and expertise to teach hands-on experimentation and critical thinking in science, math, writing, and other subjects. Saturday Academy has won seven National Science Foundation grants among other honors. Scholarships are available.**

In-home, or, as the state refers to it, "family" day care, is ubiquitous throughout Oregon and involves taking your child to someone's home for care. It can cost from $400 to $1,000 per month, with $6,000 to $7,000 per year a typical figure. In-home day-care operations must be registered with the state and can provide care for up to 10 children at a time. Be sure that you check the qualifications of anyone you hire to care for your children in his or her home and ask to see the paperwork. As with day-care centers, strict requirements for ratios of caregivers to children apply. Also, operators and employees must undergo criminal background checks, and new training requirements demand that they have an overview session, are trained in CPR, maintain a food handler's certification, and are trained to prevent child abuse and neglect. They must also carry household insurance.

Extended-Care and Summer Programs

Many Portland schools, both public and private, offer extended-care programs after and before school for children whose parents have incompatible work schedules, and these programs often run during school breaks as well. The public schools have contracts with 18 state-certified, nonprofit providers, who run programs in 62 elementary schools. Two additional schools have child care within a safe walking distance (that is, a distance that could be covered by a child in kindergarten). Your child's school can give you information about these programs, or you can call the Portland Public Schools Child Care coordinator at (503) 916-3230.

In addition to extended care within the schools, you'll find other weekday programs that take care of children until their parents can. Boys and Girls Clubs are helpful in this regard; they have four clubs in the area and run summer programs in addition to their extended-care programs. Their administrative office in Southeast Portland, at 7119 Southeast Milwaukie, (503) 232-0077, is a well-equipped facility that keeps kids busy with all kinds of wholesome activity, from basketball to photography. The number for the club is (503) 238-6868. Other locations include the Wattles Club, 9330 Harold Street, (503) 775-1549; the Blazers' Boys and Girls Club, 5250 Northeast Martin Luther King Jr. Boulevard,

(503) 282-8480; and in Hillsboro, at 560 Southeast 3rd Avenue, (503) 640-4558. You can find them online at www.bgcportland.org.

The YMCA of Columbia-Willamette has 10 regional centers and a number of in-school programs for child care, education, and extended care. The YMCA offers flexible and affordable day care and does a great job of keeping youngsters involved in stimulating and challenging activities. These fully licensed and well-staffed centers are conveniently located on both sides of the river and offer full- or part-time options for busy parents. In addition, the YMCA manages a half-dozen Child Development Centers for six-week old infants up to five-year-old children. As an added bonus, members of their child-care programs receive a 25 to 75 percent reduction in monthly membership dues at any YMCA Fitness Facility with the joining fee waived. You can reach them at (503) 327-0007 or www.ymca-portland.org.

Portland Parks and Recreation and summer day camps, both covered in the Kidstuff chapter, can also help you take care of your child. Summer day camps are a popular form of "child care." Devoted to activities such as basketball, dance, computer or language training, art lessons, theater, monitoring baby animals at the Oregon Zoo, or an array of other things, they provide care for the kids and peace of mind for their parents. *Portland Family* publishes a multipart guide to camps, and camps themselves sponsor a big exhibition, the Summer Camp and Vacation Show, at the Convention Center in the spring. Finally, Portland Parks and Rec sponsors many after-school and school-break programs throughout the city. These offerings change regularly and vary according to the season; they range from acrobatics to Zen flower arrangement. Their number is (503) 823-PLAY; call them and they will send you a nice big catalog.

i **Being a parent isn't always easy. When a crisis arises, the 24-hour Parent Helpline is there to give you support, information, and referrals: (503) 452-4789.**

Evening and Drop-In Child Care

GRANDMA'S PLACE

1505 Northeast 16th Avenue
(503) 249-7533

5845 Northeast Hoyt Street
(503) 238-0123

1730 North Flint Avenue
(503) 281-6800

8218 Northeast Sandy Boulevard
(503) 517-8888
www.grandmasplacedaycare.com

Evening and drop-in child care is always difficult to find. One agency in town, however, specializes in this kind of care, operating several centers in town—including one near the Convention Center. Grandma's Place offers part-time and temporary day-care services for young ones from just 6 weeks up to 12 years of age. Grandma's is open seven days a week, and it's open until midnight.

EDUCATION

Philosophers tell us that there is no education without growth. Oregonians have seen a lot of growth in the past decade—and that has influenced education and been an education in itself. The institutions devoted to education have also had to contend with growth. As a result they are multifaceted and diverse—they include state and private universities, community colleges, and public and private elementary, middle, and high schools.

The metro area has more than 200 public schools and a robust selection of private institutions. In both public and private schools, you may find a selection of special-needs facilities as well as experimental settings where students are challenged in different ways, from learning other languages to designing business plans. The schools in Oregon are generally well regarded, despite recent and ongoing fiscal trials. It's a testament to parents and teachers alike that the public schools remain strong in spite of the financial turmoil. Portland is also the home of Portland State University, one of seven universities run by the Oregon University System, as well as the site of a commendable list of private colleges. Among these are Reed College, Lewis & Clark, Marylhurst College, and the University of Portland. And Oregon Health and Science University holds a significant place in the Portland skyline. It is devoted to teaching and training medical professionals and research scientists, and it is responsible for innovative research in the fight against cancer and other diseases.

Community colleges play a major role in the area's educational scene. Indeed, Portland Community College has more students than any other college in the state. All the community colleges offer a broad range of programs for a broader range of students, whose reasons for attending are various and idiosyncratic. You will find newly graduated high school students who plan to transfer to a four-year college, students wishing to earn their high school diplomas, students returning to college after a number of years, students who are pursuing some kind of professional training, and students who just want to take a sculpture class or two. Besides Portland Community College, which has satellite campus sites around the area, you will also find Mount Hood Community College in Gresham, Clackamas Community College in Southeast Portland, and Clark College in Vancouver.

This section presents a snapshot of schools and colleges in the area, divided into two further sections, K–12 and Higher Education. The K–12 section is organized alphabetically into elementary, middle, and high schools, and multigrade schools in the Portland area and beyond. The Higher Education section begins with universities and four-year colleges then covers community colleges and vocational training.

K–12 Education

Ninety percent of area residents send their children to public schools, making Portland Public Schools one of the few remaining intact urban school systems, despite constant budget pressures. Changing demographic information also places pressure on the schools, for even as the area balloons in population, many families moving into the area choose the suburbs, and current projections predict enrollment declines for city schools. Although Portland's population is increasing, many new urban residents are young and childless or retired with grown children. Thus, the state legislature has pushed Portland Public Schools to cut costs, and Portland Public Schools have suffered budget cuts. These have resulted in fewer teachers, librarians, and counselors, fewer electives, ailing physical plants, and pressure to increase the student-to-teacher ratio.

Across Oregon, school budgets have been hit hard by recent economic trends. The Portland Public School system in particular has gained national notoriety for its budget troubles, especially after it looked as though more than a month would have to be cut from the school year. Attracting less notice, however, was the way that the citizens of Portland came together to support the schools. Teachers worked for free for 10 days, while local businesses accepted a small tax increase and voters in the county agreed to a temporary tax raise to protect the schools, restore the school year, and leave programs intact. Our troubles are not over, but the faith that we have in our schools creates hope and sends the message that a creative response to problems is possible.

Portland schools have many strengths. They are sometimes less crowded than suburban schools. Moreover, many schools have become the nexus for dynamic neighborhood and community development. In 1999 Multnomah County introduced a program called SUN Schools. "SUN" is an acronym for Schools Uniting Neighborhoods, and the idea behind it is to use the schools, which are natural gathering places for families, to serve their communities even more thoroughly. In this program buildings open early and stay open late to act as neighborhood centers that provide health clinics, computer labs, entertainment, or other activities for residents. They have become important neighborhood centers, points of contact that total more than the sum of their parts.

The SUN Schools program is just one of the innovative programs designed to solve persistent school-funding and other education-related troubles. Another is the charter school law, passed in 1999. This bill allows Oregon to apply for federal charter school development funds. Charter schools are independently run public schools that are taxpayer funded. They are free to set their own curricula and rules of operation. If the charter school produces students whose performances don't meet academic standards, the school's charter can be revoked and the school could be closed. There are a number of charter schools in Portland. Three established programs are the Opal School at CM2 (www.opalschool .org; 503-471-9917), which opened in 2001 and has an arts-centered curriculum; Trillium (www .trilliumcharterschool.org; 503-285-3833), which opened in 2002 and focuses on a curriculum of urban and global studies, serving K–12 students; and the Emerson School (www.emersonschool .org; 503-525-6124), which focuses on project-based learning in real-world settings. Charter schools in Oregon have had a bit of a rocky start, but their founders remain undaunted and new ones are being added every year. For a complete list of Portland charter schools, look online at www.edoptions.pps.k12.or.us.s

Portland schools should also benefit from the increased expectations of Oregonians. In 1996 the State Board of Education adopted a new set of demanding educational standards for Oregon children. The standards were developed by parents and teachers across the state, and they call for students to master six academic areas: English, mathematics, science, the social sciences, the arts, and a second language. Students are tested in grades 3, 5, 8, 10, and 12. Students who reached the curriculum goals for grade 10 would receive a Certificate of Initial Mastery (CIM); those who reach the goals for grade 12 would receive the Certificate of Advanced Mastery. The CIM was not required for graduation but is intended to serve as an academic benchmark. These standards were not without controversy, and in 2007 the state reevaluated them, deciding instead to invest in making the high school diploma more rigorous and a core measurement of learning.

Though the CIM program is being retired, the first CIM test results spurred parents, students, and teachers to work harder to raise scores, and testing scores have been on the rise ever since. These standards may have payoffs in other areas: Since 1997, Oregon high school students have consistently ranked first or second in the nation in combined SAT scores (among states where more than 50 percent of students take the SAT). Scores for the ACT test have also been high, ranking in the top five for the past several years.

The number of Portland-area schools is high enough to demand numerous school districts (see listing in this chapter). The largest is Portland Public Schools (School District 1J), a prekindergarten through twelfth-grade district with about 100 schools and 50 special-needs sites. Listed here are a few selected public and private schools in the Portland Metro area. We're highlighting schools with distinctive approaches to education such as arts or science programs or language immersion schools where students speak to each other and their teachers in a foreign language for half of their time at school. We've grouped the schools into elementary, middle, high, and multigrade schools, and we've sorted them further by whether they're public or private. Since parents may choose to send their children across town, schools are listed alphabetically rather than geographically.

i Those schooled at home have many resources available in the Portland area. City parks and recreation programs give supervised instruction in sports and other activities just for homeschoolers—even prom. Call them at (503) 823-7529 for more information. And check out Homeschoolers in Portland, a Yahoo group for pooling resources and bolstering you with moral support: http://groups.yahoo.com/group/HIP_list/.

Elementary Schools

PUBLIC ELEMENTARY SCHOOL PROGRAMS

Portland does have a flexible school choice policy, but unless you live within the boundaries for your chosen school, you'll have to apply for an administrative transfer. You can get the paperwork from the school that you are designated to attend. Special programs within schools may have their own application processes; contact the schools for more information. The Portland Public Schools Web site will let you know your designated neighborhood school, as well as link you to the Web sites of neighborhoods and others schools and programs: www.pps.k12.or.us.

BUCKMAN ELEMENTARY SCHOOL: ARTS MAGNET PROGRAM
320 Southeast 16th Avenue
(503) 916-6230
Buckman has an award-winning arts program that incorporates dance, drama, visual arts, and music into the regular curriculum. Students are encouraged to use their artistic gifts to devise interdisciplinary approaches to research projects and other academic work. The student body is astonishingly diverse, with about 10 different languages heard in the halls. The teachers are also diverse, and make use of the "multiple intelligences" approach to learning. Families are deeply involved in this beloved school.

Language Immersion Programs

AINSWORTH ELEMENTARY SCHOOL: SPANISH IMMERSION PROGRAM
2425 Southwest Vista Avenue
(503) 916-6288

ATKINSON ELEMENTARY SCHOOL: SPANISH IMMERSION PROGRAM
5800 Southeast Division Street
(503) 916-6333

BEACH ELEMENTARY SCHOOL: SPANISH IMMERSION PROGRAM
710 North Humboldt Street
(503) 916-3608

**RICHMOND ELEMENTARY SCHOOL:
JAPANESE IMMERSION PROGRAM**
2276 Southeast 41st Avenue
(503) 916-6220

**WOODSTOCK ELEMENTARY SCHOOL:
MANDARIN IMMERSION PROGRAM**
5601 Southeast 50th Avenue
(503) 916-6380
In a modern world of global awareness, the Portland School System gives its students a chance to learn about cultures through immersion in their languages. Immensely successful, these language immersion elementary schools are taught half in English and half in a foreign language. The special schooling gives students not only second language competency, but a greater cultural understanding and proficiency by grade five. These programs operate as separate schools within schools, and students must apply to get into all of them. Requirements and activities may vary in each program. For instance, children who wish to attend the immersion program at Richmond Elementary must start as kindergartners, unless they are from Japan or have lived in Japan up to the time of registration.

Year-Round Schools

ABERNETHY ELEMENTARY SCHOOL
2421 Southeast Orange Street
(503) 916-3600

PENINSULA ELEMENTARY SCHOOL
8125 North Emerald Street
(503) 916-6275
Every autumn, teachers have to spend weeks replacing all the knowledge that children have forgotten over the summer. Not at these two schools, which operate on a year-round calendar, leading to better retention and reinforcement of learning. And the yearlong calendar allows for innovation in the curriculum. At Abernethy, for example, the students have built a garden, and the teachers have integrated the garden into their science, math, history, language, and culture lessons—lessons that they can sustain beyond spring planting into midsummer harvest and maintenance. The garden also provides an arena for recreation and for service. Both schools are small, close-knit communities with active parent volunteers. An added benefit for families: They can vacation when everyone else is in school; children get the same number of days off as other Portland students, they just take them at different times.

PRIVATE ELEMENTARY SCHOOL PROGRAMS

CASCADIA MONTESSORI SCHOOL
10316 Northeast 14th Street
Vancouver, WA
(360) 256-0872
www.cascadiaschool.com
Cascadia School, for elementary school-aged children, bases its philosophy on the Montessori curriculum. The small, close-knit school encourages children to grow, educate, and challenge themselves not only in academic subject matter, but also in cultural awareness. Like all Montessori schools, children's interests are respected, and mutually respectful relationships with adults are nurtured.

CEDARWOOD SCHOOL
3030 Southwest 2nd Avenue
(503) 245-1477
www.cedarwoodschool.org
Cedarwood School, with 125 students, is based on the Waldorf philosophy; it is in the process of acquiring full Waldorf accreditation. At present they provide prekindergarten through the fifth grade and hope to have a full K–8 school in the future. The school is just south of downtown, in the Lair Hill neighborhood, making it convenient for commuting parents.

FRENCH AMERICAN SCHOOL
8500 Northwest Johnson Street
(503) 292-7776
www.faispdx.org
Since 1979 the French American School has been immersing students in the language of diplomats, and its graduates have gone on to great successes in Portland and far beyond. The

school is devoted to academic rigor, a nurturing environment, and small class sizes. There are 440 students in the school, but this number includes Gilkey Middle School. The elementary school serves prekindergarten through fifth-grade students.

THE INTERNATIONAL SCHOOL
25 Southwest Sherman Street
(503) 226-2496
The International School, which teaches 235 children ages three through grade five, offers full-immersion programs that nurture as well as challenge students. The school focuses on traditional academic areas in its small classes (the average student-to-teacher ratio is nine to two). Languages taught at the International School include Chinese, Japanese, and Spanish.

WHOLE CHILD MONTESSORI CENTER
5904 Southeast 40th Avenue
(503) 771-6366
One of a number of Montessori schools in the Portland area, Whole Child is distinguished by its excellent teachers and its beautiful children's garden. Whole Child teaches preschoolers through kindergartners; their graduates are remarkably well prepared for the first grade. Children are encouraged to follow their intellectual paths on their own, but in an atmosphere of supportive preparation that enables the children to effectively teach themselves. The well-designed garden, with its evergreens, flowers, bridges, paths, and perennials, makes a wonderful place for children to roam safely and freely, reconnecting their modern little minds to their bodies.

Middle Schools

PUBLIC MIDDLE SCHOOL PROGRAMS
DA VINCI ARTS MIDDLE SCHOOL
2508 Northeast Everett Street
(503) 916-5356
This public middle school, founded by a group of parents in 1996, serves 300 students who come from the entire metropolitan area. It's an arts magnet, and students must apply to get in; classes are a mix of age groups. Besides special instruction in visual arts, dance, music, theater, and writing, the school requires rigorous academic classes infused with aesthetic principles.

HARRIET TUBMAN MIDDLE SCHOOL
2231 North Flint Avenue
(503) 916-5630
Harriet Tubman Middle School has a special, interdisciplinary focus on the health sciences and biotechnology. It has formed community partnerships with, among others, Legacy Emanuel Hospital, Oregon Health and Science University, and the American Lung Association. Tubman students can work alongside research scientists and others from these organizations. Many electives, such as marine biology, are not available to middle school students elsewhere in the district.

PRIVATE MIDDLE SCHOOL PROGRAMS
GILKEY MIDDLE SCHOOL
8500 Northwest Johnson Street
(503) 292-9111
www.faispdx.org
Part of the French American School, this school provides bilingual education in German, French, and Spanish, but it also offers an international track in which no previous foreign language experience is required to attend. Small class sizes and an academically rigorous program are added features. (See the French American School, under Private Elementary School Programs, for more information.)

High Schools

PUBLIC HIGH SCHOOL PROGRAMS
Public high schools in the Portland area have been quietly developing innovative programs to ensure that students receive high-quality educations in a variety of modes and settings—perhaps another reason that the SAT scores of Oregonians are so good. Many of these programs accept students from other schools and even other districts, if they can meet the requirements and manage the bureaucracy of transfer.

Enrichment Experiences

Parents often want to enrich their children's education, and Portland has many resources to extend the lessons of the classroom. Besides Portland Parks and Recreation, which offers every kind of lesson you could imagine, Oregon Ballet Theater (503-227-6890), the Northwest Children's Theater and School (503-222-2190), and the Suzuki Violin School (503-246-9945) all augment basic education with their superb programs. And children adore Mad Science, which teaches science through fun demonstrations. Call them at (503) 230-8040.

BENSON HIGH SCHOOL
546 Northeast 12th Avenue
(503) 916-5100
Benson is highly regarded in Oregon for its professional and technical programs that take kids from school to work. After their sophomore year, students at Benson choose a major and supplement it with real-world experience in jobs and internships. It has been honored as a New Century School by the U.S. Department of Education—one of only six in the nation.

INTERNATIONAL BACCALAUREATE PROGRAM
The International Baccalaureate (IB) program is a demanding international college-prep program that tests students in six areas: language, second language, experimental sciences, social sciences and humanities, mathematics, and the arts. This program is more rigorous than programs based on multiple-choice tests; its graduates are skilled in higher-order reasoning and research, and their writing skills are highly prized by the colleges that accept them.

Schools that participate in the IB program are Cleveland High School (3400 Southeast 26th Avenue; 503-916-5120) and Lincoln High School (1600 Southwest Salmon; 503-916-5200) in the Portland School District. In Beaverton three schools participate: Beaverton (13000 Southwest 2nd Street; 503-259-5000), Sunset (13840 Northwest Cornell Road; 503-259-5050), and Southridge (9625 Southwest 125th Avenue; 503-259-5400). Suburban participants include Gresham High School (1200 North Main; 503-674-5500); Tigard High School (9000 Southwest Durham Road; 503-431-5400), and Tualatin High School (22300 Southwest Boones Ferry Road; 503-431-5600).

MERLO STATION HIGH SCHOOL–SCHOOL OF SCIENCE AND TECHNOLOGY
1841 Southwest Merlo Drive, Beaverton
(503) 259-5575
The School of Science and Technology (SST) routinely has the highest test scores in the state. This small special-focus program offers an outstanding and stimulating program that incorporates fieldwork and projects in its curriculum. It also has close alliances with businesses and colleges in the area. The program is built around the sciences, but it expects its graduates to be well rounded and therefore also has vigorous humanities requirements.

i If you want instruction in a foreign language to be part of your child's extracurricular activities, try Kids Like Languages, an excellent organization that will help you set up private language instruction for small groups: (503) 493-8424. Berlitz also offers language instruction; call (503) 274-0830.

RIVERDALE HIGH SCHOOL
9727 Southwest Terwilliger Street
(503) 892-0722
Riverdale High School is a public school in a tiny district in Portland, but this small school's reputation is formidable, with always-outstanding test

scores. Its challenging curriculum emphasizes preparing for college and almost every Riverdale graduate is also a college graduate. (Riverdale is also unusual in that it charges tuition—quite a lot of it.)

PRIVATE HIGH SCHOOL PROGRAMS
CENTRAL CATHOLIC HIGH SCHOOL
2401 Southeast Stark Street
(503) 235-3138
www.centralcatholichigh.org
Central Catholic High School, teaching grades 9 through 12, is a college-prep school that emphasizes moral and ethical training in addition to its academically challenging program. About 800 students attend.

NORTHWEST ACADEMY
1130 Southwest Main Street
(503) 223-3367
This independent, accredited school for grades 8 to 12 takes advantage of its downtown location to integrate the visual arts (painting, printmaking, and photography), the performing arts (jazz, dance, and theater), and media arts (film, video, sound design, and audio engineering) into its curriculum. Of course, all the traditional subjects are taught as well. The school has 60 students, who enjoy small classes (the average number of students is 15).

ST. MARY'S ACADEMY
1615 Southwest 5th Avenue
(503) 228-7181
Catholic nuns established St. Mary's in 1859, and since then it has educated more than 7,000 young women. Its long history has served it well—three times, it has received the U.S. Department of Education's Blue Ribbon award for schools of excellence, the only school in the region to be so honored. Its curriculum is academically rigorous but also imaginative, flexible, and interesting; graduating from St. Mary's is shorthand in Oregon for being well educated. And don't let the old-fashioned brick façade fool you—it is thoroughly wired, one of the most technologically advanced

schools in the city. Enrollment at St. Mary's is about 550, and the average class size is 13.

Multigrade Schools

Most people like their children's elementary schools; it's what happens afterward that they worry about. Many people feel that public middle schools are just not working, and so quite a number of schools, both public and private, are returning to a multigrade plan. Of course, some multigrade schools have always been that way: Portland has a strong network of Catholic schools such as St. Thomas More in Southwest Portland, (503) 222-6105; St. Ignatius, (503) 774-5533, in Southeast Portland; and Cathedral Catholic School, (503) 275-9370, in Northwest Portland. All offer solid academic programs and traditional values for grades K–8. But in the private schools that are not religiously affiliated, parents have responded so positively to their children's elementary education that many of the private schools have added higher grades. A fine example is the Gilkey Middle School (see separate entry), but Waldorf initiative schools such as Cedarwood (see Elementary Schools) are also adding grades. Parents and teachers find that mixing the ages together seems to work better for everyone. Not only does it help the students academically, but it fosters a sense of connection and responsibility for all.

PUBLIC MULTIGRADE SCHOOLS
Portland Public Schools maintains a number of multigrade schools or programs within schools, and the district is returning to a more widespread use of the K–8 model. Here are just a few of the notable ones; for more information visit the PPS Web site, www.pps.k12.or.us.

BEAVERTON ARTS & COMMUNICATION MAGNET
11375 Southwest Center Street
Beaverton
(503) 672-3700
www.beaverton.k12.or.us/acma
This school is the only stand-alone arts magnet

in the state, and its students must be gifted in one or more of the visual, written, performing, or other arts; a written essay and portfolio are requirements of admission. Students must also be able to work independently and in groups. And no one is getting out of math: The academic requirements are tough. Students also declare a career pathway (sort of like a major) after 8th grade, which enables them to direct their educations in a useful direction. This program focuses on all forms of the arts for students in the 6th through 12th grades.

CREATIVE SCIENCE SCHOOL
1231 Southeast 92nd Avenue
(503) 916-6336

This constructivist program for grades K–8 is based on the research of psychologist Jean Piaget. Its curriculum is fashioned to educate through activities such as observation, interaction, experimentation, and theorizing; independent thinking and problem-solving are prized very highly here. Subject periods are longer than at most elementary schools; an individual lesson might last an hour, and the particular unit may be incorporated throughout many lessons during the day. Children are encouraged to combine scientific reasoning with play. This program encourages a seamless transition between school and family life by involving parents deeply in the school.

METROPOLITAN LEARNING CENTER
2033 Northwest Glisan Street
(503) 916-5737

Portland Public School District's only K–12 school, the Metropolitan Learning Center provides a noncompetitive atmosphere with written evaluations (instead of letter grades), cooperative learning, cross-age experiences, and off-campus activities. A particular focus of the school is a healthy environment, and many lessons are devoted to this. Former governor John Kitzhaber recognized it as the first "green" school in the state. But the students and teachers at MLC are imaginative enough to understand that the "environment"

is the place we live; thus, a major focus of the school is the urban community that surrounds MLC, and it's an essential part of the curriculum.

SUNNYSIDE ENVIRONMENTAL SCHOOL
3421 Southeast Salmon Street
(503) 916-6226

The Sunnyside Environmental School, or SES, as it's known around here, is a special-focus program of Portland Public Schools in which students in mixed-age classes study the traditional subjects but with an emphasis on the natural environment. For example, a basic question throughout many courses is "How does history influence the environment and how does the environment influence history?" The environmental core curriculum, studied by all students at the same time, consists of three-year rotations focusing on rivers, mountains, and forests. SES is a small program, and its nurturing size and low ratio of students to teachers makes it very desirable. Accelerated math and Spanish are also available; community service is a key component of the curriculum as well.

What Parents Need to Know

If you're moving to Oregon with school-aged children, visit the useful Web site sponsored by the Oregon Department of Education—it features school report cards, information about Oregon's standards, and other helpful data: www.ode.state .or.us/. And even if you live here already, you'll find the parents' page of the Portland Public Schools Web site to be of infinite help, with information on everything from magnet schools to school menus: www.pps .k12.or.us.

Portland Area School Districts

General information and questions about schools in the following districts can be obtained by calling the following:

Multnomah County

Centennial SD 28JT
18135 Southeast Brooklyn Street
(503) 760-7990

David Douglas SD 40
1500 Southeast 130th Avenue
(503) 252-2900

Gresham Schools
1331 Northwest Eastman Parkway
Gresham
(503) 618-2450

Multnomah Education Service District
11611 Northeast Ainsworth Circle
(503) 255-1841

Portland Public Schools
501 North Dixon Street
(503) 916-2000

Washington County

Beaverton SD 48
16550 Southwest Merlo Road
Beaverton
(503) 591-8000

Hillsboro SD 1J
3083 Northeast 49th Place, Hillsboro
(503) 844-1500

Sherwood SD 88J
23295 South Sherwood Boulevard
Sherwood
(503) 625-8100

Tigard-Tualatin SD 23J
13137 Southwest Pacific Highway, Tigard
(503) 431-4000

Clackamas County

Canby SD 86
811 Southwest 5th Avenue, Canby
(503) 266-7861

WINTERHAVEN

3830 Southeast 14th Avenue
(503) 916-6200

Winterhaven is a wonderful K–8 public school magnet program that makes use of mixed-age classrooms, interdisciplinary intellectual approaches, and positive discipline techniques to foster personal responsibility. Winterhaven has attracted a high number of talented and gifted students who respond well to these approaches, which allow them to bloom in their own way while still being academically challenged, particularly through its focus on math, science, and technology. Community involvement is prized, and families are asked to volunteer 50 hours per year.

PRIVATE MULTIGRADE SCHOOLS

THE CATLIN GABEL SCHOOL

8825 Southwest Barnes Road
(503) 297-1894
www.catlin.edu

This distinguished coeducational school is well known for its dedication to individuality, rigorous academics, and liberal arts training. Courses educate the total person, incorporating academic excellence along with the visual and performing arts, physical education, and a strong sense of community service. Students are encouraged to devote service hours to the school and to the community; in fact one of the requirements for upper-school students is to dedicate 12 hours

Clackamas Education Service District
P.O. Box 216, Marylhurst, OR 97036
(503) 675-4000

Gladstone SD 115
17789 Webster Road, Gladstone
(503) 655-2777

Lake Oswego SD 7J
2455 Southwest Country Club Road, Lake
Oswego
(503) 636-7691

Molalla River SD 35
412 South Swiegle Avenue, Molalla
(503) 829-2359

North Clackamas SD 12
4444 Southeast Lake Road, Milwaukie
(503) 653-3600

West Linn-Wilsonville SD 3J
P.O. Box 35, West Linn, OR 97068
(503) 673-7000

Clark County, Washington
Battle Ground SD 119
11104 Northeast 149th Street

Brush Prairie
(360) 885-5300

Camas SD 117
2041 Northeast Ione Street, Camas
(360) 817-4400

Educational Service District 112
2500 Northeast 65th Avenue
Vancouver
(360) 750-7500

Evergreen SD 114
13501 Northeast 28th Street
Vancouver
(360) 604-4000

Ridgefield SD 122
2724 South Hillhurst Road, Ridgefield
(360) 887-0200

Vancouver SD 37
P.O. Box 8937, Vancouver
(360) 313-1000

Washougal SD 112-6
2349 B Street, Washougal
(360) 954-3000

of service to local agencies. Catlin Gabel has an enrollment of about 680 students in preschool through grade 12. The average class size is 17.

FRANCISCAN MONTESSORI EARTH SCHOOL & ST. FRANCIS ACADEMY
14750 Southeast Clinton Street
(503) 760-8220
www.fmes.org
Parents who send their children to Montessori preschools grow misty-eyed when they later recall the wonderful experiences their children had there. Now they can extend this effective learning atmosphere all the way through middle school. Founded in 1977, the school serves about 350 students from the Portland Metro area,

including Vancouver (it's right off Interstate 205). This environmentally and globally focused school is run by an order of Franciscan nuns. Students grow gardens and are even prepared for travel abroad. If we're lucky, they'll start a graduate school for the rest of us.

THE GARDNER SCHOOL
16413 Northeast 50th Avenue
Vancouver, WA
(360) 574-5752
www.gardnerschool.org/home.html
The Gardner School is dedicated to developing the potential of its 100 students. Howard Gardner's Multiple Intelligences model serves as a framework for individualized skill development

and interdisciplinary, thematic studies. Community partnerships provide students with real-life experiences that help them become productive, responsible, compassionate citizens. Classes are held for preschoolers through grade eight. The student-to-teacher ratio is nine to one.

OREGON EPISCOPAL SCHOOL
6300 Southwest Nicol Road
(503) 246-7771
www.oes.edu
Oregon Episcopal School (OES) is a coeducational, independent, college preparatory school where teachers challenge students in small, demanding classes. Active parent involvement is encouraged. OES holds its students to rigorous academic standards, while encouraging a free spirit as part of the joy of learning. Modern dormitories staffed by resident-faculty families provide a safe home away from home for students coming from far away rather than commuting every day. OES serves 720 students, 50 of whom are boarders. Half of these are international students, mostly from China, Japan, and other Asian countries. Most of the other boarders are from eastern and southern Oregon, California, and Washington. The schoolwide student-teacher ratio is seven to one.

PORTLAND LUTHERAN SCHOOL
740 Southeast 182nd Avenue
(503) 667-3199
Founded in 1905, this school began its life as a training school for Lutheran ministers, but over the years, its focus changed. By 1989 it was a K–12 school, and it's now the fastest-growing parochial school in the east part of the city. It offers prekindergarten through 12th grade. The elementary program is centered on traditional single-grade classrooms through the eighth grade, while the high school's main focus is a college-prep curriculum in both liberal arts and the sciences. Ninety-five percent of its graduates attend college. PLS is owned and operated by the Portland Lutheran Association for Christian Education (PLACE), a pan-Lutheran association of churches dedicated to providing quality Christian education to the young people of the Portland Metropolitan area. PLS enrollment is 440. Classes usually have 25 to 27 students, except for prekindergarten through kindergarten classes, which usually consist of 10 to 12 students.

PORTLAND WALDORF SCHOOL
2300 Southeast Harrison, Milwaukie
(503) 654-2200
www.portlandwaldorfschool.org
The Waldorf School ethos is very Portland; in fact, there are other Waldorf-based schools in the area, two of which have started up recently—Cedarwood (see Private Elementary School Programs) and Swallowtail in Hillsboro, (503) 846-0336. But the Portland Waldorf School is the original one in the area, established in 1982. Known for fostering creativity by nurturing the "head, heart, and hands" of the whole child, the Waldorf School challenges its students to develop their intellect and compassion. Kindergarten focuses on storytelling, music, movement, and artistic activity. The academic program is culturally enriched with Spanish and German, needlework, drama, drawing and painting, gardening, folk dancing, orchestra, and woodworking. Portland Waldorf has an enrollment of about 300 students and a faculty and staff of about 50 persons. The Portland Waldorf School serves students through 12th grade.

Higher Education
Higher education in Oregon has a long history—longer than anywhere else in the western United States. The Rev. Jason Lee established the Oregon Institute in his parlor in 1842; that event is now honored as the founding of what would eventually become Willamette University in Salem. Willamette also established the first western medical school, in 1866, and the first western law school, in 1883. Ever since 1842, Oregonians have been creating and nurturing high-quality independent colleges and universities.

Excellent higher education that is also affordable is a struggle for most Americans; here in Oregon we have made some progress in achieving this combination. A number of fine private and public universities, as well as a variety of smaller colleges, inhabit the region. Together this network allows students access to many academic programs. Because Portland is the state's major population center, several state universities have continuing education programs here, particularly Oregon State University and the University of Oregon, both of which offer certificate programs, for-credit classes, and graduate classes in Portland through satellites and extension programs. The University of Oregon's extension program can be reached at (503) 725-3055; Oregon State's can be found at (503) 725-2000.

Oregon's network of public community colleges stretches across the state, and in the metropolitan area, students may choose among Clackamas Community College in Oregon City, Mt. Hood Community College in Gresham, or the state's largest school, Portland Community College with its campuses in Southwest Portland, Washington County, North Portland, and Southeast Portland. These schools offer an array of educational opportunities, ranging from traditional undergraduate academics to noncredit classes in sailing, kayaking, Chinese cooking, or dog training.

The area also boasts private schools that offer a wide range of vocational and career-oriented training in religious education, the technical sciences, computer skills, and various medical and health programs, in addition to their other degrees.

The diversity of Oregon's people is clearly reflected in its high-caliber institutions, which provide undergraduate liberal arts and sciences curricula, specialized two- and four-year professional and technical training, and a wide range of graduate studies. Enrolling more than 60,000 students in the Oregon University System (OUS) alone, and employing some 11,000 tax-paying Oregonians, these schools add a combined annual budget of more than $500 million to the state's economy. They keep thousands of Oregonians from leaving the state for specialized college experiences elsewhere and also attract out-of-state students drawn to Oregon for a variety of reasons.

In addition to the OUS institutions, the state's independent institutions of higher education produce thousands of additional graduates each year. While these degrees are not cheap, they are made more affordable by financial aid, and most students at both state institutions and independent colleges depend on a wide array of direct financial assistance to meet their tuition and other costs. Among the sources of this aid are the colleges themselves, private donors, community scholarship funds, churches, foundations, corporations, and state and federal financial-aid programs. Most students at Oregon's colleges and universities receive financial assistance. Many students attend community college, which can be economical, depending on one's style of life, before they go on to finish their degrees at a four-year school.

Whether you are just out of high school, returning to school after some time off, or looking for a new way of being in the world, Portland's colleges and universities offer excellent choices and opportunities. They also offer good values, and whatever your hopes for your higher education, you are likely to find a program that suits you.

Colleges and Universities

CONCORDIA UNIVERSITY
2811 Northeast Holman Street
(503) 288-9371
A Christian liberal arts school and part of the Concordia University System, Concordia University is a small college that draws about 1,100 students from all over the world to its campus in Northeast Portland. Courses of study include psychology, biology, theology, health and fitness management, humanities, and education. Graduate degree programs within the College of Education were established in 1996. Concordia is accredited by the Northwest Association of Schools and Colleges, and it offers small classes and an opportunity to work closely with professors.

GEORGE FOX UNIVERSITY
414 North Meridian Street, Newberg
(503) 538-8383
www.georgefox.edu
Originally founded in 1891 by Quaker pioneers, this liberal arts college has been named one of America's best colleges numerous times by *U.S. News & World Report*. It includes Herbert Hoover among its alumni, though when he attended, the college was known as Friends Pacific Academy. Some things have stayed the same since President Hoover's time: The pretty residential campus is still in the town of Newberg, about a half-hour southwest of downtown Portland. It still emphasizes moral and religious as well as intellectual development. But George Fox is in every way a modern college too, with a new mission that includes working adults in its graduate, seminary, and degree-completion programs. Classes for the George Fox MBA program, which are held in Portland, are offered one night a week and occasionally on weekends at the Newberg campus. The students, faculty, and staff number about 2,700 persons.

LEWIS & CLARK COLLEGE
615 Southwest Palatine Hill Road
(503) 768-7000
www.lclark.edu
Lewis & Clark College, which sits on a lush site overlooking the Willamette River, is distinguished by its nurturing ambience, its fine and accessible faculty, and the demanding academic standards of its undergraduate, graduate, and law schools. Lewis & Clark can trace its history to 1858, when Presbyterian pioneers established Albany Academy. Then it was a tiny neighborhood school, but it moved to its present location in 1942 and changed its name to Lewis & Clark, and now it is the largest independent college in the state, with a total enrollment of around 3,000. (The undergraduate program has about 1,800 students; the Northwest College of Law, about 700; and the other graduate programs, another 500 or so.) In 1965 Northwestern School of Law was merged with Lewis & Clark College,

and in 1984, graduate programs in education, special education, and counseling psychology were consolidated into the Graduate School of Professional Studies. All programs of the college have excellent national reputations.

MARYLHURST UNIVERSITY
17600 Pacific Highway (Highway 43)
(503) 636-8141, (800) 634-9982
www.marylhurst.edu
Marylhurst, a Catholic liberal arts university, is nationally noted for being an excellent value, especially considering that no class has more than 50 students. Accredited by the Northwest Association of Schools and Colleges, Marylhurst offers its students a great deal of flexibility, with bachelor's or master's degree programs that can be completed during the weekdays, evenings, or weekends. Many returning students have completed their degrees here. If you're the type of person who never likes to leave the computer screen, Marylhurst's classes, programs, and degrees that use Web-based learning might be for you. There are, of course, regular on-site classes as well. The university also sponsors some absorbing graduate programs, such as a Master's in Art Therapy or in Interdisciplinary Studies. They have very generous life-experience credits. Though it was originally founded by Catholic sisters, Marylhurst is coeducational and accepts persons of all faiths.

NATIONAL COLLEGE OF NATUROPATHIC MEDICINE
49 Southwest Porter Street
(503) 552-1555
www.ncnm.edu
National College of Naturopathic Medicine (NCNM) has been in continual operation since 1956, making it the oldest accredited naturopathic medical school on the continent. This extremely rigorous and competitive medical school offers two postgraduate degree programs, the Doctor of Naturopathic Medicine and the Master of Science in Oriental Medicine. Applicants are expected to have a strong background

in science. Graduates are eligible to take board exams in their fields. In addition to lab and lecture courses, students are expected to devote 1,500 hours to clinical work. Students come from all over the United States and from other countries to study at NCNM, where enrollment has doubled in recent years. Each entering class is kept to 120 students, and currently only one out of every three applicants is accepted. Perhaps that's because academic worth is not the only criterion: NCNM college admissions literature states that "in addition to the educational prerequisites, candidates for admission must demonstrate to the college that they possess outstanding moral character, maturity, academic aptitude, and commitment to naturopathic medicine."

OREGON COLLEGE OF ART AND CRAFT
8245 Southwest Barnes Road
(503) 297-5544
Oregon College of Art and Craft was born in 1907 during an international movement to preserve and revive the arts and crafts that humans had practiced for a thousand years. Since then the Oregon College of Art and Craft has been training students in fiber art, metalworking, ceramics, and the production of many other useful and beautiful objects. Their book arts program is renowned the world over. The college, which rests on the grounds of an old filbert orchard, grants a Bachelor of Fine Arts degree; the training for that includes liberal arts, professional practices, and writing. The college also grants certificates in individual specialties. And there are numerous courses and programs available for those who want to simply take a pottery course or learn how to bind books. (See The Arts chapter for more information.)

OREGON EXECUTIVE MBA
200 Southwest Market Street
(503) 276-3622, (866) 996-3622
www.oemba.org
Though there are other executive MBA programs in the nation, not one of them has the firepower of Oregon's, and that's because it's the only

one made up of a consortium of universities. In 1985 Portland State, the University of Oregon, and Oregon State combined to begin this program for working mid- to senior-level managers. Because students are busy running their companies, the tough academic work is balanced by a task-oriented curriculum. Innovative assignments demonstrate in real-world terms the theory that's being taught. A chief hurdle before graduating, for example, is the completion of a major feasibility study or a business plan. Students report other advantages to this program: The peer support is good, and the chance to network, unparalleled. Classes take place on Friday and Saturday over short terms, allowing managers to earn their MBAs in two years.

OREGON HEALTH AND SCIENCE UNIVERSITY
3181 Southwest Sam Jackson Park Road
(503) 494-8311
Oregon Health and Science University (OHSU) has roots that reach back to the 1800s, but its modern history began in 1974, when the Oregon State Board of Higher Education combined extant schools of nursing, dentistry, and medicine with the Medical School Hospital, Doernbecher Children's Hospital, and various clinics to form Oregon Health Sciences Center. In 1995 the center, now called OHSU, extracted itself from the Oregon State Board of Higher Education to form a nonprofit public corporation governed by a state-appointed board. The result has been a major expansion of services and an even larger infusion of research grant money. Today OHSU educates health professionals and biomedical researchers in a variety of fields, and it provides excellent, state-of-the-art health care and research. It also devotes many resources to community service and education, including caring for the neediest patients in Oregon. And, finally, it is the largest corporate employer in the city. All things considered, few institutions have such a direct and indirect influence on the life of Portland citizens.

The main campus overlooks the city that it serves, poised atop Marquam Hill, with stunning views of the Cascades, the Willamette, and the city. The central campus is a maze of buildings connected by bridges, tunnels, stairs, and skyways, but the relatively compact nature of the hospital complex makes a visitor forget that there is another 260-acre campus west of Portland as well as many other clinics and facilities throughout the city and beyond. OHSU's programs and services extend across the state's entire 96,000 square miles, reaching into neighboring states. The main components of OHSU are the School of Dentistry, the School of Medicine, the School of Nursing, and a number of signature research institutes. One of America's first-rate academic health care and medical research centers, OHSU attracts top-ranking students from throughout the country. Graduates of the School of Dentistry regularly maintain a 97 percent first-time pass rate when they take their board exams, and no dental students in the nation have more clinical hours upon graduation. The School of Medicine has equally impressive numbers; not only do graduates attain nearly a 100 percent first-time pass rate, but the primary care education program ranks among the top 2 percent in the nation. Similar numbers are available for the School of Nursing graduates, whose master's programs also ranked in the top 2 percent. OHSU's research units are also distinguished; they include, but are not limited to, the Center for Research on Occupational and Environmental Toxicology, the Vollum Institute for Advanced Biomedical Research, the Knight Cancer Center, and the Oregon Regional Primate Research Center. OHSU offers both Masters and PhD programs in a variety of disciplines, from neuroscience to biochemistry to nursing to healthcare administration. Research funding at OHSU has almost tripled since 1995, and discoveries by its scientists are in the news daily. In fact, OHSU brings in nearly $300 million in research funding every year, making it one of the top research sites in the nation.

OREGON INSTITUTE OF TECHNOLOGY
7726 Southeast Harmony Road
Beaverton
(503) 725-3066

The Oregon Institute of Technology (OIT) offers four-year degrees, degree-completion programs, and a number of workshops and seminars on its campuses in Klamath Falls in southern Oregon, where OIT was founded, and on its campuses in Portland and Beaverton. Its degrees are granted in a broad spectrum of different engineering, science, and technological disciplines, including—but not at all limited to—health technologies, applied sciences of various kinds, communications, and environmental engineering.

PACIFIC NORTHWEST COLLEGE OF ART
1241 Northwest Johnson Street
(503) 226-4391

The Pacific Northwest College of Art (PNCA) has been training students in the visual arts since 1909, when it was an arm of the Portland Art Museum, but by 1994, PNCA was a separate institution that granted Bachelor of Fine Arts degrees in addition to its community education classes. Over the years PNCA grew so much that it had to move from its lovely Pietro Belluschi–designed building next to the museum to a large, visually stunning converted warehouse in the Pearl District. This has allowed the college to add two times the space devoted to photography, as well as providing state-of-the-art computer capability. Public galleries showcase the work of students, and the Swiggert Commons, a large space for exhibitions, installations, lectures, and other events, provides an exciting hub for aesthetic activity in the already-happening Pearl. Students here receive careful, attentive training in their specialties and are regarded for their imaginative design. They are also trained in useful and practical skills like writing, math, and professional concerns. (See The Arts chapter for more information.)

PORTLAND STATE UNIVERSITY
1721 Southwest Broadway
(503) 725-9800
www.pdx.edu

One of the seven universities and colleges of the Oregon University System, Portland State (PSU) is Oregon's urban university, responding to the needs and interests of the greater Portland area. PSU offers more than 100 undergraduate and graduate degrees in the humanities, sciences, social sciences, and professions, including doctoral degrees in education, electrical and computer engineering, environmental sciences and resources, public administration and policy, social work and social research, systems science, and urban studies and planning. PSU grants more graduate degrees than any other university in the state.

The 36 acres of the university, which straddles the southern Park Blocks downtown, are replete with big trees, fountains, ivy-covered buildings, hip students in coffee bars, and other accoutrements of a modern urban campus. Visitors will also find beautiful new buildings that house some of the most prestigious programs (such as the College of Urban and Public Affairs, which is appropriately found at the southern terminus of the new streetcar system). About 15,000 students are enrolled at Portland State, including more than 4,200 graduate students. Continuing education programs add thousands more students to the total numbers. Most students commute, but there are some dormitories and the university can assist students in finding housing, applying for financial aid, acquiring a campus job, and other staples of student life.

Extracurricular activities at the school are abundant. The PSU Vikings play 15 intercollegiate varsity sports. Men's intercollegiate sports are football, basketball, baseball, cross-country, golf, soccer, track, and wrestling. Women's sports are cross-country, basketball, soccer, softball, tennis, track, and volleyball. Baseball competes within Division I of the NCAA; all other sports compete within Division II. On the cultural front, PSU regularly sponsors events such as theater, films, guest speakers, art exhibits, and concerts. The Florestan Trio, Friends of Chamber Music, PSU Piano Recital Series, Guitar Series, and Contemporary Dance Season deliver more than 15,000 fans to PSU's Lincoln Performance Hall annually.

Like all decent universities, the programs at PSU extend beyond the tree-lined campus to serve all citizens. PSU is the epicenter of a variety of cutting-edge research and public service programs, including the Center for Black Studies, the Center for Science Education, the Center for Population Research and Census, the Center for Software Quality Research, the Center for Urban Studies, the Institute on Aging, the Institute of Portland Metropolitan Studies, and the Portland Educational Network.

REED COLLEGE
3203 Southeast Woodstock Boulevard
(503) 771-1112
www.reed.edu

Reed College looks like the cinematic version of a private college, all ivy and brick, with grassy playing fields and a picturesque stream. However, appearances can deceive: Reed College, founded in 1908, is much less traditional than it looks. One way Reed is different is that conventional letter grades for each course are recorded but not distributed. As long as you're doing satisfactory work, you don't have to worry about grades. This frees students to actually learn something, a freedom that pays off for everybody. Writer Loren Pope describes it as "the most intellectual college in the nation," one at which faculty are thrilled to teach because the students are genuinely interested in learning. A measure of the success of this approach is the rate at which Reed students win awards like Watson Fellowships and Rhodes Scholarships (31 Rhodes Scholars at last count, the second-highest tally in the nation).

Reed is a four-year liberal arts school (though the college does offer a master's degree in liberal studies as well). The standard liberal arts majors are available, but in addition, the college offers a number of interdisciplinary majors in subjects such as theater-dance and biochemistry. Its annual enrollment is about 1,400, small enough to provide an intimate environment for learning, but large enough so that everyone isn't exactly like everyone else. All Reed students take a one-year course in humanities their freshman year, and all write a senior thesis. Many departments hold weekly seminars by faculty, students, and visiting scholars, and frequent lectures and seminars further expand the opportunities for intellectual exchange. Reed's Hauser Library, with its 430,000 volumes and more than 1,500 periodical subscriptions, is worthy of mention. The periodical section is very good for a college of its size. The library, a depository for U.S. government publications, also maintains special collections of rare books, manuscripts, and archival materials.

UNIVERSITY OF PORTLAND
5000 North Willamette Boulevard
(503) 943-8000
www.up.edu
The University of Portland has been consistently ranked by *U.S. News and World Report* as a top-10 university in its class. Its 2,600 students pursue 75 undergraduate and graduate degrees, notably in the liberal arts, business, education, nursing, and engineering. Founded in 1901, the University of Portland is affiliated with the Congregation of Holy Cross, the Catholic order that also runs its sister school, the University of Notre Dame; its dedication is to the heart and spirit as well as the mind. Its reputation increases daily—with a faculty that garners substantial awards and grants (from the National Science Foundation and the National Endowment for the Arts, among others) and a 14 to 1 student-faculty ratio allowing personal contact, it's no wonder. The University of Portland sits on a dramatic bluff overlooking the Willamette; its 125-acre campus is in a pretty, residential neighborhood of North Portland. Plus, they have a phenomenal women's soccer team that's a contender for the national title nearly every year—including 2006, when they won.

WARNER PACIFIC COLLEGE
2219 Southeast 68th Avenue
(503) 517-1000
www.warnerpacific.edu
A Christian liberal arts college founded in 1937, Warner Pacific College, which serves 650 students, is in Southeast Portland near Mt. Tabor

Park. Accredited by the Northwest Association of Schools and Colleges, Warner Pacific has trained students in a Christian-centered curriculum of liberal arts for more than 60 years. Warner Pacific offers a number of education programs, including early childhood education, teacher education, and English as a second language (ESL), in addition to its four-year degrees. Warner Pacific also has an imaginative degree-completion program that is ideal for many returning students who work full-time.

Community Colleges

The Portland Metro area is blessed with no fewer than three top-notch community colleges, and they all offer state-of-the-art facilities and a wide range of academic, technical, and vocational learning opportunities. Besides the savings in tuition, the easy access, excellent instruction, and desirable teacher-to-student ratios make community colleges an attractive option.

CLACKAMAS COMMUNITY COLLEGE
19600 South Molalla Avenue
Oregon City
(503) 657-6958
www.clackamas.cc.or.us
Serving about 28,000 students annually, almost 8,000 of them full-time, Clackamas Community College (CCC) may have a lot of students, but it feels like a small college. CCC students take advantage of a variety of programs, from basic literacy and study skills to college-prep courses. Popular programs include the two-year Associate of Science degrees or the Certificates of Completion; these are granted in more than 30 areas of study. Students also may pursue the Oregon Transfer degree, an Associate of Arts degree that guarantees junior standing at any Oregon University System school (and which many non-Oregon University System schools will also honor). Transfer-degree students have more than 70 options for major study.

Because many students lack the basic skills to obtain even a high school diploma, CCC also offers personal tutoring and courses that cover fundamental academic and life skills. Some of these programs cover GED preparation and English for nonnative speakers in addition to courses in career possibilities and parenting. CCC also offers credit and noncredit courses that cover dozens of areas of personal interest at more than 100 locations.

MT. HOOD COMMUNITY COLLEGE
26000 Southeast Stark Street, Gresham
(503) 491-6422
www.mhcc.cc.or.us
Mt. Hood Community College (MHCC) enrolls approximately 27,000 students each year at its campuses. MHCC's services cover the spectrum from providing adult literacy classes to preparing students for transfer to a university or entry into highly technical fields such as microelectronics, and the college provides one- and two-year degrees and certificates in more than 100 professional, technical, and transfer programs. Academic opportunities are, naturally, also available, including the Oregon Transfer Degree, the Honors College, and the MHCC–Portland State University Co-Admission program. In addition, continuing education classes are offered to the community at locations throughout MHCC's district with topics ranging from art to aerobics, cooking to computing, investing to woodworking. Classes are offered at the 200-acre main campus, as well as at satellite campuses throughout the district.

PORTLAND COMMUNITY COLLEGE
12000 Southwest 49th Avenue
(503) 244-6111
www.pcc.edu
Portland Community College enrolls more students than any other college in Oregon—97,000 annually, full- or part-time. PCC is a two-year college that offers myriad educational opportunities. Three main campuses provide lower-division college transfer courses, two-year associate degree programs, professional and technical

career-training programs, and adult basic education courses. Several other locations offer workforce training, literacy training, and other training courses in addition to their basic academic services. And an open campus offers programs in a variety of places throughout the district. Moreover PCC also offers many community outreach services available to students and nonstudents alike. If you do decide to enroll, you may take courses at any of the campuses—it all depends on what is offered at what times. And anyone may attend PCC, even those who haven't yet finished high school.

PCC's Cascade campus sits in an urban area off North Killingsworth Street, and more than 9,000 students each year attend this city campus. It has become a focal point for rebirth in the neighborhood, for many area residents have turned to the Cascade campus for job training, college transfer, and self-improvement courses. Many community services such as child care, legal aid, neighborhood associations, and job referral services are found on the campus. Cascade also hosts the Festival of African Films each year as well as a Mardi Gras celebration; these events draw visitors from all over the area.

About 10,000 students attend the Rock Creek campus, which lies 12 miles west of town and draws many of its students from Beaverton-Hillsboro. As with all community college campuses, a multiplicity of programs is available here. One draw is the Aviation Technology Hangar, where students can have direct experience working on airplanes and helicopters.

The Sylvania Campus, PCC's administrative center, in Southwest Portland, has the largest campus. More than 26,000 students attend the programs here each year. In addition to its well-regarded basic programs, Sylvania has three specialized programs with admirable reputations: the nursing, dental, and developmental education programs. The new library and theater are focal points of the campus—that is, if you can tear your eyes from the western view, which extends over the valley to the Coast Range Mountains.

Specialized Schools

APOLLO COLLEGE
2004 Lloyd Center
(503) 288-5245
www.apollocollege.edu
The medical field is full of opportunities for people with good technical skills, and Apollo College offers associate degrees in medical laboratory technology, respiratory therapy, occupational therapy assistance, and medical radiography. You can also study in a diploma program here to become a dental or medical assistant, pharmacy technician, medical records technician, or a medical administrative assistant. Some form of financial aid is available to almost all the approximately 300 students. Job placement services are available on-site.

HEALD COLLEGE
625 Southwest Broadway, Suite 200
(503) 229-0492
www.heald.edu
One of 12 campuses in three states, Heald College of Portland, in the heart of downtown, offers associate degrees in computer business administration and computer technology as well as certificates in network technology for Cisco Systems and Microsoft Windows 2003. Accredited by the Western Association of Schools and Colleges, Heald is a nonprofit school founded in San Francisco in 1863. Its students get plenty of hands-on computer and technical experience before graduating, and then they receive ongoing job placement services. Training and internships are provided during the day and evening, and many students qualify for financial aid. No student housing is available, but counselors work with students to help them find suitable options.

INTERNATIONAL AIR ACADEMY
2901 East Mill Plain Boulevard
Vancouver, WA
(360) 695-2500
www.airacademy.com
The International Air Academy has placed 17,000 graduates in airline careers, and they can get you started in a travel career through their 20-week Airline Travel Specialist diploma program. For many students this is the first step toward becoming a certified travel consultant. Graduates of the program are qualified for a broad range of positions, including travel and tour agent and customer service agent, and for a variety of jobs in transportation, travel, and hospitality marketing. Another diploma program, the 10-week airline reservations and airport services, provides entry to jobs in reservation sales, ticket agents, and gate and ramp agent positions. Many alumni of International Air Academy are hired by major airlines as flight attendants, in customer service positions, and as schedulers or reservation agents. Founded in 1980 this school is accredited by the Accrediting Commission of Career Schools and Colleges of Technology. The majority of students qualify for financial aid, and dormitory housing is available for out-of-towners.

UNIVERSITY OF PHOENIX
12550 Southeast 93rd Avenue
Clackamas
(503) 495-2000

3600 Northwest John Olsen Place,
Suite 300, Hillsboro
(503) 495-1900

13221 Southwest 68th Parkway, Tigard
(503) 403-2900
The University of Phoenix is designed to assist working professionals with completing their undergraduate or graduate degrees, and they pay special attention to the scheduling issues that working people have by offering classes at night, on weekends, and over the Internet. Credit may be given for experience, which can lessen the time it takes to complete your degree. The University of Phoenix specializes in business, education, health care, management, nursing, and technology.

WESTERN CULINARY INSTITUTE
921 Southwest Morrison Street, Suite 400
(503) 223-2245
www.wci.edu

Every year some 600 students take their first step toward becoming artists in the kitchen at Western Culinary Institute (WCI). The 12-month course is full-time and culminates in a diploma, certification, or both. Significantly, Western Culinary Institute has formed a partnership with Le Cordon Bleu, the renowned French institute of cooking instruction. And not only does WCI offer Le Cordon Bleu certification in the culinary arts, but it recently became the first school in the United States to offer Le Cordon Bleu certification in restaurant management—quite a coup for the school. Notable chefs from around the world teach classes Monday through Friday at WCI; the curriculum emphasizes fine dining, hotel and resort cooking, and catering. Students learn hands-on at three on-site restaurants as well as through off-campus internships. Western Culinary offers financial aid to most students and assists with housing needs and part-time employment; the school claims a very high job placement rate.

WESTERN STATES CHIROPRACTIC COLLEGE
2900 Northeast 132nd Avenue
(503) 256-3180
www.wschiro.edu

Western States Chiropractic College (WSCC) is a private, nonprofit, professional school that educates students in the art, science, and philosophy of chiropractic self-healing, and its graduates are prepared to work within an interdisciplinary medical framework. Its reputation is outstanding: its graduates test very well on their board exams, and the college was the first chiropractic college ever, in 1994, to receive federal research money—nearly $1 million in grant funds from the Department of Health and Human Services. The WSCC student population numbers between 400 and 500 and comes from all parts of the United States and from several foreign countries; about one third of the students have earned a bachelor's degree before they arrive, and many are already working professionals in some other field. Originally founded as the Pacific Chiropractic College, the school was reorganized and became Western States Chiropractic College in 1932. In 1986 the college opened its 9,000-square-foot Outpatient Clinic on campus, making it the largest chiropractic facility in the Northwest.

HEALTH CARE AND WELLNESS

Portland's healing community is at the heart of a state known for exciting advances in health reform, medical research, innovative practice, and cutting-edge legislation, such as the Oregon Health Plan. Initiated through a series of laws enacted from 1989 to 1995, it provides health insurance to low-income residents. Roughly 100,000 Oregonians now have health coverage, including the working poor, seniors, people with disabilities, children, and pregnant women, although budget shortfalls have recently strained the Oregon Health Plan and continue to put pressure on the public health system.

Another notable trend suggests that Oregon and its major metropolitan center are in the forefront of a worldwide movement to integrate health-care modalities: Providence Health Plans and Kaiser Permanente both offer coverage of visits to chiropractors and acupuncturists, and Providence also works with the Community Selfcare Center located in some Wild Oats health food and nutrition outlets.

The Western States Chiropractic College, Oriental College of Oriental Medicine, National College of Naturopathic Medicine, and East-West College of Healing Arts are also important features of the health-care landscape.

Portland is also the home of influential medical research. Notably, Oregon Health and Science University's (OHSU) Brian Druker and his laboratory developed the first chemotherapy drug that specifically targets cancer cells and leaves healthy cells alone. This drug, called Gleevec, works by preventing the proteins in chronic myeloid leukemia cells from binding—and therefore from multiplying. This exciting development is widely regarded as the future for effective treatment of cancer.

If you need emergency assistance, dial 911. We have also listed other important health-care phone numbers at the end of this section. But before you reach for your phone, first check out the profiles of Portland's Health and Wellness facilities. We begin the look with hospitals; the list is ordered geographically.

HOSPITALS

Southwest Portland

OREGON HEALTH AND SCIENCE UNIVERSITY
3181 Southwest Sam Jackson Park Road
(503) 494-8311

OHSU is an internationally renowned center for research and education, as well as a complex of hospitals and clinics, that traces its beginnings to the turn of the 20th century. It is the region's only academic health center, which means that it not only teaches the next generation of physicians, nurses, and other providers, but it also engages in cutting-edge biomedical research. It is also a level-one trauma center, with Life Flight helicopters making all-too-frequent landings. Most of Oregon's state-of-the-art biomedical research and treatment goes on here, bringing hundreds of millions of dollars to Oregon's economy.

But OHSU provides other important health services to Oregon. For example, it runs Oregon's Poison Control Center (503-222-1222 or www .ohsu.edu/poison), a hotline of information and instructions about what to do in the event that dangerous substances are ingested. It conducts rural outreach programs to bring the latest in research and treatments to people across Oregon. Its Biomedical Information Communication Center (BICC) holds hundreds of thousands of books and makes the latest research available to the general public via its online catalogs.

Healthy Talks is a series of Saturday morning talks with OHSU faculty who discuss medical issues at the auditorium free of charge. The talks are also broadcast via Portland Cable Access on Channel 30.

Not everything happens at OHSU's central campus. OHSU has a number of outreach programs that connect it with the city of Portland and far beyond. These include not only patient clinics, but also programs to reduce health disparities, to help children with chronic diseases, and other important initiatives.

PROVIDENCE ST. VINCENT MEDICAL CENTER
9205 Southwest Barnes Road
(503) 216-1234
www.providence.org/oregon

Providence St. Vincent has a history in Portland dating from 1856, when five nuns arrived from Montreal to care for the natives. The Providence Health System has grown to a regional service that has 1,500 physicians in 40 specialties as well as 10,000 other health professionals. In this particular hospital there are 450 beds, 1,600 medical staff, and nearly 3,300 employees. Its specialties include a heart program, a women and children's program, and the Oregon Medical Laser Center, where lasers rather than scalpels are used in surgery. Providence St. Vincent Medical Center is also the home of the area's only inpatient mental health facility. (For information on another of Providence's hospitals in Portland, see the entry for Providence Portland Medical Center in the section on North/Northeast Portland.)

Northwest Portland

LEGACY GOOD SAMARITAN HOSPITAL & MEDICAL CENTER
1015 Northwest 22nd Avenue
(503) 413-7711
www.legacyhealth.org

Known as "Good Sam," this hospital has an average of 280 beds available each year. A Community Health Education Center, (503) 335-3500 or (503) 413-7047 (TDD), is located across the street from the hospital in the administration center. Staff provide information on a variety of health and wellness topics and treatment options. Legacy is also home to the Visiting Nurses Association, (503) 220-1000, and the Breast Health Center, (503) 335-3500, where diagnostic, educational, and support services allow women to get mammograms, receive results quickly, and obtain follow-up tests, counseling, and care.

Southeast Portland

ADVENTIST MEDICAL CENTER
10123 Southeast Market Street
(503) 257-2500
www.adventisthealthnw.org

Located in outer Southeast Portland near Mall 205 is a 302-bed hospital with a medical staff of 500 and 1,600 employees. It is part of Adventist Health, a not-for-profit health-care system of 20 hospitals throughout the western United States, all open to the general public. The hospitals and clinics are operated by the Seventh-day Adventist Church with headquarters in Roseville, California. The Adventist Health System also offers 19 clinics in the metro area. To make an appointment or find out more about available medical professionals, call the Physicians Referral Line at (503) 256-4000.

North/Northeast Portland

LEGACY EMANUEL HOSPITAL & HEALTH CENTER
2801 North Gantenbein Avenue
(503) 413-2200
www.legacyhealth.org

Besides being the largest hospital in the local Legacy Health System, this health center is also the site of one of the two level-one trauma centers in Portland. It is also the home of Legacy Emanuel Children's Hospital. To promote safety and health for children, Emanuel sponsors an annual Healthy Kids' Fair in the spring, highlighted with sales of bike helmets and car safety checks. The Children's Hospital has its own Emergency and After Hours Care. After hours call (503) 313-4684. Call (503) 413-2200 for both information and physician referral. Legacy Emanuel is also the home of the Oregon Burn Center, which specializes in treating those who have endured serious burns.

PROVIDENCE PORTLAND MEDICAL CENTER
4805 Northeast Glisan Street
(503) 215-1111
www.providence.org/oregon
Providence Health System offers graduate medical education in the Portland area at Providence Portland Medical Center and Providence St. Vincent Medical Center in two distinct programs. Portland is also home to the Earle A. Chiles Institute, a multidisciplinary center devoted to the research of heart disease, cancer, diabetes, and infectious diseases; the Robert W. Franz Cancer Research Center, which focuses on the immune system in treating breast cancer; and the Albert Starr Academic Center for Cardiac Surgery where Dr. Starr, coinventor of the artificial heart valve, and his colleagues continue to explore the field of cardiac surgery, now including heart transplants.

The campus of the Providence Portland Medical Center is also home to the Child Center at 830 Northeast 47th Avenue, (503) 215-2400. This pediatric outpatient clinic serves children with autism, seizure disorders, and mental health difficulties. The Gamma Knife Center is the newest addition to Providence. The gamma knife is a highly advanced technological tool that uses beams of gamma radiation to treat a variety of brain lesions and disorders. The Providence Resource Line is (503) 574-6595 . This line will help callers select physicians and health education classes and obtain access to various programs.

Vancouver
SOUTHWEST WASHINGTON MEDICAL CENTER
400 Northeast Mother Joseph Place
3400 Main Street, Vancouver
(503) 972-3000, (360) 256-2000
www.swmedctr.com
Southwest Washington Medical Center comprises a number of urgent-care clinics, physicians' offices, and other health-care facilities in Clark County. But its heart is the Medical Center, the first hospital in the Pacific Northwest. It has 360 beds and a level-two trauma center. The latest development at this medical complex is the Family Birth Center with 49 beds, many in private rooms with Jacuzzis.

The main medical campus is thoroughly modern, with a state-of-the-art Cancer Center, a well-designed Physician's Pavilion, and updated patient facilities. Its other clinics and centers scattered throughout Clark County offer laser eye surgery, specialized care for mothers and children, and urgent care.

SPECIALIZED HOSPITALS AND OTHER MEDICAL FACILITIES

DOERNBECHER CHILDREN'S HOSPITAL
3181 Sam Jackson Park Road
(503) 494-8311
www.ohsu.edu/health/clinics-and-services/doernbecher/

CHILD DEVELOPMENT AND REHABILITATION CENTER
(503) 494-8095
Since its founding in 1926, Doernbecher has provided the best available medical care to children in Oregon and southwest Washington, including children from families with limited incomes. Financial assistance, through the Oregon Health Plan or Oregon's Children's Health Insurance Program, assures that services here are available to all of Oregon's youth. About 30,000 children visit Doernbecher every year, some from as far

away as northern California, Idaho, Alaska, Hawaii, and Montana.

The current Doernbecher Children's Hospital opened its doors on July 14, 1998. It's a gorgeous building, and families can have private rooms with showers. Parents' lounges and a research library make stays easier for family members, and large playrooms, courtyards, and an in-house art therapy program help youngsters take their minds off their illnesses.

Doctors here not only do research but also provide a wide range of medical services from bone marrow, stem cell, and organ transplants to treating cancer, cystic fibrosis, and rare genetic diseases. The Child Research and Rehabilitation Center focuses on children with developmental disabilities, providing cutting-edge research and providing the multidisciplinary care that these children and their families require.

U.S. VETERANS HOSPITAL
3710 Southwest U.S. Veterans
Hospital Road
(503) 273-5289
www.portland.med.va.gov

This VA hospital is good news for regional vets with medical problems. Rather than dodge "Big Nurse," these men and women who served their country receive excellent care from cheerful, nurturing doctors and nurses. They may lose your files once in a while, and there's that old "hurry up and wait," but what else is new? One big plus is that this facility is professionally and literally linked to OHSU, its neighbor on Pill Hill. To get from one hospital to the other, patients and staff walk across a Sky Bridge with a terrific view of Portland, the Willamette River, and Mount Hood.

WALK-IN AND URGENT-CARE CLINICS

For Portlanders and visitors with urgent health needs, here are a few recommended walk-in clinics and urgent-care facilities. With a few exceptions, such as screenings for toxins, you won't

need to make an appointment. The first one, though, is a handy service provided by Multnomah County Health Department. With one phone call they'll direct you to the best place for your particular health needs.

MULTNOMAH COUNTY HEALTH DEPARTMENT
Health Information and Referral
(503) 988-3816 (voice and TDD)

This is an excellent resource for referrals to urgent-care facilities in your neighborhood or just about any health and wellness facility in the tri-county area. They are open Monday through Friday 8:00 a.m. to 5:00 p.m.

DOCTORS FAMILY CLINIC AND EMERGICENTER
9735 Southwest Shady Lane, Tigard
(503) 639-2800

2870 Southwest Cedar Hills Boulevard
(877) 731-3329

This urgent care center's hours are 8:00 a.m. to 8:00 p.m. Monday through Friday and 9:00 a.m. to 3:00 p.m. (6:00 p.m. in Tigard) Saturday and Sunday. Walk-ins are welcome.

LEGACY GOOD SAMARITAN URGENT CARE
1015 Northwest 22nd Avenue
(503) 413-7711

Hours for the Good Sam walk-in clinic are 9:00 a.m. to 9:00 p.m. Monday through Friday and 10:00 a.m. to 8:00 p.m. Saturday and Sunday.

NATIONAL COLLEGE OF NATUROPATHIC MEDICINE FIRST AVENUE CLINIC
2220 Southwest 1st Avenue
(503) 552-1551

The clinic offers walk-in assistance Tuesday to Friday 8:00 a.m. to noon and a number of free screenings for a variety of conditions held throughout the year. To get a schedule of screenings, call the number listed here.

HOSPICE

OREGON HOSPICE ASSOCIATION
(503) 228-2104
www.oregonhospice.org
Hospice is a program of supportive care for anyone with a terminal illness. Hospice focuses on providing a full range of physical, emotional, social, and spiritual comfort to both the patient and his or her family. The Oregon Hospice Association is the primary referral and information source in Oregon for hospice care and other options at the end of life.

SUPPORT FOR THE MENTALLY ILL

NATIONAL ALLIANCE FOR THE MENTALLY ILL OF MULTNOMAH COUNTY
3550 Southeast Woodward Street
(503) 230-8009
www.nami.org/sites/NAMIoregon
This grassroots, self-help, and advocacy organization has been in operation since 1979, helping people with mental illness and their families to live better lives. Members can attend family education programs, support groups, and general meetings. Membership includes three newsletters.

SPORTS MEDICINE

REBOUND
1 North Center Court, Suite 110
(503) 797-9585
www.reboundmd.com
Located only a limp away from the Rose Garden, home of the Portland Trailblazers, this sports medicine and neurosurgery clinic is staffed by physical therapists, neurosurgeons, and physicians whose goal it is to get you moving again. Although professional athletes are patients, Rebound is also open to those who have, for example, stretched too hard pruning a tree. Call for free, 24-hour sports injury information.

RETIREMENT

Portland is a particularly agreeable place for retirement whether you are moving here specifically for that purpose or you have lived here your whole life. And that's because civic life is still celebrated here. We have a sophisticated, affordable, and reliable mass-transit system that is sympathetic to the needs of seniors, an outstanding public library, world-class health care, a fine public parks system, and most of the other amenities that make life worth living. The temperate climate ensures that there usually won't be too many very hot or very cold days. In the interest of full disclosure, however, we should let you know that many seniors in the area spend part of the year in warmer climates such as Palm Springs and save their Portland time for the months from June through October, when the weather is especially good. However, we have noticed more and more seniors retiring to Portland permanently and choosing to live downtown, with its convenient access to the streetcar and other transportation, as well as outstanding restaurants, shopping, and the arts.

Portland seniors will find many different housing options in many different parts of the city. (Currently Washington County has the fastest-growing senior population.) You will find communities devoted solely to seniors, as well as neighborhoods that have a balance of all ages, whichever you prefer. If you live independently but are ready to give up such tasks as mowing the lawn and maintaining a house, you'll have a wide variety of choices available. And this is also true if you need more help than just having the lawn mowed. One word of caution: Portland is comparatively expensive when it comes to real estate, especially in the heart of the city, which has the most accessible services. However, if you look hard you can usually find something well priced, especially if you're looking for a row house or condominium. Many charming, well-planned, affordable housing communities are being built all across the region; some of these are close to the MAX line.

CHOOSING A RETIREMENT COMMUNITY

Our retirement communities offer independent apartment, house, or condominium living, along with support services such as weekly housekeeping. Some locations offer one or more meals per day. Many of these places contract with private home health agencies to provide extra assistance to residents for which there are additional fees. In general these retirement communities are not licensed as care facilities, but some locations offer floors or sections that are licensed to provide a higher level of care. There is no financial assistance available to help cover the cost of housing in nonlicensed retirement communities.

In the Portland area alone, there are more than 100 retirement communities—one for every taste and budget. Some have buy-in fees and long-term leases, some rent apartments by the month. Some have swimming pools, health spas, and tennis courts; others focus on providing activities such as bridge clubs, group outings, and community meals. Many offer different levels of care should you ever need them. We've listed a representative sample of housing styles here to get you started, but you can ask your Realtor, the State Office of Senior and Disabled Services, or an online service such as Senior.com for more comprehensive information. Most retirement centers will be delighted to send you a brochure and arrange a guided tour.

While many of the retirement communities are designed for seniors without serious medical problems, many of them do provide continuing care when needed. Some of the following communities are designed to meet the increasing care needs of an aging resident by providing independent apartment living supplemented with an on-site health-care facility, usually licensed by the State of Oregon Senior and Disabled Services office. The residency agreement includes a contract, and tenants pay a large entrance fee (or buy-in) in addition to monthly rates. Before making a decision on any retirement community, check with Senior and Disabled Services at (800) 282-8096. They can tell you about any complaints made against the place you are considering. If you are in the market for Alzheimer's care or other intensive, continuing-care facilities, we suggest you also check the Oregon Department of Human Services Web site—it has a comprehensive guide to long-term care and provides a list of local offices that can help you find placement (www.oregon.gov/DHS/aboutdhs/structure/spd/shtml).

Home Ownership in Senior Communities

Home ownership in a senior retirement setting is available in the following communities, which are primarily intended for independent living for persons over 55 years of age. Except for the retirement setting, the arrangements are not very different from home ownership in the community at large, and assistance in the home is the responsibility of the resident.

Portland

CLAREMONT ADULT RESORT LIVING
15800 Northwest Country Club Drive
(503) 629-5614
www.claremontgolfclub.com
Does the idea of living on the edge of a beautiful golf course sound appealing? Ten miles from Portland's city center, Claremont is one of the most exclusive adult communities in the state, with beautifully built homes selling at the higher end of the real estate market. While one doesn't have to be retired to live here (it just doesn't allow children younger than 18), most residents are 55 or older. Many are retired professionals who have active, vigorous lifestyles. The custom-planned houses have fireplaces, private outdoor terraces, spacious island kitchens, big master suites, studies, and oversize garages. There are at least 10 distinctive styles of homes to choose from. Claremont's grounds are meticulously maintained; ponds, waterfalls, streams, and fountains are everywhere; and the golf and putting course are excellent. Two elegant and comfortable clubhouses are available only to residents and guests, and a pro shop, two outdoor swimming pools, tennis and croquet courts, lawn bowling, and a fitness center are on-site. The town of Cedar Mills, which offers all the shopping opportunities one could ask for, is just a mile away.

SUMMERPLACE
2020 Northeast 150th Avenue
(503) 257-0733
Summerplace offers a combination of housing styles and apartments. There is a wide selection of houses with two bedrooms and two baths. Many seniors here pursue a variety of activities from ballroom dancing to golf, to attending the numerous spaghetti dinners and crab feeds that Summerplace holds. Besides the outdoor swimming pool, there are tennis courts and a well-equipped exercise and weight room to help residents stay in shape. Summerplace also offers its residents a variety of fun classes, ranging from woodcarving to flower arranging. Although there isn't a golf course on-site, one of the area's most popular golf clubs, Glendoveer (see the Golf chapter), is only a stone's throw away. Summerplace is located in a fairly quiet area of outer Northeast Portland off 148th Avenue, but it is close to major arterials such as Marine Drive and Glisan Street. There are numerous medical and shopping facilities and plenty of restaurants in the vicinity. Summerplace also has extensive assisted living facilities, including Alzheimer's disease care, so that families have many options for

housing. The assisted living facilities can be found at 15727 Northeast Russell Street (503-252-9361 or www.prestigecare.com/assisted.

ℹ️ A unique senior facility is emerging in the South Waterfront district: Mirabella in Portland. This innovative continuing care retirement community is designed to allow residents to "age in place"—with amenities such as a penthouse dining room atop the 30-story building. A major component is its relationship with Oregon Health and Science University, which will use its world-class researchers and caregivers to address every dimension of the aging experience in order to improve care. To learn more, call Mirabella at (503) 245-4742

Outlying Areas

KING CITY
15300 Southwest 116th Avenue
King City
(503) 639-4082
www.kingcity.com
King City, which was incorporated as a city in 1966, is widely recognized as one of the most successful adult communities in the Pacific Northwest. Its population of about 2,350 lives in 1,500 homes, apartments, condominiums, and town houses, all in a variety of sizes, styles, and prices. Twelve miles south of downtown Portland and just over the hill from the city of Tigard, King City has its own shopping center, which serves its residents and other nearby adult communities as well. The grounds are beautifully manicured and the homes are well maintained. A fine golf course is on-site, as is a modern residential center, which provides comfortable living, dining, and recreation for residents who no longer want to maintain individual homes.

Home Sharing

SHARED HOUSING
1819 Northwest Everett Street
(503) 225-9924
An Ecumenical Ministries of Oregon program, Shared Housing has proven to be invaluable to many seniors, enabling them to stay in their homes despite financial or physical limitations. This referral and matching service brings together those who need affordable housing with those who can provide it and has arranged more than 2,000 home-sharing agreements since 1982. Through the program, housing is provided in exchange for vital services such as cooking, cleaning, and yard work. Agreements can include rent only, services and reduced rent, room and board, and room and board plus salary. Shared Housing staff checks references, arranges initial meetings, and provides periodic follow-ups. There is an application fee of $10 and a one-time placement fee ranging between $25 and $60, depending on the homeowner's income.

RESOURCES FOR SENIORS

Employment

AMERICAN ASSOCIATION OF RETIRED PERSONS (AARP)
9200 Southeast Sunnybrook Boulevard, Clackamas
(866) 554-5360

AARP SENIOR EMPLOYMENT PROGRAM
4511 Southeast Hawthorne Boulevard, Suite 214
(503) 231-8078
AARP's Senior Employment Program provides temporary work experience for people 55 and older who have limited financial resources. The program focuses on giving clients an opportunity to sharpen and develop skills while searching for a permanent job. Clients are placed in nonprofit or public service agency positions for 20 hours per week to receive on-the-job training.

> # Elders in Action: from Personal Advocacy to Policy-Making
>
> Elders in Action advocates for seniors in large ways and small. Not only do they help individuals find resources in their community, but they also provide workshops on how best to use these resources, advocate for policy changes that benefit seniors, and guide businesses and local governments in making senior-friendly services and products. You can find them at 1411 Southwest Morrison, Suite 290, (503) 235-5474, or online at www.eldersinaction.org.

Home Repair and Weatherization

REBUILDING TOGETHER
5000 North Willamette Boulevard
(503) 943-7515
www.rebuildingtogetherportland.org
This nonprofit agency donates material and labor to do extensive remodeling on homes owned by low-income seniors. They accept referrals in the fall and winter and do the work in the spring, investing more than $1 million in the repair of 50 to 60 homes each year.

CITY OF BEAVERTON HOUSING REHABILITATION
4755 Southwest Griffith Drive, Beaverton
(503) 526-2588
This program provides grants and low-interest loans for roof and other repairs for low-income home owners and renters who live within the Beaverton city limits.

COMMUNITY ENERGY PROJECT
422 Northeast Alberta Street
(503) 284-6827
www.communityenergyproject.org

The Community Energy Project (CEP) helps seniors on a fixed income enjoy a warmer home and lower utility bills during the winter months. They install vinyl storm windows that roll up and down easily, weather-strip doors, caulk and eliminate drafts throughout the home, and save money and energy by insulating water heaters and pipes. The CEP also helps seniors with minor repairs and adjustments such as installing safety bars, repairing stairs, installing carbon monoxide and smoke detectors, and other services that will improve quality of life and safety. Home owners as well as renters are welcome to call, and all services and materials are provided free of cost.

HOME ACCESS AND REPAIR FOR THE DISABLED AND ELDERLY (HARDE)
Washington County
Aging Services Department
328 West Main Street, Hillsboro
(503) 846-8897
The HARDE program for low- to moderate-income seniors can provide a $3,000 grant for accessibility improvements such as ramps, wider doorways, grab bars, lower counters, and security devices. Other improvements for home owners may include heating, plumbing or electrical repairs, and roof and siding upkeep. Low-interest loans up to $25,000 are also available for qualifying residents to make needed home improvements. In some cases the repayment may be deferred as long as the senior owns and occupies the home. Renters are also eligible for help with improvements for accessibility.

HUMAN SOLUTIONS LOW INCOME ENERGY ASSISTANCE PROGRAM (LIEAP)
12350 Southeast Powell Boulevard
(503) 548-0200
www.humansolutions.org
This program, similar to the project listed above, helps low-income families and seniors stay cozy while reducing their utility bills during winter months.

Legal Help

Before you call your attorney, you may want to check *Legal Issues for Older Adults,* published by the Oregon State Bar Association. It is a fine reference guide, providing legal information on issues ranging from Medicare to age discrimination, and it includes valuable insights on safety, insurance, and landlord-tenant rights. To order, call (800) 452-8260, ext. 413, or check it out online at www.osbar.org. A printed copy costs $10, but you can download it for free.

Meals and Grocery Delivery
LOAVES AND FISHES/MEALS ON WHEELS
7710 Southwest 31st Avenue
(503) 736-6325
www.loavesandfishesonline.org
Since 1969, Loaves and Fishes and their army of caring volunteers have carried out their mission

"to enrich the lives of seniors and assist them in maintaining independence by making nutritious food, social contacts, and other resources easily available." In addition to wellness and community programs, Loaves and Fishes provides more than one million low-cost, nutritious meals to senior citizens in the Portland Metro area each year. In addition, each day Meals on Wheels delivers thousands of hot meals throughout the metro area to homebound seniors who are at least 60 years of age or have a spouse 60 or older. They have 35 sites, and you can have meals delivered or eat at the sites themselves, with transportation provided. Although the suggested donation for a meal is $2.75, no one is turned away. Besides offering balanced and carefully planned meals and fellowship, Loaves and Fishes sponsors numerous activities and parties throughout the year, especially on the holidays. Loaves and Fishes centers offer a lot more than hot meals—companionship, spiritual fellowship, and ethnic meals and celebrations make the centers a hub of activities for a wide range of elderly clients. To find your nearest Loaves and Fishes, call the central line, listed above, or take advantage of their comprehensive Web site.

Portland's Senior Centers

Southwest Portland
Neighborhood House Senior Center
7688 Southwest Capitol Highway
(503) 244-5204

Northwest Pilot Project
1430 Southwest Broadway
(503) 227-5605

Northwest Portland
Friendly House Senior Center
1816 Northwest Irving Street
(503) 224-2640

Southeast Portland
Fook Lok Woodstock Loaves & Fishes
4937 Southeast Woodstock Boulevard
(503) 771-3601

Portland Impact Senior Center
4610 Southeast Belmont Street
(503) 988-3660

Volunteers of America
537 Southeast Alder Street
(503) 235-8655

continued

North/Northeast Portland
Hollywood Senior Center
1820 Northeast 40th Avenue
(503) 288-8303

Peninsula Senior Center
7548 North Hereford Street
(503) 289-8208

Urban League of Portland
5325 Northeast Martin Luther King Jr.
Boulevard
(503) 988-5470

YWCA–St. Johns Branch
8010 North Charleston Street
(503) 721-6777

Mid-County (Outer East Multnomah County)
YWCA Mid-County District Center
2900 Southeast 122nd Avenue
(503) 988-3840

East County
YWCA East County District Center
501 Northeast Hood Street, Gresham
(503) 306-5680

Washington County
Community Senior Center of Hillsboro
750 Southeast 8th Street, Hillsboro
(503) 648-3823

Elsie Stuhr Adult Leisure Center
550 Southwest Hall Boulevard
Beaverton
(503) 643-9434

Tigard Senior Center
8815 Southwest O'Mara Street, Tigard
(503) 620-4613

Tualatin-Durham Senior Center
8513 Southwest Tualatin Road, Tualatin
(503) 692-6767

Clackamas County
Canby Adult Center
1250 South Ivy Street, Canby
(503) 266-2970

Estacada Community Center
200 Southwest Clubhouse Drive
Estacada
(503) 630-7454

Gladstone Senior Center
1950 Portland Avenue, Gladstone
(503) 655-7701

Lake Oswego Community Center
505 G Avenue, Lake Oswego
(503) 635-3758

Milwaukie Center
5440 Southeast Kellogg Creek Drive,
Milwaukie
(503) 653-8100

Molalla Senior Center
315 Kennel Street, Molalla
(503) 829-4214

Pioneer Community Center
615 5th Street, Oregon City
(503) 657-8287

Sandy Senior and Community Center
38438 Pioneer Boulevard, Sandy
(503) 668-5569

Wilsonville Senior Center,
7965 Southwest Wilsonville Road,
Wilsonville
(503) 682-3727

SENIOR CITIZENS COUNCIL OF CLACKAMAS COUNTY

19241 Beavercreek Road, Oregon City
(503) 657-1366
www.seniorcouncilofclackamasco.org
The Senior Citizens Council offers a variety of services, including grocery delivery, home care, help with medical equipment and oxygen tanks, and information and referral assistance. They also provide guardian and conservatorship services for elderly citizens who may be vulnerable.

STORE TO DOOR OF OREGON

2145 Northwest Overton Street
(503) 413-8223
www.storetodooroforegon.org
This volunteer agency shops for and delivers groceries to the disabled and senior citizens throughout most of Multnomah and Washington Counties.

Recreation and Education
Portland Area Senior Centers

Senior centers around the Portland metro area are oases of hospitality, compassion, and fun for many senior citizens. Besides offering such wide-ranging activities as ballroom dancing, bingo nights, Bible classes, and knitting and crocheting sessions, they are a place for seniors to meet longtime companions as well as to make new friends and learn about different cultures.

In addition to providing recreational and educational activities, the centers also function as information and referral sites, and periodically provide health and cholesterol screenings, tax and legal assistance, flu shots, and referrals for medical and mental health needs. At many senior centers, volunteers are available to help with a variety of in-home services, shopping and transportation, and other needs. (See box in this chapter on Portland's senior centers.)

PORTLAND PARKS AND RECREATION COMMUNITY CENTERS

1120 Southwest 5th Avenue
(503) 823-7529
www.portlandonline.com/parks
Portland Park Bureau's community centers offer a variety of programs and a good number of them are designed specifically for senior citizens. Many of the centers have swimming pools; most have fitness centers and basketball and volleyball courts. It would be impossible to list all the courses that Portland Parks offers—even classifying them takes several pages in the seasonal Portland Parks and Recreation catalog. However, to give you an idea, recent offerings included line dancing, drawing and watercolor painting classes, guitar and piano lessons, birdhouse building, stained glass, sculpting, origami, and flower arranging. Community centers provide more than instruction and classes—they are hubs of social activity. Contact the Parks office to have a complete catalog sent to you.

SENIOR RECREATION PROGRAM

Portland Parks and Recreation
426 Northeast 12th Avenue
(503) 823-4328
Activities ranging from piano lessons and ceramics classes to Native American powwows and hikes on Mount Hood are available at low cost through the Portland Parks and Recreation's Senior Recreation Program. There are also a variety of excursions and day trips planned throughout all seasons of the year. Some are close, such as trips to see the Swan Island dahlias and to ride the Canby Ferry; others are all-day affairs at the Oregon coast or treks up to Silver Star Mountain in Washington. The year-round seniors program provides many great opportunities to meet new friends while staying in good physical condition. Wilderness hikes—to destinations such as Lewis River Falls, Blue Lake, Mount Adams, and Devil Rest Trail in the Columbia Gorge—are

Elder Care Resources

What if you're a healthy senior but your spouse needs substantial care? Life can be difficult for those whose family members have chronic and debilitating diseases—but help is close at hand. Expressions, (503) 252-9361, which cares for Alzheimer's patients, is right next door to Summerplace (see the Home Ownership in Senior Communities section). It's part of a growing trend that places continuing care facilities adjacent to facilities for independent seniors, permitting families to stay together.

Adult day-care centers are another way for seniors and their families to find respite and care. Providence ElderPlace is one of a number of interdisciplinary health-care programs set up to provide comprehensive care for both body and soul to frail seniors who are still living at home. They may be reached at (503) 215-6556. You also can check with your local office of the Oregon Senior & Disabled Services Division (SDSD) to find out about similar programs.

offered every weekend during spring and summer months. The program is progressive, giving novices a chance to build up stamina and strength. Other activities include dances to big band orchestras, visits to area golf courses, art classes, yoga training, and computer classes. Activities are held at park sites throughout the city. The service will also help golfers obtain an identification card for reduced greens fees at city of Portland courses. The cost for the card is $5. A handy seasonal catalogue is available online and in print. (Be sure to check out the Portland's Parks chapter for more information on the vast offerings of this wonderful park system.)

Transportation

The senior centers in the Portland Metro area provide a wide variety of services, including help with transportation needs in their area. But they can only do so much, so many other agencies and volunteer groups have stepped up to fill the gaps in transportation services for seniors.

AMERICAN RED CROSS
3131 North Vancouver Avenue
(503) 280-1445
www.redcross-pdx.org
Providing nonemergency transportation to seniors throughout Multnomah and Washington Counties, the American Red Cross will gladly help with almost any request in return for a modest $1.50 donation. This helpful service is available on weekdays from 9:00 a.m. until 4:00 p.m., but they stay very busy and it is best to schedule your ride up to two weeks in advance.

Oregon State Services for Seniors

The Oregon Department of Human Services (DHS) is the state agency that assists older adults, persons with disabilities, and their caregivers, and they are dedicated to helping people live dignified and independent lives. The division "Seniors and People with Disabilities" (SPD) serves as a clearinghouse for all kinds of information, from how to find a nursing home to how to find discounts on travel. You can reach the state office of SPD at 500 Summer Street NE, Salem, OR 97301, (503) 945-5921, (800) 282-8096 (voice/TTY). Their Web site, http://oregon.gov/DHS/spwpd/index.shtml, is easy to use, comprehensive, and features many links to local, state, and national organizations. Listed below are local branches of SPD:

Multnomah Area Agency on Aging
421 Southwest Oak Avenue, Suite 510
3rd Floor, B161
(503) 988-6945
(503) 988-3683 (TTY)

Multnomah County Area Agency on Aging
2900 Southeast 122nd Avenue, B303
(503) 988-3040
(503) 988-5678 (TTY)

East Multnomah County Aging Services Division
600 Northeast 8th Street, Gresham
(503) 988-3840
(503) 306-5678 (voice/TTY)

Portland Mid-Area Disability Services and Area Agency on Aging Office
2900 Southeast 122nd Avenue
(503) 988-5480
(503) 306-5436 (voice/TTY)

Portland North Disability Services and Area Agency on Aging Office
4925 North Albina Avenue
(503) 988-3479

Portland Northeast Area Aging Agency
5325 Northeast Martin Luther King Jr. Boulevard, Building 322, Main Floor
(503) 988-5470

Portland Southeast Area Aging Agency
4610 Southeast Belmont Street
2nd floor
(503) 988-3660

Portland Southeast Disability Services Office and Area Agency on Aging Office
2446 Southeast Ladd Avenue
(503) 988-3288
(503) 231-0091 (voice/TTY)

Portland West Area Aging Agency
1111 Southwest 10th Avenue
(503) 988-5460

Portland West Disability Services Office and Area Agency on Aging Office
1139 Southwest 11th Avenue
(503) 988-3690

Washington County Dept. of Aging and Veterans' Services
Tigard:
11515 Southwest Durham Road
Suite E-5
(503) 968-2312
(503) 968-2713 (voice/TTY)

Beaverton:
4805 Southwest Griffith Drive, Suite B
(503) 626-4996
(503) 627-0362 (voice/TTY)

Clackamas Area Agency on Aging
2051 Kaen Road
Oregon City
(503) 655-8640

NEIGHBORHOOD HOUSE AGING SERVICES
7780 Southwest Capitol Highway
(503) 246-1663
www.nhweb.org/programs
Neighborhood House helps coordinate transportation needs to medical and dental appointments in southwestern Multnomah County.

PROJECT LINKAGE
2200 Northeast 24th Avenue
(503) 249-0471
www.metfamily.org
Through its 175 volunteers, this agency assists elderly people living in Northeast and Southeast Portland with a wide range of transportation needs, as well as yard work, housekeeping, minor bookkeeping and bill paying, shopping, and home maintenance.

RIDE CONNECTION
3030 Southwest Moody Avenue
(503) 528-1720 (office)
(503) 226-0700 (transportation services)
www.rideconnection.org
The mission of the nonprofit Ride Connection is to keep seniors mobile for as long as possible. They coordinate a network of more than 30 transportation providers so the elderly and disabled can get where they need to go. This innovative program has won many accolades for its approach to service.

Volunteer Opportunities

If you have the time, many agencies, services, and hospitals in the Portland Metro area would be grateful for your volunteer services. Check with your professional organizations too. But here are just a few places to get you started.

ELDERS IN ACTION
1411 Southwest Morrison Street
(503) 235-5474
www.eldersinaction.org

FOSTER GRANDPARENTS PROGRAM
Metro Family Services
2200 Northeast 24th Avenue
(503) 249-8215
www.metfamily.org/pages/programs.html

RETIRED AND SENIOR VOLUNTEER PROGRAM OF MULTNOMAH COUNTY
2145 Northwest Overton Street
(503) 413-7787

MEDIA

NEWSPAPERS

Daily Publications

THE COLUMBIAN
701 West 8th Street, Vancouver, WA
(360) 694-3391
www.columbian.com

By far the biggest daily newspaper in southwestern Washington, the *Columbian* started out as a weekly newspaper in 1890. In 1908 it became a daily and in 1972 grew to include a Sunday morning paper. Herbert Campbell bought the newspaper in 1921, and it has been owned by the Campbell family ever since. The *Columbian* is one of the few family-owned and -operated dailies left in the nation and is the fourth-largest newspaper in Washington, with a current daily circulation of 56,000 and a Sunday circulation of 66,000. An afternoon newspaper, the *Columbian* is published every day of the week except Saturday. It prints *TV Times* on Thursday, an entertainment guide titled *Weekend and Beyond* on Friday, a monthly real estate magazine, *Home Book,* and a weekly nonsubscriber product, *Cover Story,* as well as numerous special sections throughout the year. The *Columbian* is available at all newstands and many library branches. You can also look for it online.

THE DAILY JOURNAL OF COMMERCE
2840 Northwest 35th Avenue
(503) 226-1311
www.djc-or.com

This small paper covers everything from local small businesses to venture capital dealings around the Pacific Northwest. Founded in 1872, the *DJC* is a five-day court and commercial newspaper that is the official publisher for the city of Portland. In addition to general business news, the *DJC* publishes extensive construction industry news and data, mostly for readers in Oregon and Washington. The *DJC* is an essential resource for the business and legal community in Portland.

THE OREGONIAN
1320 Southwest Broadway
(503) 221-8327
www.oregonlive.com

Owned by the New York-based giant media conglomerate Advance Publications, the *Oregonian* casts a long shadow—not just extending over Portland but over the entire state and well beyond. Loved by some, intensely disliked by others, it seems everyone has an opinion about "the Big O." It is charged with being too conservative and pro big-business on one hand, while on the other, it is accused of leaning too far to the left. Even its critics would agree, however, that as the only major daily newspaper in Oregon, the *Oregonian,* with the largest daily circulation in the Pacific Northwest (upwards of 350,000), dominates the print media scene not only in Portland but in the entire state.

The Sunday *Oregonian* (circulation 441,000) is triple the size of the typical daily even after the considerable amount of auto, real estate, and other advertisements are culled. All the regular sections are expanded and such goodies as *Arts and Books,* the comic pages, *TV Click,* and *Parade Magazine* are included. The Friday *Oregonian* is also noteworthy for the special *Arts and Entertainment Guide,* information about everything from unique places to go hiking, biking, and bird-watching to classical music performances and public lectures. The guide also features comprehensive coverage of clubs, restaurants, movies, and Portland's live music and fine arts and literary scene. Also, the listing of restaurants and the 10-day planner—an A&E special fold-out calendar—are particularly useful.

These are challenging times for newspapers—circulation is shrinking, along with advertising revenues—and the *Oregonian* is no exception. Nevertheless, it is holding its own as it navigates the uncertain post-paper seas.

Nondailies

THE ASIAN REPORTER
922 North Killingsworth Street, Suite 1-A
(503) 283-4440
www.asianreporter.com
This weekly newspaper carries a unique blend of local, regional, national, and international news that impacts or is of interest to the area's Asian community. The *Asian Reporter* features at least three regular opinion columns and frequently profiles notable Asian personalities, including local and visiting artists, writers, and political activists. Besides featuring a variety of carefully selected wire stories, the newspaper provides in-depth coverage of issues related to schools, family, human rights, and culture. The "Arts, Culture, and Entertainment Calendar" lists and describes almost every noteworthy Asian event.

BEAVERTON VALLEY TIMES
6975 Southwest Sandburg Road
2nd Floor, Tigard
(503) 684-0360
www.beavertonvalleytimes.com
This community newspaper, dating to the early 1950s, has a circulation of approximately 18,000. It covers news, sports, and livability issues affecting Beaverton and its surrounding environs. It is distributed on Thursday.

THE BUSINESS JOURNAL OF PORTLAND
851 Southwest 6th Avenue
(503) 274-8733
www.bizjournals.com/portland
Part of the nationwide *Business Journal* chain that includes 39 newspapers, the weekly *Business Journal of Portland* was founded in 1984 and is owned by Advance Publications Inc., which also owns the *Oregonian*.

CATHOLIC SENTINEL
5536 Northeast Hassalo Street
(503) 281-1191
www.sentinel.org
Founded in 1870, the *Catholic Sentinel* is the oldest Catholic publication on the entire West Coast. A weekly tabloid with a circulation of approximately 16,200, it covers the local, regional, and national news of interest to the region's Catholic community. The *Catholic Sentinel* is the official publication for the Archdiocese of Portland, which encompasses 29,717 square miles and extends from the summit of the Cascade Mountains in western Oregon to the Pacific Ocean. It's owned and operated by the Oregon Catholic Press of Portland, which is a large publisher of religious books and liturgical materials.

GRESHAM OUTLOOK
1190 Northeast Division Street, Gresham
(503) 665-2181
www.theoutlookonline.com
Published Wednesday and Saturday, the *Outlook* reports on all the goings-on in the Gresham area and is particularly noted for its education and sports coverage. Founded in 1911, the *Gresham Outlook* is owned by the Pamplin Corporation, which has also snapped up many community newspapers and the *Portland Tribune*.

EL HISPANIC NEWS
1200 Southeast Morrison Street
(503) 228-3139
www.hispnews.com
This well-designed weekly is dedicated to the service of the Hispanic and Spanish-speaking communities of the Northwest, as well as relevant national news. The paper has pages dedicated to opinion, religion, education, health, and local news.

THE HOLLYWOOD STAR
3939 Northeast Hancock Street, #3
(503) 282-9392
www.hollywoodstarnews.com
One of the older and better-established community newspapers in town, the *Hollywood Star* does a solid job of covering the news happenings and people of central Northeast Portland, including the Hollywood, Alameda, Grant Park, Rose City Park, and Madison neighborhoods. The *Star*, which is printed at the beginning of each month, has changed hands several times over the years, and Mary De Hart, the owner since 1994, has expanded its circulation to 50,000, which is distributed by mail and newsstands. The focus is on community news, new businesses, and neighborhood livability issues.

THE JEWISH REVIEW
6680 Southwest Capitol Highway
(503) 245-4340
www.jewishreview.org
Serving Oregon and southwest Washington since 1959, this twice-a-month tabloid is published by the Jewish Federation of Portland and features a wide range of national, international, regional, and local news articles and features. The *Review* covers political and sociological issues, features a number of syndicated columns, and regularly reviews adult and children's books. Its calendar provides a good overview of the seminars, concerts, plays, and other events that are of special interest to the Jewish community.

JUST OUT
P.O. Box 14400, Portland, OR 97293-0400
(503) 236-1252
www.justout.com
This free, twice-monthly tabloid covers current events and social-political issues affecting the area's gay and lesbian community. The staff regularly reports on the Oregon State Legislature as well as on national issues. The publication also features sections containing news briefs gathered from other states and from around the globe. In each issue *Just Out* runs a comprehensive calendar, including everything from theater and chamber music events to gay roller-skating parties and discussion groups.

THE MID-COUNTY MEMO
4052 Northeast 22nd Avenue
(503) 287-8904
www.midcountymemo.com
Founded nearly 20 years ago, this monthly tabloid reports on the news, events, and personalities in outer Northeast Portland, from 82nd Avenue west to 155th Avenue and from Stark Street north to Sandy Boulevard. The *Memo*, with a circulation of about 15,000, focuses on neighborhood concerns and on livability issues, like education and crime, and also features profiles of small businesses and people who are making a difference in the Gateway and Parkrose Districts as well as covering several other smaller mid-county neighborhoods.

THE NORTHWEST EXAMINER
2066 Northwest Irving Street
(503) 241-2353
www.nwexaminer.com
As far as monthly community newspapers go, the *Northwest Examiner*, founded in 1986, is in a class by itself. It tackles controversial issues and isn't afraid of offending advertisers or business interests. Instead of the typical puff pieces about cronies and business supporters, it is full of hard news and unusual feature articles and offers a well-thought-out editorial column that addresses current neighborhood issues. The newspaper includes a section covering the bustling Pearl District. The *Examiner* also does a nice job of describing the restaurants, pubs, bistros, and other businesses on lively 21st and 23rd Avenues. The *Examiner*'s 28,000 circulation is distributed throughout the Northwest District and nearby surrounding areas.

THE PORTLAND ALLIANCE

2807 Southeast Stark Street
(503) 239-4991
www.theportlandalliance.org

Founded in 1981 and published by the Northwest Alliance for Alternative Media and Education, the *Alliance* focuses on social, political, and environmental advocacy and reports on a wide spectrum of human rights issues. This progressive, alternative, local news monthly also features a comprehensive calendar of events ranging from peace rallies to union-organizing sessions. Its editor, Dave Mazza, is an articulate leader and spokesman for progressive causes in Oregon. The newspaper's 21,000 copies are distributed throughout the Portland Metro area by the small but hardworking and versatile group of volunteers that make the *Alliance* tick.

i If you hike or bike to the summit of Mount Tabor at the east end of Southeast Hawthorne, you'll see a statue of Harvey Scott, editor of the *Oregonian* from 1865 to 1910. Scott, with his arm outstretched and finger pointed accusingly at the objects of his editorial wrath, once said, "Write so the hod carrier will understand you."

PORTLAND MERCURY

605 Northeast 21st Avenue
(503) 294-0840
www.portlandmercury.com

In addition to a sizable investigatory article in each issue, knowledgeable coverage of the local music scene, CD takes, and pithy film reviews, this weekly paper offers columns by staffers on books, television, and restaurants, as well as hilarious advice to the lovelorn by Dan Savage. The *Mercury* offers an irreverent take on all things Portland, including the other weekly.

PORTLAND OBSERVER

4747 Northeast Martin Luther
King Jr. Boulevard
(503) 288-0033
www.portlandobserver.com

Portland's oldest and largest newspaper serving the African-American community, the *Observer* was founded in 1971 and covers a broad range of issues and offers features and opinions from Portland and beyond. It's distributed on Wednesday throughout the Portland and Vancouver Metro areas. Its editor is Charles Washington, a longtime newpaper publisher.

PORTLAND TRIBUNE

629 Southwest 5th Avenue, Suite 400
(503) 226-6397
www.portlandtribune.com

This semiweekly newspaper with a daily online edition provides objective news writing, features, and columns. The *Tribune's* expertise at providing follow-up, in-depth coverage to local headlines has brought it national and regional awards. The *Portland Tribune* is a rising star on the newspaper scene and an excellent introduction to what's going on in town.

THE SELLWOOD BEE

P.O. Box 82127, Portland, OR 97282-0217
(503) 232-2326
www.readthebee.com

One of Portland's oldest community newspapers, the *Sellwood Bee* serves the Eastmoreland, Westmoreland, Sellwood, Brooklyn, and Reed neighborhoods in inner Southeast Portland. The focus of this monthly publication is news coverage of the events and people that affect the local community.

THE SKANNER

415 North Killingsworth Street
(503) 285-5555
www.theskanner.com

Founded in 1975, the *Skanner* covers the news, politics, and events affecting Portland's African-American community, with a good amount of ink devoted to the family, education, and livability issues of North and Northeast Portlanders. The *Skanner* has won a host of regional and national journalism awards and in 1996 received the Northwest Family Business Award for the small family business of the year. In 1987 The Skanner News Group published its first Seattle edition; today the combined papers have 15 employees and a readership of approximately 75,000. In addition to its regular publication, the *Skanner* prints a half-dozen special issues each year, including a black history edition in February, a career guide in June, a minority business enterprise edition in October, and a holiday issue in December.

THE SOUTHEAST EXAMINER
P.O. Box 33663, Portland, OR 97292
(503) 254-7550
www.southeastexaminer.com
Founded as the *Sunnyside Up News* in 1990 and once a sister publication to the *Northwest Examiner*, this monthly tabloid is now independently owned. The *Examiner* covers news from inner Southeast Portland, including the Industrial District, the booming Hawthorne District, and the emerging Belmont and Division Streets all the way out to 82nd Avenue. With a circulation of 24,000, of which 20,000 are home delivered, its coverage area extends roughly from Burnside Street south to Foster Road. The *Southeast Examiner* reports on a wide range of topics with a focus on neighborhood issues, arts and music, food, and history.

ST. JOHNS SENTINEL
(503) 287-3380
www.stjohnssentinel.com
This community paper reports on the news, issues, and personalities affecting North Portland and the St. Johns community. It is distributed by mail and is also available at about 40 drop sites in local neighborhoods.

STREET ROOTS
211 Northwest Davis Street
(503) 228-5657
www.streetroots.org
www.poorpeopleguide.org (resources)

This small, lively monthly newspaper gives voice to the homeless while addressing issues relating to homelessness, including health and survival. *Street Roots,* which is published the first of every month, contains news stories, columns, and editorials, and 14,000 copies are distributed throughout downtown Portland.

WILLAMETTE WEEK
822 Southwest 10th Avenue
(503) 243-2122
www.wweek.com
Founded in 1974 by Ron Buel as an alternative newspaper, *Willamette Week (WW)* has grown in size to a circulation of 80,000 and is distributed on Wednesday throughout the Portland Metro area (and well beyond) at stores, restaurants, coffee shops, and microbrew pubs. This free weekly tabloid has evolved into an upscale publication geared toward a sophisticated audience. Watch for *WW*'s "Best of Portland" issue in July; it covers everything from the best drinking fountain to the best elevator in town. Willamette Week also publishes an extensive voter's guide in election years as well as annual guides describing the area's best restaurants and brewpubs, which are lively, well written, and informative.

i Portland is a city of neighborhoods, and reading the neighborhood newspapers is indispensable for finding out the scoop on local businesses and events—as well as the political issues that might affect you directly. Find them at coffeeshops, grocery stores, restaurants, and sidewalk kiosks wherever you are.

MAGAZINES

METRO PARENT
P.O. Box 13660, Portland, OR 97213
(503) 460-2774
www.metro-parent.com
This user-friendly guide for parents offers a variety of thoughtful articles pertaining to the overall well-being of children. Besides offering

an extensive calendar of events, *Metro Parent* regularly features a directory for new parents that includes a wide assortment of support groups and resources for special-needs children. The monthly calendar is jam-packed with all kinds of stuff, ranging from children's theater to carnivals, concerts, and special exhibits that are geared toward the whole family.

NORTHWEST PALATE

P.O. Box 10860, Portland, OR
97296-0860
(503) 224-6039
www.nwpalate.com

This bimonthly, glossy, consumer magazine focuses on gourmet food, wine, entertainment, and travel in the Pacific Northwest. *Northwest Palate,* which was started as a wine newsletter nearly 20 years ago by owner/publisher/editor Cameron Nagel, is still independently owned and has now built its circulation to 45,000 with readers in all 50 states and Europe—most concentrated in Washington and Oregon. It is a well-written, indispensable guide to the local food, farm, and wine scene.

OPEN SPACES

www.open-spaces.com

Open Spaces quarterly provides intelligent commentary on the major issues facing the Pacific Northwest, giving voice to a variety of perspectives and opinions. This thoughtful magazine offers respite from the cacophony of unsubstantiated opinion that too often passes for debate in our 24/7 connected world. You should read it, even if you don't live in Portland. It also features good fiction, poetry, and other kinds of writing.

OREGON BUSINESS MAGAZINE

610 Southwest Broadway, Suite 200
(503) 223-0304
www.mediamerica.net/obm

Founded in 1981, owned by MEDIAmerica Inc., and with a circulation of 20,200, this highly polished publication covers the business scene all over Oregon and southwestern Washington. Issues regularly contain investigative business reporting, small business articles, profiles of unique people and their companies, and section pieces ranging from transportation issues and electronic commerce to education. The continuing focus of the magazine is helping large and small businesses identify and solve problems. Each year *Oregon Business* publishes special editions, which cover the fastest-growing companies in Oregon and the 100 best companies to work for.

OREGON HOME

MediAmerica Inc.
610 Southwest Broadway, Suite 200
Portland
www.mediamerica.net/oregon_home_
magazine.php

Oregon Home is a glossy magazine published bimonthly that is devoted to houses in Oregon— how they are decorated and lived in. Their company mantra is "real people, real homes," and it's true. One of the pleasures of this publication is reading it to see if anyone you know is featured in it. It happens more than you might think. You can find it by looking at supermarket checkout stands and other newsstand spots, or contact the publisher online to subscribe.

PORTLAND FAMILY MAGAZINE

P.O. Box 16667, Portland, OR 97292
(503) 255-3286
www.portlandfamily.com

This slender and wholesome-as-apple-pie magazine offers useful information for all concerned parents. Besides tackling serious issues such as education, health and wellness, and child development, *Portland Family Magazine (PFM)* keeps a calendar of events listing and describes events and fun activities that parents and their kids can enjoy together. A handsomely designed monthly with short readable stories and blurbs, *PFM* includes a column, "School Notes," with the latest info on education, and *The Spirit of Giving,* a guide for families, organizations, and individuals in need. A good resource for families, *PFM* is distributed throughout the Portland and Vancouver areas.

PORTLAND MONTHLY
623 Southwest Oak Street, Suite 300
(503) 222-5144
www.portlandmonthlymag.com

This monthly magazine provides outstanding coverage of all things Portland, from real estate and restaurants to fashion and fund-raisers. Established in 2003, it has quickly become a must-read magazine for Portlanders. They present annual issues dedicated to health care, vacations, and other themes. But they also can take on the serious issues of the day. Find it at newsstands all through town, or subscribe online.

TELEVISION

KATU-TV CHANNEL 2 (ABC)
2153 Northeast Sandy Boulevard
(503) 231-4222
www.katu.com

The slogan of this ABC affiliate, "The Power of 2," refers to its number on the dial and to a pair of weather and traffic choppers hovering over the town like two dragonflies. Not only does KATU deliver crisp and clear news reports, it also hosts a Town Hall roughly every quarter in which citizens can sound off about issues making headlines. Another feature at KATU is "The Advisory Council," a feedback loop in which viewers get a chance to talk about programming they love or hate. To participate call (503) 872-2949 or, from out of town, call (800) 777-KATU.

KGW-TV CHANNEL 8 (NBC)
1501 Southwest Jefferson Street
(503) 226-5000
www.kgw.com

This NBC affiliate is one of the first stations in the United States to offer 24-hour live news on its Web site. Perhaps the most flamboyant of all the local stations, it seems to have the biggest news staff. Maff Zaffino, an affable weather guy, is noted for his briefings on snow conditions up in the Cascade Mountains. Another popular feature is KGW's Unit 8, a consumer hotline that sends investigators out to find out who's scamming seniors, adding bogus charges to your phone

bill, or charging the government big bucks for substandard housing.

KOIN-TV CHANNEL 6 (CBS)
222 Southwest Columbia Drive
(503) 464-0600
www.koin.com

This pioneer broadcasting operation began as a radio station in 1925, sending out a signal from a single room in the Portland Hotel. By 1930 KOIN was Portland's CBS affiliate, and on October 15, 1953, KOIN-TV signed on as Portland's first VHF television station and as an affiliate of the CBS Television Network. KOIN was the first station in Portland to broadcast a one-hour newscast at 5:00 p.m. Currently KOIN is in the KOIN Tower, an easily recognizable landmark in downtown Portland.

KOPB-TV CHANNEL 10 (PBS)
7140 Southwest Macadam Avenue
(503) 244-9900
www.opb.org

The Oregon Public Broadcasting station started in 1922 as an engineering professor's 50-watt transmitter. KOPB now serves the entire state and a portion of southwest Washington as the affiliate for PBS and a venue for local issue-driven and cultural programs.

KPDX-TV CHANNEL 49 (FOX)
14975 Northwest Greenbriar Parkway
Beaverton
(503) 906-1249
www.kpdx.com

The only local programming on KPDX, a local FOX affiliate, is a news program at 10:00 p.m. But those who watch FOX's "tabloid television" to catch the goofy pratfalls and dangerous dangles broadcast by the network don't seem disappointed at the lack of local shows.

KPTV-TV CHANNEL 12 (FOX)
11 Southeast Caruthers Street
(503) 230-1200
www.kptv.com

This TV station in Portland was launched in 1952. It is a local affiliate for the Fox Network and the nation's first laboratory for digital-to-air technology. It's also known for its independent, quirky broadcasting like the popular *Good Day, Oregon*, which might feature taking your dog on a hike through the snow, how to braise chicken legs, or what's the latest hot exhibit for kids at the Oregon Museum of Science and Industry (OMSI). KPTV also gets viewer points for airing the 10 o'clock news an hour earlier than most late-night newscasts.

RADIO STATIONS

KBOO/90.7 FM
20 Southeast 8th Avenue
(503) 231-8032
www.kboo.org

The call letters KBOO were chosen because the gang organizing the station decided to go for it on Halloween 1963; they were on the air the following June. The local Pacifica affiliate, it is dedicated to innovative programming, including classical, rock, and folk. In the early 1980s, KBOO broadened its commitment to multicultural programming by adding Spanish, Asian-American, and African-American musical shows.

KBPS/89.9 FM AND 1450 AM
515 Northeast 15th Avenue
(503) 916-5828
www.allclassical.org

KBPS is Portland's classical music station. Wonderfully commercial free, the station began in the early 1980s as a project of students at Benson High School. Budget cuts to the program led to its eventual independence, and the station is now building an endowment to ensure that the works of the great composers, as well as their less famous peers, are heard throughout western Oregon forever. KBPS also broadcasts headline news from the BBC. Plus, they organize interesting concerts, contests, and other events—even music-focused tours of Europe.

KINK/102 FM
1501 Southwest Jefferson Street
(503) 241-1020
www.kink102.com

A popular station for more than 30 years, KINK is home base for local baby boomers who enjoy aging rockers, folksingers, and jazz artists as well as new releases by contemporary popsters.

KKRZ/100 FM
4949 Southwest Macadam Avenue
(503) 226-0100
www.z100portland.com

This station, known as Z-100, has been No. 1 in the local ratings competition for the past few years because of the wide appeal of its contemporary hits format.

KMHD/89.1 FM
26000 Southeast Stark Street, Gresham
(503) 661-8900

"The Jazz Station" since its start in 1984, KMHD is operated by Mt. Hood Community College in nearby Gresham. With an extensive library of more than 6,000 LPs and CDs, KMHD plays a full spectrum of jazz artists ranging from Ella Fitzgerald to Miles Davis to Horace Silver.

KNRK/94.7 FM
700 Southwest Bancroft Street
(503) 733-5470
www.947.fm

Portland's boldest champion of new rock stretches the envelope of alternative music with live broadcasts from local rock venues as well as a steady bill of edgy tunes.

KOPB/91.5 FM
7140 Southwest Macadam Avenue
(503) 293-1905
www.opb.org

The local spot on the dial for National Public Broadcasting, KOPB will connect you to *A Prairie Home Companion*, *Thistle and Shamrock*, and *Alternative Radio*, as well as local talk shows and lectures.

KPOJ/620 AM
4949 Southwest Macadam Avenue
(503) 323-6400
www.620knews.com

KPOJ is Portland's Air America affiliate and fills the

airwaves with progressive humor, observation, commentary, advice, and talk radio, with a twist.

More FM Stations
Adult Contemporary

KKCW/103 FM
500 Southwest Macadam Avenue
(503) 222-5103
www.k103.com

Album Rock 'n' Roll

KUFO/101 FM
2040 Southwest 1st Avenue
(503) 222-1011
www.kufo.com

Classic Rock

KGON/92.3 FM
700 Southwest Bancroft Road
(503) 733-5466
www.kgon.com

KLTH/FM 106.7
222 Southwest Columbia Street, Suite 350
(503) 223-0300
www.khits1067.com
Light rock, with an emphasis on 1960s and '70s.

KUPL/98.7 FM
222 Southwest Columbia Boulevard
Suite 350
(503) 733-5000
www.kupl.com

KYCH/97.1 FM
0700 Southwest Bancroft Street
(503) 223-1441
www.charliefm.com
Mixed format pop and rock.

KXJM/95.5 FM
0234 Southwest Bancroft Street
(503) 417-9595
www.jamminfm.com
"Jammin'" contemporary tunes.

KWJJ/99.5 FM
0700 Southwest Bancroft Street
(503) 223-1441
www.kwjj.com
Contemporary country music.

More AM Stations
Business News

KBNP/1410 AM
811 Southwest Naito Parkway, Suite 420
(503) 223-6769
www.kbnp.com

Christian Talk

KKPZ/1330 AM
4700 Southwest Macadam Avenue
(503) 242-1950
www.kkpz.com

News and Information

KEX/1190 AM
4949 Southwest Macadam Avenue
(503) 225-1190
www.1190kex.com

Religious

KKSL/1290 AM
4700 Southwest Macadam Avenue
(503) 242-1290
www.kksl.com

Sports Radio

KFXX/1080 AM
700 Southwest Bancroft Street
(503) 223-1441

WORSHIP

Whether you are new to town, looking for a home church, or just visiting, Portland has hundreds of places of worship, ranging from Adventist Churches to Zen Buddhist Temples and every denomination in between. The telephone book is one obvious place to help you find a church, temple, or synagogue, but other resources are also available. The *Oregonian* publishes an extensive religion section each Saturday; there you may find more information about services. Its calendar lists a wide variety of religious events, including everything from bake sales and concerts to plays, seminars, and lectures. You can also call the Ecumenical Ministries of Oregon at (503) 221-1054. This association comprises 16 denominations, has a wide range of participating members, and can serve as a good referral source as well as providing general information.

If you are in town long, you may find that some of your new friends and acquaintances don't attend church. Reports in the *Oregonian* regularly observe that Oregon residents rank lowest nationally in claiming affiliation with organized religions, which is, given Oregon's early religious history, ironic. But even as early as 1890, fewer than one quarter of Oregon's residents said they attended church regularly. Today, about 17 percent of Oregonians classify themselves as "nonreligious," compared with a national average of 7 percent, and less than one third of Oregonians claim an official religious affiliation today. It's not that they don't believe in anything, however. Only about 1 percent of Oregonians claim to be agnostic, and an even smaller percentage claims to be atheist. Apparently, a significant number of Oregonians are following their own spiritual path, even if it's not one that is readily labeled.

OVERVIEW

Oregonians tend to be a diverse lot when it comes to religion. A profusion of spiritual traditions thrives in Portland and throughout Oregon. In addition to more established churches, Oregon's mountains, plains, and forests shelter many a retreat center devoted to the practices of Native American spirituality, chi gong, western Buddhism, healing arts, and meditation. While the majority of religious persons in the state practice some form of Christianity, with Catholics and the Latter-Day Saints having the largest congregations, other faiths are also well represented. Judaism, Islam, and Buddhism all have active populations; in fact, practitioners of Buddhism can claim to have the largest following of any faith besides Christianity. The Unitarian Church and other liberal churches are quite vigorous. We have also made room for less conventional faith practices—the Wiccans and Neo-Pagans, for example, have a visible, if small, presence, and they are representative of the variety of spiritual practices found in the area and the total numbers they attract—especially if you add those 17 percent of Oregonians who are believers in spirituality but don't consider themselves religious.

In addition to their spirit of religious independence, Portlanders also are known for their tolerance and, among churchgoers, for their ecumenical spirit, both of which were strengthened in the early 1990s when a group proposed anti-gay legislation. This event mobilized the area's spiritual community to oppose it, bringing more religious coalitions together (from Catholics and Jews to Mormons and Buddhists) than any other happening in Oregon's modern history. At the forefront of the movement was the Ecumenical Ministries of Oregon, which can trace its history back more than 80 years and which from 1982 to 1992 grew from being the smallest ecumenical ministry in the nation to being the largest.

OLD-TIME RELIGION

Many of Oregon's earliest settlers from the East Coast were Christian missionaries determined to save the souls of the local Indians. At this they were unsuccessful, but they did persuade some of the soldiers, trappers, and traders who had preceded them, thus establishing the roots of Christianity and middle-class American life in the area. Arriving at Fort Vancouver in 1834, the Reverend Jason Lee, a Methodist, got right to work building churches and schools in various spots throughout the Willamette Valley, notably at Oregon City, the eventual end of the Oregon Trail. Catholic missionaries were also busy in the area. Having been invited by French Canadian settlers from Fort Vancouver, two priests, the Reverend Father Blanchet and his assistant, the Reverend Father Demers, arrived in 1838. Blanchet was a particularly talented administrator who understood the native tribes, but the Catholics also had more success with the white settlers than with the Native Americans when it came to recruitment. By the middle of the 19th century, most of the major Christian denominations were well represented in Portland. Together the various missionary sects had a significant influence on the social, political, economic, and institutional life of the state. Other forms of worship, such as Judaism and Buddhism, were also well represented, though their influence on the emerging government was less direct.

A CHOICE OF RELIGIOUS PRACTICES

Portland has the usual complement of churches, temples, synagogues, and mosques that one would expect to find in a large American city. But the varieties of religious experience in Portland have always been diverse. For example, African-American churches have a long history in the area. The earliest African Methodist Episcopal Church was the People's Church, founded in 1862 on the west side and later moving to the east side, where it became the African Methodist Episcopal Zion Church. Bethel AME was founded in the 1890s, as was Mount Olivet Baptist. **Bethel AME**, 5828 Northeast 8th Avenue, and **Mount Olivet**, 8725 North Chautauqua, are both more vigorous than ever, with many innovative programs for fostering social capital among parishioners and the community. And they are not alone: There are now more than 55 African-American churches in North and Northeast Portland.

Portland's Chinatown was at one time the second largest in the nation. The Chinese, however, endured an unimaginable amount of bigotry from the white settlers in the area and, as a result, tended to live together. Many workers, moreover, regarded their life in Oregon as merely temporary, so they did not build many buildings. Nor did they build temples. Instead they met on 2nd Avenue at a place called the Chinese Joss House. Japanese workers, who also believed their stay here to be temporary, did choose to erect a temple, the **Oregon Buddhist Church**, 3720 Southeast 34th Avenue, which is more than 100 years old. Another major temple, the **Buddhist Daihonzan Henjyoji Temple**, 2634 Southeast 12th Avenue, was founded in 1940. During the last decade, the area has seen a remarkable increase in the number of Buddhist temples built for Chinese, Korean, Cambodian, Vietnamese, and other Asian congregations. In fact, according to some recent data, it appears that the Buddhist population is slightly larger than the Jewish population in Oregon, the only state in which this may be the case.

The Mormon Church (the Church of Jesus Christ of Latter-Day Saints) has a significant presence in the Portland area and around the state, with about 100,000 practicing members and 228 congregations in Oregon.

With eight synagogues in the metro area, the Portland Jewish community is quite active. **Congregation Shaarie Torah**, 920 Northwest 25th Avenue, is Portland's only traditional synagogue; its busy, vibrant programs include education and outreach, in addition to traditional services.

Congregation Beth Israel, 1972 Northwest Flanders, a reform congregation, claims the largest membership in Oregon (about 3,000 people).

The Catholic Archdiocese of Portland is vast; it includes close to 300,000 members in 123 parishes in addition to its missions, schools, universities, and hospitals. The Catholic Church in Portland plays an active role in the greater community through a wide range of charitable services. The **St. Vincent de Paul Church and Downtown Chapel**, 601 West Burnside Street, sponsors a wide variety of activities—including community soup dinners, visitations, and open fellowships—that serve the inner-city population. The Society of St. Vincent de Paul has had a strong presence in Portland since 1869. Catholic Charities also has a significant presence and was officially established in the 1930s. This nonprofit social-service agency organizes services to the poor and needy through Catholic agencies. Programs include Adoption and Crisis Pregnancy, AIDS Ministry, Asian Social Services, Centro de Canby, Immigration Legal Services, Ministry to the Elderly, and the Refugee Resettlement.

Portland is the home to many conservative and traditional ministries. Ten different Pentecostal churches, more than 25 charismatic churches, and 15 different branches of Baptist churches minister to area residents. In spite of Oregon's low religious affiliation in general, the state ranks fifth for attendance at megachurches. Two of the most active and dynamic are **New Beginnings Christian Center**, 7600 Northeast Glisan Street, which offers a full range of adult and youth services and support groups; and **New Hope Community Church**, 11731 Southeast Stevens Road. Founded by Dale Galloway, New Hope is one of the largest and most active spiritual communities in the state, and its annual pageants and concerts draw thousands of visitors.

Portland also possesses a small, but growing, number of Muslim communities. In 1993 the Muslim Educational Trust was founded in order to educate both its Islamic members and their non-Muslim neighbors about the faith. This organization serves as a central resource for several mosques, community centers, and other Islamic resources in the area and provides outreach and education programs of its own.

Not surprisingly Portland is also regarded as a stronghold of liberal religion, even with respect to its evangelical churches, Portland is at the forefront of a new trend: "emergent" Christianity, a form that provides much of the fellowship of megachurches but with a completely different flavor, one that is mindful of history, art-embracing, and postmodern. Portland author Donald Miller is a leader in the movement, and two congregations can be found here—the Evergreen Community (www.evergreenlife.org), which meets Sunday at the Lucky Lab, a pub on Northwest Quimby (see our Brewpubs chapter), and Imago Dei, which currently meets at the Franklin High School theater.

Members of the **First Unitarian Church of Portland**, 1011 Southwest 12th Avenue, boldly express their liberal, progressive beliefs and are often at the forefront of political and socioeconomic issues. Founded in 1866, First Unitarian is the largest Unitarian Universalist congregation in the nation, with more than 1,500 members and packed Sunday morning services. Outreach programs include adult education classes and groups that serve the homeless and work for social justice, especially the causes of environmental justice, racial equality, and peace. The Reverend Dr. Marilyn Sewell, the senior Unitarian minister, is an eminent writer, speaker, and spiritual leader who is known throughout the nation.

And new ways of exploring old traditions are evolving all the time. **The Center for Spiritual Development**, directed by the Reverend Canon Marianne Wells Borg, is one of Portland's newer forums for spiritual exploration. Associated with Trinity Episcopal Cathedral, the center has a five-point program of education and outreach. In addition to long (two to three years) interfaith courses that study issues such as spirituality, justice, and religious tradition, the center also teaches different forms of spiritual practice, sponsors programs in healing, organizes pilgrimages, and hosts public lectures by acclaimed writers and speakers such as Marcus Borg, Karen Armstrong, and Huston Smith.

Readers who prefer their spirituality in less traditional forms will not be disappointed in the Portland area. All over Oregon, people are gathering to meditate, chant, align their chi, and breathe. The popular and attractive **Breitenbush Hot Springs**, (503) 854-3314, south of Portland in the Cascades, is a busy center for different New Age practices. In town, the **New Renaissance Bookshop**, 1338 Northwest 23rd (at Pettygrove), (503) 224-4929, not only provides abundant information about the breadth of spiritual practices in the area, but it also offers workshops on everything from Kabbalah to Knitting for the Goddess. Another useful resource is the free publication, *Alternatives for Cultural Creativity,* which is widely available throughout the city, especially at coffeehouses and bookstores.

i Love music? Trinity Episcopal Cathedral, at 147 Northwest 19th Avenue, (503) 222-9811, has a first-rate choir and hosts many world-class singers and musicians. On the first Sunday of the month at 5:00 p.m. from October to May, Trinity has a splendid vespers service. St. Phillip Neri Catholic Church, at Southeast 18th Avenue and Division Street, (503) 231-4955, also offers many high-quality concerts.

INDEX

ABOUT THE AUTHOR

Rachel Dresbeck, a writer and editor, has observed and written about Portland for a variety of publications. She's also an author of the *Insiders' Guide to the Oregon Coast*. She was educated at Whitman College and the University of Oregon, has taught writing and literature at Portland Community College and the University of Oregon, and now teaches writing and writes about research at Oregon Health and Science University. She lives with her husband and daughters in the Richmond neighborhood of Portland, where she studies ways in which citizens sustain their civility and community spirit against all odds.